T0297376

Handbook of Research on Security Considerations in Cloud Computing

Kashif Munir
King Fahd University of Petroleum & Minerals, Saudi Arabia

Mubarak S. Al-Mutairi
King Fahd University of Petroleum & Minerals, Saudi Arabia

Lawan A. Mohammed
King Fahd University of Petroleum & Minerals, Saudi Arabia

A volume in the Advances in Information Security, Privacy, and Ethics (AISPE) Book Series

Information Science REFERENCE
An Imprint of IGI Global

Managing Director:	Lindsay Johnston
Managing Editor:	Austin DeMarco
Director of Intellectual Property & Contracts:	Jan Travers
Acquisitions Editor:	Kayla Wolfe
Production Editor:	Christina Henning
Development Editor:	Caitlyn Martin
Cover Design:	Jason Mull

Published in the United States of America by
Information Science Reference (an imprint of IGI Global)
701 E. Chocolate Avenue
Hershey PA, USA 17033
Tel: 717-533-8845
Fax: 717-533-8661
E-mail: cust@igi-global.com
Web site: http://www.igi-global.com

Library of Congress Cataloging-in-Publication Data

Handbook of research on security considerations in cloud computing / Kashif Munir, Mubarak S. Al-Mutairi, and Lawan A. Mohammed, editors.
    pages cm
 Includes bibliographical references and index.
 ISBN 978-1-4666-8387-7 (hardcover) -- ISBN 978-1-4666-8388-4 (ebook) 1. Cloud computing--Security measures--Handbooks, manuals, etc. I. Munir, Kashif, 1976- editor.
 QA76.585.H3646 2015
 004.67'82--dc23
                        2015008172

This book is published in the IGI Global book series Advances in Information Security, Privacy, and Ethics (AISPE) (ISSN: 1948-9730; eISSN: 1948-9749)

British Cataloguing in Publication Data
A Cataloguing in Publication record for this book is available from the British Library.

All work contributed to this book is new, previously-unpublished material. The views expressed in this book are those of the authors, but not necessarily of the publisher.

For electronic access to this publication, please contact: eresources@igi-global.com.

Advances in Information Security, Privacy, and Ethics (AISPE) Book Series

ISSN: 1948-9730
EISSN: 1948-9749

MISSION

As digital technologies become more pervasive in everyday life and the Internet is utilized in ever increasing ways by both private and public entities, concern over digital threats becomes more prevalent.

The **Advances in Information Security, Privacy, & Ethics (AISPE) Book Series** provides cutting-edge research on the protection and misuse of information and technology across various industries and settings. Comprised of scholarly research on topics such as identity management, cryptography, system security, authentication, and data protection, this book series is ideal for reference by IT professionals, academicians, and upper-level students.

COVERAGE

- Risk Management
- Device Fingerprinting
- Global Privacy Concerns
- Cyberethics
- Information Security Standards
- Technoethics
- Electronic Mail Security
- Privacy Issues of Social Networking
- Security Classifications
- Access Control

IGI Global is currently accepting manuscripts for publication within this series. To submit a proposal for a volume in this series, please contact our Acquisition Editors at Acquisitions@igi-global.com or visit: http://www.igi-global.com/publish/.

Titles in this Series

For a list of additional titles in this series, please visit: www.igi-global.com

Handbook of Research on Emerging Developments in Data Privacy
Manish Gupta (State University of New York at Buffalo, USA)
Information Science Reference • copyright 2015 • 507pp • H/C (ISBN: 9781466673816) • US $325.00 (our price)

Handbook of Research on Securing Cloud-Based Databases with Biometric Applications
Ganesh Chandra Deka (Ministry of Labour and Employment, India) and Sambit Bakshi (National Institute of Technology Rourkela, India)
Information Science Reference • copyright 2015 • 434pp • H/C (ISBN: 9781466665590) • US $335.00 (our price)

Handbook of Research on Threat Detection and Countermeasures in Network Security
Alaa Hussein Al-Hamami (Amman Arab University, Jordan) and Ghossoon M. Waleed al-Saadoon (Applied Sciences University, Bahrain)
Information Science Reference • copyright 2015 • 450pp • H/C (ISBN: 9781466665835) • US $325.00 (our price)

Information Security in Diverse Computing Environments
Anne Kayem (Department of Computer Science, University of Cape Town, South Africa) and Christoph Meinel (Hasso-Plattner-Institute for IT Systems Engineering, University of Potsdam, Potsdam, Germany)
Information Science Reference • copyright 2014 • 354pp • H/C (ISBN: 9781466661585) • US $245.00 (our price)

Network Topology in Command and Control Organization, Operation, and Evolution
T. J. Grant (R-BAR, The Netherlands) R. H. P. Janssen (Netherlands Defence Academy, The Netherlands) and H. Monsuur (Netherlands Defence Academy, The Netherlands)
Information Science Reference • copyright 2014 • 320pp • H/C (ISBN: 9781466660588) • US $215.00 (our price)

Cases on Research and Knowledge Discovery Homeland Security Centers of Excellence
Cecelia Wright Brown (University of Baltimore, USA) Kevin A. Peters (Morgan State University, USA) and Kofi Adofo Nyarko (Morgan State University, USA)
Information Science Reference • copyright 2014 • 357pp • H/C (ISBN: 9781466659469) • US $215.00 (our price)

Multidisciplinary Perspectives in Cryptology and Information Security
Sattar B. Sadkhan Al Maliky (University of Babylon, Iraq) and Nidaa A. Abbas (University of Babylon, Iraq)
Information Science Reference • copyright 2014 • 443pp • H/C (ISBN: 9781466658080) • US $245.00 (our price)

Analyzing Security, Trust, and Crime in the Digital World
Hamid R. Nemati (The University of North Carolina at Greensboro, USA)
Information Science Reference • copyright 2014 • 281pp • H/C (ISBN: 9781466648562) • US $195.00 (our price)

www.igi-global.com

701 E. Chocolate Ave., Hershey, PA 17033
Order online at www.igi-global.com or call 717-533-8845 x100
To place a standing order for titles released in this series, contact: cust@igi-global.com
Mon-Fri 8:00 am - 5:00 pm (est) or fax 24 hours a day 717-533-8661

Editorial Advisory Board

List of Contributors

Table of Contents

Detailed Table of Contents

> *Subhash Chandra Patel, Indian Institute of Technology (BHU), India*
> *R.S. Singh, Indian Institute of Technology (BHU), India*
> *Sumit Jaiswal, Indian Institute of Technology (BHU), India*

This chapter discussed security risks on adoption to cloud computing, the risks related to privacy, trust, control, data ownership, data location, audits and reviews, business continuity and disaster recovery, legal, regulatory and compliance, security policy and emerging security threats and attacks.

> *Marwan Omar, Nawroz University, Iraq*

This chapter will explore and investigate the scope and magnitude of one of the top cloud computing security threats "abuse and nefarious use of cloud computing" and present some of the attacks specific to this top threat as it represents a major barrier for decision makers to adopting cloud computing model.

> *Santosh Kumar, Indian Institute of Technology, India*
> *Ali Imam Abidi, Indian Institute of Technology, India*
> *Sanjay Kumar Singh, Indian Institute of Technology, India*

This chapter presents biometrics as an authentication method and as a general security feature for cloud. This chapter provides with the stepping stone for future researches to unveil how biometrics can change the cloud security scenario.

This chapter identify the most vulnerable security threats/attacks in cloud computing, which will enable both end users and vendors to know about the key security threats associated with cloud computing and propose relevant solution directives to strengthen security in the Cloud environment. This chapter also discusses secure cloud architecture for organizations to strengthen the security.

This chapter discusses how Governance and Risk Management domain (GRM) of Cloud Controls Matrix (CSA CCM) V3 Framework from Cloud Security Alliance (CSA) and the ISO/IEC 38500:2008 standard for IT Governance can be utilized together for an effective Governance and Risk Management of Cloud Services.

Chapter 6

In this chapter, an error-resistant approach is investigated to add to low cost image authentication scheme to increase visual quality as well as improve author and user satisfaction. The image authentication includes content based digital signature that is watermarked and later diffused in the whole image before JPEG2000 coding. To tackle manipulations in the image, edge information of the image is examined to offset manipulations in the image transmission through noisy or open and unsecure channels.

Chapter 7

This chapter first provides the basic introduction to cloud computing and fuzzy logic. On the basis of extensive literature survey, this chapter discusses trust and its need, in addition to use of fuzzy logic for the purpose of trust calculation in distributed environments and cloud computing till now. At the end of this chapter, the difficulties and applications of using fuzzy logic for trust evaluation are discussed along with research directions for future.

This chapter discusses the cloud security, privacy, and ethical mechanisms required from a teacher, student, and administrator perspective.

Chapter 9

This Chapter simply contains multimedia - an integrated and interactive presentation of speech, audio, video, graphics and text, has become a major theme in today's information technology that merges the practices of communications, computing and information processing into an interdisciplinary field. The challenge of multimedia communications is to provide services that integrate text, sound, image and video information and to do it in a way that preserves the case of use and interactivity. A brief description of the elements of multimedia systems is presented.

Chapter 10

In this chapter, a new Third Party Auditor based scheme has been proposed for secured storage and retrieval of client's data to and from the cloud service provider. The scheme has been analysed and compared with some of the existing schemes with respect to the security issues. From the analysis and comparison it can be observed that the proposed scheme performs better than the existing schemes.

Chapter 11

The use of multiple cloud providers for gaining security and privacy benefits is nontrivial. As the approaches investigated in this chapter clearly show, there is no single optimal approach to foster both security and legal compliance in an applicable manner. Moreover, the approaches that are favorable from a technical perspective appear less appealing from a regulatory point of view, and vice versa.

Chapter 12

The increasing frequency of digital investigations brings with it the need to study specific scenarios in the area of forensics, both when evidence are inside the cloud and when the cloud can be used as platform to perform the investigations. This chapter highlights the problems forensics must deal with in the Cloud, highlighting specific requirements and desired functionalities, the state of the art and future issues.

Chapter 13

Despite having many advantages for IT organizations, cloud has some issues that must be consider during its deployment. The main concerns are security, privacy and trust. These issues arise during the deployment of mostly public cloud infrastructure. In this chapter, security, privacy and trust issues of cloud computing deployment in Saudi Arabia were identified and the solutions to overcome these problems were discussed.

Chapter 14

Big Data sharing brings new information security and privacy issues. Traditional technologies and methods are no longer appropriate and lack of performance when applied in Big Data context. This chapter presents Big Data security challenges and a state of the art in methods, mechanisms and solutions used to protect data-intensive information systems.

Chapter 15

This chapter presents the RBAC framework that protects the sensitive information in the cloud, specifies the privacy policies for the private cloud; and protects the data from hackers. Two scenarios has been presented. Scenario 1 deals with what if is present in a number of groups and the access rights that are given to him/her are different whereas scenario 2 deals with shareable resources be handled in this framework. Algorithm has been presented to support the scenarios.

Chapter 16

This chapter presents many technical issues regarding big data which includes heterogeneity level, lack of layout, error-handling, security, timeliness and visualization at all levels of the analysis processing from data acquisition stage to conclusion interpretation. These technical issues are more common across a large distinguish of application task area. Furthermore, these issues will acquire transformation conclusions, and will not be specified naturally by the future generation of products.

This chapter presents an efficient and reliable transparent per-file-wiping file system extension called restfs. Instead of overwriting at file level which is found in existing wiping extensions, restfs overwrites at block level to exploit the behavior of file systems for efficiency (reduction in number of block overwrites and disk writes issued) and reliability (sustainability across system crashes). restfs is design compatible with all file systems which export block allocation map of a file to VFS; however it is currently implemented for ext2 file system.

In this chapter, the current consensus of what Cloud Computing is, the confusion surrounding the different cloud computing deployment model viz., Public, Private, Hybrid and Community cloud, traditional cloud computing architecture and the relevance of reliability, fault tolerance and QoS in Clouds have been discussed.

Foreword

Security in cloud computing is a very important topic to discuss, as most of data storage and access in our world today is happening around cloud computing where remote servers are networked to provide an option to store data. To store the data in a secure manner, to access it and modify it securely is of paramount importance where data access can be private, public or hybrid. There are various security threats that could dampen the advantage that cloud computing offers. There is no doubt that cloud computing has made life easier, but security of cloud data is a very big concern. This book with various discussions around cloud computing security is thus a helpful resource.

There is a saying that prevention is better than cure. If we can act with technology foresight, most of the network related security attacks can be prevented or at least the damage can be limited. Sometimes it is a case of following basic security guidelines, but at times the attackers could get smarter. Topics like could security, abuse of cloud computing, security architecture, trust calculation using fuzzy logic, access control framework, big data challenges in cloud computing, reliable cloud computing, enhancing privacy and security in big data etc are some topics that interested me.

There is many more research that could be done in cloud computing security as there are numerous open problems when we store sensitive information in a networked environment.

Sincerely yours,

Biju Issac
CEng, FHEA, SMIEEE School of Computing, Teesside University, England, UK

Biju Issac *is a senior lecturer at the School of Computing, Teesside University, United Kingdom, and has more than 15 years of academic experience with higher education in India, Malaysia, and the United Kingdom. He has earned a PhD in networking and mobile communications, along with MCA (master of computer applications) and BE (electronics and communications engineering). He is a senior Institute of Electrical and Electronics Engineers (IEEE) member, a fellow of the Higher Education Academy, an Institution of Engineering and Technology (IET) member, and a chartered engineer (CEng). He is a CISCO-Certified Network Associate (CCNA) instructor, a Sun-Certified Java instructor, and a Lotus Notes professional. His broad research interests are in computer networks, wireless networks, computer or network security, mobility management in 802.11 networks, intelligent computing, data mining, spam detection, secure online voting, e-learning, and so forth. Dr. Issac has authored more than 60 peer-reviewed research publications.*

Preface

Today, many institutions and companies are involved in various cloud computing security researches that involve improvement of security in terms of concepts, protocols, applications, methods, and tools. To help capture the rapid growth in cloud concepts and applications and chart the future direction in this field, a resource compiling current advances in cloud computing is essential.

Cloud computing can simply be defined as services provided over the Internet, such as e-mail, Web hosting and data storage. Cloud computing has evolved from these traditionally used services to more complex services like customer relationship management tools and marketing programs.

One of cloud computing's primary advantages is drawn from economies of scale; providers of cloud computing handle all the overhead, security concerns and software or hardware updates, while providing you the core capabilities necessary to get your work done. By spreading costs over many customers, cloud computing providers can often offer services at a lower cost.

Numerous security vendors are now leveraging cloud based models to deliver security solutions. This shift has occurred for a variety of reasons including greater economies of scale and streamlined delivery mechanisms. Regardless of the motivations for offering such services, consumers are now faced with evaluating security solutions which do not run on premises. Consumers need to understand the unique nature of cloud delivered security services so that they are in a position to evaluate the services and to understand if they will meet their needs.

Users need to understand the Cloud Security mechanisms comprehensively. Comprehensive knowledge on security is required not only for researchers and practitioners, but also for policy makers, system managers, owners and administrators. The process of building and imparting security knowledge is possible through the creation of a comprehensive collection of research on the topic. Unfortunately, such a collection of research on security does not exist.

The general aim of this book is to assess the current approaches and technologies, as well as to outline the major challenges and future perspectives, related to the cloud security mechanism. It provides an overview of the state of the art, latest techniques, studies, and approaches as well as future directions in this field.

WHY CLOUD COMPUTING MATTERS?

As cloud computing is likely to benefit organizations in the long run, it is important that they embrace and adopt it as a long-term security strategy, else, risk falling behind. Although economically viable, cloud computing can turn out to be a very expensive venture if organizations fail to implement and maintain a solid security policy for their virtual environments.

With Cloud Computing, as with many new technologies and services, information security and data protection issues are intensely debated, and examined far more critically than is the case with offerings that have been around for a while. Many surveys and studies reveal that potential customers have concerns about information security and data protection which stand in the way of a wider deployment. The required trust still needs to be developed if cloud offerings are to be taken advantage of.

A study conducted by *MITSloan – Management Review* (http://sloanreview.mit.edu/article/the-impact-of-it-investments-on-profits/) showed that a net dollar of IT investment resulted in a greater than twelve-dollar increase in sales per employee, generating a compelling return on investment. So IT appears to be *beneficial*, but is cloud computing *strategic*? After all, it's hard to believe that a firm can develop competitive advantage through the use of, say, cloud-based conference-room-scheduling software or expense-reporting tools. While there are such utilitarian applications, at the other extreme, the cloud can be strategic, and potentially existential.

In most markets, winning typically requires better products, better processes, or better customer relationships, or, "value disciplines" of either *product leadership*, *operational excellence*, or *customer intimacy*. How does the cloud enable or accentuate these generic strategies?

As our world becomes increasingly connected, mobilized, and digitalized, cloud-based capabilities increasingly contribute to *product leadership*. For instance, an iPad is surely a wondrous device, but a majority of its value and infinite extensibility is unlocked by apps from the Apple App Store and the access to content and services that many of those apps in turn offer. Beyond high-tech Internet-centric products, however, cloud-enabled IT is permeating every facet of society, that record routes taken and connect to social network communities, to smart grid electric utilities, to automobiles that allow access to apps. No doubt, cloud is the embodiment of these networks, made tangible by a product-service system endpoint, whether smartphone or sedan. *Operational excellence* can be enhanced via the cloud in a variety of ways. Within the firm, time can be compressed through cloud-enabled agility, and operations can be optimized through big data analytics. *Customer intimacy* is not only enabled by the cloud, but can become frictionless as customer preferences are passively tabulated and diligently analyzed. For example, Netflix or Amazon can make recommendations based not just on one customer's past behaviors, but informed by subtle patterns and preferences identified through complex algorithms applied to tens or hundreds of millions of customers, transactions, and moments of truth. The cloud is thus inextricably interwoven with personalization and contextualization, not to mention convenience and quality of user experience.

Sure, the cloud can be mundane and tactical, easing the mechanics of running data centers or reducing costs. But more importantly, the cloud can be a source of competitive advantage through operational excellence, customer intimacy, product/service leadership, and accelerated innovation. Ultimately, the cloud is the an example of Schumpeterian creative destruction: creating wealth for those who exploit it; and leading to the demise of those that don't.

Basic common benefits of cloud computing are describes in this book are summarized as follows:

- *Costs reduction and increased in scalability* - Adding up the licensing fees for multiple users can prove to be very expensive for the establishment concerned. The cloud, on the other hand, is available at much cheaper rates and hence, can significantly lower the company's IT expenses.

- *Almost Unlimited Storage* - Storing information in the cloud gives almost unlimited storage capacity. Hence, no more need to worry about running out of storage space or increasing current storage space availability.
- *Backup and Recovery* - Since all data is stored in the cloud, backing it up and restoring the same is relatively much easier than storing the same on a physical device. Furthermore, most cloud services are usually competent enough to handle recovery of information. Hence, this makes the entire process of backup and recovery much simpler than other traditional methods of data storage.
- *Automatic Software Integration* - In the cloud, software integration is usually something that occurs automatically. This means that there is no need to take additional efforts to customize and integrate applications as per preferences. This aspect usually takes care of itself. Not only that, cloud computing allows customizing options with great ease. Hence, one can handpick just those services and software applications that will best suit particular enterprise.
- *Globalize your workforce on the cheap* - Once registered in the cloud, one can access the information from anywhere, where there is an Internet connection. This convenient feature lets one move beyond time zone and geographic location issues.

Given the increasing popularity of cloud computing, more and more organizations are migrating their data and applications to the cloud. As a result, there are many concerns for cloud service providers and users. Some of these concerns are illustrated below. Details of such concerns are explained in many chapters of this book.

- *Changes to business model* - Cloud computing changes the way in which IT services are delivered. As servers, storage and applications are provided by off-site external service providers, organizations need to evaluate the risks associated with the loss of control over the infrastructure.
- *Abusive use of Cloud computing* - Cloud computing provides several utilities including bandwidth and storage capacities. Some vendors also give a predefined trial period for use of their services. However, they do not have sufficient control over the attackers, malicious users, or spammers who can take advantage of the trials. These can often allow an intruder to plant a malicious attack and provide a platform for serious attacks. Areas of concern include password and key cracking, etc. Such threats affect the IaaS and PaaS service models.
- *Insecure interfaces and API* - Cloud providers often publish a set of APIs to allow their customers to design an interface for interacting with Cloud services. These interfaces often add a layer on top of the framework, which in turn increases the complexity of the Cloud. Such interfaces allow vulnerabilities (in the existing API) to move to the Cloud environment. Improper use of such interfaces often poses threats such as clear-text authentication, transmission of content, improper authorizations, etc. Such types of threats may affect the IaaS, PaaS, and SaaS service models.
- *Malicious insiders* - Most of the organizations hide their policies regarding the level of access granted to employees and their recruitment procedure. However, by using a higher level of access, an employee can gain access to confidential data and services. Due to the lack of transparency in the Cloud provider's process and procedure, insiders often have considerable privileges. Insider activities are often bypassed by a Firewall or Intrusion Detection system (IDS) which assumes this to be legal activity. However, a trusted insider may turn into an adversary. In such a situation, insiders can significantly affect Cloud service offerings, for example, malicious insiders can access

confidential data and gain control over the Cloud services with no risk of detection. This type of threat may be relevant to the SaaS, PaaS, and IaaS.

- *Shared technology issues/multi-tenancy nature* - In multi-tenant architecture, virtualization offers shared on-demand services which mean that the same application is shared among different users having access to a virtual machine. However, as highlighted earlier, vulnerabilities in a hypervisor allow a malicious user to gain access to and control of the legitimate users' virtual machines. IaaS services are delivered using shared resources, which may not be designed to provide strong isolation for such multi-tenant architectures. This may affect the overall architecture of the Cloud because it allows one tenant to interfere in the other's space, and may therefore, affect normal operations. This type of threat affects IaaS.
- *Data loss and leakage* - Data may be compromised via either deletion or modification. Due to the dynamic and shared nature of the Cloud, such threats could prove to major issues leading to data theft. Examples of such threats may be lack of authentication, authorization, and audit control, weak encryption algorithms, weak keys, risk of association, unreliable data center, and lack of disaster recovery. This threat is applicable to SaaS, PaaS, and IaaS.
- *Service hijacking* - Service hijacking may redirect the client to an illegitimate website. User accounts and service instances could in turn create a new base for attackers. Phishing attacks, fraud, exploitation of software vulnerabilities, reused credentials, and passwords may provide channels opportunities for hijacking. This threat can affect IaaS, PaaS, and SaaS.
- *Risk profiling* - Cloud offerings make organizations less involved with ownership and maintenance of hardware and software. This offers significant advantages. However, these make them unaware of internal security procedures, security compliance, hardening, patching, auditing, and logging processes and expose the organization to greater risk.
- *Identity theft* - Identity theft is a form of fraud in which, a person pretends to be someone else, to access resources or obtain credit and other benefits. The victim (of the identity theft) can suffer adverse consequences and losses and be held accountable for the perpetrator's actions. Relevant security risks here, include weak password recovery workflows, phishing attacks, key loggers etc. This affects SaaS, PaaS, and IaaS as well.

OBJECTIVE

The general aim of this book is to assess the current approaches and technologies, as well as to outline the major challenges and future perspectives, related to the cloud security mechanism. It provides an overview of the state of the art, latest techniques, studies, and approaches as well as future directions in this field.

TARGET AUDIENCE

This book is expected to get a large amount of attention in the cyber security realm. This will cover all emerging negative uses of technologies which will allow individuals to gain insight so they can better defend these new attacks. This can be used by training organization, intelligence community, researchers, scholars, postgraduate students and developers who are interested in Cloud Security Management.

APPROACH

This handbook incorporate the basic concepts of cloud computing security as well as design techniques, architecture and application areas. It also addresses advanced security issues such as digital forensic, big data, access control and fault tolerance etc. The chapters are organized as follows:

Chapter 1: "Cloud Computing Security Issues" This chapter discussed security risks on adoption to cloud computing, the risks related to privacy, trust, control, data ownership, data location, audits and reviews, business continuity and disaster recovery, legal, regulatory and compliance, security policy and emerging security threats and attacks.

Chapter 2: "Cloud computing security: Abuse and nefarious use of cloud computing" This chapter will explore and investigate the scope and magnitude of one of the top cloud computing security threats "abuse and nefarious use of cloud computing" and present some of the attacks specific to this top threat as it represents a major barrier for decision makers to adopting cloud computing model.

Chapter 3: "Cloud Security Using Ear Biometrics" This chapter presents biometrics as an authentication method and as a general security feature for cloud. This chapter provides with the stepping stone for future researches to unveil how biometrics can change the cloud security scenario.

Chapter 4: "Secure Architecture for Cloud Environment" This chapter identify the most vulnerable security threats/attacks in cloud computing, which will enable both end users and vendors to know about the key security threats associated with cloud computing and propose relevant solution directives to strengthen security in the Cloud environment. This chapter also discusses secure cloud architecture for organizations to strengthen the security.

Chapter 5: "Governance and Risk Management in the Cloud with Cloud Controls Matrix V3 and ISO/IEC 38500:2008" This chapter discusses how Governance and Risk Management domain (GRM) of Cloud Controls Matrix (CSA CCM) V3 Framework from Cloud Security Alliance (CSA) and the ISO/IEC 38500:2008 standard for IT Governance can be utilized together for an effective Governance and Risk Management of Cloud Services.

Chapter 6: "Authentication and Error Resilience in Images Transmitted through Open Environment" In this chapter, an error-resistant approach is investigated to add to low cost image authentication scheme to increase visual quality as well as improve author and user satisfaction. The image authentication includes content based digital signature that is watermarked and later diffused in the whole image before JPEG2000 coding. To tackle manipulations in the image, edge information of the image is examined to offset manipulations in the image transmission through noisy or open and unsecure channels.

Chapter 7: "Trust Calculation using Fuzzy Logic in Cloud Computing" This chapter first provides the basic introduction to cloud computing and fuzzy logic. On the basis of extensive literature survey, this chapter discusses trust and its need, in addition to use of fuzzy logic for the purpose of trust calculation in distributed environments and cloud computing till now. At the end of this chapter, the difficulties and applications of using fuzzy logic for trust evaluation are discussed along with research directions for future.

Chapter 8: "Advances in Information, Security, Privacy & Ethics: Use of Cloud computing For Education" This chapter discusses the cloud security, privacy, and ethical mechanisms required from a teacher, student, and administrator perspective.

Chapter 9: "Networked Multimedia Communication Systems" This Chapter simply contains multimedia - an integrated and interactive presentation of speech, audio, video, graphics and text, has become a major theme in today's information technology that merges the practices of communications, computing and information processing into an interdisciplinary field. The challenge of multimedia communications is to provide services that integrate text, sound, image and video information and to do it in a way that preserves the case of use and interactivity. A brief description of the elements of multimedia systems is presented.

Chapter 10: "Data Security Issues and Solutions in Cloud Computing" In this chapter, a new Third Party Auditor based scheme has been proposed for secured storage and retrieval of client's data to and from the cloud service provider. The scheme has been analysed and compared with some of the existing schemes with respect to the security issues. From the analysis and comparison it can be observed that the proposed scheme performs better than the existing schemes.

Chapter 11: "Improving Privacy and Security in Multicloud Architecture" The use of multiple cloud providers for gaining security and privacy benefits is nontrivial. As the approaches investigated in this chapter clearly show, there is no single optimal approach to foster both security and legal compliance in an applicable manner. Moreover, the approaches that are favorable from a technical perspective appear less appealing from a regulatory point of view, and vice versa.

Chapter 12: "Hard clues in soft environments The Cloud's influence on digital forensics" The increasing frequency of digital investigations brings with it the need to study specific scenarios in the area of forensics, both when evidence are inside the cloud and when the cloud can be used as platform to perform the investigations. This chapter highlights the problems forensics must deal with in the Cloud, highlighting specific requirements and desired functionalities, the state of the art and future issues.

Chapter 13: "Security Challenges for Cloud Computing Development Framework in Saudi Arabia" Despite having many advantages for IT organizations, cloud has some issues that must be consider during its deployment. The main concerns are security, privacy and trust. These issues arise during the deployment of mostly public cloud infrastructure. In this chapter, security, privacy and trust issues of cloud computing deployment in Saudi Arabia were identified and the solutions to overcome these problems were discussed.

Chapter 14: "Big Data Security: Challenges, Recommendations and Solutions" Big Data sharing brings new information security and privacy issues. Traditional technologies and methods are no longer appropriate and lack of performance when applied in Big Data context. This chapter presents Big Data security challenges and a state of the art in methods, mechanisms and solutions used to protect data-intensive information systems.

Chapter 15: "Access Control Framework for Cloud Computing" *This* chapter presents the RBAC framework that protects the sensitive information in the cloud, specifies the privacy policies for the private cloud; and protects the data from hackers. Two scenarios has been presented. Scenario 1 deals with what if is present in a number of groups and the access rights that are given to him/her are different whereas scenario 2 deals with shareable resources be handled in this framework. Algorithm has been presented to support the scenarios.

Chapter 16: "Big Data-An Emerging Field of Data Engineering" This chapter presents many technical issues regarding big data which includes heterogeneity level, lack of layout, error-handling, security, timeliness and visualization at all levels of the analysis processing from data acquisition stage to conclusion interpretation. These technical issues are more common across a large distinguish of application task area. Furthermore, these issues will acquire transformation conclusions, and will not be specified naturally by the future generation of products.

Chapter 17: "Achieving Efficient Purging in Transparent per-file Secure Wiping Extensions" This Chapter presents an efficient and reliable transparent per-file-wiping file system extension called restfs. Instead of overwriting at file level which is found in existing wiping extensions, restfs overwrites at block level to exploit the behavior of file systems for efficiency (reduction in number of block overwrites and disk writes issued) and reliability (sustainability across system crashes). restfs is design compatible with all file systems which export block allocation map of a file to VFS; however it is currently implemented for ext2 file system.

Chapter 18: "Reliability, Fault Tolerance and Quality-of-Service in Cloud Computing: Analysing Characteristics" In this Chapter, the current consensus of what Cloud Computing is, the confusion surrounding the different cloud computing deployment model viz., Public, Private, Hybrid and Community cloud, traditional cloud computing architecture and the relevance of reliability, fault tolerance and QoS in Clouds have been discussed.

Acknowledgment

We extend our thanks to the many people who contributed to the preparation of this book. In particular, we heartily thanks all the contributing authors. We greatly appreciate reviewers for their helpful and insightful comments, thorough technical reviews, constructive criticisms, and many valuable suggestions.

We are indebted to the management and staff of IGI Global for their valuable contribution, suggestions, recommendations, and encouragements from inception of initial ideas to the final publication of the book. In particular, we would like to thanks Allison McGinniss for her initial contributions and support. And most importantly, we are grateful to Caitlyn Martin for the great help received from her throughout the final stages.

Deep appreciation goes to Dr. Biju Issac for providing us with constructive and comprehensive foreword.

The editors wish to acknowledge University of Hafr Al-Batin, Saudi Arabia for their support in providing the various facilities utilized in the process of production of this book.

This work was supported by Deanship of Scientific Research program of the University of Hafr Al-Batin, Saudi Arabia.

Kashif Munir
King Fahd University of Petroleum & Minerals, Saudi Arabia

Mubarak S. Almutairi
King Fahd University of Petroleum & Minerals, Saudi Arabia

Lawan A. Mohammed
King Fahd University of Petroleum & Minerals, Saudi Arabia

Chapter 1
Security Issues in Cloud Computing

Subhash Chandra Patel
Indian Institute of Technology (BHU), India

R.S. Singh
Indian Institute of Technology (BHU), India

Sumit Jaiswal
Indian Institute of Technology (BHU), India

ABSTRACT

Cloud computing is a computing style in which scalable and flexible IT functionalities are delivered as a service to external customers using Internet technologies. As cloud computing continues to gain more momentum in the IT industry, more issues and challenges are being reported by academics and practitioners. Cloud computing is not a revolutionary idea; Instead, it is an evolutionary concept that integrates various existing technologies to offer a useful new IT provisioning tool. In this chapter, security risks are discussed on adoption to cloud computing, the risks related to privacy, trust, control, data ownership, data location, audits and reviews, business continuity and disaster recovery, legal, regulatory and compliance, security policy and emerging security threats and attacks.

INTRODUCTION

Recently Cloud computing has emerged as an obliging paradigm for delivering and managing services over the internet. The boom of Cloud computing is quickly changing the concept of information technology, and utility computing exists into a reality by ultimately turning the long-held promise. It realizing the utility computing model since it is heavily driven by industry vendors. It drew attention of business owners with its ability to reduced overhead of provisioning plan, and its low cost service provisioning facilities. It allows enterprises to start with small scale and dynamically increases their resources simultaneously with the increase of their service demand. Cloud computing promises to deliver reliable services through next-generation datacenters built on virtualized compute and storage technologies. Users will be able to access applications and data from a

DOI: 10.4018/978-1-4666-8387-7.ch001

Cloud anywhere in the world following the pay-as you-go financial model (Shawish & Salama, 2014). A Cloud is datacenter hardware and software that the vendors use to offer the computing resources and services. It represents both the cloud & the provided services. With such speedy progressing of the Cloud Computing and emerging in most of the enterprise business and scientific research areas, it becomes crucial to understand all aspects about this technology. The aim of this chapter is to provide a complete overview on the Cloud Computing through a comprehensive descriptions and discussion of all aspects of this technology and respective risks.

The security of the data across the Cloud is gaining a great interest due to its sensitivity. Similarly the Service Level Agreement that drives the relation between the provider and the consumer becomes also of a great significance. This chapter discusses the Cloud security related aspects in terms of the Service Level Agreements, service cost, service pricing, and security issue and challenges facing the new paradigm also; such as security, availability and resources management; should be carefully considered in future research in order to guarantee the long-term success of Cloud Computing.

BACKGROUND

Cloud Computing has accelerated business and technological initiatives that promise to provide services at comparably low infrastructure and operating costs. The rapid growth of cloud computing is a good example (Onwubiko, 2010). The popularity of Cloud services has increased immensely over the past few years. Cloud computing is a large-scale distributed computing paradigm that is driven by economies of scale, in which a pool of abstracted, virtualized, dynamically-scalable, managed computing power, storage, platforms, and services are delivered on demand to external customers over the Internet (Giordanelli &

Mastroianni, 2010). It's a set of approaches that can help organizations quickly, effectively add and subtract resources in almost real time. It has a revolution in the way it will change the way we deploy technology and how we think about the economics of computing (Irakoze, 2013). It is an Internet-based computing solution where shared resources/services are provided like electricity distributed on the electrical grid. It is a computing model providing web-based software, middleware and computing resources on demand, in which services, resources, and applications are provided on metered basis over the Internet (Patel, Umrao, & Singh, 2012). Cloud applications extend their accessibility through the Internet by using large data centers' and powerful servers that host web applications and services. Anyone with a suitable Internet connection and a standard Internet browser can access a cloud application (Hung & Lin, 2013). Rapid evolution of cloud computing technologies can easily confuse its definition perceived by the public. Yet, there are five key attributes to distinguish cloud computing from its conventional counterpart as shown in figure 1:

- Service-based
- Scalable and elastic
- Shared
- Metered by usage
- Uses Internet technologies

Services and Deployment Models of Cloud Computing

The cloud computing provide basically three type of services as shown in figure 1.

Software as a service (SaaS) in which the cloud service provider provides applications and software over a network. SaaS uses the Web to deliver applications that are managed by a third-party vendor and whose interface is accessed on the clients' side. Most SaaS applications can be run directly from a Web browser, without any downloads or installations required Google Docs,

Figure 1. Relationship between various models and characteristic of cloud
(*Source: http://mrbool.com/cloud-computing-and-security-issues/29894#ixzz3D066UQJx*)

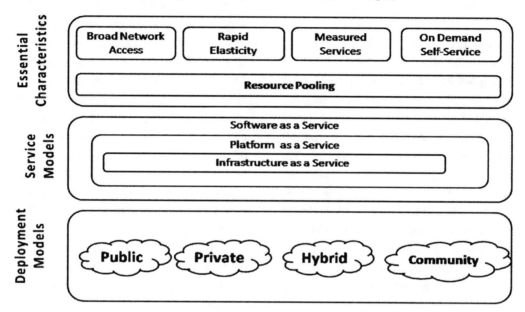

Facebook, Gmail, Yahoo are the example of SaaS (Patel, Umrao, & Singh, 2012).

Platform as a Service (PaaS) provides application or development platform in which user can create their own application that run on the cloud. PaaS allows you to create applications using software components that are controlled by a third-party vendor, PaaS is highly scalable, and users don't have to worry about platform upgrades or having their site go down during maintenance, for example of PaaS are Microsoft's Azure, Google's App Engine(App Engine), Yahoo Pig (Patel, Umrao, & Singh, 2012).

Third type of cloud service is *Infrastructure as a service (IaaS),* the whole cloud infrastructure, including servers, routers, hardware based load-balancing, firewalls, storage and other network equipment is provided by the IaaS provider i.e. Amazon S3, Amazon EC2 (Patel, Umrao, & Singh, 2012).

The cloud computing can be deployed as *public cloud, private cloud, hybrid cloud* and *community cloud.* Public clouds are publicly available and can serve multiple tenants, examples of public

Cloud: Google App Engine, Microsoft Windows Azure, IBM Smart Cloud and Amazon EC2 while private cloud is typically a tailored environments with dedicated virtualized resources for particular organization examples of private clouds are Eucalyptus, Ubuntu Enterprise Cloud – UEC, Amazon VPC (Virtual Private Cloud), VMware Cloud Infrastructure Suite, Microsoft ECI data center. Similarly, community cloud is tailored for a particular group of customers Google Apps for Government, Microsoft Government Community Cloud are the example of community cloud. Hybrid cloud is composed of multiple clouds like Windows Azure (capable of Hybrid Cloud), VMwarevCloud (Hybrid Cloud Services) (Patel, Umrao, & Singh, 2012).

Cloud service is based on Web Services and Web Services are based on Internet. Internet has many inherent security flaws because of its openness, and it also has many other attacks and threats. Therefore, cloud services will face a wide range of security issues (Patel, Umrao, & Singh, 2012).

SECURITY ISSUES IN CLOUD COMPUTING

With the growing popularity of cloud computing, security issues are showing in figure 2, which show the importance of a gradual upward trend has become an important factor restricting the development (Ming & Yongsheng, 2012). There comes an increasingly frequent cloud computing security incident. According to international data corporation (IDC)'s survey, 87.5% of users worry about security issues in cloud computing. Obviously, security ranked first as the greatest challenge or issue of cloud computing. Gartner 2009-year survey also stated that 70% of respondents believe that the recent CTO of cloud computing without the use of the primary reasons is that there is data security and privacy concern.

The cloud computing is a recent development, insights into critical aspects of security can be gathered from reported experiences of early adopters and also from researchers analyzing and experimenting with available service provider platforms and associated technologies (Jansen, Grance, 2011and Chandrarcddy, Mahesh,2012). The issues are organized into several general categories: trust, architecture, identity management, software isolation, data protection, and availability. Because cloud computing has grown out of an merging of technologies, including service oriented architecture, virtualization, Web 2.0, and utility computing, many of the security issues involved can be viewed as known problems cast in a new setting.

Trust- Trust is a complex concept for which there is no universally accepted scholarly definition. *"Taking someone into trust or trusting fully on someone is very difficult and dangerous in any scenario especially in cloud computing environments"*. Evidence from a contemporary,

Figure 2. Security issues in cloud computing
(Source: IDC Enterprise Panel, August 2008)

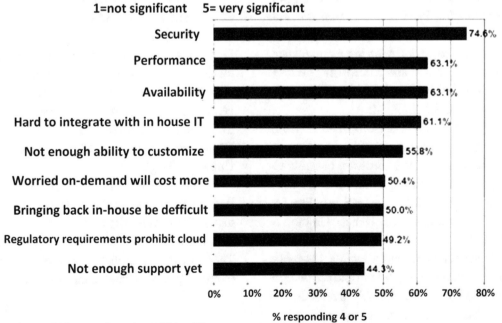

Rate the challenges/issues as scribed to the 'cloud'/on-demand model

1=not significant   5= very significant

Challenge	% responding 4 or 5
Security	74.6%
Performance	63.1%
Availability	63.1%
Hard to integrate with in house IT	61.1%
Not enough ability to customize	55.8%
Worried on-demand will cost more	50.4%
Bringing back in-house be defficult	50.0%
Regulatory requirements prohibit cloud	49.2%
Not enough support yet	44.3%

% responding 4 or 5

Source: IDC Enterprise Panel, August 2008, n=244

cross-disciplinary collection of scholarly writing suggests that a widely held definition of trust is as follows: *"Trust is a psychological state comprising the intention to accept vulnerability based upon positive expectations of the intentions or behavior of another"*. (Pearson, Casassa, Mont, & Crane, 2005 and Rousseau, Sitkin, Burt & Camerer, 1998).

This definition does not yet fully capture the dynamic and varied refinements involved. For example: letting the trustees take care of something the trustor cares about (Baier, 1986), the subjective probability with which the trustor assesses that the trustee will perform a particular action. The expectation that the trustee will not engage in opportunistic behavior, a belief, attitude, or expectation concerning the likelihood that the actions or outcomes of the trustee will be acceptable or will serve the trustor's interests (Gambetta,1988, Nooteboom, 2007, Sitkin, & Roth, 1993). Trust is a broader notion than security as it includes subjective criteria and experience. Correspondingly, there exist both *hard (security-oriented) and soft trust (i. e. non-security oriented trust) solutions* (Pearson, 2012 and Wang & Lin, 2008). *"Hard"* trust involves aspects like authenticity, encryption, and security in transactions, whereas *"soft"* trust involves human psychology, brand loyalty, and user friendliness (Singh, and Morley, 2009) Some soft issues are involved in security; an example of soft trust is reputation, which is a component of online trust that is perhaps a company's most valuable asset (Osterwalder, 2001). Brand image is associated with trust and suffers if there is a breach of trust or privacy. People often find it harder to trust on-line services than off-line services, often because in the digital world there is an absence of physical cues and there may not be established centralized authorities (Best, Kreuger & Ladewig, 2005 and Chang, Dillon & Calder, 2008). The distrust of on-line services can even negatively affect the level of trust accorded to organizations that may have been long respected as trustworthy (Jaeger, Fleischmann,

2007). There are many different ways in which on-line trust can be established: security may be one of these some would argue that security is not even a component of trust: Nissenbaum (1999) argues that the level of security does not affect trust. On the other hand, an example of increasing security to increase trust comes from people being more willing to engage in ecommerce if they are assured that their credit card numbers and personal data are cryptographically protected (Giff, 2000). There can be differing phases in a relationship such as building trust, a stable trust relationship and declining trust. Trust can be lost quickly: as Nielsen (1999) states *"It [trust] is hard to build and easy to lose: a single violation of trust can destroy years of slowly accumulated credibility"*. Various approaches have targeted to measurement of factors that influence trust and the analysis of related causal relationships (Huynh, 2008). Many trust metrics have traditionally relied on a graph and have dealt with trust propagation (Ziegler, & Lausen 2004). When assessing trust in relation to cloud computing, it may be useful to distinguish between social and technological means of providing *persistent and dynamic trust*, as all of these aspects of trust can be necessary (Pearson, Casassa Mont, Crane, 2005).

Persistent Trust

Persistent trust is trust in long-term underlying properties or infrastructure; this arises through relatively static social and technological mechanisms.

Dynamic Trust

Dynamic trust is trust specific to certain states, contexts, or short-term or variable information; this can arise through context-based social and technological mechanisms. Persistent social-based trust in a hardware or software component or system is an expression of confidence in technological-based trust, because it is assurance about implementation and operation of that component or system. In particular, there are links between social-based trust and technological-based trust through the vouching mechanism, because it is important to know who is vouching for something as well as what they are vouching; hence social-based trust should always be considered (Pearson, 2012).

The interactions between different service domains driven by service requirements can be expected to be very dynamic/transient and intensive. Thus, a trust management framework should be developed to efficiently capture a generic set of parameters required for establishing trust and to manage evolving trust and interaction/sharing requirements (Takabi, James, Joshi & Joon, 2013). Furthermore, the customers' behavior can evolve rapidly, thereby affecting established trust values. Efficient techniques are needed to manage evolving trust. This suggests a need for a trust management approach to support the establishment, negotiation and maintenance of trust to adaptively support policy integration (Shin & Gail, 2005 and Zhang & Joshi, 2009). There exist some critical questions that need to be answered: How do we establish trust and determine access mapping to satisfy inter-domain access requirements? How do we manage and maintain dynamically changing trust values and adapt the access requirements as trust evolves? One of the solutions to get ride-off security risk concern with trust is the Service Level Agreement. A service-level agreement is a negotiated agreement between two parties, where one is the customer and the other is the service provider. This can be a legally binding formal or an informal "contract" (for example, internal department relationships).

Insider Access- Most companies focus their resources and defensive strategies on protecting the perimeter from outsider attacks but often the greatest damage can be done by someone already inside these defenses (Brad, 2009). System administrators can be a company's most trusted ally or their worst nightmare depending on their motivation or personal interest. Data processed or stored outside an organization's physical boundary, its firewall, and other security controls bring an inherent level of risk technologies (Jansen, Grance, 2011 and Chandrareddy, Mahesh 2012 and Cappelli, Moore, Trzeciak & Shimeall, 2009). Moving data and applications to an external cloud computing environment expands the insider security risk not only to the service provider's staff, but also potentially among other customers using the service. The insider security threat is a well-known issue for most organizations and, despite the name, applies as well to outsourced cloud services technologies (Jansen & Grance, 2011 and Chandrareddy & Mahesh,2012). Insider threats go beyond those posed by current or former employees to include organizational affiliates, contractors, and other parties that have received access to an organization's networks, systems, and data to carry out or facilitate operations. Incidents may involve various types of fraud, sabotage of information resources, and theft of information. Incidents may also be caused unintentionally technologies (Jansen &Grance, 2011and Chandrareddy & Mahesh, 2012). For example, an internal denial of service attack against the Amazon Elastic Compute Cloud (EC2) was demonstrated that involved a service user creating an initial 20 accounts and launching virtual machine instances for each, when using those accounts to create an additional 20 accounts and machine instances in an iterative fashion to grow and consume resources exponentially (Jansen & Grance, 2011 and Chandrareddy & Mahesh 2012 and Slaviero 2009).

Composite Services- Cloud services can be composed with other cloud services through nesting and layering (Jansen & Grance, 2011and Chandrareddy & Mahesh,2012). For instance, a SaaS provider could build its services upon those of a PaaS or IaaS cloud. Cloud service providers that subcontract some services to third-party service providers should raise concerns, including the scope of control over the third-party, the responsibilities involved, and the remedies and recourse available should problems occur. Trust is often not transitive, requiring that third-party arrangements be disclosed in advance of reaching an agreement with the service provider, and that the terms of these arrangements are maintained throughout the agreement or until sufficient notification can be given of any anticipated changes (Janse & Grance, 2011and Chandrareddy & Mahesh 2012 and Brodkin, 2008). Liability and performance guarantees can become a serious issue with composite cloud services. The Linkup, an online storage service that closed down after losing access to a significant amount of data from its 20,000 customers, illustrates such a situation. Because another company, Nirvanix, hosted the data for The Linkup, and yet another, Savvies, hosted its application and database, direct responsibility for the cause of the failure was unclear (Jansen & Grance, 2011 and Chandrareddy &Mahesh, 2012 and Brodkin, 2008).

Visibility- Migration to cloud services gives up control to the service provider for securing the systems on which the organization's data and applications operate. To avoid creating gaps in security, management, procedural, and technical controls must be applied commensurately with those used for internal organizational systems. The task is formidable, since metrics for comparing the security of two computer systems are an ongoing area of research (Jansen & Grance, 2011 and Chandrareddy & Mahesh, 2012 and Jansen, 2009). Moreover, network and system level monitoring by the user is generally outside the scope of most service arrangements, limiting visibility and the means to audit operations directly. To ensure that policy and procedures are being enforced throughout the system lifecycle, service arrangements should contain some means for gaining visibility into the security controls and processes employed the service provider, as well as their performance over time (Jansen, Grance, 2011 and Chandrareddy & Mahesh, 2012)

Risk- "*Risk is the possibility that an event will occur and adversely affect the achievement of objectives*". The types of risks (e.g., security, integrity, availability, and performance) are the same with systems in the cloud as they are with non-cloud technology solutions (LLP, Chan, Leung & Pili, 2012). An organization's level of risk and risk profile will in most cases change if cloud solutions are adopted (depending on how and for what purpose the cloud solutions are used). This is due to the increase or decrease in likelihood and impact with respect to the risk events (inherent and residual) associated with the CSP that has been engaged for services. Some of the typical risks associated with cloud computing are:

Disruptive force- When an industry member adopts cloud solutions, other organizations in the industry could be forced to follow suit and adopt cloud computing (LLP, Chan, Leung & Pili, 2012).

Residing in the same risk ecosystem as the CSP and other tenants of the cloud- When an organization adopts third-party-managed cloud solutions, new dependency relationships with the CSP are created with respect to legal liability, the risk universe, incident escalation, incident response, and other areas. The actions of the CSP and fellow cloud tenants can impact the organization in various ways. Consider the following:

Legally, if the CSP neglects or fails in its responsibilities, it could have legal liability implications for the CSP's customer organizations. But if a cloud customer organization fails in its responsibilities, it is less likely there would be any legal implications to the CSP (LLP, Chan, Leung & Pili, 2012). Cloud service providers and their customer organizations are likely to have separate enterprise risk management (ERM) programs to address their respective universe of perceived risks. Only in a minority of cases (involving very high-dollar contracts) will CSPs attempt to integrate portions of their ERM programs with those of their customers. The universe of risks confronting an organization using third-party cloud computing is a combination of risks the individual organization faces along with a subset of the risks that its CSP is facing (LLP, Chan, Leung & Pili, 2012)

Lack of transparency- A CSP is unlikely to disclose detailed information about its processes, operations, controls, and methodologies. For instance, cloud customers have little insight into the storage location(s) of data, algorithms used by the CSP to provision or allocate computing resources, the specific controls used to secure components of the cloud computing architecture, or how customer data is segregated within the cloud.

Reliability and performance issues- System failure is a risk event that can occur in any computing environment but poses unique challenges with cloud computing. Although service-level agreements can be structured to meet particular requirements, CSP solutions might sometimes be unable to meet these performance metrics if a cloud tenant or incident puts an unexpected resource demand on the cloud infrastructure (Babu, & Sekhar, 2013).

Vendor lock-in and lack of application portability or interoperability- Many CSPs offer application software development tools with their cloud solutions. When these tools are proprietary, they may create applications that work only within the CSP's specific solution architecture. Consequently, these new applications (created by these proprietary tools) might not work well with systems residing outside of the cloud solution. In addition, the more applications developed with these proprietary tools and the more organizational data stored in a specific CSP's cloud solution, the more difficult it becomes to change providers (Rustan, 2012 and Babu & Sekhar, 2013).

Security and compliance concerns- Depending on the processes cloud computing is supporting, security and retention issues can arise with respect to complying with regulations and laws such as the *Sarbanes-Oxley Act of 2002* (Pincus, & Rego, 2008), the *Health Insurance Portability and Accountability Act of 1996* (HIPAA), and the various data privacy and protection regulations like *USA PATRIOT Act*, the EU Data Protection Directive, Malaysia's *Personal Data Protection Act 2010*, and India's *IT Amendments Act* are enacted in different countries. In the cloud, data is located on outside of the organization's direct control. Depending on the cloud solution used (SaaS, PaaS, or IaaS), a cloud customer organization may be unable to obtain and review network operations or security incident logs because they are in the possession of the CSP. The CSP may be under no obligation to reveal this information or might be unable to do so without violating the confidentiality of the other tenants sharing the cloud infrastructure (LLP, Chan, Leung & Pili, 2012).

High-value cyber-attack targets- The consolidation of multiple organizations operating on a CSP's infrastructure presents a more attractive target than a single organization, thus increasing the likelihood of attacks. Consequently, the inherent risk levels of a CSP solution in most cases are higher with respect to confidentiality and data integrity (LLP, Chan, Leung & Pili, 2012).

Risk of data leakage- A multi-tenant cloud environment in which user organizations and applications share resources presents a risk of data leakage that does not exist when dedicated servers and resources are used exclusively by an organization. This risk of data leakage presents an additional point of consideration with respect to meeting data privacy and confidentiality requirements (LLP, Chan, Leung & Pili, 2012).

IT organizational changes- If cloud computing is adapted to a significant degree, an organization needs fewer internal IT personnel in the areas of infrastructure management, technology deployment, application development, and maintenance. The morale and dedication of remaining IT staff members could be at risk as a result (LLP, Chan, Leung & Pili, 2012).

Cloud service provider viability- Many cloud service providers are relatively young companies, or the cloud computing business line is a new one for a well-established company. Hence the projected longevity and profitability of cloud services are unknown. At the time of publication, some CSPs are restricting their cloud service offerings because they are not profitable. Cloud computing service providers might eventually go through a consolidation period. As a result, CSP customers might face operational disruptions or incur the time and expense of researching and adopting an alternative solution, such as converting back to in-house hosted solutions (LLP, Chan, Leung & Pili, 2012).

Risk Management- A risk management process must be used to balance the benefits of cloud computing with the security risks associated with the agency handing over control to a vendor. A risk assessment should consider whether the agency is willing to trust their reputation, business continuity, and data to a vendor that may insecurely transmit, store and process the agency's data (Cyber Security Operations Centre, 2012). With cloud-based services, some subsystems or subsystem components are outside of the direct control of the organization that owns the information and authorizes use of system. Many people feel more comfortable with risk when they have more control over the processes and equipment involved. At a minimum, a high degree of control provides the option to weigh alternatives, set priorities, and act decisively in the best interest organization when faced with an incident. In choosing between an in-house solution and a cloud-based implementation, the associated risks need to be assessed in detail. Assessing and managing risk in systems that use cloud services can be a challenge. Ideally, the level of trust is based on the amount of direct control the organization is able to exert on the external service provider with regard to employment of security controls necessary for the protection of the service and the evidence brought forth as to the effectiveness of those controls (Jansen & Grance, 2011). However, verifying the correct functioning of a subsystem and the effectiveness of security controls as extensively as with an organizational system may not be feasible, and the level of trust must be based on other factors.

Architecture- The architecture of the software systems used to deliver cloud services comprises hardware and software residing in the cloud. Many of the "simplified" interfaces and service abstractions belie the inherent complexity that affects security. For instance, how will cloud architecture from one provider integrate with an organization's other third party solutions? If a company leverages cloud services from multiple providers how will this impact system integration and overall architecture? (Cloud Security Toolkit, 2012). The physical location of the infrastructure is determined by the service provider as is the implementation of reliability and scalability logic of the underlying support framework. Virtual machines (VMs) typically serve as the abstract unit of deployment and are loosely coupled with the cloud storage architecture. Applications are built on the programming interfaces of Internet-accessible services and typically involve multiple intercommunicating cloud components controls (Jansen & Grance, 2011).

Attack Surface- A hypervisor or virtual machine monitor is an additional layer of software between an operating system and hardware platform, needed to operate multi-tenant VMs and applications hosted thereupon. Besides virtualized resources, the hypervisor normally supports other programming interfaces to conduct administrative operations, such as launching, migrating, and terminating VM instances. Compared with a non-virtualized implementation, the addition of a hypervisor causes an increase in the attack surface (Jansen & Grance, 2011). The complexity in VM environments can also be more challenging than their traditional counterpart, giving rise to conditions that undermine security (Kalpana, 2012). For example, paging, check pointing, and migration of VMs can leak sensitive data to persistent storage, subverting protection mechanisms in the hosted operating system. The hypervisor itself can also be compromised. A zero-day exploit in the HyperVM virtualization application purportedly led to the destruction of approximately 100,000 virtual server based Websites hosted at Vaserv. com (Garfinkel & Rosenblum, 2005).

Virtual Network Protection - Most virtualization platforms have the ability to create software-based switches and network configurations as part of the virtual environment to allow VMs on the same host to communicate more directly and efficiently. For example, the VMware virtual networking architecture supports same-host networking in which a private subnet is created for VMs requiring no external network access. Traffic over such networks is not visible to the security protection devices on the physical network, such as network-based intrusion detection and prevention systems (Vieira, Alexandre, Carlos Westphall & Carla Westphall, 2009). To avoid a loss of visibility and protection against intra-host attacks, duplication of the physical network protections may be required on the virtual network.

Ancillary Data - While the focus of protection is placed mainly on application data, service providers also hold significant details about the service users' accounts that could be compromised and used in subsequent attacks. While payment information is one example, other, more subtle information sources can be involved. For example, a database of contact information stolen from Salesforce.com, via a targeted phishing attack against an employee, was used to launch successful targeted email attacks against users of the service (McMillan & Krebs, 2007). The incident illustrates the need for service providers to promptly report security breaches occurring not only in the data it holds for its service users, but also the data it holds about them. Another type of ancillary data is VM images. A VM image entails the software stack, including installed and configured applications, used to boot the VM into an initial state or the state of some previous checkpoint. Sharing VM images is a common practice in some cloud computing environments. Image repositories must

be carefully managed and controlled to avoid problems. The provider of an image faces risks, since an image can contain proprietary code and data. An attacker may attempt to examine images to determine whether they leak information or provide an avenue for attack (Wei, Zhang, Ammons, Bala & Ning, 2009). This is especially true of development images that are accidently released. The reverse may also occur—an attacker may attempt to Supply a VM image containing malware to users of a cloud computing system (Jensen, Schwenk, Gruschka & Iacono, 2009). For example, researchers demonstrated that by manipulating the registration process to gain a first-page listing, they could readily entice cloud users to run VM images contributed to Amazon EC2 (Slaviero, 2009).

Client-Side Protection- A successful defence against attacks requires both a secure client and a secure Website infrastructure. With emphasis typically placed on the latter, the former can be easily overlooked. Web browsers, a key element for many cloud computing services, and the various available plug-ins and extensions for them are notorious for their security problems (Slaviero, 2009; Kerner, 2010). Moreover, many browser add-ons do not provide automatic updates, increasing the persistence of existing vulnerabilities. The increased availability and use of social media, personal Webmail, and other publicly available sites also has associated risks that can impact the security of the browser, its underlying platform, and cloud service accounts negatively through social engineering attacks. For example, spyware reportedly installed in a hospital via an employee's Yahoo Webmail account sent out more than 1,000 screen captures containing financial and other confidential information to the originator before it was discovered (McMillan, 2009). Having a backdoor Trojan, keystroke logger, or other type of malware running on a client does not bode well for the security of the cloud or other Web-based services (Frei, Duebendorfer, Ollmann & May, 2008). Organizations need to employ measures to secure the client side as part of the overall architecture. Banks are beginning to take the lead in deploying hardened browser environments that encrypt network exchanges and protect against keystroke logging (Dunn, 2010).

Server-Side Protection- Virtual servers and applications, much like their non-virtualized counterparts, need to be secured in IaaS clouds. Following organizational policies and procedures, hardening of the operating system and applications should occur to produce VM images for deployment. Care must also be taken to make adjustments for the virtualized environments in which the images run. For example, virtual firewalls can be used to isolate groups of VMs from other groups hosted, such as production systems from development systems or development systems from other cloud-resident systems. Carefully managing VM images is also important to avoid accidently deploying images containing vulnerabilities.

Identity Management- One recurring issue is that the organizational identification and authentication framework may not easily integrate into the cloud. Extending or changing the existing identity management framework to support cloud services may be difficult and may result in additional expense. Data sensitivity and privacy of information have increasingly become a concern for organizations, and unauthorized access to information resources in the cloud is a major issue. One reason is that an organization's identification and authentication framework may not naturally extend into the cloud and may require effort to modify the existing framework to support cloud services (R. Chow et al., 2009). The alternative of having two different systems for use authentication, one for internal organizational systems and another for external cloud-based systems is a complication that can become unworkable over time. Identity federation, popularized with the introduction of service oriented architectures, is one solution that can be accomplished in a number of

ways, such as with the Security Assertion Mark-up Language (SAML) standard surface (Jansen & Grance, 2011).

Authentication- A growing number of cloud service providers support the SAML standard and use it to administer users and authenticate them before providing access to applications and data. SAML provides a means to exchange information, such as assertions related to a subject or authentication information, between cooperating domains. SAML request and response messages are typically mapped over the Simple Object Access Protocol (SOAP), which relies on XML for its format. With Amazon Web Services, for example, once a user has established a public key certificate, it is used to sign SOAP requests to the EC2 to interact with it. SOAP message security validation is complicated and must be carried out carefully to prevent attacks. XML wrapping attacks involving the manipulation of SOAP messages have been successfully demonstrated against Amazon's EC2 services (Gajek, Jensen, Liao & Schwenk, 2009; Gruschka & Iacono, 2009). A new element (i.e., the wrapper) is introduced into the SOAP Security header; the original message body is then moved under the wrapper and replaced by a bogus body containing an operation defined by the attacker. The original body can still be referenced and its signature verified, but the operation in the replacement body is executed instead.

Access Control- Besides authentication, the capability to adapt user privileges and maintain control over access to resources is also required, as part of identity management. Standards like the eXtensible Access Control Mark-up Language (XACML) can be employed to control access to cloud resources, instead of using a service provider's proprietary interface. XACML focuses o n the mechanism for arriving at authorization decisions, which complements SAML's focus on the means for transferring authentication and authorization decisions between cooperating entities[(Jansen & Grance, 2011; Keleta & Eloff,

2005). XACML is capable of controlling the proprietary service interfaces of most providers, and some service providers, such as salesforce.com and Google Apps, already have it in place. Messages transmitted between XACML entities are susceptible to attack by malicious third parties, making it important to have safeguards in place to protect decision requests and authorization decisions from possible attacks, including unauthorized disclosure, replay, deletion and modification (Keleta & Eloff, 2005).

Software Isolation- High degrees of multi-tenancy over large numbers of platforms are needed for cloud computing to achieve the envisioned flexibility of on-demand provisioning of reliable services and the cost benefits and efficiencies due to economies of scale. To reach the high scales of consumption desired, service providers have to ensure dynamic flexible delivery of service and isolation of user resources. Multi-tenancy in cloud computing is typically done by multiplexing the execution of VMs from potentially different users on the same physical server (Ristenpart, Tromer, Shacham & Savage, 2009). It is important to note that applications deployed on guest VMs remain susceptible to attack and compromise, much the same as their no virtualized counterparts. This was dramatically exemplified recently by a botnet found operating out of Amazon's EC2 cloud computing environment (McMillan, 2009; Whitney 2009).

Hypervisor Complexity-The security of a computer system depends on the quality of the underlying software kernel that controls the confinement and execution of processes. A hypervisor or virtual machine monitor (VMM) is designed to run multiple guest VMs, hosting operating systems and applications, concurrently on a single host computer and to provide isolation between the guest VMS (Jansen & Grance, 2011). A VMM can, in theory, be smaller and less complex than an operating system. Small size and simplicity make it easier to analyze and improve the quality of security, giving a VMM the potential to

be better suited for maintaining strong isolation between guest VMs than an operating system is for Isolating processes (Karger, 2008). In practice, however, modern hypervisors can be large and complex, comparable to an operating system, which negates this advantage. For example, Xen, an open source x86 VMM, incorporates a modified Linux kernel to implement a privileged partition for input/output operations, and KVM, another open source effort, transforms a Linux kernel into a VMM (Shah, 2008). Understanding the use of virtualization by a service provider is a prerequisite to understanding the risks involved.

Attack Vectors. Multi-tenancy in VM-based cloud infrastructures, together with the subtleties in the way physical resources are shared between guest VMs, can give rise to new sources of threats. The most serious threat is that malicious code can escape the confines of its VMM and interfere with the hypervisor or other guest VMs. Live migration, the ability to transition a VM between hypervisors on different host computers without halting the guest operating system, and other features provided by VMM environments to facilitate systems management, also increase software size and complexity and potentially add other areas to target in an attack. Several examples illustrate the types of attack vectors possible. The first is mapping the cloud infrastructure. While seemingly a daunting task to perform, researchers have demonstrated an approach with Amazon's EC2 network (Ristenpart, Tromer, Shacham & Savage, 2009). By launching multiple VM instances from multiple user accounts and using network probes, assigned IP addresses and domain names were used to identify service location patterns. Building on that information and general technique, the plausible location of a specific target VM could be identified and new VMs instantiated to be eventually co-resident with the target. Once a suitable target location is found, the next step for the guest VM is to bypass or overcome containment by the hypervisor or to takedown the hypervisor and system entirely. Weaknesses in the available programming interfaces and the processing of instructions are common targets for uncovering vulnerabilities to exploit (Ferrie, 2009). For example, vulnerability was discovered in a VMware routine handling FTP requests, allowing specially crafted requests to corrupt a heap buffer in the hypervisor, which could allow the execution of arbitrary code (Shelton, 2005). Similarly, a serious flaw that allows an attacker to write to an arbitrary out-of-bounds memory location was discovered in the PIIX4 power management code of VMware by fuzzing emulated I/O ports (Ormandy, 2007). A denial of service vulnerability was also uncovered in a virtual device driver, which could allow a guest VM to crash the VMware host along with other VMs active there (VMSA-2009). More indirect attack avenues may also be possible. For example, researchers developed a way for an attacker to gain administrative control of VMware guest VMs during a live migration, employing a man in-the-middle attack to modify the code used for authentication (Oberheide, Cooke & Jahanian, 2008). Memory modification during migration presents other possibilities such as the potential to insert a VM-base root-kit layer below the operating system (S. King et al. 2006). Another example of an indirect attack is monitoring resource utilization on a shared server to gain information and perhaps perform a side-channel attack, similar to attacks used in other computing environments (Ristenpart, Tromer, Shacham, & Savage, 2009). For example, an attacker could determine periods of high activity, estimate high-traffic rates, and possibly launch keystroke timing attacks to gather passwords and other data from a target server.

Data Protection- Data stored in the cloud typically resides in a shared environment collocated with data from other customers. Organizations moving sensitive and regulated data into the cloud, therefore, must account for the means by which access to the data is controlled and the data is kept secure (Jansen & Grance, 2011).

Data-Isolation- Data can take many forms. For example, for cloud-based application devel-

opment, it includes the application programs, scripts, and configuration settings, along with the development tools. For deployed applications, it includes records and other content created or used by the applications, as well as account information about the users of the applications. Access controls are one means to keep data away from unauthorized users; encryption is another. Access controls are typically identity-based, which makes authentication of the user's identity n important issue in cloud computing. Database environments used in cloud computing can vary significantly. For example, some environments support a multi-instance model, while others support a multi-tenant model. The former provides a unique database management system running on a VM instance for each service user, giving the user complete control over role definition, user authorization, and other administrative tasks related to security. The latter p provides a predefined environment for the cloud service user that is shared with other tenants, typically through tagging data with a user identifier. Tagging gives the appearance of exclusive use of the instance, but relies on the service provider to maintain a sound secure database environment. Various types of multi-tenant arrangements exist for databases. Each type pools resources differently, offering different degrees of isolation and resource efficiency (Jacobs & Aulbach, 2007 and Wainewright, 2008). Other considerations also apply. For example, certain features like data encryption are only viable with arrangements that use separate rather than shared databases. These sorts of tradeoffs require careful evaluation of the suitability of the data management solution for the data involved. Requirements in certain fields, such as healthcare, would likely influence the choice of database and data organization used in an application. Privacy sensitive information, in general, is a serious concern (Pearson, 2009). Data must be secured while at rest, in transit, and in use, and access to the data controlled. Standards for communications protocols and public key certificates allow data transfers to be protected using cryptography. Procedures for protecting data at rest, however, are not as well standardized, making interoperability an issue due to the predominance of proprietary systems. The lack of interoperability affects data availability and complicates the portability of applications and data between cloud service providers. Currently, the responsibility for cryptographic key management falls mainly on the cloud service subscriber. Key generation and storage is usually performed outside the cloud using hardware security modules, which do not scale well to the cloud paradigm. Work is ongoing to identify scalable and usable cryptographic key management and exchange strategies for use by government, which could help to alleviate the problem eventually. Protecting data in use is an emerging area of cryptography with few practical results to offer, leaving trust mechanisms as the main safeguard (Greenberg, 2009).

Data-Sanitization-The data sanitization practices that a service provider implements have evident significances for security. Sanitization is the removal of sensitive data from a storage device in various situations, such as when a storage device is removed from service or moved elsewhere to be stored. It also applies to backup copies made for recovery and restoration of service, and residual data remaining upon termination of service. In a cloud computing environment, data from one subscriber is physically commingled with the data of other subscribers, which can complicate matters. For example, with the proper skills and equipment, it is possible to recover data from failed drives that are not disposed of properly by service providers (Jansen & Grance, 2011).

Data Location One of the most common compliance issues facing an organization is data location. Use of an in-house computing centre allows an organization to structure its computing environment and know in detail where data is stored and the safeguards used to protect the data. In contrast, a characteristic of many cloud computing services is that the detailed information of the location of an organization's data is unavailable

or not disclosed to the service subscriber. This situation makes it difficult to ascertain whether sufficient safeguards are in place and whether legal and regulatory compliance requirements are being met. External audits and security certifications can, to some extent, alleviate this issue, but they are not a panacea. Once information crosses a national border, it is extremely difficult to guarantee protection under foreign laws and regulations. For example, the broad powers of USA Patriot Act have raised concern with some foreign governments that the provisions would allow the U.S. government to access private information, such as medical records, outsourced to American companies. Constraints on the transborder flow of unclassified sensitive data, as well as the requirements on the protection afforded the data, have become the subject of national and regional privacy and security laws and regulations (Eisenhauer, 2005). The main compliance concerns with transborder data flows include whether the laws in the jurisdiction where the data was collected permit the flow, whether those laws continue to apply to the data post-transfer, and whether the laws at the destination present additional risks or benefits (Eisenhauer, 2005). Technical, physical and administrative safeguards, such as access controls, often apply. For example, European data protection laws may impose additional obligations on the handling and processing of European data transferred to the U.S. (Shimanek, 2000).

Availability In simple terms, availability means that an organization has its full set of computing resources accessible and usable at all times. Availability can be affected temporarily or permanently, and a loss can be partial or complete. Denial of service attacks, equipment outages, and natural disasters are all threats to availability (Jansen & Grance, 2011).

Temporary Outages- Despite employing architectures designed for high service reliability and availability, cloud computing services can and do experience outages and performance slowdowns (Leavitt, 2005). Several examples illustrate this point. In February 2008, Amazon's Simple Storage Service (S3) and EC2 services suffered a three-hour outage that, in turn, affected Twitter and other startup companies using the services (Krigsma, 2008; Miller, 2008). In June 2009, a lightning storm caused a partial EC2 outage that affected some users for 4 hours. Similarly, a database cluster failure at Salesforce.com caused an outage for several hours in February 2008, and in January 2009, another brief outage occurred due to a network device failure (Ferguson, 2009; Goodin, 2009). In March 2009, Microsoft's Azure cloud service experienced severe degradation for about 22 hours due to networking issues related to an upgrade (Clarke, 2009). At a level of 99.999% reliability, 8.76 hours of downtime is to be expected in a year. The level of reliability of a cloud service and also its capabilities for backup and recovery should be taken into account in the organization's contingency planning to address the restoration and recovery of disrupted cloud services and operations, using alternate services, equipment, and locations. Cloud storage services may represent a single point of failure for the applications hosted there. In such situations, a second cloud service provider could be used to back up data processed by the primary provider to ensure that during a prolonged disruption or serious disaster at the primary, the data remains available for immediate resumption of critical operations (Jansen & Grance, 2011).

Prolonged and Permanent Outages- It is possible for a service provider to experience serious problems, like bankruptcy or facility loss, which affect service for extended periods or cause a complete shutdown. For example, in April 2009, the FBI raided computing centres in Texas and seized hundreds of servers, when investigating fraud allegations against a handful of companies that operated out of the centres (Zetter, 2009). The seizure disrupted service to hundreds of other businesses unrelated to the investigation, but who had the misfortune of having their computer operations collocated at the targeted centres. Other examples are the major data loss experienced by magnolia, a bookmark repository service, and the abrupt failure of Omnidrive, an on-line storage provider, who closed without warning to its users in 2008 (Calore & Magnolia, 2009 and Gunderloy, 2008).

Denial of Service- A denial of service attack involves saturating the target with bogus requests to prevent it from responding to legitimate requests in a timely manner. An attacker typically uses multiple computers or a botnet to launch an assault. Even an unsuccessful distributed denial of service attack can quickly consume a large amount of resources to defend against and cause charges to soar. The dynamic provisioning of a cloud in some ways simplifies the work of an attacker to cause harm. While the resources of a cloud are significant, with enough attacking computers they can become saturated (Jensen, Schwenk, Gruschka & Iacono, 2009). For example, a denial of service attack against Bit Bucket, a code hosting site, caused an outage of over 19 hours of downtime during an apparent denial of service attack on the underlying Amazon cloud infrastructure it uses (Brooks, 2009 and Metz, 2009). Besides publicly available services, denial of service attacks can occur against private services, such as those used in cloud management. For example, a denial of service attack occurred against the cloud management programming interface of the Amazon Cloud Services involved machine instances replicating themselves exponentially (Slaviero, 2008). Internally assigned no routable addresses, used to manage resources within the service provider's network, and may also be used as an attack vector. A worst-case possibility that exists is for elements of one cloud to attack those of another or to attack some of its own elements (Leavitt, 2009).

Value Concentration-The bank robber Willie Hutton is often attributed with the claim that he robbed banks "because that is where the money is" (Shimanek, 2000). In many ways, data records are the currency of the 21st century and cloud-based data stores are the bank vault, making them an increasingly preferred target. Just as an economy of scale exists in robbing banks instead of individuals, a high payoff ratio also exists for successfully compromising a cloud. Finesse and circumvention was Willie's trademark and that style works well in the digital world of cloud computing. For instance, a recent exploit targeted a Twitter employee's email account by reportedly answering a set of security questions and then using that information to access company files stored on his organizational Google Apps account (Infosecurity Magazine, 2009 and Sutter, 2009). A similar weakness was noted in Amazon Web Services (AWS) (Garfinkel, 2007). A registered email address and valid password for an account are all that is required to download authentication credentials from the AWS Web dashboard, which in turn grant access to the account's resources. Since lost passwords can be reset by email, an attacker controlling the mail system, or passively eavesdropping on the network thru which email containing a password reset would pass, could effectively take control of the account. Having data collocated with the data of an organization with a high threat profile could also lead to denial of service, as an unintended casualty from an attack targeted against that organization. Similarly, indirect effects from an attack against the physical resources of a high-profile organization's service provider are also a possibility. For example, IRS facilities are continually targeted by would be attackers (Katz, 2010).

Comparative Analysis for Strengths and Limitations of Some of the Existing Security Scheme

The table 1 shows the comparison between various proposed methods and list the Strengths and Limitations of Some of the Existing Security Scheme

Attacks on Cloud Computing

In the following, we present a selection of security attacks related to Cloud Computing. Each attack is explained briefly and accompanied with a short discussion on potential or real-world measured impacts.

XML Signature-A well known type of attacks on protocols using XML Signature for authentication or integrity protection is *XML Signature Element Wrapping* (Ristenpart, 2007) (henceforth denoted shortly as wrapping attack). This of course applies to Web Services and therefore also for Cloud Computing. Since the discovery of wrapping attacks by McIntosh and Austel in 2005 have be published a number of further variations, Counter measures and again attacks circumventing these countermeasures. For example, in (Gruschka & Iacono, 2009) a method – called *inline approach* – was introduced to protect some key properties of the SOAP message structure and thereby hinder wrapping attacks, but shortly later in (Google, ——Browser security handbook, 2009) it was shown how to perform a wrapping attack anyhow. However, mostly due to the rare usage of WS -Security in business applications these attacks remained theoretical and no real-life wrapping attack became public, until in 2008 it was discovered that Amazon's EC2 services were vulnerable to wrapping attacks (Jensen, Gruschka & Herkenh¨oner, 2009). Using a variation of the attack presented before an attacker was able to perform arbitrary EC2 operations on behalf of a legitimate user. In order to exploit the SOAP message security validation vulnerability of EC2, a signed SOAP request of a legitimate, subscribed user needed to be intercepted. Since the vulnerability in the SOAP request validation allows interfering any kind of operation and having it executed, it does not matter what kind of request

Table 1. Comparative analysis for strengths and limitations of some of the existing security scheme

Security Scheme	Suggested Approach	Strengths	Limitations
Data Storage security (Wang, C., Wang, Q., Ren, K., Lou, W., 2009)	Uses homomorphism token with distributed verification of erasure-coded data towards ensuring data storage security and locating the server being attacked.	1. Supports dynamic operations on data blocks such as: update, delete and append without data corruption and loss. 2. Efficient against data modification and server colluding attacks as well as against byzantine failures.	1. Supports dynamic operations on data blocks such as: update, delete and append without data corruption and loss. 2. Efficient against data modification and server colluding attacks as well as against byzantine failures.
User identity safety in cloud computing	Uses active bundles scheme, whereby predicates are compared over encrypted data and multiparty computing.	Does not need trusted third party (TTP) for the verification or approval of user identity. Thus the user's identity is not disclosed. The TTP remains free and could be used for other purposes such as decryption.	Active bundle may not be executed at all at the host of the requested service. It would leave the system vulnerable. The identity remains a secret and the user is not granted permission to his requests.
Trust model for interoperability and security in cross cloud (Pal, Khatua, Chaki & Sanyal, 2012)	1. Separate domains for providers and users, each with a special trust agent. 2. Different trust strategies for service providers and customers. 3. Time and transaction factors are taken into account for trust assignment.	1. Helps the customers to avoid malicious suppliers. 2. Helps the providers to avoid cooperating/serving malicious users.	Security in a very large scale cross cloud environment is an active issue. This present scheme is able to handle only a limited number of security threats in a fairly small environment.
Virtualized defence and reputation based trust management	1. Uses a hierarchy of DHT-based overlay networks, with specific tasks to be performed by each layer. 2. Lowest layer deals with reputation aggregation and probing colluders. The highest layer deals with various attacks.	Extensive use of virtualization for securing clouds.	The proposed model is in its early developmental stage and needs further simulations to verify the performance.
Secure virtualization (Lombardi, Pietro, 2011).	1. Idea of an Advanced Cloud Protection system (ACPS) to ensure the security of guest virtual machines and of distributed computing middleware is proposed. 2. Behaviour of cloud components can be monitored by logging and periodic checking of executable system files.	A virtualized network is prone to different types of security attacks that can be launched by a guest VM. An ACPS system monitors the guest VM without being noticed and hence any suspicious activity can be blocked and system's security system notified.	System performance gets marginally degraded and a small performance penalty is encountered. This acts as a limitation towards the acceptance of an ACPS system.
Safe, virtual network in cloud environment [81]	Cloud Providers have been suggested to obscure the internal structure of their services and placement policy in the cloud and also to focus on side-channel risks in order to reduce the chances of information leakage.	Ensures the identification of adversary or the attacking party and helping us find a far off place for an attacking party from its target and hence ensuring a more secure environment for the other VMs.	If the adversary gets to know the location of the other VMs, it may try to attack them. This may harm the other VMs in between.

the attacker has at its disposal. The instantiation of a multitude of virtual machine to send spam mails is just one example what an attacker can do—using the legitimated user's identity and charging his account.

Browser Security-In a Cloud, computation is done on remote servers. The client PC is used for I/O only, and for authentication and authorization of commands to the Cloud. It thus does not make sense to develop (platform dependent) client software, but to use a universal, platform independent tool for I/O: a standard Web browser (Chauhan, Malhotra, Pathak & Singh, 2012). This trend has been observed during the last years, and has been categorized under different names: Web applications, Web 2.0, or Software-as-a-Service (SaaS). Modern Web browsers with their AJAX techniques (JavaScript, XMLHttpRequest, Plugins) are ideally suited for I/O. But what about security? A partial answer is given in (Fletcher, 2010), where different browser security policies (with the notable exception of TLS) are compared for the most important browser releases. With a focus on the *Same Origin Policy* (SOP), this document reveals many shortcomings of browser security. If we additionally take into account TLS, which is used for host authentication and data encryption, these shortcomings become even more obvious. Web browsers can not directly make use of XML Signature or XML Encryption: data can only be encrypted through TLS, and signatures are only used within the TLS handshake. For all other cryptographic data sets within WS-Security, the browser only serves as a passive data store. Some simple workarounds have been proposed to use e.g. TLS encryption instead of XML Encryption, but major security problems with this approach have been described in the literature and working attacks were implemented as proofs-of concept. Our goal is to propose provably secure solutions using TLS, but at the same time encourage the browser community to adapt XML based cryptography for inclusion in the browser core (Chauhan, Malhotra, Pathak & Singh, 2012).

Attacks on Browser-based Cloud Authentication- The realization of these security issues within browser-based protocols with Cloud Computing can best be explained using Federated Identity Management (FIM) protocols: Since the browser itself is unable to generate cryptographically valid XML tokens (e.g. SAML tokens) to authenticate against the Cloud, this is done with the help of a trusted third party. The prototype for this class of protocols is Microsoft's Passport (Kormann & Rubin, 2000), which has been broken by Slemko (Slemko, 2001). If no direct login is possible at a server because the browser does not have the necessary credentials, an HTTP redirect is sent to the Passport login server, where the user can enter his credentials (e.g. username/ password). The Passport server then translates this authentication into a Kerberos token, which is sent to the requesting server through another HTTP redirect. The main security problem with Passport is that these Kerberos tokens are not bound to the browser, and that they are only protected by the SOP. If an attacker can access these tokens, he can access all services of the victim. Whereas Passport used a REST type of communication, its successors MS Cardspace and the SAML family of protocols definitively belong to the world of Web Services. However, the same security problems persist: Groß (Groß, 2003) analyzed SAML browser profiles, and one of the authors of this paper described an attack on MS Cardspace (Gajek, Schwenk, Steiner & Xuan, 2008 & 2009), which can also be applied to the SAML browser profiles (both token and artefact profiles).To resume: Current browser-based authentication protocols for the Cloud are not secure, because (a) the browser is unable to issue XML based security tokens by itself, and (b) Federated Identity Management systems store security tokens within the browser, where they are only protected by the (insecure) SOP (Jensen, Schwenk, Gruschka & Iacono, 2009).

Secure Browser-based Authentication- However, the situation is not hopeless: If we integrate TLS and SOP in a better way, we can secure FIM protocols. In previous work, we identified four methods to protect (SAML) tokens with the help of TLS.

- TLS Federation- In this approach, the SAML token is sent inside an X.509 client certificate. The SAML token thus replaces other identification data like distinguished names. The certificate has the same validity period as the SAML token (H¨uhnlein & Schwenk, 2008).
- SAML 2.0 Holder-of-Key Assertion Profile- Here again TLS with client authentication is used, but the client certificate does not transport any authorization information. Instead, the SAML token is bound to the public key contained in this certificate, by including this key in a Holder-of-Key assertion (Scavo, 2009).
- Strong Locked Same Origin Policy - Whereas the previous approaches relied on the server authenticating (in an anonymous fashion) the client, in this approach we strengthen the client to make reliable security decisions. This is done by using the server's public key as a basis for decisions of the Same Origin Policy, rather than the insecure Domain Name System (Schwenk & Gajek, 2008).
- TLS session binding. By binding the token to a certain TLS session, the server may deduce that the data he sends in response to the SAML token will be protected by the same TLS channel, and will thus reach the same (anonymous) client who has previously sent the token.

Future Browser Enhancements- Even with the workarounds using TLS, the browser is still very limited in its capacities as an authentication center for Cloud Computing. Whereas many Web Service functionalities can be added within the browser by simply loading an appropriate

JavaScript library during runtime (e.g. to enable the browser to send SOAP messages), this is not possible for XML Signature and Encryption, since the cryptographic keys and algorithms require much higher protection2. Therefore it would be desirable to add the following two enhancements to the browser security API (Jensen, Schwenk, Druschka & Iacono, 2009).

XML Encryption: Here standard APIs could easily be adapted, because only a byte stream has to be encrypted/decrypted, and no knowledge of XML is necessary. However, a naming scheme to access cryptographic keys "behind" the API must be agreed upon. DOM or (mostly) SAX based processing of XML data can be handled by a JavaScript library, since the decrypted data will be stored in the browser and is thus in any case accessible by a malicious (scripting) code (Jensen, Schwenk, Druschka & Iacono, 2009).

XML Signature: This extension is non-trivial, because the complete XML Signature data structure must be checked inside the API. This means that the complete <ds:Signature> element must be processed inside the browser core, including the transforms on the signed parts, and the two-step hashing. In addition, countermeasures against XML wrapping attacks should also be implemented. In addition, the API should be powerful enough to support all standard key agreement methods specified in WS-Security family of standards natively, since the resulting keys must be stored directly in the browser. This could be done e.g. by enhancing known security APIs, e.g. PKCS#11 (Jensen, Schwenk, Druschka & Iacono, 2009).

Cloud Malware Injection Attack- A first considerable attack attempt aims at injecting a malicious service implementation or virtual machine into the Cloud system. Such kind of *Cloud malware* could serve any particular purpose the adversary is interested in, ranging from eavesdropping via subtle data modifications to full functionality changes or blockings (Jensen, Schwenk, Druschka & Iacono, 2009). This attack requires the adversary to create its own malicious service implementation module (SaaS or PaaS) or virtual machine instance (IaaS), and add it to the Cloud system. Then, the adversary has to trick the Cloud system so that it treats the new service implementation instance as one of the valid instances for the particular service attacked by the adversary. If this succeeds, the Cloud system automatically redirects valid user requests to the malicious service implementation, and the adversary's code is executed (Jensen, Schwenk, Gruschka, Iacono, 2009). A promising countermeasure approach to this threat consists in the Cloud system performing a service instance integrity check prior to using a service instance for incoming requests. This can e.g. be done by storing a hash value on the original service instance's image file and comparing this value with the hash values of all new service instance images. Thus, an attacker would be required to trick that hash value comparison in order to inject his malicious instances into the Cloud system (Jensen, Schwenk, Druschka & Iacono, 2009).

Metadata Spoofing Attack- As described in (Jensen, Schwenk, Druschka & Iacono, 2009), the *metadata spoofing attack* aims at maliciously reengineering a Web Services' metadata descriptions. For instance, an adversary may modify a service's WSDL so that a call to a deleteUser operation syntactically looks like a call to another operation, e.g. setAdminRights. Thus, once a user is given such a modified WSDL document, each of his deleteUser operation invocations will result in SOAP messages that at the server side look like—and thus are interpreted as—invocations of the setAdminRights operation. In the end, an adversary could manage to create a bunch of user logins that are thought to be deleted by the application's semantics, but in reality are still valid, and additionally are provided with administrator level access rights. For static Web Service invocations, this attack obviously is not so promising for the adversary, as the task of deriving service invocation code from the WSDL description usually is done just once, at the time of client code

generation (Jensen, Schwenk, Druschka & Iacono, 2009). Thus, the attack here can only be successful if the adversary manages to interfere at the one single moment when the service client's developer leeches for the service's WSDL file. Additionally, the risk of the attack being discovered assumably is rather high, especially in the presence of sound testing methods. These restrictions tend to fall away in the Cloud Computing scenario. As the Cloud system itself has some kind of WSDL repository functionality (comparable to a UDDI registry (Clement, Hately, Riegen & Rogers, 2004) new users most assumably will gather for a service's WSDL file more dynamically. Thus, the potential spread of the malicious WSDL file—and thus the probability for a successful attack—rises by far. Similar to the hash value calculation discussed for the Cloud malware injection attack, in this scenario a hash-based integrity verification of the metadata description files prior to usage is required. For instance, an XML digital signature performed on the WSDL by the original service implementer would ensure its integrity. If the WSDL is additionally extended with a ash value on the service instance's image file, this also ensures a cryptographically strong binding between the WSDL and the original service image.

Flooding Attacks- A major aspect of Cloud Computing consists in outsourcing basic operational tasks to a Cloud system provider. Among these basic tasks, one of the most important ones is server hardware maintenance. Thus, instead of operating an own, internal data center, the paradigm of Cloud Computing enables companies (users) to *rent* server hardware on demand (IaaS). This approach provides valuable economic benefits when it comes to dynamics in server load, as for instance day-and-night cycles can be attenuated by having the data traffic of different time zones operated by the same servers (Jensen, Schwenk, Druschka & Iacono, 2009). Thus, instead of buying sufficient server hardware for the high workload times, Cloud Computing enables a dynamic adaptation of hardware requirements to the actual workload occurring. Technically, this achievement can be realized by using virtual machines deployed on arbitrary data-centre servers of the Cloud system. If a company's demand on computational power rises, it simply is provided with more instances of virtual machines for its services. Under security considerations, this architecture has a serious drawback. Though the feature of providing more computational power on demand is appreciated in the case of valid users, it poses severe troubles in the presence of an attacker. The corresponding threat is that of *flooding attacks*, which basically consist in an attacker sending a huge amount of nonsense requests to a certain service. As each of these requests has to be processed by the service implementation in order to determine its invalidity, this causes a certain amount of workload per attack request, which—in the case of a flood of requests—usually would cause a Denial of Service to the server hardware (cf. Jensen, Gruschka & Luttenberger, 2008). In the specific case of Cloud Computing systems, the impact of such a flooding attack is expected to be amplified drastically. This is due to the different kinds of impact.

Direct Denial of Service- When the Cloud Computing operating system notices the high workload on the flooded service, it will start to provide more computational power (more virtual machines, more service instances...) to cope with the additional workload (Jensen, Schwenk, Druschka & Iacono, 2009). Thus, the server hardware boundaries for maximum workload to process do no longer hold. In that sense, the Cloud system is trying to work *against* the attacker (by providing more computational power), but actually—to some extent—even *supports* the attacker by enabling him to do most possible damage on a service's availability, starting from a single flooding attack entry point. Thus, the attacker does not have to flood all servers that provide a certain service in target, but merely can flood a single, Cloud-based address in order to perform a full loss of availability on the intended service (Jensen, Schwenk, Druschka & Iacono, 2009).

Indirect Denial of Service- Depending on the computational power in control of the attacker, a side effect of the direct flooding attack on a Cloud service potentially consists in that other services provided on the same hardware servers may suffer from the workload caused by the flooding (Jensen, Schwenk, Druschka & Iacono, 2009). Thus, if a service instance happens to run on the same server with another, flooded service instance, this may affect its own availability as well. Once the server's hardware resources are completely exhausted by processing the flooding attack requests, obviously also the other service instances on the same hardware machine are no longer able to perform their intended tasks. Thus, the Denial of Service of the targeted service instances is likely to cause a Denial of Service on all other services deployed to the same server hardware as well. Depending on the level of sophistication of the Cloud system, this side-effect may worsen if the Cloud system notices the lack of availability, and tries to "evacuate" the affected service instances to other servers (Jensen, Schwenk, Druschka & Iacono, 2009). These results in additional workload for those other servers, and thus the flooding attack "jumps over" to another service type, and spreads throughout the whole computing Cloud (Jensen & Schwenk, 2009). In the worst case, an adversary manages to utilize another (or the very same) Cloud Computing system for hosting his flooding attack application. In that case, the *race in power* (Jensen, Gruschka & Luttenberger, 2008) would play both Cloud systems off against each other; each Cloud would provide more and more computational resources for creating, respectively fending, the flood, until one of them eventually reaches full loss of availability.

SUMMARY OF THE CHAPTER

As cloud computing can seen as new paradigm which is set to revolutionize the way we use the Internet. There are many new technologies emerging at rapid rate. Here, we presented a selection of issues of Cloud Computing security. We investigated ongoing issues i.e Trust, Risk Management, Architecture, Identity Management, Software Isolation, Data Protection and Availability with application of XML Signature and the Web Services security frameworks (attacking the Cloud Computing system itself), discussed the importance and capabilities of browser security in the Cloud Computing context (SaaS), raised concerns about Cloud service integrity and binding issues (PaaS), and sketched the threat of flooding attacks on Cloud systems (IaaS). As we showed, the threats to Cloud Computing security are numerous, and each of them requires an in-depth analysis on their potential impact and relevance to real-world Cloud Computing scenarios.

REFERENCES

Act, A. (1996). Health insurance portability and accountability act of 1996. *Public Law*, *104*, 191.

Babu, M. S., & Sekhar, M. C. (2013). Enterprise Risk Management Integrated framework for Cloud Computing. *International Journal of Advanced Networking & Applications*, *5*(3), 1939–1950.

Baier, A. (1986). Trust and antitrust. *Ethics*, *96*(2), 231–260. doi:10.1086/292745

Best, S. J., Krueger, B. S., & Ladewig, J. (2008). The effect of risk perceptions on online political participatory decisions. *Journal of Information Technology & Politics*, *4*(1), 5–17. doi:10.1300/J516v04n01_02

Böhm, M., Koleva, G., Leimeister, S., Riedl, C., & Krcmar, H. (2010). Towards a generic value network for cloud computing. In Economics of Grids, Clouds, Systems, and Services. (pp. 129-140). Springer Berlin Heidelberg. doi:10.1007/978-3-642-15681-6_10

Brad, R., (2009, April). Protecting Against Insider Attacks. *GIAC (GCIH) Gold Certification*. SANS Institute InfoSec Reading Room.

Brodkin, J. (2008, August). Loss of customer data spurs closure of online storage service. *Network World*.

Brooks, C. (2009). *Amazon EC2 Attack Prompts Customer Support Changes*. Tech Target.

Bruegger, B. P., Hühnlein, D., & Schwenk, J. (2008). *TLS-Federation-a Secure and Relying-Party-Friendly Approach for Federated Identity Management* (pp. 93–106). BIOSIG.

Calore, M. (2009, January). Ma.gnolia suffers major data loss, site taken offline. *Wired*.

Cappelli, D. M., Moore, A. P., Trzeciak, R. F., & Shimeall, T. J. (2008). *Common Sense Guide to Prevention and Detection of Insider Threats. CERT Insider Threat Study Team*. Carnegie Mellon University.

Chandrareddy, J. B., & Mahesh, G. U. (2012). Cloud Zones: Security and Privacy Issues in Cloud Computing", Asian Journal of Information Technology 11(3), 83-93- ISSN-1682-3915-

Chang, E., Dillon, T., & Calder, D. (2008, May). Human system interaction with confident computing. The mega trend. In *Human System Interactions, 2008 Conference* (pp. 1-11).

Chow, R., Golle, P., Jakobsson, M., Shi, E., Staddon, J., Masuoka, R., & Molina, J. (2009, November). Controlling data in the cloud: outsourcing computation without outsourcing control. In *Proceedings of the 2009 ACM workshop on Cloud computing security.* (pp. 85-90). doi:10.1145/1655008.1655020

Clarke, G. (2009, March 16). Microsoft's Azure Cloud Suffers First Crash. *The Register*.

Clement, L., Hately, A., von Riegen, C., & Rogers, T. (2004). *UDDI Version 3.0. 2, UDDI Spec Technical Committee Draft*. OASIS UDDI Spec TC.

Cloud Security Toolkit, Cloud Security 101. (2012, February). Healthcare Information and Management Systems Society

Dunn, J. E. (2010). Ultra-secure Firefox Offered to UK Bank Users. *Techworld*.

Eisenhauer, M. P. (2005). *Privacy and Security Law Issues in Off-shore Outsourcing Transactions* (pp. 15). Atlanta, Georgia: Hunton & Williams.

Ferguson, T. (2009). Salesforce.com outage hits thousands of businesses. *CNET*. Retrieved from http://news. cnet. com/8301-1001_3-10136540-92. html

Ferrie, P. (2007). *Attacks on more virtual machine emulators*. Symantec Technology Exchange.

Fletcher, K. K. (2010). Cloud Security requirements analysis and security policy development using a high-order object-oriented modeling. Master of science, Computer Science, Missouri University of Science and Technology, 13.

Frei, S., Duebendorfer, T., Ollmann, G., & May, M. (2008). *Understanding the web browser threat*. *TIK*. ETH Zurich.

Gajek, S., Jager, T., Manulis, M., & Schwenk, J. (2008). A browser-based kerberos authentication scheme. In *Computer Security-ESORICS 2008* (pp. 115–129). Springer Berlin Heidelberg. doi:10.1007/978-3-540-88313-5_8

Gajek, S., Jensen, M., Liao, L., & Schwenk, J. (2009, July). Analysis of signature wrapping attacks and countermeasures. In *Web Services, 2009. ICWS 2009. IEEE International Conference.* (pp. 575-582). IEEE. doi:10.1109/ICWS.2009.12

Gajek, S., Schwenk, J., & Chen, X. (2008). On the insecurity of Microsoft's identity metasystem cardspace. *Horst Görtz Institute for IT-Security, Tech. Rep. HGI TR-2008-004*.

Gajek, S., Schwenk, J., Steiner, M., & Xuan, C. (2009). Risks of the CardSpace protocol. In *Information Security*. (pp. 278–293). Springer Berlin Heidelberg. doi:10.1007/978-3-642-04474-8_23

Gambetta, D. (2000). Can we trust trust. *Trust: Making and breaking cooperative relations,* (pp. 213-237).

Garfinkel, S. L. (2007). An evaluation of Amazon's grid computing services: EC2, S3, and SQS.

Garfinkel, T., & Rosenblum, M. (2005). *When Virtual is Harder than Real*. HotOS.

Gellman, R. (2012, August). Privacy in the clouds: risks to privacy and confidentiality from cloud computing. In *Proceedings of the World privacy forum*.

Giff, S. (2000). The Influence of Metaphor, Smart Cards and Interface Dialogue on Trust in eCommerce. *MSc project*.

Giordanelli, R., & Mastroianni, C. (2010). *The cloud computing paradigm: Characteristics, opportunities and research issues. Istituto di Calcolo e Reti ad Alte Prestazioni*. ICAR.

Goodin, D. (2011). Salesforce.com outage exposes cloud's dark linings.

Greenberg, A. (2009, July 13). IBM's blindfolded calculator. *Forbes*.

Groß, T. (2003, December). Security analysis of the SAML single sign-on browser/artifact profile. In *Computer Security Applications Conference, 2003. Proceedings. 19th Annual.* (pp. 298-307). IEEE. doi:10.1109/CSAC.2003.1254334

Gruschka, N., & Iacono, L. L. (2009, July). Vulnerable cloud: Soap message security validation revisited. In *Web Services, 2009. ICWS 2009. IEEE International Conference.* (pp. 625-631).

Gruschka, N., & Iacono, L. L. (2009, July). Vulnerable cloud: Soap message security validation revisited. Proceedings of *Web Services, 2009. ICWS 2009. IEEE International Conference on* (pp. 625-631).

Gunderloy, M. (2008, January 13). Who Protects Your Cloud Data?, Web Worker Daily.

Horwath, C., Chan, W., Leung, E., & Pili, H. (2012). Enterprise Risk Management for Cloud Computing. *Thought Leadership in ERM, Committee of Sponsoring Organizations of the Treadway Commission (COSO) research paper*, (pp. 3-32).

Huynh, T. D. (2009, March). A personalized framework for trust assessment. In *Proceedings of the 2009 ACM symposium on Applied Computing* (pp. 1302-1307). ACM. doi:10.1145/1529282.1529574

Irakoze, I. (2013). Cloud-Based Mobile Applications.

Jacobs, D., & Aulbach, S. (2007, March). *Ruminations on Multi-Tenant Databases*, 103, 514–521. BTW.

Jaeger, P. T., & Fleischmann, K. R. (2013). Public libraries, values, trust, and e-government. *Information technology and Libraries, 26*(4), 34-43.

Jansen, W. (2010). *Directions in security metrics research*. Diane Publishing.

Jansen, W., & Grance, T. (2011). Guidelines on security and privacy in public cloud computing. *NIST* publication. (pp.144, 800).

Jensen, M., Gruschka, N., & Herkenhöner, R. (2009). A survey of attacks on web services. *Computer Science-Research and Development, 24*(4), 185–197. doi:10.1007/s00450-009-0092-6

Jensen, M., Gruschka, N., & Luttenberger, N. (2008, March). The impact of flooding attacks on network-based services. In *Availability, Reliability and Security, 2008. ARES 08. Third International Conference.* (pp. 509-513). doi:10.1109/ARES.2008.16

Jensen, M., & Schwenk, J. (2009, March). The accountability problem of flooding attacks in service-oriented architectures. In *Availability, Reliability and Security, 2009. ARES'09. International Conference.* (pp. 25-32). doi:10.1109/ARES.2009.11

Jensen, M., Schwenk, J., Gruschka, N., & Iacono, L. L. (2009, September). On technical security issues in cloud computing. In *Cloud Computing, 2009. CLOUD'09. IEEE International Conference.* (pp. 109-116). doi:10.1109/CLOUD.2009.60

Jensen, M., Schwenk, J., Gruschka, N., & Iacono, L. L. (2009, September). On technical security issues in cloud computing. In *Cloud Computing, 2009. CLOUD'09. IEEE International Conference.* (pp. 109-116). doi:10.1109/CLOUD.2009.60

Kalpana, P. (2012). Cloud Computing–Wave of the Future. *International Journal of Electronics Communication and Computer Engineering, 3*(3).

Kandukuri, B. R., Paturi, V. R., & Rakshit, A. (2009, September). Cloud security issues. In *Services Computing, 2009. SCC'09. IEEE International Conference.* (pp. 517-520). doi:10.1109/SCC.2009.84

Karger, P. A. (2009, March). Securing virtual machine monitors: what is needed? In *Proceedings of the 4th International Symposium on Information, Computer, and Communications Security* (p. 1). ACM. doi:10.1145/1533057.1533059

Katz, N. (2010, February 18). Austin Plane Crash: Pilot Joseph Andrew Stack May Have Targeted IRS Offices. Says FBI. *CBS News.*

Keleta, Y., Eloff, J. H. P., & Venter, H. S. (2005). *Proposing a Secure XACML architecture ensuring privacy and trust. Research in Progress Paper.* University of Pretoria.

Kerner, S. M. (2010). Mozilla Confirms Security Threat from Malicious Firefox Add-Ons, eSecurity Planet, February 5, 2010.

King, S. T., & Chen, P. M. (2006, May). SubVirt: Implementing malware with virtual machines. In *Security and Privacy, 2006 IEEE Symposium.* (pp. 14).

Kormann, D. P., & Rubin, A. D. (2000). Risks of the passport single signon protocol. *Computer Networks*, *33*(1), 51–58. doi:10.1016/S1389-1286(00)00048-7

Kosko, B. (1986). Fuzzy cognitive maps. *International Journal of Man-Machine Studies*, *24*(1), 65–75. doi:10.1016/S0020-7373(86)80040-2

Kowalski, E., Conway, T., Keverline, S., Williams, M., Cappelli, D., Willke, B., & Moore, A. (2008). Insider threat study: Illicit cyber activity in the government sector. *US Department of Homeland Security, US Secret Service, CERT, and the Software Engineering Institute (Carnegie Mellon University), Tech. Rep.*

Krebs, B. (2007, November 6). Salesforce.com Acknowledges Data Loss. *The Washington Post*, 8-10.

Krigsma, M. (2008, February 15). Amazon S3 Web Services Down. Bad, Bad News for Customers, ZDNET.

Leavitt, N. (2009). Is cloud computing really ready for prime time? *Computer*, *42*(1), 15–20. doi:10.1109/MC.2009.20

Levien, R. (2009). Attack-resistant trust metrics. In *Computing with Social Trust.* (pp. 121–132). Springer London. doi:10.1007/978-1-84800-356-9_5

Li, H., Pincus, M., & Rego, S. O. (2008). Market reaction to events surrounding the Sarbanes-Oxley Act of 2002 and earnings management. *The Journal of Law & Economics*, *51*(1), 111–134. doi:10.1086/588597

Lombardi, F., & Di Pietro, R. (2011). Secure virtualization for cloud computing. *Journal of Network and Computer Applications*, *34*(4), 1113–1122. doi:10.1016/j.jnca.2010.06.008

McMillan, R. (2007, November 6). Salesforce.com warns customers of phishing scam. *PC Magazine, IDG News Network.*

McMillan, R. (2009). *Hackers find a home in Amazon's EC2 cloud. Infoworld.* IDG News Network.

McMillan, R. (2009, September 17). Misdirected Spyware Infects Ohio Hospital. *PC Magazine, IDG News Service.*

Metz, C. (2009). *DDoS attack rains down on Amazon cloud.* The Register.

Miller, R. (2009, June 11). Lightning Strike Triggers Amazon EC2 Outage. *Data Center Knowledge.*

Miller, R. (2013). Major outage for Amazon S3 and EC2. *Data Center Knowledge.*

Nielsen, J. (1999). *Trust or bust: Communicating trustworthiness in web design.* Jacob Nielsen's Alertbox.

Ning, G., Jiamao, L., & Xiaolu, C. (2006, January). *Theory and Practice R & D of Web Services.* (pp. 10). Machinery Industry Press.

Nissenbaum, H. (1999). Can trust be secured online? A theoretical perspective.

Nooteboom, B. (2007). Social capital, institutions and trust. *Review of Social Economy*, *65*(1), 29–53. doi:10.1080/00346760601132154

Oberheide, J., Cooke, E., & Jahanian, F. (2008, February). Empirical exploitation of live virtual machine migration. In *Proc. of BlackHat DC convention.*

Onwubiko, C. (2010). Security issues to cloud computing. In *Cloud Computing* (pp. 271–288). Springer London. doi:10.1007/978-1-84996-241-4_16

Ormandy, T. (2007). *An empirical study into the security exposure to hosts of hostile virtualized environments.*

Osterwalder, D. (2001). Trust through evaluation and certification? *Social Science Computer Review, 19*(1), 32–46. doi:10.1177/089443930101900104

Overby, S. (2010, April). How to Negotiate a Better Cloud Computing Contract. *CIO.*

Pal, S., Khatua, S., Chaki, N., & Sanyal, S. (2011). A new trusted and collaborative agent based approach for ensuring cloud security. *arXiv preprint arXiv:1108.4100.*

Patel, S. C., Umrao, L. S., & Singh, R. S. (2012). Policy-based Framework for Access Control in Cloud Computing. In *International Conference on Recent Trends in Engineering & Technology (ICRTET2012).* (pp. 142-146).

Pearson, S. (2009, May). Taking account of privacy when designing cloud computing services. In *Proceedings of the 2009 ICSE Workshop on Software Engineering Challenges of Cloud Computing* (pp. 44-52). IEEE Computer Society. doi:10.1109/CLOUD.2009.5071532

Pearson, S., Casassa, M., Mont, & Crane, S. (2005, March 18). *Analysis of Trust Properties and Related Impact of Trusted Platforms.* Trusted Systems Laboratory. HP Laboratories, Bristol.

Pearson, S., Mont, M. C., & Crane, S. (2005). Persistent and dynamic trust: analysis and the related impact of trusted platforms. In *Trust management* (pp. 355–363). Springer Berlin Heidelberg. doi:10.1007/11429760_24

Provos, N., McNamee, D., Mavrommatis, P., Wang, K., & Modadugu, N. (2007, April). The ghost in the browser analysis of web-based malware. In *Proceedings of the first conference on First Workshop on Hot Topics in Understanding Botnets.* (pp. 4).

Provos, N., Rajab, M. A., & Mavrommatis, P. (2009). Cybercrime 2.0: When the cloud turns dark. *Communications of the ACM, 52*(4), 42–47. doi:10.1145/1498765.1498782 PMID:21218176

Ristenpart, T., Tromer, E., Shacham, H., & Savage, S. (2009, November). Hey, you, get off of my cloud: exploring information leakage in third-party compute clouds. In *Proceedings of the 16th ACM conference on Computer and communications security.* (pp. 199-212). doi:10.1145/1653662.1653687

Ristenpart, T., Tromer, E., Shacham, H., & Savage, S. (2009, November). Hey, you, get off of my cloud: exploring information leakage in third-party compute clouds. In *Proceedings of the 16th ACM conference on Computer and communications security.* (pp. 199-212). doi:10.1145/1653662.1653687

Rousseau, D., Sitkin, S., Burt, R. & Camerer, C. (1998). Not so Different after All: A Crossdiscipline View of Trust. *Academy of Management Review, 23*(3), pp. 393-404.

Rustan, J. (2012). The Risks in the Cloud. *Foster Rapid Innovation in Computational Science and Information Management.*

Scavo, T. (2009). SAML V2. 0 Holder-of-Key Assertion Profile Version 1.0. OASIS, 2009.

Schwenk, J., Liao, L., & Gajek, S. (2008). Stronger bindings for saml assertions and saml artifacts. In *Proceedings of the 5th ACM CCS Workshop on Secure Web Services (SWS'08). (pp. 11-20).*

Security Within a Virtualized Environment: A New Layer in Layered Security. *Reflex Security.* retrieved http://www.vmware.com/files/pdf/partners/security/securityvirtualizedwhitepaper.pdf

Shah, A. (2008). Kernel-based Virtualization with KVM. *Linux Magazine, 86,* 37–39.

Shawish, A., & Salama, M. (2014). Cloud Computing: Paradigms and Technologies. In Intercooperative Collective Intelligence: Techniques and Applications (pp. 39-67). Springer Berlin Heidelberg.

Shelton, T. (2005). *Remote Heap Overflow.* ID: ACSSEC-2005-11-25 - 0x1, http://packetstorm-security.org/0512- advisories/ACSSEC-2005-11-25-0x1.txt

Shimanek, A. E. (2000). Do You Want Milk with Those Cookies: Complying with the Safe Harbor Privacy Principles. *The Journal of Corporation Law, 26,* 455.

Shin, D., & Ahn, G. J. (2005). Role-based privilege and trust management. *Computer Systems Science and Engineering, 20*(6), 401.

Singh, S., & Morley, C. (2009, November). Young Australians' privacy, security and trust in internet banking. In *Proceedings of the 21st Annual Conference of the Australian Computer-Human Interaction Special Interest Group: Design: Open 24/7.* (pp. 121-128). doi:10.1145/1738826.1738846

Sitkin, S. B., & Roth, N. L. (1993). Explaining the limited effectiveness of legalistic "remedies" for trust/distrust. *Organization Science, 4*(3), 367–392. doi:10.1287/orsc.4.3.367

Slaviero, M. (2009). BlackHat Presentation Demo Vids: Amazon, part 4 of 5. *AMIBomb.* Retrieved fromhttp://www. sensepost. com/blog/3797. html

Slaviero, M. (2009, August 8). BlackHat presentation demo vids: Amazon, part 4 of 5. *AMIBomb.*

Slemko, M. (2001). Microsoft passport to trouble.

Sutter, J. D. (2009). Twitter Hack Raises Questions about 'Cloud Computing'. *CNN.*

Takabi, H., Joshi, J. B., & Ahn, G. J. (2010, July). Securecloud: Towards a comprehensive security framework for cloud computing environments. Proceedings of Computer Software and Applications Conference Workshops (COMPSACW), 2010 IEEE 34th Annual. (pp. 393-398).

Twitter Email Account Hack Highlights Cloud Dangers. (2009, July 23). *Infosecurity Magazine.* Retrieved from http://www.infosecurity-magazine.com/view/2668/twitteremail-account-hack-highlights-cloud-dangers-/

Vieira, K., Schulter, A., Westphall, C., & Westphall, C. (2009). Intrusion detection for grid and cloud computing. *IT Professional,* (4): 38–43.

Virtualization-Aware Security for the Cloud. (2010). VMware vShield Product brochure. Retrieved from http://www.vmware.com/files/pdf/vmware-vshield_br-en.pdf>

VMware Hosted Products and Patches for ESX and ESXi. (n. d.). VMware Security Advisory. http://www.vmware.com/security/advisories/VMSA-2009-0006.html

Wainewright, P. (2010). Many degrees of multi-tenancy. *ZDNET.*

Wang, C., Wang, Q., Ren, K., Cao, N., & Lou, W. (2012). Toward secure and dependable storage services in cloud computing. *Services Computing. IEEE Transactions, 5*(2), 220–232.

Wang, Y., & Lin, K. J. (2008). Reputation-oriented trustworthy computing in e-commerce environments. *IEEE Internet Computing*, *12*(4), 55–59. doi:10.1109/MIC.2008.84

Wayne, A., & Jansen, (2011) "Cloud Hooks: Security and Privacy Issues in Cloud Computing", NIST, *Proceedings of the 44th Hawaii International Conference on System Sciences*. (pp. 1530-1605)

Wei, J., Zhang, X., Ammons, G., Bala, V., & Ning, P. (2009, November). Managing security of virtual machine images in a cloud environment. In *Proceedings of the 2009 ACM workshop on Cloud computing security*. (pp. 91-96). doi:10.1145/1655008.1655021

Whitney, L. (2009). Amazon EC2 cloud service hit by botnet, outage. *CNET News, 11*.

Zalewski, M. Browser security handbook, 2008.

Zetter, K. (2009, April). FBI defends disruptive raid on Texas data centers. *Wired*. Retrieved from http://www.wired.com/threatlevel/2009/04/data-centers-ra

Zhang, Y., & Joshi, J. (2009). *Access control and trust management for emerging multidomain environments*. (pp. 421–452). Emerald Group Publishing.

Ziegler, C. N., & Lausen, G. (2004, March). Spreading activation models for trust propagation. In *e-Technology, e-Commerce and e-Service, 2004. EEE'04*. (pp. 83-97). IEEE. doi:10.1109/EEE.2004.1287293

KEY TERMS AND DEFINITIONS

Access Control: access control is the selective restriction of access to a place or other resource. The act of accessing may mean consuming, entering, or using. Permission to access a resource is called authorization.

Authentication: is the function of specifying access rights to resources related to information security and computer security in general and to access control in particular.

Cloud Computing: Cloud computing is an Internet-based computing solution which provides the resources in an effective manner. In the cloud, many computers are configured to work together where the resources are allocated on demand. Cloud computing allows the customers to access resources through the internet from anywhere at any time without thinking about the management and maintenance issues of the resources. Resources of cloud computing can be provided dynamically.

Internet: The Internet is a global network connecting millions of computers. More than 100 countries are linked into exchanges of data, news and opinions.

Privacy: is the ability of an individual or group to seclude themselves, or information about themselves, and thereby express themselves selectively. The boundaries and content of what is considered private differ among cultures and individuals, but share common themes. When something is private to a *person*, it usually means there is something to them inherently special or sensitive. The domain of privacy partially overlaps security, including for instance the concepts of appropriate use, as well as protection of information. Privacy may also take the form of bodily integrity.

Security Policy: Security policy is a definition of what it means to *be secure* for a system, organization or other entity. A computer security policy defines the goals and elements of an organization's computer systems. The definition can be highly formal or informal. Security policies are enforced by organizational policies or security mechanisms. A technical implementation defines whether a computer system is *secure* or *insecure*. These formal policy models can be categorized into the core security principles of: Confidentiality, Integrity and Availability.

Security: In Computing, the extent to which a computer system is protected from data corruption, destruction, interception, loss, or unauthorized access. The prevention of and protection against assault, damage, fire, fraud, invasion of privacy, theft, unlawful entry, and other such occurrences caused by deliberate action.

Service Level Agreement: A service-level agreement (SLA) is a contract between a network service provider and a customer that specifies, usually in measurable terms, what services the network service provider will furnish. Many Internet service providers (ISP)s provide their customers with an SLA.

Virtualization: Virtualization is a key technology to create cloud computing platform. Unused resources can be effectively utilized, based on the requirement resources can be scaled using this technology compared to physical resource scaling. Entire existing OS along with all its application also can be moved to a virtual machine or vice versa also possible. Virtualization is simulating hardware and/or software to run on top of hardware and/or software.

Chapter 2

Cloud Computing Security:
Abuse and Nefarious Use
of Cloud Computing

Marwan Omar
Nawroz University, Iraq

ABSTRACT

The focus of this chapter is to highlight and address security challenges associated with the use and adoption of cloud computing. The chapter will describe how cloud computing has become an emerging and promising computing model that provides on-demand computing services which eliminates the need of bearing operational costs associated with deploying servers and software applications. As with any technology, cloud computing presents its adopters with security and privacy concerns that arise from exposing sensitive business information to unauthorized access. Also, this chapter will explore and investigate the scope and magnitude of one of the top cloud computing security threats "abuse and nefarious use of cloud computing" and present some of the attacks specific to this top threat as it represents a major barrier for decision makers to adopting cloud computing model. Finally, this chapter aims to serve as an introductory research effort to warrant more extensive research into this top threat and help researchers make recommendations to business organizations as to whether or not their data are vulnerable to such threat when deciding to join the cloud.

INTRODUCTION

Cloud computing is one of the revolutionary technologies that is expected to dominate and reshape the information technology industry in the near future (Rashmi, Sahoo, &.Mehfuz, 2013). This emerging computing technology provides highly scalable computing resources (e.g. information, applications, and transactions) in a way that is accessible, flexible, on-demand, and at a low cost (Eludiora, Abion, Oluwatope, Oluwaranti, Onime, &Kehinde, (2011); it provides unique opportunities for organizations to run business with efficacy and efficiency by allowing businesses to run their applications on a shared data center thus eliminating the need for servers, storage, processing power, upgrades, and technical teams. Furthermore; in cloud computing model, business organizations do not need to purchase any software products or services to run business because they can simply

DOI: 10.4018/978-1-4666-8387-7.ch002

subscribe to the applications in the cloud; those applications normally are scalable and reliable and ultimately allow business leaders to focus on their core business functions to enhance performance and increase profitability (Alam, Doja, Alam, & Malhotra (2013)).

Many organizations have become interested in the cloud computing concept due to many compelling benefits presented by this emerging computing paradigm (Aslam, Ullah, & Ansari (2010). Cloud computing vendors are offering scalable services and applications via centralized data centers utilizing thousands of server computers which provide easy access to computing resources anytime and anywhere (Aslam, Ullah, & Ansari (2010); the capability of cloud computing to quickly scale and provide access to computing services and resources anytime and anywhere, allowing organizations to quickly respond to changing business needs without the expenditures of time, space, money, personnel, and other resources needed for traditional infrastructures for example, New York newspaper organization were able to convert 11 million scanned and archived hard copies into pdf files in 24 hours by renting 100 servers from amazaon's cloud services at a cost to the organization was approximately $250. alternative methods for the conversion would have required cost and taken weeks or even months to complete. (Mongan, 2011).

While cloud computing offers enormous potential for reducing costs and increasing an organization's ability to quickly scale computing resources to respond to changing needs, there are risks associated with cloud computing (Alshammari, (2014)). Specifically, cloud computing may mean that an organization relinquishes control, resulting in exposure to breaches in confidentiality, losses in data integrity and availability. However; as with any technology, cloud computing has its own disadvantages such as releasing control of maintaining confidentiality, integrity, and availability of sensitive business data. In general, most cloud computing consumers want to be assured that cloud providers have effective security policies and controls in place to comply with data protection standards and meet regulatory compliance requirements prior to making a decision to migrate their data or applications to the cloud.

BACKGROUND

Cloud Deployment Models

According to cloud security alliance (2009) there are three cloud deployment models regardless of the service model adopted (SaaS, PaaS, and IaaS):

Public cloud: this is also called external cloud sometimes and it basically involves an organization that sells readily available cloud services to the general public. Business organizations with sensitive corporate data are reluctant to adopt this model because it increases the threat of exposing confidential data to unauthorized access by third parties and potential cyber criminals. The advantage of using the public cloud is that an organization itself does not have to manage the cloud computing infrastructure nor maintain operational activities. The disadvantage of utilizing the services from a public cloud provider is that it is entirely dependent upon another business entity that is offering resources through public cloud (Baber & Chauhan, 2011).

Private cloud: also referred to as internal cloud which means that cloud infrastructure and services are explicitly made available for a single organization. This deployment model can be located on premise or off site as it can also be managed by the organization itself or can be outsourced to a third party. Privately-hosted cloud services tend to be more costly but safer than other deployment models because organizations can retain control of their sensitive data and applications and implement their own security measures. The advantage for maintaining the private cloud is that an organization can retain full control of all the computing resources (e.g. applications, data, and systems) related to a cloud infrastructure. The disadvantage of such a deployment model is that an organization has to invest significantly in computing and storage resources and bear the cost of maintaining all software and computing platforms.

Community cloud: organizations who share the same concerns and goals (e.g. security controls, privacy concerns, organizational mission, and regulatory compliance requirements) can join this deployment model to share the cloud infrastructure which could exist on-premise or off-premise as it could be managed by a third party as well.

Hybrid cloud: this deployment model can span two or more other deployment models such as private, public, or community. In this model, data and applications are still standardized and enabled by a proprietary technology. The benefit of this model is that it offers a blend of cost effectiveness and scalability without exposing sensitive business data to external threats. This is possible because the hybrid model allows organizations to maintain their mission-critical applications in a private cloud (which provides security and control of in-house computing resource) and migrate their non-critical applications and platforms to the public cloud. Data availability, control, and performance are some of the disadvantages that can arise from adopting the hybrid cloud model. Figure 1 below is a visual model defined by the National Institute of Standards and Technology (NIST) illustrating the three cloud service models and the four deployment models, each business organization may choose to implement any of those models depending on their business needs and the sensitivity level of information residing in their systems:

Cloud Computing Service Models

The cloud security alliance guide (2009) states that the cloud computing technology comprises three fundamental classifications which are commonly referred to as "SPI Model" where "SPI" refers to "Software", "Platform", "Infrastructure" respectively (the cloud security alliance guide, 2009). Below is a definition of each service model:

1. Software as a Service (SaaS): in this model, the cloud provider has control of the underlying cloud infrastructure such as servers, operating system, processing, storage, and even the applications capabilities. Cloud provider has the responsibility of managing application capabilities while allowing cloud customers to use and access the application capabilities from their own devices via a thin client interface such as a web browser. Cloud subscribers who adopt this service model will generally have the least control over cloud applications while they have very limited freedom in changing user specific configuration settings (the cloud security alliance guide, 2009); a good example for this type of service model is the Gmail application which is a web-based e-mail provided by Google as a SaaS.

2. Platform as a Service (PaaS): this computing model is similar to the previous one in that cloud consumers do not have any control over the underlying cloud infrastructure such as network, servers, storage, processing, and applications. This model allows cloud customers to deploy their own application (created by customer) onto the cloud infrastructure that enables them to control and mange those applications. Furthermore; cloud clients do not need to purchase or manage the cloud computing infrastructure while they are provided with capabilities to develop and use software applications. For example, Google has a PaaS that allows clients to run their web applications on the Google App Engine using an internet browser such as Internet Explorer (Choo, 2010).

3. Infrastructure as a Service (IaaS): this is the foundation of cloud services because it

Figure 1. NIST Visual Model of Cloud Computing Definition, Cloud Security Alliance, 2009

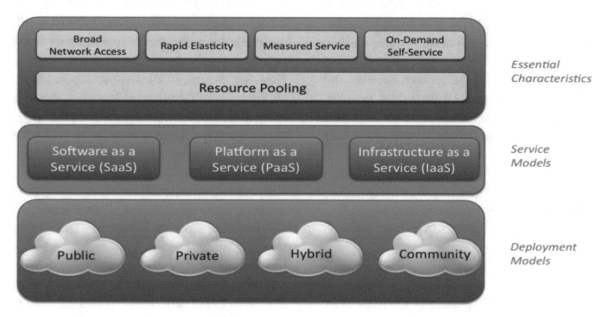

Visual Model Of NIST Working Definition Of Cloud Computing
http://www.csrc.nist.gov/groups/SNS/cloud-computing/index.html

provides capabilities for cloud consumers to deploy fundamental computing resources such as operating systems, applications, servers, bandwidth, storage, and processing. As with the other two models, this model does not demand cloud consumers to manage or control the underlying cloud infrastructure. For example, Amazon EC2 allows individuals and businesses to run their own applications on machines that can be rented with preconfigured and selected operating system (Choo, 2010).

Cloud Computing Threats

Security researchers as well as industry experts strongly predict that cloud computing will be the "next big thing" due to its compelling cost saving advantage and on-demand web based nature which allows business organizations to focus on their core business competencies; however, these computing possibilities do not come risk free because they expose organization's sensitive data to cyber threats and open the door for new attack vectors (Arora, P, Chaudhry, R, Satinder, W., & Ahuja, P., 2012). In fact; migrating to the cloud magnifies risks to confidential data because business information resources are exposed to third parties (cloud providers) who themselves may pose a risk from their internal employees and thereby increasing the possibility of insider threat. Moreover; the real threat arises from the fact that service provider has the privilege of accessing sensitive business data and may be allured to misuse or abuse this privilege or even access data in an unauthorized manner. Therefore cloud consumers have to take the risk of entrusting service providers with their sensitive information assets and hope that the cloud service providers have security measures in place to restrict employee access to information thereby reduce risk of insider threat to a minimum (Gharshi, R., Suresha. (2013)). One of the unique security risks associated with the use of cloud services is that of virtualization;

cloud computing utilizes virtual machines to run different multiple instances on the same physical machine (Subashini&Kavitha, 2011). Those instances have to be isolated to prevent malicious hackers from eavesdropping or taking control of host machine. Although cloud providers such as Amazon have VM monitors in place to detect such malicious or illegal activity; however, this security measure cannot fully address the security requirements necessary to block or prevent compromised VMs from extracting and leaking information to cyber criminals.

Top Cloud Computing Security Threat: Abuse and Nefarious use of Cloud Computing

According to Cloud Security Alliance (2010), abuse and nefarious use of cloud computing is considered as the top security threat to cloud computing because cloud providers do not enforce any strong registration process where any person with a valid credit card can register to receive cloud services; this huge flaw in the registration system coupled with weak fraud detection capabilities lends cloud computing models such as IaaS and PaaS to malicious attacks by criminals who can leverage those technologies and target cloud providers. To make matters worse, and according to Cloud Security Alliance (2010), some cloud service providers offer readily available free limited trial period of cloud services which presents a perfect opportune time for cyber criminals to join the cloud and possibly misuse and abuse their access privilege to cloud services. Cloud computing model by its very nature involves multiple data centers across possibly multiple locations and each data center is dedicated to many customers and their data needs; this in turn makes investigating and detecting unauthorized or inappropriate activity significantly difficult in a cloud environment.

Attackers can exploit this threat and launch an attack called "cloud computing malware injection attack" by creating their own implementation

module (e.g. PaaS or SaaS) within the cloud environment and trick the cloud system to treat that malicious instance as a valid instance for the particular service module; once adversary is capable of doing this trick, the cloud system will automatically redirect valid user requests to the service module run by attackers (Jensen, Schwenk, Gruschka, Iacono, 2009). As a case in point, hackers can host malicious data and possibly convince users of Amazon Elastic Cloud Compute (EC2) to run images on a virtual machine by giving the image a name that sounds official such as "Fedora-core" (Chen, Paxson, & Katz, 2010). In fact; Ristenpart, Tromer,Shacham, and Savage (2009) were able to use the Amazon EC2 service as a case study and demonstrated information leak by first mapping internal cloud infrastructure, identify the possible location of a target virtual machine, and then continue to create instances of Virtual Machines (VM) until one is created adjacent to the target VM; once the target VM has been located and identified, hackers can compromise that VM and use it to leak information (Da Silva et al, 2013). They showed that investing a few dollars to buy an instance of a VM with Amazon EC2 service can have a % 40 chance of successfully placing a malicious VM on the same physical machine as the target customer. Moreover; cyber hackers can masquerade themselves as legitimate cloud users and abuse this feature to launch spam campaigns, run botnets, and brute force attacks. Figure 2 below shows different components of security requirements within a cloud platform which makes security a more challenging task for cloud providers given that there are four deployment methods and three cloud computing models.

Applicability of "Abuse and Nefarious Use of Cloud Computing" to "PaaS":

The threat of abusing cloud services is somewhat unique in that it involves the risk of insider threat as well as the risk posed by cyber criminals to join

Figure 2. complexity of security in a cloud environment- Subashini & Kavitha, 2011

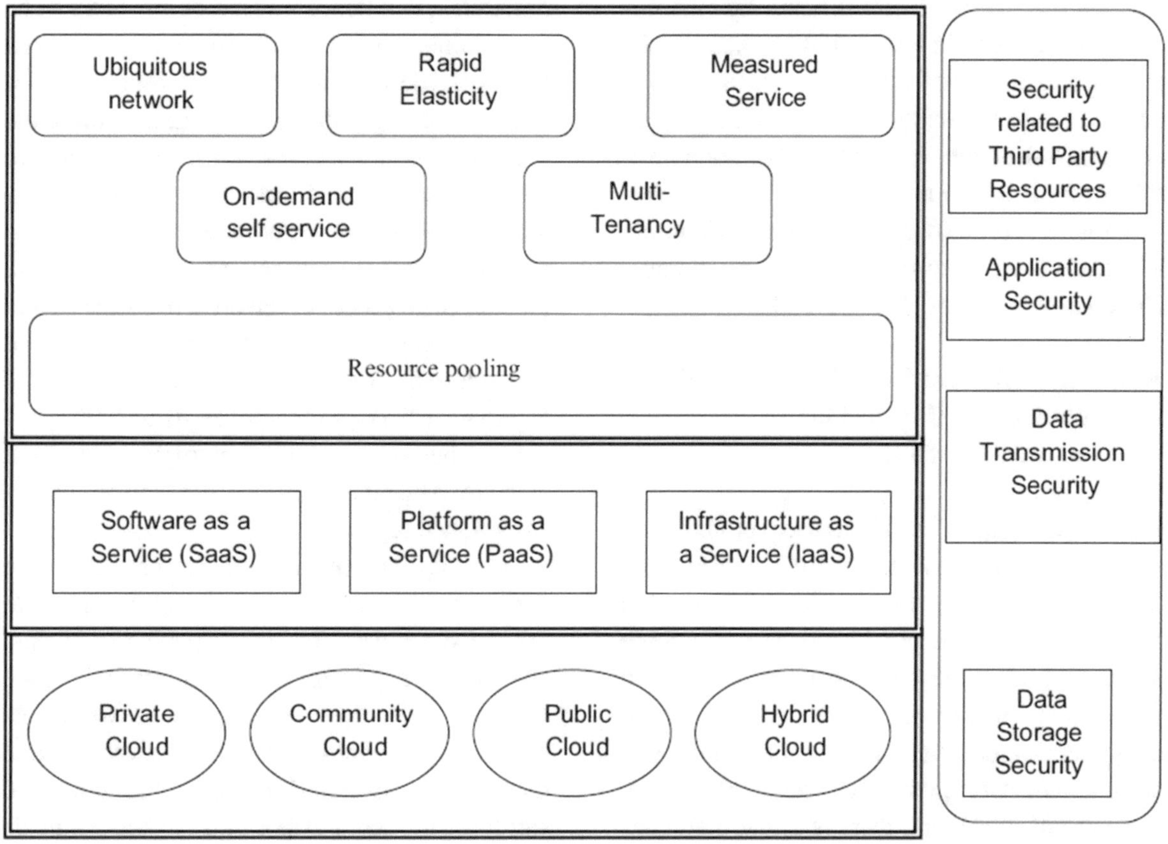

the cloud and misuse its services; cloud providers can be a big risk on organizational information assets if they do not enforce stringent security procedures to regulate employee access to sensitive business data. With the increased adoption of cloud services, cloud provider employees are prone to be targeted by malicious hackers given the fact that "PaaS" model involves storing and processing sensitive organizational resources such as intellectual property, trade secrets, and customer confidential information on the provider's servers; therefore cloud providers have to practice due diligence to minimize the risk of insider threat and detect unauthorized access from internal employees (Blumenthal, 2011). The other security risks stems from the fact that " PaaS" is readily available for the public which provides an opportunity for hackers to try the service with

the intent of circumventing provider's security controls and ultimately compromise sensitive business data illegally; arguably, "PaaS" can be used as a "Hacking as a Service" because cloud computing is increasingly becoming an ecosystem that involves numerous services, interactions, interdependencies, and its many deployment models with different structures (SaaS,PaaS,IaaS).

PaaS is particularly susceptible to nefarious cyber threats because it allows "legitimate" cloud customers to deploy their own- created applications on a platform that is supported by the cloud provider. For example, many cloud vendors (e.g. Google App Engine& Sun Microsystems) facilitate the deployment of applications and APIs that are written in Java, Python, or .Net on their computing platform (Chakraborty, Ramireddy, Raghu, & Rao, (2010)).Furthermore; Cloud providers allow their customers to deploy and control their applications and configure the hosting environment, this feature, in turn, could be exploited by attackers to inject malicious code into the hosting environment and eventually infect the underlying cloud infrastructure. A representative example of this threat is the Amazon EC2 cloud based service that was used by cyber criminals whom ran a botnet called "Zeuscrimeware" for command and control purposes (Danchev, 2009)

Attacks Relating to "Abuse and Nefarious Use of Cloud Computing" Threat

Host hopping attacks: this attack exploits one of the most defining characteristics of cloud computing: resource sharing; this attack can be launched by hackers if cloud provider does not enforce strict mechanism to isolate shared resources such as memory, storage, and reputation of different customers or hosts (ENISA, 2011). Failing to separate tenants (customers) can certainly facilitate this type of attack and thereby allow malicious hackers to hop on other hosts to compromise other customers' data and gain illegal access to it. This attack can be particularly dangerous for public clouds and the PaaS model where multiple clients share the same physical machine. Attackers can cause severe damage that could range from compromising sensitive customer data to interrupting service for cloud providers and distorting their image and reputation.

Malicious Insider and abuse of privileges: the shared and multi-tenancy nature of cloud computing creates a fertile ground for insider threat and promotes risk of "privilege abuse" to confidential customer information. Hosting sensitive information from multiple clients on the same physical machine certainly entices users with high privilege roles such as system administrators and information security managers to abuse their privileged access to clients' sensitive data and the possibility of leaking or selling that information

to competitors or other parties of interest. The possibility, and hence impact, of this risk can be further amplified if cloud provider does not enforce strict definition of roles and responsibilities or does not apply the "need to know" principle (ENISA, 2011). Also, it's worth noting that with the increased adoption of cloud computing services; cloud computing employees are becoming a target of cyber criminals as an effort to gain unauthorized access to sensitive business data in the cloud. Unfortunately, most organizations that experience this type of insider attacks choose not to publicize the issue and "sweep it under the rug" due to reputation and customer trust concerns; not to mention that they may face legal and regulatory compliance issues.

Identity theft attacks: malicious hackers can easily set up accounts with cloud providers to use cloud resources by simply paying for the usage without any restrictions or limits from cloud vendors on resource consumption or workloads. Attackers can exploit this advantage to use and compromise customer's critical information and sell it for a price. Furthermore; cyber criminals could also set up rogue clouds and entice individuals to host their sensitive data and provide cloud computing services such as e-mail applications. Once individuals entrust their confidential data with rogue cloud providers, their identity is at risk and can be compromised and thereby can lead to identity theft and financial fraud.

Service engine attacks: the service engine is a highly customized platform that sits above the physical layer and characterizes the underlying cloud architecture; this service engine is normally controlled by cloud provider to manage customer resources but it can be rented by potential customers who wish to use and adopt the IaaS model. hackers can abuse this feature by subscribing to the IaaS model and renting a virtual machine that would be hosted and controlled by the service engine; then they can use the VM to hack the service engine from the inside and use the service engine to their advantage where it may contain sensitive business information through other VMs from other cloud subscribers. In other words, hackers can escape the isolation feature that separates data belonging to different cloud customers and possibly breach and compromise their confidential data. (ENISA, 2011)

CONCLUSION

The foregone discussion explored the security aspects of cloud computing; specifically shed light on one of the top cloud computing security threats "abuse and nefarious use of cloud computing". The research indicated that cyber criminals have already exploited and misused cloud computing due to weak registration procedures of obtaining cloud computing services and lack of effective security controls; also, hackers are able to abuse cloud services by obtaining unauthorized and illegal access to other customer's confidential data residing on the same cloud platform. As a result, scholars are encouraged to conduct more extensive research to reveal more information about the risks and impact of this threat on sensitive business data; additionally, cloud security providers need to implement and deploy more proactive security techniques to prevent unauthorized and illegal access to sensitive organizational information residing on the cloud.

REFERENCES

Alam, B., Doja, M. N., Alam, M., & Malhotra, S. (2013). Security issues analysis for cloud computing. *International Journal of Computer Science and Information Security*, *11*(9), 117–125.

Alshammari, H. (2014). Privacy and security concerns in cloud computing. *International Journal of Computer Science and Information Security*, *12*(3), 1–4.

Aslam, U., Ullah, I., & Ansari, S. (2010). Open source private cloud computing. *Interdisciplinary Journal of Contemporary Research in Business*, 2(7), 399-399-407

Baber, M., & Chauhan, M. (2011). A Tale of Migration to Cloud Computing for SharingExperiences and Observations, Proceedings of the *2nd International Workshop on Software Engineering for Cloud Computing 2011*. Retrieved from http://delivery.acm.org.ezproxy.apollolibrary.com

Bisong, A., & Rahman, S. M. (2011). An Overview of the Security Concerns in Enterprise Cloud Computing. *International Journal of Network Security & Its Applications*, *3*(1), 30–45. doi:10.5121/ijnsa.2011.3103

Blumenthal, M. S. (2011). Is security lost in the clouds? *Communications & Stratégies*, *81*(1), 69–86.

Chakraborty, R., Ramireddy, S., Raghu, T. S., & Rao, H. R. (2010). The information assurance practices of cloud computing vendors. *IT Professional Magazine*, 12(4), 29-29-37

Chen, Y., Paxson, V., & Katz, R. H. (2010). What's new about cloud computing security. *Technical Report No. UCB/EECS-2010-5*. Retrieved from http://www.eecs.berkeley.edu/Pubs/TechRpts/2010/EECS-2010-5.html

Choo, K. (2010). Cloud computing: Challenges and future directions. *Trends & Issues in Crime & Criminal Justice*, (400), 1-6

Da Silva, C. M. R., da Silva, J. L. C., Rodrigues, R. B., do Nascimento, L. M., & Garcia, V. C. (2013). Systematic mapping study on security threats in cloud computing. *International Journal of Computer Science and Information Security*, *11*(3), 55–64.

Danchev, D. (2009). Zeus crimeware using Amazon's EC2 as command and control server. *ZDnet*. Retrieved from http://blogs.zdnet.com/security/?p=5110

Eludiora, S., Abiona, O., Oluwatope, A., Olu-waranti, A., Onime, C., & Kehinde, L. (2011). A user identity management protocol for cloud computing paradigm. *International Journal of Communications, Network and System Sciences*, 4(3), 152-152-163

Cloud Computing: Benefits, Risks, and Recom-mendations. (2009). European Network and In-formation Security Agency. Retrieved from http://www.enisa.europa.eu/act/rm/files/deliverables/cloud-computing-risk-assessment

Gharshi, R. S. (2013, July). Enhancing Security in Cloud Storage using ECC Algorithm. *Inter-national Journal of Science and Research*, 2(7).

Jensen, M., Schwenk, J., Gruschka, N., & Iacono, L. (2009). On Technical Security Issues in Cloud Computing. Proceedings of *2009 IEEE Interna-tional Conference on Cloud Computing*. (pp.109-116). doi:10.1109/CLOUD.2009.60

Mongan, K. (2011). Cloud computing the storm is coming. *Accountancy Ireland*, 43(3), 58-58-60.

Rashmi, .G.Sahoo, .S.Mehfuz (2013, August). Securing Software as a Service Model of Cloud Computing: Issues and Solutions. *International Journal on Cloud Computing: Services and Ar-chitecture*, Vol.3, No.4.

Ristenpart, T., Tromer, E., Shacham, H., & Sav-age, S. (n. d.). Hey, you, get off of my cloud: Exploring information leakage in third-party compute clouds. Proceedings of the *16th ACM conference on Computer and communications security CCS'09*. doi:10.1145/1653662.1653687

Security guidance for critical areas of focus in cloud computing. (2009). *Cloud Security Alliance*. Retrieved from http://www.cloudsecurityalliance.org

Subashini, S., & Kavitha, V. (2011). A survey on security issues in service delivery models of cloud computing. *Journal of Network and Com-puter Applications*, 34(1), 1–11. doi:10.1016/j.jnca.2010.07.006

Top Threats to Cloud Computing. (2010). *Cloud Security Alliance*. Retrieved from http://www.cloudsecurityalliance.org/topthreats/csathreats.v1.0.pdf

KEY TERMS AND DEFINITIONS

IaaS: Infrastructure as a Service, also known as "utility computing," "infrastructure util-ity" "instance computing" where the physical infrastructure is composed of virtual instances of required resources. Examples for providers: Amazon EC2, GoGrid.

PaaS: Platform as a Service, also describe by Redmonk analyst Stephen O'Grady* as "fabric* computing", where the underlying physical and logical architecture are abstracted. Examples: Google App Engine, Microsoft Azure.

SaaS: Software as a Service, which refers to Internet-based access to specific applications. Example: Salesforce.com, Workstream.

Chapter 3
Cloud Security Using Ear Biometrics

Santosh Kumar
Indian Institute of Technology, India

Ali Imam Abidi
Indian Institute of Technology, India

Sanjay Kumar Singh
Indian Institute of Technology, India

ABSTRACT

Cloud computing has created much enthusiasm in the IT world, institutions, business groups and different organizations and provided new techniques to cut down resource costs and increase its better utilization. It is a major challenge for cloud consumers and service providers equally. Establishing one's identity has become complicated in a vastly interconnected cloud computing network. The need of a consistent cloud security technique has increased in the wake of heightened concerns about security. The rapid development in cloud data storage, network computing services, accessing the cloud services from vendors has made cloud open to security threats. In this chapter, we have proposed an approach based on Ear Biometric for cloud security of individual consumers and vendors. This approaches started to get acceptance as a genuine method for determining an individual's identity. This chapter provides with the stepping stone for future researches to unveil how biometrics can change the cloud security scenario as we know it.

1. INTRODUCTION

Cloud computing security is an evolutionary offshoot of computer security, information security and security of internet based computation, whereby shared resources, different relevant software and information is provided to computers and other devices on demand. Cloud computing has rapidly become one of the most prominent concept in the IT world due to its innovative model of computing as based on their utility. It promises increased flexibility, scalability and reliability, while promising decreased operational and support costs. However, many potential cloud users are

DOI: 10.4018/978-1-4666-8387-7.ch003

reluctant to move to cloud computing on a large scale due to the unaddressed security issues present in cloud computing. In October 2009 paper representation "Effectively and Securely using the Cloud Computing Paradigm" by Peter Mell and Tim Grance of United States National Institute of Standards and Technologies (NIST) has given the definition of cloud computing: "Cloud computing is a model for enabling ubiquitous, convenient, on demand network access to shared pool of configurable computing resources(e.g., networks, servers, storage, applications, and services) and applications as services that can be rapidly provisioned and released with minimal management effort or service provider interaction" (Mell, & Grance, 2009). Cloud security emphasizes on the main objective of the a broad set of policies for different issues, new trend of technologies and to control deployments to protected cloud database like shared resources, different essential software, information of different organizations (academics, Industries and different Vendors) and provide a complete level of security to infrastructure (may be very complex) of cloud computing.

1.1 Characteristics of Cloud Computing Model

In cloud computing, the shared pool of resources is incorporated through virtualization or job scheduling techniques. Virtualization is a process to create the set of logical resources whether it may be hardware platform, operating system, network resources and other shared resources usually implemented by the software based components acting like physical resources. In general software resources is known as hypervisor which imitates as a set of resources and gives permission to the operating system software (logical resources) running on a virtual machine separated from the underlying hardware resources. Following are essential characteristics of cloud computing model. The National Institute of Standards and Technology (NIST)'s definition of cloud computing identifies "five essential characteristics".

1.1.1 On-Demand Self-Service

On demand self–service enables consumer to use the cloud computing as needed without human interaction between users and service providers. With the help of on demand self service characteristics, consumer can schedule the different cloud services such as computation and storages as their requirement. In addition to valuable and satisfactory to the consumer, the self service interear must be user friendly to access the different cloud resources and effective means to manage the service offerings. The main advantage of on-demand self-service provides better and eases and elimination of human interaction provides efficiencies to both the consumer and vendor of cloud service (Mell, & Grance, 2009).

1.1.2 Broad Network Access

For cloud computing to be successful alternative to the in house data centre it requires the high bandwidth communication internet communication links and capabilities are available over the network and accessed through standard mechanisms that promote use by heterogeneous thin or thick client platforms (e.g., mobile phones, tablets, laptops, and workstations). One of the principal economics explanations for cloud computing is that lowered cost of high bandwidth network communication to the cloud provides access to a bigger pool of shared resources that sustain efficient level of utilization. In addition many organizations utilizes the three–tier based architecture to provide the communication between cloud and consumer's laptop, printer, communication devices like mobile phones and PDAs to wide area networks. Following are the elements in the three tier architecture of cloud computing.

- Access Switch: it connects the desktops device to aggregation switches.
- Aggregation switches: it emphasizes on switches the flow control.
- Routers: Core router and switches that provides the connection mechanism for WAN and manage the traffic control.

1.1.3 Resource Pooling

The provider's computing resources are pooled to serve multiple consumers using a multi-tenant model, with different physical and virtual resources dynamically assigned and reassigned according to consumer demand. There is a sense of location independence in that the customer generally has no control or knowledge over the exact location of the provided resources but may be able to specify location at a higher level of abstraction (e.g., country, state, or datacenter).

1.1.4 Rapid Elasticity

Rapid elasticity refers to the ability to cloud expand or reduce allocate resources quickly and efficiently to meet the requirements of the self services characteristics of cloud computing. Capabilities can be elastically provisioned and released, in some cases automatically, to scale rapidly outward and inward commensurate with demand. To the consumer, the capabilities available for provisioning often appear to be unlimited and can be appropriated in any quantity at any time.

1.1.5 Measured Service

Cloud systems automatically control and optimize resource use by leveraging a metering capability at some level of abstraction appropriate to the type of service (e.g., storage, processing, bandwidth, and active user accounts). Resource usage can be monitored, controlled and reported, providing transparency for both the provider and consumer of the utilized service.

1.2 Cloud Computing Service Based Layer

Cloud computing refers to the fundamental infrastructure which can be make available different services to customer via defined interear. There are different layer of cloud computing services that refers to different type of services model. Each service layer provides the separate capability apart from administration and management of service layer. Depending on the services offered their deployment models it can be believed to consist of three layers as follows (Pearson, Siani, & Yee, 2013).

- Infrastructure as a service (IaaS).
- Plate form as a service (PaaS).
- Software as a service (SaaS).

1.2.1 Infrastructure as a Service (IaaS)

Infrastructure as a service model is a basic cloud computing service model. The providers of infrastructure as a service offer resources as services including computers which may be physical or virtual machines and different operating systems over distributed network. The offered resources can be managed through as service application programming interear. The hypervisor (hypervisor providing services that allow multiple computer operating systems (Xen, Kernel based virtual Machine) runs the virtual machine as the guest computer. Pool of Pools of hypervisors within the cloud operational support-system can support large numbers of virtual machines and the ability to scale services up and down according to customers' varying requirements.

1.2.2 Platform as a Service (PaaS)

In platform as a service, the cloud providers deliver different platform including programming language execution environment, operating system, databases and web server. It emphasizes on the delivery of a solution of stack for software development including runtime environment and its life time management. It gives flexibility to users or consumers to develop new application programming interear (API) deployed and configurable remotely. Examples include Microsoft Azure, Google App Engine and Force.com.

1.2.3 Software as a Service (SaaS)

To delivery of application as service which is available on demand and paid for on a per use basis. In simple multi-tenancy, each consumer has its own resources that are separated out from those of others consumers. A more efficient form is fine grained multi tenancy, where all the resources are shared except that consumer data and access capability are segregated within the application.

1.2.4 Anything as a Service

According to (Armbrust, 2009), infrastructure as a service and platform as a service are comparable. These are connected together arguing that the gap between these models is not hard enough yet. In addition to the three service delivery models, this chapter describes one particular approach known as anything-as-a-Service (XaaS) (Armbrust, 2009) (Banerjee, Friedrich, Bash, & Goldsack, 2010), (Bhaskar, Admela, Dimitrios,& Goeleven, 2011), (Chao-Chi, 2011) which refers to the fact that cloud systems are able to support and offer anything or everything in the form of services, ranging from large resources to personal specific and granular requirements.

1.2.5 Data-as-a-Service (DaaS)

Data as a Service (DaaS) is a cousin of software as a service. Data as a service is based on the concept that the product, data in this case, can be provided on demand to the user regardless of geographic or organizational separation of provider and consumer. Data as a Service brings the

notion that data quality can happen in a centralized place, cleansing and enriching data and offering it to different systems, applications or users, irrespective of where they were in the organization or on the different locations.

1.2.6 Routing-as-a-Service (RaaS)

Routing-as-a-Service (RaaS) is framework for tenant-directed route control in data centers in cloud computing scenario, Data center is most important key infrastructure for "on-line service providers" (OSP) to provide always on demand and responsive services to end-users of cloud. Normally consist of 1,000- 100,000' number of servers, data centers are designed to handle tremendous computations, large storage and quick service delivery. However, the computational resources in a data center are not used monolithically. Often the resources are multiplexed between different tenants clients of the data center resources so they can simultaneously perform computations, store data, and provide services to end-users. Therefore RaaS-based implementation provides a route control platform for multiple tenants to perform route control independently with little administrative involvement and for the landlord to set the overall network policies (Al-Aqrabi, Liu, & Xu, 2012) (Chao-Chih, Lihua, Albert, Greenberg, Chen-Nee, & Prasan, 2011).

1.2.7 Security-as-a-Service (SecaaS)

Security-as-a-service (SECaaS) is an outsourcing based model for security management in cloud computing. Normally, it involves applications like anti-virus software delivered over the internet however the term can also refer to security management provided in-house by an external organization. Security as a service (SECaaS) is a business model in which a large service provider integrates their security services into a corporate infrastructure on a subscription basis more cost effectively than most individuals or corporations can provide on their own, when total cost of owner-ship is considered. These security services often include authentication, anti-virus, anti-malware/spyware, intrusion detection, and security event management, among others (Al-Aqrabi, Liu, & Xu, 2012), (James, & Wayman, 2001). Following table 1 demonstrates that responsibility and shared responsibility of different cloud service layers which is given to various types of cloud, service providers, users and cloud consumer/customer.

1.3 Cloud Deployment Approaches

Cloud deployment methodologies demonstrate the definite of Cloud environments the way the Cloud delivery models (i.e. software, platforms and infrastructures as services) which are deployed by the Cloud providers (vendors) to make the cloud provisions available to cloud consumers. The deployment models where can be either internally or externally implemented recapitulated in the NIST presentation as follows:

- Private: A cloud infrastructure managed solely for an organization which being accessible only within private network and being operated by organization or third party organization.

- Public: Public clouds are cloud services offered by third parties but hosted and supervised by the service providers (Vendors). It is publically accessible cloud infrastructure.
- Community Cloud: Shared infrastructure for specific community.
- Hybrid Cloud: it is composition of two or more cloud.
- Virtual private Cloud: It consists on using virtual private network (VPN) connectivity to create virtual private or semi-private clouds and resorting to secure pipes supplied by VPN technology and by assigning isolated resources to customers. A virtual private network seats on top of any model previously described, likewise a VPN that is built upon other networks. Hence, it is a particular case of private cloud existing within any other. This model allows entities to use cloud services without worrying about operating in shared or public environments. An example of this model is Amazon VPC. Figure 1 demonstrates cloud delivery Models and Cloud deployment model as follow in figure1 (Lenk, FZI Karlsruhe, Klems, Nimi and Tai, 2009)

Table 1. Responsibility of cloud service layer

So. No	Name of Cloud Computing Layer	Responsibility of Cloud Service Layer	CP	SP	CC/C
1	IaaS (Infrastructure as a service)	Virtual Machine security			R
		Secured VM images repository	R		
		Securing VM boundaries	R		
		Hypervisor security			
2	PaaS (Plate form as a service)	SOA	SR		SR
		API Security		R	
3	Software as a Service security	SaaS security	SR	SR	
		Web application security	R		

Where, R=Responsible, SR=Shared responsibility, CP=Cloud Provider, SP=Service Provider, CC/C=Cloud Consumer/Customer, SOA: service-oriented architecture related security.

Figure 1. Cloud delivery models and cloud deployment model

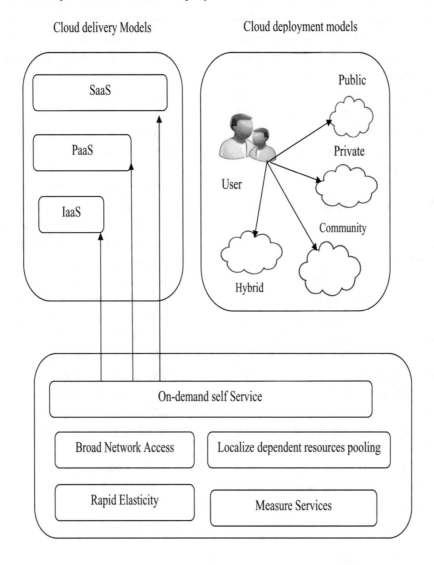

2. LITERATURE REVIEW

In traditional cloud authentication approach, a login and password are the primary means for authenticating users. A login and password is a combination of the most universally used method for authentication however, this approaches are not secure. It may be breached by existing hacking tools (Maninder, & Sarbjeet, 2012).There are several traditional approach listed below:

OTP is a 'One Time Password' (OTP) approach wherein a password is provided upon request by user for accessing the resources. OTP can prevent the possibility of a password being stolen and reused (Rubin, 1995). The allotted password is valid for only one login session or transaction time out and can only be used once. The most important inadequacy that is addressed by OTPs is that in comparison to static passwords, they are not vulnerable to replay attacks. These systems are not cheap and more reliable for system protection. Users of OTP systems are still susceptible to one kind of system attack known as man-in-the-middle attacks.

For cloud secure data storage and accessibility by authorized user, Govinda K. and N. Yannick proposed an effective and flexible for cloud secure data storage and accessibility by using face as biometric traits (Govinda, & Yannick, 2012). (Yang, & Lai, 2013) proposed a cloud service model under a multi-tenant architecture (MTA) using identity management and Role-Based Access Control and propose and design a Role-Based Multi-Tenancy Access Control (RB-MTAC). The RB-MTAC applies identity management to determine the user's identity and applicable roles, since different users possess different functional roles with respective privileges for processing. Such role-based assignments can easily and efficiently manage a user's access rights to achieve application independence and data isolation for improving the processing performance of cloud multi-tenant services and hardening the security and privacy of cloud applications. (Yassin, 2012) proposed a method of two-factor authentication scheme based on Schnorr digital signature and feature extraction from fingerprint to overcome the weakness of user and password based cloud authentication and their issues. (Jivanadham, 2013) proposed an authentication scheme known as cloud cognitive authenticator (CCA). It applies one round zero knowledge protocol (ZKP) for authentication. CCA is an API designed for cloud environment that integrates bio-signals, ZKP and CCA improves security in a public cloud by providing bi-level authentication. It also provides encryption and decryption of user ids. Electro dermal responses are used for first level authentication. The main advantage of CCA compared to other existing models is that it provides two levels of authentication combined with the encryption algorithm. Following table 2 illustrates the advantages and disadvantages of cloud authentication methods.

3. ISSUES AND CHALLENGES OF CLOUD COMPUTING SECURITY

Movement of various data and business operations in the cloud presents various security concerns, risks and threats issues associated with the movement of data and access control mechanisms. The nature of cloud presents one of its own unique challenges that are previously strange to traditional ways of computing. The main issue is not about the security mechanisms being applied on data being stored in a remote location; rather it is about "How much the environment is safe?" As the businesses grow, so do their dependence on cloud for storing their sensitive data and applications on it. Thus in the coming time, the concern for making the cloud environment safe will grow. Risks are defined on basis the nature of threats and possibility of attacks (Jansen, & Grance, 2011). The major issues concerned for security are data confidentiality, data Integrity, data Availability, trust Issues (Al-Aqrabi, 2012), (Jackson, 2010).

3.1. Data Confidentiality

The term, confidentiality ensures that only the entity who is properly authenticated and authorized by the access control policies laid down by the enterprises are able to access the data and different applications (within their levels of controls). It is the most important need of any enterprise to maintain the confidentiality of its business data and authorized user database. The hierarchy of different cloud access controls defines the order of levels of access by the individuals based on their levels of security clearance. Thus confidentiality can be achieved partially by access control mechanisms (if not fully when stored without encrypted). But still, major obstacle lies in distributing and

Table 2. Comparison of cloud authentication methods

S.N.	Method /Scheme	Year Advantages	Disadvantages	Future Directions
1.	Authentication in the Clouds: A Framework and its Application to Mobile Users (Chow, 2010)	2010 Authentication is done on the clients" behavior hence theft of the device is not a threat	Authentication score is checked against a certain threshold. Hence a best result depends on application.	The flexibility of the system provides support to latest and evolving Cloud authentication systems
2.	Two Factor Authentication (Shen, 2010)	2010 It is robust and efficient against phishing and replay attacks	Theft of mobile phone leads to breach of security	Need to design a system that will authenticate the user with the feature other than possession of Mobile phone.
3.	A strong user authentication framework for cloud computing (Choudhury, 2011)	2011 Identity management, Mutual authentication and Session key agreement.	Password and Smartcard Verification is done by the local system. Performance unknown	Providing formal security proof
4.	Consolidated authentication model (Kim, & Hong, 2011)	2012 Secure protocols allow the credentials to freely roam in cloud computing environment	Credential store is the repository for credentials, posing serious threat of being hacked.	Design and implementation of the proposed scheme.
5.	Single Sign On (Dinesha, 2012)	2011 Central server Supplies credential to the application server. Hence no multiple authentication for different applications	If the central server is hacked then entire server is hacked	Security measures for central authentication server to be reviewed
7.	Multidimensional Password generation (Quorica, 2009)	2012 Multiple levels of authentication	Overhead is more in multilevel authentication	Security levels need to be strengthened.
8.	Face Recognition System (FRS) on Cloud Computing for User Authentication (Wang, Ku, & Wang, 2011)	2013 This technique is simple and easy to implement	It will not work in the absence of camera also face features might become different depending on lighting conditions, time of the day.	Work can be done in the direction of removing its limitations such as face recognition after ageing, makeup, jewelry.
9.	ALP: An Authentication and Leak Prediction Model for Cloud Computing Privacy by (Tereza Cristina, Melo de, & BritoCarvalho, 2013)	2013 It solves the issue of privacy preservation by authentication & confidentiality approach for redacted trees that uses the previous privacy patterns	The approach is based on the previous information, so it cannot cover new attack patterns	In this approach the clustered documents are organized as trees. However, there is a possibility of extending the same approach to graphs and forests as well.

implementing permission hierarchy. In a scenario where lack of access control mechanisms prevails, business data must be stored encrypted form of data. However, there must be strong measures of establishing the access control policies. Even if, in case of whether data is being encrypted or not, there must be a strong and a well established methodologies of implementing individually attribute based access control mechanisms. However, there prevails a significant lack of any particular strong access control method apart from authentication through passwords, individual personal questions or any cookies based technique. Therefore, existing scenario of current access control mechanisms makes the data storage in the cloud vulnerable to threats and possible account breaches because the existing policies do not present any strong authentication mechanism apart from just passwords or individual security questions, which makes it highly possible of attacks being deployment through Social Engineering (Zissis, & Lekkas, 2012), (Li, Tian, Wei, & Sun, 2012).

3.2. Data Integrity

Integrity refers to presenting the data in same initial form as it was earlier (before any authorized modification) thus by preventing any unauthorized modification or deletion. Integrity is important for any crucial data from perspective of enterprise or individual one. Data integrity can be checked (if not prevented fully) by hash check mechanisms through Message Authentication Codes (MAC's). Hash functions bear uniqueness for every different message. It is a one way function. Through this, it is easy to calculate message digest for any given data, however vice-versa is not possible making Hash functions a secure way to compute data integrity. Also monitoring of access logs of entities helps in preventing unauthenticated data access (Mather, Kumaraswamy, & Latif, 2009). Despite of the above mechanisms keeping data integrity into check, better mechanisms for preventing data unauthorized access should be deployed. Although data can be encrypted to make it non-intelligent and MAC mechanisms can be deployed to check the message digest of data (to ensure data integrity), it is on the first place very necessary to restrict the access of the entities to the sensitive data. Proper authentication and authorization techniques must be implemented before allowing the entity gain access the data.

3.3. Data Reliability and Availability

The uptime of the data by CSP (cloud data provider) should be as per their SLA (Service Level Agreement) and comply the terms and conditions agreed by the cloud service provider (in absence of any clearly mentioned SLA, it must be as per negotiated with the customer earlier). Since data in being cloud is on the verge of being accessed anytime, anywhere and by multiple accessing devices on different platforms, data must be readily available without any constraint towards multiple business locations. It is a major challenge to implement proper access control policies on individual entities before granting the access towards the data and different software and hardware resources in the cloud, when requests for verification and validation of access permissions come dynamically from multiple locations in real time scenario. Cloud providers (vendors) still are deficient in round-the-clock service, these results in frequent outages. It is important to monitor the service being provided using internal or third-party tools. It is vital to have plans to supervise usage, SLAs, performance, robustness, and business dependency of these services. Data back-up is also a major challenge to the cloud computing. In order to avoid such problems with back-up, especially when it comes to crucial data, never assume that someone else is automatically protecting. When deciding to move your data to the cloud, make sure your service provider has a back-up methodology or a disaster recovery setup. Even better, make your own arrangements to back up your data.

3.4. Identity and Access Management

There is a difference between authenticating any entity for the accessing the resources in the cloud and authorization of any entity defining its access clearance level. Hereby, it is important to note that authorization is a major factor in deciding the access permissions of any entity in the cloud than just by simple authentication. Proper authorization mechanism can be implemented by various authentication attributes of entity which in turn corresponds to different security clearance levels. Higher level of security clearance corresponds to more access permissions. Therefore, in the cloud scenario, better access control policies can be deployed apart from just mere passwords (which includes character or numeric strings) and also include attributes based on "different individual credentials".

3.5. Trust Over CSP (Cloud Service Provider)

Trust is a factor which makes an entity to believe over credibility of CSP over the services as promised in SLA (Service Level Agreement). Trust is defined when *"an entity A is considered to trust another entity B when entity A believes that entity B will behave exactly as expected and required"* (ITU, 2001) Trust involves putting the faith in the CSP's ability to properly manage the data/resources and its ability of enforcement of its security policies. Trust generates by the time being reputation of any CSP and its promises to

ensure the security policies. More any CSP announces the proposed security policies, better it will be in condition to implement it and gain trust of business organizations.

3.6. Other Cloud Security Challenges and Requirement

Based on a survey conducted by IDC in 2008, the major challenges that prevent Cloud Computing from being adopted are recognized by organizations are as follows (table 3):

3.7. Security Technology in the Cloud Computing Environment

There are numerous concrete securities technologies in cloud computing however, this security does not provide competence level of security to cloud's databases, different users, consumers, organizations, academic and service providers. However, if we regard cloud computing as an extension of the existing IT technologies, it possible to divide some of them by each component of cloud computing and apply to access control and user authentication are representative as security technologies used for platforms. Access

Table 3. Security challenges and requirements

Security Challenges		Security Requirement
System Reliability		Security integration and various technologies
Privacy and data protection		Privacy protection mechanism
Data isolation		Virtualization concept
Cloud Interoperability		Interoperability is to realize the seamless fluid data across clouds and between cloud and local applications.
Other Challenges	Security management	Regulations and supervisions require selection of cloud computing operator of high credit
	Cloud costing model	Cloud consumers must consider the tradeoffs amongst computation, communication and integration. While migrating to the Cloud can significantly reduce the infrastructure cost, it does raise the cost of data communication, i.e. the cost of transferring an organization's data to and from the public and community Cloud and the cost per unit of computing resource used is likely to be higher (Ramgovind, Eloff,& Smith, 2010).

control is the technology that controls a process in the operating system not to approach the area of another process (Un et al. 2009). There are DAC (Discretionary Access Control), MAC (Media Access Control), and RBAC (Role-Based Access Control). Discretionary access control helps a user establish the access authority to the resources that he/she owns as he/she pleases. Media access control establishes the vertical/horizontal access rules in the system at the standard of security level and area for the resources and uses them. Role-based access control gives an access authority to a user group based on the role the user group plays in the organization not to a user. It is widely used because it is fit for the commercial organizations. Numerous technologies used to authenticate a user are id/password, public key infrastructure, multi-factor authentication, SSO (Single Sign On), MTM (Mobile Trusted Module) and i-Pin (Dikaiakos et al., 2009), (Onwubiko, 2010), (Feng et al., 2011). In addition, security issues to cloud computing are listed as follows (Onwubiko, 2010) (Hamlen, Kantarcioglu, Khan,& Thurai singham, 2010):

- Privacy Issues
- Data Ownership and Content Disclosure Issues
- Data Location
- Control Issues
- Regulatory and Legislative Compliance
- Forensic Evidence Issues
- Auditing Issues
- Business Continuity and Disaster Recovery Issues
- Trust Issues
- Emerging Threats to Cloud
- Security Policy Issues

Therefore, security issues for many of these systems and technologies are applicable to cloud computing. For example, the network that interconnects the systems in a cloud has to be secure. Furthermore, virtualization paradigm in cloud computing environment consequences numerous security concerns. Mapping the virtual machines to the physical machines has to be carried out securely. Data security involves encrypting the data as well as ensuring that appropriate policies are enforced for data sharing. Furthermore, resource allocation scheme and memory management of algorithms have to be very secure. Finally, data mining techniques may be applicable to malware detection in clouds (Jain, Pankanti, & Prabhakar, 2004).

4. CLOUD SECURITY

With the growing popularity of cloud computing, security issues are showing the importance of a gradual upward trend has become an important factor restricting the development. There comes an increasingly frequent cloud computing security incident. According to international data corporation (IDC)'s survey, 87.5% of users worry about security issues in cloud computing. Obviously, security ranked first as the greatest challenge or issue of cloud computing. Gartner2009-year survey also stated that 70% of respondents believe that the recent CTO of cloud computing without the use of the primary reasons is that there is data security and privacy concern (Feng, & Zhang, 2011).

4.1. Types of Cloud Security Methods

Cloud computing has become known as a resource sharing platform, which permits different service providers (vendors) to deliver software as services to consumers. In a cloud computing environment, the entire data reside over a set of networked resources, enabling the data to be accessed through virtual machines. However, for many security sensitive applications such as critical data processing and e-business application, we must emphasize on afford necessary security safeguard for mitigating the threats in the shared open cloud infrastructures.

4.2. Security Technology in Cloud Computing Environment

There are numerous concrete securities technologies in cloud computing however, this security does not provide competence level of security to cloud's databases, different users, consumers, organizations, academic and service providers. However, if we regard cloud computing as an extension of the existing IT technologies, it possible to divide some of them by each component of cloud computing and apply to access control and user authentication are representative as security technologies used for platforms. Access control is the technology that controls a process in the operating system not to approach the area of another process (Un et al., 2009).There are DAC (Discretionary Access Control), MAC (Media Access Control), and RBAC (Role-Based Access Control). Discretionary access control helps a user establish the access authority to the resources that he/she owns as he/she pleases. Media access control establishes the vertical/horizontal access rules in the system at the standard of security level and area for the resources and uses them. Role-based access control gives an access authority to a user group based on the role the user group plays in the organization not to a user. It is widely used because it is fit for the commercial organizations. Numerous technologies used to authenticate a user are id/password, public key infrastructure, multi-factor authentication, SSO (Single Sign On), MTM (Mobile Trusted Module), and i-Pin (Dikaiakos et al., 2009).

5. BIOMETRIC SYSTEM

Biometric system is a pattern recognition based system. It acquires biometric data from an individual, extracts a salient feature set from the data, compares feature set against the feature set(s) stored in the database, and executes an action based on the result of the comparison (Jain, Flynn, & Ross, 2008). Establishing one's identity has become complicated in a vastly interconnected cloud network. The need of a consistent cloud security based technique has increased in the wake of heightened concerns about security. Biometrics is the science of establishing the identity of an individual based on their physical, chemical and behavioral traits. Nowadays numerous biometric methods are used and deployed for authentication which means the process of ensuring correct identification of the user including three categories bellow:

- Something users know, e.g. Password, PIN.
- Something users have, e.g. ATM, Smart cards.
- Something users are, e.g. Fingertips, the iris.

The need of a consistent cloud security based technique has increased in the wake of heightened concerns about security. It is a reliable and suitable methodology of identifying individuals. It can be defined as an automated methodology to uniquely identify humans using their behavioral or physiological characteristics (Rong, & Cheng, 2012). The widespread implementation of biometric recognition requires strong privacy protection against possible misuse, loss or theft of the biometric data. Existing techniques and methodologies for privacy-preserving biometric identification primarily rely on conventional cryptographic primitives such as homomorphic encryption and unconscious transfer, which inevitably introduces tremendous cost to the system and are not applicable to practical large-scale applications (Yuan, & Shucheng, 2013). The data leakage and security attacks can be caused by inadequate authentication (Vu, Pham, &Truong, 2012). Cloud services are paid services, so to identify an authorized user is a major concern in cloud computing.

5.1. Biometric Characteristic

Biometrics offers a natural and reliable solution to certain aspects of identity management by utilizing fully automated or semi-automated schemes to recognize individuals (Human or Animal) based on their inherent physical and/or behavioral characteristics (Fig. 2). With the help of physiological and behavioral characteristics currently used for automatic identification include fingerprints, iris, voice, retina, hand, ear, handwriting, keystroke, and finger shape (Fig. 2). However, this is only a partial list as new measures (such as ear gait, shape, optical skin reflectance, head resonance and body odor) are being produced all of the time. Due to the broad range of characteristics used in identification or verification, the imaging requirements for the technology vary greatly. Here always one

question arises: Which biometric characteristic is best? The ideal biometric characteristic has five qualities: robustness, distinctiveness, availability, accessibility and acceptability are discussed below (Pun, & Moon, 2004):

- **Robustness:** By "robust", we mean unchanging on an individual over time.
- **Distinctive:** By "distinctive", we mean showing great variation over the population.
- **Available:** By "available", we mean that the entire population should ideally have these measuring multiples.
- **Accessible:** By "accessible", we mean easy to image using electronic sensors.
- **Acceptable:** By "acceptable", we mean that people do not object to having this measurement taken from them.

Figure 2. Biometric characteristics (1): Physiological Characteristics (2): Behavioral Characteristics

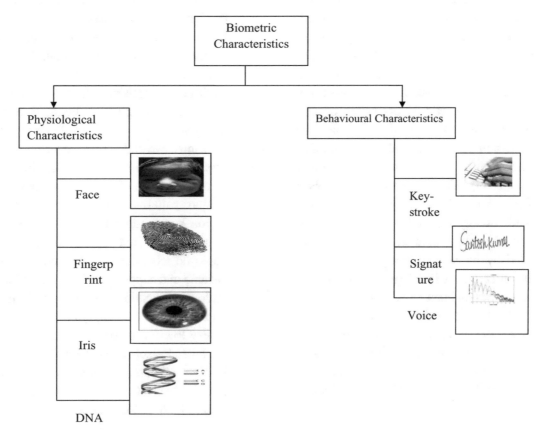

Several different aspects of human physiology, chemistry or behaviour characteristics can be used for biometric authentication. The selection of a particular biometric for use in a specific application involves a weighting of several factors. Biometric traits are classified as follows:

5.2. Different Biometrics Techniques

- **Fingerprint Recognition:** Fingerprint is a pattern of ridges and valleys on the surear of the fingertip whose formation is determined during the first seven month fetal development. It has been empirically determined that the fingerprints of same twins are different (Shen et al., 2010). Fingerprint recognition refers to the automated method of verifying a match between two human fingerprints. The dryness of fingers, soiled fingers can affect the system and it can show error. One problem with large scale fingerprint recognition systems is that they require a huge amount of computation resources. Finally, fingerprints of small fraction of population may be unstable for automatic identification because of genetic factors aging; occupational reason like manual works may have large number of cuts and bruises on their fingerprints that keep changing (Jain & ross, 2008) (Wayman, 2000), (Jantz, 1997).

- **Face Recognition**: It is non –intrusive methodology and facial attributes are probably the most common biometric feature used by humans to recognize one other. In order that a facial recognition system works well in practice as (1) face detection: It should automatically detect whether a face is present in the in acquired image. (2) face location: To locate the face if there is in the used face database. (3) Recognition of Face: To recognize the face from a general viewpoint from any posture/profile.

- **Voice Recognition:** Voice is a combination of different physiological or behavioral biometric characteristics. The physiological features of an individual's voice are based on their shape and size of appendages (vocal tracts, mouth structure and cavities of nasal and lips). Voice recognition is used to authenticate user's identity based on patterns of voice pitch and speech style. However a user's voice can be easily recorded and may use by unauthorized user. A disadvantages of voice based recognition is that human's speech features are very sensitive to a number of factor such as noise and voice signal quality is typically degraded in the quality by the communication channel.

- **Signature Recognition**: Signature recognition is used to authenticate user's identity based on the traits of their unique signature. It is behavioral biometrics that changes over a period of time. It is influenced by the physical and emotional conditions of the signatures (Ramgovind, Eloff, & Smith, 2010).

- **Retinal Recognition:** Retinal recognition is for recognizing people by the pattern of blood vessels on the retina. However, it is very intrusive and expensive technique.

- **Iris Recognition:** Iris recognition is a method of identifying people based on unique patterns within the ring-shaped region surrounding the pupil of the eye. The accuracy and rapidity of at present deployed iris-based recognition system is capable and support the feasibility of large scale identification systems based on iris information. Iris recognition systems have a very low False Accept Rate (FAR) and the False Reject Rate (FRR) of system can be high compared to other biometrics traits like fingerprints, voice, retinal and ear (Jain, Flynn, & Ross, 2008).

- **Hand Geometry Recognition:** The palms of human hands include pattern of ridges and numerous valleys like fingerprints. Hand geometry biometrics is the foundation on the geometric shape of the hand. However, this technique has some drawbacks like not ideal for children as with increasing age there hand geometry tend to change, not valid for persons suffering from arthritis, since they are not able to put the hand on the scanner properly.
- **Palm Recognition:** Palm recognition is based on ridges, principal lines and wrinkles on the surear of the palm. This technique is very expensive and not appropriate for children as there lines of palm change once they are fully grown up. All the above techniques tend to tell us that none of it is feasible & not much useful due to its various drawbacks. To overcome drawbacks of all these security techniques and to provide proper security for user authentication in cloud computing.

5.3. Biometrics System Technology

Biometric technologies are automated methods of verifying or recognizing the identity of a living person based on a physiological or behavioral characteristic (Al-Aqrabi, Liu, & Xu, 2012) (Vu, Pham, &Truong, 2012). There are two key words in this definition: "automated" and "person". The word "automated" differentiates biometrics from the larger field of groups of people (Jackson, 2010) or to probabilistically link persons to groups, but biometrics is interested only in recognizing people as individuals. All of the measures used contain both physiological and behavioral components, both of which can vary widely or be quite similar across a population of individual's human identification science. A generic biometric system can be demonstrated as having four main modules in fig. 3.

- **Sensor as Acquisition Module:** In biometric system a suitable biometric reader or scanner is required to capture the raw biometric data of individuals. For example, fingerprint images, an optical fingerprint (minutiae points) sensor can be used to capture the friction, ridge shape and size of individual fingerprint.
- **Pre-processing:** The related biometrics preprocessing technologies, including: noise removing from capture image, edge sharpening, image restoration, image segmentation, pattern extraction and dis-classification etc. Some preprocessing steps before feature extraction are noise filtering (for example with Gaussian windows (Jain, Flynn, & Ross, 2008) and re-sampling. Resampling is carried out in some systems in order to obtain a shape-based representation consisting of equidistant points. Other systems avoid the resampling step as some discriminative speed characteristics are lost in the process (Ketabdar, 2005).
- **Feature Extraction Module:** In biometric system basic elements in pattern recognition system, and some introduction of pattern recognition systems on biometrics such as fingerprint, palm-print, hand, ear, iris, and ear, as well as dental, DNA and retina recognition. In quality assessment and feature extraction, it determines the quality and suitability of biometric data acquired by the sensor in assessed. The obtained data is subjected to a signal enhancement algorithm in order to improve its quality. In order to facilitate matching or comparison of the raw digital representation is usually further processed by feature extractor to generate a compact but expressive representation called feature set. For example the position and orientation of minutiae points in a fingerprint image would be computed in feature extraction module.

- **Matching Process Module:** The features extracted in the previous (IIIrd stage) stage have to be compared against those stored in the database (template databasc) in order to establish the identity of the input biometric characteristics. In simplest form, matching involves the generation of a match score by comparing the feature sets pertaining to two images. The match score indicates the similarity between two images.
- **Decision Process Module**: In the decision stage, the match score(s) generated in the matching module are used to make a final decision. In the identification mode of operation, the output is a list of potential matching identities sorted in terms of their match score.

5.4. Biometric System Process

Depending on the application context, biometrics system may operate either in the verification or identification mode.

- **Verification Process:** In the verification mode, where the subject (people) claims an identity, the input image is compared against that of the claimed identity via their respective feature sets in order to validate the claim. It is used for positive recognition where the main objective is to prevent multiple subjects from using the same identity.
- **Identification Process:** In the identification mode, where the subject (people/object) does not claim an identity, the input

Figure 3. General biometric system

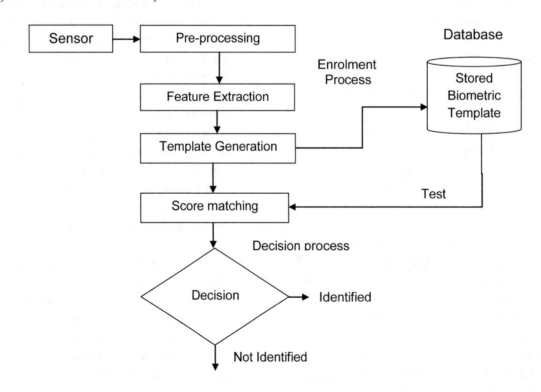

ear image is compared against a set of labeled (it is used to indicate that the identity of the images in the database is known) ear images in a database in order to determine the best match and, therefore, its identity. Identification is a critical component in the negative recognition application where the system establishes whether the person is who she denies to be. The main scope of the negative recognition is to prevent a single person from using the multiple identities.

5.5. Feature Extraction using Principal Component Analysis

The ear recognition algorithms are based on Principle Component Analysis (PCA). PCA reduces the dimensionality of each ear image by exploiting similarities between all ear images. Thus, PCA seeks to extract a set of images (eigenears) that combine linearly to describe all ear images. Given M ear images arranged as column vectors Γ_1, Γ_2, Γ_3, Γ_4,.......... Γ_M. The average ear

$$\Psi = \frac{1}{M} \sum_N^M \Gamma n$$

is subtracted from each image $\Phi_i = \Gamma_i - \Psi$. Next we joining the ear images into a single matrix $A = [\Phi_1 \Phi_2 \Phi_3 .... \Phi_M]$ PCA find a set of orthonormal vectors that best represents the data. These vectors are the eigenvectors U_k of the covariance matrix $C = AA^T$. In Eigenspace terminology, each ear image is projected by the top M' significant eigenvectors u_k to obtain weights $w_k = u_k^T (\Gamma_i - \Psi)$ that best linearly weight the eigenears into a representation of the original image. Knowing the weights of the training images and a new test ear image, a nearest neighbor approach determines the identity of the ear (Pentland, Moghaddam, & Starner, 1994). Eigenears

has the advantage of being simple and fast at the cost of low accuracy when pose, expression, and illumination vary significantly. An Eigenspace model Ω may be defined for set $S = \{S_1, S_2, S_3, ..., S_N\}$ of N training images (observations) (Turk, & Pentland,1991):

$$\Omega = \Omega(\mu, U, \lambda, S) \tag{1}$$

For a set $S = \{S_1, S_2, S_3, ..., S_N\}$ of N training images, the average vector image μ and the deviation matrix Φ of each image from the average image μ is given by:

$$\Phi = (S - \mu) \tag{2}$$

The covariance matrix C is given by:

$$C = \frac{1}{N} \sum_{i=1}^N \Phi_i \Phi_i^T = AA^T \tag{3}$$

where $A = [\Phi_1 \Phi_2 \Phi_3 .... \Phi_M]$ and Φ^T is the transpose matrix of Φ. The eigenvectors of the product $L = A^T A$ are obtained as:

$$Lv_i = A^T A v_i = \lambda_i v_i, \quad L_{ij} = (\Phi_i)^T \Phi_j \tag{4}$$

Premultiplying both sides by matrix A.

$$AA^T A v_i = \lambda_i A v_i \tag{5}$$

where v_i and λ_i are respectively the N eigenvectors and N eigenvalues of matrix L and $A v_i$ and λ_i are respectively the eigenvectors and eigenvalues of the covariance matrix $C = AA^T$

The eigenvectors $u_i = A v_i$ of matrix C are the eigenears that are obtained by projection of the deviation matrix Φ on the eigenvectors v_i of L

$$u_i = \sum_{j=1}^{N} v_i \Phi_j, i = 1, 2, 3........, N \qquad (6)$$

6. EAR BIOMETRIC SYSTEM

Ear Recognition is non–intrusive methodology and attributes are probably the most common biometric feature used by humans to recognize one other. Ear Detection should automatically detect whether an ear is present in the acquired image and to locate the ear if there is in the used ear database. Finally recognize the ear from a general viewpoint from any posture/profile (Ayman et al., 2013).

Identifying people by their ear as biometrics has recently received significant attention in the literature. Several reasons account for this trend: (1) ear recognition does not suffer from numerous problems associated with other non-intrusive biometrics, such as ear recognition. (2) It is the most competent candidate for combination with the ear in the context of multi-pose ear recognition. (3) The ear can be used for human recognition in surveillance videos where the ear may be occluded (cover – non-cover) completely or in part. In addition, the ear appears to degrade little with age. Even though at present ear detection and recognition systems have accomplished a certain level of maturity, their achievement is limited to control indoor conditions (Abaza et al., 2013). Ear as biometrics has a prosperous and stable feature that is preserved from birth to old age (Yuizono et al., 2002), (Burge, & Burger, 2002). It does not suffer from facial expression of human.

6.1. Ear Recognition as Biometric System

Ear recognition as a biometric system may be demonstrated as a characteristic pattern recognition system where the input ear image is reduced to a set of features that is subsequently used to compare against the feature sets of other images in order to determine its identity. The External anatomy of human's ear is shown in figure 4.

The forensic science literature demonstrates that ear development after the first four months of birth is highly linear. The rate of stretching is approximately five times greater than normal during the period from four months to the age of eight, after which it is constant until around the age of seventy when it again increases (Abaza Ayman et al., 2013).

Figure 4. External anatomy of the ear

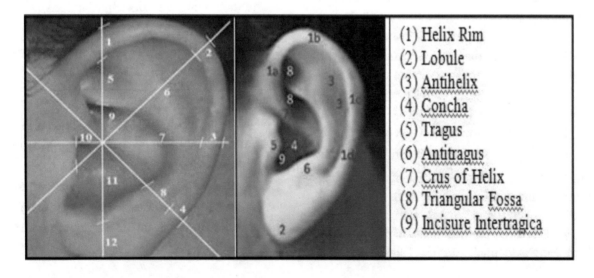

Ear recognition system may be accomplished using 2-D images of the ear which is completed during acquisition stage or 3-D point clouds that capture the three-dimensional details of the ear surear. The salient stages of a classical ear recognition system are illustrated in Figure 5.

6.1.1. Ear detection and Segmentation

The first and primary stage involves localizing the position of the ear in an image. Here, a rectangular boundary is typically used to indicate the spatial extent of the ear in the given image. Ear detection is a critical component since the errors in this stage can challenge the utility of the biometric system.

6.1.2. Ear Normalization and Enhancement

In this stage, the detected or segmented ear image is subjected to an enhancement process that improves the loyalty of the image. Furthermore, the ear image can be subjected to certain geometric or photometric corrections in order to facilitate feature extraction and matching. In some cases,

a curve that tightly fits the external contour of the ear may be extracted (Abaza Ayman, Ross, Christin, Harriso, & Nixon, 2013).

6.1.3. Ear Feature Extraction

At the same time as the segmented ear can be directly used during the matching stage, most systems extract a salient set of features to represent the ear. Feature extraction refers to the process in which the segmented ear is reduced to a mathematical model (feature vector) that summarizes the discriminatory information.

6.1.4. Matching Process

The features extracted in the previous (IIIrd stage) stage have to be compared against those stored in the database (template database) in order to establish the identity of the input ear. In simplest form, matching involves the generation of a match score by comparing the feature sets pertaining to two ear images. The match score indicates the similarity between two ear images.

Figure 5. Block diagram of a general Ear Recognition System

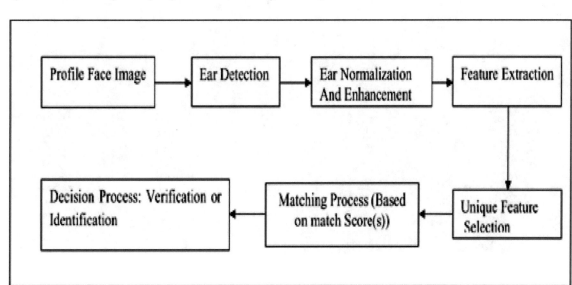

6.1.5. Decision Process

In the decision stage, the match score(s) generated in the matching module are used to make a final decision. In the identification mode of operation, the output is a list of potential matching identities sorted in terms of their match score.

6.2. Ear Database Acquisition and Preparation

The ear images are acquired using a 12 Megapixel digital camera under different lighting conditions with illumination changes. All left and right ear images are captured at distance 25-30 centimeter and save it in JPEG file format. The ear database included 1200×2 with 120 subjects with 10 images per subject (5 left and 5 right ear images). For training purpose, 4 images of each subject are used for training and the remaining 6 images are used for testing. In the processing step the ear part is manually coped color images to a size of 1402 x1900 pixels as shown in figure 6.

6.3. Implementation of Proposed Ear Recognition System for Cloud Security

We have proposed a framework, based on biometric methodology known as ear recognition system for cloud computing which provides a competent level of security to cloud and not accessed by imposter or unauthorized cloud users, consumers and numerous service providers (vendors). The proposed framework consists of following parts:

6.4. Enrollment Process of people to Face Recognition System for Cloud Security

Initially, users are requested to enroll first on to the cloud server over internet communication, whenever they want to access cloud resources (figure 7). Following steps enroll a user on the cloud server (Singh, & Singh, 2012):

- User has to fill the enrollment form which is provided by a cloud service provider

Figure 6. Sample dataset of human ear images

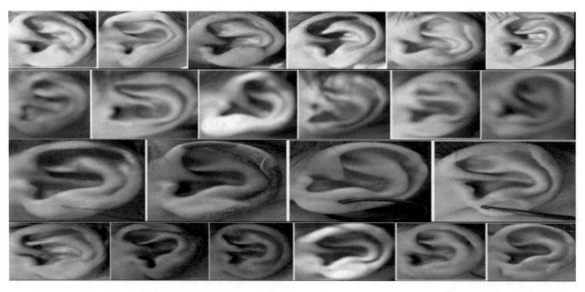

Figure 7. User registration in Cloud using ear recognition system

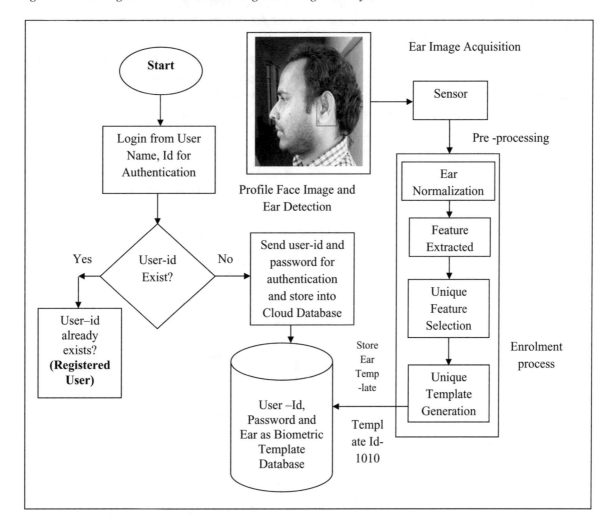

(vendor). It contains detail information about the users like user-id, password, name, address etc.

- User has to provide valid email-id (as user-name) and a valid password to cloud server database.
- If user-id already exists in cloud user database, it requires alternative email-id to be sent. This information is stored in the database and act as a level-1 security measure.
- In Ear recognition system, sensor module (e.g. digital camera or webcam) ac-

quires Ear image from user's frontal face, normalize all the Ear images of database and extract unique salient features from it (figure 5). The process of normalization and feature extraction (using Principal Component Analysis is already mentioned before).

- Then form a unique biometric template from the extracted features (e.g. Id1:1001) and store into biometric template database. This process is known as biometrics enrollment process.

- The stored templates are used as biometric passwords to access the cloud resources. These essentially act as a level-2 security layer.
- After providing valid user-id, password and storing their Ear biometric template as a level 2 password by user, the registration on cloud server is completed. The complete registration procedure is illustrated in figure 7.

6.5. Authentication Process of User for Accessing Cloud Services

This section provides a methodology for communication between user and cloud network, whenever registered user wants to access cloud resources on the cloud server. Following are the steps to login on to the cloud server (figure 8):

- First, user must enter valid user-id and level-1 valid password in his/her login inter-

Figure 8. Registered user registration in Cloud using ear recognition system

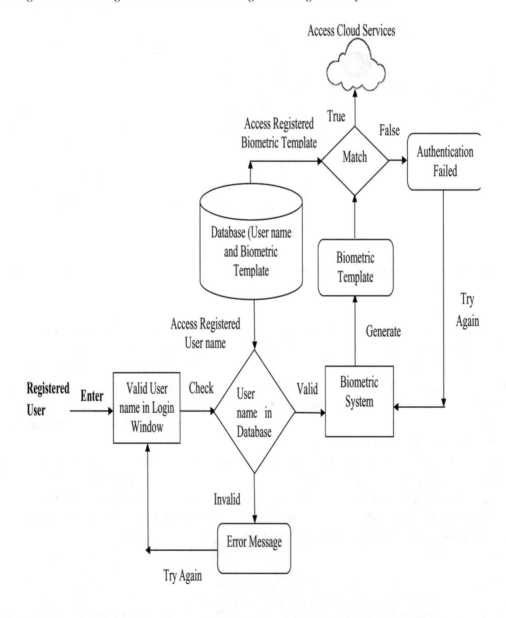

face window. After a successful verification from level-1, the user's Ear as image is captured by web camera or high resolution digital camera.

- Ear recognition as biometric system now employs the level-2 security check. Features are extracted from the input Ear image (using the same techniques during enrollment) and matched aginst the templates which are already stored in the database.
- After a succesflly match based on a matching score (performed in the previous step), the user gets access to the cloud. In case of a non-match in level-2, the user authentication fails but the whole template verification process is performed again (for a limited number of attempts).
- Thus in this proposed framework two layers of security is employed (level-1 for user-id/password matching and level-2 for Ear image based authentication).

7. CONCLUSION AND FUTURE DIRECTION

Cloud computing is not fully mature and still a lot needs to be explored in this direction. Security issues have been and are one of the biggest threats for user/service provider on a cloud network. Clouds services are used by both large and small scale organizations alike as the advantages, it provides are huge. Being a global phenomenon, it comes with a fair share of disadvantages as well. Its immunity towards security threats takes a dip on larger cloud networks. Service Providers, researchers and IT security professionals are working on security issues associated with cloud computing. This proposed system, in comparison to other recognition systems so far is more advantageous and result-oriented because it does not work on presumptions, it is unique and provides fast and contactless authentication.

In future, we aspire and aim to improve the ear data acquisition technique. It will improve the user identification process using Ear recognition system vastly. Thus, to leading us one step closer towards a threat free and secure cloud computing network.

REFERENCES

Abaza, A., Ross, A., Hebert, C., Harrison, M. A. F., & Nixon, M. S. (2013). A Survey on Ear Biometrics. *ACM Computing Surveys*, *45*(2), 1–35. doi:10.1145/2431211.2431221

Al-Aqrabi, H., Liu, L., Xu, J., Hill, R., Antonopoulos, N., & Zhan, Y. (2012, April). Investigation of IT security and compliance challenges in Security-as-a-Service for cloud computing.15th *IEEE International Symposium on Object/Component/Service-Oriented Real-Time Distributed Computing Workshops*. (pp. 124-129). doi:10.1109/ISORCW.2012.31

Amazon Virtual Private Cloud. (2012). Amazon.com. Retrieved from http://aws.amazon.com/vpc/

Armbrust, M., Fox, A., Griffith, R., & Anthony, D. Joseph, Katz R. H., Konwinski A., Lee G., Patterson D. A., Rabkin A., S. Ion and Zaharia M., (2009). Above the clouds: A Berkeley view of cloud computing. *EECS Department, University of California, Berkeley*.

Banerjee, P., Friedrich, R., Bash, C., Goldsack, P., Huberman, B., & Manley, J. et al. (2010). Everything as a Service: Powering the New Information Economy. *IEEE Computer*, *44*(3), 36–43. doi:10.1109/MC.2011.67

Bhaskar, P. R., Admela, J., Dimitrios, K., & Goeleven, Y. (2011). Architectural requirements for cloud computing systems: An enterprise cloud approach. *Journal of Grid Computing*, 3–26.

Burge, M., & Burger, W. (2002). Ear biometrics in Computer Vision, *In Proceedings of International Conference of Pattern Recognition*. (pp. 822-826).

Chao-Chih, C., Lihua, Y., & Albert, G., Greenberg, Chen-Nee C., Prasant M. (2011). Routing-as-a-Service (RaaS): A framework for tenant-directed route control in data center, *In Proceedings of 30th IEEE international conference of INFOCOM*. (pp. 1386-1394).

Chow, R., Jakobsson, M., Masuoka, R., Molina, J., Niu, Y., Shi, E., & Song, Z. (2010, October). Authentication in the clouds: a framework and its application to mobile users. *In Proceedings of the 2010 ACM workshop on Cloud computing security workshop*. (pp. 1-6). doi:10.1145/1866835.1866837

Data as a service. (2014, December 11). Wikipedia. Retrieved from http://en.wikipedia.org/wiki/Data_as_a_service

Dikaiakos, M. D., Katsaros, D., Mehra, P., Pallis, G., & Vakali, A. (2009). Cloud Computing: Distributed Internet Computing for IT and Scientific Research. *IEEE Internet Computing*, *13*(5), 10–13. doi:10.1109/MIC.2009.103

Dinesha, H. A. (2012). Multi-level Authentication Technique for Accessing Cloud Services. *In Proceedings of IEEE Computing, Communication and Applications (ICCCA)*. (pp. 1-4). doi:10.1109/ICCCA.2012.6179130

Feng D.G., Zhang, et al. (2011). Research on Cloud Computing Security. *Journal of Software*, 71–82.

Hamlen, K., Kantarcioglu, M., Khan, L., & Thuraisingham, B. (2010). Security Issues for Cloud Computing. *International Journal of Information Security and Privacy*, *4*(2), 39–51. doi:10.4018/jisp.2010040103

Jackson, C. (2010). *8 Cloud Security Concepts You Should Know*. Network World.

Jain, A. K. Flynn Patrick, Ross Arun A. (2008). Handbook of Biometrics. New York, Springer.

Jain, A. K., Pankanti, S., Prabhakar, S., & Hong, L. (2004), Biometrics: a grand challenge. *Proceedings of 17th International Conference on Pattern Recognition*, 2, (pp. 935-942).

James, L., Wayman. (2001). Fundamentals of biometric authentication technologies. *International Journal of Imaging and Graphics*, *1*(93). doi:10.1142/S0219467801000086

Jantz, R. L. (1987). Anthropological dermatoglyphic research. *Annual Review of Anthropology*, *16*(1), 161–177. doi:10.1146/annurev.an.16.100187.001113

Jantz, R. L. (1997). Variation among European populations in summary finger ridge count variables. *Journal of Annual Human Biology*, *24*(2), 97–108. doi:10.1080/03014469700004842 PMID:9074746

Jivanadham, L. B., Islam, A. K. M. M., Katayama, Y., Komaki, S., & Baharun, S. (2013). Cloud Cognitive Authenticator (CCA): A public cloud computing authentication mechanism. *In Proceedings of International IEEE Conference on In Informatics, Electronics & Vision (ICIEV)* (pp. 1-6). doi:10.1109/ICIEV.2013.6572626

Kim, J., & Hong, S. (2011). One-Source Multi-Use System having Function of Consolidated User Authentication. Proceedings of *JCICT & The first Yellow Sea International Conference on Ubiquitous Computing*.

Lenk, A., Klems, M., Nimis, J., Tai, S., & Sandholm, T. (2009, May). What's inside the Cloud? An architectural map of the Cloud landscape. *In Proceedings of the 2009 ICSE Workshop on Software Engineering Challenges of Cloud Computing*, 23-31. IEEE Computer Society. doi:10.1109/CLOUD.2009.5071529

Li, H., Tian, X., Wei, W., & Sun, C. (2012). A Deep Understanding of Cloud Computing Security. In Network Computing and Information Security. (pp. 98-105). Springer Berlin Heidelberg.

Mell, P., & Grance, T. (2009, October 7). The NIST Definition of Cloud Computing. *National Institute of Standards and Technology*. Retrieved from www.csrc.nist.gov

Miller, B. (1988). *Everything you need to know about biometric identification. Personal Identification News*. Washington, DC: Warfel &Miller, Inc.

Onwubiko, C. (2010). Security issues to cloud computing. In Cloud Computing. (pp. 271-288). London: Springer.

Pearson, S., & Yee, G. (Eds.). (2013). *Privacy and Security for cloud Computing. In series Computer Communications and Networks*. New York: Springer London Heidelberg. doi:10.1007/978-1-4471-4189-1

Pentland, A., Moghaddam, B., & Starner, T. (1994).View-Based and Modular Eigen spaces for Face Recognition. *Proceedings of the IEEE Computer Vision and Pattern Recognition, Seattle*, Washington. (pp. 84-91). doi:10.1109/CVPR.1994.323814

Pun, K. H., & Moon, Y. S. (2004). Recent advances in ear biometrics. In *Proceedings of the Automatic Ear and Gesture Recognition*, 164–169.

Ramgovin, S., Eloff, M.M., Smith, E. (2010). *The* Management of Security in Cloud Computing. *In proceedings of the IEEE Cloud Computing.* (pp. 1-7).

Rong, C., & Cheng, H. (2012). A Secure Data Access Mechanism for Cloud Tenants. *In Proceedings of the Cloud Computing, GRIDs, and Virtualization*.

Rubin, A. D. (1995, June). Independent One-Time Passwords. *USENIX UNIX Security Symposium*, Salt Lake City, Utah.

Shen, Z., Li, L., Yan, F., & Wu, X. (2010). Cloud Computing System Based on Trusted Computing Platform. *Proceedings of Intelligent Computation Technology and Automation*, *1*, 942–945.

Singh, M., & Singh, S. (2012). Design and Implementation of Multi-tier Authentication Scheme in Cloud, International *Journal of Computer Science Issues*.

Turk, M., & Pentland, A. (1991). Eigenfaces for Recognition. *Journal of Cognitive Neuroscience*, *3*(1), 71–86. doi:10.1162/jocn.1991.3.1.71 PMID:23964806

Turk, M., & Pentland, A. (1991) Face Recognition Using Eigenfaces, *IEEE Conference on Computer Vision and Pattern Recognition*, Maui, Hawaii, USA, 586-591

Un, S., Jho, N. S., Kim, Y. H., & Choi, D. S. (2009). Cloud computing security technology. *ETRI*, *24*(4), 79–88.

Vu, Q. H., Pham, T. V., Truong, H. L., Dustdar, S., & Asal, R. (2012, March). Demods: A description model for data-as-a-service. DEMODS: A Description Model for Data-As-A-Service, IEEE 26th Conference on Advanced Information Networking and Applications. (pp. 605–612). doi:10.1109/AINA.2012.91

Wang, P., Ku, C. C., & Wang, T. C. (2011). *A New Fingerprint Authentication Scheme Based on Secret-Splitting for Enhanced Cloud Security*, 183-196.

Wayman, J., Jain, A. K., Maltoni, D., & Maio, D. (2005). An introduction to biometric authentication systems. In Biometric Systems, 1-20). Springer London. doi:10.1007/1-84628-064-8_1

Yang, S. J., Lai, P. C., & Li, J. (2013). Design Role-Based Multi-tenancy Access Control Scheme for Cloud Services, *International Symposium on Biometrics and Security Technologies (ISBAST),* (pp. 273-279. doi:10.1109/ISBAST.2013.48

Yassin, A. A., Hai, J., Ibrahim, A., & Deqing, Z. (2012). Anonymous Password Authentication Scheme by Using Digital Signature and Finger-print in Cloud Computing, *In Proceedings of the Cloud and Green Computing (CGC).* (pp. 282–289). doi:10.1109/CGC.2012.91

Yuan, J., Yu S. (2013). Efficient privacy-preserving biometric identification in cloud computing, Proceedings of *IEEE INFOCOM.* (pp. 2652–2660).

Yuizono, T., Wang, Y., Satoh, K., & Nakayama, S. (2002). Study on individual recognition for ear images by using genetic local search, In *Proceedings of the Congress on Evolutionary Computation.* (pp. 237–242). doi:10.1109/CEC.2002.1006240

KEY TERMS AND DEFINITIONS

Cloud Computing Security: It is an evolutionary offshoot of computer security, information security and security of internet based computation, whereby shared resources, different relevant software and information is provided to computers and other devices on demand.

Biometric System: It is a pattern recognition based system. It acquires biometric data from an individual, extracts a salient feature set from the data, compares feature set against the feature set(s) stored in the database, and executes an action based on the result of the comparison.

Biometric Traits: Class of phenotypic characteristics (e.g., face or stripe pattern) used as source for constructing a biometric profile.

Biometrics: Biometrics" means "life measurement" but the term is usually associated with the use of unique physiological characteristics to identify an individual.

Biometric Profile: Information used to represent an individual or group in an information system.

Ear Recognition: is non–intrusive methodology and attributes are probably the most common biometric feature used by humans to recognize one other.

Verification Process: One to One matching process: Biometrics can also be used to verify a person's identity. For example, one can grant physical access to a secure area in a building by using finger scans or can grant access to a bank account at an ATM by using retinal scan.

Identification Process: In identification mode, where the subject (people/object) does not claim an identity, the input ear image is compared against a set of labeled (it is used to indicate that the identity of the images in the database is known) ear images in a database in order to determine the best match and, therefore, its identity.

Principal Component Analysis: It is unsupervised dimension reduction approach for large database size. It is used to find the Eigen values for face recognition.

Chapter 4
Secure Architecture for Cloud Environment

Kashif Munir
Malaysia University of Science and Technology, Malaysia

Sellapan Palaniappan
Malaysia University of Science and Technology, Malaysia

ABSTRACT

Cloud computing is set of resources and services offered through the internet. Cloud services are delivered from data centers located throughout the world. Enterprises are rapidly adopting cloud services for their businesses, measures need to be developed so that organizations can be assured of security in their businesses and can choose a suitable vendor for their computing needs. In this chapter we identify the most vulnerable security threats/attacks in cloud computing, which will enable both end users and vendors to know about the key security threats associated with cloud computing and propose relevant solution directives to strengthen security in the cloud environment. This chapter also discusses secure cloud architecture for organizations to strengthen the security.

INTRODUCTION

With Cloud Computing becoming a popular term on the Information Technology (IT) market, security and accountability has become important issues to highlight. There are a number of security issues/concerns associated with cloud computing but these issues fall into two broad categories: Security issues faced by cloud providers (organizations providing Software-, Platform-, or Infrastructure-as-a-Service via the cloud) and security issues faced by their customers.[1] In most cases, the provider must ensure that their infrastructure is secure and that their clients' data and applications are protected while the customer must ensure that the provider has taken the proper security measures to protect their information(Philip Wik, 2011).

Cloud computing has emerged as a way for IT businesses to increase capabilities on the fly without investing much in new infrastructure, training of personals or licensing new software.

NIST defines Cloud computing as a "model for enabling ubiquitous, convenient, on demand network access to a shared pool of configurable computing resources that can be rapidly provisioned and delivered with minimal managerial

DOI: 10.4018/978-1-4666-8387-7.ch004

effort or service provider interaction"(Mell P, Grance T, 2011) . It follows a simple "pay as you go" model, which allows an organization to pay for only the service they use. It eliminates the need to maintain an in-house data center by migrating enterprise data to a remote location at the Cloud provider's site. Minimal investment, cost reduction, and rapid deployment are the main factors that drive industries to utilize Cloud services and allow them to focus on core business concerns and priorities rather than dealing with technical issues. According to (Ponemon, 2011), 91% of the organizations in US and Europe agreed that reduction in cost is a major reason for them to migrate to Cloud environment.

As shown in Figure. 1, Cloud services are offered in terms of Infrastructure-as-a- service (IaaS), Platform-as-a-service (PaaS), and Software-as-a-service (SaaS). It follows a bottom-up approach wherein at the infrastructure level; machine power is de- livered in terms of CPU consumption to memory allocation. On top of it, lies the layer that delivers an environment in

terms of framework for application development, termed as PaaS. At the top level resides the application layer, delivering software outsourced through the Internet, eliminating the need for in-house maintenance of sophisticated software [6]. At the application layer, the end users can utilize software running at a remote site by Application Service Providers (ASPs). Here, customers need not buy and install costly software. They can pay for the usage and their concerns for maintenance are removed (Kashif & Sellapan, 2012).

SECURITY CONCERNS OF CLOUD COMPUTING

While the benefits of the cloud increase with experience, the challenges of cloud show a sharp decrease as organizations gain expertise with cloud.

Security remains the most-often cited challenge among Cloud Beginners (31 percent) but decreases to the fifth most cited (13 percent) among Cloud Focused organizations as shown in Figure 2. As

Figure 1. Cloud Computing represented as a stack of service (Kashif & Sellapan, 2012)

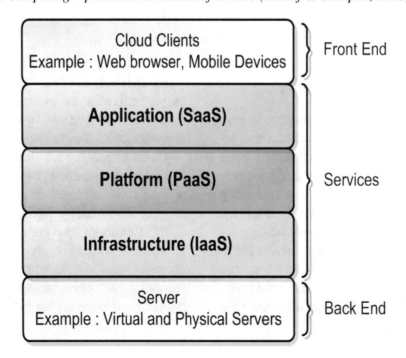

Figure 2. Cloud Security Survey

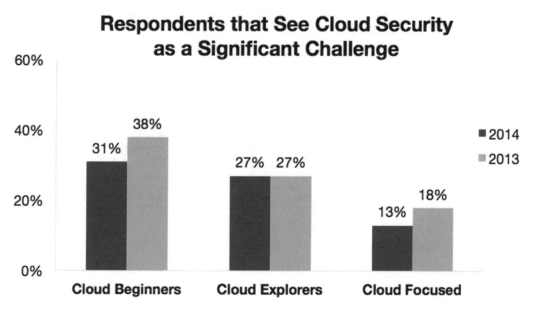

Source: RightScale 2014 State of the Cloud Report

organizations become more experienced in cloud security options and best practices, the less of a concern cloud security becomes. Concerns about cloud security declined in 2014 among both Cloud Beginners and Cloud Focused respondents (Kim Weins, 2014).

While the benefits of the cloud increase with experience, the challenges of cloud show a sharp decrease as organizations gain expertise with cloud. Security remains the most-often cited challenge among Cloud Beginners (31 percent) but decreases to the fifth most cited (13 percent) among Cloud Focused organizations. As organizations become more experienced in cloud security options and best practices, the less of a concern cloud security becomes. Concerns about cloud security declined in 2014 among both Cloud Beginners and Cloud Focused respondents.

VULNERABILITIES IDENTIFIED IN CLOUD COMPUTING

Recent incidents involving clouds have not helped the perception on its security. This section outlines some recent incidents that explain the vulnerabilities of cloud computing. These vulnerabilities range from outages to hacking attempts that inconvenienced end users and organizations using the services.

Table 1 was published by the Open Security Foundation, a non-profit organization providing security information and a list of incidents.

THREAT MODEL FOR CLOUD

An abstract view of threat model for Cloud computing is shown in Figure 3. Cloud clients are facing two types of security threats viz; external and internal attacks.

External network attacks in the cloud are increasing at a notable rate. Malicious user outside the Cloud often performs DoS or DDoS attacks to affect the availability of Cloud services and resources. Port scanning, IP spoofing, DNS poisoning, phishing are also executed to gain access of Cloud resources. A malicious user can capture and analyze the data in the packets sent over this network by packet sniffing. IP spoofing occurs

Table 1. Recent Cloud Incidents (Cloud Age, 2010)

Type	Date	Organization	What Happened?
hack	2012-01-21	DreamHost	DreamHost Database Hack Forces Mass Password Reset
outage	2011-04-21	Amazon Web Services	Companies left staggering or totally knocked out because of server problems in the Amazon datacenter
outage	2011-04-21	Sony	Play Station Network outages
outage	2011-03-25	Twitter, Inc.	Twitter Experiences Delays in Delivering to Facebook and SMS
outage	2011-03-25	Heroku	Heroku Users Experience HTTP 503 Errors
outage	2011-03-25	Twitter, Inc.	Twitter Experiences Tweet Delivery Delay
outage	2011-03-25	Heroku	Heroku Shared Database Experienced Hardware Failure
outage	2011-03-25	Heroku	Heroku Users Unable to Provision New Dedicated Databases

Figure 3. Threat model for Cloud computing.

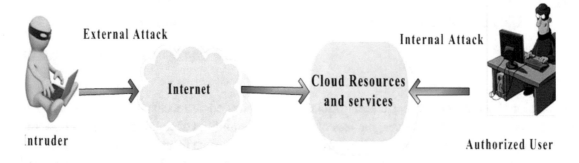

when a malicious user impersonates a legitimate users IP address where they could access information that they would not have been able to access otherwise. Availability is very important. Not having access to services when needed can be a disaster for anyone especially in the case of being denied service. This can occur when exhaustion of the host servers causes requests from legitimate consumers to be denied. This can cost a company large amounts of money and time if the services they depend on to operate are not available.

Internal attacker (authorized user) can easily get access to other user's resources without being detected. An insider has higher privileges and knowledge (related to network, security mechanism and resources to attack) than the external

attacker. Therefore, it is easy for an insider to penetrate an attack than external attackers.

VULNERABILITIES IN CLOUD ENVIRONMENT

This section presents summary of major Cloud specific vulnerabilities, which pose serious threats to Cloud computing in Table 2.

THREATS TO CLOUD COMPUTING

In this section, Researcher presents summary of threats relevant to the security architecture of

Table 2. Effects of vulnerabilities in the Cloud and consequent effects

Vulnerabilities	Effects
Vulnerabilities in virtualization	Bypassing the security barriers can allow access to underlying hypervisor.
Vulnerabilities in Internet protocol	Allow network attacks like ARP spoofing, DoS/DDoS etc
Unauthorized access to management interface	An intruder can gain access control and can take advantage of services to harbor attacks. Access to administrative interface can be more critical.
Injection vulnerabilities	Unauthorized disclosure of private data behind applications.
Vulnerabilities in browsers and APIs	Allow unauthorized service access

Cloud services and their solution directives in Table 3.

ATTACKS ON CLOUD COMPUTING

This section presents the summary of attacks on cloud and their directive solution in Table 4.

SECURE CLOUD ARCHITECTURE

In this chapter Researcher discuss proposed cloud security architecture shown in figure 4, which protect organization against security threats and attacks. The key points for this architecture based on our analysis of existing Single Sign-on (SSO) security technology.

Defense in Depth Security Approach

As enterprise networking technology has evolved, so too has enterprise security. What began simply as setting up a perimeter around the network via fairly basic security tools like firewalls and email gateways, has evolved into adding an array of virtual private networks (VPNs), virtual local area network (VLAN) segmentation, authentication,

Table 3. Summary of threats to Cloud and solution directives

Threats	Affected Cloud Services	Solution Directives
Change the business model	SaaS, PaaS and IaaS	Provide control and monitoring system on offered services.
Abusive use	PaaS and IaaS	Stronger registration and authentication. Comprehensive monitoring of network traffic.
Insecure interfaces	SaaS, PaaS and IaaS	Ensure strong authentication and access control mechanism with encrypted transmission.
Malicious insiders	SaaS, PaaS and IaaS	Provide transparency for security and management process. Use compliance reporting and breach notification.
Shared technology	IaaS	Use strong authentication and access control mechanism for administrative task. Inspect vulnerability and configuration.
Data loss and leakage	SaaS, PaaS and IaaS	Use secure APIs, encryption algorithms and secure keys. Apply data retention and backup policies.
Service hijacking	SaaS, PaaS and IaaS	Use security policies, strong authentication mechanism and activity monitoring.
Risk profile	SaaS, PaaS and IaaS	Disclose partial logs, data and infrastructure detail. Use monitoring and alerting system for data breaches.

Table 4. Summary of attacks to Cloud and solution directives

Attack Type	Service Affected	Mitigation Techniques
Zombie attack, DoS/DDoS attack	SaaS, PaaS, IaaS	Better authentication and authorization. IDS/IPS.
Attacks on virtualization, VM Escape and attack on a hypervisor	IaaS	Use of secure hypervisor. Monitor activities at hypervisor. VM isolation required.
Malware-injection Attack	PaaS	Check service integrity using a hash function. Strong isolation between VMs. Web service security. Use secure web browsers and APIs.
Man-in-the Middle(MitM) attack	SaaS, PaaS, IaaS	Proper configuration of SSL required.
Metadata spoofing attack	SaaS, PaaS	Strong isolation between VMs.
Phishing attack	SaaS, PaaS, IaaS	Identify the spam mails.

Figure 4. Secure Cloud Architecture (Kashif and Sellapan, 2013)

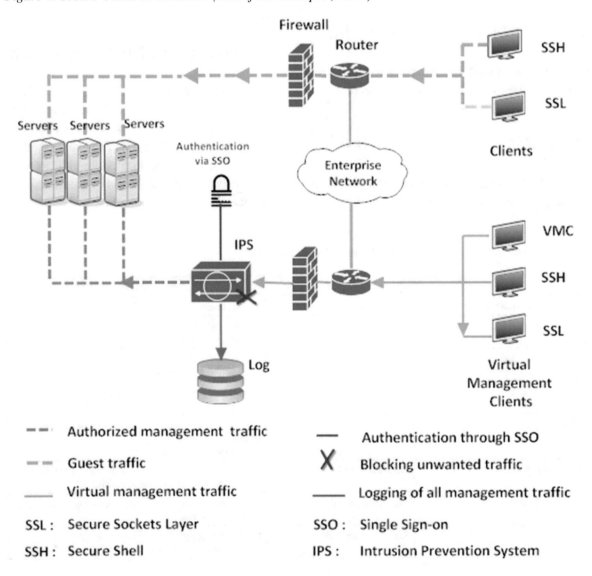

and intrusion detection systems (IDS)—necessary to handle the consistently growing number of threats to the corporate network.

Virtual firewall appliances should be deployed instead of first-generation firewalls. This allows network administrators to inspect all levels of traffic, which includes basic web browser traffic, to peer-to-peer applications traffic and encrypted web traffic in the SSL tunnel .Intrusion Prevention Systems (IPS) should be installed to protect networks from internal threats from insiders.

Increase Availability

Availability is a reoccurring and a growing concern in software intensive systems. Cloud systems services can be turned offline due to conservation, power outages or possible denial of service invasions. Fundamentally, its role is to determine the time that the system is up and running correctly; the length of time between failures and the length of time needed to resume operation after a failure. Availability needs to be analyzed through the use of presence information, forecasting usage patterns and dynamic resource scaling (M. Armbrust, *et al*, (2010). Access to cloud service should be available all the time, even during maintenance. This makes critical business data stored in the cloud to be always available to cloud users, reducing network down time, thereby increasing business profits. This can be done by implementing high availability technologies such as active/active clustering, dynamic server load balanced and ISP load balancing within the network infrastructure.

Data Privacy

Cloud data privacy problem will be found at every stage of the life cycle. For the data storage and use, (Miranda Mowbray and Siani Pearson, 2009) proposed a client-based privacy management tool that provides a user-centric trust model to help users control their sensitive information during the cloud storage and use.

Data loss prevention (DLP) tools can help control migration of data to the cloud and also find sensitive data leaked to the cloud. Data loss prevention (DLP) is a strategy for making sure that end users do not send sensitive or critical information outside of the corporate network. DLP help a network administrator control what data end users can transfer.

Data Integrity

As a result of large scale data communication cost, the users don't want to download data but verify its correctness. Therefore, users need to retrieve the little cloud data through some kinds of agreements or knowledge's which are the probability of analytical tools with high confidence level to determine whether the remote data integrity. User can do the increase and decrease of the data capacity in the cloud server with the help of CSP (cloud service provider) in his request. This storage level must be with flexible and durability condition as far as its entire design or structure is concerned. Thus it should be claimed extra storage space concerning future process in data exchange (Kashif and Sellapan, 2013).

Virtual Machine Protection

You can't just install your firewall or antivirus software on a cloud-based virtual machine. Physical firewalls aren't designed to inspect and filter the vast amount of traffic originating from a hypervisor running 10 virtualized servers. Because VMs can start, stop and move from hypervisor to hypervisor at the click of a button, whatever protection you've chosen has to handle these activities with ease. Plus, as the number of VMs increases in the data center, it becomes harder to account for, manage and protect them. And if unauthorized people gain access to the hypervisor, they can take advantage of the lack of controls and modify all the VMs housed there.

These virtual machines are vulnerable like their physical counterparts. Hence, to adequately protect virtual machines, they should he isolated from other network segments and deep inspection at the network level should be implemented to prevent them both from internal and external threats. Illegal internal access should be restricted by implementing intrusion prevention systems and unauthorized external access should be protected by using secure remote access technologies like IPSec or SSL VPN (Kashif and Sellapan, 2013).

SECURE PROTOCOL – A PROPOSAL

To limit most of the above mentioned threats, we proposed a secure protocol scheme based on Beller-Chang-Yacobi's protocol [30]. We will mention the main drawback of the scheme and show some counter measures against the drawback. We will consider three entities in our model: Set of users (*A*), Enterprise Network (*B*), and Intrusion Prevention System which serves as certification authority (*CA*).

Let *A* be the set of users and $\mu \in A$, for every $\mu \exists$ a pair of public and secret keys $(P\mu, S\mu)$

Where $P\mu \equiv a^{S\mu} \left(mod\ N \right)$

Where *N* is a large prime and α is a generator for the multiplicative group *GF (N)*, both *N* and α are made public. The secure enterprise network router *B* also has a pair of $\left(P_B, S_B \right)$,

Where $P\mu \equiv a^{SB} \left(mod\ N \right)$

The *CA* issues certificate for each user and *B* as well as P_μ and P_B. We define the certificate as follows:

$$Sig_{CA}(\mu) \equiv (h\ (\mu,\ P\mu))^{1/2} \left(Mod\ N_{CA} \right)$$

$$Sig_{CA} (B) \equiv \left(h \left(B, N_B, P_B \right) \right)^{1/2} (Mod\ N_{CA})$$

Where *h* is a one-way hash function known to the public. N_B is the product of two large primes associated with *B*. Similarly N_{CA}. N_B and N_{CA} are made public (their prime factors must be kept secret). Lastly, we can use any secret key encryption algorithm such as IDEA, DES, or Rijndael. Summary of the steps:

$\mu \Rightarrow B \left(request\ for\ service \right)$
$\mu \Leftarrow B \left(B, N_B, P_B, Sig_{CA}(B) \right)$
$\mu\ checks\ if \left(h \left(B, N_B, P_B \right) \right) \equiv Sig^2_{CA} (B) \left(mod\ N_{CA} \right)$
$\mu \Rightarrow B \left(e_2,\ e_3 \right)$
$B\ extracts\ x\ from\ e_2\ and\ use\ it\ to\ decrypt\ e_3\ and\ check\ if$
$h(\mu,\ P\mu) \equiv Sig^2_{CA}(\mu) \left(mod\ N_{CA} \right)$
$\mu \Leftrightarrow B \left(using\ session\ key\ sk \right)$

Note that the numbers e_2, e_3 are defined as:

$$e_2 = x^2 \left(mod\ N_B \right)$$
$$e_3 = encrypt\ x\ (\mu,\ P\mu,\ Sig_{CA}(\mu))$$

x is a random number between 1 and $N_B - 1$. *B* extracts *x* from e_2 as and uses e_3 as follows:

$$x \equiv \left(e_2 \right)^{1/2} \left(mod\ N_B \right)$$
$$(\mu,\ P\mu,\ Sig_{CA}(\mu)) = decryptx \left(e_3 \right)$$

It is easy to see that μ and *B* can respectively calculate:

$$\Re \equiv P_B^{S\mu} \left(mod\ N \right), sk = encrypt\Re \left(x \right)$$
$$\Re \equiv P_\mu^{SB} \left(mod\ N \right),\ sk = encrypt\Re \left(x \right)$$

sk is now the session key for μ and *B*.

Analysis

The major problem with Belleret. al. scheme is concern with *replay* attacks. For instance, an attacker T can obtain the public key and the digital signature of μ i.e $(\mu, P_\mu Sig_{CA}(\mu))$. T can then impersonate μ and initiate the protocol with B. Next we show how this can be prevented in three different ways:

Method 1 (Using Nonce)

Recall that $\oplus$ denotes bit-wise exclusive-or operation, and CA is a mediator between B and μ, we consider the following steps:

$$\mu \Rightarrow CA: \{AI_\mu, \ I_B\}P_{CA}$$
$$CA \Rightarrow \mu: \{AI_\mu, \ IB, \ (n_{CA})K_\mu\}$$
$$\mu \Rightarrow B\{AI_\mu, I_B, \mu n_1, \mu n_2 (n_{CA}) \ K_\mu\}P_{CA}$$
$$B \Rightarrow CA: \{AI_\mu, \ I_B, \mu n_1, \mu n_2 (n_{CA}) \ K_\mu\}P_{CA}$$
$$B \Rightarrow CA: \{I_B, \ AI_\mu,, \ Bn_1, \ Bn_2(n_{CA})K_B\}P_{CA}$$
$$CA \Rightarrow B: \{\mu n_1, \ K_{\mu B}Å \oplus \mu n_2\}K_\mu, \ \{Bn_1, \ K_{\mu B} \oplus Bn_2\}K_B$$
$$B \Rightarrow \mu: \{\mu n_1, \ K_{\mu B} \oplus \mu n_2\}K_\mu, \ \{f_1(r\mu), \ rB\}K_{\mu B}$$

$$B \Leftarrow \mu \left\{ f_2 \left(rB \right) \right\} K_{\mu B}$$

where K_μ, K_B, $K_{\mu B}$ denote a session key between CA and μ, CA and B, and μ and B respectively. n_{CA} denote a nonce issued by CA. P_{CA} denotes CA's public key. AI_μ, and I_B denote anonymity ID of μ, and ID of B respectively. $\mu n_1, \mu n_2, Bn_1, Bn_2$ are random numbers generated by μ and B. $(r\mu)$ is a challenge and $f(r\mu)$ is the response encrypted using the session key $K_{\mu B}$.

Note that AI_μ is the anonymity of user μ, it should contain some secret information only known and can only be used be used by CA alone.

Method 2 (One-Time Signature)

One-time signature can be used instead of normal signature. We assume that μ has stored a precomputed signature S, as well as the pair of one-time

(P_μ^*, S_μ^*) keys. To sign a message M, μ uses a hash function h i.e. $h(M)$ and then computes the one-time signature:

$$\gamma = \ S \left(h \left(M \right) \right)$$

The signature of M consists of the concatenation of P_μ^*, S, and Υ. CA can then verify P_μ^*, S, and Υ with respect to P_μ using a verification algorithm V. First, CA uses V and P_μ to check whether S is a signature of P_μ, CA then computes $f = h(M)$ to check whether Υ is a signature of with respect to P_μ^*. The verification can be written as:

$$V1 \ P_\mu(P_\mu^*, S)$$
$$V2 P_\mu^*, (h(M), \gamma)$$

Note that the hash function is also a one-way hash function. Therefore, even if an attacker attempt to replay an old $P\mu^*$ and forge Υ for a new M^*, this will amount to either attacking the one-time signature, i.e. $h(M^*)$ which is different from all previously hashed values or finding a new M^* such that $h(M) = h(M^*)$. Since h is one-time this implies $h(M)$ will never be equal to $h(M^*)$.

Method 3 (Timestamp)

The main drawback of method 1 and 2 is time consuming. Therefore in some situations whereby charges are considered to be less, a timestamp approach can be used. This can be achieved as follows:

$$\mu \Rightarrow CA: \ (ts \ \| \ r\mu)^e \left(mod \ N \right)$$

Where τs is timestamp, $\|$ denotes concatenation, $r\mu$ is the random number generated by μ and e is the encryption exponent. In this case, CA should have the means of checking the timeless of the timestamp. Note that τs may include date, time, expiring date etc.

SECURING CLOUD COMPUTING

Cloud computing is currently facing numerous problems. These security issues have significantly impacted the development and popularization of cloud computing. Therefore, steps need to be taken to secure the cloud computing environment and actively carry out relevant cloud security key technology research. Secure cloud computing environment is shown in Figure 5.

Firewall

Cloud computing can greatly increase security in the configuration of a firewall by limiting the form of open port. Among them, the Web server group opens ports 80 (HTTP port) and 443 (HTTPS port) to the world, while the application server group only opens port 8000 (special application service ports) for the Web server group. The database server group only opens port 3306 (MySQL port) for the application server group. At the same time, the three groups of network servers open port 22 (SSH port) for customers, and by default, refuse other network connections. This mechanism significantly improve security (Bikram, B, 2010).

Figure 5. Secure Cloud Computing Environment

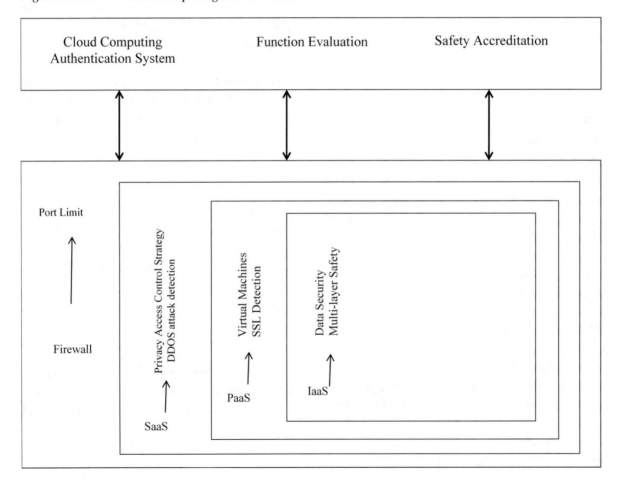

Security Measures of SaaS

In cloud computing, SaaS providers offer users the full application and components, and guarantee program and components' security. The proposing security functions have two main aspects:

Priority access control strategy: SaaS providers offer identity authentication and access control functions usually the user name and password verification mechanism. Users should know enough about the provider they have chosen, in order to eliminate the threat to the security of the cloud applications' internal factors. At the same time, cloud providers should notify users about the need to change their passwords on time, choose passwords of high strength, define the length of the password, and refrain from using the old password to strengthen the security of the user account.

Common network attack prevention: Rely on the existing mature network attack defensive measures for DDOS attack, providers can use several methods: for example, configuring a firewall, blocking the Internet Control Message Protocol (ICMP) and any unknown protocol; shutting down unnecessary TCP/IP services, or even configuring the firewall to refuse any request from the Internet. For utilization type attack, providers can monitor the service of TCP regularly and update software patches on time. The traditional network attack has been studied for a long time, and there are very mature products that can be employed. In fact, cloud providers can make full use of these products to ensure the computing clouds' security (Boss, G et al., 2010).

Security Measures of PaaS Layer

In cloud computing, security measures of PaaS layer are two aspects: Virtual machine technology application: Using the advantages of virtual machine technology, providers can set up virtual machines in the existing operating system. At the same time, they can also set access restrictions. Common users can operate computer hardware

only through promoting operating permissions. This is good distinguished between the ordinary users and administrators, even if the user has been attacked, there will be no damage to the server.

Defense for an SSL attack: In the event of an SSL attack or if it is imminent, the user must strengthen the prevention methods. Providers should offer the corresponding patch and measures, so the user can patch-in the first time, and ensure that the SSL patch works quickly. At the same time, using the firewall to close some port to prevent common HTTPS attacks, strengthening management authority, making security certificates difficult to attain also qualify as good defending methods (Jamil, D., Zaki, H., 2011).

Security Measures of IaaS Layer

Generally, IaaS is not visible for ordinary users, and the management and maintenance personnel also rely entirely on the cloud providers. The most important part is that of the security of data storage locations. Cloud providers should convey all the pertinent details about the country where the server is located and the legal aspects regarding the operation of data without any conflicts with the local law to all users.. Data encryption is not reliable for combinations of different user data, but also reducing the efficiency of data, providers need to separate user data stored in different data server (Zhang, S., Zhang, S., Chen, X, 2010). Separating the user data storage locations can prevent data separation chaos. With regard to data backup, it is important to get regular backups of critical and confidential data so that in the event of hardware failure, data can be easily recovered and the recovery time can also be guaranteed.

CONCLUSION

In this chapter we have discussed the characteristics of a cloud security that contains threats/attacks and vulnerabilities. Organizations that are implementing cloud computing by expanding their on-premise infrastructure, should be aware of the security challenges faced by cloud computing. This chapter has discussed the proposed secure cloud architecture to strengthen the security in organization. A high level design of the Cloud based SSO solution has been developed, which involved designing a new architecture. The new architecture consist only the authentication mechanism on the SSO Server, resulting in moving computation and storage to the Cloud. Single sign-on greatly enhances the usability of the Cloud environment by allowing users to authenticate once to access applications on multiple machines. Such capabilities may lead to greater acceptance of these solutions in large community. Cloud server can activate and retire resources as needed, dynamically update infrastructure elements, and move workloads to improve efficiency without having to worry about creating new infrastructures.

At the same time, cloud computing security is not just a technical problem, it also involves standardization, supervising mode, laws and regulations, and many other aspects, cloud computing is accompanied by development opportunities and challenges, along with the security problem be solved step by step, cloud computing will grow, the application will also become more and more widely.

This chapter has discussed the proposed secure cloud architecture to strengthen the security in an organization. A high level design of the Cloud-based SSO solution has been developed, which also involved designing new architecture. The new architecture consists only of the authentication mechanism on the SSO Server, resulting in moving computation and storage to the Cloud. Single Sign-On greatly enhances the usability of the Cloud environment by allowing users to authenticate themselves once to access applications on multiple machines. Such capabilities may lead to greater acceptance of these solutions in a large community. Cloud servers can activate and retire resources as needed, dynamically update infrastructure elements, and move workloads to improve efficiency without having to worry about creating new infrastructures.

Future Work

In future, the proposed architecture may be modified with the advancement of security technologies used for implementing this physical cloud security architecture. By considering the contributions from several IT industries worldwide, it is obvious that cloud computing will be one of the leading strategic and innovative technologies in the near future.

Other research opportunities include the modification of the model to suit other areas of cloud computing applications. As security and trust play a critical role in other cloud computing domains, the hypotheses can be extended to be tested in these domains. This would provide a generalized view of security mechanisms, perception and trust in cloud computing.

There is a great scope of future work with this research. This research can be extended to get IT user perceptions of cloud security by targeting the method of comparison between various groups and organizations. This research can be used for comparisons of current trends, IT user perceptions, and risk awareness against the future IT user population by surveying and other methods. This research can also be used for pre- and post-tests by asking questions like IT user perceptions versus reality.

On the other hand, we suggest that future research should be directed towards the management of risks associated with cloud computing. Developing risk assessment helps organizations make informed a decision as to whether cloud computing is currently suitable to meet their business goals with an acceptable level of risks. However, managing risks in cloud computing is a challenging process that entails identifying and assessing risks, and taking steps to reduce it to an acceptable level. We plan to pursue research in finding methods for qualitative and quantitative risk analysis in cloud computing. These methods should enable organizations to balance the identified security risks against the expected benefits from cloud utilization.

REFERENCES

A Security Analysis of Cloud Computing (2009). Cloudcomputing.sys. Retrieved from http://cloud-computing.sys- con.com/node/1203943

Armbrust, M., Fox, A., Griffth, R., et al. (2009). Above the clouds: A Berkeley View of Cloud Computing. EECS Department University of California Berkeley. Retrieved from http://www.eecs.berkeley.edu/Pubs/TechRpts/2009/EECS-2009-28.pdf

Armbrust, M., Stoica, I., Zaharia, M., Fox, A., Griffith, R., & Joseph, A. D. et al. (2010). A view of cloud computing. *Communications of the ACM*, *53*(4), 50–58. doi:10.1145/1721654.1721672

Bikram. B (2009). Safe on the Cloud. A Perspective into Security Concerns of Cloud Computing, 4, 34-35.

Boss, G., Malladi, P., Quan, D., et al. (2010). *IBM Cloud Computing White Book*. Retrieved from http://www-01.ibm.com/software/cn/Tivoli/ao/reg.html

Cloud Computing and Security. (2010). A Natural Match. *Trusted Computing Group*. http://www.trustedcomputinggroup.org

Cloud Security Questions? Here are some answers (2010). Cloudcomputing.sys. http://cloudcomputing.sys-con.com/node/1330353

Controlling Data in the Cloud (2009). Outsourcing Computation Without Outsourcing Control. Retrieved from http://www.parc.com/content/attachments/ControllingDataInTheCloud- CCSW-09.pdf

Dutta, R. (2009). *Planning for Single SignOn*. [White Paper]. MIEL e-Security Pvt

Grimes, J., Jaeger, P., & Lin, J. (2011). Weathering the Storm: The Policy Implications of Cloud Computing [Online]. Retrieved from ischools.org/images/iConferences/CloudAbstract13109FINAL.pdf

Grobauer, B., Walloschek, T., & Stocker, E. (2011). Understanding Cloud Computing Vulnerabilities. *Security & Privacy, IEEE*, *9*(2), 50–57. doi:10.1109/MSP.2010.115

Jamil, D., & Zaki, H. (2011). Cloud Computing Security. *International Journal of Engineering Science and Technology*, *3*(4), 3478–3483.

Jensen, M., Gruschka, N., et al. (2008). The impact of flooding Attacks on network based services. Proceedings of the *IEEE International conference on Availiabilty, Reliability and Security.*

Jensen, M., Sehwenk, J., et al. (2009). On Technical Security Issues iCloud Computing. Proceedings of *International conference on cloud Computing.*

34. Kashif, M., & Sellapan, P. (2012, December). *Security Threats\Attacks present in Cloud Environment*. International Journal of Computer Science and Network Security, 12(12), 107-114. Retrieved from http://paper.ijcsns.org/07_book/201212/20121217

La'Quata Sumter, R. (2010). Cloud Computing: Security Risk Classification. ACMSE Oxford, USA.

Mathisen (2011, May 31-June 3). Security Challenges and Solutions in Cloud Computing. Proceedings of 5th IEEE International Conference on Digital Ecosystems and Technologies. Daejeon, Korea.

Mell, P., & Grance, T. (2011). The NIST definition of cloud computing (draft). *National Institute of Standards and Technology.* http://csrc.nist.gov/publications/drafts/800–145/Draft-SP-800-145_cloud-definition.pdf.

Mowbray, M., & Pearson, S. (2009, June 16-19). A client-based privacy manager for cloud computing. Proceedings of *Fourth International Conference on Communication System Software and Middleware (ComsWare).* Dublin, Ireland. doi:10.1145/1621890.1621897

Mukhin, V., & Volokyta, A. (2011, September 15-17). Security Risk Analysis for Cloud Computing Systems. Proceedings of the *6th IEEE International Conference on Intelligent Data Acquisition and Advanced Computing Systems: Technology and Applications.* Prague, Czech Republic.

Okuhara, M., et al. (2009). Security Architecture for Cloud Computing. *Fujitsu.* www.fujitsu.com/downloads/MAG/vol46-4/paper09.pdf

Overview of Security processes. (2008, September). *Amazon Web Services.* Retrieved from http://aws.amazon.com

Ponemon (2011, April). Security of cloud computing providers study. *CA Technologies.* http://www.ca.com/~/media/Files/ IndustryResearch/security-of-cloud-computing-providers-final-april-2011.pdf

Schreiber, T. (2004). *Session Riding a Widespread Vulnerability in Today's Web Applications.* [White Paper]. Retrieved from http://www.securenet.de/papers/Session_Riding.pdf

Swamp Computing a.k.a. Cloud Computing. (2009, December 28). Web Security Journal.

Top 7 threats to cloud computing (2010). *HELP NET SECURITY.* Retrieved from http://www.net-security.org/secworld.php?id=8943

Tripathi & Mishra, A. (2011, September 14-16). Cloud computing security considerations. Proceedings of *IEEE conference signal processing, communication and computing.* Xi'an, Shaanxi, China.

Wayne, A. Jansen (2011). Cloud Hooks: Security and Privacy Issues in Cloud Computing. Proceedings of *44th Hawaii International Conference on System.*

What cloud computing really means. InfoWorld (2007). *Infoworld.* Retrieved from http://www.infoworld.com/d/cloud-computing/what-cloud-computing-really-means-031?page=0,0

Wik, P. (2011, November). Thunderclouds: *Managing SOA-Cloud Risk. Service Technology Magazine.*

Zhang, S., Zhang, S., & Chen, X. (2010). Cloud Computing Research and Development Trend. Proceedings of Second International Conference on Future Networks, ICFN 2010. (pp. 93). doi:10.1109/ICFN.2010.58

KEY TERMS AND DEFINITIONS

Cloud Computing: A computing term or metaphor that evolved in the late 2000s, based on utility and consumption of computer resources.

Privacy: The ability of an individual or group to seclude themselves, or information about themselves, and thereby express themselves selectively.

Protocol: In information technology, a protocol is the special set of rules that end points in a telecommunication connection use when they communicate. Protocols specify interactions between the communicating entities.

Secure Architecture: Focusing on information security throughout the enterprise.

Security: The degree of resistance to, or protection from, harm. It applies to any vulnerable and valuable asset, such as a person, dwelling, community, nation, or organization.

Single Sign-On: (SSO): A property of access control of multiple related, but independent software systems. With this property a user logs in once and gains access to all systems without being prompted to log in again at each of them.

Threat: A possible danger that might exploit a vulnerability to breach security and thus cause possible harm.

Vulnerability: A weakness which allows an attacker to reduce a system's information assurance.

Chapter 5
Governance and Risk Management in the Cloud with Cloud Controls Matrix V3 and ISO/IEC 38500:2008

Abhik Chaudhuri
Tata Consultancy Services, India

ABSTRACT

Cloud based services are gaining popularity across the globe and there is a growing interest to adopt the cloud for operational efficiency, green computing initiatives and service agility. However, concerns of security and risks in the Cloud are important constraints to reaping the benefits of Cloud Computing. Controlling the threats and vulnerabilities of Cloud based IT Services are prime necessities with proper policies and guidance from the Business Leadership or Board. While Business is concentrating on cost reduction as a primary enabler for adopting Cloud based Services, there is a growing need for exercising effective Governance and Risk Management to mitigate security risks and to exercise control over data in the Cloud. This chapter discusses how Governance and Risk Management domain (GRM) of Cloud Controls Matrix (CSA CCM) V3 Framework from Cloud Security Alliance (CSA) and the ISO/IEC 38500:2008 standard for IT Governance can be utilized together for an effective Governance and Risk Management of Cloud Services.

INTRODUCTION

Cloud Computing is gradually gaining significance as an effective IT Service Delivery methodology with every passing year and there is growing interest among the Business Owners and IT Service Providers to embrace the Cloud. According to Gartner Inc.'s Hype Cycle for Cloud Computing (2013), Cloud Computing is gradually moving towards the Slope of Enlightenment, as shown in Figure 1, with its growing popularity and two key technology concepts related to the Cloud – Virtualization and Software as a Service (SaaS) are approaching the Plateau of Productivity. However, Cloud based IT Services are not free from security threats and vulnerability issues. In

DOI: 10.4018/978-1-4666-8387-7.ch005

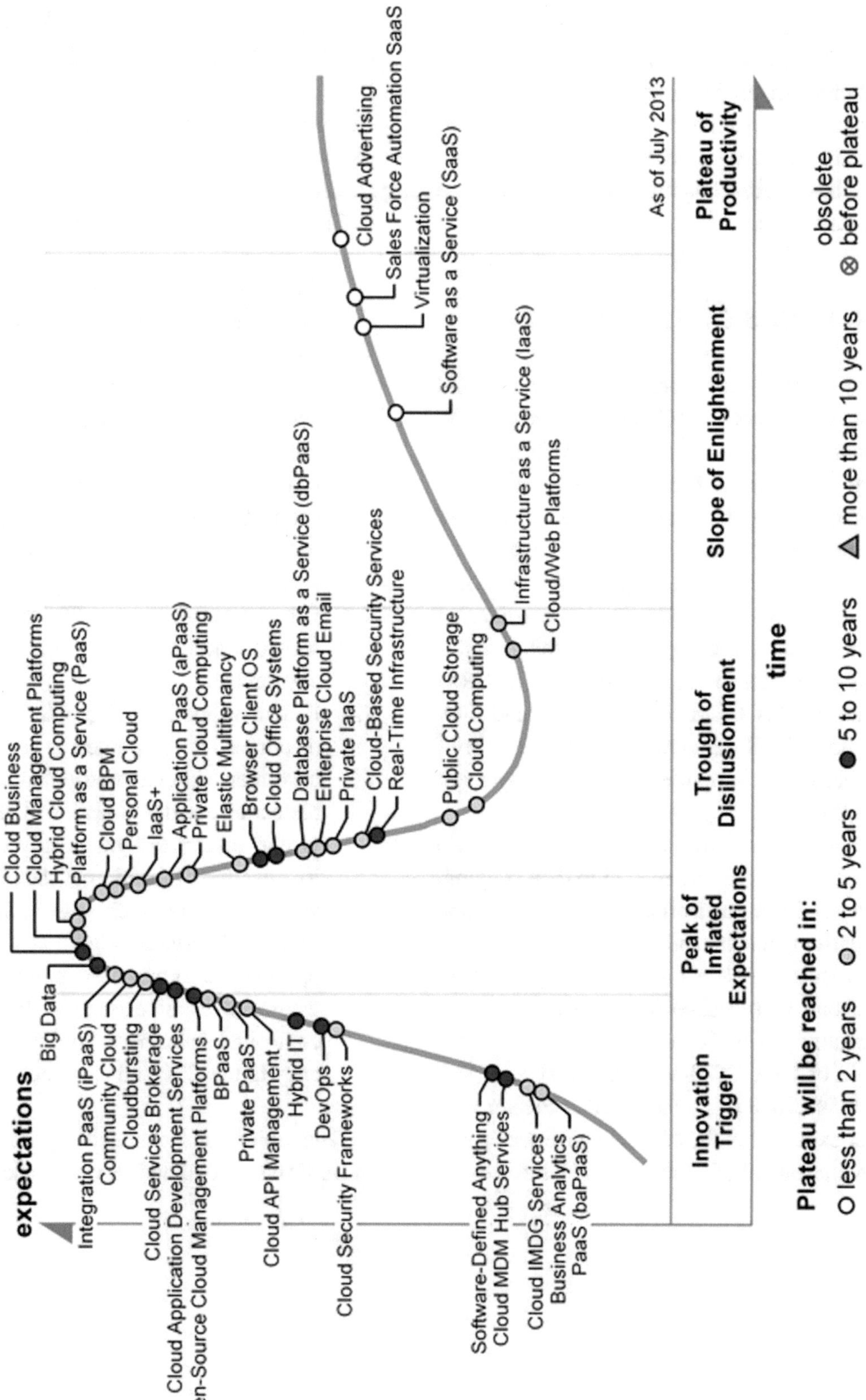

Figure 1. Hype Cycle for Cloud Computing (Gartner, 2013).

fact, if an organization overlooks the risks from security threats while moving to the Cloud and if it does not have proper governance mechanism to mitigate the risks then the Return on Investment in Cloud can have a negative impact that can reduce the tangible benefits and might even lead to a catastrophe.

MAIN FOCUS OF THE CHAPTER

We start with a brief description of the essential characteristics of Cloud Computing, basic Cloud Computing Service Models and the Cloud Computing Deployment Models to understand the characteristics of these models. Then we discuss about the critical areas of focus for a secured cloud environment and the inherent risks. We also cover the security risks of Virtualization considering the current trends of popularity of this technology as an enabler for Cloud adoption. The GRM domain of CSA CCM V3 framework and ISO/IEC 38500:2008 standard are discussed in brief with focus on Governance and Risk Management in the Cloud.

We also discuss the issues of data ownership in the Cloud, the issues related to data copying, deleting and movement of data across geographical boundaries to understand the role of the Business Owner/Board of Directors in defining an effective Cloud Governance mechanism. A 'Cloud Governance Matrix' compliant with GRM domain of CSA CCM V3 framework and ISO/IEC 38500:2008 is provided in this chapter with proper explanation for effective governance and risk management of Cloud based IT services.

ESSENTIAL CHARACTERISTICS OF CLOUD COMPUTING

According to Mell and Grance (2011), NIST (National Institute of Standards and Technology, U.S.A.) has ascribed five essential characteristics to Cloud Computing. These are:

1. On-demand self-service - The Cloud Service Provider (CSP) should have the ability to automatically provision computing capabilities, such as server and network storage, as needed without requiring human interaction with the CSP.
2. Rapid elasticity - The computing capabilities should be rapidly and elastically provisioned with minimal response time, to scale out or scale in quickly.
3. Broad network access - The cloud network should be accessible anywhere and by almost any device.
4. Resource pooling - The CSP's computing resources can be pooled to serve multiple customers using a multi-tenant model with allocation and de-allocation of physical and virtual resources dynamically on demand irrespective of location of the physical and virtual resources (across geographies).
5. Measured service - Cloud systems should provide a utility based computing experience where the resource usage can be monitored, controlled and reported providing transparency to the CSP and customer.

The ubiquitous connectivity coupled with dynamic nature of cloud services makes the static security perimeters of customer organizations ineffective and requires effective governance. Details of governance and risk management measures are described later in this chapter.

CLOUD COMPUTING SERVICE MODELS

The cloud computing service models, as per ISACA (2009), consist of three basic service models namely Infrastructure as a Service (IaaS), Platform as a Service (PaaS) and Software as a Service (SaaS) depicted in Table 1 below.

IaaS

As shown in Table1, IaaS has the capability to provision processing, storage, networks and other fundamental computing resources to offer the customer the ability to deploy and run arbitrary software which can include operating systems and applications.

A customer opting for IaaS puts these IT operations into the hands of a third party CSP. The critical risks to be considered for this Cloud Service delivery model are service interruption due to security breach, virus attack or other operational constraints like data centre connectivity failure, server boot failure, data corruption etc. If any organization opts for IaaS from a CSP then the service level agreements should have proper clause to cover the above mentioned risk and mitigation options should be kept ready to minimize the impact.

PaaS

PaaS provides computing platform and solution stack as a service on the cloud infrastructure. This service delivery model facilitates deployment of applications for the user without the requirement of buying and managing the underlying hardware, software and provisioning hosting capabilities. PaaS allow developers to build applications on the platform with programming languages and tools

Table 1. Cloud Computing Service Models (ISACA, 2009).

Service Model	Definition	To Be Considered
Infrastructure as a Service (IaaS)	Capability to provision processing, storage, networks and other fundamental computing resources, offering the customer the ability to deploy and run arbitrary software, which can include operating systems and applications. IaaS puts these IT operations into the hands of a third party.	Options to minimize the impact if the cloud provider has a service interruption
Platform as a Service (PaaS)	Capability to deploy onto the cloud infrastructure customer-created or acquired applications created using programming languages and tools supported by the provider	• Availability • Confidentiality • Privacy and legal liability in the event of a security breach (as databases housing sensitive information will now be hosted offsite) • Data ownership • Concerns around e-discovery
Software as a Service (SaaS)	Capability to use the provider's applications running on cloud infrastructure. The applications are accessible from various client devices through a thin client interface such as a web browser (e.g., web-based e-mail).	• Who owns the applications? • Where do the applications reside?

that are supported by application development frameworks, middleware capabilities, and functions such as database, messaging, and queuing.

Some of the key considerations for PaaS implementation are confidentiality, data ownership, availability, privacy and legal liabilities related to data movement across geographical boundaries, data security, and concerns over e-discovery.

SaaS

SaaS is a software delivery model in which software and its associated data are hosted in the cloud and are accessed by users from various client devices through a thin client interface such as a web browser. The CSP has a responsibility for security of the software and secured maintenance of users' data.

CLOUD COMPUTING DEPLOYMENT MODELS

There are four primary cloud deployment models according to ISACA (2009) - Private Cloud, Public Cloud, Community Cloud and Hybrid Cloud. The cloud deployment model and the corresponding cloud infrastructure characteristics with necessary considerations are shown in Table 2. While choosing the cloud service and deployment model an organization should consider the necessity of opting for that service and model, the benefits that can be derived from it and the risks that need to be addressed.

Private Clouds are operated solely for an organization and the cloud infrastructure can reside on-premise or off-premise. The cloud infrastructure may be managed by the organization or handed

Table 2. Cloud Computing Deployment Models (ISACA, 2009).

Service Model	Definition	To Be Considered
Private cloud	• Operated solely for an organization • May be managed by the organization or a third party • May exist on-premise or off-premise	• Cloud services with minimum risk • May not provide the scalability and agility of public cloud services
Community cloud	• Shared by several organizations • Supports a specific community that has shared mission or interest. • May be managed by the organizations or a third party • May reside on-premise or off-premise	• Same as private cloud, plus: • Data may be stored with the data of competitors.
Public cloud	• Made available to the general public or a large industry group • Owned by an organization selling cloud services	• Same as community cloud, plus: • Data may be stored in unknown locations and may not be easily retrievable.
Hybrid cloud	A composition of two or more clouds (private, community or public) that remain unique entities but are bound together by standardized or proprietary technology that enables data and application portability (e.g., cloud bursting for load balancing between clouds)	• Aggregate risk of merging different deployment models • Classification and labeling of data will be beneficial to the security manager to ensure that data are assigned to the correct cloud type.

over to a third party. This deployment model can be of minimum risk if external influences and vulnerabilities are identified and mitigation plans are put in place.

Public Clouds are owned by CSPs and made available to general public or organizations with features of multi-tenancy. Data in public clouds can be stored in locations across geographies unknown to the customer. Data ownership and data privacy are key concerns for the customer that needs to be addressed by the CSPs.

Community Clouds are shared by several community groups and may be managed by the organizations or a third party CSP. One of the key concerns for this deployment model is data privacy. This is because data in a community cloud may be stored with the data of competitors and any issue of data loss, data theft or security breach can have detrimental effects. Along with legislative and regulatory requirements, all community cloud member groups and organizations will need to comply with other policies, strategies and frameworks.

A Hybrid Cloud is a composition of two or more cloud deployment models (private, community or public) that remain as unique entities but are bound together by standardized or proprietary technology that enables data and application portability. This deployment model can provide load-balancing between clouds to provide scalability as per demand without stretching the resources of the individual clouds. Data movement between clouds is a critical factor of importance in this type of deployment. Classification and labeling of data can be a risk mitigation strategy in such a scenario to ensure confidentiality, integrity and privacy.

CRITICAL AREAS OF FOCUS FOR A SECURED CLOUD ENVIRONMENT

Cloud Security Alliance (CSA, 2011) has identified the critical areas of focus for Cloud Computing in the "Security Guidance for Critical Areas of Focus in Cloud Computing V3.0".

Here we discuss the critical areas (not exhaustive) in brief to highlight the risks for effective operations and governance in the Cloud.

Physical Security

Traditional physical security will not be effective in a cloud environment irrespective of the service or deployment option chosen by an organization. While choosing the CSP for cloud service, the customer organization needs to evaluate the traditional security of a CSP and the enhanced security features in the Cloud. Critical evaluation of physical location of the data center facility and the documentation of critical risk and recovery factors are important 'need-to-check' activities that need to be performed before moving to the Cloud. Data Center Perimeter Security should be evaluated and high-risk areas of the facility should be secured. Some factors for consideration during evaluation of physical security for the facility are –

1. Risks of seismic activity of physical location
2. Historical records of natural disaster at the physical location
3. Accessibility of the facility's location
4. The facility should not be at a location with high crime rate or political/ social unrest

Business Continuity Planning

The CSP should have proper measures in place to ensure business continuity with minimal impact during any kind of service disruption. These measures should be over and above the commitments to main the agreed Service Level Agreement (SLA) with the customer. Periodic BCP drills at all the locations maintained by the CSP are mandatory and these reports should be shared with the customer for their decision making regarding the opted cloud service. The customer should also conduct an onsite assessment of the CSP's facility to confirm and verify the asserted controls used to maintain the continuity of the service.

Data Centre Operations

Data Centers are the backbone of the Cloud Infrastructure and are primary enablers for a CSP's service delivery to the customers. Physical access to information assets and functions at the data centers by users and support personnel should be restricted with proper segregation of duty and periodic audits. The applications running in the data center that contain regulated information (governed under an information security or application security standard) should be audited. The result of these physical audit findings undertaken by the CSP should be published to the customers for their knowledge. Multi-tenancy at the data centers require special attention from the customers regarding how their data and applications are hosted and secured from loss, theft and breach of access.

Backup and Disaster Recovery

Efficient Cloud storage for business requires proper backup and disaster recovery services (DR). Cloud Backup necessitates reliable data replication at multiple physical locations and it might be across geographical boundaries based on the CSP's cloud infrastructure setup. However, this might have legal implications regarding data management and data privacy. The CSP may adhere and certify against BS 25999, the British Standard for Business Continuity Management (BCM) and the customer can verify the scope of the certification and the assessment details before choosing the CSP.

Incident Response

Customers should verify with the CSPs the measures that have been put in place to enable efficient and effective handling of security incidents that involve resources in the cloud. It is necessary to have proper capabilities of security incident detection, analysis, containment, and recovery engineered into the service offering. The customer as well as the CSP can work together to implement these capabilities at both ends for proper ad efficient Incident Handling and Response. Forensic capabilities can be embedded in the cloud infrastructure without compromising the privacy of co-tenants to ensure robust security. Legal and Regulatory implications may adversely affect the incident handling process by placing limitations so it will be wise for an organization to include representatives from its legal department on the Incident Response team to provide guidance as and when necessary.

Security Event and Information Management

Implementation of security event and information management (SIEM) can ensure a secured cloud environment by increasing the visibility on security events and risks related to it on a real-time basis and by taking appropriate action. SIEM provides an early warning system to the Cloud customers. The SIEM features can be customized with proper configurations of the audit policies and rule responses based on the organization's need of monitoring and logging of security events in the Cloud. SIEM can be designed to provide variety of reports (executive/technical/audit) to effectively communicate the risk levels and the state of security of the cloud infrastructure. Cloud customers using SIEM can identify the threats and vulnerabilities in the cloud infrastructure and take corrective measures for better security and control of the cloud environment. SIEM can be tuned to generate event logs with time-stamps for forensic investigations or requirements from regulatory and law enforcement agencies. The logged data should be stored securely preferably with encryption.

Identity, Entitlement, and Access Management

The concept of identity, entitlement and access management (IdEA) for cloud services has additional dimensions than the requirements of traditional computing, because a cloud service has to leverage multiple identities and attributes from external sources to make better risk based decision about granular access to system, process and data in the cloud. To provide a secured cloud environment it is necessary to obtain identity and attributes from multiple sources and then make authorization or access management decisions based on entitlement rules as required by the business following a defined entitlement process. Proper access management process should be set up by the Business Leadership to govern access to the following five architectural layers of the cloud infrastructure - network layer, system layer, application layer, process layer and data layer. For identity federation in the cloud, Security Assertion Markup Language (SAML), an XML-based OASIS open standard, can be used for exchanging authentication and authorization data between security domains. Specific authorization and access control model can be adopted for safe and secure access to contents in the cloud. For example, in an enterprise centric authorization model the enterprise is the Policy Decision Point (PDP) and the CSP acts as the Policy Enforcement Point (PEP).

Encryption and Key Management

A cloud premise is characterized by highly scalable and on-demand service environment. Data encryption in large volumes in such an environment is a true challenge but again, the organizations opting for a cloud service cannot ignore the aspects of data security and protection in the cloud. For data deployments in the cloud, con-cepts like content aware encryption and format preserving encryption can be used. However, an organization moving data to the cloud should understand the complexity in encrypting all its data assets. Alternative approaches to encryption can be considered like establishing access control mechanism for data access with segregation features. Key management is an important aspect in public cloud environments specifically when data has to be removed or deleted while exiting that environment. In such cases local key management is required that allows revoking the key from the key management system to assure that any data or traces remaining in the public cloud system cannot be decrypted.

Data Loss Prevention

Theft or loss of sensitive data is a cause of concern for the organizations operating in the Cloud. Data Loss Prevention (DLP) is an important information protection and control strategy that helps to protect against security risks through all stages of data lifecycle - data in motion, data in use and data at rest. The embedded characteristics of a DLP strategy are the C-I-A triad, data origin verification and access control. In a multi-tenant cloud service, the CSP should have proper mechanism to differentiate the data discovery requirements of various customers so that individual customers' data are protected and accessed through proper access control features. In-built forensic capabilities in a DLP mechanism can help in post-incident discovery scenarios. The DLP requirements for the CSP and the customers will vary but the underlying binder should be secured and appropriate use of data. Copying and creating multiple back up of data by CSPs across geography is often used as a DLP strategy but this path to data sovereignty has growing legal and socio-political concerns that needs to be addressed.

Data Security Lifecycle in the Cloud

Data security lifecycle spans from creation to destruction of data controlled through the lifecycle by setting up specific policies of creation, storage, access, usage, sharing and destroying. Data classification, data labeling and enterprise digital rights management are key responsibilities of the Business Leadership for effective and efficient data management in the Cloud. Data discovery tools should be used to scan all locations in the Cloud where organization data has been stored. This can help to prevent data loss at the acceptable level as defined by business. While using virtual private storage, data should be encrypted locally before moving it to the Cloud with proper access control and key management. All files and folders should be properly encrypted to prevent loss or theft.

Compliance and Audit Management

The distributed and virtualized nature of Cloud provides new challenges as organizations migrate from traditional data centers to a more distributed framework in the cloud. There are regulatory requirements for the CSPs and the customers to demonstrate compliance with evidence in a periodic manner. Compliance to external requirements for businesses migrating to the Cloud is mandatory corporate obligation and the Business Leadership should perform period audits for assurance and disclosure. Controls should be implemented to address cross-border or multi-jurisdictional issues with data movement, ownership and other concerns. CSP might require ISO/IEC 27001 or ISO/IEC 27002 based audits for mission critical services. For some customers and CSPs there might be regulatory requirements to provide Service Organization Control (SOC) 2 Report that focuses on a business's non-financial reporting controls related to security, availability, processing integrity, confidentiality, and privacy of the operating environment in the Cloud.

VIRTUALIZATION ROUTE TO THE CLOUD

Virtualization has gained popularity in recent years as an enabler of Cloud Computing to implement Cloud infrastructure in a short span of time. As depicted earlier in Figure 1, the Hype Cycle for Cloud Computing (Gartner, 2013) shows that virtualization is gradually moving towards the Plateau of Productivity with its wider acceptance among CSPs and businesses.

Virtualization is a software technology that uses a physical resource, such as a server, and divides it into virtual resources called virtual machines (VMs). Virtualization helps to consolidate physical resources, simplify deployment and administration, and reduce power and cooling requirements. Virtualization of IT systems has many advantages, and that is why it has become so popular. Apart from improving IT service agility, virtualization technology reduces the infrastructure cost of ownership by reducing the total number of physical servers. As a result the operating expenses are reduced considerably with a fewer number of physical servers. Recent trends indicate urgency amongst the Business Leaderships for cost savings in IT investments and for embracing 'Green IT' initiatives. Virtualization of IT systems is playing a significant role in cost savings as wells as Green Computing.

As shown in Figure 2, VMs are encapsulated into files, making it possible to rapidly save, copy and provision a VM. Fully configured systems, applications, OSs and virtual hardware may be moved, within seconds, from one physical server to another for zero-downtime maintenance and continuous workload consolidation.

SECURITY RISKS IN VIRTUAL IT SYSTEMS

The security risks in virtual IT systems can be broadly classified as below:

Figure 2. Architectural overview of Virtual IT Systems.

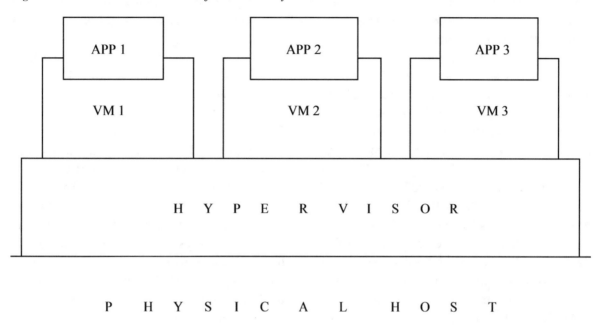

Architectural vulnerability —The layer of abstraction between the physical hardware and the virtualized systems running the IT services is a potential target of attack. As the guest OS is subjected to the same security risks as a physical system, proper security measures (e.g., antivirus agents, spyware filters, IDs) should be installed on all VMs.

Software vulnerability —The most important software in a virtual IT system is the hypervisor. The hypervisor intercepts the hardware resource requests from the virtual machines that reside on it and translates the requests to a format that can be understood by the physical hardware. Any security vulnerability in the hypervisor software will put VMs at risk of failure. A single instance of replicating malware can cause a single point of failure by rapidly exploiting all hypervisors in the networked IT environment. Proper lockdown of privileges and controlled access to virtual environments should be ensured to reduce single point of failure through malicious software (Chaudhuri, A., Solms, S.H. & Chaudhuri, D., 2011).

Configuration risks — Due to the ease of cloning and copying images, a new infrastructure can be deployed very easily in a virtual environment. This introduces configuration drift; as a result, controlling and accounting for the rapidly deployed environments becomes a critical task.

If the host computer is compromised, it can provide direct access to all VMs on the server. An intruder can reconfigure, move and copy the VMs, putting sensitive data at risk. If any malware intrudes the virtualization layer, it can gain access to all VMs on the host computer including the production VMs, causing increased security risk.

GOVERNANCE AND RISK MANAGEMENT IN THE CLOUD: ROLE OF THE BOARD

Cloud Services have to comply with policies, procedures, laws, regulations, industry standards and requirements of multiple jurisdictions for assurance and adherence to corporate obligations.

This is not possible without Governance initiative of the Board or Top Management of an organization that has opted for Cloud services.

Enterprise Risk Management, Compliance and Audit assurance are responsibilities of the Board/ Top Management for effective Governance in the Cloud. The Board should provide a strategic direction while opting for Cloud Services, identify the changes required to meet the performance objectives, ensure data and business related IT assets are secure and risks are managed in a controlled environment (Chaudhuri, 2011). To achieve these, proper Service Level agreements (SLAs) are required with the CSPs, so the Board should define the SLAs in alignment with business requirements of the organization. The Board should organize, manage and review service level agreements and contractual arrangements with the CSPs and third party service providers on a periodic basis. Operational level agreements within the various business units for Cloud services can also help to implement the organization's security policies and to maintain the state of security and incident response to the desired level.

The governing body should play a leadership role in developing strategies for obtaining value from Cloud based IT Services that it has opted for. Policies and procedures for establishing effective internal control in the Cloud is a primary requisite that should be addressed in the very beginning.

According to ISACA (2013), the Board of Directors should ask the following questions and have proper answers to ensure Governance of Cloud based IT Services -

1. Do management teams have a plan for cloud computing? Have they weighed the value and opportunity costs?
2. How do current cloud plans support the enterprise's mission?
3. Have executive teams systematically evaluated organizational readiness for operations in the Cloud?
4. Have management teams considered what existing investments might be lost in their cloud planning?
5. Do management teams have strategies to measure and track the value of cloud return versus risk?

Organizational-level initiatives are required to establish the data protection policies for Cloud environments. Disaster recovery and backup policies should be clearly defined and should mention critical factors such as acceptable data loss, acceptable downtime, guest-level backups and host-level backups. These should be included in the service agreement with the CSP. An internal audit program should be developed, specifically for the Cloud IT system. The Board should provide directives for preventive and detective measures via well-defined monitoring and auditing policies and their execution with proper follow-up action.

The Board can utilize industry accepted standards and frameworks to establish control for compliance with all internal policies and external legal, regulatory requirements. Cloud Controls Matrix V3 Framework and ISO/IEC 38500:2008 standard can be used for establishing Governance and Risk management (GRM) in the Cloud. Here we discuss in brief about the Framework and ISO Standard and show how we can utilize these to achieve the desired state of IT service in the Cloud.

OVERVIEW OF GRM DOMAIN OF CSA CLOUD CONTROLS MATRIX V3 FRAMEWORK

The Cloud Security Alliance's (CSA, 2013) Cloud Controls Matrix (CCM) V3 Framework provides fundamental security principles to guide cloud vendors and to assist prospective cloud customers in assessing the overall security risk of a cloud service. The CSA CCM version 3 provides a controls framework in multiple domains with customized relationship to other industry-accepted security standards, regulations, and controls frameworks such as the ISO 27001/27002, ISACA COBIT, PCI, NIST, Jericho Forum, NERC CIP. It also provides internal control direction for service organization control reports attestations provided by CSPs.

The CSA CCM V3 framework can be used to strengthen existing information security control environments and to identify and reduce consistent security threats and vulnerabilities in the cloud. It provides standardized security and operational risk management and security measures implemented in the cloud.

Governance and Risk Management (GRM) domain of CSA CCM V3 has 12 control specifications as explained below and shown in Table 3. For a business opting for a cloud service these controls should be implemented to mitigate the security risks. And for a CSP these control specifications are essential requirements to ensure the customers that its cloud service offerings are secured.

Here we discuss the 12 GRM control specifications and the corresponding security measures.

GRM-01: Baseline Requirements

For efficient Governance and Risk management, CSA CCM V3 Framework proposes baseline security requirements to be established for the cloud infrastructure that is developed or acquired, organizationally-owned or managed, physical or virtual, with appropriate security features for the applications, infrastructure system and network components. The defined security features should comply with applicable legal, statutory and regulatory compliance obligations. Any deviation from standard baseline configurations must be authorized with appropriate change management policies and procedures prior to deployment, provisioning, or use. Compliance with security baseline requirements must be reassessed at least annually unless an alternate frequency has been established and authorized based on the business need.

Table 3. GRM domains of CSA CCM V3 and Control IDs.

Governance and Risk Management Control Domain	CCM V3.0 Control ID
Baseline Requirements	GRM-01
Data Focus Risk Assessments	GRM-02
Management Oversight	GRM-03
Management Program	GRM-04
Management Support/Involvement	GRM-05
Policy	GRM-06
Policy Enforcement	GRM-07
Policy Impact on Risk Assessments	GRM-08
Policy Reviews	GRM-09
Risk Assessments	*GRM-10*
Risk Management Framework	*GRM-11*
Risk Mitigation / Acceptance	*GRM-12*

GRM-02: Data Focus Risk Assessments

Data Governance in the cloud should be a primary area of focus for the business to maintain privacy in a controlled environment. Risk assessments associated with data governance requirements should be conducted at planned intervals and should consider the following:

- Awareness of where sensitive data is stored and transmitted across applications, databases, servers, and network infrastructure in the cloud
- Compliance with defined data retention periods and end-of-life disposal requirements
- Data classification and protection from unauthorized use, access, loss, destruction, and falsification

The CSP should provide necessary infrastructure support towards data governance of its customers and to prevent any form of data loss, theft or infringement.

GRM-03: Management Oversight

Managers should be responsible for maintaining awareness of security policies, procedures and standards that are relevant to their area of responsibility and ensure compliance.

GRM-04: Management Program

An Information Security Management Program (ISMP) should be developed, documented, approved, and implemented that includes administrative, technical, and physical safeguards to protect assets and data from loss, misuse, unauthorized access, disclosure, alteration, and destruction. The security program should include the following areas along with other necessary areas that relate to the characteristics of the business:

- Risk management
- Security policy
- Organization of information security
- Asset management
- Human resources security
- Physical and environmental security
- Communications and operations management
- Access control
- Information systems acquisition, development, and maintenance

GRM-05: Management Support/Involvement

Executive and line management should take formal action to support information security through clearly-documented direction and commitment, and ensure that the action has been assigned.

GRM-06: Policy

Information security policies and procedures are required to be established and made readily available for review by all impacted personnel and external business relationships. Information security policies must be authorized by the organization's Business Leadership/Board and supported by a strategic business plan and information security management program that includes defined information security roles and responsibilities for business leadership.

GRM-07: Policy Enforcement

A formal disciplinary or sanction policy should be established for employees regarding violation of security policies and procedures. Employees should be made aware of what action might be taken in the event of a violation, and disciplinary measures must be stated in the policies and procedures.

GRM-08: Policy Impact on Risk Assessments

Risk assessment results should include updates to security policies, procedures, standards, and controls to ensure that they remain relevant and effective.

GRM-09: Policy Reviews

The organization's business leadership/Board should review the information security policy at planned intervals or as a result of changes to the organization to ensure alignment with the security strategy, effectiveness, accuracy, relevance, and applicability to legal, statutory, or regulatory compliance obligations on a continuous basis.

GRM-10: Risk Assessments

Formal risk assessments aligned to the enterprise-wide framework should be performed at least annually or at planned intervals, to determine the likelihood and impact of all identified risks using qualitative and quantitative methods. The likelihood and impact associated with inherent and residual risk should be determined independently, considering all risk categories (e.g., audit results, threat and vulnerability analysis, and regulatory compliance).

GRM-11: Risk Management Framework

Organizations should develop and maintain an enterprise risk management framework to mitigate risk to an acceptable level.

GRM-12: Risk Mitigation/Acceptance

Risks should be mitigated to an acceptable level as required by the business. Acceptance levels should be established based on risk criteria and

documented in accordance with reasonable resolution time frames and executive approval.

OVERVIEW OF ISO/IEC 38500:2008 STANDARD FOR IT GOVERNANCE

ISO/IEC 38500:2008, the standard for Corporate Governance of Information Technology, is an advisory standard that provides a framework of principles for Senior Management and Board of Directors to use while evaluating, directing, and monitoring the use of IT in their organizations (ISO, 2008). In addition to providing broad guidance on the role of a governing body for effective IT Governance, it encourages organizations to use appropriate standards and frameworks for effective governance of IT. This Standard can be utilized by the Business Leadership for IT Governance in the Cloud.

The framework comprises definitions, principles and a model as shown in Figure 3. It sets out six principles for good corporate governance of IT. The directors and top management should evaluate, direct, and monitor IT activities in the Cloud based on these six principles:

1. Responsibility
2. Strategy
3. Acquisition
4. Performance
5. Conformance
6. Human behavior

The practical implications of each of the six principles for ISO/IEC 38500:2008 for aligning Business and IT Services in the Cloud are explained here:

Principle 1: Responsibility

The standard emphasizes that people must understand, accept, and have sufficient authority to perform their responsibilities provided by the

Figure 3. ISO/IEC 38500:2008 Model for corporate governance of IT (© 2008, International Organization for Standardization (ISO). Used with permission.).

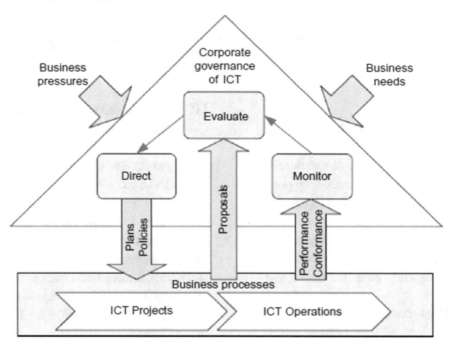

business. It spans the total set of responsibility for the use of IT, beginning with responsibility for developing a business strategy that takes into account the market impact and opportunity associated with cloud based IT Services from the CSPs. Irrespective of the IT team being internal to the organization or a third-party, the Board of Directors should clearly define the roles and responsibilities of the IT team and the business owners for the accountability and ownership of important decisions and tasks for IT operations in the Cloud. The staff should be trained for the skills and tools in accordance with their assigned roles and responsibilities. Larger enterprises should have an IT executive committee acting on behalf of the board to evaluate, direct, and monitor the use of IT in the Cloud to advise the board on critical issues.

Principle 2: Strategy

This principle applies to the full spectrum of IT related plans that include business plans defining the use of IT and the supply plans. The scope spans the established capabilities and proposed capabilities for operating in the Cloud and to derive the benefits from it. The IT capabilities like the human resources and the IT infrastructure should be planned appropriately to support the IT strategy for controlled and secured operations in the Cloud. The Business Leadership should understand the needs of moving to the Cloud and address all concerns related to data security, privacy and confidentiality concerns, availability concerns, data movement across geographical boundaries and compliance and legal issues. Proper risk assessment and evaluation of IT plans is mandatory before execution. The Board should provide oversight of development, establishment and ongoing support for the IT operations in the Cloud with policy decisions and consensus decision making. The Board should endorse policy for security standards in the Cloud and ensure that the Business can operate in a trusted environment.

Principle 3: Acquisitions

This principle applies to current and future use of IT and for migration to the cloud. It relates to any decisions to commit resources—IT infrastructure, human, financial, and other—to the use of IT. It applies in the context of decisions regarding maintenance and use of existing IT systems, decisions about creation of new business capability, decisions about the Cloud Service model that can be most beneficial for the Business and the IT capabilities required for Cloud based services, decisions about development of divestiture of IT skills to support the business and IT capabilities, sourcing decisions, decision on choosing the right CSP and the adoption of strategic plans for cloud based IT services where the strategy will require a significant investment in IT.

Principle 4: Performance

The Business leadership and Board should set up a performance measurement process for IT using proper metrics for verification and validation of IT's alignment with business. Effective governance is established when IT supports the business with the requisite capacity and capability as required by business. Policies and plans should be established by the top management for business continuity measures with special attention to the security and risk management of data and applications in the Cloud and to ensure account-

ability for achieving the goals. Regular evaluation of the effectiveness of the controls established for the Cloud Services and performance of the organization's IT system comprising of Cloud and non-Cloud components is a prime responsibility of the director and senior management.

Principle 5: Conformance

The Board should ensure ethical use of IT in compliance with all internal policies and external legal and regulatory requirements. Privacy, confidentiality, intellectual property rights, and security should be included in the strategic plan for IT operations in the Cloud. The top management should define appropriate policies and procedures and these should be implemented, enforced, monitored, and audited periodically as an organization initiative toward conformance and compliance.

Principle 6: Human Behavior

IT is implemented, managed, and used by the people in various roles as stakeholders, specialists, managers, users, customers, and business partners beyond borders. Any proposed change in the use and application of IT specifically in a Cloud based Service environment will require significant cultural and behavioral change within the enterprise and with customers and business partners. Directors should clearly communicate goals and ensure integrity in a multicultural IT environment. IT activities and work practices should be monitored to ensure appropriate use of IT.

The Business Leadership can evaluate, direct and monitor the use of IT in the Cloud based on the above six principles. They can guide and influence behavior and decision making by establishing policies that correlate to each of the six principles.

"CLOUD GOVERNANCE MATRIX" FOR GOVERNANCE AND RISK MANAGEMENT

ISO/IEC 38500:2008 Standard and CSA CCM V3's GRM Control Domain can be utilized together for an effective Governance and Risk Management of Cloud Services. While ISO/IEC 38500:2008 provides a high-level standard for IT Governance in the Cloud, the Cloud Controls Matrix (CSA CCM) V3 Framework's GRM Control Domain provides additional insight to assess the overall security of a cloud service and to take necessary action for risk mitigation.

Combining ISO/IEC 38500:2008 and CSA CCM V3's GRM Control Specifications enables framing a "Cloud Governance Matrix", as shown in Table 4 for effective Governance and Risk Management in the Cloud. The six principles of ISO/IEC 38500:2008 have been mapped to the 12 Control IDs of CSA CCM V3 GRM control domain in the Cloud Governance Matrix and each of the mappings is explained here:

Responsibility

ISO/IEC 38500:2008 stresses on the clarity regarding responsibility and accountability to enable effective Governance of IT. Irrespective of the IT team being internal to the organization or a third-party service provider or CSP, the board

of directors should clearly define the roles and responsibilities of the IT team and the business application teams for the accountability and ownership of important decisions and tasks. CSA CCM V3 GRM control domain entrust responsibility through control specifications for Control IDs GRM-01, GRM-02, GRM-03, GRM-04, GRM-05, GRM-07, GRM-08, GRM-09, GRM-10 and GRM-11. GRM-06 specifies that Information Security Policies must be authorized by the organization's Leadership and supported by a strategic business plan. An information security management program (ISMP) inclusive of defined information security roles and responsibilities for business leadership should be in place. Executive and line management should also take formal action to support information security through clearly documented direction and commitment. Managers should be responsible for maintaining awareness and compliance with respect to security policies, procedures and standards that are relevant to their area of responsibility.

Strategy

ISO/IEC 38500:2008 considers Strategy as the key to the current and future use of IT in an organization. A business should strategize the migration to the Cloud, maximize the benefits from the Cloud with proper risk mitigation and establish necessary controls for operating in the

Table 4. Cloud Governance Matrix

CSA CCM V3 / ISO/IEC 38500:2008	GRM-01	GRM-02	GRM-03	GRM-04	GRM-05	GRM-06	GRM-07	GRM-08	GRM-09	GRM-10	GRM-11	GRM-12
Responsibility	√	√	√	√	√		√	√	√	√	√	
Strategy	√	√	√	√		√		√		√	√	√
Acquisitions				√								
Performance		√		√	√		√	√		√		√
Conformance		√		√	√		√	√	√	√		√
Human behavior		√		√	√		√	√	√	√		√

Cloud. CSA CCM V3 GRM domain also mentions the strategic needs of operations in the Cloud like establishing baseline security requirements, conducting risk assessments associated with data governance requirements, data classification and protection from unauthorized use, establishment, authorization and use of information security policies and procedures. The Control IDs for GRM domain specifications that relate to the Strategy principle of ISO/IEC 38500:2008 are GRM-01, GRM-02, GRM-03, GRM-04, GRM-06, GRM-08, GRM-10, GRM-11 and GRM-12.

Acquisitions

This ISO/IEC 38500:2008 principle applies to the context of decisions regarding maintenance and continued use of existing IT systems, sourcing decisions and adoption of strategic plans where the strategy will require a significant investment in IT like migration of IT function to the Cloud. CSA CCM V3 control specification for GRM-04 also advises to set up an Information Security Management Program (ISMP) that should include Information systems acquisition to protect assets and data from loss, misuse, unauthorized access, disclosure, alteration, and destruction in the Cloud.

Performance

According to ISO/IEC 38500:2008, regular evaluation of the performance of the organization's IT system is a prime responsibility of the Director and Senior Management. When opting for a Cloud service, the business organization can define Key Performance Indicators and set up Service Levels in agreement (SLAs) with the CSP for performance measurement on a continuous basis. Assigning service credits and penalty with the SLAs can help both sides to maintain the required level of service in the Cloud. CSA CCM V3 GRM domain also mentions about performance reviews of IT systems and any proposed deviation from standard baseline configurations in the Cloud must be authorized

following change management policies and procedures prior to deployment, provisioning or use. The Control IDs for GRM domain specifications that relate to the Performance principle of ISO/IEC 38500:2008 are GRM-02, GRM-04, GRM-05, GRM-07, GRM-08, GRM-10 and GRM-12.

Conformance

The Business Leadership should ensure ethical use of IT in the Cloud in compliance with all internal policies and external legal and regulatory requirements. Privacy, confidentiality, intellectual property rights and security should be the key components of the strategic plan for Cloud based IT operations. The top management should define appropriate policies and procedures and these should be implemented, enforced, monitored, and audited periodically as an organization initiative toward conformance and compliance. As per CSA CCM V3 GRM domain, baseline security requirements must comply with applicable legal, statutory and regulatory compliance obligations. Formal risk assessments should be performed at least annually or at planned intervals to determine the likelihood and impact of all identified risks. Risk assessments associated with data governance requirements should also be conducted at planned intervals. The key specifications for conformance are for Control IDs GRM-02, GRM-04, GRM-05, GRM-07, GRM-08, GRM-09, GRM-10 and GRM-12.

Human Behavior

IT operations in the Cloud is implemented, managed, and used by the people in various roles as stakeholders, specialists, managers, users, customers, and business partners beyond borders. Any proposed change in the use and application of IT will require significant cultural and behavioral change within the organization and with customers and business partners. The following Control IDs from CSA CCM V3 GRM domain requires human behavior as key consideration for governance and risk management in the Cloud: GRM-02, GRM-04, GRM-05, GRM-07, GRM-08, GRM-09, GRM-10 and GRM-12. Training sessions should be conducted for all employees to ensure secured use of the Cloud. A formal disciplinary or sanction policy should be established by the Business Leadership for employees who have violated security policies and procedures. Disciplinary measures must be stated in the policies and procedures and all employees should be made aware of what action might be taken in the event of a violation.

DERIVING BENEFITS FROM THE CLOUD GOVERNANCE MATRIX

While migrating to the Cloud or opting for Cloud based IT services the Board or Business Leadership should understand that Governance and Risk Management responsibilities cannot be handed over to the CSPs and these have to be exercised as organization initiatives for the benefits of business. To reap the benefits of on-demand service agility of the Cloud, the Cloud service recipients (customers) have to continuously evaluate, direct and monitor the security levels, policies and access rights of the Cloud services with some centralized control. This is possible by referring the Cloud Governance Matrix which maps the desirable behavior expressed in the six principles of ISO/IEC 38500:2008 to each of the twelve Control Specifications of CSA CCM V3 GRM Control Domains.

The Cloud Governance Matrix can be utilized by the organizations to prepare a Cloud roadmap and migration plan for their IT services. Using ISO/IEC 38500:2008 together with CSA CCM V3 GRM domain specifications provides an integrated Governance and Risk Management approach and helps to reduce the risk exposure of the CSPs and the cloud based IT services of the customer organizations.

By using the Cloud Governance Matrix the auditors can provide independent assurance of compliance to the Board for the Cloud Services and adherence to internal policies derived from internal directives or external legal, regulatory, and contractual requirements. It is important for the auditors and the Board to consider not only control weaknesses but also opportunities for improvement. These Cloud audits can help the Board and top management to confirm that corrective actions have been taken in a timely manner to address the compliance gaps.

CONCLUSION

The need for Cloud Governance and Cloud Risk Management are becoming much more apparent with increase in complex multi-cloud and multi-tenant service model adoptions and emerging issues like security threats, data ownership, cross-border data movement, identity and access management, compliance, regulatory requirements and legal liabilities. While ISO/IEC 38500:2008 provides answers regarding "what behavior is appropriate for effective use of Cloud based IT services ?", the CSA CCM V3 GRM domain based Control Specifications provide the answers regarding "What needs to be done for business information security control and risk management in the Cloud?" As depicted in this article, the Board of Directors can leverage ISO/IEC 38500:2008 and CSA CCM V3 GRM domain to govern and manage risks in the Cloud. By utilizing the Cloud Governance Matrix an organization can ensure successful deployment of IT services in the Cloud that is safe, secure, reliable and compliant.

DEDICATION

I would like to dedicate this chapter to my parents, wife and cute little daughter Aishani.

REFERENCES

Chaudhuri, A. (2011). Enabling Effective IT Governance: Leveraging ISO/IEC 38500: 2008 and COBIT to Achieve Business–IT Alignment. *EDPACS*, *44*(2), 1–18. doi:10.1080/07366981.2011.599278

Chaudhuri, A., Solms, S. H., & Chaudhuri, D. (2011). Auditing Security Risks in Virtual IT Systems. *ISACA Journal*, *1*, 16.

Corporate governance of information technology. (2008). International Organization for Standardization IEC 38500:2008-s. Retrieved from http://www.iso.org/iso/catalogue_detail?csnumber=51639

Security Guidance for Critical Areas of Focus in Cloud Computing V3.0. (2011). *CSA*. Retrieved from http://www.cloudsecurityalliance.org/guidance/csaguide.v3.0.pdf

CSA. (2013). Cloud Controls Matrix v3.0: Cloud Security Alliance. Retrieved from https://cloudsecurityalliance.org/download/cloud-controls-matrix-v3/

Hype Cycle for Cloud Computing. (2013). Gartner Inc. Retrieved from https://www.gartner.com/doc/2573318/hype-cycle-cloud-computing-

Cloud Computing: Business Benefits With Security, Governance and Assurance Perspectives. (2009). *ISACA*. Retrieved from http://www.isaca.org/Knowledge-Center/Research/ResearchDeliverables/Pages/Cloud-Computing-Business-Benefits-With-Security-Governance-and-Assurance-Perspective.aspx

Cloud Governance: Questions Boards of Directors Need to Ask. (2013). ISACA. Retrieved from http://www.isaca.org/Knowledge-Center/Research/ResearchDeliverables/Pages/Cloud-Governance-Questions-Boards-of-Directors-Need-to-Ask.aspx

Mell, P., & Grance, T. (2011). The NIST Definition of Cloud Computing. *National Institute of Standards and Technology*. Retrieved from http://csrc.nist.gov/publications/nistpubs/800-145/SP800-145.pdf

ADDITIONAL READING

Becker, J., & Bailey, E. (2014). A Comparison of IT Governance & Control Frameworks in Cloud Computing. Twentieth Americas Conference on Information Systems, Savannah, Georgia, USA. Retrieved May 12, 2014, from http://www.cob.unt.edu/itds/faculty/becker/BCIS5520/Readings/AMCIS-0674-2014_ITCloudGovernance_FINAL.pdf

Becker, J. D., & Bailey, E. IT Controls and Governance in Cloud Computing. Retrieved May 18, 2014 from http://cob.unt.edu/itds/faculty/becker/BCIS5520/Assignments/Class_13_IT_Governance_in_the_Cloud.pdf

Boyles, R. (n.d.). Why Do You Need Governance in the Cloud? Project and Service Governance. [Web log comment]. Retrieved May 11, 2014 from https://www-304.ibm.com/connections/blogs/aim/entry/why_do_you_need_governance_in_the_cloud_project_and_service_governance2?lang=en_us (2014, June 12).

CCM v3 Info Sheet. (2013). Retrieved May 18, 2014 from https://downloads.cloudsecurityalliance.org/initiatives/ccm/CCM_v3_Info_Sheet.pdf

Chaudhuri, A., Chaudhuri, D., & Davis, R. E. (2009). Managing Sarbanes-Oxley Section 404 Compliance in ERP Systems Using Information Security Control Reports. ISACA Journal Online, 6.

Crowe Horwath, L. L. P. (2012). COSO Enterprise Risk Management for Cloud Computing. Retrieved May 14, 2014, from http://www.coso.org/documents/Cloud%20Computing%20Thought%20Paper.pdf

CSA. (2010). Domain 12: Guidance for Identity & Access Management V2.1. Retrieved May 18, 2014 from https://cloudsecurityalliance.org/guidance/csaguide-dom12-v2.10.pdf

CSA. (2012). Security Information and Event Management Implementation Guidance. Retrieved May 18, 2014 from https://downloads.cloudsecurityalliance.org/initiatives/secaas/SecaaS_Cat_7_SIEM_Implementation_Guidance.pdf

CSA. (2012). SecaaS Implementation Guidance, Category 2: Data Loss Prevention. Retrieved May 18, 2014 from https://downloads.cloudsecurityalliance.org/initiatives/secaas/SecaaS_Cat_2_DLP_Implementation_Guidance.pdf

Doe, N. P., Sitti, M., & Suganya, V. (2014). An Efficient Approach to prevent Data Breaches in Cloud. *International Journal of Scientific & Engineering Research*, 5(5), 630–634. http://www.ijser.org/researchpaper%5CAn-Efficient-Approach-to-prevent-Data-Breaches-in-Cloud.pdf Retrieved June 8, 2014

Durrani, U., Richardson, J., & Pita, Z. (2014). Lean Configuration Management Systems Implementation For The Governance: A Cloud Computing Case Study. *Journal of Information Technology Management*, 25(1), 43.

Haff, G. (2011). Cloud governance is about more than security. Retrieved May 21, 2014 from http://www.cnet.com/news/cloud-governance-is-about-more-than-security/

Jin, B. W., & Lee, K. W. (2014). A Design of Access Control Framework for User Identification Based on Personal Cloud. Advanced Science and Technology Letters, 49, 17-21. Retrieved May 16, 2014 from http://onlinepresent.org/proceedings/vol49_2014/4.pdf

Ma, X. (2014). On the feasibility of data loss insurance for personal cloud storage. In Proceedings of the 6th USENIX conference on Hot Topics in Storage and File Systems (pp. 2-2). USENIX Association. Retrieved May 16, 2014 from https://www.usenix.org/system/files/conference/hotstorage14/hotstorage14-paper-ma.pdf

Merrill, T., & Kang, T. (2014). Cloud Computing: Is Your Company Weighing both Benefits & Risks? Retrieved May 19, 2014 from http://www.acegroup.com/us-en/assets/privacy-network-security-cloud-computing-is-your-company-weighing-both-benefits-risks.pdf

NIST. (2009). Federal Cloud Computing Governance Framework. Retrieved May 16, 2014 from http://csrc.nist.gov/groups/SMA/ispab/documents/minutes/2009-12/cloud-computing-government-tic.pdf

Prakash, S. (2011). Risk Management in Cloud Computing. Retrieved May 14, 2014, from http://www.cio.com/article/679638/Risk_Management_in_Cloud_Computing

Savage, M. (2011). Cloud risk management: CSA on its Cloud Controls Matrix. Retrieved May 12, 2014, from http://searchcloudsecurity.techtarget.com/news/1280099645/Cloud-risk-management-CSA-on-its-Cloud-Controls-Matrix

Sommer, T., Nobile, T., & Rozanski, P. (2014). The Conundrum of Security in Modern Cloud Computing. *Communications of the IIMA*, 12(4), 2.

Wallace, S. (2012). Community Cloud Governance – An Australian Government perspective. Retrieved May 12, 2014 from http://www.finance.gov.au/sites/default/files/community_cloud_governance_better_practice_guide.pdf

Yin, L. (2013). The Analysis of Critical Technology on Cloud Storage Security. *International Conference on Computer Sciences and Applications*, Wuhan, China. doi:10.1109/CSA.2013.14

KEY TERMS AND DEFINITIONS

Cloud Controls Matrix: Cloud Controls Matrix (CCM) is a Framework from Cloud Security Alliance that provides fundamental security principles to guide cloud vendors and to assist prospective cloud customers in assessing the overall security risk of a cloud service.

Cloud Governance Matrix: It maps the six governance principles of ISO/IEC 38500:2008 to the 12 Control IDs of CSA CCM V3 GRM control domain to provide a unified matrix for Governance and |Risk Management of Cloud Services.

Cloud Services: A cloud service is any computing resource that is provided over the Internet. The three basic cloud service models are Infrastructure as a Service (IaaS), Platform as a Service (PaaS) and Software as a Service (SaaS).

Hype Cycle: The Hype Cycle branded by Gartner Inc. represents the evolving maturity, adoption and social application of emerging technologies.

SIEM: Security information and event management (SIEM) is a term for software products and services that combines security information management and security event management and is mostly tool based technology that provides real-time analysis of information system security alerts.

SLA: Service Level agreement (SLA) is a contract between a service provider (e.g. - a Cloud Service Provider) and the end user that defines the level of service expected by the end user from the service provider.

Virtualization: Virtualization is a software technology that uses a physical resource, such as a server, and divides it into virtual resources called virtual machines (VMs). Virtualization helps to consolidate physical resources, simplify deployment and administration, and reduce power and cooling requirements.

Chapter 6
Authentication and Error Resilience in Images Transmitted through Open Environment

Qurban A Memon
UAE University, UAE

ABSTRACT

Nowadays data compression and authentication are believed to be vital to image transmission through heterogeneous infrastructure or storage at a centralized place. Though compression and authentication have independently grown to be matured technologies, but currently integration of these technologies is understood to be a key factor in handling tampering in images transmitted through unsecure channels like cloud. In this chapter, an error-resistant approach is investigated to add to low cost image authentication scheme to increase visual quality as well as improve author and user satisfaction. The image authentication includes content based digital signature that is watermarked and later diffused in the whole image before JPEG2000 coding. To tackle manipulations in the image, edge information of the image is examined to offset manipulations in the image transmission through noisy or open and unsecure channels. The edge image is sent along with JPEG2000 coded image to determine corrupted coefficients. The simulation results are conducted on test images for different values of bit error rate to judge confidence in error concealment within the received images.

INTRODUCTION

Nowadays, it is widely understood that data compression is not only essential to speed up the transmission rate but also to provide other gains like low storage. In order to counter data manipulations and tampering during transmission, the image authentication has turned out to be equally important. But the drawback of compressed data transmission is that the compressed data are susceptible to channel impairments.

The two common standards to compress and code images before transmission and storage are JPEG and JPEG2000. The JPEG standard

DOI: 10.4018/978-1-4666-8387-7.ch006

is based on the discrete cosine transform (DCT) while JPEG2000 is based on the Wavelet transform. JPEG is the older standard and still widely used. The JPEG2000 is the newer standard. The original standard for digital images (IS 10918-1, popularly referred to as JPEG) was developed long time ago. Due to major advancement in computer technology and related research, it was decided by professional community that it is the timely need not only to find a standard that can make the digital image files as small as possible, but also find a new standard that can handle many more aspects. This was motivated by the fact that the JPEG2000 is better at compressing images (up to 20 per cent plus), and that it can allow an image to be retained without any distortion or loss. The communication and multimedia industry are shifting towards JPEG2000 standard for image transmission and storage. However, the JPEG2000 is still under improvements to reach the point where it could have its significant place in the world of imaging and telecommunications.

Data compression reduces the use of channel bandwidth; however compressed data are more vulnerable to channel noise. Therefore, the transmitted data must be resilient to channel noise and other impairments due to channel coding of binary bits (S. Khalid, 2009; L. Hanzo, et al, 2001; Y. Wang, Q. Zhu, 1998; Q. Memon, 2006). Several techniques have been proposed in the literature to address the problem of transmission errors by making transmitted data more robust to channel noise and to conceal corrupted data at the receiver. The authors (Mairal, C., Agueh, M., 2010) present a scalable scheme for robust JPEG 2000 images and video transmission to multiple wireless clients, using an adaptive bandwidth estimation tool. The objective seems to select suitable image layers and resolution for each wireless client, depending upon estimated bandwidth. The authors (Phadikar, A., Maity, S., 2010) propose JPEG200 compatible compressed domain algorithm using integer wavelet, and region-of-interest coding functionality. To find region-of-interest (ROI), threshold based

image segmentation and morphological operations are used together to find ROI. Using simulation results, the authors claim that the scheme provides acceptable performance improvement with various lost blocks in ROI. In another research (Martinez-Ruiz, M., et al, 2010), the authors present the results of an initiative to transmit imagery content through a Link-16 tactical network using JPEG2000 compatible approach that involves wavelets to compress images. Specifically, the JPEG2000 code-stream is mapped into Link-16 free-text messages. The most important part of the JPEG2000 compressed image is transmitted through a more error resistant (and anti-jamming) Link-16 packed structure and the remaining of the image in less robust data structures but at higher data rates. The results claimed are preliminary and dependent on Link-16 network resources.

Cloud computing lets businesses to develop applications without installation and allows consumers to access their data at any computer with Internet access. This technology has provided more efficient computing environment by centralizing storage, memory, and processing by offering resources encapsulation in the form of dynamic, scalable, and virtualized services over Internet. This has led to huge development of digital applications such as telemedicine. With regard to provision of easily accessible and reconfigurable resources such as virtual systems and applications with low cost, it has attracted many researchers. On the other side, it also exposes to risks. For example, having a contract with a cloud computing service provider exposes clients to various risks of dealing indirectly with different entities for data handling, and computation. Data authentication and user authorization as well as information ownership are the main security issues that need to be addressed when considering cloud-based imaging services. It has turned out that encryption of data objects that are stored or exchanged in this environment is the most suitable measure of data security. In this arena, there exist research works that protect the right of service providers, and/or customers. As an example, a customer wants to verify the seller of the image and that the purchased image is in fact bought from the legal one. In this case, digital signature comes as a useful tool. In section two, literature review is presented to highlight state of the art recent works related to authentication of JPEG2000 transmission. But before that, it seems necessary to summarize wavelet transform as it is one of the primary components in JPEG2000 standard.

Wavelet Transform and JPEG2000

The need for high compression as well as artifacts free imaging has made JPEG2000 a capable and sustaining algorithm that can replace the current JPEG which is applied and used till today (P. Shelkens, A. Skodras, T. Ebrahimi, 2009). In order to understand JPEG2000 steps, a block diagram of the JPEG2000 standard is shown in Figure 1. The brief discussion of each step is provided below.

Level Offset: It brings an offset to the range of intensity values of the pixels from (0, 255) to (-128, 127). This offset will result in more efficient compression during wavelet transform since pixel intensity will be symmetric around zero.

Color Transform: This step transforms a color image to gray level image and two complementary images. In fact, these three images are constructed by linear combination of three primary colors red, green, and blue. The three images are considered to be gray level images of intensity that range from -128 to 127 pixel intensity.

Wavelet Transform: This transforms the pixel intensity values to wavelet coefficients. This transformation confines the image energy that is distributed uniformly among the pixels into fewer wavelet coefficients. Typically, 93% of the image energy is concentrated into 13% of the wavelet coefficients.

Quantization: This step divides each coefficient by a specific number and then rounds the result to the nearest integer. This will eliminate typically most wavelet coefficients of higher frequency (higher *subband*) since they will be rounded to zeros. This action uses the fact that human visual system is less sensitive to patterns of high spatial frequency.

Block Code: This step uses Huffman coding to further compress the image data by converting the decimal values of the coefficients to binary bits. The coefficient values with highest probability of occurrence are coded by fewer bits while coefficients with lower probability of occurrence are coded by more bits.

The discrete version of Wavelet Transform in two dimensions is called two dimensional discrete wavelet transform (2-D DWT). The implementation requires digital filers and down-samplers. With two-dimensional scaling and wavelet functions, the one dimensional fast wavelet transform (1-D FWT) of the rows of $f(x, y)$ is followed by 1-D FWT of the resulting columns. Specifically, the rows of the input $f(x, y)$ are convolved with the filters h_φ and h_ψ then down sampled by a factor of 2. Both sub-images are then convolved again by columns with the filters h_φ and h_ψ and down sampled by a factor of 2 to get the four quart-size output sub-images. In the reconstruction process, the sub-images are then up-sampled by 2 and convolved with the two one-dimensional filters in two operations one for the sub-images' columns and the other is for the sub-images' rows. Adding the results is going to yield the reconstruction of

Figure 1. Block diagram of JPEG2000 Standard

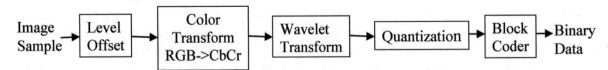

the original image. The mathematical operation to obtain wavelet coefficients from the image pixels is given by (S. Mallat, 1989):

$$W_\varphi(j_o,m,n) = \frac{1}{\sqrt{MN}} \sum_{x=0}^{M-1} \sum_{y=0}^{N-1} f(x,y)\, \varphi_{j_o,m,n}(x,y)$$

$$W_\psi^i(j,m,n) = \frac{1}{\sqrt{MN}} \sum_{x=0}^{M-1} \sum_{y=0}^{N-1} f(x,y)\, \psi_{j,m,n}^i(x,y) \qquad , i = \{H,V,D\}$$

(1)

where $\phi_{j_0,m,n}(x,y)$ is the approximation wavelet function, and $\psi_{j,m,n}^i(x,y)$ is the detail wavelet function. The superscript i could be H for the horizontal detail image, V for vertical, and D for diagonal. The subscripts m and n are the location indices of the wavelet coefficient in the detail image, j is the level of wavelet decomposition (*sub-band*), and M and N are the number of rows and columns in the image respectively.

In JPEG2000, typically images are decomposed into five to seven wavelet levels to accomplish higher compression ratio. The wavelet functions used in JPEG2000 typically belong to the first member of the Cohen-Daubechies-Feauveauthe family (A. Cohen, et al, 1992). For reconstruction of the image, the inverse wavelet transform is used at the receiver from the received wavelet coefficients. The inverse wavelet transform is described mathematically as follows (S. Mallat, 1989):

$$f(x,y) = \frac{1}{\sqrt{MN}} \sum_m \sum_n W_\varphi(j_o,m,n)\, \varphi_{j_o,m,n}(x,y)$$
$$+ \frac{1}{\sqrt{MN}} \sum_{i=H,V,D} \sum_{j=j_0} \sum_m \sum_n W_\psi^i(j,m,n)\, \psi_{j,m,n}^i(x,y)$$

(2)

where first term relates to approximation coefficients and the second term relates to horizontal, vertical and diagonal coefficients. In the next section, literature review of is presented that discusses approaches typically used for image authentication, encryption and/or error correction at the receiver.

LITERATURE REVIEW

A number of research works can be found that target JPEG2000 of images for the purpose of authentication, error-handling reception and/or encryption. These works can be combined into groups like digital signature, watermarking, scrambling and encryption, etc. The objective is to see how each has matured, and how much have they penetrated into real life applications. Some of these well-known approaches are presented below:

Digital Signature

A number of research works can be found that use signature driven authentication of data. For example, the authors (Sun, Q., 2005) investigate the invariant features, which are generated from fractionalized bit-planes during Embedded Block Coding with Optimized Truncation (EBCOT) procedure in JPEG2000. These are then coded and signed by the sender's private key to generate one crypto signature (hundreds of bits only) per image, regardless of the image size. The authors state that in addition to the original image, only two inputs are needed to generate the JPEG2000 image signature in a content-based way: the private key and the lowest authentic bit-rate (LABR). In this way, if a JPEG2000 image signature is generated with LABR value, a new image with compression (CBR) will be authentic as long as CBR is greater than LABR and the new image is derived from defined acceptable manipulations or transcoded from a compressed JPEG2000 image. In another research work (Koide, M., Keiichi, K, 2010), the approach is based on the aggregate signature developed by Boneh et al. (2003). In this approach, the user produces single signatures on each of the packets with his secret key. The user then stores them on the server with the JPEG 2000 code stream constructed from the signed packets. When the JPEG 2000 image data are sent to a client using JPEG2000 interactive protocol (JPIP), the server produces an aggregate signature from single signatures that match the client-requested data. Next, the server delivers the aggregate signature and image data to the client side. In every transmission, the client verifies the aggregate signature with the author's public key, and verifies whether the image data is valid or not. When all client-requested data has been delivered, the client produces a new aggregate signature from the aggregate signatures that are sent in each transmission. In this way, the extra verification of the new aggregate signature shows the client the validity of the requested image. If the signature is valid, all of the received data are proved to be the author's JPEG 2000 original image.

The authors (Wen, J., et al, 2009) discuss a scheme, where scalability and robustness is achieved by truncating bit planes of wavelet coefficients into two portions in JPEG2000 codec based on lowest compression bit rate (CBR). The invariant features, which are generated from upper portion, are signed by the sender's private key to generate a crypto-signature. By embedding the signature in upper portion, the scheme has the ability for content authentication as long as the final transmitted bit rate of the image is not less than the lowest CBR. Data that are used to recover the original image are hidden in lower portion in a reversible way, and therefore if entire bit stream is transmitted, the recovery data can be extracted and the degradation introduced by signature embedding can be recovered. Similarly, in the work by authors (Yan, S., Lin, Q., 2010), the two types of data (Data D in level LL, and Data A in other high-frequency sub-bands are first selected from EBCOT coding and then encrypted (using for

example a stream cipher). Finally, the encrypted data are combined with the other unselected plain data to form the output bit stream.

In another work (Zahia, B., et al, 2008), a secure encryption scheme is proposed, where only some sensitive precincts of the entire image are encrypted. Thus, the code stream is parsed to select only packets containing code-blocks which belong to the selected precincts. The remaining packets are sent without encryption. The formatter receives non encrypted and encrypted packets and works to reconstruct a compliant partially permuted/encrypted code stream. The block packets processing is used to only encrypt code blocks or to permute and encrypt them. The permutation of code blocks contributing in the selected precincts is introduced to improve the security level.

Watermarking

The authors in their work (Tsai, P., et al, 2012) select LL coefficients as authentication code (AC) since root nodes preserve the most important energy. To embed AC in image with imperceptibility, AC is further scaled and rearranged into bit planes. The embedding procedure inserts the AC bit plane into multi-resolution images according to progressive image transmission. Three AC bit planes will be embedded into HH, HL and LH sub-bands, respectively. To carry the authentication bit, each embedding coefficient will be modified. To achieve multi-resolution image authentication, the more important AC bit planes are embedded into the earlier encoded bits. Similarly, the less important AC bit plane is inserted into the later encoded bits. After that, the more important authentication bit is embedded into the more important and the earlier encoded bits. To verify multi resolution image integrity, the embedded AC will be extracted from the low resolution images.

The author in (Lim, S., et al, 2009) employ Dugad technique (R. Dughad, et al, 1998) as a robust watermarking technique. This approach attempted to resolve security issues in medical images by adding watermark technology to JPEG2000 compression. Dugad technique is a widely known watermarking algorithm using the wavelet transform. Thus, the watermarks are embedded in the areas with higher coefficients than threshold T_1 among all the sub-bands leaving out low pass sub-band. Instead of using Gaussian sequence, image is used instead in this approach. In another work (Inoue, H., et al, 2000), authors embed watermarks to the lowest frequency components in such a way that that the embedded watermark can be extracted without access to the original image. An important feature quoted for this approach is that the data of 256 bits and over can be embedded into one standard image. The authors claim that this method is robust against common signal processing such as JPEG compression, additive noise, smoothing, reduction of grayscale level and scaling, etc.

In another research work (Chao-yang, Z., 2011), the authors apply watermarking scheme on binary text images using singular value decomposition. This is done by aiming at the binary text image's characteristics of being a simple pixel, complex texture and bad immunity of information concealment. In this approach, a digital watermarking embedment location choosing method based upon compatible roughness class has been proposed. The proposed method divides binary text images into different equivalence classes, which are further divided into different subclasses according to each pixel's degree and texture changes between blocks. The authors (Kung, C., et al, 2009) propose a watermarking and image authentication scheme. The robust watermarking scheme is performed in the frequency domain (with DCT coefficients). It is used to prove the ownership, and the second step is the signature process, which can be used to prove the integrity of the image. The input of the signature process is

the edge properties extracted from the image. In work (Sun, Q., Zhang, Z., 2006), the main features of the proposed authentication system include integration of both content based (semi-fragile) authentication and code-stream based (complete) authentication into one unified system. This gives users more freedom to choose a proper type of authentication according to their specific requirements in the application.

Scrambling and Encryption

Recently, a great deal of concern has been raised regarding the security of an image transmitted or stored over public channels. The authors (Sathishkumar, G., et al, 2012) have proposed a new image encryption algorithm using random pixel permutation based on chaos logistic maps and prime modulo multiplicative linear congruential generators. The chaos is effectively spread into the encrypted image through permutation and transformation of pixels in the plain image. In another work (Joshi, S., et al, 2012), a neural network based encryption has been suggested as a part of encryption and decryption. The image to be encrypted is read pixel by pixel and the transformation is done on these pixels using permutation, substitution and impurity addition. Two levels of encryption are used to obtain high level of image encryption. At the receiving end, it uses neural network to obtain the original image. An encryption algorithm is also investigated by Yu, Z., et al, 2010, where authors use the wavelet decomposition to apply encryption on high-frequency for the sub-band image. After that, wavelet reconstruction is introduced in order to spread the encrypted part throughout the whole image. A second encryption process follows to complete the encryption process.

Scrambling has also been investigated by many authors to secure image transmission. In the work (Musheer A., et al, 2011), an image scrambling scheme based on two-dimensional coupled Logistic systems and Arnold Cat map is proposed, where non-overlapping blocks of pixels are permuted at multiple levels, in which the size of blocks depends on the level of scrambling. Additionally, the control parameters of scrambling are randomly generated to strengthen the security of algorithm. The authors (Khade, P., Narnaware, M., 2012) discuss practical approach for image scrambling and encryption using 3D Arnolds cat Map to R, G, and B components. Another variant of Arnold Transform for image encryption has been proposed by Tang, Z. and Zhang, X. (2011), where authors achieve encryption by dividing the image into random overlapping square blocks, generating random iterative numbers and random encryption order, and scrambling pixels of each block using Arnold transform. In another work (Li, S., et al 2008), the authors use fast image scrambling algorithm using a multidimensional orthogonal transform and a cipher image. The security is achieved by a large number of multi-dimensional orthogonal sequences.

Noise Removal

Once data is received at the receiver, errors are detected and if possible, they are also corrected. In this subsection, different types of errors detection and concealment schemes are briefly discussed. The objective here is to highlight respective capabilities and weaknesses.

Error detection methods can be divided into systematic methods or non-systematic methods (Lin, S., Costello, D., Jr., 1983). The systematic methods can be applied by simply letting the transmitter to add known number of check bits with the transmitted data. The receiver then analyzes the received data by applying the same scheme and then makes a comparison between its output and the received checking bits. In non-systematic method, the transmitter applies a transform on the original message and then encodes it. Error detection scheme could be selected based on the knowledge of the communication channel. Common channel models include either memory-less

models where errors occur randomly and with a certain probability, or dynamic models where errors occur primarily in bursts. Consequently, error-detecting codes can generally be categorized as random-error-detecting and burst-error-detecting. Some codes can also be suitable for a mixture of random errors and burst errors. Each of these carries a computational cost.

In multimedia communications, there are several contradictory system design requirements, such as the minimum use of channel bandwidth while the transmitted data are more resilient to channel noise. Thus, the transmitted data must be made resilient to noise and other impairments by for example use of channel coding the binary bits (S. Khalid, 2000). The channel coding requires transmission of more bits. Research in this category that have been proposed in the literature address the problem of transmission errors by making the transmitted data more robust to channel noise and to conceal corrupted data at the receiver. These techniques have been classified into three groups depending on the approach employed by the encoder and decoder. The first technique is Forward Error Concealment (FEC) at which the encoder plays the major role by making the source data more immune to transmission errors either through source and channel coding such as Reed-Solomon channel coding and multi description coding (MDC). The main purpose in the forward error concealment technique is to decrease the effect of errors that could occur in the transmitting channels to a minimum in order to cancel the need of error concealment in the decoder. Two types of distortion could be observed at the decoder when using the forward error concealment technique: the first one is the noise that is related to the quantization introduced by the waveform coder; and the second one is the transmission errors distortion. The second technique is error concealment by post processing such as the Spatial Predictive Concealment (SPC) technique. In error concealment by post processing technique, the decoder plays the major role in concealing errors without depending on additional data from the encoder. This could be achieved by using different methods such as estimation and interpolation, spatial and temporal smoothing. The third technique is interactive error concealment (IEC) in which the encoder and decoder work cooperatively through a feedback channel to minimize the impact of transmission errors. The idea here is based on the assumption that if a backward channel from the decoder to the encoder is available, better performance can be achieved if the encoder and decoder can cooperate in the process of error concealment, either at the source coding or at the transport level. According to the feedback information from the decoder, the coding parameters at the source coder can thus be adapted. The aforementioned algorithms require that the corrupted region be identified prior to respective error concealment.

Edge detection is the most useful approach in detecting valuable or important changes in the value of the intensity. This kind of detection is achieved using first order or second order derivative of intensity values. In case of images, the first order derivative is the gradient and in the case of 2-D, function *f(x, y)* is defined as the vector of gradients. When there is a change in the intensity, the direction of the gradient vector can be determined by calculating the angle of the maximum rate of change. The second order derivative for the images is the Laplacian. The Laplacian of a 2-D function $f(x, y)$ is:

$$\nabla^2 f(x,y) = \frac{\partial^2 f(x,y)}{\partial x^2} + \frac{\partial^2 f(x,y)}{\partial y^2} \qquad (3)$$

It is very rare to use the Laplacian for direct edge detection. The Laplacian is a second derivative, and its sensitivity to noise is very high and unacceptable. Thus, it can be said that the purpose of the edge detection is to detect location in the image where the intensity has changed in a rapid way by either one or two of the following criteria:

a. Detect a location in the image where the magnitude of the first order derivative of the intensity is greater than a certain threshold.

b. Detect a location in the image where the second order derivative of the intensity has a zero crossing.

A brief discussion about well-known edge detectors is presented below:

a. Sobel Edge Detector: The Sobel approximation takes the difference between rows and columns in 3 by 3 matrix and is considered as the first order derivative. The middle row and the middle column are multiplied by 2 to avoid the smoothing.

b. Prewitt Edge Detector: The Prewitt detector is very similar to the Sobel detector but much simpler with somehow more noisy results.

c. Robert Edge Detector: The Robert Edge Detector is one of the oldest and the simplest edge detectors in the digital image processing. This detector is very limited. It is not symmetric and cannot detect edges that are with angle $45°$ or its multiples. These disadvantages are reasons of using this detector less than others, however, it is still found to be useful in some applications where the simplicity and the speed are major factors (e.g, some hardware implementations).

d. Laplacian of Gaussian (LoG) Detector: The name LoG (Laplacian of Gaussian) detector came from the idea of convolving the image with $\nabla^2 G(x,y)$ where $G(x, y)$ is defined as:

$$G(x,y) = e^{-\frac{x^2+y^2}{2\sigma^2}}$$

which is the same as convolving the image with smoothing function first, then computing the Laplacian of the result. This is because the second derivative is a linear operation. This convolution blurs the image with a degree of blurring determined by the value of σ.

e.   Canny Edge Detector: Canny Detection method (J. Canny, 1986) is the most powerful method. Canny approach was based on three basic objectives:

   i.   The detector should detect all the edges with no false detection. And at the same time the detected edge should be very close to the correct edge.

   ii. Edge location should be very accurate. That means the difference between the point marked as an edge and the center of the true edge should be minimized as much as possible.

   iii. No multi responses for one edge. The detector should give one edge point for each detected edge and should never identify multiple edges in the case of existence of just a single edge.

It can be easily proven using experiments that the canny edge detector outperforms other edge detection methods.

As discussed before, edge detectors are very useful in detecting the important change in the value of the intensity. This means that whenever there is a detection of an edge, at that area there is going to be an important difference between the pixels. Moreover, one of the reasons that could make this variation high is the existence of high frequency (noise) at that area. The property of edges in the image to identify high level intensity changes (to reflect data manipulations, tampering, etc.) is used in the proposed approach presented in section three.

Summary of Issues

It can be easily summarized that in multimedia communication and data storage, though compression is very much desired but it remains suscep-

tible to noise and/or data tampering. The area of compressed data transmission through open channels is still active in research, and needs further investigation. Additionally, the authentication of transmitted data is equally important to justify all image transmission related activities. Recently, protection of image data transmitted or stored over open channels is also getting serious attention. In infrastructure as-a-service environment in cloud computing, encryption, access control and monitoring can reduce the threat of information access, whereas in platform-as-a-service environments, customers have fewer ways to do any monitoring or protection of content. Similarly, in software as a service, users are at the mercy of vendors. Though independent digital signature and watermarking techniques has grown to be mature technologies, but the current state of the art approaches do not completely solve the problem of unauthorized copying or provide protection from digital data privacy. Furthermore, there exist many image editing applications that enable easy manipulation of image data, and this problem becomes serious in applications like medical imaging and area surveillance. Related and well-known approaches presented in previous section are tabulated in Table 1, for the purpose of quick look on respective strengths and weaknesses.

In this work, an approach is investigated that collectively addresses security and privacy of (compressed) image data transmitted through open channels. Integrating noise removal with image authentication as one approach, compatible with JPEG2000 standard is the main contributions of this work.

The rest of the chapter is organized as follows. The next section presents the proposed approach based on JPEG2000. In the following section, experimental setup is detailed along with results. The results presented in this are discussed and compared in the next section. The standardization review is presented next followed by conclusions.

Table 1. Well-known Approaches in the Area of Image Authentication

	Research Title References [11-12, 14, 16-17, 21-25, 28- 29]	JPEG2000		Application
			Compatible Flexibility	
1	A Secure and Robust Digital Signature Scheme for JPEG2000 Image Authentication (2005)	Yes	Public key infrastructure based crypto signature	Lossy
2	Scalable Authentication for Various Representations of JPEG 2000 Images (2010)	Yes	Public key infrastructure based scalable authentication	Lossless
3	A Reversible Authentication Scheme for JPEG2000 Images (2009)	Yes	Public key infrastructure based crypto hash	Lossy
4	A new selective encryption technique of JPEG2000 code stream for medical images transmission (2008)	Yes	Some processing steps added to JPEG2000	Lossy
5	Watermarking for Multi-resolution Image Authentication (2012)	Yes	Some processing steps added to JPEG2000	Progressive image transmission
6	An Improved Binary Image Watermarking Algorithm Based on Singular Value Decomposition (2011)	No	Independent watermarking insertion and extraction algorithm	Lossy
7	A Robust Watermarking and Image Authentication Scheme used for Digital Content Application (2009)	No	Independent watermarking insertion and extraction algorithm	Lossy
8	A Standardized JPEG2000 Image Authentication Solution based on Digital Signature and Watermarking (2006)	Yes	Lossy/lossless/complete signature modules are embedded to JPEG2000	Lossy/Lossless
9	Image Encryption Using Random Pixel Permutation by Chaotic Mapping (2012)	No	Independent scrambling algorithm for authentication	Lossless
10	A Novel Neural Network Approach for Digital Image Data Encryption/Decryption (2012)	No	Neural network based independent decryption algorithm	Lossless
11	Practical Approach for Image Encryption /Scrambling using 3D Arnolds Cat Map (2012)	No	Independent image encryption algorithm	General
12	Secure Image Encryption without Size Limitation using Arnold Transform and Random Strategies (2011)	No	Independent image encryption algorithm	General

PROPOSED APPROACH

In this section, an approach is presented that achieves two major objectives in image transmission: (i) embeds authentication in JPEG2000 image before transmission, (ii) uses edge image to help in identifying corrupted regions in the wavelet domain, at the receiver. Pictorially, the approach is drawn as shown in Figure 2. Each of the steps, as shown in Figure 2, is discussed in detail as follows:

Edge Extraction: At the transmitter, the N_L-scale wavelet transform is applied as a first step in JPEG2000 coding standard, and the edge image is extracted from these wavelet coefficients. Though, the size of the edge image is significantly lower than the JPEG2000 coded image, it can be further coded for the purpose of size reduction and encryption (to withstand channel distortion). The reduction in size can be achieved using lossless compression of the edge image. The lossy approach can't be used here as the lossless edge image is to be used for error concealment in the received image. For the purpose of edge detection, Canny edge detector (J. Canny, 1986) with convenient thresholds is applied to the wavelet transformed image. The resulting binary edge image undergoes scrambling and lossless compression before transformation through noisy channel, as discussed below.

Scrambling: In literature (Musheer, A., et al, 2011), it has been shown that block level scrambling provides better results than pixel based scrambling in noisy channels, and that it is

Figure 2. Block diagram of Proposed Algorithm

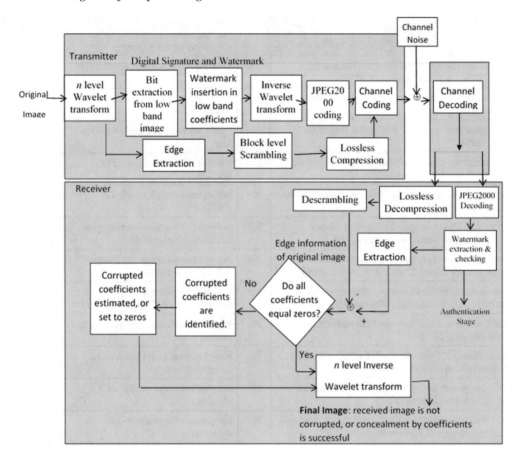

computationally efficient. For the same purpose, sub-bands of the edge image are decomposed into non-overlapping blocks of pixels, with block size dependent on the level of scrambling. In the next step, these blocks are permuted using 2-D Arnold transform, and these permutations again depend on the level of scrambling. The 2-D Arnold transform is given as (Musheer, A., et al, 2011):

$$\begin{bmatrix} x' \\ y' \end{bmatrix} = \begin{bmatrix} 1 & b \\ a & 1+ab \end{bmatrix} \begin{bmatrix} x \\ y \end{bmatrix} \mod (N) \qquad (4)$$

where N is the order of the image matrix, and a, b being positive control parameters are further randomly generated through 2-D coupled logistic map, given below:

$$x_1(n+1) = \mu_1 \, x_1(n) \, (1- x_1(n)) + \gamma_1 \, x^2_2(n)$$
$$x_2(n+1) = \mu_2 \, x_2(n) \, (1- x_2(n)) + \gamma_2 \, (x^2_1(n)$$
$$+x_1(n)x_2(n))$$

$$(5)$$

This logic map has three coupling terms to show its complexity. It is easily shown (Musheer, A., et al, 2011), that the map is chaotic if $2.75 <$ $\mu_1 \le 3.4$, $2.7 < \mu_2 \le 3.45$, $0.15 < \gamma_1 \le 0.21$, $0.13 <$ $\gamma_2 \le 0.15$. Thus, the chaotic sequence in equation (5) is generated for $0 < x_1, x_2 < 1$, and then a, and b are generated through x_1 and x_2. Once a, and b are generated, then equation (4) is applied on blocks of each sub-band of the edge image, up to k-level scrambling, to get the overall scrambled image.

Since the steps of this scrambling are deterministic, it seems easy to apply it in reverse order to descramble image at the receiver. It should be noted that since higher subbands of the edge image contain relatively little visual information about the edge, hence for effective results, scrambling can only be applied to lower band subbands and leaving higher subbands untouched.

Lossless Compression: There exist many compression algorithms in literature, which deal with two-dimensional binary data. Since the objective of this step is to reduce the size of overhead that results due to transmission of the encrypted edge image, any lossless compression scheme that reduces the size of this overhead can be used. Since higher subbands of the edge image contain a lot of zeros, the lossless compression of these bands would yield a bigger compression gain. In this approach, run length encoding is adopted for simplicity and efficiency. The idea is pick up identical patterns present in the binary edge image and represent them as *nd*, where *n* is the number of consecutive occurrences, and *d* is the data string.

For practical purposes, since run length encoding is simple in terms of packet generation for transmission, the lossless compression step can be embedded in scrambling process. In the receiver, the reverse approach is to be adopted, where these *nd* representations are replaced by corresponding binary data before initiating descrambling.

Embedding Authentication: In order to present digital signature extraction and watermark insertion into image, it is seems reasonable to define parameters. For simplicity, we assume image and block of square size. Let original image $f(x, y)$ be of size $N \times N$, and its low band subband be represented as $LL_n(i, j)$, where n represents the decomposition scale of the image and i, j are indices of the image band in the range $0 \leq i \leq N/2^n$ and $0 \leq j \leq N/2^n$. In order to extract digital signature from the image, it is proposed to divide the lowest image subband into blocks S_k ($k=1, 2, 3, ..,$

M) to enable bit extraction across whole subband image. The total extracted number of bits is $M \times L$, where L is number of bits generated per block. Moreover, it seems satisfying for customers and image providers to have content dependent digital signature extracted from within the image rather than selecting external bits as digital signature, and sent separately across the channel. These extracted bits are later inserted as watermark in the same subband. The approach of digital signature extraction and its insertion as watermark may also help in detecting channel manipulation of bits at the receiver. This issue will be addressed again, once receiver process is discussed.

Digital Signature: The digital signature extraction is based on two main points: (a) any low band image coefficient cannot be made larger or smaller without causing significant perceptional changes to the image, thus all similarly looking blocks (whether watermarked, un-watermarked, or attacked) in the wavelet transformed low band image will have same signature bits (b) a variable threshold is used in generating bits from the low band image blocks in such a way that 50% of the projections lie on either side of the threshold to ensure maximum information content in extracted bits. The adaption of the threshold is done to counter changes in information content from block to block due to data manipulations, for example certain image processing operations such as histogram stretching, watermarking, noise adding, compression, filtering, etc. In order to extract bits from low band subband, a secret key K (to be chosen, say by image provider or author) is used to generate L random sequences with values uniformly distributed in the interval $\{0, 1\}$. These matrices are later smoothed out by a low pass filter, and made zero mean to represent subband variations only. Later, image block S_k, as a vector, is projected on each zero mean smoothed random pattern L_i, and then its absolute value is compared with a threshold to generate corresponding bit c_i, as follows:

$$c_i = 1, if \left| S_k - L_i \right| > 0$$
$$c_i = 0, if \left| S_k - L_i \right| < 0 \tag{6}$$

Based on this approach, it can be easily seen that (i) resulting projected values change with a change in K (ii) resulting projected values change if S_i is dissimilar than S_j where $i \neq j$. Thus, bits c_i are sensitive to key K and vary continuously with subband block S_k.

Watermarking: As described above, the signature bits that are extracted from LL_n are inserted back as watermark in the lowest subband. This is ensured by using a quantization process, and mean amplitude of the lowest subband. Furthermore, it is desired that inserted watermark be extracted without having access to the original image, and that process be robust against common image processing application such as JPEG compression. Mathematically, watermarking process can be described as:

$$LL'_n = W_F \left(LL_n, c, K \right) \tag{7}$$

where LL'_n, W_F, LL_n, c, K represent watermarked subband, watermark (forward) coding process, unwatermarked subband, signature bits and key respectively. Similarly, the inverse process can be described as:

$$c' = W_R \left(LL'_n, K \right) \tag{8}$$

where c' and W_R represent recovered bits and watermark (reverse) coding process respectively. Finally, c and c' go through similarity index check using a threshold T_2 to determine whether correct watermark has been recovered.

For embedding watermarking bits into the subband, the procedure starts as follows:

i. Select embedded intensity as a quantization step size B_t, and calculate the mean m_k of each block S_k. Set $b_k = int [m_k/B_t]$.

ii. Compute the difference $diff_k$ as:

$$diff_k = abs \left(b_k - trunc \left[\frac{m_k}{B_t} \right] \right)$$

iii. Modify b_k using c_k, b_k and $diff_k$ as:

If b_k is an odd number and $c_k = 0$, OR if b_k is an even number and $c_k = 1$, then

$$b'_k = \begin{cases} b_k + 1 & for \quad diff_k = 0 \\ b_k - 1 & for \quad diff_k = 1 \\ else \quad b'_k = b_k \end{cases}$$

iv. Update wavelet coefficients of block S_k of $LL_n (i, j)$ as:

$$LL_{nk} \left(i, j \right) = LL_{nk} \left(i, j \right) + \left(b'_k . B_t - m_k \right)$$

where $LL_{nk} (i, j)$ stands for wavelet coefficient (i, j) of block S_k in lowest subband.

v. Compute and save new mean m_t of $LL'_n (i, j)$, and construct watermarked image using inverse wavelet transform.

Once the image arrives at the receiver, the watermarked bits are extracted as follows:

i. The mean m_r of the received lowest subband $LL_n^- (i, j)$ is calculated, and difference is computed as:

$$\partial_m = m_r - m_t$$

ii. The received lowest subband $LL_n^- (i, j)$ is decomposed into blocks S_k^- and mean m_k^- is calculated.

iii.   Compute the quantization value as:

$$B_r = \text{int}\left[\left[m_{\tilde{k}} - \frac{\delta_m}{B_t}\right]\right]$$

iv.   Extract the embedded bit as:

If B_t is even, then $c_k = 0$, else $c_k = 1$

JPEG2000 and Channel Coding: Once the watermarked image is available, it is ready for JPEG2000 coding (with *n* number of decomposition levels) and transmission through noisy channel. Furthermore, scrambled and lossless compressed edge image is also ready for transmission through the same channel. As the size of the compressed edge image is significantly lower than the original image, it can be coded using robust channel coding schemes to void distortion due to noise. Thus it is assumed that it is correctly received at the receiver. So at the receiver, watermarked-noisy-compressed image and noise free lossless-compressed edge image are received. The channel noise assumed is the burst noise i.e., the two-state Markov channel model is used to represent bursty noise channel. This noise adds to the transmitted data before it reaches the receiver.

Receiver operations: The receiver steps follows exactly as shown in Figure 2. Once edge is extracted from wavelet coefficients image, it is termed as extracted edge image respectively. Next extracted edge image is subtracted from the received edge image of the original image. If the difference between the received edge image and the extracted edge image is zero or below a certain threshold level then the received image is correct or corruption is unobjectionable. In the case where the received edge image differs from the extracted edge image at different regions, these regions

are marked as corrupted regions. In JPEG2000, the corrupted regions will have different sizes since the wavelet coefficients at different levels represent different sizes of blocks in the reconstructed image. The block sizes can range from 2 by 2 pixels to 32 by 32 pixels, and generally this depends how many levels of wavelet transform are computed at the transmitter. The spatial pattern of the corrupted region may help to determine if the corrupted region is in the horizontal, vertical, or diagonal sub-band.

Concealing errors at higher sub-band: This step deals with existence of the corrupted regions or blocks in received wavelets coefficients. The location of the corrupted block in the received wavelet coefficients may be used to determine the location of the wavelet coefficient within the sub-band. Effectively, all of these sub-bands may be processed in parallel to determine corrupted wavelet coefficients. Once it is possible to locate the corrupted wavelet coefficients, then their values may be set to zero if the coefficients belong to higher sub-bands at higher level lower level or may be estimated by adjacent coefficients if the coefficients belong to higher sub-bands at lower level. Then the image is reconstructed. The loss of image information by setting the values of the wavelet coefficients to zero is unobjectionable especially for coefficients located at higher sub-bands.

Concealing errors at lower sub-band: If the corrupted coefficients are in the lower sub-band then it is proposed to estimate their values from the neighborhood of affected coefficients. For example, if the corrupted coefficients are the approximation coefficients, then it is proposed to estimate their values using the uncorrupted adjacent approximation coefficients.

Concealment in the spatial domain (Optional): After estimating the values of the corrupted coefficients in the wavelet domain, the image is constructed. There are two possibilities: the first is that the image is completely corrected by estimating the values of the coefficients in the wavelet domain; the second possibility is that some of the corrupted regions are still present, so if desired, the corrupted regions may be further concealed in the spatial domain. This optional step is not shown in Figure 2. To conceal the persistent corrupted regions, the edge information of the original image is again used to estimate corrupted pixels. The edge information is expected to classify regions based on intensities. Each corrupted pixel may be estimated by the median intensity of the neighboring uncorrupted pixels located in the same region. By doing so, the original edges and boundaries are preserved. Preserving the edge information of the corrupted image using median filter enhances the subjective quality of the recovered received image.

EXPERIMENTAL SETUP AND RESULTS

A set of five 1024×1024 8-bit monochrome images were selected based on various image details to test the approach presented in the previous section. The following Figure 3 shows these images: *woman* and *pirate* images (with low image detail), *boat* and *goldhill* (with medium level of detail) and *baboon* image (with large image detail). All of these images were transformed using an arbitrary five-scale (N_L=5) wavelet transform with implicit quantization μ_0 =8 and ε_0 = 8.5.

A canny edge detector with convenient thresholds was applied on wavelet coefficients sub-images in order to extract the edge image. The resulting binary image, termed as 'edge_image' undergoes scrambling, as follows. It should be noted here that, as discussed in previous section, only lowest subband undergoes scrambling. Once initial block size is selected, at each level the blocks are permuted using the equation 4. The arbitrary values (to be used in equation 5) for initial conditions and parameters for secret key selected were: x_0=0.0215, y_0=0.5734, μ_1=2.93, μ_2=3.17, γ_1=0.197, γ_2=0.139, and t=100. The values a and b are then generated using equation (4). The final scrambled image is reached once number of

Figure 3. Test images (a) woman (b) pirate (c) boat (d) goldhill and (e) baboon

levels starting from $y=1$ reaches $log_2(Y)-1$, where Y is the initial block size.. All variables were set to double with 15-digit precision, and decimal fractions of the variables are multiplied by 10^{14}. The scrambled subbands levels together with remaining binary edge image subbands were then losslessly compressed using run length coding.

The next step on the transmission side is to embed authentication in the image. As discussed in the previous section, only lowest subband is to be used for digital signature extraction and watermark insertion. For signature extraction, first the lowest subband image is divided into blocks of arbitrary size of 8x8 pixels, thus generating 16 blocks. Using an author name as secret key, $L=32$ random sequences were generated with values uniformly distributed in the interval {0, 1}, followed by smoothing, and zero mean steps. Each subband block is finally projected onto each random sequence (and using equation 6) to generate a total of $16x32 = 512$ signature bits. In order to insert these signature bits back into lowest subband as a watermark, the quantization step size was arbitrarily selected as $B_t = 10$. Using the watermarking algorithm stated in previous section, the wavelet coefficients of each block in the lowest subband are modified. The mean m_t of resulting coefficients in the lowest band is also saved. Finally, inverse wavelet transform is applied on the modified wavelet coefficients together with remaining subbands to generate watermarked image.

The watermarked image finally undergoes JPEG2000 coding using an arbitrary five-scale ($N_L=5$) wavelet transform, with implicit quantization $\mu_0. = 8$ and $\varepsilon_0 = 8.5$. The resulting JPEG2000 coded image together with mean value m_t and edge image were channel coded before transmission. The size of wavelet coefficients for the JPEG2000 approximation of resulting watermarked image together with mean value is 252KB, whereas edge image size (after lossless compression) is ~3KB only. Since edge image is required

to be with zero distortion at the receiver, this is coded with robust channel coding technique to withstand noise in the channel. This step adds up to 7KB extra to the edge image. The added noise to the channel is the burst noise, which was simulated by two-state Markov channel model. After generating the two-state Markov noise, this noise (with bit error rate equal to 0.004, 0.006, 0.009, and 0.0095 to represe different noise scenario) was added logically to the binary Huffman coded data. The method of addition was done simply by applying the exclusive OR logical operation and the result was an image with noise distortion. The image mixed with noise is transmitted using JPEG2000 protocols and is the one received at the receiver.

After data is channel decoded, two images are available. One undergoes lossless decompression, followed by descrambling exactly in reverse order of transmission. Since this image was channel coded using a robust channel code, hence there was no distortion in the received edge image. On the other end, the second image was JPEG2000 decoded, followed by watermark extraction. Using the algorithm stated in previous section, the watermark bits were extracted. The method used to validate authentication of received image included number of mismatched bits exceeding a predefined threshold T_2. It was found out that in all cases of noise (for all images), the bits were recovered with an average of 96.8% accuracy. It must be noted here that distortion in the received image included noise in the channel, imprecision added due to watermark, and JPEG2000 coding/compression. With various levels of compression, it was noted that as compression rate increased, watermark bit extraction success rate decreased.

However, higher scale decomposition used in wavelet transform improved the success rate as bits diffused from lowest scale to full image size. The quantization step size also affected the quality of the watermarked image i.e., the higher the quantization level, higher the degradation observed in all of the test images.

Once watermark authentication is completed, edge image from received wavelet coefficients is computed. This image is termed as 'extracted_ edge_image'. This new extracted_edge_image is then subtracted from the received 'edge_image' to determine the corrupted regions resulting due to distortion in transmission channel. As an example, the Figure 4(a) shows the received image reconstructed after passing through noisy transmission channel with $BER = 0.009$. The Figure 4(b) shows the displayed wavelet coefficients of the received image, the Figure 4(c) shows the edge extraction of displayed wavelet coefficients, and the Figure 4(d) shows the location of the corrupted regions resulting by subtracting the received coefficients of extracted_edge_image from the received coefficients of original_edge_image.

In order to minimize distortion in the reconstructed image, error concealment method was adopted to handle corrupted regions in wavelet coefficients domain. In this work, selective corrupted regions are processed for error concealment, though the approach can be extended to all subbands. As an implementation, all corrupted coefficients for all sub-bands on level 5 are estimated using a median filter (Qurban, M., Takis, K., 1995) on 3x3 neighborhood of the corrupted coefficient. The filter selection and its neighborhood size were arbitrary. The rest of corrupted coefficients on the higher sub-bands were simply set to zero. Once corrupted region coefficients are identified and estimated, the inverse wavelet transform is applied to reconstruct image. This approach was repeated on all five test images

Figure 4. (a) Top left: Original image received with BER=0.009 (b) Top right: The displayed wavelet coefficients (c) Bottom left: Edge extraction of received wavelet coefficients (d) Bottom right: Result of subtracting extracted_edge_image from the received edge_image

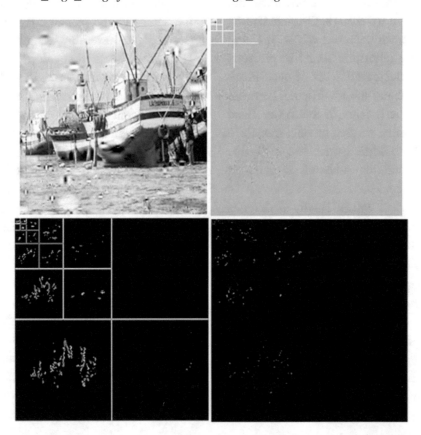

with different bit error rates, and the result for one image is shown in Figure 5. It seems clear that the proposed approach does conceal errors introduced in the noisy channel.

In order to judge quality of reconstructed images, root mean square error (*rms*) and peak signal-to-noise ratio (PSNR) were calculated for test images against different BER values. Mathematically, this is described as:

$$PSNR = 10\log_{10}\left(\frac{255^2}{mse}\right) \qquad (9)$$

where *mse* stands for mean square of the difference between the original and reconstructed image. From results shown in Table 2, it is clear that almost all distortion due to channel noise have been removed due to error concealment and quality images restored. It can easily be inferred

Figure 5. The received and concealed images for Pirate image: Top (left) and (right) for BER=0.004; Middle: (left) and (right) for BER=0.006; Bottom: (left) and (right) for BER=0.009

Table 2. The rms and PSNR values for concealment method used on test images

Image Type	Received Image		Concealed Image	
Woman image	RMS	PSNR (dB)	RMS	PSNR (dB)
BER=0.004	5.22	33.71	1.12	46.79
BER=0.006	6.33	32.14	0.91	48.30
BER=0.009	9.74	28.43	2.81	38.88
BER=0.0095	10.1	26.96	3.17	36.92
Pirate image				
BER=0.004	11.62	26.88	1.61	43.59
BER=0.006	13.51	25.61	2.10	36.31
BER=0.009	12.82	25.99	2.91	41.32
BER=0.0095	13.84	24.76	3.19	39.89
Boat image				
BER=0.004	8.51	29.61	2.01	41.81
BER=0.006	11.68	26.42	2.51	37.12
BER=0.009	17.30	23.43	2.85	39.69
BER=0.0095	18.42	23.10	3.12	38.77
Goldhill image				
BER=0.004	9.23	28.78	3.91	36.16
BER=0.006	9.35	28.72	1.83	42.39
BER=0.009	10.65	27.59	2.31	40.47
BER=0.0095	10.97	26.89	2.95	39.29
Baboon image				
BER=0.004	7.45	30.69	2.35	40.52
BER=0.006	8.53	29.52	3.15	38.59
BER=0.009	10.52	27.63	3.42	37.25
BER=0.0095	12.46	26.81	3.49	36.58

from Table 2 that as BER increases, *rms* values get increased. However, after concealment, these values are largely reduced. Likewise, PSNR values improved after concealment, with improvement ranging from 9-15 decibels.

COMPARATIVE DISCUSSION AND FUTURE DIRECTIONS

The objective of this research was to supplement transmission of JPEG2000 image data with authentication and error handling capability. Image authentication method proposed in this approach was to counter unauthorized manipulations in the image. The lowest subband was used to extract signature bits and place watermark inside. The purpose behind content driven signature extraction was simplicity as opposed to different signature taken from the author or the publisher. It was found out that as number of decomposition levels increases, so is the diffusion rate of this watermark within the whole image after reconstruction. The authentication level at the receiver can be adjusted based on how much percentage of error is allowed.

The edge image was used to tackle channel distortion. In order to ensure minimum overhead on transmission, and noise free reception at the receiver, it was scrambled, lossless compressed and then followed by channel coding. Though it causes overhead, but it provides tradeoff with respect to visual quality of the image. Besides, this overhead is minimal as total overhead amounts to few kilo bytes. This step is optional and can be removed if channel has least noise distortion.

The advantages gained through proposed approach can be compared, for example, with different approaches described in literature. In the work (Sun, Q, 2005), the authors discuss digital signature extraction scheme for semi-fragile content through combination of hashing, public/private key for digital signature, and transmission of watermarked image along with cryptographic signature. The approach proposed in our paper is generic and more flexible than the one described by Sun, Q, 2005, because it is independent of public/private infrastructure, and carries noise concealment ability. Similarly, the approach (Zahia, B., et al, 2008) targets only medical images and encrypts some of the JPEG2000 coded image data using permutations, and remaining image data is not processed.

This approach only fits some local network applications that secure only partial content. Likewise, the approach described by Wen, J., et al, 2009, embeds watermark in the JPEG coded image using private key and lowest compression bit rate. There is no immunity against noise or how the encrypted image is degraded by noise. Additionally, there is no way to know regions where degradation or tampering may have occurred. The authors (Tsai, P., et al, 2012) propose watermarking scheme for progressive image transmission along with compensation mechanism to reduce embedding distortion. The approach considers low band coefficients, and uses it as an authentication code to be embedded into other bands. It fails to consider effects of noise during transmission and how this noise affects compensation algorithms

proposed by Tsai, P., et al, 2012. The approach is not generic and fits only an specific application.

Most of the medical organizations do not have much IT resources for managing the increasing volume of medical imaging data. Cost and security have turned out to be main factors for managing data storage and access. An important driver of cloud storage is the observation that as CTs and MRI studies increase in size, longer times are required to transfer them to imaging workstations. With recent advancements (Q. Memon, 2013) medical record sharing is enabling medical records to be shared across different healthcare establishments, starting with public hospitals and progressively to healthcare establishments in the private sector. Patient data can now be easily stored in virtual archives that are accessible by different healthcare providers, thus facilitating data sharing and significantly reducing storage requirements. The data sharing is expected to reduce the cost for patients as doctors can now view the results of any recent X-rays, CT scans etc. across autonomously managed heterogeneous healthcare information systems. Among the potential driving forces for the increased use of cloud computing in medical imaging are raw data management and image processing and sharing demands, all of which require high-capacity data storage and computing. To meet these demands, a secure cloud-based medical imaging exchange can improvise access to current and historical imaging studies. For improved degree of satisfaction, cloud storage clients need to implement their own measures for ensuring high integrity of the imaging data using any of the image protection scheme such as proposed in this chapter.

The medical image exchange is also useful in research applications involving multiple investigators at different clinical institutions, and in large-scale data processing applications such as those in clinical medicine. One of the challenges facing medical image processing today is the development of benchmarks that allow image processing algorithms to be run and compared under common measures. Though cloud can contribute to such benchmarks by facilitating their creation as well as their widespread availability, but such databases combine different datasets necessary for the assessment of image processing algorithms (e.g., in segmentation, de-noising, registration, fusion). As discussed before, cloud is prone to data integrity hazards, so secure data transfer in cloud computing is still a challenge in such an environment. The available protection on imaging data represents a trade-off between the cloud provider's better defenses against attack and the greater consequences of a successful attack. The solution proposed in this chapter can alleviate concerns of both clients and owners of the medical image data. While all clouds are based upon the Internet, a private cloud can encrypt data during transmission and be available only to authorized users.

STANDARDIZATION REVIEW

In this section, an effort is made to highlight standardization efforts made by different international bodies in coming up with recommendations on image storage and transmission to fulfill user expectations while image is being accessed on open and unsecure platform, such as cloud.

As discussed in section one, the application areas for JPEG include: Internet, Digital Photography, Medical Imaging, Wireless imaging, Document imaging, Remote sensing and GIS, Digital Cinema, Image archives and databases, Surveillance, Printing and scanning, Facsimile, etc. The newer version JPEG 2000 (available at http://www.jpeg.org/jpeg2000/index.htnl) has 12 parts in its standard. Part 1 addresses core coding system with part2 on extensions. Part 3, 4, 5, and 6 address motion JPEG2000, conformance, reference software, and compound image file format respectively. Part 7 was abandoned, while part 8

addresses JPEg2000 secured (JPSEC). It addresses security aspects for JPEG2000 standard. While part 9 and 10 discuss JPIP (interactive protocols and API), and volumetric imaging (JP3D) respectively, the part 11 and 12 discuss wireless applications (JPWL) and base media file format (common with MPEG-4).

For security aspects to ensure safe transactions, secured bit streams and protection of contents, the JPEG 2000 Secured (JPSEC) or Part 8 of the standard describes tools and solutions in terms of specifications. The tool examples include encryption (including partial or encryption with different strengths), data integrity (including semi-robust mechanisms), authentication of source, conditional access to portion of an image, and ownership protection, etc. Different methods defined in the standard include Digital signature, Watermarking, Encryption, Scrambling, Key generation and management, Identification and registration, and others. These methods are to be enabled in JPSEC by means of a central authority, also known as registration authority (JPSEC RA). The authority carries a role on the Internet for those who want to register their JPSEC related items. It acts as a point of contact for registration related activities such as reviewing, maintaining and distributing important information related to JPSEC items.

Part 8 became an International Standard (ISO/IEC 15444-8) in July 2006. This was confirmed by a Press Release of 47th WG1 meeting, San Francisco, USA, held in January 19-23, 2009, hosted by US national body with delegates from 10 countries. It is currently available for download from ITU-T as Recommendation T.807.

2KAN is a research and development project, partly funded by Information Society Technologies theme of the European Commission's Fifth Framework Program. Its objective is to address the new work items being developed within JPEG 2000 Standard, with aim of maintaining a European presence in this process.

One of the active body based in part on the US National Institute of Standards and Technology's Special Publication 800-145, have released a document called "The NIST Definition of Cloud Computing." The body is known as Organization for the Advancement of Structured Information Standards (OASIS) and has two technical committees working on cloud-centric issues. The first committee "The IDCloud Technical Committee" is developing recommendations pertinent to security issues in identity in order to make sure people using cloud resources are who they say they are. The group is also developing guidelines for vulnerability mitigation, which is considered important as cloud computing platform is open, and distributed architecture. The second committee "The Symptoms Automation Framework Technical Committee" is putting up efforts to prepare procedures in making sure cloud-computing providers understand consumer requirements such as quality of service (QoS) and capacity.

CONCLUSION

An image authentication approach was proposed in this research that embedded content driven digital signature as a watermark before JPEG2000 coding. A separate edge image data was integrated with image authentication as a supplement to offset effects of noisy channel on image transmission. Effectively, this added edge image data turned out to be very small, of about 0.78% fraction of the actual image data. The approach provides system robustness, security, and better visual quality, and suitable for use in error prone platform like cloud. Three advantages were clearly noted: (a) the selected data for scrambling and that for signature extraction and watermarking was small resulting in reduced computational complexity (b) data rate remains unchanged as effectively individual coefficients in selected subbands were replaced by equivalently by same number of new modified values (c) error or tampering concealed by this approach is significant compared to overhead cost of about 0.78% on transmission.

ACKNOWLEDGMENT

The author would like to express sincere thanks to the Research Affairs unit of College of Engineering at United Arab Emirates University for financial support of this project under grant code number UAEU-EE-21N151.

REFERENCES

Cohen, A., Daubechies, I., & Feauveau, J. C. (1992). Biorthogonal bases of compactly supported wavelets. *Communications on Pure and Applied Mathematics*, *45*(5), 485–560. doi:10.1002/cpa.3160450502

Chao-yang, Z. (2011). An Improved Binary Image Watermarking Algorithm Based on Singular Value Decomposition. *Proceedings of International Symposium on Intelligence Information Processing and Trusted Computing*. Hubei, China. doi:10.1109/IPTC.2011.70

Boneh, D., Gentry, C., Lynn, B., & Shacham, H. (2003). Aggregate and Verifiably Encrypted Signatures from Bilinear Maps. In E. Biham (Ed.), *Advances in Cryptology*. Lecture Notes in Computer Science Heidelberg: Springer. doi:10.1007/3-540-39200-9_26

Inoue, H., Miyazaki, A., & Katsura, T. (2000). A Digital watermark for Images Using the Wavelet Transform. *Integrated Computer-Aided Engineering*, *7*(2), 105–115.

Canny, J. (1986). A Computational Approach to Edge Detection. *IEEE Transactions on Pattern Analysis*, 8(6), 679–698.

Joshi, S., Udupi, V., & Joshi, D. (2012). A Novel Neural Network Approach for Digital Image Data Encryption/Decryption. Proceedings of *IEEE International Conference on Power, Signals, Controls and Computation*, Kerala, India. doi:10.1109/EPSCICON.2012.6175229

Khade, P., & Narnaware, M. (2012). Practical Approach for Image Encryption/Scrambling using 3D Arnolds Cat Map. *Advances in Communication, Network, and Computing*, 108, 398–404.

Koide, M., & Keiichi Iwamura, K. (2010). Scalable Authentication for Various Representations of JPEG 2000 Images. In *proceedings of 17th International Conference on Image Processing*, Hong Kong. doi:10.1109/ICIP.2010.5650709

Kung, C., Chao, S., Yan, Y., & Kung, C. (2009). A Robust Watermarking and Image Authentication Scheme used for Digital Content Application. *Journal of Multimedia*, 4(3), 112–119. doi:10.4304/jmm.4.3.112-119

Hanzo, L., Cherriman, P., & Streit, J. (2001). *Wireless Video Communications*. NY: IEEE. doi:10.1109/9780470547083

Lim, S., Moon, H., Chae, S., Yongwha Chung, Y., & Pan, S. (2009). JPEG 2000 and Digital Watermarking Technique Using in Medical Image. *Proceedings of* 3rd *International Conference on Secure Software Integration and Reliability Improvement*, Shanghai, China. doi:10.1109/SSIRI.2009.45

Li, S., Wang, J., & Gao, X. (2008). The Fast Realization of Image Scrambling Algorithm using Multi-Dimensional Orthogonal Transform. Proceedings of Congress on Image and Signal Processing, Sanya, China. doi:10.1109/CISP.2008.433

Lin, S., & Costello, D. Jr. (1983). *Error Control Coding: Fundamentals and Applications*. NJ: Prentice Hall.

Mairal, C., & Agueh, M. (2010). Scalable and robust JPEG 2000 images and video transmission system for multiple wireless receivers. *Proceedings of Latin-American Conference on Communications*. Paris, France. doi:10.1109/LATINCOM.2010.5641128

Martinez-Ruiz, M., Artes-Rodriguez, A., Diaz-Rico, J. A., & Fuentes, J. B. (2010). New initiatives for imagery transmission over a tactical data link. A case study: JPEG2000 compressed images transmitted in a Link-16 network method and results. Proceedings of Military Communications Conference, San Jose, CA, USA. doi:10.1109/MILCOM.2010.5680102

Musheer Ahmad, A., Haque, E., & Farooq, O. (2011). A Noise Resilient Scrambling Scheme for Noisy Transmission Channel. *Proceedings of International Conference on Multimedia, Signal Processing and Communication Technologies*, Aligarh, India.

Schelkens, P., Skodras, A., & Ebrahimi, T. (2009). *The JPEG 2000 Suite*. NJ: Wiley Series. doi:10.1002/9780470744635

Phadikar, A., & Maity, S. P. (2010). Roi based error concealment of compressed object based image using QIM data hiding and wavelet transform. *IEEE Transactions on Consumer Electronics*, 56(2), 971–979. doi:10.1109/TCE.2010.5506028

Memon, Q. (2006). A New Approach to Video Security over Networks. *International Journal of Computer Applications in Technology*, 25(1), 72–83. doi:10.1504/IJCAT.2006.008670

Qurban, M., & Takis, K. (1995). Block median filters. Proceedings of *International Symposium on OE/Aerospace Sensing and Dual Use Photonics*, Orlando, FL, USA.

Memon, Q. (2013). Smarter Healthcare Collaborative Network. In K. Pathan Al-Sakib, M. Monowar Muhammad, Md. Fadlullah Zubair (Eds.), Building Next-Generation Converged Networks: Theory and Practice (451–474). Florida: CRC Press.

Dugad, R., Ratakonda, K., & Ahuja, N. (1998). A New Wavelet-based Scheme for Watermarking Images. *Proceedings of International Conference on Image Processing*, Chicago, IL, USA. doi:10.1109/ICIP.1998.723406

Khalid, S. (2000). *Introduction to Data Compression*. New York: Morgan Kaufmann Publishers.

Mallat, S. (1989). A Theory for Multiresolution Signal Decomposition: The Wavelet Representation. *IEEE Transactions on Pattern Analysis and Machine Intelligence*, *11*(7), 674–693. doi:10.1109/34.192463

Sathishkumar, G., Ramachandran, S., & Bagan, K. (2012). Image Encryption Using Random Pixel Permutation by Chaotic Mapping. *Proceedings of IEEE Symposium on Computers and Informatics*. Penang, Malaysia.

Sun, Q., & Zhang, Z. (2006). A Standardized JPEG2000 Image Authentication Solution based on Digital Signature and Watermarking". Proceedings of China Communications, Beijing, China.

Tang, Z., & Zhang, X. (2011). Secure Image Encryption without Size Limitation using Arnold Transform and Random Strategies. *Journal of Multimedia*, *6*(2), 202–206. doi:10.4304/jmm.6.2.202-206

Tsai, P., Hu, Y., Yeh, H., & Shih, W. (2012). Watermarking for Multi-resolution Image Authentication. *International Journal of Security and Its Applications*, *6*(2), 161–166.

Wen, J., Wang, J., Feng, F., & Zhang, B. (2009). A Reversible Authentication Scheme for JPEG2000 Images. *Proceedings of Ninth International Conference on Electronic Measurement & Instruments*. Beijing, China. doi:10.1109/ICEMI.2009.5274015

JPEG2000. (2014, April 14) Retrieved from www.jpeg.org/jpeg2000/index.html

Wang, Y., & Zhu, Q. (1998). Error control and concealment for video communication: A Review. *Proceedings of the IEEE*, *86*(5), 974–996. doi:10.1109/5.664283

Yan, S., & Lin, Q. (2010). Partial Encryption of JPEG2000 Images Based on EBCOT. *Proceedings of International Conference on Intelligent Control and Information Processing*, China. doi:10.1109/ICICIP.2010.5565304

Yu, Z., Zhe, Z., Haibing, Y., Wenjie, P., & Yunpeng, Z. (2010). A Chaos-Based Image Encryption Algorithm Using Wavelet Transform. *Proceedings of International Conference on Advanced Computer Control*, China.

Zahia, Z., Bessalah, H., Tarabet, A., & Kholladi, M. (2008). A new selective encryption technique of JPEG2000 codestream for medical images transmission. *Proceedings of International Conference on Telecommunications and Informatics*. US.

KEY TERMS AND DEFINITIONS

BER: Short for *bit error rate*. In a digital transmission, BER is the percentage of bits with errors divided by the total number of bits that have been transmitted, received or processed over a given time period.

Data Compression: Storing data in a format that requires less space than usual.

Digital Signature: A digital code that can be attached to an electronically transmitted message that uniquely identifies the sender.

Encryption: The translation of data into a secret code. Encryption is the most effective way to achieve data security.

JPEG: JPEG stands for the *Joint Photographic Experts Group standard* - a standard for storing and compressing digital images.

JPEG2000: JPEG2000 is a new standard for image compression method and file format. JPEG2000 is an image coding system that uses state-of-the-art compression techniques based on wavelet technology.

Watermarking: It is a pattern of bits inserted into a digital image, audio or video file that identifies the file's copyright information (author, rights, etc.).

Chapter 7
Trust Calculation Using Fuzzy Logic in Cloud Computing

Rajanpreet Kaur Chahal
Panjab University, India

Sarbjeet Singh
Panjab University, India

ABSTRACT

Cloud Computing is the latest rage in the world of technology. It has vast potential that can be tapped to the advantage of mankind. But there are some challenges which need to be resolved in order to fully utilise its potential. One of these challenges is trust evaluation. Since services are provided by service providers to clients, there has to be some notion of trust between them. This chapter first provides the basic introduction to cloud computing and fuzzy logic. On the basis of extensive literature survey, this chapter discusses trust and its need, in addition to use of fuzzy logic for the purpose of trust calculation in distributed environments and cloud computing till now. Trust calculation using fuzzy logic has been explained through the use of various models. At the end, the difficulties and applications of using fuzzy logic for trust evaluation are discussed along with research directions for future.

INTRODUCTION

Cloud Computing is emerging as a promising way to change the perception of technology as we have today. Zhang et al. (2010) have defined cloud computing as "a model for enabling convenient, on-demand network access to a shared pool of configurable computing resources that can be rapidly provisioned and released with minimal management effort or service provider interaction." It is based on the premise of "why buy when you can rent". In simple words, it provides the consumers or users with an opportunity to use the resources provided by another party on pay-per-use basis. That is, users don't need to buy or install the hardware or software at their end. Instead they can use the services installed by another party and pay them as per their use. This results in reduction in the costs incurred by the users. While this arrangement has many benefits, it also has some drawbacks. One major question that arises is – which Cloud Service

DOI: 10.4018/978-1-4666-8387-7.ch007

Provider (CSP) should a user choose? Or framed in another way – which Cloud Service Provider should a user trust?

The basic objectives of this chapter are:

- To describe the issue of trust evaluation in cloud computing.
- To understand the basics and importance of fuzzy logic.
- To describe various approaches for calculation of trust using fuzzy logic.
- To highlight latest happenings particularly in cloud computing.
- To identify the opportunities and challenges.
- To identify new research directions.

BACKGROUND

Trust in Cloud Computing

Trust can be defined as the extent to which one partner is willing to participate in a given action with another partner considering the risks and incentives involved (Ruohomaa and Kutvonen, 2005). Reputation is defined as a perception a partner creates through past actions about his intentions and norms (Mui et al., 2002). In the context of cloud computing, "trust" may mean the degree of faith a consumer or user has on the goodwill of a Cloud Service Provider. "Trust" may also mean the level of confidence a Cloud Service Provider has on its users. Taking this notion to a different level, "trust" can also mean the degree of belief a user has in the goodwill of other users of the same CSP. Another related concept to that of trust is reputation. Reputation of a CSP may be defined as the collective trust all the users have on that CSP based on their past interactions with it. Reputation can also be used as a measure of trust. A user may trust a CSP based on its reputation.

Need of Trust

When users want to use a cloud service, they first search for the CSPs meeting their requirements. The next step is to assess the trustworthiness of the CSP which may be based on individual experience or reputation or both. Users while using any service need to be fully assured about the security of their data. The users' apprehensions about the security of their data in cloud environment arise out of several factors. Some of them are:

- Transfer of control: Data, infrastructure, resources and applications are situated with the cloud provider and he is the one entrusted with the responsibility of managing users, access control, security policies and their enforcement. The user, therefore, relies on the provider for ensuring data security, confidentiality, integrity and availability.
- Involvement of a third party: Dealing with a third party always involves risks. The core issue regarding trust is the levels of trust. Many cloud computing providers trust their customers and implement security on the assumption that those inside the cloud are good and those outside are evil but what if those inside are evil?
- Multi-tenancy: A Cloud Service Provider typically has a number of clients/tenants. These tenants share a pool of resources and may have conflicting goals. The issue here is how to deal with the conflict of interests. Do the tenants get along each other nicely? If not, then how can we isolate them?

Categories of Trust Functions

Following are the different categories of trust functions (Chakrabarti, 2007):

- Subjective vs Objective: If an entity's performance or accuracy or quality of information can be objectively measured without any dispute or conflict, then the trustworthiness of such an entity is objective. If the same depends on individual situations and other subjective factors, then such an entity's trustworthiness is subjective.

- Transaction-based vs Opinion-based: If the truthfulness or trustworthiness of an entity is measured based on individual transactions, then such a trust is called transaction-based. If an entity's trustworthiness is measured based on the opinions of other entities in the environment, then such a trust is called opinion-based.

- Complete vs Localized information: Trust evaluation functions that work by assuming that each and every entity in the system can gain access to all the transaction or opinion information are called global trust functions. On the other hand, trust functions that work on the assumption that every entity has access to incomplete and varied transaction or opinion information are called localized trust functions.

- Rank-based vs Threshold-based: Trust evaluation functions which pre-define a threshold value of trustworthiness to arrive at trust decisions are called threshold-based. Whereas the trust functions which compare the trustworthiness value of an entity with other entities and return a relative ranking of that entity are called opinion-based.

Introduction to Fuzzy Logic

There are two major classifications of logic. One is Boolean logic and the other is fuzzy logic. Boolean logic deals with only two values – true and false or 0 and 1. In Boolean logic, the membership or belongingness of an entity in a set is precisely defined, i.e. it either belongs to the set or it does not (Bai and Wang, 2006). For example, a child of age 5 years clearly belongs to the set 'young' and a person of age 70 years definitely belongs to the set 'old'. But what about a person who is 30 years old? He may be considered 'young' for one context and 'old' for another. In simple words, his membership in the set 'young' is neither 0 nor 1. In such situations, fuzzy logic proves helpful.

Fuzzy logic was conceived by Lotfi Zadeh. It has the potential to deal with subjectivity, uncertainty and imprecision. The basic concepts of fuzzy logic are explained in the following sections.

Membership Functions

In fuzzy logic, an object or entity can belong to a set to varying degrees. A membership function describes the degree to which an object is a member of the set (Mendel, March 1995). Lets assume we have an object x and a set A. Membership function of x with respect to set A will then be given by $\mu_A(x)$, and its value ranges from 0 to 1. This can be represented mathematically as follows:

$$A = \{(x, \mu_A(x)) \mid x \in X, \mu_A(x) : X \rightarrow [0,1]\}$$

As shown above, a fuzzy set is represented in the form of an ordered tuple $(x, \mu_A(x))$. X here is the universe of discourse and A is the fuzzy set to which x belongs.

Let us consider the previous example of sets 'young' and 'old'. Suppose we represent them as fuzzy sets Y and O respectively. Now, a person who is 30 years old may have a membership of 0.9 in set Y and that of 0.1 in set O, instead of having a membership of 1 or 0 in any one of these sets.

Fuzzy Set Operators

There are three fuzzy set operators (Zadeh, June 1965):

1) Union
2) Intersection
3) Complement

Union: The union of two fuzzy sets $f_A(x)$ (Figure 1) and $f_B(x)$ (Figure 2) is defined as- Union $(f_A(x)$ and $f_B(x))$ = max $(f_A(x), f_B(x))$. This is depicted in Figure 3.

Intersection: The intersection of two fuzzy sets $f_A(x)$ and $f_B(x)$ shown in Figure 1 and 2 respectively is defined as- Intersection $(f_A(x)$ and $f_B(x))$ = min $(f_A(x), f_B(x))$. This is depicted in Figure 4.

Complement: Complement of $f_A(x)$ (Figure 1) is defined as: Complement $(f_A(x))$ = 1- $f_A(x)$. This is shown in Figure 5.

Similarly, complement of $f_B(x)$ (Figure 2) is defined as: Complement $(f_B(x))$ = 1- $f_B(x)$. This is shown in Figure 6.

Fuzzy Logic Operators

There are three fuzzy logic operators (Chevrie and Guély, 1998)-

1) AND
2) OR
3) NOT

AND: AND operator is used for the conjunction of two antecedents of a rule and is evaluated as

Figure 1. $f_A(x)$

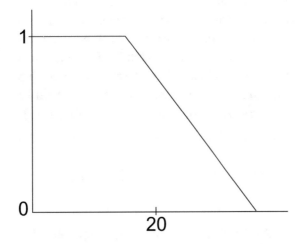

Figure 2. $f_B(x)$

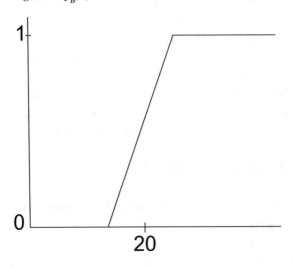

Figure 3. Union $(f_A(x)$ and $f_B(x))$ = max $(f_A(x), f_B(x))$

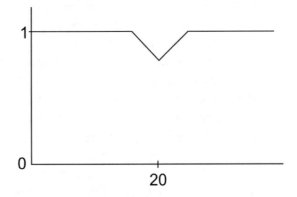

Figure 4. Intersection $(f_A(x)$ and $f_B(x))$ = min $(f_A(x), f_B(x))$

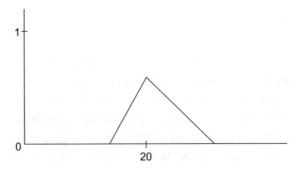

Figure 5. Complement $f_A(x) = 1 - f_A(x)$

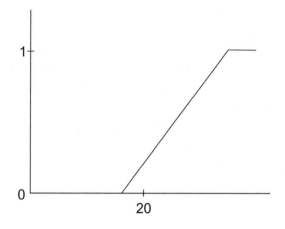

Figure 6. Complement $f_B(x) = 1 - f_B(x)$

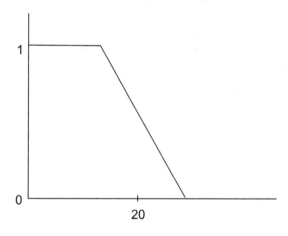

$$\mu_{A \cap B}(x) = \min\left[\mu_A(x), \mu_B(x)\right]$$

OR: OR operator is used for the disjunction of two antecedents of a rule and is evaluated as

$$\mu_{A \cup B}(x) = \max\left[\mu_A(x), \mu_B(x)\right]$$

NOT: Not is evaluated as

$$\mu_{\bar{A}}(x) = 1 - \mu_A(x)$$

Fuzzy Rules

The essence of fuzzy logic lies in its simplicity. Fuzzy logic works in the form of simple IF-THEN rules which are essentially conditional statements (Mendel, March 1995). These rules are described using linguistic variables.

A fuzzy rule can be represented as:

IF x is A THEN y is B

Here, *x* and *y* are the linguistic variables and *A* and *B* are the linguistic values. A fuzzy rule has two parts- antecedent and consequent. The first part of rule '*IF x is A*' is known as antecedent and the second part '*THEN y is B*' is known as the consequent. It is also possible to have a rule with multiple antecedents and consequents. Examples of rules with multiple antecedents are:

IF x is A AND y is B THEN z is C

IF x is A OR y is B THEN z is C

AND and *OR* in the above examples are the logical operators combining two antecedents.

Rules with multiple consequents are of the following form:

IF x is A

THEN y is B;

z is C

Hedges

Hedge causes variations to the shape of the fuzzy set and hence modifies the membership function (Mendel, March 1995). In simple words, we can say that a hedge converts a fuzzy set into another fuzzy set. The term '*very*' in the above examples is a hedge. Other examples of hedges are 'somewhat', 'rather', 'more', 'less', 'quite' etc. The two most commonly used hedges are 'very' and 'somewhat/rather'. The hedge 'very' strengthens the fuzzy membership of an object and is defined as:

$$\tau(x) = x^2$$

where $x = \mu(t)$ is the membership function.

The hedge 'somewhat' or 'rather' weakens the fuzzy membership of an object and is defined as:

$$\tau(x) = x^{1/2}$$

where $x = \mu(t)$ is the membership function.

Example: Suppose we have defined the membership function for the variable 'hot' as depicted in Figure 7.

Now, we want to represent the membership function for 'Extremely hot' and 'Fairly hot'. 'Extremely' and 'Fairly' are the hedges and we can model these using 'concentration' and 'dilation' as described above. The figure 8 shows the membership functions for 'Extremely Hot', 'Hot', 'Fairly Hot'.

Fuzzy Inference Process

The flowchart given in Figure 9 summarizes the whole process of fuzzy inference. Fuzzy inference is defined as a process that, using fuzzy logic, traces a given input to an output (MathWorks). All the elements discussed in the previous sections, i.e. membership functions, operators and fuzzy rules are used in this process.

Figure 7. Membership function for 'Hot'

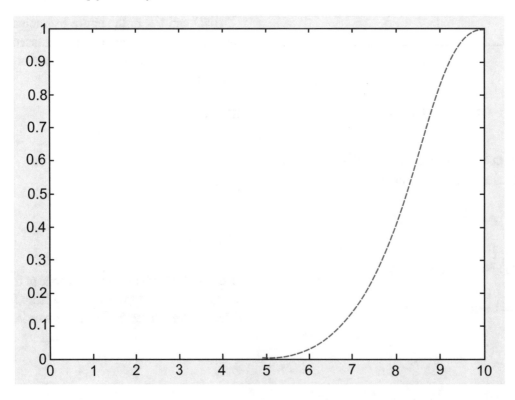

Figure 8. Membership function for 'Hot' after using hedges

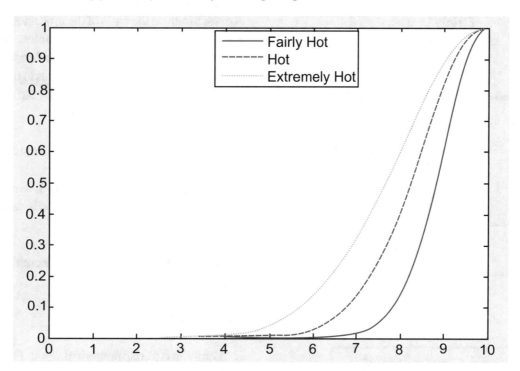

Step 1: Fuzzification

The first step involves taking the crisp inputs and fuzzifying them to know the degree to which they belong to the fuzzy sets.

Step 2: Rule evaluation

The fuzzified inputs are applied to the rule antecedents and the truth value is calculated. If a rule has multiple antecedents, then a single value is obtained by evaluating the AND and OR operators as explained in the above sections. This single value (truth value) is then applied to the membership function of the rule consequent. There are two methods of correlating antecedent truth value with the consequent membership function. These are clipping and scaling. Clipping involves using the level of the antecedent truth value to chop the consequent membership function. Scaling, on the

other hand, uses the rule antecedent's truth value to adjust the original membership function of the rule consequent.

Step 3: Aggregation of rule outputs

Since there are a number of fuzzy rules and each fired rule gives its own output, the next step is to aggregate the outputs from all the fuzzy rules to arrive at a single fuzzified output. This process takes a list of scaled or clipped consequent membership functions as an input and produces one fuzzy set for each output variable as the output.

Step 4: Defuzzification

Defuzzification is the final step in fuzzy inference process. It takes the aggregate output fuzzy set as input and produces a crisp number as output. There are many methods available for de-

Figure 9. Fuzzy inference process

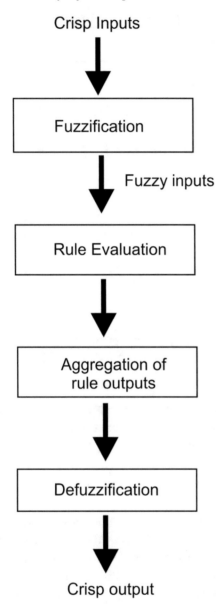

deals with deciding the tip to be given to a waiter at a restaurant on the basis of the food and service. Therefore, we have two input variables, namely, food and service and one output variable named tip.

The input variables take the values in the range 0 to 10 and the output is a value between 0 and 1. The rules used in this system are:

Rule 1: If service is poor or food is rancid, then tip is cheap.
Rule 2: If service is good, then tip is average.
Rule 3: If service is excellent or food is delicious, then tip is generous.

Now, the steps mentioned above are followed as explained below:

Step 1: Fuzzification

The input is a crisp numerical value. This input is then fuzzified according to the membership function of that input. This fuzzified value is then applied to the rules. Suppose, a customer gives a value of 8 for the input variable 'food'. When this value is fuzzified, it will yield a value between 0 and 1. Say, the membership function defined for 'food' returns a value of 0.7 for a numerical value of 8. This is shown in Figure 10:

Step 2: Rule Evaluation

i) Since we have two input variables, these variables have to be combined in some way before evaluating rules. This can be done by using either AND or OR operator. In this example, we use OR operator. OR operator picks up the maximum value from the two inputs. Figure 11 shows the application of OR operator for Rule 3.

The value 0.0 is achieved by applying the service value 3 to its membership function. OR returns 0.7 as the result.

fuzzification. Some of them are centroid method, weighted average method, max-membership, mean-max membership, center of sums, center of largest area and first (or last) of maxima. Out of all these, centroid method is the most common. It is also known as center of area or center of gravity method.

Example: There is a famous tipping problem which is solved using fuzzy logic. The problem

Figure 10. Fuzzy value for input variable 'food'

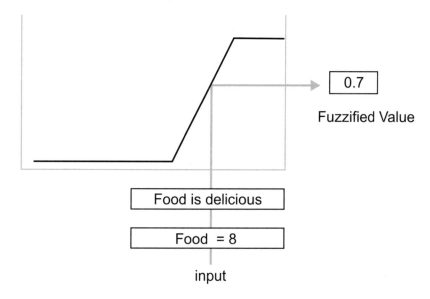

Figure 11. Combining the two inputs

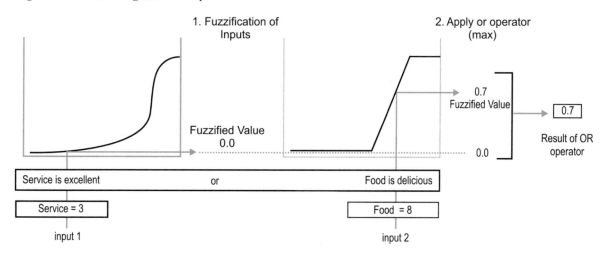

ii) Now, we have the value of antecedent. Next we use the implication method to arrive at the fuzzy set for consequent. The method used for this is *min*. It truncates the output fuzzy set as shown in Figure 12.

Step 3: Aggregation of Rule Outputs

After the output for each rule is evaluated as explained, all these outputs are combined or aggregated to arrive at a single value. This is done using *max* method as shown in Figure 13.

Figure 12. Applying the implication method

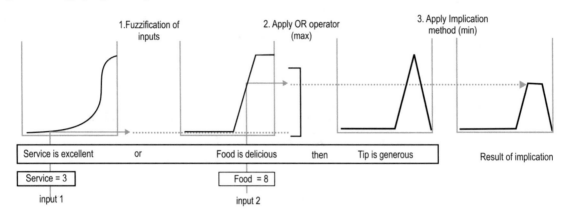

Figure 13. Aggregating rule outputs

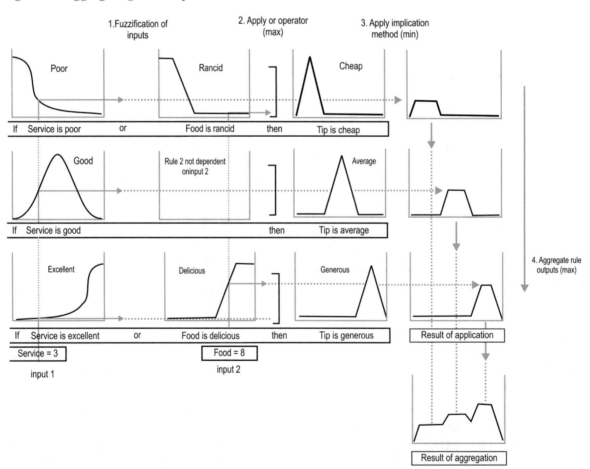

Step 4: Defuzzification

The last step defuzzifies the output of Step 3 i.e. the aggregated output to produce a single crisp value. There are many methods available for defuzzification but in this example, centroid method is used which returns the centre of area under the curve. This is illustrated in Figure 14.

TRUST CALCULATION USING FUZZY LOGIC

Various models used for assessing the trustworthiness and reputation of a system based on fuzzy logic are described in this section.

Use of Fuzzy Logic in Loosely Connected Communities

SPORAS

It is a reputation mechanism proposed by Zakaria and Maes (2000) for loosely connected communities. It has also been discussed by Carbo et al (2003).

SPORAS calculates the reputation using the following formulae:

$$R_i = R_{i-1} + \frac{1}{\theta} \cdot \phi(R_{i-1}) \cdot (W_i - R_{i-1}) \qquad (1)$$

where R_i = Reputation rating at time i,

R_{i-1} = Previous Reputation

W_i = Purchase Rating

θ = number of ratings considered $(\theta > 1)$. Higher the value of θ, lesser the change in reputation. ϕ is defined with a purpose to slow down modifications for very reputable customers. It is calculated as follows:

$$\phi(R_{i-1}) = 1 - \frac{1}{1 + e^{\frac{-(R_{i-1} - D)}{\sigma}}} \qquad (2)$$

Where D = maximum possible reputation value, and σ is chosen in such a way that ϕ remains

Figure 14. Defuzzification using centroid method

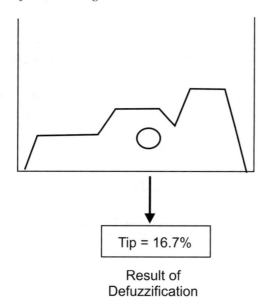

5. Defuzzify the aggregate output (centroid)

Tip = 16.7%

Result of Defuzzification

above 0.9 when reputation values are below $\frac{3}{4}$ of D.

SPORAS also measures the reliability of reputations. Reliability here means accuracy of estimations. Reliability is measured in terms of Reputation Deviation (RD) as follows:

$$RD_i^2 = \frac{[\lambda \cdot RD_{i-1}^2 + (W_i - R_{i-1})^2]}{\theta} \qquad (3)$$

Here λ is known as the forgetting factor and it is computed using θ i.e. the effective number of ratings.

$$\lambda = \frac{\theta - 1}{\theta} \qquad (4)$$

Since $\theta > 1$, the forgetting factor will always be $1 > \lambda \geq \frac{1}{2}$.

REGRET

Sabater and Sierra (2001) proposed another model called REGRET that shows improvement in the outcomes achieved by SPORAS under specific conditions. It has also been discussed by Carbo et al (2003). This model takes into account the freshness of information. Based on a time-dependent function ρ, a high relevance is given to recent ratings as compared to older ratings. That is, ρ gives a higher value to the reputation ratings held at a time closer to the present value of time.

The reputation rating at time i, denoted as R_i, is calculated using the weighted mean of the last θ ratings. This is depicted below:

$$R_i = \sum_{j=i-\theta}^{j=i} \rho(i, j) \cdot W_j \qquad (5)$$

Where $\rho(i, j)$ is a normalised value calculated as follows:

$$\rho(i, j) = \frac{f(j, i)}{\sum_{k=i-\theta}^{k=i} f(k, i)} \qquad (6)$$

Here, $i \geq j$ and they may denote time or number of the rating. For example, a time-dependent function f can be of the following form:

$$f(j, i) = \frac{j}{i} \qquad (7)$$

Like SPORAS, REGRET also measures reliability of the estimations. But in a different way. The formula used in computing reputation deviation is as follows:

$$DT_i = 1 - \sum_{j=i-\theta}^{j=i} \rho(i, j) \cdot |W_j - R_i| \qquad (8)$$

To calculate reliability, REGRET combines the above value of deviation with another measure called Number of Impressions (NI), where $0 < NI < 1$. It is used to decide if the number of impressions, i, attained is sufficient or not.

REGRET establishes another parameter known as intimate level of interactions, represented as *itm*. It establishes the minimum threshold of experiences needed to obtain close relationships. Any further increase in interactions will not lead to increase in reliability. The equation given below shows the intimate level of interactions with a given agent:

$$if\,(i \in [0, itm]) \rightarrow NI =$$
$$\sin\left(\frac{\pi}{2 \cdot itm} \cdot i\right), Otherwise \rightarrow NI = 1 \qquad (9)$$

Use of Fuzzy Logic in Multi-Agent Systems

AFRAS

AFRAS stands for A Fuzzy Reputation Agent System. Carbo et al. (2003) developed this model for multi-agent system consisting of seller, buyer, recommender or facilitator. The model has the following principles:

- Reputation serves as a measure to predict or forecast the future conduct of a merchant. If all the merchants behave consistently, then mean error in the reputation forecasts keeps on decreasing.
- Variations in reputation have to be adjusted depending on the overall success or failure of forecasts. If the gross success in the past forecasts is very high, then variations in reputation have to be small and vice versa.
- Reliability of each reputation rating should also be adjusted dynamically. If the reputation of a merchant is by no means similar to the contentment resulting from a purchase, then the reliability of this new reputation should be reduced accordingly.

These principles are applied to two fuzzy sets, namely, reputation R of a merchant and satisfaction S resulting from a purchase with the corresponding merchant. The new reputation of a merchant is calculated using weighted aggregation of these two sets. In weighted arithmetic mean, $\sum W_i = 1$ and $\forall W_i \geq 0$. The weights used in this model are:

$$W_1 = \frac{2-W}{2} \; ; \; W_2 = \frac{W}{2} \qquad (10)$$

Where, W_1 and W_2 denote the contribution of the last experience and that of previous reputa-tion in the calculation of new reputation respectively.

The equation for calculation of new reputation using weighted arithmetic mean can be written as follows:

$$R_i = R_{i-1} \cdot W_2 + S_i \cdot W_1 \qquad (11)$$

Substitute the values of W_1 and W_2 in the above equation as follows:

$$R_i = \frac{R_{i-1} \cdot W + S_i \cdot (2-W)}{2} \qquad (12)$$

It can be rewritten as:

$$R_i = R_{i-1} + \frac{(S_i - R_{i-1}) \cdot (1-W)}{2} \qquad (13)$$

The value of weight W has significant importance for the management of reputation. It can be regarded as the remembrance of the previous experiences. If W has a low value, that means old experiences are nearly forgotten. If W has a high value, that means old experiences are recalled. If the remembrance in an instant i is denoted as ρ_i, the previous equation would become:

$$R_i = R_{i-1} + \frac{(S_i - R_{i-1}) \cdot (1-\rho_i)}{2} \qquad (14)$$

Depending upon how remembrance grows or decreases, adaptive behaviour of reputation updating also changes.

Remembrance, ρ_i is calculated as follows:

$$\rho_i = \frac{\rho_{i-1} + \Delta(R_{i-1}, S_i)}{2} \qquad (15)$$

Where ρ_i = new remembrance

ρ_{i-1} = previous remembrance

$\Delta(R_{i-1}, S_i)$ = similarity between previous reputation and satisfaction provided

The similarity is measured by the support matching between both the fuzzy sets. This is done through mass assignment theory developed by J.F. Baldwin.

From the above equation, two things can be inferred:

- If the prediction matches the rating, i.e. $\Delta \approx 1$, then remembrance would increase by $1/2 + \rho/2$
- If the prediction is not at all similar with the rating, i.e. $\Delta \approx 0$, then remembrance was of no use and its relevance will be halved in future predictions.

The results of equations (14) and (15) satisfy the first two principles of the model described in the starting. But the third principle relating to adjustment of reliability is not yet satisfied. For this, the values of R_i and S_i to the jth square of the respective fuzzy set are used:

$$R_i^j = R_{i-1}^j + \frac{(S_i^j - R_{i-1}^j) \cdot (1 - \rho_i + f(S_i, R_{i-1}, j))}{2}$$

(16)

Where, f is the forgetting factor calculated according to the similarity degree between R and S as follows:

$$f(S_i, R_{i-1}, j) = \phi_j \cdot (1 - \Delta(S_i, R_{i-1}))$$

(17)

The forgetting factor f is damped according to a damping factor ϕ which depends on the relative positions of previous reputation and satisfaction fuzzy sets.

ϕ_j in the above equation is a damping factor that calculates the value of normalised relative distance of point j of set R_{i-1}^j to the square of R_{i-1} closest to S_i.

Following points need to be considered for defining damping function:

- Minimum distance between the previous reputation fuzzy set R_{i-1}^j and any square of the satisfaction fuzzy set S_i is $\min_{k=1,...,4}\{R_{i-1}^j - S_i^k\}$.
- Minimum distance from reputation fuzzy set to satisfaction fuzzy set is $\min_{l=1,...,4}\{\min_{k=1,..4}[R_{i-1}^l - S_i^k]\}$.

Calculating the difference between these results, an increasing linear function from the proximity of reputation fuzzy set to the farther points associated with satisfaction fuzzy set is obtained. To normalise this difference in the range [0,1], it is divided with the minimum distance of farthest point of reputation fuzzy set with the satisfaction fuzzy set as shown in Box 1.

The distance function given above can be intensified with the help of a function:

Box 1.

$$D = \frac{\min_{k=1,...,4}\{R_{i-1}^j - S_i^k\} - \min_{l=1,...,4}\{\min_{k=1,..,4}[R_{i-1}^l - S_i^k]\}}{\max_{l=1,...,4}\{\min_{k=1,...,4}[R_{i-1}^l - S_i^k]\} - \min_{l=1,...,4}\{\min_{k=1,...,4}[R_{i-1}^l - S_i^k]\}} \quad (18)$$

$$\phi = \frac{1}{1 + e^{D \cdot 100}} \tag{19}$$

Substituting the above value for damping function in Eq. (17), we get the forgetting factor as:

$$f(S_i, R_{i-1}, j) = \frac{1}{1 + e^{D \cdot 100}} \cdot (1 - \Delta(R_{i-1}, S_i)) \tag{20}$$

The model now satisfies all the three stated principles.

Model Incorporating Trust, Distrust, and Insufficient Trust

Griffiths (2006) has proposed a model to deal with the issue of trust in multi-agent systems. The threat or risk involved in failure while cooperating with one another can be estimated by utilising the trust of capable partners. The heavy load of work and study has been done and executed on the positive side of trust leaving behind the negative facet of distrust. Distrust is a notion that a party or an agent would act against the best interests of another. The authors have used Marsh's view pertaining to the significance of distrust and how distrust can be a coherent part in the decision making process. Additionally, a new notion of undistrust is introduced which is better defined as positive trust but not sufficient for cooperation. The notion of untrust and undistrust can be significant in reasoning process involving cooperation, but otherwise they are not sufficient in obtaining a concrete conclusion. This can be best exhibited with an example wherein in an absence of trusted agents, an agent may select to perform interaction with an untrusted or an undistrusted party only if the cost incurred due to it is negligible.

Interaction histories: Retrospective interactions and past interaction occurrences are maintained by agents, as trust is a value derived through previous experiences by an individual agent.

Rather than containing the scope of interactions to success or failure, partial success or success with deviated characteristics are also included and are observed as a trusted interaction. For example, an agent committed for providing an output may provide it with delay or less details comparatively. This doesn't make the agent a complete failure in terms of trust but might decrement its performance level. Therefore, it is an agent's prerogative to take it beyond the scope of traditional expectation of success and failure. Different dimensions of the view of trust such as quality and cost of task imposed for its initiation apart from its success is also taken into consideration. Assessment of trust is ensured by evaluating the agent's experience in each of the dimensions of trust in the multi-dimensional model. An agent's expectation has been said to be met or not met depending upon the agent's each interaction in each dimension of the multidimensional aspect of trust. Every interaction history is maintained at each dimension for number of successful and unsuccessful interaction so as to seek whether expectations were met or not. Experience (e_α^d) can be calculated by using the values I_α^{d+} and I_α^{d-}, which denote interactions for which expectations were met and not met respectively. These values are maintained by an agent. The formula for calculating experience is:

$$e_\alpha^d = \frac{I_\alpha^{d+} - I_\alpha^{d-}}{I_\alpha^{d+} + I_\alpha^{d-}} \tag{21}$$

From this information, value of trust factor or trustworthiness of others can be estimated by the agent. These are crisp values in the interval [-1,1] and in order to reason about trust these are required to be translated into fuzzy values.

Purging old interactions: The resultant outcome of each agent's interaction is maintained by using a window of experiences that is created for each other agent. This window is restricted by the fact that there exists an upper limit on the frequency of interactions that are monitored and recorded for any specific agent. The window operates in First In First Out (FIFO) fashion and when it becomes full, the earliest or oldest experiences are removed to make way for the new ones. To address the change of reliable agents turning unreliable, an agent removes expired experiences from its interaction windows after the lapse of a specific fixed time. This removal of expired experiences occurs even in the case when the window is not full. The delay happening between the occurrence of an interaction and its subsequent removal from the interaction window is known as Purge lag. It also has a direct impact on the swiftness of the agent's trust evaluation response to the modifications in its environment. The interaction details do not persist for long in case of a small purge, which signifies that trust assessment quickly responds to changes. The small purge also decrements the range of experiences that can be used to evaluate trust. Sufficient experience is necessary for the calculation of trust. The confidence level in the experience for a specific dimension is based upon the total number of interactions on which it is dependent upon.

$$confidence_{\alpha}^{d} = I_{\alpha}^{d+} + I_{\alpha}^{d-} \qquad (22)$$

If the confidence level is below a predefined threshold level, then a value of untrust or undistrust will be affiliated for the success dimension or a default value will be used in case of other dimensions.

Fuzzy trust: Fuzzy terms are defined for experiences in each of the dimensions in which the agents capture and maintain their interactions. The dimensions chosen for this model are cost, success and quality. Fuzzy variables are defined with the help of fuzzy terms and to represent experience, fuzzy variables are defined for each

trust dimension. So the fuzzy variables for experience for the chosen dimensions are E_{α}^{s}, E_{α}^{c} and E_{α}^{q} for success, cost and quality dimensions for agent α respectively. The universe of discourse of these fuzzy variables is [-1,1]. For each fuzzy variable, following terms are defined: negative big, negative medium, negative small, zero, positive small, positive medium and positive big. Since the main aim is to calculate trustworthiness of agent α, so trust t is also defined as a fuzzy variable on universe of discourse [-1,1] with following associated fuzzy terms: high distrust, distrust, undistrust, untrust, trust and high trust. Next, fuzzy inference rules are defined for each dimension. These rules take experiences as antecedents and produce trust as consequent. An example of rules used in the system is shown in Figure 15.

Determining Trustworthiness: The main prerequisite for evaluating the trustworthiness of an agent is whether there are sufficient number of previous interactions to reason about the trust value of the agent. The model does not employ the concept of partial success of interactions, so all the previous interactions would have been either successful or failure. The success dimension is therefore used to represent if there is sufficient information available to reason about trustworthiness of the agent. If the success dimension does not contain a sufficient number of interactions, then the agent is assigned a value of either untrust or undistrust depending on the previous interactions being overall positive or negative. That is, depending upon whether the value of e_{α}^{d} is positive or negative.

Thus, the first step in assessing the trustworthiness of an agent α is to determine if there is sufficient confidence or not, i.e. to check whether

$$confidence_{\alpha}^{s} \geq \min Confidence.$$

Figure 15. An example of fuzzy rule set (Griffiths, 2006)

(R$_{UT}$1)   **if** *confidence* $\frac{d}{\alpha}$ < *minConfidence* **and** E_α^d is *positive* **then** T_α is *untrust*

(R$_{UT}$2)   **if** *confidence* $\frac{d}{\alpha}$ < *minConfidence* **and** E_α^d is *negative* **then** T_α is *undistrust*

-

-

-

(R$_T$1)   **if** E_α^d is *negativeBig* **then** T_α is *highDistrust*

(R$_T$2)   **if** E_α^d is *negativeMedium* **then** T_α is **very** *distrust or undistrust*

(R$_T$3)   **if** E_α^d is *negativeSmall* **then** T_α is *undistrust*

(R$_T$4)   **if** E_α^d is *zero* **then** T_α is *undistrust or untrust*

(R$_T$5)   **if** E_α^d is *positiveSmall* **then** T_α is *untrust*

(R$_T$6)   **if** E_α^d is *positiveMedium* **then** T_α is **very** *trust or untrust*

(R$_T$7)   **if** E_α^d is *positiveBig* **then** T_α is *highTrust*

-

-

-

(R$_R$n)   **if** T_α is *highTrust* **and** F_α^c is *medium* **and** F_α^q is *very high* **then** R_α is *high*

(R$_R$m)   **if** T_α is **low** *distrust* **and** F_α^c is *medium* **and** F_α^q is *high* **then** R_α is *low*

If there is not sufficient confidence, then the trust value of agent α, represented as T_α, is assigned a value of either untrust or undistrust with a membership degree that is determined by the level of confidence and value of experience as given by rules $R_{UT}1$ and $R_{UT}2$ in Figure 15.

In case there is sufficient experience to calculate the trust, then fuzzy inference method is used. In order to evaluate the trustworthiness of the potential interaction partners, fuzzy inference rules for each of the trust dimensions is considered. Each rule is considered in turn. Whenever there is a match between the input supplied, i.e. E_α^d, and the rule antecedent, that rule is fired. If for a particular dimension, there is insufficient experience to calculate trust, then the agent uses default experience value for that dimension. This default value is determined by the agent's trust position or character.

Untrust and Undistrust: If the trust level assigned to an agent is untrust or undistrust, the conclusion for an agent's suitability cannot be made as the trust level being considered is not sufficient in such cases. Henceforth, every untrust or undistrust assigned agent should not be considered for selection. This can be a problem in hostile or dynamic environment as majority agents may either be distrusted, untrusted or undistrusted and not considered for cooperation thus causing deadlock. Therefore, in order to avoid such situations these untrusted and undistrusted agents are included for proportional interactions. In case of absence of trusted agents consisting of required capabilities, then with some probability known as rebootstrap rate, the agent possessing the highest trust level amongst the set of untrusted and undistrusted agents will be chosen.

Selecting cooperative partner: Fuzzy rules are introduced which in combination of trust and decision factors assign a rating for each alternative interaction partner. Each of these F_i values are crisp in nature and can be fuzzified to obtain a singleton set. A set of inference rules consisting of fuzzy trust and fuzzy decision factors as antecedents and rating for an agent as conclusion, are defined. For example, the authors have used the cost and quality from an agent α, denoted by F_α^c and F_α^q respectively, as the factors. Suppose the fuzzy terms low, medium and high are defined for the above mentioned factors under the universe of discourse presented by the domain and scope of suitable advertised cost and quality values. Similarly, we also have terms low, medium, high and reject defined for ratings, under universe of discourse [0,1]. Then a set of rules is defined shown by $R_R n$ and $R_R m$. Rule $R_R n$ states that an agent is said to have high rating provided it is trusted, has medium advertised cost and a high advertised quality. Same way rule $R_R m$ states that an agent is said to have low rating if it has low distrust, has a medium advertised cost and high advertised quality. Each of these rules is applied in parallel using Mamdani min-max inference for calculating trust. This provides with a crisp rating value for agent by defuzzifying the fuzzy rating.

Boot strapping: In case of insufficient experience for reasoning, each agent undergoes a boot strapping phase in which partner agents are selected in random fashion by exploration method. Bootstrapping phase provides the distrusted, undistrusted, untrusted and trusted agents with an equal chance of being selected.

Use of Fuzzy Logic in Peer-To-Peer Systems

Fuzzy Trust for Peer-To-Peer Based Systems

The trust model given by Azzedin et al. (2007) combines the first-hand and second-hand information to evaluate other peers' trustworthiness in the system. First-hand information refers to direct experience of a peer with another peer, whereas second-hand information refers to the reputation of a peer.

In this model, each peer x has a set of recommenders (R_x) and a set of trusted associates (T_x) The peer x believes its associates blindly and uses them to evaluate the honesty of its recommenders. The peer x's recommenders are kept in a table called Recommender Trust Table (RTT_x) where each recommender is described using a two-tuple entry (honesty, accuracy). For the purpose of monitoring transactions that peer x carried out with other peers, x creates another table called Direct Trust Table (DTT_x).

Calculating honesty and accuracy: The peer x selects one of its recommenders z randomly and initially considers it to have maximum accuracy irrespective of the target peer, i.e. $A_x(z,t,c)=1$, which means x regards z as having utmost accuracy for context c at time t. Second, z's recommendation error as perceived by x for context c at time t is equal to zero since z is a new recommender and has not given any recommendations so far, i.e. $\psi_{RE_x}(z,t,c)=0$. Third, z is regarded as having maximum consistency, i.e. $C_x(z,t,c)=1$.

It means x regards z to be consistent for context c at time t. The objective of peer x is to have only truthful and meticulous recommenders in set R_x.

Let $C_x(z, y, t, c)$ denote the consistency of recommender z as perceived by x for context c at time t, and $RE_k(z, y, t, c)$ be the recommendation provided by z for peer y to peer k for context c at time t, where $k \in T_x$. This recommendation is given from the Direct Trust Table of z i.e. DTT_z because that is the reputation of peer y according to z.

Let

$$TL_{\min}(x, z, y, t, c) = \min_{k \in T_z} \{RE_k(z, y, t, c)\},$$

and

$$TL_{\max}(x, z, y, t, c) = \max_{k \in T_x} \{RE_k(z, y, t, c)\}$$

Where TL is the Trust Level ranging from very untrustworthy to very trustworthy given by the range 1 to 5.

Let $\Delta_{RE_x}(z, y, t, c)$ be the difference between $TL_{\max}$ and $TL_{\min}$ calculated as follows:

$$\Delta_{RE_x}(z, y, t, c) = TL_{\max}(x, z, y, t, c) - TL_{\min}(x, z, y, t, c) \quad (23)$$

If recommender z is consistent, then the value of $\Delta_{RE_x}(z, y, t, c)$ calculated by the above equation will be lower than a minute value $\in_{RE}$. Now, $C_x(z, y, t, c)$ can be computed as follows:

$$C_x(z, y, t, c) = \begin{cases} 0 & if \ \Delta_{RE_x}(z, y, t, c) > \in_{RE} \\ 1 & otherwise \end{cases}$$

$$(24)$$

If $C_x(z, y, t, c) = 0$, then z is fraudulent and will be removed from R_x so that it does not influ-

ence the recommendation system. If $C_x(z, y, t, c) = 1$, then z is consistent but nothing can be said about its honesty. To determine whether z is honest or not, another filter called accuracy is applied. This filter is used to identify consistent but dishonest recommenders so that their recommendations can be adjusted before they are used to compute the reputation of y.

When x wants to assess the reputation of y, it will enquire its recommenders about reputation of y for context c at time t. When z gives its recommendation for y, i.e. $RE_x(z, y, t, c)$, this recommendation has to be adapted according to recommender z's accuracy before it can be used by x to evaluate the reputation of y. For this purpose, a shift function is used. This function is represented as S and uses the overall accuracy of z irrespective of the target peer to correct $RE_x(z, y, t, c)$ as shown below:

$$S(A(x, z, t, c), RE_x(z, y, t, c)) = \begin{cases} RE_x(z, y, t, c) + 4(1 - A(x, z, t, c)) & if \ \psi_{RE}^* < 0 \\ RE_x(z, y, t, c) - 4(1 - A(x, z, t, c)) & if \ \psi_{RE}^* \geq 0 \end{cases}$$

$$(25)$$

where ψ_{RE}^* is equal to ψ_{RE} obtained in the last transaction event, since monitoring is done every n^{th} transaction.

Let $ITL_x(y, t, c)$ be the Instantaneous Trust Level of y given by x for context c at time t. This value is obtained by x by monitoring its current transaction with y. The $ITL_x(y, t, c)$ of the transaction is determined by the Transaction Monitor proxy of $x (TM_x)$. Different TM proxies may assign a transaction to distinct trust levels, since each TM proxy is governed by the associated peer. TM proxies identify if any abuses have taken place by analyzing the transaction or its records. Since it is difficult to monitor each and every transaction, the process of obtaining $ITL_x(y, t, c)$ is carried out after every n^{th} transaction. Once the transaction is complete and x determines $ITL_x(y,t,c)$, $\psi_{RE_x}(z,y,t,c)$ can be calculated as follows:

$$\psi_{RE_x}(z,y,t,c) = RE_x(z,y,t,c) - ITL_x(y,t,c)$$

(26)

where $\psi_{RE_x}(z,y,t,c)$ is recommendation error of z as perceived by x when z provides recommendation about y for context c at time t.

$|\psi_{RE_x}(z,y,t,c)|$ has a value between 0 to 4 since $RE_x(z,y,t,c)$ and $ITL_x(y,t,c)$ are in the range 1 to 5. The above value can be computed only if $ITL_x(y,t,c)$ is acquired.

Finally, the accuracy of recommender z for peer x when z gives recommendation regarding y for context c at time t can be calculated as:

$$A_x(z,y,c) = -\frac{1}{4}|\psi_{RE_x}(z,y,t,c)| + 1$$

(27)

If $|\psi_{RE_x}(z,y,t,c)| = 0$, then $A_x(z,y,t,c) = 1$, which means that z has maximum accuracy as far as x is concerned.

If $|\psi_{RE_x}(z,y,t,c)| = 4$, then $A_x(z,y,t,c) = 0$, which means that z is completely wrong about y as far as x is concerned.

So, $A_x(z,y,t,c)$ has a value in the interval [0,1].

From the above discussion, it is safe to conclude that largest recommendation error results in minimum accuracy and smallest recommendation error results in maximum accuracy.

Also, is the accuracy of z regarding y and $A_x(z,t,c)$ is the overall accuracy of z as far as x is concerned irrespective of the target peer. Similarly, $\psi_{RE_x}(z,y,t,c)$ is the recommendation error of z regarding y and $\psi_{RE_x}(z,t,c)$ is the overall recommendation error as far as x is con-

cerned regardless of the target peer. $A_x(z,y,t,c)$ will be used to update $A_x(z,t,c)$ and $\psi_{RE_x}(z,y,t,c)$ will be employed to upgrade $\psi_{RE_x}(z,t,c)$ as explained in 'Trust Evolution' section below.

Calculation of trust and reputation: For calculating trust and reputation, following points were considered:

- Trust and reputation may deteriorate with time. For instance, a peer x trusts peer y at a level q on the basis of its past interactions 3 years ago. The present trust level will probably be lesser than this unless they have interacted on a regular basis since then.
- The peers may create associations and consequently they would trust their associates more than the other peers.
- The trust that x has on y is a result of direct experience of x with y as well as reputation of y. So, the trust evaluation model should be able to combine both the direct trust and the reputation.
- The model should be flexible enough to allow both direct trust and reputation to weigh differently as the situation demands.

Let $\Gamma(x,y,t,c) =$ behaviour trust between two entities x and y for context c and time t.

$\Theta(x,y,t,c) =$ direct trust between x and y for context c and time t.

$\Omega(y,t,c) =$ reputation of y for context c and time t.

Trust changes with time and number of experiences as explained above in the first point. To model this aspect, the authors have multiplied the trust levels in DTT_x by a decay function represented as $Y(t - \tau_{xy}((t),c)), TF_{xy}(c)$ where,

$t =$ current time

$\tau_{xy}((t),c) =$ time of last interaction between x and y for context c

$TF_{xy}(c) =$ transaction frequency between x and y for context c

Behaviour trust and Direct trust can be calculated using the following equations:

$$\Gamma(x,y,t,c) = \alpha\,\Theta(x,y,t,c) + \beta\,\Omega_x(y,t,c) \tag{28}$$

$$\Theta(x,y,t,c) = \\ Y(t - \tau_{xy}((t),c), TF_{xy}(c))\,DTT_x(y,t,c) \tag{29}$$

Reputation can be calculated as:

$$\Omega_x(y,t,c) = \\ \frac{1}{|R_x|}\sum_{z \in R_z} Y(t - \tau_{zy}((t),c), TF_{xy}(c))\,S(x,y,z,t,c) \tag{30}$$

The reputation of y is computed using the above equation for all recommenders $z \in R$ and $z \neq y$.

Trust Evolution: In this section, the process for updating direct trust, accuracy and recommendation errors is discussed. Assume that after carrying out the trust evaluation, peer x indulges in interaction with peer y. The transaction is monitored by TM_x and TM_y proxies. The TM_x and TM_y proxies are responsible for determining $ITL_x(y,t,c)$ and $ITL_y(x,t,c)$ respectively. Since a *TM* proxy is governed by the associated peer, TM_x and TM_y proxies might rate the same transaction differently.

$ITL_x(y,t,c)$ denotes the *ITL* of y as perceived by x for context c at time t and $DTT_x(y,t,c)$ denotes the DTT_x entry representing the level of trust that x has on y for context c at time t on the basis of direct interaction of x with y.

Let δ be a real number between 0 and 1. The direct trust between x and y can be updated as follows:

$$DTT_x(y,t,c) = \\ \delta DTT_x(y,t,c) + (1-\delta)ITL_x(y,t,c) \tag{31}$$

X calculates the accuracy and consistency of its recommenders as described earlier. The overall recommendation error of recommender z as far as x is concerned can be updated using the following formula:

$$\psi_{RE_x}(z,t,c) = \\ \delta\,\psi_{RE_x}(z,t,c) + (1-\delta)\,\psi_{RE_x}(z,y,t,c) \tag{32}$$

Where $\psi_{RE_x}(z,t,c) =$ overall recommendation error of z irrespective of the target peer in the context of peer x.

$\psi_{RE_x}(z,y,t,c) =$ recommendation error of z when z provides recommendation regarding y for context c at time t.

The average accuracy measure can be updated using the following formula:

$$A_{RTT_x}(z,t,c) = \\ \delta\,A_{RTT_x}(z,t,c) + (1-\delta)A_x(z,y,t,c) \tag{33}$$

Where $A_x(z,y,t,c) =$ accuracy of recommender z as observed by x on the basis of recommendation given by z for y based on the current transaction.

$A_{RTT_x}(z,t,c) =$ accuracy of recommender z on the basis of all previous recommendations maintained at RTT_x.

The method for updating consistency of recommenders is entirely different. The equation for updating is shown below:

$$C_{RTT_x}(z,t,c) = \min\left(C_{RTT_x}(z,t,c), C_x(z,y,t,c)\right)$$

$$(34)$$

Where $C_x(z,y,t,c)$ = consistency of recommender z on the basis of its recommendation regarding y given to x for context c at time t.

$C_{RTT_x}(z,t,c)$ = consistency of z on the basis of all previous recommendations provided by z maintained at RTT_x.

FuzzyTrust Reputation System

Song et al. (2005) have proposed a reputation system called FuzzyTrust for evaluating a peer's reputation in a Peer to Peer (P2P) system. The authors have identified the following requirements for a P2P reputation system:

- The system must evaluate reputation locally and then aggregate the reputation globally.
- It must be able to precisely measure and monitor the local parameters affecting reputation.
- It must be able to filter out false opinions given by malicious peers to downgrade a well-behaved peer.

Before proposing the system, the authors analyzed the eBay transaction data to understand the important characteristics of transactions. These characteristics were recognised as follows:

- Small users and Super users: There are two types of users. Super users are those that have a large number of transaction partners and conduct more transactions. Small users, on the other hand, are those that have a few transaction partners and conduct few transactions.
- Unsteady transactions by small users: The time span between two adjacent transac-

tions by small users is long and unstable, whereas the same is short and stable for super users.
- Skewed transaction amount: A large number of small transactions co-exist with a small number of large transactions but the total amount transacted is dominated by the large transactions.

FuzzyTrust Architecture: After analyzing the above characteristics, the system has been designed to incorporate the following design criteria:

- The reputation system must take into account the unbalanced transaction amount between users as the bandwidth consumption for exchanging local trust outcomes for hot spots would be remarkably high as compared to small users. Hot spots are the situations in which super users engage in majority of the transactions whereas small users engage in very few transactions.
- Since small users have a lesser impact on the overall transacted amount, the same evaluation cycle cannot be applied to both small users and super users. Super users should be updated frequently as compared to small users.
- Since the transaction amount is skewed, large transactions should be evaluated more frequently than small transactions.

The system performs two major steps:

1. Local-score computation: The peers monitor the local parameters and perform fuzzy inference on these parameters to arrive at local trust score. The fuzzy inference system can adapt to the variations in these parameters and can handle uncertainties. These local parameters can be quality of goods, delivery time, payment time etc. The process for calculating local trust scores is depicted in Figure 16.

Figure 16. The FuzzyTrust system determines the local trust scores by performing fuzzy logic inferences on local parameters

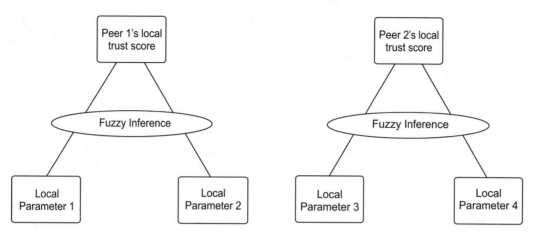

2. Global reputation aggregation: The FuzzyTrust system collects the local outcomes from all peers and aggregates them to create a global reputation for each peer. The fuzzy inference mechanism is then used to arrive at aggregation weights for global reputation. The weights are derived using three variables- peer's reputation, transaction amount and transaction date. The process is shown in Figure 17.

The fuzzy inference rules used with the prototype FuzzyTrust system are as follows:

1) If transaction time is new and transaction amount is very high, then aggregation weight is very large.
2) If transaction time is very old or transaction amount is very low, then aggregation weight is small.

Figure 17. The FuzzyTrust system performs weight inference in global reputation aggregation

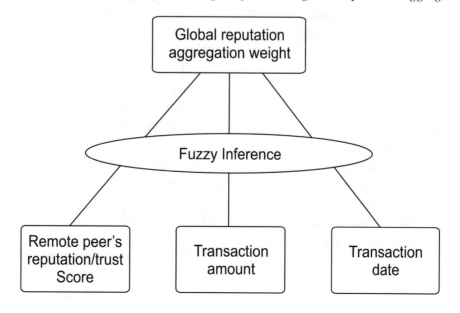

3) If transaction amount is high and peer's reputation is good, then aggregation weight is very large.
4) If transaction amount is low and peer's reputation is good, then aggregation weight is medium.
5) If peer's reputation is bad, then aggregation weight is very small.

The global reputation is calculated using the following formula:

$$R_i = \sum_{j \in S} \left(\frac{w_j}{\sum_{j \in S} w_j} t_{ji} \right) = \frac{\sum_{j \in S} w_j t_{ji}}{\sum_{j \in S} w_j} \qquad (35)$$

Where R_i = global reputation of peer i

S = set of peers with whom peer i transacted

T_{ji} = local trust of peer i rated by peer j

w_j = aggregation weight of t_{ji}

The process for global reputation aggregation runs multiple times till each R_i converges to a stable global reputation for each peer i.

TRUST CALCULATION USING FUZZY LOGIC IN CLOUD COMPUTING

Trust Calculation for IaaS Based E-Learning System

Various trust and reputation systems are in place for varied online services. But there is dearth of such models in the field of cloud computing. Alhamad et al. (2011) have made an effort in this regard. Since it is very difficult to evaluate cloud metrics generally, the authors have done so for IaaS-based e-learning system. IaaS is one of the models of cloud computing. The factors identified by the authors that affect the trustworthiness of an

IaaS-based system are scalability, usability, availability and security. These parameters are rated for different Cloud Providers and using fuzzy logic, a decision about the trust value of these providers is arrived at. The process is explained in Figure 18:

Step 1: The first step involves defining fuzzy sets for the four input factors and the output. The output is trust value of the providers.

Step 2: The next step involves setting the weights for the four factors. These weights can be provided by the users who wish to enquire about the trustworthiness of the providers. If the users don't provide these weights, then the fuzzy inference system treats all factors equally.

Step 3: The third step involves determining the membership degree of each input factor. Using the membership function, each input is assigned to the relevant degree of fuzzy sets of input.

Step 4: The next step is to design fuzzy rules. Fuzzy rules combine the input factors and determine the output accordingly. The authors have designed the rules based on discussions and an online survey.

Step 5: This step involves providing the inputs to a fuzzy inference engine. The authors have used Sugeno fuzzy inference engine for this model.

Step 6: Final step consists of defuzzification. Defuzzification takes in the fuzzy output value and produces a crisp value as an output. This model uses the centroid method for defuzzification purpose.

A sample of rules used in this model are shown in Table 1.

TMFC Model

TMFC is a trust management model developed on fuzzy set theory by Sun et al. (2011). It incorporates the concepts of direct trust measurement

Figure 18. Trust evaluation for cloud providers

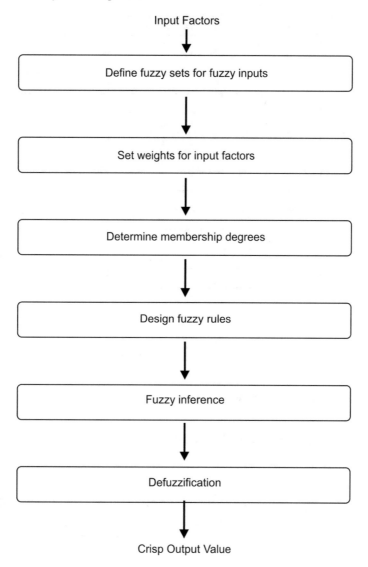

and computing, connecting, trust chain and recommended trust. These concepts are explained below:

Trust: Trust between two nodes can be formed either through direct interaction between the two or through recommendations given by trusted entities. The trust is assessed through trust degree and is described through the trust relation. Trust on a node depends on the performance of that node measured in multiple dimensions.

Direct Trust Relation: It is the relation between a trustor and a trustee. The node establishing direct trust relation is known as the trustor and the one which is being trusted is called the trustee. This relation is formed on the basis of direct interaction between the two nodes. The direct trust relation is of two types – inter-domain direct trust relation and intro-domain direct trust relation.

Inter-domain Direct Trust Relation: The direct trust relation in which the cloud service provider acts as the trustee is known as inter-domain direct trust relation. It is depicted by a solid arrow line in Figure 19. This relation can be described using

Table 1. Sample of rule set (Alhamad et al., 2011)

Scalability	Availability	Security	Usability	Trust
L	L	L	L	VP
M	L	L	M	P
M	M	L	M	G
L	M	M	L	P
M	L	M	M	G
H	L	L	H	P
M	M	M	M	G
H	H	L	H	G
L	H	H	L	G
H	L	H	H	VG
H	M	M	H	G
M	H	M	M	G
H	M	H	H	VG

Where L = Low,
M = Medium,
H = High,
VP = Very Poor,
P = Poor,
G = Good,
VG = Very Good
This model can be extended to include other input factors as well.

Figure 19. Oriented recommended trust chain in cloud

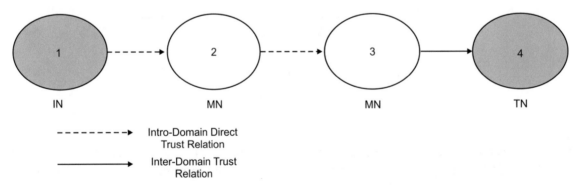

inter-domain direct trust evaluation set. To define this set, five attributes of the trustee provider, namely, reliability(r), availability(a), integrity(it), maintainability(m) and safety(s), are considered. All these attributes decay with time and have values between zero and one. After considering the time factor and related calculations, the values of these attributes are denoted as r(t), a(t), it(t), m(t) and s(t). These attribute values constitute a vector $Vd(I) = (r(t), a(t), s(t), it(t), m(t))$.

The inter-domain direct trust evaluation set is calculated from the inter-domain trust evaluation attribute factor ψ_1. ψ_1 can be calculated as follows:

$$\psi_1 = Vd(I) \circ Wd(I)^T \qquad (36)$$

$$\xi(\Delta t) = e^{-\Delta t^l} = e^{-|tp-ts|^l} \text{, k is an integer} \qquad (38)$$

Where, $Wd(I) = (w_1, w_2, w_3, w_4, w_5)$ is the weight vector.

Intro-domain Direct Trust Relation: It is a direct trust relation in which the cloud service provider is not the trustee and is depicted by a dashed arrow line in Figure 19. It is also described using trust evaluation set based on time-decaying evaluation attributes. This set is regularly updated based on the times of interaction. The evaluation attributes considered for intro-domain trust evaluation set are - network Flow created by interaction (F), current network's Bandwidth (B), n^{th} interaction's Successful communication times (S), n^{th} interaction's Tentative communication times (T), and time consumed (t). As in case of inter-domain trust evaluation set, intro-domain trust evaluation set is also calculated from the intro-domain trust evaluation attribute factor ψ_2 using the following equation:

$$\psi_2 = \xi(\Delta t)\,\varphi_2(n-1) \qquad (37)$$

$\xi(\Delta t)$ is the time-decaying function and $\varphi_2(n)$ is the interaction feedback factor discussed next.

Time-Decaying Function: It is represented as ξ and is defined over the domain time. It has values in the range [0,1] and is calculated as:

$\Delta(t) = |tp - ts|$ is the time interval, where tp refers to the present time and ts refers to the initiatory time, and

l is an integer that determines the decay speed of comprehensive interaction degree within the time interval $\Delta(t)$.

Interaction Feedback Factor: It is represented as $\varphi_2(n)$ and its value lies between 0 and 1. It indicates the level of last n times of interaction among two nodes and is computed automatically after the nth transaction is completed, using the following function (Box 2).

Where, k = parameter that adjusts $\varphi_2(n)$ and enables it to be of reasonable size,

λ = punishment factor determined by trustor based on its contentment from the interaction. Its value lies in the range [0,1] and is used to punish the trustee that is unreliable or provides low-quality services immediately.

$\Delta(t)$ = time interval between ending times of two adjoining transactions/interactions.

$F(n)$ = network flow created by n^{th} transaction.

Direct Trust Expression: The assessment of a trustee's trustworthiness in both the inter-domain and intro-domain direct trust relations is done using Trust Valuation Set or Trust Valuation Vector. Its value is computed using membership function.

Box 2.

$$\varphi_2(n) = \begin{cases} \lambda \cdot \dfrac{F(1)}{B(1) \cdot t(1)} \cdot \dfrac{S(1)}{T(1)}, & \text{if } n = 1, \\[4mm] \lambda \cdot \left[(1 - \xi(\Delta t)) \cdot \left(\dfrac{F(n-1)}{B(n-1) \cdot t(n-1)} \cdot \dfrac{S(n-1)}{T(n-1)} \right)^{\frac{1}{k}} \right. \\[4mm] \left. + \xi(\Delta t) \cdot \left(\dfrac{Fa(n)}{B(n) \cdot t(n)} \cdot \dfrac{S(n)}{T(n)} \right)^{\frac{1}{k}} \right] & (k \neq 0), \text{ if } n \in \{2, 3, ...\} \end{cases} \qquad (39)$$

This set indicates the extent to which the trustor has faith on the trustee at each trust level. The membership function is defined as:

Let X be the universe of discourse consisting of all entities in the cloud network and A be the mapping from X to the interval [0,1] as shown below:

$$A : X \rightarrow [0,1], \quad x \mapsto \mu_A(x) \in [0,1]$$

Then, $A = \{(x, \mu_A(x)) \mid x \in X\}$ is known as the fuzzy subset on X and $\mu_A(x)$ is known as the membership function of A. All the fuzzy subsets on X are represented using natural language and each fuzzy subset defines a trust set having a corresponding trust degree.

The trust of x_0 on x_l where $x_i \in X$, can be represented using the trust evaluation vector $V = \{v_0, v_1, ..., v_m\}$. Here, each value v_j is the membership degree of trustee x_i in the trust subset T_i, which can be determined by using ψ_1 or ψ_2 with the already defined membership functions. These membership functions are shown in Table 2:

Recommended Trust Relation: Recommended trust relationship exists only between two non-adjacent nodes. This relationship is developed between an initial node (IN) and a terminal node (TN). The IN is the one which initiates the establishment of a recommended trust relation and the TN is the ultimate entity on which trust is being done. This relation is created on the basis of indirect interaction experience and knowledge

Table 2. Membership functions (Sun et al., 2011)

Natural Language Name	Membership Function
Complete Trust	$\mu_{T1}(x) = \begin{cases} 0, & if\ x = 1, \\ e^{-\frac{x^q}{p}}, & if\ 0 \leq x < 1 \end{cases}$
Relative Trust	$\mu_{T2}(x) = \begin{cases} 0, & if\ x = 0,1\ , \\ e^{-\frac{(x-0.25)^q}{p}}, & if\ 0 < x < 1 \end{cases}$
Uncertainty	$\mu_{T3}(x) = \begin{cases} 0, & if\ x = 0,1\ , \\ e^{-\frac{(x-0.5)^q}{p}}, & if\ 0 < x < 1 \end{cases}$
Relative Distrust	$\mu_{T4}(x) = \begin{cases} 0, & if\ x = 0,1\ , \\ e^{-\frac{(x-0.75)^q}{p}}, & if\ 0 < x < 1 \end{cases}$
Complete Distrust	$\mu_{T5}(x) = \begin{cases} 0, & if\ x = 0, \\ e^{-\frac{(x-1)^q}{p}}, & if\ 0 < x \leq 1 \end{cases}$

The membership degrees of these five fuzzy subsets can be calculated after bringing in the trust evaluation attribute factor. These values can then be combined to form a trust evaluation set.

given to IN by the middle nodes (MNs) about the TN. The recommended trust relation has the following features:

- Only the middle node that is the last one in the recommended trust chain can give recommendation information about the terminal node.
- For simplicity, middle nodes and the initial node enquire only one of their adjoining nodes in the network.

Trust Chain: It is a way to express the oriented and ordered Recommended and Direct trust relations. A trust chain is depicted in the Figure 19:

Connection and Incorporation of Trust: Work done by Zadeh in the field of fuzzy logic is internationally acclaimed and most researchers use the operators defined by Zadeh in their work related to fuzzy logic. Most famous of these operators are AND and OR, represented as $\wedge$ and $\vee$ respectively. However, these operators have certain drawbacks in terms of information loss, data loss and inaccurate calculations. So in this model, the authors have used more general fuzzy operators known as Einstein operators. Suppose we have two trust evaluation sets $V_i = \{x_1, x_2, ..., x_k, ...,x_n\}$ and $V_j = \{y_1, y_2, ..., y_k, ..., y_n\}$. The Einstein operators on these sets can be defined as:

$$x_k \ \varepsilon \bullet \ y_k = \frac{x_k y_k}{1+(1-x_k)(1-y_k)},$$
$$x_k \ \varepsilon + \ y_k = \frac{x_k + y_k}{1+x_k y_k} \tag{40}$$

Consider a specific chain out of a total of n trust chains. Let this chain be m^{th} trust chain. Suppose, the IN i i.e. the cloud user wants to calculate the trust valuation set of TN j i.e. the cloud service provider. When IN successfully receives all the trust evaluation sets sent by the nodes on this m^{th} trust chain, it will calculate the $V_{i,j}(m)$ by using the following equation:

$$V_{i,j}(m) =$$
$$V_{i,i+1}(m) \ \varepsilon \bullet \ V_{i+1,i+2}(m) - - - V_{k,k+1}(m) \ \varepsilon \bullet$$
$$V_{k+1,k+2}(m) - - - V_{j-3,j-2}(m) \ \varepsilon \bullet V_{j-2,j-1}(m),$$
$$i \le k \le j-3 \tag{41}$$

Since it is possible for the middle nodes to transmit falsified recommendation information about the provider to the cloud user for their own vested interests, the credibility of the trust evaluation sets received from the trust chains in which such malicious nodes are located should be reduced. Such deceitful behaviour can be revealed using trust evaluation similarity. There are three popular methods to measure similarity – cosine similarity, adjusted cosine similarity and correlation similarity. For this model, correlation similarity has been used. So, trust evaluation similarity, $sim(i,j)$, of the two sets V_i and V_j about the TN from i^{th} and j^{th} chain is calculated using the equation given in Box 3.

If there are in total n trust chains between the IN and TN, then the trust evaluation set V_i about TN coming from i^{th} chain will be compared on the basis of similarity with the trust evaluation sets about TN coming from the rest $n-1$ chains, and finally it will be adjusted as follows:

$$V(i)^* = \frac{\sum_{k=1}^{m} sim\ (i,k)\ V(i)}{\sum_{k=1}^{m} sim\ (i,k)} \tag{43}$$

Suppose that there are n trust chains between IN (user) and TN (provider). After receiving trust evaluation sets about TN from all the n trust chains, IN can calculate comprehensive trust evaluation set V about TN j by using:

$$V = V(1)^* \ \varepsilon + V(2)^* - - - - - \varepsilon + V(n)^* \tag{44}$$

Box 3.

$$sim(i,j) = \begin{cases} 1 - \dfrac{1}{n}\sum_{k=1}^{n} |\, x_k - y_k \,|, \; if \; \forall x_k = \dfrac{1}{n}\sum_{k=1}^{n} x_k \; or \; \forall y_k = \dfrac{1}{n}\sum_{k=1}^{n} y_k, \\[3em] \dfrac{\displaystyle\sum_{k=1}^{n}\left(x_k - \dfrac{1}{n}\sum_{k=1}^{n} x_k \right) \cdot \left(y_k - \dfrac{1}{n}\sum_{k=1}^{n} y_k \right)}{\sqrt{\displaystyle\sum_{k=1}^{n}\left(x_k - \dfrac{1}{n}\sum_{k=1}^{n} x_k \right)^2} \cdot \sqrt{\displaystyle\sum_{k=1}^{n}\left(y_k - \dfrac{1}{n}\sum_{k=1}^{n} y_k \right)^2}}, \; otherwise \end{cases} \tag{42}$$

Through experiments, the TMFC model has proved to ensure high trust accuracy rate even when the percentage of malicious middle nodes is as high as 55%.

Trust Fuzzy Comprehensive Evaluation

Li et al. (2012) have proposed a new transaction framework for cloud based on trust and a new algorithm known as Cloud Service Discovery Algorithm based on fuzzy comprehensive evaluation of trust.

Trust Based Transaction Framework

The transaction framework depicted in Figure 20 is divided into two subsystems: Service Trust Subsystem and User Trust Subsystem.

Service Trust Subsystem: It consists of Service Trust Domains wherein exist different service providers and agents. Outside these domains is the Cloud Information Service Center, abbreviated as CISC. CISC is a trusted third party which acts as a trust management center for all the providers.

Algorithm 1. TMFC Algorithm

```
Input: all inter-domain and intro-domain direct trust evaluation attributes'
values.
Output: comprehensive trust evaluation set V.
Begin:
Set weights for the factors in Wd(I);
Compute ψ₁ by Eq. (36);
Compute ξ by Eq. (38);
Compute ψ₂ by Eq. (37);
Establish trust levels and their membership functions.
Find out all the direct trust evaluation sets;
For the mᵗʰ (1 ≤ m ≤ n) trust chain do
    Compute the trust evaluation set of mᵗʰ trust chain by Eq. (41);
    Compute the trust evaluation similarity by Eq. (42);
    Find out the adjusted trust evaluation set by Eq. (43);
Compute the comprehensive trust evaluation set by Eq. (44);
End
```

Figure 20. Trust based transaction framework

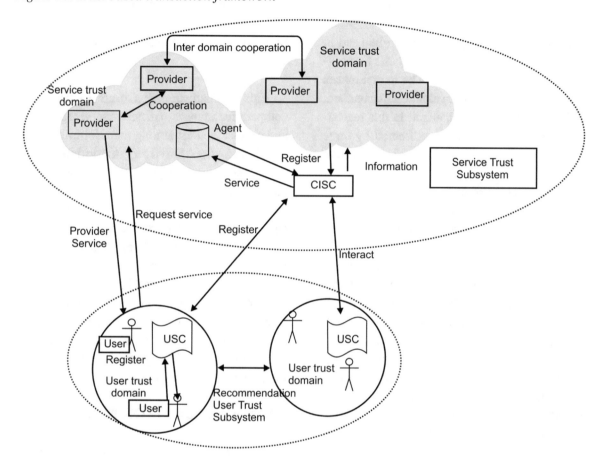

User Trust Subsystem: It consists of User Trust Domains wherein exist users and User Service Center (USC).

CISC and USC can exchange data with each other. The transactions are also differentiated into two types, namely, inner domain transactions and cross domain transactions. Different strategies are used for evaluating trust for both types of interactions. The transactions occurring between a user and a provider or coordination between providers in different domains are known as cross-domain transactions. When a user wishes to transact with a provider, it first investigates the transaction history with the provider. If the efficacious number in the trade context is greater than the direct trust threshold, then the direct trust in the local trust table is used for making trust decision, else trust

recommendation request is broadcast within the user's recommendation set and integrated trust value in combination with the direct trust value is computed. This is the process used for evaluation of trust in cross-domain transactions. The process followed for inner domain transactions is different. When a user takes an initiative to find a transaction partner on its own, it will first scan its local trust records and select the partner with greatest direct trust. In the passive trade context, a user will agree to deal with the selected partner as long as it is not in the transaction refusing list. After the transaction, the direct trust score will be computed and updated. If the partner turns out to be unreliable, then the user will add it into the transaction refusing list and will refrain from dealing with it in future.

Cloud Service Discovery Process

Cloud Service Discovery model can be used in order to satisfy the cloud users' requests for trustworthy and credible services. The model makes use of the following trust evaluation mechanism.

Trust Evaluation Mechanism: In this mechanism, Cloud Providers are represented by three attributes as $CP = \{pID, pName, pTrust\}$ where,

pID denotes the provider's unique ID,
$pName$ denotes the provider's name, and
$pTrust$ denotes the service's trust value.

The mechanism considers trust to be sensitive to transaction context. In other words, when different services are provided by the same provider, there may be variations in the quality and reliability of the services. So, in order to describe trust more accurately, a multi-dimensional vector is used to represent $pTrust$. The model is explained by considering three services – computation service, network transmission service and storage service. Hence, $pTrust$ is represented as $pTrust = \{cpuT, bwT, storeT\}$ where,

$cpuT$ = computation trust,
bwT = network trust, and
$storeT$ = storage trust

To solve complicated things, Fuzzy Comprehensive Evaluation (FCE) method is very efficacious. Since cloud services involve multiple facets, the problem of assessing trust of cloud providers can aptly be solved using comprehensive evaluation. So, comprehensive trust evaluation is done based on FCE as follows:

Step 1: Determine the set of evaluation factors E.
Step 2: Establish the weight vectors W. The model should be flexible enough to allow users to set different weights for different factors according to their requirements.
Step 3: Create judgement set J.

Step 4: Based on the membership functions, create judgement matrix M.
Step 5: Compute comprehensive evaluation result $R = W \times M$.

This mechanism helps users to perform a comparative analysis of different service providers and choose the best among them for transaction.

Cloud Service Discovery Algorithm:

All the concepts discussed above are used in the algorithm to select the best provider out of many. The algorithm uses multi-dimensional trust vector to represent a provider's trustworthiness providing a variety of services. Then FCE method is used to sort services based on their trust value. The algorithm is given in Figure 21.

Through experiments, this model has proved to be more successful in trust accuracy and transaction success rates than simple behaviour feedback model and domain based model when number of malicious nodes increases.

Fuzzy Modified VIKOR Method

Alabool and Mahmood (2013) have developed a model for selecting a Cloud Infrastructure Service (CIS) based on its trust value. The model employs a group decision making approach based on multiple criteria using a hybrid of fuzzy sets and modified VIKOR method. Deciding which CIS is trustworthy is an onerous task. It requires two components:

- Understanding the main factors that impact the trustworthiness of a CIS through a trust quality model.
- Developing a method for the trust evaluation of CIS.

With the exponential growth of cloud computing and the number of Cloud Service Providers (CSPs), it has become difficult for both the CSPs and the CSRs (Cloud Service Requesters) to choose a CIS which can be trusted. This model,

Figure 21. Cloud service discovery algorithm (Li et al., 2012)

```
Cloud Service Discovery Algorithm.

CServDiscover (pList, serviceType)
{`
Boolean found = false;
providerList choseproviders;
choseproviders = (serviceType, plist);
/*Trust Fuzzy comprehensive evaluate on providers in the list and return the credible
provider list in their comprehensive trust value descending order */

While (!found&choseproviders.iterator().hasNext())
        {
        Provider p = (choseprovdiers) iter.next();
        Found = AskForService(p, service Type);
        /*Send service request to the chosen provider */
        }
    }
Trust Fuzzy Evaluation Algorithm.

providerList PFuzzyJudge (serviceType, plist)
{
Vector a = setWeightVector(serviceType);
//set weight vector according to request service type
Matrix r = setTrustJudgeMatrix(plist);
/*construct trust judgment matrix according to weight vector */

List idList = generateJudgeResult(a,r);
/*calculate comprehensive evaluation result based on the weighted mean method and
return the credible providers id in the trust value descending order */
providerList resultList = Sort(plist, idList);
/*sort plist according to the comprehensive avaluation result and return the sorted list */
}
```

however, helps both parties to assess the trust degree of a CIS. CSRs can use this information to select a trustworthy CIS, whereas, CSPs can use this information to further improve their services.

Modified VIKOR method:

VIKOR method is considered as one of the best methods for reaching an optimized and compromise solution. It can be used for making decisions from a set of conflicting alternatives based on multiple criteria. These criteria can be further conflicting or non-commensurable. VIKOR sorts the alternatives based on degree of closeness to the ideal solution.

The VIKOR method uses a measure known as aggregating function (L_p) to deal with multiple criteria. The alternatives are represented as A_i. The degree of closeness between the ideal solution and an alternative (L_p^j) can be calculated as:

$$L_p^j = \left\{ \sum_{i=1}^{n} \left[\frac{W_i \left(F_i^* - F_{ij} \right)}{F_i^* - F_i^-} \right]^p \right\}^{1/p} \tag{45}$$

$1 \leq p \leq \infty \; ; \; j = 1, 2, \ldots, J$

Where, J = total number of alternatives

F_{ij} = evaluation result of criteria *i* for alternative A_j

VIKOR uses two measurements known as Concordance (S_j) and Discordance (Q_j), which are calculated as follows:

$$L_j^{p=1} = S_j = \sum_{i=1}^{n} \left[\frac{W_i\,(F_i^* - F_{ij})}{F_i^* - F_i^-} \right] \qquad (46)$$

for $j = 1, 2, \ldots, m$

$$L_j^{p=\infty} = Q_j = \left\{ Max_i \left[\frac{W_i\,(F_i^* - F_{ij})}{F_i^* - F_i^-} \right] \right\} \qquad (47)$$

for $j = 1, 2, \ldots, m$

'Concordance' refers to matching between CSR requirements and CIS features and 'Discordance' refers to mismatching between the same. These are the ways through which various CSP alternatives are ranked by numerous methods.

VIKOR index F_j is calculated using concordance and discordance values alongwith the weights. There are two types of weights used. One is Criteria weight (W_i) and the other is Maximum group utility weight (v). W_i represents the importance of the relative criteria whereas v represents the weight of largest group's usefulness value. F_j is then calculated as:

$$F_j = v \left[\frac{(S_j - S^*)}{(S^- - S^*)} \right] + (1-v) \left[\frac{(Q_j - Q^*)}{(Q^- - Q^*)} \right] \qquad (48)$$

Where, $S^* = \min_j S_j$,

$S^- = \max_j S_j$,

$Q^* = \min_j Q_j$,

$Q^- = \max_j Q_j$

$\min_j S_j$ denotes the best alternative providing maximum group usefulness for the 'most' and $\min_j Q_j$ represents the minimum of individual useless for the 'opponents'. S^* and Q^* are known as the positive-ideal values, and, S^- and Q^- are known as the negative-ideal values.

The traditional VIKOR method and the modified VIKOR method can be differentiated on the fact that the values of performance deviations that are observed between the status quo and the ideal point cannot be specified by the traditional VIKOR method. Because of this reason:

- For deriving absolute relations on index values, $S^* = 0$, $S^- = 1$; $Q^* = 0$, $Q^- = 1$ From Eq. (48) given above, we can say that, if $v > 0.5$ then S is more emphasised than Q and if $v < 0.5$ then Q is more emphasised than S.
- $v = 1$ represents an approach for peak group usefulness whereas $v = 0$ represents an approach for least individual regret.

Removing the weights (W_i) from Eq. (47) and using Eq. (48), the modified indices can be calculated as follows:

$$Q_j^{\text{mod}} = \left\{ Max_i \left[\frac{(F_i^* - F_{ij})}{F_i^* - F_i^-} \right] \right\} \qquad (49)$$

for $j = 1, 2, ..., m$

$$F_j^{\mathrm{mod}} = $$
$$v[(S_j - 0)/(1 - 0)] + (1 - v)[(Q_j - 0)/(1 - 0)]$$
$$(50)$$

F_j^{mod} can be simplified as:

$$F_j^{\mathrm{mod}} = v(S_j) + (1 - v)Q_j \qquad (51)$$

Finally, the following two constraints are used to improvise the alternatives for a compromise solution:

Constraint 1: Admissible advantage

$$F(CIS^{(2)}) - F(CIS^{(1)}) \geq R \qquad (52)$$

where, $CIS^{(1)}$ = the alternative 1,

$CIS^{(2)}$ = the alternative 2

R^{mod} is represented as:

$$R^{\mathrm{mod}} = (Max_j F_j^{\mathrm{mod}} - Min_j F_j^{\mathrm{mod}})/(m - 1) \qquad (53)$$

where, m = total number of alternatives

Constraint 2: Admissible decision making stability

$CIS^{(1)}$ is best-ranked in S_j or/and Q_j^{mod} tables based on F_j^{mod} ranking.

Only if both these constraints are satisfied by $CIS^{(1)}$, it can be called the compromise solution. Otherwise, following measures are used to arrive at a compromise solution:

If constraint 1 is not satisfied, then $(CIS^{(1)}, CIS^{(2)}, ..., CIS^{(e)})$ will be the compromise solution.

If constraint 2 is not satisfied, then $CIS^{(1)}, CIS^{(2)}$ will be the compromise solution.

Fuzzy modified VIKOR method for cloud service selection:

The modified VIKOR method is combined with fuzzy logic to help evaluate the trustworthiness of a CIS. This helps:

- The CSRs to choose a trustworthy CIS from a set of alternatives.
- The CSPs to improve their CIS in order to reach the ideal trust level.

The model consists of nine steps which are explained below:

Step 1: Recognise
  ○ A set of M alternatives of CIS: CIS = $\left\{CIS_1, CIS_2, ..., CIS_m\right\}$
  ○ A set of N criteria for evaluating trust of CIS: C = $\left\{C_1, C_2, ..., C_n\right\}$
  ○ A set of P decision makers who evaluate the trust degree of CIS: DM = $\{DM_1, DM_2, ..., DM_p\}$
  ○ A set of fuzzy rating of CIS_i and C_j where $x = 1, 2, ..., m$ and $y = 1, 2, ..., n$:

$$L = \{l_{ij}, \ i = 1, 2, ..., m \ ; \ j = 1, 2, ..., n\}$$

Step 2: Since fuzzy logic involves use of simple linguistic variables, in this step the linguistic variables and the appropriate membership functions are defined.

The authors have used the linguistic variables shown in Table 3 for weights of criteria:

Table 4 shows the linguistic variables for the fuzzy rates of alternatives against criteria:

Step 3: In this step, the importance weight for each criteria and fuzzy rates of alternatives are calculated. Let the fuzzy rating of ith

Table 3. Illustrating weights of criteria using linguistic variables (Alabool and Mahmood, 2013)

Linguistic Variables	Fuzzy Number
Very Low	(0.00,0.00,0.25)
Low	(0.00,0.25,0.50)
Medium	(0.25,0.50,0.75)
High	(0.50,0.75,1.00)
Very High	(0.75,1.00,1.00)

Table 4. Illustrating fuzzy rates for alternatives against criteria using linguistic variables (Alabool and Mahmood, 2013)

Linguistic Variables	Fuzzy Number
Worst	(0.00,0.00,2.50)
Poor	(0.00,2.50,5.00)
Fair	(2.50,5.00,7.50)
Good	(5.00,7.50,10.00)
Best	(7.50,10.0,10.0)

alternative against j^{th} criteria for k^{th} decision maker be $l_{ijk} = \left(l_{ijk1}, l_{ijk2}, l_{ijk3}\right)$ and the importance weight of jth criteria given by k^{th} decision maker be $w_{ijk} = \left(w_{ijk1}, w_{ijk2}, w_{ijk3}\right)$. These values can be calculated as follows:

$$w_j = \frac{1}{k} \sum_{k=1}^{k} [w_{jk}] \qquad (54)$$

$$l_{ij} = \frac{1}{k} \sum_{k=1}^{k} [l_{ijk}] \qquad (55)$$

Using both these values, a decision making matrix is built which is then used to solve the CIS selection problem.

$$D = \begin{bmatrix} l_{11} & l_{12} & \cdots & l_{1n} \\ l_{21} & l_{22} & \cdots & l_{2n} \\ \vdots & \vdots & \ddots & \vdots \\ l_{m1} & l_{m2} & \cdots & l_{mn} \end{bmatrix}, W = \begin{bmatrix} w_1 \\ w_2 \\ \vdots \\ w_n \end{bmatrix} \qquad (56)$$

Step 4: Defuzzification is performed using the Center of Area (CoA) method to defuzzify the two matrices and arrive at a crisp value by using the equation given below:

$$\frac{\int \mu(x) \cdot x dx}{\int \mu(x) dx} \qquad (57)$$

The steps explained next are used to find the ranking index using VIKOR:

Step 5: For all the criteria, calculate the top F_i^* values and the least F_i^- values, where $i = 1,2, ..., n$ and n is the total number of criteria. Assume the ith criteria represents a benefit, then

$$F_i^* = \max_i F_{ij} \qquad (58)$$

$$F_i^- = \min_i F_{ij} \qquad (59)$$

Step 6: Calculate the values of concordance S_j using Eq. (46) and discordance Q_j^{mod} using Eq. (49) for alternative A_j.

Step 7: Compute F_j^{mod} i.e. the VIKOR index using Eq. (51)

Step 8: In this step, alternatives are ranked and sorted based on the S_j, Q_j^{mod} and F_j^{mod} values using the increasing order strategy. These results are then classified into three tables.

Step 9: Finally, the alternatives for the compromise solution will be improved using the two constraints explained previously.

Hierarchical Fuzzy Inference System for Service Selection

Figure 22 shows the general architecture of the system proposed by Qu and Buyya (2014).

It consists of two major steps:

1) Using fuzzy membership functions to represent a user's perceptions of different QoS requirements.
2) The service deployment process through submission of requirements, discovery of service, evaluation of trust, service selection and deployment.

The major components of the system are:

Web Interface: Users and cloud brokers submit their service requirements and requests through the web interface. They also provide their perceptions of the requirements through this component.

It works with the help of perception manager and request manager and is linked to the perception database.

Service Discovery: This component includes service matchmaker and compatibility checker. It is responsible for retrieving services from the IaaS service repository in accordance with the user's requirements and filtering out services that are incompatible with the user's policies or platforms.

Trust Evaluation Service: It is the main component of the system and includes QoS evaluator, rule generator and fuzzy inference engine. It measures the trustworthiness of the services selected by the service discovery component based on the user's requirements and the past benchmark data of the services. It produces a list of services alongwith their trust values as output. The users and brokers can then select a service with maximum trust value meeting their specifications.

Figure 22. Architecture of hierarchical fuzzy inference system

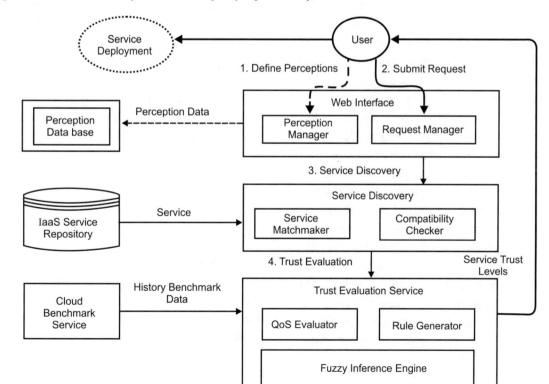

Cloud Benchmark Service: This service carries out the task of monitoring different clouds' performances for various QoS parameters through benchmark applications run on virtual machines located dynamically. The results of these tests are then made open to the public. Through these results, users and brokers can easily compare the services of various cloud service providers on the basis of different QoS parameters.

Capturing Requirements and Preferences:

Requirements: In order to search for compatible services, the users must first submit their requirements and preferences to the system. The system allows two types of requirements to be defined - numerical requirements and linguistic requirements. The system even allows for a combination of both these types of requirements to be submitted to the system. Numerical requirements are the one in which users submit the numerical values of different parameters and expect the service to provide values greater than the submitted values during operation. Linguistic requirements, on the other hand, are the ones in which users submit the values of parameters in natural language form such as high, medium, low etc. These values are described using fuzzy linguistic descriptors and since these involve natural language, users find these requirements easy to describe.

QoS parameters/attributes: Various QoS parameters used include performance (CPU and memory), assurance, elasticity, security, cost etc. Users can also add the parameters specific to their concern. The leaf parameters can further be classified into dynamic and static attributes. Dynamic attributes are the ones which vary with performance. Examples of these are CPU performance, memory performance, disk performance, network performance, availability, failure rate etc. Static attributes are the ones whose performances can be considered static compared to the dynamic attributes. Examples of static attributes are security, cost etc.

QoS inputs and membership functions: For the purpose of trust evaluation, the system first con-

tacts the cloud benchmark service for benchmark results and then analyses these results to deduce QoS inputs for the hierarchical fuzzy inference system depending upon the requirements of the user. The following discussion explains the process of retrieving benchmark results and then deriving QoS inputs for both the linguistic requirements and numerical requirements.

a) Retrieving benchmark results: Since benchmark results are used for trust evaluation, these results should be retrieved very carefully taking into account factors such as expected running time of virtual machines and startup time of virtual machine. If a user wishes to deploy a virtual machine on Tuesday from 10 AM to 4 PM, then the benchmark results recorded on nearest Tuesday or weekday within the same time 10 AM to 4 PM should be retrieved. Also, if a virtual machine is to be used for a long time, then results pertaining to large time window should be retrieved and if a virtual machine is to be used for short span of time, then results pertaining to a small time window should be retrieved.

b) Numerical Requirements: in case of numerical requirements, the system computes the QoS inputs of the ith service for j^{th} parameter or attribute using the following equation:

$$p_{i,j} = \frac{n^{satisfy_{i,j}}}{n^{total_{i,j}}} \qquad (60)$$

The numerator in the above equation represents the number of benchmark results satisfying the numerical requirements and the denominator represents the total number of retrieved benchmark results.

c) Linguistic requirements: For these requirements, the system finds the statistical indicators of benchmark results as the QoS inputs. The examples of indicators are mean, median etc. In this model, triangular membership functions have been used to represent linguistic requirements. For immature users, the system provides an option of using default values for each parameter.

Modeling preferences: Preferences are modelled at two levels in the system – attribute level and requirement level. At attribute level, users can indicate their preferences for important attributes by assigning them higher values, for example, high for CPU and memory, and low for disk. At the requirement level, users can select an importance level to be assigned to their different requirements. These importance levels can be very important, important, neutral, unimportant, very unimportant. For a user who considers security to be most important and is willing to sacrifice on performance requirement, the importance level attached to the security requirement can be very important, whereas the level attached to the per-

formance requirement can be unimportant. This aspect is implemented in the system through the use of hedges, which are functions that modify the original membership function. The importance levels for the two types of requirements can be defined as follows:

$$Numerical : d = \begin{cases} satisfactory \ (x)^{a_i} \\ unsatisfactory \ (x)^{\frac{1}{a_i}} \end{cases}$$

$$(61)$$

$$Linguistic : d = \begin{cases} f(x)^{a_i} & if \ x \le peak \\ f(x)^{\frac{1}{a_i}} & if \ x > peak \end{cases} \quad (62)$$

Where, *satisfactory(x)* and *unsatisfactory(x)* are the membership functions shown in Figure 23 and *f(x)* is a triangular membership function shown in Figure 24, peak is the value of *x* at its

Figure 23. Numerical requirements
(Qu and Buyya, 2014)

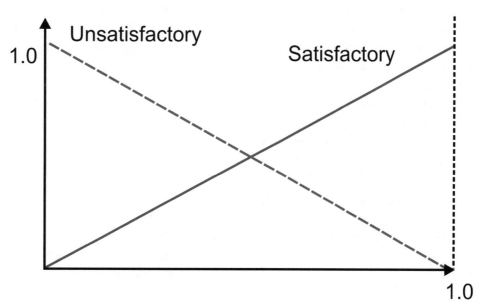

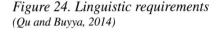

Figure 24. Linguistic requirements
(Qu and Buyya, 2014)

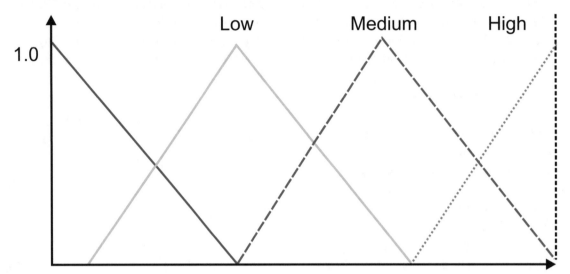

maximum membership point and a_i is the importance coefficient of the ith importance level.

The importance levels with importance coefficients are given in Table 5:

Working of the Hierarchical Fuzzy Inference System: Figure 25 shows the overall system which consists of three types of inference modules. One is higher level inference module for non-leaf attributes. The inputs to these modules are the corresponding outputs of sub-inference modules. For leaf attributes, there are two modules – linguistic inference module and numerical inference module, depending on whether the requirements are linguistic or numerical.

The input membership functions for higher level inference modules are the membership functions depicted in Figure 23. For leaf level modules, the input membership functions used

are discussed in the section 'Capturing requirements and preferences'. The output membership functions for all the modules are the ones shown in Figure 23. According to the generated hierarchy of attributes, the system creates the hierarchical fuzzy inference system for each query dynamically.

All inference modules make use of the same inference engine. The system uses 'Product' for AND operator, 'Max' for OR and Aggregation operator, and 'Center of Maxima' as the defuzzification method. Center of Maxima computes the crisp output value t (trust) using the following formula:

$$t = \frac{\sum_{i=1}^{n} x_i \mu_i}{\sum_{i=1}^{n} \mu_i} \qquad (63)$$

Where, n = membership functions of each output variable,

x_i = value of ith membership function at maximum membership point, and

μ_i = membership degree for i^{th} membership function

Table 5. Importance levels (Qu and Buyya, 2014)

Importance Level	Importance Coefficient
Very Important	½
Important	2/3
Neutral	1
Unimportant	3/2
Very Unimportant	2

Figure 25. Overview of hierarchical fuzzy inference mechanism

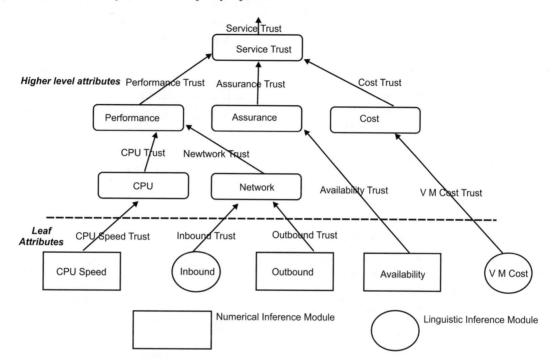

If-Then Rules: Depending upon the user requirements and the rule generation strategy used, the system automatically creates fuzzy rules for each inference module. This system uses pessimistic strategy in which the output trust value is satisfactory only if all the input factors are satisfactory. Rules generated for the three types of modules are explained below:

a) Higher level inference modules: The trust values of the corresponding sub-attributes act as input to these modules. Assume attribute D consists of sub-attributes E and F. Then, the rules generated will be:

R1: If Etrust is satisfactory AND Ftrust is satisfactory, then Dtrust is satisfactory

R2: If Etrust is not_satisfactory OR Ftrust is not_satisfactory, then Dtrust is not_satisfactory

b) Numerical inference modules: The input to this module is the value that is achieved from analysing benchmark results. Assume user defines its requirements for attribute D

in numerical terms, then the rules generate will be:

R3: If D is (importance level) satisfactory, then Dtrust is satisfactory

R4: If D is (importance level) not_satisfactory, then Dtrust is not_satisfactory

c) Linguistic inference modules: The input to this module is also the single value that is achieved after analysing benchmark results. Assume user defines its requirements for attribute D in linguistic terms, then rules generated will be:

R5: If D is atleast (importance level) medium, then Dtrust is satisfactory

R6: If D is atmost (importance level) low, then Dtrust is not_satisfactory

'atleast' and 'atmost' in the above rules are hedges that are defined as follows:

$$d_{atleast} = \begin{cases} f(x) & if \ x \leq peak \\ 1 & if \ x > peak \end{cases} \qquad (64)$$

$$d_{atmost} = \begin{cases} 1 & if \ x \le peak \\ f(x) & if \ x > peak \end{cases} \quad (65)$$

Where, peak is the *x* value at the maximum membership point of the membership function.

This model has proved to be time efficient and linearly scalable through experiments. Moreover, it has been successful in selecting the best service out of a number of alternatives depending on the user requirements and can be used by both the

experienced and inexperienced users because of the use of linguistic variables and option of using default settings for attributes.

COMPARISON OF DIFFERENT MODELS

Table 6 shows a brief comparison of all the models discussed in this chapter.

Table 6. Comparison of different models

Name of Model	Year	Strengths	Weaknesses	Environment
SPORAS	2000	Reputation is updated recursively. Very high reputations held previously have little impact on reputation updates in the future. While evaluating the new reputation, it takes into account the most recent ratings and ignores the old ones. Until a specific confidence level is attained, the modification applied to the reputation rating keeps on reducing with an increase in the number of ratings considered for reputation assessment. Once the confidence level is achieved, modification becomes constant. Reliability of reputations is also measured.	Model treats all new users very unfavourably. The optimum performance of such model is solely dependent on the linguistic fuzzy sets received and fed as input. The model lacks dealing with security issues in communication, in case of a newcomer. As the system updates value based on remembrance from past variable instances, constant invariable behaviour of other merchants introduces distorting factors predictions about malicious one	Loosely Connected Communities
REGRET	2001	Freshness of information is given more importance by giving more weightage to recent ratings as compared to older ratings. Measures reliability of estimations. After a minimum threshold of experiences, further increase in the number of interactions does not increase reliability.	The model is mainly dependent on peer reviews and opinions which are subject to individual preferences and objections. In real world scenario, presence of more than one malignant peer is possible wherein peer opinions alone cannot be trusted or relied upon.	Loosely Connected Communities
AFRAS	2003	The similarity level between predictions and outcomes changes the reliability of future predictions. Reputation acts as the means to predict future behaviour. It represents real behaviour and is adapted based on success or failure of predictions. Reliability of reputation is adapted according to the accuracy of predictions. Models remembrance, sociability, susceptibility and shyness into agents' behaviour. Filters out malicious agents.	It shows improvement over REGRET model only when the merchants' behaviour changes significantly i.e. they show 30% variability. Below that level, it has performance nearly similar to that of REGRET.	Multi-Agent Systems
FuzzyTrust	2005	The use of DHT overlay network guarantees fast and secure dissemination of reputation information. Decreased message overhead when global reputation is aggregated. Very efficient in recognising malicious peers. It takes into account the skewed transactions, distinction between small users and super users, bandwidth consumption, and transaction interval.	The model can be further improved by including peer anonymity and secure storage of global reputation.	Peer-to-Peer Systems

continued on following page

Table 6. Continued

Name of Model	Year	Strengths	Weaknesses	Environment
Model incorporating trust, distrust and insufficient trust	2006	System is flexible – system designer can specify the rules. Each agent maintains an interaction window and filters out old interactions after a certain time period. Responsiveness of an agent's trust assessments to the changing environment can be adjusted by adjusting the time interval between entry of interaction in interaction window and its removal.	In absence of a trusted agent, the system uses a trial and hit mechanism citing it as a better option to try and fail rather than abstain from trying. Such approaches are not feasible and acceptable in high priority and sensitive cases.	Multi-Agent Systems
Fuzzy Trust for peer-to-peer based systems	2007	The system considers decay of trust with time. It has the ability to assign different weights to direct trust and reputation. It takes into account the honesty, accuracy and consistency of the peers which recommend about the reputation of other peers.	The system leaves the calculation of local score completely on the local peer itself and makes no effort to model it.	Peer-to-Peer Systems
Trust calculation for IaaS based e-learning system	2011	It has scope for further extension by incorporating additional parameters for evaluating trust. It provides a sound basis for selecting parameters for IaaS-based cloud system. Expert knowledge has been used for selecting parameters affecting the system.	It is Iaas – specific model and mainly focused on e-learning systems. Its deployment to other e-commerce systems is still to be discussed. Only four input factors scalability, availability, security, and usability are considered whereas cases which use additional factors for inputs are not discussed in this model.	Cloud-Computing (e-learning system)
TMFC	2011	The model maintains a high trust accuracy rate even when the number of malicious middle nodes increases. The model is successful in preventing the cheating behaviour of middle nodes.	The model needs further study and evaluation to justify its rationality and practicability.	Cloud-Computing
Trust Fuzzy Comprehens-ive Evaluation	2012	It can be used in large-scale distributed cross-cloud environments. It provides higher value of trust accuracy and transaction success rate, and retains high performance even if number of malicious nodes increases. It classifies the service providers on the basis of the service types provided by them. The developed algorithm is very efficient in quickly finding the credible transaction partners.	The model is still to be inspected upon the attributes and trust degree measurement which can vary depending upon real world simulation conditions. The security demands in a cloud service are yet to be detailed and discussed.	Cloud-Computing
Fuzzy modified VIKOR method	2013	The method solves multiple decision making problems involving conflicting criteria. It helps the CSPs to improve the gaps in their infrastructure. It helps the CSPs to determine how much improvement is needed to reach the desired trust level. It aids the CSPs to price their infrastructure services according to the values of the criteria.	It needs to be extended to include the mismatch that can occur between the user requirements and the service provided by CSPs. Common trust criteria such as integrity, privacy etc have not been included in the model.	Cloud-Computing
Hierarchical Fuzzy Inference System for Service Selection	2014	It takes into account the variations in the performance of cloud services leading to more cost efficiency for users. The model has the provision of balancing the requirements of the users with their budget while selecting a cloud service. The model is quite extensive. It takes into account 11 attributes for trust evaluation. It is linearly scalable and time efficient.	Both evaluation accuracy and quality of ranking show a decrease when number of linguistic requirements increase.	Cloud-Computing

SUMMARY, CONCLUSION, AND FUTURE SCOPE

This chapter discusses the issue of trust calculation using fuzzy logic in distributed as well as cloud environments. For this purpose, first an introduction to cloud computing is provided and the importance of trust is highlighted. Since trust is a complex concept and depends on various facets, it cannot be calculated using classical or Boolean concepts. There are a number of factors to be considered which may make an entity trustworthy to varying degrees. For instance, an entity can be fully trustworthy, somewhat trustworthy, average trustworthy, untrustworthy, completely untrustworthy. Therefore, to model trust, we need various degrees of trust to which entities can be assigned. Consequently, fuzzy logic is the appropriate choice for trust calculation. Keeping this in view, this chapter provides basic introduction to fuzzy logic and its basic concepts. After making the reader familiar with the basic knowledge, this chapter discusses the use of fuzzy logic for trust calculation using various models proposed till date. In addition to cloud computing specific models, models pertaining to other similar environments have also been discussed to provide an opportunity to the readers to understand the power of fuzzy logic and extend it to the field of cloud computing.

Trust calculation using fuzzy logic can be useful in:

- Identification of malicious users in an environment.
- Intrusion detection.
- Selection of the best provider from the alternatives based on its trust value.
- Classification of cloud service providers into various categories depending upon their trustworthiness.

- Can be applied to Mobile Ad-hoc Networks (MANET) also for selecting a route with maximum trust value.

Cloud Computing has a complex architecture. Its architecture varies depending upon the deployment model, i.e. whether it is a private, public or hybrid cloud, as well as on the service model, i.e. SaaS, PaaS or IaaS. An application may use any of these models. Moreover, each client has specific requirements and may calculate trustworthiness depending on the satisfaction of these requirements. This calls for variations of trust calculation method to suit the particular application and client. Additionally, a cloud environment consists of multiple parties. These are cloud broker, cloud auditor, consumer, cloud service provider and cloud carrier. Therefore, calculating trust keeping in mind only one or a few parties would not give a true estimate. Hence, we need to take into account multiple parties involved. Also, information from these sources can be incomplete, vague and uncertain. When this information is aggregated to arrive at a final trust value, the vagueness and uncertainty may increase further. This further reinforces the choice of fuzzy logic for trust calculation.

Future research may be aimed at creating trust calculation models for a particular deployment model or service model, and models incorporating multiple parties for trust evaluation. Selection policies, having their roots in trust calculation system, can be created for the cloud consumers and brokers to enable automation of cloud deployment. Efforts are needed to prevent reputation attacks, since a number of trust evaluation mechanisms rely on the reputation of a peer or agent. Also, some sort of method is needed to prevent collusion between different agents or parties, as such a collusion may lead to fabrication of wrong information.

REFERENCES

Alabool, H. M., & Mahmood, A. K. (2013). Trust-Based Service Selection in Public Cloud Computing Using Fuzzy Modified VIKOR Method. *Australian Journal of Basic and Applied Sciences*, *7*(9), 211–220.

Alhamad, M., Dillon, T., & Chang, E. (2011). A Trust-Evaluation Metric for Cloud applications. *International Journal of Machine Learning and Computing*, *1*(4), 416–421. doi:10.7763/IJMLC.2011.V1.62

Azzedin, F., Ridha, A., & Rizvi, A. (2007). Fuzzy Trust for Peer-to-Peer Based Systems. World Academy of Science,Engineering and Technology, 123-127.

Bai, Y., & Wang, D. (2006). Fundamentals of Fuzzy Logic Control – Fuzzy Sets, Fuzzy Rules and Defuzzifications. In Y. Bai, D. Wang, & H. Zhuang, Advanced Fuzzy Logic Technologies in Industrial Applications (pp. 17-36). Springer London.

Carbo, J., Molina, J., & Davila, J. (2003). Trust Management Through Fuzzy Reputation. *International Journal of Cooperative Information System*, *12*(1), 135–155. doi:10.1142/S0218843003000681

Chakrabarti, A. (2007). Managing Trust in the Grid. In A. Chakrabarti, Grid Computing Security (pp. 218-221). Springer-Verlag Berlin Heidelberg. doi:10.1007/978-3-540-44493-0_10

Chevrie, F., & Guély, F. (1998). *Fuzzy Logic. Cahier Technique no. 191*. France: Groupe Schneider.

Griffiths, N. (2006). A Fuzzy Approach to Reasoning with Trust, Distrust and Insufficient Trust. *Proceedings of the 10th international conference on Cooperative Information Agents*. (pp. 360-374). Springer-Verlag Berlin Heidelberg. doi:10.1007/11839354_26

Li, W., Ping, L., Qiu, Q., & Zhang, Q. (2012). Research on Trust Management Strategies in Cloud Computing Environment. *Journal of Computer Information Systems*, *8*(4), 1757–1763.

MathWorks. (n. d.). *MathWorks*. Retrieved from www.mathworks.in: http://www.mathworks.in/help/fuzzy/fuzzy-inference-process.html

Mendel, J. (1995, March). Fuzzy Logic Systems for Engineering: A Tutorial. *Proceedings of the IEEE*, (pp. 345-377). doi:10.1109/5.364485

Mui, L., Mohtashemi, M., & Halberstadt, A. (2002). A Computational Model of Trust and Reputation. *Proceedings of the 35th Annual Hawaii International Conference on System Sciences*. IEEE. doi:10.1109/HICSS.2002.994181

Qu, C., & Buyya, R. (2014). A Cloud Trust Evaluation System using Hierarchical Fuzzy Inference System for Service Selection. Proceedings of *IEEE 28th International Conference on Advanced Information Networking and Applications*. (pp. 850-857). IEEE Computer Society.

Ruohomaa, S., & Kutvonen, L. (2005). Trust Management Survey. In P. Herrmann, V. Issarny, & S. Shiu, Trust Management. (pp. 77-92). Springer Berlin Heidelberg. doi:10.1007/11429760_6

Sabater, J., & Sierra, C. (2001). Regret: a reputation model for gregarious societies. *Proceedings of the Fifth International Conference on Autonomous Agents*. (pp. 194-195). New York: ACM. doi:10.1145/375735.376110

Song, S., Hwang, K., Zhou, R., & Kwok, Y.-K. (2005). Trusted P2P Transactions with Fuzzy Reputation Aggregation. *IEEE Internet Computing*, *9*(6), 24–34. doi:10.1109/MIC.2005.136

Sun, X., Chang, G., & Li, F. (2011). A Trust Management Model to enhance security of Cloud Computing Environments. *Second International Conference on Networking and Distributed Computing*. (pp. 244-248). IEEE Computer Society. doi:10.1109/ICNDC.2011.56

Zadeh, L. (1965, June). Fuzzy Sets. *Information and Control*, 8(3), 338–353. doi:10.1016/S0019-9958(65)90241-X

Zakaria, G., & Maes, P. (2000). Trust Management through Reputation Mechanisms. In Applied Artificial Intelligence. (pp. 881-907). doi:10.1080/08839510050144868

Zhang, Q., Cheng, L., & Boutaba, R. (2010). Cloud computing: State-of-the-art and Research Challenges. *Journal of Internet Services and Applications*, 1(1), 7–18. doi:10.1007/s13174-010-0007-6

KEY TERMS AND DEFINITIONS

Cloud Computing: Cloud Computing refers to a pool of shared resources which can be accessed by a number of people across the globe through Internet.

Fuzzy Logic: It is a type of logic which deals with incomplete, vague and imprecise information. It uses degrees of truth rather than the precise values of 0 or 1 to arrive at a conclusion.

Multi-Agent Systems: These systems consist of a number of intelligent agents that interact and cooperate with each other in an environment. These agents are autonomous to a certain degree and work together to solve a particular problem.

P2P Systems: P2P stands for Peer-to-Peer systems. Such systems consist of multiple entities with each entity possessing the same capabilities. The system allows each entity to act as a client as well as a server.

Reputation: In the context of computing, reputation refers to the public image or opinion regarding the abilities of an entity.

Trust: Trust between any two parties can be defined as the faith or belief that one party has on the credibility of the other party.

Chapter 8
Advances in Information, Security, Privacy & Ethics:
Use of Cloud Computing For Education

Joseph M. Woodside
Stetson University, USA

ABSTRACT

The future of education lays in the hand of Cloud Computing given the benefits of learning delivery, costs reduction, and innovation. At the same time, the threat of cyber-attacks and security breaches are also mounting for education based organizations and are a prime target given the amount and type of personal information available. This manuscript discusses the cloud security, privacy, and ethical mechanisms required from a teacher, student, and administrator perspective.

INTRODUCTION

The future of education lays in the hand of Cloud Computing, with easy to configure hardware and software components. Utilizing Cloud Computing to their advantage, teachers, administrators, and students are able to deliver content and learn much more effectively within an integrated environment. Given the ability to access anytime anywhere, this enables teachers, administrators and students to target individual needs of students and customize educational delivery. Instead of maintaining all systems separately at each institution and in order to eliminate infrastructure that is dated by 10-20 years at most institutions, Cloud Computing offers the flexibility to delivery current learning technology for the 21st century.

In an effort to reduce costs, increase efficiency and availability, increase enrollment, and innovate with technology many educational institutions are moving to a Cloud Computing model. At the same time, the threat of cyber-attacks and security breaches are also mounting for education based organizations and are a prime target given the amount and type of personal information available. In recent example cases, financial and legal costs are estimated in the millions of dollars with several hundred thousand student and personnel records compromised. In another instance at a state university, some 30,000 student's social security numbers were compromised. It is estimated that many data breaches in education go undetected more than in other industries, and the impact is often realized in the forms of enrollments and endowments.

DOI: 10.4018/978-1-4666-8387-7.ch008

Learning Objectives

This chapter includes the cloud security, privacy, and ethical mechanisms required from a teacher, student, and administrator perspective. For cloud security, the paper outlines the access strategies, service-oriented architectures, and implementation components required to successfully utilize cloud computing in education. For privacy and ethical considerations, several federal laws have been passed to develop a minimum standard for protection of records, and must be developed with flexibility of changing technology and regulations, along with established techniques for privacy preservation.

CLOUD COMPUTING

Cloud computing enables convenient on demand access to an elastic set of shared computing resources. Generally cloud computing is broken into 3 categories of software as a service (SaaS), infrastructure as a service (IaaS) and platform as a service (Paas). SaaS is anticipated to grow the fastest and is typically what users see and interact with directly. The cloud computing market is anticipated to be nearly $200 Billion in 2020 according to Forrester, up from $58 Billion in 2013 (Seeking Alpha, 2015).

SaaS

Software as a Service (SaaS) is software that can be deployed over the Internet and is licensed to customers typically on a pay-for-use model. In some cases a service may be offered at no charge if supported from other sources such as advertisements. SaaS is quickly growing and double-digit growth of 21% is anticipated, with a forecast of $106B in 2016 (Seeking Alpha, 2015).

Cloud computing support SaaS by providing a scalable and virtualized services to the end-user via a simple web browser. A third party manages the computing infrastructure, and provides the software as a service (SaaS). Salesforce.com, Google Apps, Amazon, and Facebook provide have cloud computing offerings. Cloud computing allows organizational to reduce IT capital costs, and buy computing on an as needed basis. There are economies of scale through shared use of systems and resources by multiple customers. Cloud computing reduces the entry barriers by eliminating software distribution and site installation requirements. This also permits organizations to develop new business models and sources of revenue through on demand services (Woodside, 2010).

SOA is used as the access point for all systems through web services and XML is utilized for the data representation. SOA promises improved agility and flexibility for organizations to deliver value-based services to their customers. A service is the application of knowledge for co-creation of value between interacting entities. Service systems involve people, technology, and information. Service science is concerned with understanding service systems, and improve and design services for practical purposes. SOA includes Web service, technology, and infrastructures, and is a process that add value, reuse, information, and overall value to the business. SOA provides a commodization of hardware and software providing organizations with improved architectures and which support IT service flexibility. The SOA approaches are utilized to develop SaaS from IaaS (Woodside, 2010).

IaaS

Infrastructure as a Service (IaaS) is a method for deploying infrastructure such as servers, storage, network and operating systems. These infrastructure services are offered on-demand in a secure environment. This allows customers to utilize resources on-demand instead of purchasing the resources up front. There are a few technologies IaaS utilizes including virtualization, enterprise information integration (EII) and service oriented architecture (SOA). Virtualization creates a virtual version of a computing platform, storage, or network. Unlike SaaS users are responsible for managing the operating system components along with data and middleware (Seeking Alpha, 2015).

Additional technologies supporting IaaS include EII which describes the combination of various sources of data into a unified form without requiring all sources be contained within a data warehouse and also integration complexity reductions. The enterprise unified view must consume data that is available real-time via direct system access, and semantic resolution must occur across systems. Semantic integration or an ontology is a higher level natural language approach to combine differing pieces of information together, and in support of real-time events. A semantic information model can be constructed using Web Ontology Language (OWL) developed by W3C. (Woodside, 2010).

Most real-time architectures consist of the required data sources and a virtual or mediated data schema which is then queried by the end user or application. The systems are typically build on a XML data model and query language. EII reduces data access time, while Enterprise Application Integration (EAI) allows system updates as part of the business process to occur. Both these technologies are utilized as a best practice and combined into the concept of Enterprise Integration (EI). The EI architecture supports heterogeneous data sources such as relational and non-relational databases, flat files, XML, transactional systems, and content management systems. Information transparency is provided through the virtual data access services layer which permits real-time programming services. This architecture adheres to SOA, where business processes exist as distinct services which communicate through known interfaces. This also helps promote code re-use and more flexible IT infrastructure by allowing focus on business logic, and leaving the data tasks to the EII layer (Woodside, 2010).

PaaS

Platform as a Service (PaaS) is generally considered the most complex of the three categories of cloud computing. PaaS is a computing platform which also allows the instantiation of web-based software applications without the added complexity of purchasing and maintaining software and infrastructure. Based on market studies, PaaS is anticipated to reach $44 Billion in revenue by 2020, with 16% of overall cloud services by 2018 (Seeking Alpha, 2015). Some of the advantages to PaaS include efficiency of development and deployment cycles, capacity on demand, portability between platforms, simplified mobile application creation, and increased business value (Mehta, 2015).

Cloud Computing in the Classroom

New generations of touch enabled devices which interact via wireless networks have created a new form of learning also called the Classroom in the Cloud. Students now have an entire computing ecosystem in the palm of their hand through mobile devices such as smartphones, tablets, and laptops. Administration and installation of the infrastructure is easily setup through a wide spectrum wireless network which permits connectivity across locations with resource and Internet access using a specified user key or account. Using a Cloud-based implementation further saves administrative and maintenance costs, allowing platform and service based storage and systems. Distance learning or joint classroom learning is also enabled from local or international partners. Virtual networking, web conferencing, and whiteboard technology can be utilized to display the assignments, homework, or in class materials (Lieberman, 2013).

K-12 Cloud Computing

Cloud computing in K-12 is forecasted to comprise 25% of the technology budget and increase to 35% within the next four years. Educational institutions are leverage cloud computing, which utilizes remotely hosted servers to help reduce technology costs and reduce administration and content management costs. Other key advantages include backup capability to auto-save content to avoid any loss of documents and all accessible through the cloud. Storage also allows use of all types of content and files such as eBooks, apps, music, documents, and photos. Accessibility of information is key with access from anywhere and any device such as portable or mobile devices. The Cloud also allows collaboration between users to update, edit, or exchange ideas simultaneously. Less resources are utilized printing hard copy content, with all documents accessible electronically. Assignments and grading can also all be done online with real-time grading and quizzing (Weaver, 2013).

In a recent example, all Lincoln Nebraska Public Schools students in grades 3-12 will receive Chromebook computing devices at an approximate cost of $300 each, which rely on cloud computing and include word processing, spreadsheet and educational applications in the cloud vs. locally installed on the devices. The plan took approximately four years to date, with a 10-year $50 million plan. This plan is expected to cover nearly 40,000 students and become the largest program in the state. The name of the plan is CLASS for Connected Learning for the Achievement of Students and Staff - Technology Plan. Digital curriculum, assessments, learning goals, student collaboration, research and lab scheduling has driven the need for devices to be rolled out to all students (Anderson, 2015).

Higher Education Cloud Computing

In higher education end-users are also driving the use of the Cloud. In higher education end users or students are digitally focused and mobile adept. In a CDW survey, colleges are moving to the Cloud to increase efficiency, improve employee mobility, increase innovation, improve IT staff availability,

reduce IT costs, and enable new service offerings. For applications, email, word processing, messaging, conference, communication and collaboration tools were commonly moved to the Cloud to increase employee and students productivity (Daley, 2013).

At Fairfield University, a 70 year old private institution with 5000 students, they have transformed their organization and the classroom through technology in order to remain competitive and enroll students. These technologies allow students to engage with campus activities, measure student participation and satisfaction, maintain calendars, and access the centralized portal through their cloud and mobile devices. Staff at the University have enjoyed a cloud system for streamlining various hiring and HR paperwork processes such as W-2s and paystubs. Fairfield University has also introduced an innovative classroom, one that students are looking to more closely replicates the way they use digital tools and cloud-computing outside of the classroom (Castle, 2015).

While cloud computing has many potential applications and benefits to universities, administrators will be required to educate and engage all faculty members on cloud technologies. Some examples of cloud computing at universities include campus mail and learning management system software. Unfortunately some surveys suggest that most universities will not have deployed more advanced cloud computing applications by 2019. In addition, many technology officers are still unclear on the security of clouds and uneasy with trusting third parties or vendors (Florence, 2015).

CYBER ATTACKS IN EDUCATION

Cases and Impact

It is estimated that many data breaches in education go undetected more than in other industries, and the impact is often realized in the forms of enrollments and endowments. Traced to the year 1998, a cyber attack at the University of Maryland has resulted in the loss of 309,079 student and personnel records, and estimated to result in millions of dollars in legal and related costs. The University of Maryland case unfortunately is not an isolated incident. Indiana University had 146,000 student data records vulnerable due to a staff error. North Dakota University identified 291,465 students and 784 employees whose information was on a hacked server (O'Neil, 2014). At Iowa State University, 29,780 student social security numbers were breached with data ranging from 1995-2012 (Jackson, 2014).

On average, data breaches cost $111 per record, similar to the $136 per record found in other industries. Costs to address these breaches include consultants, lawyers, call centers, websites, mailings, identity theft protection, credit checks, security projects, and legal suits. Indiana University has incurred costs of $75000 for their call center, while North Dakota State University incurred costs of $200,000 on identity theft services and call center. Another Maricopa County Community College District incurred costs estimated at $17.1 million after adding in consultant work to fix their security and legal services (O'Neil, 2014).

Methods

The image of the individual hacker in the basement no longer holds true. These individuals are being replaced by increasingly sophisticated governments and organized crime groups which create the biggest threat for education. These groups work 24/7 to compromise sensitive research, student information, and intellectual property. Methods for these attacks include passwords, social media, phishing, smartphones, and denial of service. For passwords, weak policies and ability to download sensitive information unprotected to portable devices is a common area of concern, along with outdated anti-virus software across campus devices. For social media, hackers often impersonate friends or employers that students may access and install virus or other malware tools unintentionally. Phishing utilizes personal information from Facebook, LinkedIn and other publically available sites to send a personalized communication in hopes of stealing information or installing malware. Smartphones are another common area of risk, given the wide usage and often insecure connectivity over wireless networks along with loss or theft of devices (Zalaznick, 2013). In a recent example in Kansas, distributed denial of service (DDoS) attacks also inundate a network and overwhelm the system with traffic 100 times the usual volume, causing a shut-down of state exams (Herold, 2014).

CLOUD COMPUTING EDUCATIONAL MODEL

Security Strategies

While schools see Cloud-computing as a way to gain efficiencies and improved performance, they must consider the challenges unique to each environment vs. a one-size-fits-all Cloud approach. Security is of critical importance and remains challenging as schools utilize wireless access. Approximately 33% of higher education identified potential security breaches as the biggest barrier to cloud adoption. Common components of security include browser, data, network, denial of service, location, and team monitoring (Cisco, 2012). In discussing security methods, or the tools and techniques used to prevent security issues, there are three main categories: 1. authentication and authorization, 2. prevention and resistance, and 3. detection and response (Baltzan, 2012).

Authentication and authorization deals primary with people, which is often the greatest source of security breaches. This includes people both inside the organization who may misuse or distribute their access, and people outside the organization and may include social engineering to learn access information. The danger can be diverse and can come from outsiders who are unauthorized to get the information, from insiders who are authorized users, or even from the patient himself with the misuse of technology (Baltzan, 2012).

Access threats can concern inappropriate access but can also involve modification of records which can be done by mistake, for fraud or malice. The access topic has two main perspectives: one regarding the role and the other one concerning the devices that are allowed to access the records, since both these aspects can have important implications. Disclosure threats, including data at rest and data in transit, can result in release of information due to allowance of data disclosure beyond what was intended by the act of sharing, motivated by financial gain, or to embarrass the individual (Kruger &Anschutz, 2013).

In summary, anyone with potential access information could pose a potential threat to the security of the information. Strong information security policies and security plans such as password and logon requirements can help prevent these types of issues. Authentication confirms the user's identity, whereas authorization provides a user with appropriate permissions to the environment. Smart cards, tokens, and biometrics are types of devices that improve authentication of the user and implemented in conjunction with passwords (Baltzan, 2012).

All the advantages that the information technology is bringing to the system come with multiple challenges regarding the data security and privacy. The traditional approach for data protection, the perimeter approach that described the internal network of an organization as a perimeter defined network, is nowadays obsolete due to the extended usage of mobile devices. Not only that the perimeter can no longer be defined, but the perimeter-only security ignores the inside threat that exists when an organization's staff or others with access to the organization's information

maliciously or non-maliciously access or leak information (Kruger and Anschutz, 2013).

Prevention and resistance deals primarily with data and technologies including encryption, content filtering and firewalls. A firewall is a hardware or software device that analyzes information to detect unauthorized use. Content filtering prevents uses software to prevent emails and spam from being received or transmitted. Encryption requires a special key to decode the information and make the information readable; this is used for secure information such as financials or other protected information (Baltzan, 2012).

Detection and response deals primarily with attacks by analyzing suspicious activity such as password attempts or file access. Intrusion detection software will monitor and alert if patterns are detected and can even shut down part of the network as warranted (Baltzan, 2012). Organizational users need advanced tools similar to malicious users and the advanced tools being used to compromise the systems. Security Intelligence and event monitoring systems analyze network, user, application, and datasets to identify trends, behaviors, and incidents (LogRhythm, 2012).

For dataset inputs these include firewall, network, system, application, rules and other event logs. These logs are then normalized to a standard format for review. Once standardized, the data is analyzed for patterns, and alerts are generated for user review. Examples of analysis methods include aggregation and categorization of logs and events, time of events and directions, statistical log, source and host information, and top items within various categories for further detailed drill-down and analysis. Examples of analysis output include the ability to detect unusual application behaviors, unusual network connections, user behavior, network baseline deviations, and compromised credentials. Other methods analyze historical data to recreate scenarios for auditing, and also generate detailed and summary reporting output for security professionals, compliance officials, or other end users to review. Organizations are beginning to establish a security center in which monitoring and investigations occur (LogRhythm, 2012).

Physical, organizational, and technical safeguards must also be in place to ensure security. Physical safeguards include protecting facility access against unauthorized entry, as well as security workstations, transportation, and storage of media and information. However physical safeguards also apply well behind the walls of an organization. Organizational safeguards include consultant or contractor agreements, customer requirements, and policies and procedures (Iron Mountain, 2010).

Technical safeguards include unique user identification, automatics logoff, encryption, having a responsible person to authorize and verify passwords, strong passwords, locking accounts after invalid logins, and deactivating employee accounts after termination. From a mobile perspective endpoint access should also be verified and permitted or prevented from accessing the network, including monitoring and notification of an unauthorized device. Wireless threats should be detected and prevented through security policies and location tracking. Security compliance should be kept by administrators to verify personally owned and operated devices to ensure compliance (Iron Mountain, 2010).

Service-Oriented Architectures

Service-oriented architecture (SOA) is the design that permits the existence of the Cloud. The premise behind SOA is that all activity between devices are known as services which fit together in a standard way, ensuring the compatibility of the system. Cloud-computing can be categorized into three general categories of software as a service (SaaS), platform as a service (PaaS), and

infrastructure as a service (IaaS). Examples of SaaS may include Office 365 for word-processing or productivity software or Apple iCloud for class scheduling to common calendar. In PaaS, vendor provides the platform components such as a computer, operating system and database, examples may include Azure, Oracle Database, or Amazon EC2. Student and administrative data can be stored on these systems and hosted remotely. IaaS consists of computing or data resources, educational organizations can utilize a service such Amazon's Simple Storage Service to increase data capacity on demand (Kroenke, 2014).

Web or Cloud applications are commonly deployed using a three-tier architecture of a server, database, and user. The user tier contains the devices and web browsers to access the web pages and display content. The server tier runs the applications and resources by managing traffic and sending and receiving web content. The database tier stores and retrieves data for the web applications and content (Kroenke, 2014).

Legal, Privacy, and Ethical Considerations

Student privacy is enforced by strict regulations and risk must be limited due to legal and compliance penalties (Cisco, 2012). With all the educational breaches the public is only notified of less than 50% of data breaches due to high risk of reputation damage. Often in other industries the cost can be tied directly to sales, though in education the costs are harder to quantify (O'Neil, 2014). Educational institutions have an obligation to protect privacy and provide ethical notification of individual impacts.

With educational data many key legal, privacy and ethical considerations are present. For example, who is legally liable for computer systems, and in cases where Cloud-computing systems are compromised, or employees or students have direct liability to loss of information. Privacy considerations include the notion that privacy is not guaranteed and public information need outweighs individual rights. In an educational setting a significant amount of personal information is collected on individuals, such as for financial aid purposes, medical insurance, grade reports, employment, and housing information. Mobile devices and remote connectivity to educational resources is also recorded and may track location and usage history (Sharda, 2014).

In an effort to address these key considerations, privacy preserving analytics may be utilized to help protect information. Organizations such as Google, Facebook, Twitter and others employ similar techniques to safeguard user information. The capability of utilizing analytics to de-identify and anonymize data helps minimize risk for misuse of information both from a privacy, legal, ethical and security standpoint (Sharda, 2014).

CONCLUSION

Trends and Future Directions

The trend is clear for educational use of Cloud-computing, and the desire to improve efficiencies and learning capabilities. However despite the capabilities, caution must be exercised to ensure proper security protocols are established within the given Cloud-computing architecture. Care must also be given to individuals to ensure their information is protected and to limit impacts to the individual as well as the educational institution. There are still many improvements that educational organizations can make with regard to security and privacy, though we are beginning to reach a turning point where the attention, resources, and strategic importance of Cloud-computing and the associated security and privacy considerations must be realized for educational organizations to be successful in the 21st century.

Many cloud computing trends have taken an enterprise-oriented direction. Many enterprise workloads have begun moving to the cloud,

some technologies include AWS, Google Compute Engine, Microsoft Azure, and Rackspace. Containers are also being released to speed the deployment of application components allowing faster operationalization of cloud services. Price is another important trend that is continuing to drive low-cost infrastructures and applications. Companies such as Amazon, Azure, SoftLayer and Google will continue to maintain a top tier but also are competing with low-cost providers such as Digital Ocean now the 3rd largest hosting provider in the world based on a startup low-price model. Security is also coming to the forefront, and vendors will begin incorporating more software-defined security to protect the enterprise work and feed business intelligence to end users including surveillance agents to help in monitoring. Lastly the Internet of Things (IoT) and Big Data promise to make changes with increasing numbers of internet connected devices and increasing amounts of data generation. This promises to drive cloud computing vendors and capabilities (Babcock, 2014).

One of the latest trends that is also helping to drive cloud-computing is wearable tech such as smart watches and glasses. Shipments of 100 million wearable devices are estimated in 2014, with 485 million by 2018. To further educational learning opportunities these devices must also be incorporated into the classroom and a tremendous area of growth potential within an innovative classroom environment. With BYOT and cloud-computing in education, instead of demanding students turn off or put away technology devices, BYOT and cloud-computing captures the students use and interest of technology within an educational context (Woodside and Amiri, 2014).

The initial items released under wearable tech included watches and eye lenses, followed by fitness and health monitoring devices, then smart watches with an example being Samsung's Android powered Galaxy Gear smart watch. The smart watch allowed connections to a smartphone, health, and fitness patterns. The most recent notable entry was Google Glass, an eyewear with connection to a smartphone, GPS, voice activation, camera and video recording. These devices utilize demonstrated technology such as Wi-Fi, Bluetooth Smart, Near Field Communication and GPS (Woodside and Amiri, 2014).

When implementing a cloud computing and wearable technology strategy, a few of the best practices include development of a formal set of policies including governance, compliance, equitable access to technology, and acceptable usage. The second component includes device management and ensuring compatibility between all devices and development of the appropriate infrastructure to accommodate the increase in demand of traffic and user connectivity. The last area is security, and verifying all devices contain up to date anti-virus software and patches to prevent unauthorized access or loss of data (Woodside and Amiri, 2014).

Acceptable Usage: Existing policies must be reviewed to ensure they are compatible with cloud-computing and modified as appropriate. Individuals are still bound by acceptable use guidelines whether on personal or provided devices. Also device usage time can be restricted and not permitted at all times. Acceptable personal computing devices may include laptops, netbook, tablet, cell phone, smart phone, e-reader, iPad, iPod. Gaining devices with Internet access are not permitted (Woodside and Amiri, 2014).

Technical Support Levels: In most cases, cloud-computing support is the responsibility of the individual, and they are expected to be knowledgeable on the device's usage. The company or educational facility personnel to not provide direct support for devices. This is primarily due to the range of devices and resources necessary to provide complete support (Woodside and Amiri, 2014).

Network and Software Access: Individuals are provided with Internet access and wireless access which may be filtered, and also reduced for bandwidth. Individuals may download and install any additional applications, components, or storage as

they see fit, granted any do not conflict with the ethics and acceptable use policies. This is viewed similar to public access in coffee shops, hotels, or other public access points permitted (Woodside and Amiri, 2014).

Technology Ethics and Acceptable Usage: For acceptable use, this is using technology as a privilege to improve the skills, knowledge and abilities students will require in the 21st century. One important component of cloud-computing is acceptable online behavior and safety (Woodside and Amiri, 2014).

Lost or Stolen Devices: Personal devices are used at one's own risk, loss or damage would need to be covered by the individual. Due to lack of secure storage, theft is often cited as a top reason students did not bring personal devices (Woodside and Amiri, 2014).

Staff Training: While in some cases instructors were not provided with direct training, after implementation recommends providing professional development to learn best practices and have an interactive community to share insights and expertise. An entrepreneurial spirit is encouraged along with experimentation to achieve the best results of cloud-computing and share those results with others to continuously improve (Woodside and Amiri, 2014).

Device Management: In order to ensure compatibility and consistent user experience across devices, organizations should utilize open standards. One such open web standard HTML5 is intended to allow cross-platform usage with a promise of write once and run anywhere, for example a Windows, Apple, or Android user could all access the same application across devices and platforms. This allows the developers to focus on the features and functionality rather than the conversion between platforms. Along with operating systems, screen sizes, resolutions, aspect rations, orientations, cameras, GPS, accelerometers and other features may vary by user and device. HTML5 is designed to accommodate these items through dynamically adapting to platforms variables and delivering a consistent experience. Currently the major browsers Internet Explorer, Firefox, Opera, Safari, and Chrome support HTML5 and CSS3, with full readiness varying (Woodside and Amiri, 2014).

Security: In order to ensure adequate security is in place for user of mobile devices, security methods must be employed. In discussing security methods, or the tools and techniques used to prevent security issues, there are three main categories: 1. authentication and authorization, 2. prevention and resistance, and 3. detection and response (Woodside and Amiri, 2014).

A recent initiative begun by The University of Texas at San Antonio is to create an Open Cloud Institute. This Institute would help develop degree programs in cloud computing along with working with industry partners. An initial investment has been made of $9 million, to include 4 endowed professors, 2 faculty researchers, and 10 graduate students. This combination aims to create a leadership role with key industry partners and recruit the top academics in the areas of cloud computing research (UTSA, 2015).

In upcoming years and decades many educators foresee a "virtual class" to include the nation's best teachers, professionally produced footage, TedTalks, interactive games, simulations, and formal real-time assessments for student results. Other innovations to classrooms include flipped learning, blending learning, student-centered learning, project-based learning, and self-organized learning. In flipped-learning the student learns fundamental knowledge outside of the classroom typically through videos, then once in the classroom works on projects, problems, and critical-thinking activities. In blended learning, students complete a portion of the course, this is projected to impact K-12 students to a greater extent with a projection of half of all high-school classes being offered online by 2019. In a recent TedTalk Sugata Mitra earned a $1 million award for a discussion around a school built in the cloud (Godsey, 2015).

REFERENCES

Anderson, J. (2015). Lincoln school district to become largest in state to provide computers to all students from elementary grades up. *OMaha World-Herald*.

Babcock, C. (2014). 9 Cloud Trends for 2015. *InformationWeek*.

Baltzan, P., & Phillips, A. (2012). *Business Driven Technology*. New York, NY: McGraw-Hill Irwin.

Castle, L. (2015). *Creating a New IT at Fairfield University*. Mobile Enterprise.

Cloud 101: Developing a Cloud-Computing Strategy for Higher Education. (2012). *Cisco*.

Daly, J. (2013). The State of Cloud Computing in Higher Education. *EdTechMagazine*.

Florence, L. (2015). *Universities struggle to effectively implement cloud-based technologies*. The Daily Texan.

Godsey, M. (2015). The Deconstruction of the K-12 Teacher. *The Atlantic*.

Herold, B. (2014). Kansas Suspends State Tests Following Cyber Attacks. *Education Week*.

HIPAA Best Practices Checklist: Best Practices That Go Beyond Compliance to Mitigate Risks. (2010). Iron Mountain.

IBM Cloud Services (Part I).(2015). Seeking Alpha.

Jackson, S. (2014) Data breach could affect 30,000 Iowa State students. *The Des Moines Register*.

Kroenke, D. M. (2013). *Experiencing MIS*. Boston, MA: Pearson.

Kruger, D., & Anschutz, T. (2013). A new approach in IT security. *Healthcare Financial Management Association*, *67*(2), 104–106. PMID:23413677

Lieberman, B. (2013). *Testing the Waters: Mobile and Cloud Computing for Education*. Intel.

Mehta, M. (2015). The Wisdom of the PaaS Crowd. *Forbes*.

O'Neil, M. (2014). Data Breaches Put a Dent in Colleges' Finances as Well as Reputations. *The Chronicle*.

Security Intelligence: Can "Big Data Analytics Overcome Our Blind Spots? (2012). LogRhythm.

Sharda, R., Dursun, D., & Turban, E. (2014). *Business Intelligence A Managerial Perspective on Analytics*. Boston, MA: Pearson.

UTSA announces creation of Open Cloud Institute. (2015 The University of Texas at San Antonio.

Weaver, D. (2015). *Six Advantages of Cloud Computing in Education*. Technology in the Classroom.

Woodside, J. M. (2010). A BI 2.0 Application Architecture for Healthcare Data Mining Services in the Cloud. Proceedings of *The World Congress in Computer Science, Computer Engineering & Applied Computing - International Data Mining Conference*.

Woodside, J. M., Allabun, N., & Amiri, S. (2014). Bring Your Own Technology (BYOT) to Education. Proceedings of The 5th International Multi-Conference on Complexity. Informatics and Cybernetics.

Woodside, J. M., & Amiri, S. (2014). Bring Your Own Technology (BYOT) to Education. *Journal of Informatics, Systems, and Cybernetics*, *12*(3), 38–40.

Zalaznick, M. (2013). *Cyberattacks on the rise in higher education*. University Business.

KEY TERMS AND DEFINITIONS

Classroom: A physical or virtual room where student education occurs.

Cloud Computing: Enables convenient on demand access to an elastic set of shared computing resources.

Education: The process of receiving or providing instruction and learning.

Ethics: A set of moral policies that governs behavior.

Legal: A set of law policies that governs behavior.

Privacy: The ability to have personal information used appropriately and without ongoing observation.

Security: A set of processes and techniques for ensuring appropriate access by individuals or systems in an effort to prevent harm.

Chapter 9
Networked Multimedia Communication Systems

Piyush Kumar Shukla
University Institute of Technology RGPV, India

Kirti Raj Bhatele
University Institute of Technology RGPV, India

ABSTRACT

This Chapter simply contains multimedia - an integrated and interactive presentation of speech, audio, video, graphics and text, has become a major theme in today's information technology that merges the practices of communications, computing and information processing into an interdisciplinary field. The challenge of multimedia communications is to provide services that integrate text, sound, image and video information and to do it in a way that preserves the case of use and interactivity. A brief description of the elements of multimedia systems is presented. User and network requirements are discussed together with the pocket transfer concept. About Multimedia communication standards a general idea is also given. Multimedia transport over ATM and IP networks discussed in brief. The issues pertaining to multimedia digital subscriber lines are outlined together with multimedia over wireless, mobile and broadcasting networks as well as digital TV infrastructure for interactive multimedia services.

INTRODUCTION

The precedent years have seen an expansion in the usage and the field of digital media. Industry is making considerable investments to deliver digital audio, image and video information to consumers and customers. A novel infrastructure of digital audio, image and video recorders and players, on-line services, and electronic commerce is quickly being deployed. Abreast major corporations are converting their audio, image and video archives to an electronic form. Digital media offers several discrete advantages over analog media: the quality of digital audio, image and video signals is higher than that of their analog counterparts. Editing is easy because one can access the exact discrete locations that should be changed. No loss of fidelity happens while copying. A copy of digital media is alike to the original. Digital audio, image and videos are easily transmitted over networked information systems. These advantages have opened up numerous new

DOI: 10.4018/978-1-4666-8387-7.ch009

possibilities. Multimedia consists of Multimedia data and set of interactions. Multimedia data are casually considered as the collection of three M's: multi-source, multi-type and multi-format data. The interactions among the multimedia components consist of intricate relationships without which multimedia would be a simple set of visual, audio and other data. Multimedia and multimedia communication can be seen worldwide as a hierarchical system. The multimedia software and applications offer a direct interactive environment for users. Whenever a computer in need of information from far-off computers or distant servers with that scenario, multimedia information must travel through computer networks. As the amount of information involved in the transmission of video and audio can be significantly huge, the multimedia information must be compressed before it can be transported through the network in order to lessen the communication delay. Limited delay and jitters like constraints are used to make sure a reasonable video and audio outcome at the receiving end. That is why, communication networks are undergoing constant up gradation and improvements in order to provide multimedia communication capabilities. In order to connect local terminal computers and other equipment with each other, Local area networks are used and wide area networks and the Internet connect the various local area networks together. Improved standards are constantly being developed in order to provide a worldwide information expressway over which multimedia information will travel. Multimedia communications is the field referring to the representation, storage, retrieval and dissemination of machine-process able information expressed in multiple media, such as text, image, graphics, speech, audio, video, animation, handwriting, data files. With the advent of high capacity storage devices, powerful and yet economical computer workstations and high speed integrated services digital networks, providing a variety of multimedia communications services is becoming not only technically but also economically feasible.

In addition, the broadband integrated services, digital network (BISDN) has been given special attention as a next generation communication network infrastructure which will be capable of transmitting full motion picture and high speed data at 150 and 600 MB/s and voice as well as data throughout the world (Mouftah, 1992). At first, the concept of multimedia communication modeling will be described, together with user and network requirements, packet transfer concept as well as multimedia terminals. The second part deals with multimedia communication standards. Finally, we will concentrate on multimedia communications over networks. Multimedia transfer over ATM networks is described. This is followed by multimedia over IP networks. Special issues relating to multimedia over wireless will be discussed.

Improvement in the quality of video and audio is always being demanded. The increasing demands pose great challenges in developing multimedia applications in the areas of content creation, usage and sharing of media experiences. Additional challenges come from communication systems; handovers between different networks are especially challenging in mobile devices. We identify and analyze the requirements that a distributed multimedia application may enforce on the communication network. Due to the vastness of this field, we do not claim that this list is exhaustive, but we have tried to include all the important aspects (from our view point) that have significantly impacted the enhancements to the basic Internet architecture and its associated protocols. Recent advances in communications technologies have witnessed a growing and evolving multimedia content delivery market based on information gathering, manipulation, and dissemination. It is a fact that personal communications, computing, broadcasting, entertainment, etc. have turned into streams of multimedia content, and the various communication and network technologies have become the means to carry that content to a wide variety of terminals. Unlike traditional communication systems, a fundamental challenge for present and future communication systems is the ability to transport multimedia content over a variety of networks energy-efficiently at different channel conditions and bandwidth capacities with various requirements of quality-of-service. There are many issues need to be addressed such as signal processing, collaborations, power management, flexible delivery, specialization of new content, dynamic access, telecommunications, networking, etc., due to the multi-disciplinary nature of the applications in advanced multimedia communications.

The objective of this chapter is to carry together the state of the art research contribution that describes original and unpublished work addressing the new emerging techniques on multimedia communications. Particularly, we solicit research papers on addressing challenging issues existing for enabling mobile multimedia communications over heterogeneous infrastructure for realizing next generation networking and computing. For example, ubiquitous multimedia is a requirement in next generation networks, such as multimedia adaption in wireless network; multimedia services in ubiquitous circumstance; improving distributed multimedia communication through location awareness, action awareness, user awareness, etc. On the other hand, due to the limited computational power, memory and battery energy in wireless and portable terminals, power efficient design also plays important role in next generation mobile multimedia applications. The table consisting of some of the frequently used acronyms in the field of Networked Multimedia communication is given below in table 1.

MULTIMEDIA COMMUNICATION

Multimedia Communication is simply the transfer of information or data over the network, in which the information or data may be, consist of one or more of the following types: Text, images, audio and video, etc. Applications in medicine, education, travel, real estate, banking, insurance, ad-

ministration and publishing are emerging at a fast pace. These applications are characterized by large multimedia documents that must be communicated within very short delays. Computer-controlled cooperative work, whereby a group of users can jointly view, create, edit and discuss multimedia documents, is going to be characteristic of many transactions (Cox, 1998). Some glamorous applications in multimedia processing include: distance learning, virtual library access and living books. The students learn and interact with instructors remotely via broadband communication network in distance learning. Virtual library access means that we instantly have access to all of the published material in the world, in its original form and format, and can browse, display, print and even modify the material instantaneously. Living books supplement the written word and the associated pictures with animations and hyperlink access to supplementary material (Rosenberg, 1992). Applications that are enabled or enhanced by video are often seen as the primary justification for the development of multimedia networks depicted by figure 1 given below.

Much of the work on packet video has considered fairly homogenous networking scenario (Bojkovic, 1996). It would be a proper if a single type of video service dominated in the networks. However, it is not a valid assumption for the traffic issues. First, video will not constitute a uniform service with easily determined behavior and requirements. Secondly, video will not share resources with streams of only the same type. This means that multiplexing in the network should be evaluated for a heterogeneous mix of traffic types. In business areas, there is a potential need for various kinds of new communication system, such as high-speed data networks between geographically distributed local area networks (LAN's) high definition still picture communication and TV conferencing or corporate cable TV services. The new paradigm of the BISDN application system as a result of the integration of multimedia processing by workstations and multimedia communication by BISDN is shown in Figure 2.

Table 1. Different Acronyms used in the field Networked multimedia communication

S.No	Acronym	Description
1.	ADPCM	Adaptive Differential Pulse Code Modulation
2.	ADSL	Asymmetric Digital Subscriber Line
3.	AE	Area Directors
4.	ATDM	Asynchronous Time-Division Multiplex
5.	ATM	Asynchronous Transfer Mode
6.	AV	Audiovisual
7.	BISDN	Broadband Integrated Services Digital Networks
8.	CATV	Cable Television
9.	CLEC	Competitive Local Exchange Carriers
10.	CTI	Complete Timing Information
11.	DBS	Direct Broadcast Satellite
12.	DDL	Description Definition Language
13.	DSL	Digital Subscriber Line
14.	DSM	Digital Storage Media
15.	GSM	GSM Global System for Mobile
16.	HDTV	High Definition Television
17.	HFC	Hybrid Fiber Coax
18.	IAB	Internet Architecture Board
19.	IEC	International Electro technical Commission
20.	IESG	Internet Engineering Steering Group
21.	IETF	Internet Engineering Task Force
22.	IPN	Integrated Packet Network
23.	ISOC	Internet Society
24.	JPEG	Joint Photographic Experts Group
25.	LMDS	Local Multipoint Distribution Service
26.	MBS	Mobile Broadband System
27.	MVPD	Multichannel Video Program Distribution
28.	NTI	Null Timing Information
29.	NTSC	National Television System Committee
30.	PAL	Phase Alternating Line
31.	PCM	Pulse Code Modulation
32.	PVR	Packet Voice Receiver
33.	PVT	Packet Voice Transmitter
34.	QoS	Quality of Service
35.	RFC	Request for Comments
36.	SHDSL	Single pair High speed DSL
37.	SIF	Standard Source Input Format
38.	TCP	Transmission Control Protocol
39.	TR	Technical Report
40.	UDP	User Datagram Protocol
41.	UMTS	Universal Mobile Telecommunication System

Figure 1. Multimedia communication

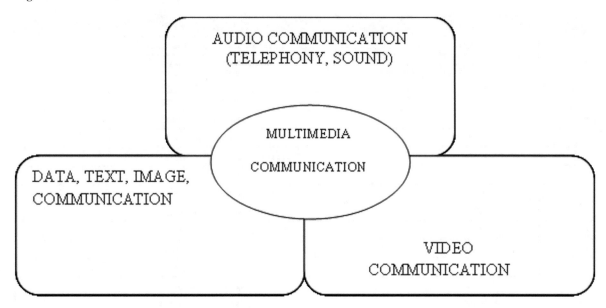

Figure 2. Elements involve in Multimedia communication systems in person to person communication and person to machine modes

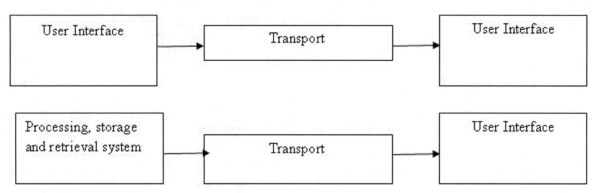

A multimedia communication model is strongly influenced by the manufacturer-dependent solutions for personal computers and workstations including application software on the one hand and by the intelligent network concept on the other (Jayant, 1993). A layered model for future multimedia communication comprises five constituents:

1. Partitioning of complex information objects into distinct information types for the purpose of easier communication, storing and processing. This comprises data, video or audio taking into account the integration of different information types not being excluded.

2. Standardization of service components per information type, possibly with several levels of quality per information type.

3. Creation of platforms at two levels: a network service platform, and a multimedia communication platform. The first level hides the transport networks and network building blocks from an application designer's or

user's point of view. The second level provides communication support on the basis of information structure and information exchange building blocks for a large number of applications.

4. The definition of "generic applications" for multiple uses in various multimedia environments and different branches meeting common widespread needs.

5. Specific applications: electronic shopping, tele training and remote maintenance, based on special information building blocks and utilizing the network service platform, the multimedia communication platform as well as including generic applications.

With regards to the capability of the available resources in each case, the multimedia communication applications must be scalable in order to run in a constant manner across different network and terminal types and capabilities.

There are two key communication modes in which multimedia systems are generally used: person-to-person communications and person-to-machine communications. The key elements of multimedia systems are presented in Figure 2. As it can be seen both these modes have a lot of commonality, as well as some differences.

In the person-to-person mode shown in Figure 2, there is a user interface that provides the mechanisms for all users to interact with each other and a transport layer that moves the multimedia signal from one user location to some or all other user locations associated with the communications. The user interface creates the multimedia signal and allows users to interact with the multimedia signal in an easy-to-use manner. The transport layer preserves the quality of the multimedia signals so that all users receive what they perceive to be high-quality signals at each user location. Examples of applications for the person-to-person mode are teleconferencing, video phones, distance learning and shared workspace scenarios. In the person-to-machine mode, shown in Figure 2, there

is again a user interface for interacting with the machine, along with a transport layer for moving the multimedia signal from the storage location to the user, as well as a mechanism for storage and retrieval of multimedia signals that are either created by the user or requested by the user. The storage and retrieval mechanisms involve browsing and searching to find existing multimedia data. Also, storage and archiving in order to move user-created multimedia data to the appropriate place for access by others. Examples of applications for the person-to-machine mode include creation and access of business meeting notes, access of broadcast video and document archives from a digital library or other repositories.

MULTIMEDIA COMMUNICATION OVER NETWORKS

There are basically nine types of communication networks that are used to provide multimedia communication services. With the increase in transfer of multimedia information over the past few decades has resulted in many new multimedia processing and communication systems, being put into service. The increasing availability of optical fiber channels and rapid advancement in VLSI circuits and systems has fostered a tremendous interest in developing sophisticated multimedia services with an acceptable cost. Today's fiber technology offers a transmission capacity that can easily handle high bit rates. This leads to the development of networks which integrate all types of information services. By basing such a network on packet switching, the services (video, voice and data) can be dealt with in a common format. Packet switching is more flexible than circuit switching in that it can emulate the latter while vastly different bit rates can be multiplexed together. In addition, the network's statistical multiplexing of variable rate sources may yield a higher fixed capacity allocation.

1. Packet Video

Asynchronous transfer of video signals which often is referred to as "packet video" can be defined as the transfer of video signals over asynchronously time-division multiplex (ATDM) networks, such as IP and ATM. The video may be transferred for instantaneous viewing or for subsequent storage for replay at a later time. The previous case has requirements on pacing so that the received video data can be displayed in a perceptually continues sequence. The last case can be seen as a large data transfer with no inherent time-constraints. Apart from the requirement on pacing, there may also be bounds on the maximum transfer delay from camera to monitor, if the video is a part of an interactive conversation or conference. These limits are set by human perception and determine when the delay starts to the information exchange. Parts of the signal may be lost or corrupted by errors during the transfer. This will reduce the quality of the reconstructed video and if the degradation is serious enough, it may cause the viewer to reject the service. Thus, packet video common topics are to perform coding and make sure the asynchronously transfer of video signals under quality constraints.

The synchronous transfer mode combines the circuit switched routing of telephony networks with the asynchronous multiplexing of packet switching. This is accomplished by establishing a connection (fixed route) through the network before accepting any traffic. The information is then sent in 53-octet long cells. The switches route calls according to address information contained in each cell's 5-octet header. Traffic on a particular link consists of randomly interleaved cells belonging to different calls. The network guarantees that all cells of a call follow the same route and hence, get delivered in the same order as sent. The intention is that ATM networks should be able to guarantee the quality of service in terms of cell loss and maximum delay, as well as maximum delay variations.

The internet protocol differs in two major respects from ATM as there is no pre-established route and the packets are variable length (up to 65535 octets). IP does not give any guarantees on the delivery of the packets and they may even arrive out of order if the routing decision changes during the session. These issues will be addressed by the introduction of IP in conjunction with the resource reservation protocol RSVP. IP often called Internet Protocol (version 6), packets contain a 24-bit flow identifier in addition to the source and destination addresses which can be used in routers for operations like scheduling and buffer management to provide service guarantees. Delay and some loss are inevitable during transfers across both ATM and IP networks. The delay is chiefly caused by propagation and queuing. The queuing delay depends on the dynamic load variations on the links and must be equalized before video can be reconstructed. Bit errors can occur in the optics and electronics of the physical layer through thermal and impulsive noise. Loss of information is mainly caused by multiplexing overload of such magnitude and duration that buffers in the nodes overflow.

2. Multimedia Transport over ATM Networks

As previously stated, multimedia it denotes the integrated manipulation of at least some information represented as continues media data, as well as some information encoded as discrete media data (text and graphics). Multimedia communication deals with the transfer, protocols, services, and mechanisms of discrete media data and continues media data (audio, video) in/over digital networks. Such communication requires that all involved components be capable of handling a well-defined quality of services (QoS). The most important QoS parameters are required capacities of the involved resources, compliance to end-to-end delay and jitter as timing restrictions, and restriction of the loss characteristics. A protocol designed to reserve capacity for continuous media data, transmitted in conjunction with the discrete media data over, for example an asynchronous transfer mode - local area network (ATM-LAN) is certainly a multimedia communication issue (Orzessek & Sommer, 1998). The success of ATM for multimedia communications depends on the successful standardization of its signaling mechanisms, its ability to attract the development of the native ATM applications, and the integration of the ATM with other communications systems. The integration of ATM into the Internet world is under investigation. If there will be ATM applications such as video on demand, then there is also the need for a "side-by-side" integration of ATM and Internet protocols. It can be very well understood that the ATM/BISDN in wired networks is behind the success of wireless ATM (WATM). When ATM networks become a standard in the wired area, the success of WATM will be realized.

3. Video Over Wireless ATM Networks

Wireless ATM (WATM) has become the direct result of the ATM "anywhere" movement because of the success of ATM on wired networks. WATM can be seen as a solution for next-generation personal communication networks, or a wireless extension of the BISDN networks. There has been a great deal of interest recently in the area of wireless networking. Issues such as bit error rates and cell loss rates are even more important when transmitting video over a wireless network. A very high performance wireless local area network which operates in the 60 GHz millimeter waveband can experience cell loss rates of 10^{-4} to 10^{-2}. To provide adequate picture quality to the user, some form of error correction or concealment must be employed. One option is to use the MPEG-2 error resilience techniques and to modify the MPEG-2 standard slightly when it is used over wireless ATM networks. This technique is known as macro blocker synchronization (Zhang, 1997). In macro

block resynchronization the first macro block in every ATM cell is coded absolutely rather than differentially. This allows for resynchronization of the video stream much more often than would be possible if resynchronization could only take place at the slice level. It would be relatively simple to incorporate this method with the existing MPEG-2 coding standard by adding an interworking adapter at the boundary between the fixed and wireless network (E. Ayanoglu). A second proposal for improving error resilience in wireless network is to use forward error correction (FEC) methods. In addition, improve performance can be achieved by using a two layer scalable MPEG-2 coding scheme rather than one layer (Ayanoglu, 1993).

4. Multimedia Over IP Networks

Multimedia has become a major subject or theme in today's information technology that combines the practices of communications, computing, and information processing into an interdisciplinary field. In this Internet era, IP based data networks have emerged as the most important infrastructure, reaching millions of people anytime, anywhere. They serve as an enabling technology that creates a whole new class of applications to enhance productivity, reduce costs, and increase business agility. Anticipating that multimedia over IP will be one of the major driving forces behind the emerging broadband communications of the 21st century; we address the challenges facing the delivery of multimedia applications over IP in a cost effective, ubiquitous, and quality guaranteed manner.

5. Packet Voice

In Packet voice, the phenomenon of packets witching offer several potential advantages in terms of performance when compared to circuit-switched networks. Major advantage is efficient utilization of channel capacity, particularly for "bursty" traffic. Well not as bursty as interactive data, speech exhibits some burstiness in the form of talks parts

(Brady, 1990). It is actually on the sensitivity of the speech detector average talk's part duration depends but it is well known that individual speakers are active only about 35-45 percent in typical telephone conversations. Although by sending voice packets only during talk's parts, packet switching offers a natural way to multiplex voice calls as well as voice with data. Another major advantage is that call blocking can be a function of the required average bandwidth rather than the required peak bandwidth. In addition, packet switching is flexible. For instance, packet voice is quite capable of sustaining priority traffic and point to multipoint connections. Network capabilities in traffic control, accounting and security are enhanced as the packets are processed in the network. Continuous speech of acceptable quality must be reconstructed from voice packet that experience variable delays through the network. Imposing an additional delay is all required for compensating of the variable delay component in the reconstruction process. Hence, packet should be delivered with low average delay and delay variability. Speech can tolerate a certain amount of distortion (e.g., compression, clipping) but is sensitive to end-to-end delay. The exact amount of maximum tolerable delay is subject to debate. It is generally accepted to be in the range of 100-600 ms. For example, the public telephone network has a maximum specification of 600 ms. In order to minimize packetization and storage delays, it has been proposed that voice packets should be relatively short, on the order of 200-700 bits, and generally contain less than 10-50 ms of speech (Listanti, Villani & Gold, 1983). Network protocols should be simplified to shorten voice packet headers (e.g., on the order of 4-8bytes), although timestamps and sequence numbers are likely needed. Since a certain amount of distortion is tolerable, error detection, acknowledgements, and retransmissions are unnecessary in networks with low-error rates. Flow control can be exercised end-to-end by blocking calls. In addition, network switches can possibly discard packets under heavy traffic conditions. In this case, embedded coding has been proposed whereby speech quality degrades gracefully with the loss of information (Bially, 1980).

6. Integrated Packet Networks

The economies and flexibility of integrated networks make them very attractive and packet network architectures have the potential for realizing these advantages. However, the effective integration of speech and other signals such as graphics, image and video into an integrated packet network (IPN) can rearrange network design properties. Although processing speeds will continue to increase, it will also be necessary to minimize the nodal per-packet processing requirements imposed by the network design. Data signals must generally be received error-free in order to be useful. The inherent structure of speech and image signals and the way in which they are perceived allows for some loss of information without significant quality improvement. This presents the possibility of purposely discarding limited information to achieve some other goal, such as the control of temporary congestion. One of the goals in integrated packet network is to construct a model which considers the entire IPN (transmitters, packet multiplexers and receivers) as a system to be optimized for higher speeds and capabilities (Patr, DaSilva & Frost, 1989).

In summary, the advantages gained by taking a total system approach to integrated packet network are as follows:

1. A powerful overload control mechanism is provided.
2. The structure of speech is effectively exploited.
3. Extremely simple per-packet processing for overload control is allowed.
4. Only one packet per speech segment is required.

5.   Receiver speech synchronization is simplified.
6.   Reduced per-packet error processing at packet multiplexers is possible.

7. Video Transmission over IP Networks

The problem of sending video over IP has essentially two main components: video data compression and design of communication protocols as illustrated in Figure 3 (Servetto & Nahrstedt, 2001).

One approach consists of designing a low bit rate coder, protecting the resulting bit stream with channel codes and using one of the standard Internet transport protocols to transmit the resulting data stream. If the source bit rate is low enough and the channel is not too congested, then it is possible to use TCP, in which case no errors occur and therefore there is no need for channel codes. Otherwise, user datagram protocol (UDP) is used with a constant packet injection rate, and low-redundancy channel codes are used to protect against infrequent lost packets.

8. Multimedia Over Digital Subscriber Lines

The Internet is responsible for changing the way we work, live and spend time with all its applications. However, today the Internet is confronted with a major problem. Increasing demand for access has produced bottlenecks and huge congestion, which resulted degraded internet speed. These restrictions has simply forced the existing technology of traditional telephony to new and innovative

heights with the emergence of Asymmetric Digital Subscriber Line (ADSL) technology. With the advent of the High speed ADSL simply eliminate bottlenecks, granting all subscribers quick and reliable access to Internet content. Telecom service providers have yet to realize the full potential of ADSL. Traditional telephone and Internet services are only the beginning, while the ability to offer broadcast video services is a reality. Cable TV operators are beginning to offer voice and data services. There is increasing competition from Competitive Local Exchange Carriers (CLEC) and other carriers, making it imperative that traditional telecom service provides video services. By offering a range of services, established service providers can generate additional revenue and protect their installed base. Direct Broadcast Satellite (DBS) providers, particularly in Europe and Asia, are offering a compelling Multichannel Video Program Distribution (MVPD) service (Merriman, 2000).

A key factor contributing to the successful deployment of Asymmetric Digital Subscriber Line (ADSL) access systems has been the facility for overlying data services on top of existing voice service without interfering with the voice service. For the users this basically offers:

1.   Always-on service capability. There is no need to dial up as the Internet Protocol (IP) connection is always available and the office networking model in which network resources are available all the time.
2.   Virtual second voice line. Unlike when the user is connected through a modem, the voice line remains available for incoming and outgoing calls. For the operator, the

Figure 3. Structure of a video streaming system

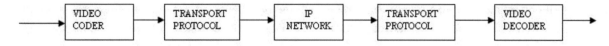

service overlay allows ADSL to be installed throughout the network, irrespective of what types of narrow band switches are installed. After the initial success of ADSL, it became apparent that it could be used to offer multiple phone lines together with a greater range of services (e.g., Virtual Private Networks VPN) targeted at specific markets. This has been made possible by the high bandwidth of ADSL, backed up progress in voice compression, echo canceling and digital signal processing technologies. ADSL offers a high data bandwidth, of which a portion can be used to offer additional voice services integrated with the data services. Symmetric Digital Subscriber Line (DSL) techniques, such as Single pair High Speed DSL (SHDSL) cannot be deployed as an overlay to existing analog telephone services, so the delivery of voice and data services using a single facility requires voice to be carried directly on the DSL link. The techniques used to transport voice and data in an integrated way over DSL-whether ADSL or SHDSL - are referred to as Voice over DSL (VoDSL). With VoDSL, two main market segments are of interest to service providers. The first is small to medium sized businesses, a significant percentage of which need to be able to send and receive data of around 500 kbit/s. The voice needs of these customers are typically met by 4 to 12 outgoing plane lines. Using, for example, Adaptive Pulse Code Modulation (ADPCM) voice coding, at peak times these phone lines consume only 128 to 256 kbit/s of the ADSL bandwidth, which is typically in excess of 2 Mbit/s downstream and more than 500 kbit/s upstream. The second market interested in VoDSL services is residential users who will appreciate the extra two to four voice lines that VoDSL offers (Verhoeyen, 2000). ADSL will be delivering multimedia services

to millions of users. The transmission of digital multimedia data requires the existing systems to be augmented with functions that can handle not only ordinary data. In addition, the high volume of multimedia data can be handled efficiently only if all available system services are carefully optimized.

9. Internet Access Networks

Asymmetric digital subscriber line (ADSL) offers asymmetric rates of transfer of data to and from the Internet. The uplink rates can go up to 768 Kbit/s and down links rates are 6-8 Mbit/s, depending on the length and condition of the local loop - the wiring between the customer's premises and the telco central office. Cable companies bring analog TV signals over optical filters to their neighborhood distribution points, a head ends, whence the signals are distributed to residences by coaxial cables. The combination of fiber and coaxial cable, which can carry high-speed data as well as TV signals, is known as hybrid fiber coax (HFC). Each distribution point typically serves 200-500 residences. The extent of the network of a cable TV operator is measured in terms of homes passed - that is, the number of homes adjacent to which the operator's cable passes, regardless of whether those homes have been signed up as customers. Realistically, cable modems are capable of passing data upstream at speeds of 200 kbit/s to 2 Mbit/s, and downstream at speeds up to about 10 Mbit/s. Cable modems, capable of operating at higher speeds than ADSL, have some serious drawbacks. The cable link to a residence is shared among many users, so that if many of them decide to log onto the Internet at the same time, achievable communications speeds may plunge. Because the lines are shared, a hacker may be able to drop on a neighbor's connection to the Internet or on an intranet - a security problem that may be serious to some users. Consequently, a customer who happens to be a road warrior will be unable get access into the Internet at airports or hotels through his laptop computer at his usual data rate. If he is able to connect at all, it will be through a dial-up modem at a much lower speed.

MULTIMEDIA COMMUNICATION SYSTEM ARCHITECTURE

A multimedia communication system consisting of both the communication protocols which are used to transport the real-time data and also the distributed computing system (DCS) within which any applications using these protocols must execute (Constantine & Papandreou, 1998). The presented architecture attempts to integrate these communications protocols with the DCS in a swift fashion in order to ease the writing of multimedia applications. Two issues are recognized as being necessary to the success of this integration: namely the synchronization of related real-time data streams and the management of heterogeneous multimedia hardware. The synchronization problem is solved by defining explicit synchronization properties at the presentation level and by providing control and synchronization operations within the DCS which operate in terms of these properties. The heterogeneity problems are addressed by separating the

data transport semantics (protocols themselves) from the control semantics (protocol interfaces). The control semantics are implemented using a distributed, typed interface, scheme within the DCS (i.e., above the presentation layer), whilst the protocols themselves are implemented within the communication subsystem. The interface between the DCS and communications subsystem is referred to as the Orchestration interface and can he considered to lie in the presentation and session layers. There are three types of Multimedia Communication System Architecture depicted in Figure 4 given below.

AUDIO-VIDEO CONFERENCING

The emergence of videoconferencing as a new means of communication with many applications such as tele meeting, remote education or telemedicine is quite evident. When two or more people communicate synchronously by means of audio, video and very often, using data applications such as electronic whiteboards or chat then it is known as a videoconference. Videoconferencing plays a very significant role in the various application fields as it is a direct way of supporting cooperation. It allows simultaneous communication

Figure 4. Types of multimedia communication system architectures

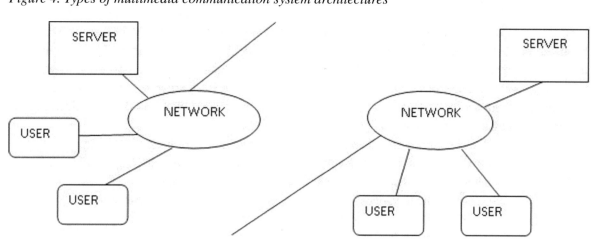

for geographically dispersed participants, and it accomplishes this task without imposing a rigid structure on the communication, thus leading to interactions that resemble as close as possible natural communication in a face-to-face situation. Videoconferencing communication is thus a key issue in multimedia cooperative systems (Bellido, Fernández & Pastor, 1996).

The mounting facilities available in videoconferencing systems are also important. From systems that allowed a uni-directional communication between two sites, we are now in a situation where it is possible to have several users engaged in a N to M communication. The potential utility of videoconferencing has increased with the help of systems electronic whiteboards, transfer of documents and window sharing. The term multimedia conferencing has been proposed to illustrate the merging of the different data applications to basic audio and video communication. In the project LEVERAGE [Lev01], for instance, a multimedia conferencing system has been developed, to support task-based foreign language learning, collaboration and interaction between students present in Paris, Madrid and Cambridge. The EDUBA project (Pastor, Fernández & Bellido, 1995) is another example where Videoconferencing is used in learning scenarios.

Till recently, the finest way to access to videoconferencing (or multimedia conferencing) has been the use of equipment based on the H.320 standard [H.320]. The equipments and protocols needed to support videoconferencing over narrowband ISDN (Integrated Services Digital Networks) is simply defined by the H.320 is an ITU (International Telecommunications Union) standard. The quality of videoconferencing (Okubo, 1997) is improving day by day with the deployment of broadband network technologies and advances in the techniques for audio and video compression. Below there is a analysis and comparison among different alternatives available to support videoconferencing over broadband networks is given. Specifically, the ITU recommendations H.321, H.310 and H.323 ([H.321], [H.310] and [H.323].

1. First Standard

The standard H.320 has been considered as the very starting point for the current development of videoconferencing systems. It is the first standard ("Recommendation" in ITU terminology) to provide a total system for videoconferencing, allowing the interoperation of equipment built by different manufacturers. H.320 is supported by narrow-band ISDN (N-ISDN), which provides digital channels with different bandwidths: 64 kbit/s (B channel), 384 kbit/s (H0 channel) and 1536/1920 kbit/s (H11/H12 channel) [27]. The Recommendation stipulates several other Recommendations in which constituent elements, such as audio coding, video coding, multimedia multiplexing and system control, are defined. For audio coding, G.711 [G.711] is the basic standard, but other Recommendations define different qualities with different bandwidth requirements. For video coding and compression, ITU-T defines the H.261 standard, which can work from 64 kbit/s to 2 Mbit/s in multiples of 64 kbit/s.

2. ATM for Videoconferencing Systems

The advent of broadband network technology has created the requirement to use these technologies to support videoconferencing which requires high bandwidth. As ATM is the chosen technology for future broadband ISDN, therefore the ITU-T concentrated on the standardization of videoconferencing systems in ATM environments. Some characteristics of ATM make it an excellent supporting infrastructure for videoconferencing systems, among them (S Okubo, 1997):

1. Flexibility in bandwidth usage
2. Availability of high bandwidths
3. Service integration
4. Variable bit rate capability
5. Use of Cell Loss Priority
6. Multipoint distribution
7. Flexible multiplexing

However, there are also some drawbacks:

1. Cell loss
2. Cell delay variation (Jitter)
3. Packetization delay

3. Adapting to Broadband Networks

The H.321 simply defines the technical specifications for adapting H.320 terminals to broadband ISDN environments. This recommendation allows the interworking of terminals over broadband ISDN and terminals over narrowband ISDN. To facilitate interworking, the basic technologies used for audio and video codification and compression are also G.711 and H.261, the same as in H.320 (*ITU-T Recommendation H.320, ITU-T Recommendation H.321*).

4. Taking Full Advantage of Broadband

Recommendation H.310 has been recently approved. H.310 covers the requirements for systems and terminals to carry out audiovisual communications over ATM networks. These recommendation defines uni-directional and bi-directional terminals and classifies different types of terminals, depending on the ATM Adaptation Layer used (AAL1 or AAL5). H.310 standard apart from covering conversational services such as videoconferencing does also covers retrieval, messaging, video-on-demand, broadcast TV, video transmission and surveillance services (*ITU-T Recommendation H.310*).

H.321 is integrated in H.310 as one of the operating modes, providing interworking with other networks. H.310 also solves some of the limitations of H.321 by defining a Native ATM mode. Though it keeps the basic H.261 and G.711 as the coding for interoperability in video and audio respectively, it also defines the use of MPEG audio and video, which will provide a better quality in Native Mode operation (*ITU-T*

Recommendation G.711). The H.310 protocol reference model, which consists of the following protocol, stacks (*ITU-T Recommendation G.711, ITU-T Recommendation H.261*):

1. Out-of-band network access signaling stack for DSS2 signals.
2. In-band communication control stacks for H.245 messages [H.245], in charge of logical channel signaling and capabilities exchange.
3. H.320/H.321 interoperation mode stack using H.221 multimedia multiplex.
4. H.310 native mode stack using H.222.1/H.222.0 multimedia multiplex.
5. T.120 stack for data applications.

MULTIMEDIA COMMUNICATION STANDARDS

A multimedia standard is likely to provide support for a large number of applications. These applications render into specific set of requirements which may be very different from one another. One theme common to most applications is the need for supporting interactivity with different kinds of data. Communications mean standards but the production of standards for multimedia communications is beset by the problem that the many industries having a stake in it have radically different approaches to standardization. Standards play a major role in the multimedia revolution because they provide interoperability between hardware and software provided by multiple vendors. Some of the multimedia communication standards are discussed below:

1. MPEG-1 (Coding of Moving Pictures and Associated Audio))

The MPEG-1 is actually the first standard developed by the group and was the coding of the combined audio-visual signal at a bit rate around 1.5 Mbit/s. This was aggravated by the hope that was becoming apparent in 1988 to store video signals on a compact disc with a high quality comparative to VHS cassettes. Coding of video in 1988 at a such low bit rates had become possible all because of the decades of research in video coding algorithms. The video coding algorithms however, had to be applied to sub sampled pictures – a single field from a frame and only half of the samples in a line - to show their effectiveness. Also coding of audio, as separate from speech, allowed reduction by 1/6 of the PCM bitrate, typically 256 Kbit/s for a stereo source, with virtual transparency. When audio and video streams are encoded with the constraint of having a common time base, resulted into a single stream by the MPEG system layer. MPEG-1 formally known as ISO/IEC 11172 is standardized in five parts. The first three parts as Systems, Video and Audio. Two more parts complete the suite of MPEG-1 standards. Conformance Testing, which specifies the methodology for verifying claims of conformance to the standard by manufacturers of equipment and producers of bit streams, and Software Simulation, a full C-language implementation of the MPEG-1 standard (encoder and decoder) (ISO/IEC IS 13818-1).

2. MPEG-2 (Generic Coding of Moving Pictures and Associated Audio)

The MPEG-2 families of standards simply summarize the compression technologies and bit stream syntax that enables transmission of audio and video in broadband networks. Although these standards also describe the aspects needed to multiplex programs, enable clock synchronization and setup logical network links carrying video and audio content. MPEG-2 is, in many cases, associated only with video compression, which is certainly one of the most important parts of its functionality (Tseng & Anastassiou, 1996). In total, there are eight different parts of the MPEG-2, covering the different aspects of digital video and audio delivery and representation. Table 2 contains the different MPEG-2 parts.

MPEG-2 can be seen as a superset of the MPEG-1 coding standard and was designed to be backward compatible to MPEG-1 and every MPEG-2 compatible decoder can decode a valid MPEG-1 bit stream. Many video coding algorithms were integrated into a single syntax to meet the diverse applications requirements.

3. MPEG-4 (Coding of Audio-Visual Objects)

Multimedia communication is the possibility to communicate audiovisual information that is natural, synthetic, or both, is real time and non real time, supports different functionalities responding to user's needs, flows to and from different sources simultaneously, does not require the user to bother with the specifics of the communications channel, but uses a technology that is aware of it, gives users the possibility to interact with the different

Table 2. Comparison in between the traditional and multimedia communication

S.No	Characteristics	Data Transfer	Multimedia Transfer
1	Data rate	Low	High
2	Traffic pattern	Burst	Stream oriented, highly burst
3	Reliability requirements	No loss	Some loss
4	Latency time requirements	None	Low (for example: 20ms)
5	Mode of communication	Point to Point	Multipoint
6	Temporal relationship	None	Synchronized transmission.

information elements, lets the user to present the results of his interaction with content in the way suiting his needs.

In order to reach its own target, MPEG-4 follows an object based representation approach where an audio visual scene is coded as a composition of objects, natural as well as synthetic, providing the first powerful hybrid playground. Therefore, the objective of MPEG-4 is to provide an audiovisual representation standard supporting new ways of communication, access, and interaction with digital audiovisual data, and offering a common technical solution to various service paradigms -Telecommunications, broadcast, and interactive – among which the borders are disappearing. MPEG-4 will supply an answer to the emerging needs of application fields such as video on the Internet, multimedia broadcasting, content-based audiovisual database access, games, audiovisual home editing, advanced audiovisual communications, notably over mobile networks, teleshopping, remote monitoring and control (ISO/ IEC JTC1/SC29/WG11). The fully backward compatible extensions under the title of MPEG-4 Version 2 were frozen at the end of 1999, to acquire the formal International Standard Status early 2000. Some work, on extensions in specific domains, is still progress. MPEG-4 builds on the proven success of three fields:

1. Digital television,
2. Interactive graphics applications (synthetic content),
3. Interactive multimedia (World Wide Web, distribution of and access to content).

4. MPEG-4 VTC and JPEG-2000 Image Compression Standards

The rising use of multimedia communication systems and image compression requires higher performance and new features. JPEG-2000 is an emerging standard for still image compression. It is not only intended to provide rate distortion and subject image quality performance superior to existing standards, but also to provide functionality that current standards can either not address efficiency or not address at all. The compression advantages in JPEG-2000 are a direct result of the inclusion into the standard of a number of advanced and attractive features including progressive recovery, lossy /lossless compression, and region of interest capabilities. These features lay the foundation for JPEG- 2000 to provide tremendous benefits to a range of industries. Some of the applications that will benefit directly from JPEG-2000 are: image archiving, Internet, Web browsing, document imaging, digital photography, medical imaging and remote sensing (Koenen & Pereira, 2000).

Functionally, JPEG-2000 includes many advanced features:

Image compression must not only reduce the necessary storage and bandwidth requirements, but also allow extraction for editing, processing and targeting particular devices and applications. JPEG-2000 allows extraction of different resolutions, pixel fidelities and regions of interest, components, and more, all from a single compressed bit stream. This allows an application to manipulate or transmit only the essential information for any target device from any JPEG-2000 compressed source image.

1. Component precision: 1 to 127 bits/sample (signed or unsigned).
2. Each component may have different precision and sub sampling factor.
3. Image data may be stored compressed or uncompressed.
4. Lossy and lossless compression.

Progressive recovery by fidelity or resolution

1. Tiling
2. Error resilience
3. Region of interest coding
4. Random access to image in spatial domain
5. Security

Some of the technology highlights for JPEG-2000 are:

1. Wavelet sub-band coding
2. Reversible integer-to-integer and nonreversible real to real wavelet transforms
3. Reversible integer-to-integer and nonreversible real to real multi component transforms
4. Bit-plane coding
5. Arithmetic coding
6. Code stream syntax similar to JPEG
7. File format syntax.

5. MPEG-7 Standardization Process of Multimedia Content Description

MPEG-7 formally named "Multimedia Content Description Interface" is the standard that describes multimedia content so users can search, browse and retrieve the content more efficiently and effectively than they could by using existing mainly text-based search engines (ISO/IEC JTC1/SC29/WG11, Doc.N3752). It is a standard for describing the features of multimedia content. The word "features" or "descriptions" represent a rich concept that can be related to several levels of abstraction. Descriptions vary according to the types of data. Furthermore, different types of descriptions are necessary for different purposes of categorization. MPEG-7 will specify a standard set of descriptors that can be used to describe various types of multimedia information. Also, MEPG-7 will standardize ways to define other descriptors as well as structures for the descriptors and their relationships. This description will

be associated with the content to allow fast and efficient searching for material of user's interest. A language to specify description schemes i.e. a description definition language (DDL) will be standardized, too. Audiovisual (AV) material that has MPEG-7 data associated with it can be indexed and searched for. This material includes: still pictures, graphics, 3D models, audio, speech, video and information about how these elements are combined in a multimedia presentation. Special cases of these general data types may include facial expressions and personal characters (ISO/IEC N4041, *MPEG-21*). There are people who want to use the audiovisual information for various purposes. However, before the information could be used, it must be located. At the same time, the increasing availability of potentially interesting material makes this search more difficult. This challenging situation led to the need of a solution to the

Problem of quickly and efficiently searching for various types of multimedia material of interest to the user. MPEG-7 standard wants to answer to this need, providing this solution (Okubo, 1997). MPEG-7 is rather different from the other MPEG standards, because it does not define a way to represent data with the objective to reconstruct the data as faithfully as possible, like MPEG-1, MPEG-2 and MPEG-4 did. The increasingly pervasive role that audiovisual sources are destined to play in our lives and the growing need to have these sources further processed make it necessary to develop forms of audiovisual information representation that go beyond the simple waveform or sample-based, frame-based (such as MPEG-1 and MPEG-2) or even object-based (such MPEG-4) representations. This necessitates forms of representation that allow some degree of interpretation of the information's meaning, which can be passed onto, or accessed by, a device or a computer code. The people active in defining MPEG-7 standard represent broadcasters, equipment and chip manufacturers, digital content creators and managers, telecommunication service provides, publishers and intellectual property rights managers as well as researchers.

6. MPEG-21 Multimedia Framework

The objectives behind initiating MPEG-21 are as follows:

1. In order to understand if and how various components fit together.
2. To discuss which new standards may be required, if gaps in the infrastructure exist and, once the above two points have been reached.
3. To actually accomplish the integration of different standards.

The digital market place, which is founded upon ubiquitous international communication network such as the Internet, rewrites existing business models for trading physical goods with new models for distributing and trading digital content electronically. In this new market place, it is becoming increasingly difficult to separate the different intellectual property rights which are associated with multimedia content (ISO/IEC JTC1/SC29/WG11, Doc.N3752).

The latest MPEG project MPEG-21 Multimedia Frameworks has been started with the prime objective to enable transparent and augmented use of multimedia resources across a wide range of networks and devices. The basic elements of the framework are:

1. Digital Items, structured digital objects with a standard representation, identification and metadata within the MPEG-21 framework.
2. Users of all entities that interact in the MPEG-21 environment or make use of MPEG-21 Digital Items.

The meaning of User in MPEG-21 is very broad and is by no means restricted to the end user. Therefore an MPEG-21 user can be anybody who creates content, provide content, archive content, rates content, enhances or delivers content, aggregates content, syndicates content, sells content to end users, consumes content, subscribe to content, regulate content, facilitates or regulates transactions that occur from any of the above. The work carried out so far has identified seven technologies that are needed to achieve the MPEG-21 goals. They are (ISO/IEC JTC1/SC29/WG11, Doc.N3752):

1. Digital Item Declaration: a uniform and flexible abstraction and interoperable schema for declaring Digital Items
2. Content Representation: how the data is represented as different media.
3. Digital Item Identification and Description: a framework for identification and description of any entity regardless of its nature, type or granularity.
4. Content Management and Usage: the provision of interfaces and protocols that enable creation, manipulation, search, access, storage, delivery, and reuse of content across the content distribution and consumption value chain.
5. Intellectual Property Management and Protection: the means to enable content to be persistently and reliably managed and protected across a wide range of networks and devices.
6. Terminals and Networks: the ability to provide interoperable and transparent access to content across networks and terminal installations.
7. Event Reporting: the metrics and interfaces that enable Users to understand precisely the performance of all reportable events within the framework.

DISTRIBUTED MULTIMEDIA SYSTEMS

Distributed Multimedia Systems is an area of active commercialization and research. This technology can be seen as the next generation technology for computers and communication networks. A distributed multimedia system combines a variety of multimedia information resources over a network into an application used by the client. In this manner, the user can access different remote information sources and services. The system is based on the interaction between the user and the application. The user can control the data flow. Which means that multimedia system is made interactive as if it were on the same system? Therefore this type of system is different from the conventional broadcast system. In such services typified by Cable television, clients can neither control the programs they view nor schedule the viewing time of the programs to suit their preferences. The user in such systems is flooded with irrelevant information, without a possibility to choose only the information of the interest. This kind of distributed environment is capable of serving a large number of end users to concurrently access a large number of repositories of stored data and also with the option of manipulating the environment by making the broadcast interactive. The enormous communication bandwidth required, the Quality of Service (QOS) demanded a careful design of the system in order to maximize the number of concurrent users while minimizing the cost needed to obtain it. The main component of a distributed multimedia system consists of major 3 components: Information (content) providers, a wide area network, and a multimedia client. There are many design issues in building each of the components. The breakthrough achieved in Digital Information Compression has helped to transmit the digital information in real time.

1. Architecture of Distributed Multimedia System

A distributed multimedia system consists of three different basic components: an Information server, a wide area network and a multimedia client on the user site. The user interface or the multimedia client deals with the issues related to presentation and manipulation of multimedia objects and the interaction with the user. The network provides the communication mechanism between the user and the server. The server is responsible for managing multimedia databases and also composing general multimedia objects for the user. The composition of the object is a complex process of integrating and synchronizing multimedia data for transport, display and manipulation. The system usually consists of multiple users, servers and networks as depicted in the figure 5.

2. User Terminal

A Multimedia terminal consists of a computer with a special hardware such as a microphone, high-resolution graphics display, stereo speakers, and a network interface. The user interacts with the system via a computer keyboard, mouse or a hand held remote control. Many of the user terminals still resemble traditional computers. Because of this, additional development work is required before the terminals can meet the requirements of the multimedia data and the user. Because of the large size of the multimedia objects and real - time requirements the multimedia terminal or the network should include large data buffers. To restore the temporal relationship of a data stream, stream handlers should be connected to the data buffers. To synchronize the possible multiple data streams and to control the stream handlers, synchronization and streaming manager is required. Since multimedia data objects are large,

Figure 5. Architecture of distributed multimedia system

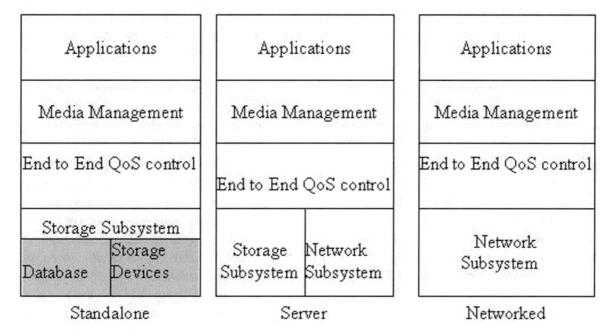

the terminal should also include compression and decompression hardware. Well some of these issues would be discussed later on.

3. Network and Communication

Multimedia communication differs from the traditional communication. The multimedia traffic requires transfer of large volumes of data at very high speeds, even when the data is compressed. Especially for interactive multimedia communication the network must provide low latency. Continuous media as video and audio require guarantees of minimum bandwidth and maximum end-to-end delay. The variation in delay referred to as jitter, and loss of data must also be bound. Traditional networks are used to provide error-free transmission. However, most multimedia applications can tolerate some errors in transmission due to corruption or packet loss without retransmission or correction. In some cases, to meet real-time delivery requirements or to achieve synchronization, some packets are

even discarded. Some of the differences in the traditional and multimedia communication are given in the table 2 given below:

The increasing popularity of the Internet and the fact that the infrastructure already exists suggest that the Internet could be used for distributed multimedia systems. The telephone and common antenna TV (CATV) cable networks are also a possibility to support interactive multimedia at user homes due to their wide deployment. From the above discussion we have noted that the Traditional networks do not suit multimedia communication. Transmission characteristics of existing Ethernet and Internet Protocols (CSMA/ CD, TCP/IP) do not support the low latency, high bandwidth requirements of the audio video based applications. Ethernet only provides a bandwidth of 10 Mbps. This is inadequate for most multimedia applications. Moreover its access time is not bound and its latency and jitter are unpredictable. New protocols which are considered for carrying multimedia data include the 100 Mbps Ethernet Standard, Distributed Queue dual bus (DQDB),

Fiber Distributed Data Interface (FDDI) and Asynchronous Transfer mode (ATM). The first three have bandwidths of the order of 100 Mbps. ATM enables a bandwidth of 155 – 622 Mbps depending on the characteristics of the network.

FDDI in its synchronized mode has low access latency and low jitter. FDDI also guarantees a bounded access delay and a predictable average bandwidth for synchronous traffic. However, Due to its high cost FDDI is at the moment used primarily for the backbone networks. Asynchronous Transfer Mode (ATM) is rapidly emerging as the future protocol for multimedia communication. ATM provides great flexibility in the bandwidth allocation by assigning fixed length packets called cells, to support virtual connections. ATM can also increase the bandwidth efficiency by buffering and statistically multiplexing burst traffic at the expense of cell delay and loss. For the Internet, the Internet Engineering Task Force (IETF) is working on a TCP/IP interface for ATM.

4. Multimedia Server

Current personal computers, workstations and servers are designed to handle traditional forms of data. Their performance is optimized for a scientific or transaction – oriented type of workload. These systems do not perform well for multimedia data, requiring fast data retrieval and guaranteed real time capabilities. The I/O capacity is usually a severe bottleneck. Some of the requirements for Multimedia Server are as follows:

1. Minimal Response time: A crucial factor for the success of multimedia services is the response time seen by the client. The server must be able to minimize response time to live unto the expectations of the user.
2. Fast Processing Capability: To guarantee fast response time, clients should be processed fast and data access rates should be minimized.
3. Reliability and availability: Like any other server, multimedia server must be reliable. The larger the number of users and volume of data handled by the server, the more difficult is to guarantee reliability. To provide fault tolerance special hardware and software mechanisms must be employed. Since client requests may arrive at any time, the time the server is unavailable should be minimized.
4. Ability to sustain guaranteed number of streams: Another important factor is the maximum number of data streams the server can simultaneously handle. This affects the total number of clients the server can serve.
5. Real-time delivery: To be able to deliver multimedia data, the server should support real-time delivery. This poses profound requirements on the resource scheduling at the operating system level. The server should be able to guarantee real-time delivery for individual streams as well as for all the streams combined together. For this accurate real-time operating systems have to be developed.
6. High storage capacity: To be able to store multimedia data and a large variety of information the server must have a large storage capacity. To sustain the delivery requirements of multimedia data, the server may be required to compress and encode video and image data prior to transport or storage. The performance of compression and signal processing should be optimized. This might require special hardware.
7. Quality of Service (Qos) requirements: The Quality of Service (Qos) is a set of parameters describing the tolerable end-to-end delay, throughput, and the level of reliability in multimedia communication and presentation. Qos requirements of clients are an important factor that affects the usage of the server. The server should be able to provide and adapt itself to different QoS require-

ments, according to the characteristics of the client's terminal, the network connection and the requested data type.

8. Exploit user access patterns: The server should also be able to trap and exploit dynamic user behavior, minimizing system load and network traffic. For example, by analyzing data access rates and times, popular data could be distributed closer to users in periods of low network load.

9. Ability to handle different types of traffic: A multimedia server should be able to serve multiple real-time data streams simultaneously, but it must also be able to provide satisfactory service to non-real-time data. It should be able to handle control data encountered when loading new data from other servers or storage repositories, billing and accounting data and communication between intelligent personal agents. Agents are autonomous programs selecting and managing data according to user preferences.

10. Cost effectiveness: A very important requirement governing the future of multimedia servers is the cost effectiveness. The server must be affordable.

5. Current Trends in Distributed Multimedia Systems

Some of the Distributed Multimedia Systems are as follows:

1. Video on Demand: The consumer can select a video or any program on demand. The application consists of Interactive features like forward, rewind and pause.

2. News and Reference Services: News on Demand is similar to VOD but it provides sophisticated news retrieval and reference services that combine live and achieved video, access to textual data and still photog-

raphy from various sources. The information is delivered based on a filtering criteria kept by the user.

3. Interactive shopping and electronic commerce: Home shopping will provide a customizable shopping environment. Customers will be effectively and rapidly focus on the products and services that are of interest to them.

4. Entertainment and games: Interactive entertainment may become a frequently used service. Games will consist of simple applications that will be downloaded to the set top device thus not incurring the significant cost associated with the use of server and network facilities.

5. Distance Learning: Educational interactive programming and distance learning are areas where the research is going on. Current indications are there that these may become popular but not have sufficient commercial use to the providers.

SOME OF THE ADVANCE PROJECTS IN THE WORLD CREATING A REVOLUTION IN THE FIELD OF NETWORKED MULTIMEDIA SYSTEMS

Research programs on future Internet architecture in the United States are administrated by the National Science Foundation (NSF) directorate for computer and Information Science and Engineering (CISE). The Future Internet Architecture (FIA) program of the National Science Foundation (NSF) is built on the previous program, Future Internet Design (FIND). FIND funded about 50 research projects on all kinds of design aspects of the future Internet. FIA is the next phase to pull together the ideas into groups of overall architecture proposals. Some of the Advance Projects are as follows:

1. Named Data Networking (NDN)

The Named Data Networking (NDN) project is led by the University of California, Los Angeles with participation from about 10 universities and research institutes in the United States. The initial idea of the project can be traced to the concept of content-centric networks (CCNs) by Ted Nelson in the 1970s. After that, several projects such as TRIAD at Stanford and DONA from the University of California at Berkeley were carried out exploring the topic. In 2009 Xerox Palo Alto Research Center (PARC) released the CCNx project led by Van Jacobson, who is also one of the technical leaders of the NDN project (**Named Data Networking Project**).

2. Mobility First

The Mobility First (Mobility First Future Internet Architecture Project) project is led by Rutgers University with seven other universities. The basic motivation of Mobility First is that the current Internet is designed for interconnecting fixed endpoints. It fails to address the trend of dramatically increasing demands of mobile devices and services. The Internet usage and demand change is also a key driver for providing mobility from the architectural level for the future Internet. For the near term, Mobility First aims to address the cellular convergence trend motivated by the huge mobile population of 4 to 5 billion cellular devices; it also provides mobile peer-to-peer(P2P) and info station (delay-tolerant network[DTN]) application services which offer robustness in case of link/network disconnection. For the long term, in the future, Mobility First has the ambition of connecting millions of cars via vehicle-to-vehicle (V2V) and vehicle-to-infrastructure (V2I) modes, which involve capabilities such as location services, geo routing, and reliable multicast. Ultimately, it will introduce pervasive system to interface human beings with the physical world, and build a future

Internet around people. The challenges addressed by Mobility First include stronger security and trust requirements due to open wireless access, dynamic association, privacy concerns, and greater chance of network failure.

3. NEBULA

NEBULA (NEBULA Project) is another FIA project focused on building cloud-computing-centric network architecture. It is led by the University of Pennsylvania with 11 other universities. NEBULA envisions the future Internet consisting of a highly available and extensible core network interconnecting data centers to provide utility-like services. Multiple cloud providers can use replication by themselves. Clouds comply with the agreement for mobile "roaming" users to connect to the nearest data center with a variety of access mechanisms such as wired and wireless links. NEBULA aims to design the cloud service embedded with security and trustworthiness, high service availability and reliability, integration of data centers and routers, evolvability, and economic and regulatory viability. NEBULA design principles include, reliable and high-speed core interconnecting data centers, parallel paths between data centers and core routers, secure in access and transit, policy-based path selection mechanism, authentication enforced during connection establishment. With these design principles in mind, the NEBULA future Internet architecture consists of the following key parts:

1. The NEBULA data plane (NDP), which establishes policy-compliant paths with flexible access control and defense mechanisms against availability attacks.
2. NEBULA virtual and extensible networking techniques (NVENT), which is a control plane providing access to application selectable service and network abstractions such as redundancy, consistency, and policy routing

3. The NEBULA core (NCore), which re- dundantly interconnects data centers with ultrahigh-availability routers

4. *4WARD*

4WARD (The FP7 4WARD Project) is an EU FP7 project on designing a future Internet architecture led primarily by an industry consortium. The fund- ing is over 45 million dollars for a 2-year period. The key 4WARD design goals are:

1. To create a new "network of information" paradigm in which information objects have their own identity and do not need to be bound to hosts (somewhat similar to the goal of the NDN project)
2. To design the network path to be an active unit that can control itself and provide re- silience and failover, mobility, and secure data transmission
3. To devise "default-on" management capa- bility that is an intrinsic part of the network itself
4. To provide dependable instantiation and interoperation of different networks on a single infrastructure.

Thus, on one hand, 4WARD promotes the innovations needed to improve single network architecture; on the other hand, it enables multiple specialized network architectures to work together in an overall framework.

5. Future Internet Research and Experimentation (FIRE)

FIRE (FIRE: Future Internet Research and Experi- mentation) is one of the European Union's research projects on test beds and is like a counterpart of GENI in the United States. FIRE was started in 2006 in FP6 and has continued through several con- secutive cycles of funding. FIRE involves efforts from both industry and academia. It is currently in

its "third wave" focusing on providing federation and sustainability between 2011 and 2012. Note that the FIRE project's research is built on the previous work on the GEANT2 (Gigabit European Academic Networking Technology) project [11], which is the infrastructure test bed connecting over 3000 research organizations in Europe. FIRE also expects not only to change the Internet in techni- cal aspects but also in socio-economic terms by treating socio-economic requirements in parallel with technical requirements.

SUMMARY

In the field of telecommunication network, research is focused on post ISDN architectures and capabilities such as an integrated packet network and broadband ISDN. The economics and flexibility of integrated networks make them very attractive, and above all the packet network architectures have the potential for realizing these advantages. However, the effective incorporation of speech and other signals such as graphics, image and video into an integrated packet network (IPN) can rearrange network design priorities. Although processing speeds will continue to increase, it will also be necessary to minimize the nodal per-packet processing requirements imposed by the network design. This is a motivation for new switching concepts like fast packet switching and ATM. Data signals must generally be received error free in order to be useful, but the inherent structure of speech and image signals and the way in which they are perceived allows for some loss of infor- mation without significant quality impairment. This allows the possibility of purposely discarding limited information to achieve some other goal, such as the control temporary congestion. Multi- media communication standards have to depend on compromises between what is technologically feasible and what is theoretically possible. The success of the Standards in the market place is possible only if the cost performance ratio is well balanced. This is specifically true in the field of audio/video coding where a large variety of innovative coding algorithms exist, but may be too complex for implementation. Over the Internet, streaming of video faces many technological as well as business challenges and new codec's, protocols, players and subsystems are developed and came into existence to address them. Since its inception in early 1990s, the concept of streaming media has gone through a dramatic growth and transformation from a novel technology into one of the mainstream manners in which people experience the Internet today. The arrival of concept of streaming media comes at a time when basic multimedia technologies have already established themselves on desktop PCs. Streaming media is a technology that enabled the user to experience a multimedia presentation on-the-fly while it was being download from the Internet. The provision, bandwidth on demand with strict QoS guarantees is a fundamental property of ATM networks that makes them especially suitable for carrying real time multimedia traffic. Statistical multiplexing of VBR connections within the backbone network allows effective aggregation and capacity engineering. Anticipating that multimedia over IP will be one of the major driving forces behind the emerging broadband communications, addressing the challenges facing the delivery of multimedia applications over IP are a great importance. In order for the Internet to allow applications to request network packet delivery characteristics according to their needs, sources are expected to declare the offered traffic characteristics. Admission control rules have to be applied to ensure that requests are accepted only if sufficient network resources are available. Moreover, service-specific policing actions have to be employed within the network to ensure that nonconforming data flows do not affect the QoS commitments for already active data flows. One generic framework that addresses both the video coding and networking challenges

associated with Internet video is scalability. Any scalable Internet video coding solution has to enable a very simple and flexible streaming framework. The fine-grained scalable framework strikes a good balance between coding efficiency and scalability while maintaining a very flexible and simple video coding structure.

With the advent of common uses of the Internet, the demands for real-time and low-rate voice over IP applications are growing rapidly. Since the delivery of packets is not guaranteed in the IP networks, it is necessary to deal with the audible artifacts, which are caused by burst packet losses. Packet loss degrades the speech quality of the analysis-by-synthesis coders seriously since the loss parameters not only affect the current speech frame, but also produce the so-called error propagation problem resulting from corrupted filter memory. This packet loss problem can be solved by using different model parameters. Digital Subscriber line (DSL) technology offers unprecedented scalability for interactive video services. It is the basis for the point-to-point architecture that is the key to providing a combination of interactive video and broadcast services. The implementation of video services is a high priority for telecom providers. Delivering voice services over digital subscriber line offers a lucrative opportunity for both established and emerging services. Data broadcasting in support of multimedia applications requires efficient use of bandwidth resources in order to maximize the availability of play out content. From the data delivery point of view, the digital TV infrastructure provides a broadband digital distribution network, data transport protocols and digital terminals on the user premises. A number of advances in the network technology have proved a boon to the advances in Distributed Multimedia Systems. Some of the Advance Projects related to the development of the Networked Systems are discussed in the last section of the chapter.

REFERENCES

Ayanoglu, E. (1993). Performance improvement in the broadband networks using forward error correction for lost packets recovery. *Journal of High-Speed Networks*, *1*, 287–303.

Ayanoglu, E. (1996). Forward error control for MPEG-2 video transport in a wireless ATM LAN. *Proceedings of IEEE ICIP*, *2*, 833–836.

Bellido, L., & Fernández, D. & Pastor. (1996). Architectural Issues for Multimedia Cooperative Systems. *Proceedings of the 3rd International Workshop on Protocols for Multimedia Systems (PROMS)*. (pp. 33-47).

Bially, T., Gold, B., & Seneff, S. (1980). A technique for adaptive voice flow control in integrated packet networks. *IEEE Transactions on Communications*, *28*(3), 325–333. doi:10.1109/TCOM.1980.1094677

Bojkovic, Z. S. (1995). Image decomposition and compression in digital multimedia systems. *Proceedings of IX Int. Conference on signal processing applications and technology, ICSPAT*. Boston, USA. (pp.940-944).

Bojkovic, Z. S. (1996). Multimedia communication system: modeling, standardization, requirements. *Proceedings of International Conference on multimedia technology and digital telecommunication services, ICOMPT*. Budapest, Hungary. (pp. 5-13)

Brady, P. (1990). A model for generating on-off patterns in two-way communications. *The Bell System Technical Journal*, *48*(7), 2445–2472. doi:10.1002/j.1538-7305.1969.tb01181.x

Chang, Znati, T.F. (n. d.). ADVANCES IN DISTRIBUTED MULTIMEDIA SYSTEMS.

Constantine, A. Papandreou. (1998). Architecture of a multimedia communication system for technical documentation in a modern factory. In Computers in Industry. (pp. 83–93). Elsevier.

Cox, R. V., Haskell, B. G., LeCun, Y., Shahraray, B., & Rabiner, L. (1998). On the applications of multimedia processing to communications. *Proceedings of the IEEE*, *86*(5), 755–824. doi:10.1109/5.664272

FIRE. Future Internet Research and Experimentation. (2014). Retrieved from http://cordis.europa.eu/fp7/ict/fire

Gold, B. (1977). Digital speech networks. *Proceedings of the IEEE*, *65*(12), 1630–1658. doi:10.1109/PROC.1977.10806

Homma, T. (1995). MPEG contribution: Report of the adhoc group on MPEG-2 applications for multi-view point pictures. *ISO/IEC SC29/WG11 Doc*. 861.

ISO/IEC N4041. (2001). *MPEG-21 Overview*, Singapore. Retrieved from https://itscj.ipsj.or.jp/sc29/open/29view/29n43211.doc

ISO/IEC IS 13818-1. *Generic coding of moving pictures and associated audio, Part 1: System*, 1995. Retrieved from https://www.iso.org/iso/iso_catalogue/catalogue.../catalogue_tc_browse.html

ISO/IEC JTC1/SC29/WG11, Doc. N4030. (2001, March). *MPEG-4 Overview v18.0*, Singapore.

ISO/IEC JTC1/SC29/WG11, Doc.N3752. (2000). *Overview of the MPEG-7 standard*, La Baule. Retrieved from https:// 193.226.6.174/IT2002/pdf/L3.pdf

G.711 *ITU-T Recommendation G.711: Pulse code modulation (PCM) of voice frequencies* (1988). Retrieved from https://www.itu.int/rec/T-REC-G.711

H.261 *ITU-T Recommendation H.261: Video codec for audiovisual services at p x 64 kbit/s* (March 1993). Retrieved from https://www.ece.cmu.edu/~ece796/documents/Intro_H26x.doc

ITU-T Recommendation H.261, Video codec for audiovisual services at px64 kbit/s. (n. d.). Retrieved from https://www.itu.int/rec/T-REC-H.261-199303-I/en

H.310 *ITU-T Recommendation H.310: Broadband audio-visual communications systems and terminal equipment* (1996). Retrieved from https://www.ece.cmu.edu/~ece796/documents/H323V2NC-final.DOC

H.321 *ITU-T Recommendation H.321: Adaptation of H.320 Visual Telephone Terminals to B-ISDN Environments* (1996). Retrieved from https://www.itu.int/rec/T-REC-H.321-199603-S/en

Jayant, N. (1993). High quality networking of audio-visual information. *IEEE Communications Magazine, 31*(9), 84–95. doi:10.1109/35.236275

Karlsson, G. Asynchronous transfer of video. *SICS Research Report R95:14, Sweden.*

Koenen, R., & Pereira, F. (2000). *MPEG-7: A standardized description of audiovisual content. Signal Processing Image Communication, 16*(1-2), 5–13. doi:10.1016/S0923-5965(00)00014-X

Listanti, M., & Villani, F. (1983, February). An X.25 compatible protocol for packet voice communications. *Computer Communications, 6*(1), 23–31. doi:10.1016/0140-3664(83)90172-X

Merriman, P. (2000). *Video over DSL architecture* (pp. 250–257). Alcatel Telecommunications Review.

Minoli, D. (n. d.). Optimal packet length for packet voice communication. *IEEE Transactions on Communications, COM-27*, 607–611.

MobilityFirst Future Internet Architecture Project. (2013). Retrieved from http://mobilityfirst.winlab.rutgers.edu

Mouftah, H. T. (1992). Multimedia communications: An overview. *IEEE Communications Magazine, 30*, 18–19.

Named Data Networking Project. (2014). Retrieved from http://www.nameddata.net

NEBULA Project. (2013). Retrieved from http://nebula.cis.upenn.edu

Ni, J., Yang, T., & Tsang, D. H. K. (1996). CBR transportation on VBR MPEG-2 video traffic for video-on-demand in ATM networks. *Proceedings of the IEEE, ICC*, Dallas, Texas, USA. (pp. 1391–1395).

NSF Future Internet Architecture Project. (2013). Retrieved from http://www.nets-fia.net

NSF NeTS FIND Initiative. (2013). Retrieved from http://www.nets-find.net

Okubo, S., Dunstan, S., Morrison, G., Nilsson, M., Radha, H., Skran, D. L., & Thom, G. (1997). ITU-T Standardization of Audiovisual Communication Systems in ATM and LAN Environments. *IEEE Journal on Selected Areas in Communications, 15*(6), 965–982. doi:10.1109/49.611153

Okubo, S., Dunstan, S., Morrison, G., Nilsson, M., Radha, H., Skran, D. L., & Thom, G. (1997). ITU-T standardization of audiovisual communication systems in ATM LAN environments. *IEEE Journal on Selected Areas in Communications, 15*(6), 965–982. doi:10.1109/49.611153

Orzessek, M., & Sommer, P. (1998). *ATM and MPEG-2. Integrating digital video into broadband networks.* Upper Saddle River: Prentice Hall PTR.

Orzessek, M., & Sommer, P. (2006). *ATM and MPEG-2 integration of digital video into broadband networks. Prentice Hall PTR.* Upper Saddle River: New Jersy.

Pastor, E., Fernández, D., & Bellido, L. (1995). Cooperative Learning Over Broadband Networks. *6th Joint European Networking Conference (JENC6)*, Tel-Aviv.

Patr, D. W., DaSilva, L. A., & Frost, V. S. (1989). Priority discarding of speech in integrated packet networks. *IEEE Journal on Selected Areas in Communications*, 7(5), 644–656. doi:10.1109/49.32328

Pereira, F. (2004). . *Signal Processing Image Communication*, *15*, 269–270.

Puri, A. (1993). *Video coding using the MPEG-2 compression standard.* (pp. 1701–1713). Boston: SPIE/VCIP.

Rosenberg, J., Kraut, R. E., Gomez, L., & Buzzard, C. A. (1992). Multimedia communications for users. *IEEE Communications Magazine*, *30*(5), 20–36. doi:10.1109/35.137476

Servetto, S. D., & Nahrstedt, K. (2001). Broadcast quality video over IP. *IEEE Transactions on Multimedia*, *3*(1), 162–173. doi:10.1109/6046.909603

Sidron, J., & Gotal, J. S. (1988). PARIS: An approach to integrated high speed private networks. *International Journal of Digital Analog Cable System*, *1*(2), 77–85. doi:10.1002/dac.4520010208

Skodras, A. N., Christopoulos, C. A., & Ebrahimi, T. (2000). JPEG2000: the upcoming still image compression standard. *Proceedings of the 11th Portuguese Conference on Pattern Recognition*, Porto, Portugal. (pp. 359-366).

The FP7 4WARD Project. (2014). Retrieved from http://www.4ward-project.eu/

Tseng, B. L., & Anastassiou, D. (1996). Multi view point video coding with MPEG-2 compatibility. *IEEE Transactions CSVT*, 6, 414-419.

Verhoeyen, M. (2000). *Delivering voice services over DSL* (pp. 244–249). Alcatel Telecommunications Review.

Wolf, L. C., Griwadz, C., & Steinmetz, R. (1997). Multimedia communication. *Proceedings of the IEEE*, *85*(12), 1915–1933. doi:10.1109/5.650175

Zhang, Y. (1997). MPEG-2 video services for wireless ATM networks. *IEEE Journal on Selected Areas in Communications*, *15*(1), 119–128. doi:10.1109/49.553683

ADDITIONAL READING

Baileym, C. W., Jr. (2007). Intelligent Multimedia Computer Systems: Emerging Information Resources in the Network Environment.

Borko Furht. (2009). *Handbook of multimedia for Digital Entertainment and Arts*. Springer.

KEY TERMS AND DEFINITIONS

Asynchronous Transfer Mode: *ATM* is a high-speed networking standard designed to support both voice and data communications.

Internet: Global computer network providing a variety of information and communication facilities, consisting of interconnected networks using standardized communication protocols.

Multimedia: Multimedia means that computer information can be represented through audio, video, and animation in addition to traditional media (i.e., text, graphics drawings and images).

Network: A of interconnected (cable and/or wireless) computers and peripherals that is capable of sharing and between many .

Protocols: Protocol is the special set of rules that end points in a telecommunication connection use when they communicate.

Terminal: In data communications, a terminal is any device that terminates one end (sender or receiver) of a communicated signal.

Chapter 10
Data Security Issues and Solutions in Cloud Computing

Abhishek Majumder
Tripura University, India

Sudipta Roy
Assam University, India

Satarupa Biswas
Tripura University, India

ABSTRACT

Cloud is considered as future of Information Technology. User can utilized the cloud on pay-as-you use basis. But many organizations are stringent about the adoption of cloud computing due to their concern regarding the security of the stored data. Therefore, issues related to security of data in the cloud have become very vital. Data security involves encrypting the data and ensuring that suitable policies are imposed for sharing those data. There are several data security issues which need to be addressed. These issues are: data integrity, data intrusion, service availability, confidentiality and non-repudiation. Many schemes have been proposed for ensuring data security in cloud environment. But the existing schemes lag in fulfilling all these data security issues. In this chapter, a new Third Party Auditor based scheme has been proposed for secured storage and retrieval of client's data to and from the cloud service provider. The scheme has been analysed and compared with some of the existing schemes with respect to the security issues. From the analysis and comparison it can be observed that the proposed scheme performs better than the existing schemes.

INTRODUCTION

Cloud Computing is a new computing model that distributes the computation on a resource pool. The resource pool which contains a large amount of computing resources offers services to the clients.

These services are provided to the cloud users as utility services. The utility services are generally described as XaaS (X as a Service) where X can be software, platform or infrastructure.

Many organizations deal with the storage, retrieval and maintenance of huge amount of

DOI: 10.4018/978-1-4666-8387-7.ch010

data. In traditional computing environment, the organization has to maintain an infrastructure for storing the data. With the use of cloud computing services, the organization gets relieved from the burden of maintaining the infrastructure. But, when the cloud clients are storing their data, users are unaware of its physical storage location. As a result, one of the biggest concern of cloud computing is its data security. It is not clear how safe the client's data is and ownership of data is also unclear when these services are used. Cloud service providers claim that the stored data are completely safe. But, it is too early to comment on the reliability issues claimed by them. The stored data may suffer from damage during data transition to or from the cloud service provider by intrusion. Therefore, data security is the prime threat of modern technological era that each of the cloud service providers are facing. Data security involves encrypting the data as well as ensuring that suitable policies are imposed for sharing those data. The issues which need to be considered for ensuring data security in cloud environment are: data integrity, data intrusion, service availability, confidentiality and non-repudiation (Mahmood, 2011; Alzain et al., 2012; You et al., 2012).

For ensuring data security in cloud environment many schemes have been proposed. Varalakshmi et al., (2012), proposed a third party broker based scheme. Here a third party broker has been introduced to reduce the computational burden on client side and to increase the security of the system by not relying on the cloud service provider. The third party broker performs the activities of partitioner, hash key generator, encryptor, decryptor, local database manager and verifier. S. Kumar et al., (2011), proposed a meta data encryption based scheme for checking the integrity of stored data. In this scheme the verifier creates the meta data and encrypts it to reduce the computational overhead on the client side. At the time of integrity checking the verifier compares the decrypted

meta data with the stored meta data. P. Kumar et al., (2011), proposed a hidden markov model and clustering based approach for intrusion detection in cloud environment. The scheme uses a data mining techniques for securing the cloud computing network. Hemant et al., (2011), proposed a governance body based scheme for solving the security issues of cloud computing. In this scheme all the transaction between the cloud server and the clients goes through the central server or governance body. Double encryption is used on each transaction. Shuai Han et al. proposed a third party auditor (TPA) scheme for ensuring data storage security in cloud computing. In this scheme, the cloud service performs additional functionality of TPA for making the system more trustful. Alzain et al., (2011) proposed Multi-clouds Database Model (MCDB). The model has been developed for handling data security issues in multi cloud environment. A redundancy based approach (Alzain et al., 2012) has been proposed for improving the security of MCDB model. The scheme uses Shamir's secret sharing algorithm (Shamir, 1979) and triple modular redundancy (TMR) to enhance the security of MCDB model.

In this chapter a new Third Party Auditor based scheme has been proposed. The entities used in the scheme are: Client/Data owner, Third Party Auditor (TPA) and Cloud Service Provider (CSP). It uses Whirlpool hash algorithm (Stallings, 2006) to maintain data integrity. A comparative study of the proposed scheme has been carried out with respect to some of the existing schemes. It has been observed that the proposed scheme performs better than the existing schemes.

The organization of the chapter is as follows. Next section discusses different data security issues. Various data security models, a Third Party Auditor based scheme and its comparison with other existing schemes have been discussed in the subsequent sections.

DATA SECURITY ISSUES

With the popularity of cloud computing the users store more and more amount of data in cloud environment. Therefore, there is an immense increase in data seeking activity of the users from the cloud service providers. This increase can give rise to serious security concerns in cloud environment. In this section, a detailed discussion on the data security issues in cloud computing have been presented.

In cloud environment, there is a critical need to securely store, manage, share and scrutinize enormous amount of data. It is very important that the cloud is secured enough to maintain the security of data. Exact physical localization of user data in virtual cloud atmosphere is among some of the prime challenges in cloud computing. The major security challenge with clouds is that the owner of the data may not have complete knowledge of where their data are stored. Data security involves encryption of the data and it ensures that suitable policies are imposed for sharing those data. While developing a scheme for data security in cloud environment many security issues need to be considered. Some of these security issues are (Mahmood, 2011; Alzain et al., 2012; You et al., 2012):

- **Data Integrity:** Data integrity is maintenance of accuracy and consistency of the stored data. It is indicated by absence of change in stored data between two consecutive updates of any data record by some legitimate user. In cloud environment, the data stored in the cloud storage may be modified by some attacker during its transmission and reception to and from the cloud storage provider. The risk of such attacks from both inside and outside the cloud provider exists. Therefore, mechanisms to detect any modification of the stored data should be present in the data storage and retrieval system of the cloud.

- **Data Intrusion:** Data intrusion is the process of getting access to the private data of a user by any undesired person using some backdoor or trap. In cloud computing system, the user accesses the stored data using his account. Therefore, data intrusion is another security risk that may occur with a cloud service provider. If any intruder can gain access to the account password, he will be able to do any kind of unwanted changes to the account's private documents. Undesirable alteration of user data may also occur due to intrusion. So, data intrusion is an important issue in cloud environment.

- **Service Availability:** The principle of service availability is that the service has to be available to the authorized users all the times. Since cloud service providers offer different kind of services to their customers, service availability is a major issue in cloud services. It is mentioned in some cloud providers licensing agreement, that the service may be unavailable anytime due to some unforeseen reason. If all valuable business documents are stored in the cloud and the cloud suddenly goes down, can all the important documents be recovered intact? It is also important to know whether the company, where user is storing his vital information, is financially steady and will not suddenly vanish taking all the valuable information with it.

- **Confidentiality:** Confidentiality ensures that only the sender and the intended receivers are able to access the contents of the message. Large amount of data is stored in the cloud storage. The data should be kept secured and should not be exposed to anyone at any cost. Therefore, confidentiality of data is another important security issue associated with cloud computing.

- **Non-Repudiation:** Non-repudiation restricts the sender of the message from making any claim that he has not sent the message. Since in cloud environment there are large numbers of message transfers between the users, it has to guarantee that the sender cannot deny the ownership of the file sent. Therefore, non-repudiation is a major concern for data security.

DATA SECURITY SOLUTIONS

Because of rapid increase in security threats, now-a-days, researchers and enterprises have highly concentrated on ensuring data security in cloud computing environment. Several schemes have been proposed by the researchers for securing the stored data in cloud storage server. In this section some of the existing schemes for data security have been discussed:

Third Party Broker Based Scheme

Third party broker based scheme (Varalakshmi et al., 2012) has been designed mainly to check the integrity of the data items by using encryption algorithm. In this scheme the system is divided into three entities: clients, storage servers and broker. Broker acts as an interface between client and storage servers. Broker consists of partitioner, encryptor, decryptor, hash key generator, verifier and local database manager. Client stores encrypted data in storage server and queries the data through broker for checking its integrity. When the client requests for data storage, the request handler of the broker receives it. After that the files are encrypted using encryption algorithm and sent to the partitioner. The partitioner partitions the received client files into multiple segments. These segments are processed by the hash key generator to generate hash key for each segment using SHA algorithm. Then the database stores the client's file identity, encrypted segments, sequence numbers of the segments, hash key for encrypted segments and IP address of corresponding virtual

machine in which the encrypted segments are stored. This information is required for checking integrity of the data stored in the cloud. When the client wants to retrieve the file from CSP, it will send the request to request handler. Request handler will send the request to the verifier. With the identity of the client's file, verifier retrieves the corresponding details from the database and sends the retrieval request to the respective virtual machines (VMs). Then the broker will generate the hash value of that encrypted segments which is retrieved from VMs and compare the generated hash value with already stored hash value. If all the hash values match, verifier concludes that the file is intact. If there is some modification in the stored file, the hash values will not match. All the encrypted segments will be combined based on their sequence number. Then, the combined files will be decrypted using reverse of encryption algorithm and sent to the client.

Meta Data Encryption Based Scheme

Meta data encryption based scheme (S. Kumar et al., 2011) has been proposed with an objective to reduce the computational and storage overhead while ensuring security of the data. It does not involve encryption of the whole data. Only few bits of data per data block are encrypted which reduces the computational overhead of the clients. In this scheme, the verifier does not store any data. It needs to store only a single cryptographic key and two functions which generate a random sequence. Before storing the file at the archive, the verifier pre-processes the file and appends some metadata to the file. The integrity of the file can be verified by using the metadata. Let, the file F consists of n number of file blocks each having m bits in them. For each data block, the function g generates a meta data containing a set of k bit positions within the m bits. The function $g(i,j)$ gives the jth bit in the ith data block. Verifier chooses the value of k which is a secret known only to him. Therefore, from each data block a set of k bits are generated. In total for all n blocks the metadata size is n×k bits. Let m_i represents the k bits of metadata for the ith block. Each of the metadata m_i is encrypted by using a suitable algorithm to give a new modified metadata M_i. A function h is used to generate a k bit integer α_i for each ith block. The verifier keeps the function secret. For generating M_i the output of a function h is added with m_i. So M_i can be computed as:

$$M_i = m_i + \alpha_i$$

All the generated meta data bit blocks are concatenated together. This concatenated meta data will be appended to the file F before storing it at the cloud server. At the time of verification, verifier compares the challenge and the response. Let, the verifier wants to check the integrity of nth block. A challenge is thrown to the cloud server by the verifier specifying block number i, a bit number j generated by g and the position at which metadata of the ith block is appended. The cloud server responds to the challenge by sending back the meta data. The verifier will use α_i to decrypt the metadata sent by the cloud. After that the corresponding bit in the decrypted meta data is compared with the bit which is sent by the cloud. If both the bits match, integrity is preserved.

Hidden Markov Model and Clustering Based Approach

P. Kumar et al., (2011), proposed a scheme for security in cloud computing using Hidden Markov Model (HMM) and clustering. The scheme performs intrusion detection based on the probability of the behaviour. Clustering is introduced into the system for fast and efficient data access. It also provides a compact view of data in cloud environment. It is used for fraud detection (Shrivastava et al., 2008). For data security, Firewall gateway is deployed to block the SSH service. SSH service is used for gaining access to the server from anywhere in the world. It simply drops the packets that come from any IP address which is not known to it. For ensuring stronger data security the scheme also uses HMM. HMM model monitors the user behaviour continuously. If any malicious activity is detected by filter network after getting input from the HMM, the system administrator immediately takes action. It is the responsibility of the system administrator to keep the data safe. In this scheme, the cloud computing environment is connected to the external network through plug–in. It can help the proposed model to backup the data regularly. These backups can be used for data recovery in case of emergency. It can be easily connected with any other cloud environment if needed. As a result, the load on the server of a cloud can be minimized. The main advantage of this scheme is that, with the help of HMM the cloud environment can protect itself from attack even though the intruder uses stolen ID and password of a legitimate user.

Governance Body Based Scheme

Hemant et al., (2011) have introduced a new governance body based scheme where a central sever will maintain a router table. The router table will contain cloud id, user id, the actual server id to which the user is connecting, server name, total time of synchronization, packet size, lease time, source IP and destination IP. It will also contain the packet transfer rate which is the actual amount of data flow. With the help of router table the central server can back track to the user and server. The user side will contain personal firewall. These application level firewalls will not only check the undesirable web sites based on their IP addresses but they will also keep track if the packets are malicious. They can record the activities of the user. The connectivity between user and the central server will be encrypted using SSL encryption standards. Different security algorithms can be used with SSL for enhancing the security of the system. When any user wants to connect to a particular server, his information gets stored in the router table. In case, the user is unable to connect to the server, the server can be easily backtracked from the central server's routing table.

Third Party Auditor (TPA) Scheme

The traditional network architecture consists of three entities which are users, cloud service provider and third party auditor (TPA). Users have large data files to be stored in the cloud. They are active participants and can be individual customers or organizations. Cloud service provider has sufficient storage space as well as computation resources for maintaining the stored data. But users cannot completely rely on the cloud providers for safety of their data. Therefore, to ensure the safety of stored data TPA is used. It is powerful than the cloud customers and keeps every day data access in control. It provides trustful authentication to the user who stores their data in the cloud. Upon receiving request from the user, TPA can review and interpret the stored data in the cloud on behalf of the user. It can also provide a log report to the user. In this scheme (Han et al., 2011) the authors have proposed a new architecture for cloud storage, where the third party auditor and the cloud service provider have been combined together forming an advanced cloud service provider. The RSA has been used to encrypt the data flow between servers. It uses Bilinear Diffie-Hellman algorithm for exchanging keys. Users and cloud service provider can communicate with each other using a message header without a third party auditor. When a cloud storage server receives a request from a user, it will create a pair of user public key, user secret key and user's identity in certain server. After that the server will save the user's information in the user list and will send the user secret key, user's ID in certain server and server ID to the user. The cloud storage server will also send a copy of the keys to the trustful organization server. Trustful organization servers are maintained by trustful organizations to act as a watchdog for every ac-

cess key in cloud service provider. It comprises of few number of servers. The users and cloud service provider cannot get any authentication information from trustful organization without a certain module. Trustful organization server will maintain all the keys stored in cloud storage servers. Before sending the data files to the cloud service provider the user will create a message header. The header will contain: cloud server ID (SID), check code of SID (SIDCC), time to live (TTL), user ID in certain cloud server (CUID), check code for CUID (SIDCC) and check code of the message header (HCC). The message header along with the file will be encrypted and sent to the cloud server. When the cloud server receives the data file, it will save the file and search SID both in the server list and trustful organization's server. If SID is found it will communicate with SID server to get user public key (UPK) of the user. Use of the message header eliminates the need of a separate TPA. On the other hand, upon receiving a data download request from the user, the storage server will check the check code of the message header (HCC), check code for cloud server ID (SIDCC) and check code for user ID in certain cloud server (CUIDCC). If all these codes are correct it will locate the server using the cloud server ID and send the unique client ID to the server. The server will check its user list and sends back user public key (UPK) of the user. If the server indicated by the SID fails to respond, the request will be sent to the trustful organization's server and it will perform the same work as done by the server.

Multi-Cloud Database Model (MCDB)

According to Alzain et al. (2011), shifting from single cloud to multi cloud is very important for ensuring the security of user's data. Authors suggested that, there are three main security factors of data (data integrity, data intrusion and service availability) that needs to be considered as the major concern for cloud computing. They have proposed a new model called Multi-clouds Database Model (MCDB). Shamir's secret sharing algorithm [12], which is based on polynomial interpolation, has been incorporated in the scheme. In Shamir's secret sharing algorithm, a data D is shared into n pieces in such a way that D is easily reconstruct able from k pieces, but even complete knowledge of k-1 pieces reveals absolutely no information about D. Multi-clouds Database Model (MCDB) uses data bases management system (DBMS) for managing and controlling the communication between the cloud service providers and the client. When the user sends some data to the cloud the DBMS receives the data and divides it into n parts using Shamir's secret sharing algorithm. Each of the part is stored in different cloud service provider. The authors have suggested that cloud computing should not end with a single cloud. Therefore, DBMS replicates the data among several clouds. Division of the data depends upon the number of cloud service providers. MCDB model has been compared with Amazon cloud service which is single cloud. This model guarantees the security and privacy of the data in multiple clouds using multi shares technique instead of single cloud.

Redundancy Based Approach

Alzain et al. (2012) proposed a Multi-clouds Database Model employing both secret sharing approach and triple modular redundancy (TMR). Shamir's secret sharing approach ensures security of the stored data in the cloud. On the other hand, triple modular redundancy (TMR) is a type of passive hardware redundancy. In TMR technique, three identical modules execute the same task in parallel. If one of the three modules was faulty, the other two modules will mask and hide the result of the faulty module. This model also uses sequential method in which single hardware module is used and the software is executed three times to perform the same operation. The output will be based on majority voting. TMR is used

with sequential method to improve the reliability of the system and multi shares technique to improve the security of the system. The sequential voting method decreases the number of execution cycles. The cloud manager divides the data into n shares and stores them in different clouds. Then it will generate a random polynomial function of the same degree for every value of the valuable attribute which the clients want to hide from untrusted clouds. The data store will not store the polynomials. The polynomials are generated by the data store at the beginning and end of query processing. When the cloud manager receives a query, it will rewrite n queries for each of the n clouds. To retrieve the shares from clouds, shares from three clouds will pass through the voter inside cloud manager. The output will be the output of majority of the voters.

PROPOSED SCHEME

In this section the proposed Third Party Auditor Based scheme has been presented. The proposed scheme uses the following three entities:

- **Client/Data Owner:** They are the participants who have data to be stored in the cloud for maintenance and computation. Data owner can be individual customers or organization.
- **TPA:** It has the skills that the cloud users do not have. It verifies the stored data in the cloud storage server to check whether the cloud server has manipulated the user data or not.
- **CSP:** Cloud Storage Servers are managed by Cloud Storage Provider, which has a huge storing space and flexible resources to keep up the client's data.

The architecture of the proposed scheme is shown in Figure 1. The client or data owner stores his file in the cloud to get relieved from the bur-

Figure 1. Proposed architecture

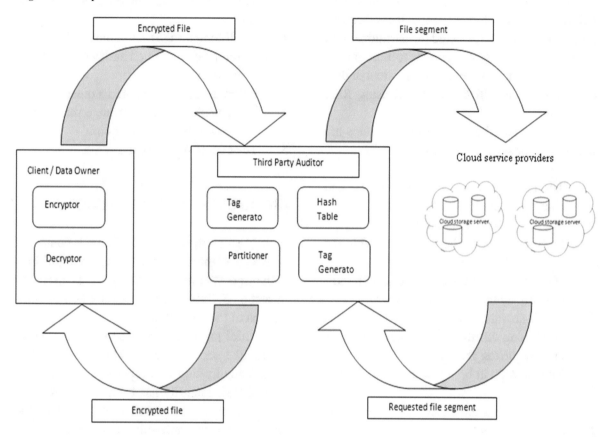

den of storage and computation. In this scheme encryption and decryption is done with the help of RSA algorithm. Client or data owner encrypts the digitally signed data by using RSA algorithm before storing it at the cloud servers. The RSA encryption is the most widely used public key cryptography algorithm in the world. Then the file will be sent to the TPA. The TPA has access to the cloud service provider environment and understands the service level agreement (SLA) that is in between the customer and the provider. By this way the TPA is reliable and independent (Shah et al., 2007). In the proposed architecture the TPA will have four components: Tag Generator, Partitioner, Hash Table and Hash Generator. The partitioner will divide each data file into number of data blocks. Hash generator will generate hash value for each data block individually using Whirl-

pool hash algorithm (Stallings, 2006). Whirlpool hash algorithm is based on 512 bit block cipher, whose structure is similar to Rijndael (Advanced Encryption Standard). It uses 512 bit-keys. In this scheme Whirlpool algorithm is used because there is not any known successful attack made against the algorithm and higher performance can be achieved. After generating the hash values they will be stored in a hash table along with the sequence numbers that are generated using the Tag generator. The data is then sent for storage in the cloud storage servers. Same data blocks will be stored in multiple cloud service providers. At the time of verification, CSPs are requested to send the encrypted file segments. When the CSPs respond with the requested blocks, data integrity is checked by the TPA. The TPA will compute the hash value of each of the block and compare the stored hash value with newly computed hash values. If they mach, the file is intact otherwise not. If the file is not tempered the partitioner will rearrange the file blocks according to the sequence number. The file will be sent to the client or data owner. Then, it will be decrypted using RSA decryption algorithm.

In the proposed scheme following steps are performed for storing the files in the CSP:

1. The client will digitally sign the file and encrypt it using RSA algorithm.
2. The file will be sent to TPA.
3. Partitioner inside the TPA will divide the file into blocks.
4. Hashing will be done for each block individually by the hash generator.
5. The hash values will be stored in the hash table along with the sequence number generated by the tag generator.
6. The blocks will be sent to multiple CSPs.

Following steps are executed for retrieving files from the server:

1. TPA will download the file blocks from the CSPs.
2. It will compute the hash values for the blocks and compare the stored hash values with the new values.
3. If they are same, file is intact otherwise not.
4. The partitioner will rearrange the file and will send it back to the client.
5. The client will decrypt the file.

ANALYSIS AND COMPARISON

In this section the proposed scheme is compared with some of the existing data security algorithms with respect to the data security issues discussed in section 3. Table 1 shows a summarized comparison of the algorithms.

In third party broker based scheme security issues like data integrity, data intrusion, data confidentiality and non-repudiation have been solved. Data integrity has been solved by comparing the previously stored hash values with the newly computed hash values. Another security

Table 1. Comparative study

Data Security Issues \ Algorithm	Third Party Broker Based Scheme	Meta Data Encryption Based Scheme	Governance Body Based Scheme	Redundancy Based Approach	Multi-Cloud Database Model	Hidden Markov Model and Clustering Based Approach	Third Party Auditor (TPA) Scheme	Proposed Scheme
Data Integrity	Yes	Yes	Yes	Yes	Yes	No	No	Yes
Data Intrusion	Yes	Yes	No	Yes	Yes	Yes	Yes	Yes
Service Availability	No	No	Yes	Yes	Yes	Yes	No	Yes
Data Confidentiality	Yes	No	Yes	Yes	Yes	Yes	Yes	Yes
Non-Repudiation	Yes	No	Yes	No	No	Yes	Yes	Yes

risk called data intrusion that may occur with a CSP is solved in this case by storing the hashes for different file segments separately with their sequence numbers. It is very easy to detect the tempered file segment. Service availability remains unsolved in this scheme. If the broker goes down, the data cannot be recovered. The risk of attack exists in the broker. Data confidentiality is achieved by encrypting the data before storing it in cloud service provider. Client's name is stored inside the broker. Therefore, broker helps to preserve non-repudiation.

In meta data encryption based scheme, the issue of data integrity has only been solved. Data integrity is preserved by generating the metadata before storing those at the cloud server. In case of verification, the previously generated meta data can be compared with the new one. In case, any intruder gains access to the cloud server. He can easily modify the data but at the time of verification the modification in the data will be detected. As a result, the issue of data intrusion has been solved. Service availability remains unsolved in this scheme, that is, in any case if the cloud server goes down, the data cannot be recovered at any cost. The data is stored inside cloud server in unencrypted from which does not preserve confidentiality. In this scheme, no record is maintained for the client who wants to store his file in the cloud server. As a result, non repudiation is an unsolved issue in this scheme.

In governance body based scheme, hashing is done in SSL technology. It helps to maintain the integrity of data. Confidentiality is achieved by using dual SSL technology. Another security risk called data intrusion that may occur with a cloud service provider (CSP) is unsolved in this scheme. Authentication through conventional SSL can be weak and vulnerable to man-in-the-middle attack. In this scheme, the issue of service availability is solved by using the central server. This server acts as a backup server. So, if the server goes down, the failure can be avoided. Non-repudiation is

satisfied using the central server, which stores all the necessary information about a user in its routing table.

In multi-cloud database model the data is stored in multiple clouds. So, there is a higher possibility that the integrity of the data is preserved. But there is no mechanism to check the integrity of the stored data. This model maintains confidentiality by encrypting the data using Shamir's secret sharing algorithm and storing it in multiple cloud service providers. Data intrusion is prevented in this scheme because if an intruder tries to know the stored hidden information in the cloud, he has to retrieve it from three different CSPs. It makes data intrusion difficult for the intruders. This scheme enhances service availability since data is replicated in three different clouds. If one cloud goes down data can be retrieved from other clouds. The problem of non-repudiation has not been taken care of in this scheme.

Since redundancy based approach is an advanced version of the MCDB model it enhances the data security features of MCDB. In this scheme TMR technique replicates the encrypted data in three clouds at the time of storing. At the time of data retrieval the correct data is obtained by using voting technique. By this way, the scheme ensures that the data retrieved is not tempered and thus enhances data integrity. Like MCDB, this scheme will also maintain data confidentiality using Shamir's secret sharing algorithm. In this scheme TMR technique is used to resolve the data intrusion in a more effective manner than MCDB. Using TMR it is very easy to detect the faulty cloud and find out where the intrusion has taken place. Like MCDB this scheme also replicates the data in multiple clouds and therefore it increases the data availability of the system. This scheme does not take any measure to solve the problem of non-repudiation.

In HMM and clustering based approach, HMM model is used to monitor the user behaviour continuously by system administrator. As a result, the data is safe in the cloud environment. But there is no mechanism to ensure the integrity of the stored data. HMM model can be used to detect intrusion based on the portability of behaviour. Firewall gateway is also used in this scheme to prevent data intrusion. Firewall gateway can block any anonymous port with live IP address which is not in its knowledge. As a result, intrusion is not possible in this scheme. Data can be kept confidential using this scheme, as every traffic is sent to the administrator via email notification. Service availability is solved with the help of plug-in, which helps the environment to connect with another network. Non-repudiation is not possible as the firewall gateway contains the list of authenticated IP addresses.

In third party auditor scheme, data intrusion problem have been solved because only the authenticated user can have access to the information. The users are given permission to access the stored data through the authentication modules which are given by the trustful organization. Any intruder cannot have access to the valuable data without proper permission. Confidentiality is achieved as the data file is encrypted with user secret key. After encryption, the data file is sent for storing in the cloud service provider. Service availability and data integrity problems are not considered in this scheme. If the CSP goes down, the data cannot be recovered. The risk of attacks exists in the cloud storage provider. The data stored in the cloud may suffer from any damage during transition to or from the cloud storage provider. But, no measures have been taken in this scheme to ensure the integrity of data. Non-repudiation is not possible here, because when a user sends a request, the user's information is added in cloud storage server's user list.

The proposed scheme solves all the security issues considered in this chapter. It stores the hash values of the encrypted segments. At the time of data retrieval the hash value of the retrieved data will be compared with the stored hash value. In this way integrity of the data will be checked. Data intrusion is not possible in this case, because any intruder cannot gain access to the entire file since the file is segmented into blocks after encryption. In the proposed scheme the issue of service availability is addressed because if one CSP goes down data can be retrieved from the other CSP where the data is replicated. Data confidentiality has also been achieved by encrypting the file before storing it to the cloud storage provider. Non-repudiation is fulfilled by the use of digital signature.

CONCLUSION AND FUTURE RESEARCH DIRECTIONS

In this chapter, a detailed discussion on various security issues in cloud computing environment has been presented. The major security issues are data integrity, data intrusion, service availability, data confidentiality and non-repudiation. For addressing these security issues some of the schemes have already been proposed. But all the existing schemes fulfil only few of the security issues. For solving these security issues a third party auditor based scheme has been proposed in this chapter. A detailed analysis of the proposed scheme is carried out. The proposed scheme has been compared with the other existing algorithms. It has been observed that the proposed scheme outperforms all the data security algorithms, discussed in this chapter, with respect to the security issues. The problem with this scheme is that the scheme works only for static storage of data. It cannot handle the data that needs to be dynamically changed. Enabling the proposed scheme to handle dynamic data remains as future work.

REFERENCES

Alzain, M. A., Pardede, E., Soh, B., & Thom, J. A. (2012). Cloud Computing Security: From Single to Multi-Cloud. In *Proceedings of 45th Hawaii International Conference on System Science.* (pp. 5490-5499). Maui, HI: IEEE. doi:10.1109/HICSS.2012.153

Alzain, M. A., Soh, B., & Pardede, E. (2011). MCDB: Using Multi Cloud to Ensure Security in Cloud Computing, In *Proceedings of IEEE 9th International Conference on Dependable, Autonomic & Secure Computing.* (pp. 784-791). Sydney, NSW: IEEE. doi:10.1109/DASC.2011.133

Alzain, M. A., Soh, B., & Pardede, E. (2012). A New Approach Using Redundancy Technique to Improve Security in Cloud Computing, In *Proceedings of International Conference on Cyber Security, Cyber Warfare & Digital Forensic.* (pp. 230-235). Kuala Lumpur: IEEE. doi:10.1109/CyberSec.2012.6246174

Han, S., & Xing, J. (2011). Ensuring Data Storage Security Through a Novel Third Party Auditor Scheme in Cloud Computing, In *Proceedings of IEEE International Conference on Cloud Computing & Intelligence Systems.* (pp. 264-268). Beijing, China: IEEE. doi:10.1109/CCIS.2011.6045072

Hemant, P., Chawande, N. P., Sonule, A., & Wani, H. (2011). Development of Servers in Cloud Computing to Solve Issue Related to Security and Backup, In *Proceedings of IEEE International Conference on Cloud Computing & Intelligence System.* (pp. 158-163). Beijing, China: IEEE. doi:10.1109/CCIS.2011.6045052

Kumar, P., Nitin, V., Shah, K., Shukla, S. S. P., & Chauhan, D. S. (2011). A Novel Approach for Security in Cloud Computing using Hidden Markov Model and Clustering. In *Proceedings of Information & Communication Technologies.* (pp. 810–815). Mumbai, India: IEEE. doi:10.1109/WICT.2011.6141351

Kumar, S., & Saxena, A. (2011). Data Integrity Proofs in Cloud Storage. In *Proceedings of Third International Conference on Communication Systems and Networks.* (pp. 1-4). Bangalore, India: IEEE.

Mahmood, Z. (2011). Data Location and Security Issues in Cloud Computing. In *Proceedings of International Conference on Emerging Intelligent Data and Web Computing.* (pp. 49-54). Tirana: IEEE. doi:10.1109/EIDWT.2011.16

Shah, M. A., Baker, M., Mogul, J. C., & Swaminathan, R. (2007). Auditing to Keep Online Storage Services Honest. In Proceedings of HotOS. (pp. 1-5). Berkeley, California.

Shamir, A. (1979). How to share a secret. *Communications of the ACM, 22*(11), 612–613. doi:10.1145/359168.359176

Shrivastava, A., Kundu, A., Surat, S., & Majumdar, A. K. (2008). Credit Card Fraud Detection Using Hidden Markov Model. *IEEE Transactions on Dependable and Secure Computing, 5*(1), 37–48. doi:10.1109/TDSC.2007.70228

Stallings, W. (2006). The Whirlpool secure hash function. *Cryptologia, 30*(1), 55–67. doi:10.1080/01611190500380090

Varalakshmi, P., & Deventhiran, H. (2012). Integrity Checking for Cloud Environment Using Encryption Algorithm. In *Proceedings of International Conference on Recent Trends in Information Technology.* (pp. 228-232). Chennai, Tamil Nadu: IEEE. doi:10.1109/ICRTIT.2012.6206833

You, P., Peng, Y., Liu, W., & Xue, S. (2012). Security Issues and Solutions in Cloud Computing. In *Proceedings of 32nd International Conference on Distributed Computing System Workshops.* (pp. 573-577). Macau, China: IEEE. doi:10.1109/ICDCSW.2012.20

ADDITIONAL READING

Abadi, D. J. (2009). Data Management in the Cloud: Limitations and Opportunities. *IEEE Data Eng. Bull.*, *32*(1), 3–12.

Almorsy, M., Grundy, J., & Müller, I. (2010, November). An analysis of the cloud computing security problem. In *Proceedings of APSEC 2010 Cloud Workshop*. Sydney, Australia.

Almulla, S. A., & Yeun, C. Y. (2010, March). Cloud computing security management. In *Proceedings of Second International Conference on Engineering Systems Management and Its Applications.* (pp. 1-7). Sharjah: IEEE.

AlZain, M. A., Pardede, E., Soh, B., & Thom, J. A. (2012, January). Cloud computing security: from single to multi-clouds. In *Proceedings of 45th Hawaii International Conference on System Science (HICSS).* (pp. 5490-5499). Maui, HI: IEEE. doi:10.1109/HICSS.2012.153

Blunsom, P. (2004). Hidden markov models. *Lecture notes, August, 15*, 18-19.

Boneh, D., Boyen, X., & Goh, E. J. (2005). Hierarchical identity based encryption with constant size ciphertext. In *Advances in Cryptology–EUROCRYPT 2005* (pp. 440–456). Springer Berlin Heidelberg. doi:10.1007/11426639_26

Celesti, A., Tusa, F., Villari, M., & Puliafito, A. (2010, June). Security and cloud computing: intercloud identity management infrastructure. In *Proceedings of 19th IEEE International Workshop on Enabling Technologies: Infrastructures for Collaborative Enterprises.* (pp. 263-265). Larissa: IEEE. doi:10.1109/WETICE.2010.49

Chen, D., & Zhao, H. (2012, March). Data security and privacy protection issues in cloud computing. In Proceedings of *2012 International Conference on Computer Science and Electronics Engineering.* (Vol. 1, pp. 647-651). Hangzhou: IEEE. doi:10.1109/ICCSEE.2012.193

Chow, R., Golle, P., Jakobsson, M., Shi, E., Staddon, J., Masuoka, R., & Molina, J. (2009, November). Controlling data in the cloud: outsourcing computation without outsourcing control. In *Proceedings of the 2009 ACM workshop on Cloud computing security* (pp. 85-90). Chicago, IL: ACM. doi:10.1145/1655008.1655020

Christodorescu, M., Sailer, R., Schales, D. L., Sgandurra, D., & Zamboni, D. (2009, November). Cloud security is not (just) virtualization security: a short paper. In *Proceedings of the 2009 ACM workshop on Cloud computing security.* (pp. 97-102). Chicago, IL: ACM. doi:10.1145/1655008.1655022

Dai Yuefa, W. B., Yaqiang, G., Quan, Z., & Chaojing, T. (2009, November). Data security model for cloud computing. In *Proceedings of the International Workshop on Information Security and Application. (pp. 141-144). Qingdao, China: Academy Publisher.*

Dawoud, W., Takouna, I., & Meinel, C. (2010, March). Infrastructure as a service security: Challenges and solutions. In *Proceedings of 7th International Conference on Informatics and Systems.* (pp. 1-8). Cairo: IEEE.

de Chaves, S. A., Westphall, C. B., & Lamin, F. R. (2010, March). SLA perspective in security management for cloud computing. In Proceedings of *Sixth International Conference on Networking and Services.* (pp. 212-217). Cancun: IEEE. doi:10.1109/ICNS.2010.36

Dhage, S. N., & Meshram, B. B. (2012). Intrusion detection system in cloud computing environment. *International Journal of Cloud Computing, 1*(2), 261–282. doi:10.1504/IJCC.2012.046711

Dikaiakos, M. D., Katsaros, D., Mehra, P., Pallis, G., & Vakali, A. (2009). Cloud computing: Distributed internet computing for IT and scientific research. *IEEE Internet Computing, 13*(5), 10–13. doi:10.1109/MIC.2009.103

Dillon, T., Wu, C., & Chang, E. (2010, April). Cloud computing: issues and challenges. In Proceedings of *International Conference on Advanced Information Networking and Applications*. (pp. 27-33). Perth, WA: IEEE.

Dubey, A. K., Namdev, M., & Shrivastava, S. S. (2012, September). Cloud-user security based on RSA and MD5 algorithm for resource attestation and sharing in java environment. In Proceedings of *CSI Sixth International Conference on Software Engineering (CONSEG)*. (pp. 1-8). Indore: IEEE. doi:10.1109/CONSEG.2012.6349503

Fox, A., Griffith, R., Joseph, A., Katz, R., Konwinski, A., Lee, G., et al. (2009). Above the clouds: A Berkeley view of cloud computing. Dept. Electrical Eng. and Comput. Sciences, University of California, Berkeley, Rep. UCB/EECS, 28, 13.

Gampala, V., Inuganti, S., & Muppidi, S. (2012). Data Security in Cloud Computing with Elliptic Curve Cryptography. [IJSCE]. *International Journal of Soft Computing and Engineering*, 2(3), 138–141.

Grobauer, B., Walloschek, T., & Stocker, E. (2011). Understanding cloud computing vulnerabilities. *IEEE Security and Privacy, 9*(2), 50–57. doi:10.1109/MSP.2010.115

Hay, B., Nance, K., & Bishop, M. (2011, January). Storm clouds rising: security challenges for IaaS cloud computing. In Proceedings of *44th Hawaii International Conference on System Sciences*. (pp. 1-7). Kauai, HI: IEEE. doi:10.1109/HICSS.2011.386

Huang, D., Zhou, Z., Xu, L., Xing, T., & Zhong, Y. (2011, April). Secure data processing framework for mobile cloud computing. In *Proceedings of Conference on Computer Communications Workshops*. (pp. 614-618). Shanghai: IEEE. doi:10.1109/INFCOMW.2011.5928886

Hwang, K., Kulkareni, S., & Hu, Y. (2009, December). Cloud security with virtualized defense and reputation-based trust mangement. In *Proceedings of Eighth IEEE International Conference on Dependable, Autonomic and Secure Computing*. (pp. 717-722). Chengdu: IEEE. doi:10.1109/DASC.2009.149

Hwang, K., & Li, D. (2010). Trusted cloud computing with secure resources and data coloring. *IEEE Internet Computing, 14*(5), 14–22. doi:10.1109/MIC.2010.86

Jadeja, Y., & Modi, K. (2012, March). Cloud computing-concepts, architecture and challenges. In *Proceedings of International Conference on Computing, Electronics and Electrical Technologies*. (pp. 877-880). Kumaracoil: IEEE.

Jansen, W. A. (2011, January). Cloud hooks: Security and privacy issues in cloud computing. In *Proceengs of 44th Hawaii International Conference on System Sciences (HICSS)*. (pp. 1-10). Kauai, HI: IEEE. doi:10.1109/HICSS.2011.103

Jasti, A., Shah, P., Nagaraj, R., & Pendse, R. (2010, October). Security in multi-tenancy cloud. In *Proceedings of International Carnahan Conference on Security Technology*. (pp. 35-41). San Jose, CA: IEEE.

Jensen, M., Schwenk, J., Gruschka, N., & Iacono, L. L. (2009, September). On technical security issues in cloud computing. In Proceedings of *IEEE International Conference on Cloud Computing*. (pp. 109-116). Bangalore: IEEE. doi:10.1109/CLOUD.2009.60

Kandukuri, B. R., Paturi, V. R., & Rakshit, A. (2009, September). Cloud security issues. In *Proceedings of International Conference on Services Computing*. (pp. 517-520). Bangalore: IEEE.

Kaufman, L. M. (2010). Can public-cloud security meet its unique challenges?. *IEEE Security & Privacy, 8*(4), 0055-57.

Khan, K. M., & Malluhi, Q. (2010). Establishing trust in cloud computing. *IT Professional, 12*(5), 20–27. doi:10.1109/MITP.2010.128

Ko, R. K., Jagadpramana, P., Mowbray, M., Pearson, S., Kirchberg, M., Liang, Q., & Lee, B. S. (2011, July). TrustCloud: A framework for accountability and trust in cloud computing. In *Proceedings of IEEE World Congress on Services*. (pp. 584-588). Washington, DC: IEEE. doi:10.1109/SERVICES.2011.91

Kolodner, E. K. et al. (2011, November). A cloud environment for data-intensive storage services. In *Proceedings of third international conference on Cloud computing technology and science (Cloud-Com)*. (pp. 357-366). Athens: IEEE. doi:10.1109/CloudCom.2011.55

Kulkarni, G., Gambhir, J., Patil, T., & Dongare, A. (2012, June). A security aspects in cloud computing. In *Proceedings of 3rd International Conference on Software Engineering and Service Science (ICSESS)*. (pp. 547-550). Beijing: IEEE.

Li, H. C., Liang, P. H., Yang, J. M., & Chen, S. J. (2010, November). Analysis on cloud-based security vulnerability assessment. In *Proceeding of IEEE 7th International Conference on e-Business Engineering (ICEBE)*. (pp. 490-494). Shanghai: IEEE.

Li, W., & Ping, L. (2009). Trust model to enhance security and interoperability of cloud environment. In *Proceedings of* First International Conference on Cloud Computing. (pp. 69-79). Beijing, China: Springer Berlin Heidelberg. doi:10.1007/978-3-642-10665-1_7

Li, X. Y., Zhou, L. T., Shi, Y., & Guo, Y. (2010, July). A trusted computing environment model in cloud architecture. In *Proceedings of International Conference on Machine Learning and Cybernetics*. (Vol. 6, pp. 2843-2848). Qingdao: IEEE. doi:10.1109/ICMLC.2010.5580769

Liu, Q., Wang, G., & Wu, J. (2014). Time-based proxy re-encryption scheme for secure data sharing in a cloud environment. *Information Sciences, 258,* 355–370. doi:10.1016/j.ins.2012.09.034

Liu, W. (2012, April). Research on cloud computing security problem and strategy. In *Proceedings of Consumer Electronics, Communications and Networks. 2nd International Conference on* (pp. 1216-1219). IEEE. doi:10.1109/CECNet.2012.6202020

Lori, M. K. (2009). Data security in the world of cloud computing. *IEEE Security and Privacy, 7*(4), 61–64. doi:10.1109/MSP.2009.87

Luo, S., Lin, Z., Chen, X., Yang, Z., & Chen, J. (2011, December). Virtualization security for cloud computing service. In Proceedings of *International Conference on Cloud and Service Computing (CSC)*. (pp. 174-179). Hong Kong: IEEE.

Pal, S., Khatua, S., Chaki, N., & Sanyal, S. (2011). A new trusted and collaborative agent based approach for ensuring cloud security. *arXiv preprint arXiv:1108.4100*.

Paquette, S., Jaeger, P. T., & Wilson, S. C. (2010). Identifying the security risks associated with governmental use of cloud computing. *Government Information Quarterly, 27*(3), 245–253. doi:10.1016/j.giq.2010.01.002

Park, N. (2011). Secure data access control scheme using type-based re-encryption in cloud environment. In Semantic Methods for Knowledge Management and Communication (pp. 319-327). Katarzyniak, R.K., Chiu, T.-F., Hong, C.-F., Nguyen, N.-T. (Eds.). Germany: Springer Berlin Heidelberg. doi:10.1007/978-3-642-23418-7_28

Pearson, S., & Charlesworth, A. (2009). Account-ability as a way forward for privacy protection in the cloud. In *Proceedings of First International Conference on Cloud computing* (pp. 131-144). Bejing, China: Springer Berlin Heidelberg. doi:10.1007/978-3-642-10665-1_12

Popovic, K., & Hocenski, Z. (2010, May). Cloud computing security issues and challenges. In *Proceedings of the 33rd international convention MIPRO.* (pp. 344-349). Opatija, Croatia: IEEE.

Ramgovind, S., Eloff, M. M., & Smith, E. (2010, August). The management of security in cloud computing. In *Proceedings of Information Security for South Africa Conference.* (pp. 1-7). Sandton, Johannesburg: IEEE. doi:10.1109/ISSA.2010.5588290

Rimal, B. P., Choi, E., & Lumb, I. (2009, August). A taxonomy and survey of cloud computing systems. In *Proceedings of Fifth International Joint Conference on INC, IMS and IDC.* (pp. 44-51). Seoul: IEEE. doi:10.1109/NCM.2009.218

Sabahi, F. (2011, May). Cloud computing security threats and responses. In *Proceedings of 3rd International Conference on Communication Software and Networks (ICCSN).* (pp. 245-249). Xi'an: IEEE.

Sabahi, F. (2011, May). Virtualization-level security in cloud computing. In Proceedings of *3rd International Conference on Communication Software and Networks.* (pp. 250-254). Xi'an: IEEE.

Sangroya, A., Kumar, S., Dhok, J., & Varma, V. (2010). Towards analyzing data security risks in cloud computing environments. In Proceedings of 4th International Conference *on Information Systems, Technology and Management.* (pp. 255-265). Bangkok, Thailand: Springer Berlin Heidelberg. doi:10.1007/978-3-642-12035-0_25

Sato, H., Kanai, A., & Tanimoto, S. (2010, July). A cloud trust model in a security aware cloud. In *Proceedings of 10th IEEE/IPSJ International Symposium on Applications and the Internet (SAINT).* (pp. 121-124). Seoul: IEEE. doi:10.1109/SAINT.2010.13

Shaikh, F. B., & Haider, S. (2011, December). Security threats in cloud computing. In Proceedings of *International Conference for Internet technology and secured transactions.* (pp. 214-219). Abu Dhabi: IEEE.

Shen, Z., Li, L., Yan, F., & Wu, X. (2010, May). Cloud computing system based on trusted computing platform. In *Proceedings of International Conference on Intelligent Computation Technology and Automation (ICICTA),* (Vol. 1, pp. 942-945). Changsha: IEEE. doi:10.1109/ICICTA.2010.724

Shen, Z., & Tong, Q. (2010, July). The security of cloud computing system enabled by trusted computing technology. In Proceedings of *2nd International Conference on Signal Processing Systems.* (Vol. 2, pp. 11-15). Dalian: IEEE. doi:10.1109/ICSPS.2010.5555234

Somani, U., Lakhani, K., & Mundra, M. (2010, October). Implementing digital signature with RSA encryption algorithm to enhance the Data Security of cloud in Cloud Computing. In Proceedings of *1st International Conference on Parallel Distributed and Grid Computing* (pp. 211-216). Solan: IEEE. doi:10.1109/PDGC.2010.5679895

Srinivasan, M. K., Sarukesi, K., Rodrigues, P., Manoj, M. S., & Revathy, P. (2012, August). State-of-the-art cloud computing security taxonomies: a classification of security challenges in the present cloud computing environment. In *Proceedings of the International Conference on Advances in Computing, Communications and Informatics*. (pp. 470-476). *Kerala, India:* ACM. doi:10.1145/2345396.2345474

Stolfo, S. J., Salem, M. B., & Keromytis, A. D. (2012, May). Fog computing: Mitigating insider data theft attacks in the cloud. In *Proceedings of IEEE Symposium on Security and Privacy Workshops (SPW)*. (pp. 125-128). San Francisco, CA: IEEE. doi:10.1109/SPW.2012.19

Subashini, S., & Kavitha, V. (2011). A survey on security issues in service delivery models of cloud computing. *Journal of Network and Computer Applications*, *34*(1), 1–11. doi:10.1016/j.jnca.2010.07.006

Sudha, M. (2012). Enhanced security framework to ensure data security in cloud computing using cryptography. *Advances in Computer Science and its Applications, 1*(1), 32-37.

Sultan, N. (2010). Cloud computing for education: A new dawn? *International Journal of Information Management*, *30*(2), 109–116. doi:10.1016/j.ijinfomgt.2009.09.004

Sun, D., Chang, G., Guo, Q., Wang, C., & Wang, X. (2010, September). A dependability model to enhance security of cloud environment using system-level virtualization techniques. In *Proceedings of First International Conference on Pervasive Computing Signal Processing and Applications (PCSPA)*. (pp. 305-310). Harbin: IEEE. doi:10.1109/PCSPA.2010.81

Sun, D., Chang, G., Sun, L., & Wang, X. (2011). Surveying and analyzing security, privacy and trust issues in cloud computing environments. *Procedia Engineering*, *15*, 2852–2856. doi:10.1016/j.proeng.2011.08.537

Takabi, H., Joshi, J. B., & Ahn, G. J. (2010, July). Securecloud: Towards a comprehensive security framework for cloud computing environments. In *Proceedings of 34th Annual Computer Software and Applications Conference Workshops*. (pp. 393-398). Seoul: IEEE. doi:10.1109/COMPSACW.2010.74

Tan, X., & Ai, B. (2011, August). The issues of cloud computing security in high-speed railway. In Proceedings of *International Conference on Electronic and Mechanical Engineering and Information Technology (EMEIT)*. (Vol. 8, pp. 4358-4363). Harbin, Heilongjiang: IEEE. doi:10.1109/EMEIT.2011.6023923

Tribhuwan, M. R., Bhuyar, V. A., & Pirzade, S. (2010, October). Ensuring data storage security in cloud computing through two-way handshake based on token management. In *Proceedings of International Conference on Advances in Recent Technologies in Communication and Computing*. (pp. 386-389). Kottayam: IEEE. doi:10.1109/ARTCom.2010.23

Tripathi, A., & Mishra, A. (2011, September). Cloud computing security considerations. In *Proceedings of International Conference on Signal Processing, Communications and Computing*. (pp. 1-5). Xi'an: IEEE.

Wang, C., Ren, K., Lou, W., & Li, J. (2010). Toward publicly auditable secure cloud data storage services. *IEEE Network*, *24*(4), 19–24. doi:10.1109/MNET.2010.5510914

Wang, C., Wang, Q., Ren, K., & Lou, W. (2010, March). Privacy-preserving public auditing for data storage security in cloud computing. In *Proceedings of IEEE INFOCOM* (pp. 1–9). San Diego, CA: IEEE. doi:10.1109/INFCOM.2010.5462173

Wei, J., Zhang, X., Ammons, G., Bala, V., & Ning, P. (2009, November). Managing security of virtual machine images in a cloud environment. In *Proceedings of the 2009 ACM workshop on Cloud computing security* (pp. 91-96). Chicago, IL: ACM. doi:10.1145/1655008.1655021

Wen, F., & Xiang, L. (2011, December). The study on data security in Cloud Computing based on Virtualization. In *Proceedings of International Symposium on IT in Medicine and Education (ITME)*. (Vol. 2, pp. 257-261). Cuangzhou: IEEE.

Xu, J. S., Huang, R. C., Huang, W. M., & Yang, G. (2009). Secure document service for cloud computing. In Proceedings of First International Conference *on Cloud Computing*. (pp. 541-546). Beijing, China: Springer Berlin Heidelberg. doi:10.1007/978-3-642-10665-1_49

Yan, L., Rong, C., & Zhao, G. (2009). Strengthen cloud computing security with federal identity management using hierarchical identity-based cryptography. In *Cloud Computing* (pp. 167–177). Springer Berlin Heidelberg. doi:10.1007/978-3-642-10665-1_15

Yang, J., & Chen, Z. (2010, December). Cloud computing research and security issues. In *Proceedings of International Conference on Computational Intelligence and Software Engineering (CiSE)*. (pp. 1-3). Wuhan: IEEE.

Yildiz, M., Abawajy, J., Ercan, T., & Bernoth, A. (2009, December). A layered security approach for cloud computing infrastructure. In *Proceedings of 10th International Symposium on Pervasive Systems, Algorithms, and Networks (ISPAN)*. (pp. 763-767). Kaohsiung: IEEE. doi:10.1109/I-SPAN.2009.157

Yu, S., Wang, C., Ren, K., & Lou, W. (2010, March). Achieving secure, scalable and fine-grained data access control in cloud computing. In *Proceedings of INFOCOM*. (pp. 1-9). San Diego, CA: IEEE. doi:10.1109/INFCOM.2010.5462174

Yu, X., & Wen, Q. (2010, December). A view about cloud data security from data life cycle. In *Proceeding of International Conference on Computational Intelligence and Software Engineering (CiSE)*. (pp. 1-4). Wuhan: IEEE. doi:10.1109/CISE.2010.5676895

Zhang, Q., Cheng, L., & Boutaba, R. (2010). Cloud computing: state-of-the-art and research challenges. *Journal of Internet Services and Applications, 1*(1), 7-18.

Zhang, X., Du, H. T., Chen, J. Q., Lin, Y., & Zeng, L. J. (2011, May). Ensure Data Security in Cloud Storage. In Proceedings of *International Conference on Network Computing and Information Security (NCIS)*. (Vol. 1, pp. 284-287). Guilin: IEEE.

Zhang, X., Wuwong, N., Li, H., & Zhang, X. (2010, June). Information security risk management framework for the cloud computing environments. In *Proceedings of 10th International Conference on Computer and Information Technology (CIT)*. (pp. 1328-1334). Bradford: IEEE. doi:10.1109/CIT.2010.501

Zhou, M., Zhang, R., Xie, W., Qian, W., & Zhou, A. (2010, November). Security and privacy in cloud computing: A survey. In *Proceedings of Sixth International Conference on Semantics Knowledge and Grid (SKG)*. (pp. 105-112). Beijing, China: IEEE. doi:10.1109/SKG.2010.19

Zissis, D., & Lekkas, D. (2012). Addressing cloud computing security issues. *Future Generation Computer Systems, 28*(3), 583–592. doi:10.1016/j.future.2010.12.006

KEY TERMS AND DEFINITIONS

Data Consistency: It is the property of the database to ensure that a consistent view of each data item is shown to every user, which includes visible changes resulting from user's own transactions and other users' committed transactions.

Clustering: In data mining Clustering is a technique used to partition a set of data elements into sub-classes or cluster. A cluster is a collection of objects having some similarity. Some of the clustering techniques are: k-means clustering and expectation maximization (EM) clustering. For more information on Clustering, see Appendix.

Decryption: In cryptography, decryption is the process to decode the data that has been encoded into some secret format.

Encryption: The process of encoding a message into a form so that it can only be read by an authorized party is known as encryption. Encryption algorithms can be classified into two categories, Symmetric key encryption and Asymmetric key encryption. In symmetric key encryption same key is used for encryption as well as decryption. This type of encryption algorithms incur less computational cost but sharing of the key is the major problem. In Asymmetric key encryption, two keys are used: private key and public key. Public key is known to every sender. When a sender wants to send data to the receiver, the data will be encrypted using public key of the receiver. On receiving the encrypted data, the receiver will decrypt it using his private key.

Hidden Markov Model (HMM): It is a Markov model with hidden states. HMM is used to model a system which is assumed as a Markov process having unobserved states. HMM is used in many areas such as, signal processing and in speech processing.

Resource Pool: A resource pool is a collection of a single or multiple types of resources. The resources may be CPU, memory, storage and network.

Virtual Machine: It is a program or operating system. It provides an environment that is not physically existent but resides into another environment. The virtual machine is known as guest, on the other hand the environment in which the virtual machine resides is known as guest. It is often used to create an environment different from the host environment. It emulates a computer system. Specialized hardware, software or both may be required for implementation of virtual machine (VM).

APPENDIX

There are plenty of applications of clustering algorithms. Few of them are discussed as follows:

- *Marketing*: Customers having similar purchasing behavior can be grouped together based on a database of their past buying records. These grouping can be used to make some business decisions.
- *Biology*: Animals as well as plants can be classified into groups considering some features.
- *Libraries*: Clustering algorithms can also be used for ordering the book in libraries.
- *Insurance*: Clustering algorithms can be used to find out group of motor vehicle policy holders having very high claim rate. According the terms and conditions of insurance policy are decided.
- *Earthquake studies*: Clustering algorithms can be applied on a database of past history records of earthquake to classify a give region into different earthquake prone zone.

Clustering algorithms have to satisfy the following requirements:

- It should be scalable.
- It should be capable of dealing with different types of attributes.
- It should be capable of finding clusters of arbitrary shape.
- It should require minimum amount of domain knowledge for determining input parameters.
- It should be capable of handling outliers and noise.
- It should be insensitive to the order in which inputs are recorded.
- It should be highly dimensional.
- It should be highly interpretable and usable.

There are several difficulties with clustering. Some of the difficulties are:

- All the requirements are not fulfilled by the clustering algorithms.
- It may create problem while handling large amount of data items having large dimensions.

Clustering algorithms can be classified into four categories:

- Exclusive Clustering: In this type of clustering the data are grouped in such a way that a datum from one cluster can't be a part of another cluster.
- Overlapping Clustering: In this type of clustering fuzzy set is used for clustering the data. Each of the data item may be a member of two or more clusters with different membership values.
- Hierarchical Clustering: In this type of clustering union of two nearest clusters are carried out.
- Probabilistic Clustering: In this type of clustering the membership of each data item is given as a probability.

Chapter 11
Improving Privacy and Security in Multicloud Architectures

Piyush Kumar Shukla
University Institute of Technology RGPV, India

Mahendra Kumar Ahirwar
University Institute of Technology-RGPV, India

ABSTRACT

In this chapter we described the concept of multicloud architecture in which locally distributed clouds are combined to provide combined services of locally distributed clouds to the users. We started with basic of cloud computing and reached to multicloud through single cloud. In this chapter have described four architectural models for multicloud. Architecture models are Repetition of applications, Partition of System architecture into layers, Partition of Security features into segments and Distributing of data into fragments with these models security of the data resides in the datacenters of the cloud computing must be increased which leads to reliability in data storing of data.

CLOUD SERVICE MODELS

The services provided by the cloud computing are divided into three universally accepted categories these are Infrastructure-as-a-Service (IaaS), Platform-as-a-Service (PaaS) and Software-as-a-Service (SaaS). Basically these three service models are interrelated to each other and designed 3-tiers architecture.

Infrastructure-as-a-Service (IaaS): This is first and base layer of 3-tier architecture. It is used to provide network for connecting users and servers and also provides virtual machines to start, stop, access and configure virtual servers and storage blocks. Pay-per-use service is implemented at this layer of 3-tier architecture. Examples of IaaS are Amazon EC2, Windows Azure, Rack space, Google Compute Engine etc. Infrastructure-as-a-Service like Amazon Web Services provides virtual server instance API) to start, stop, access and configure their virtual servers and storage. In the enterprise, cloud computing allows a company to pay for only as much capacity as is needed, and bring more online as soon as required. Because

DOI: 10.4018/978-1-4666-8387-7.ch011

this pay-for-what-you-use model resembles the way electricity, fuel and water are consumed; it's sometimes referred to as utility computing.

Platform-as-a-Service (PaaS): This is second or middle layer of 3-tier architecture. In this model a platform is provided to users which typically include operating system, programming languages, execution environments, databases, queues and web servers. Examples are AWS Elastic Beanstalk, Heroku, Force.com and Google App Engine. Platform-as-a-service in the cloud is defined as a set of software and product development tools hosted on the provider's infrastructure. Developers create applications on the provider's platform over the Internet. PaaS providers may use APIs, website portals or gateway software installed on the customer's computer. Force.com, (an outgrowth of Salesforce.com) and GoogleApps are examples of PaaS. Developers need to know that currently, there are not standards for interoperability or data portability in the cloud. Some providers will not allow software created by their customers to be moved off the provider's platform.

Software-as-a-Service (SaaS): This is third or upper layer of 3-tier architecture. This model provides "On-demand software's" to users without installation setup and running of the applications. Users have to pay and use it through some client. Examples are Google Apps and Microsoft office 365. In the software-as-a-service cloud model, the vendor supplies the hardware infrastructure, the software product and interacts with the user through a front-end portal. SaaS is a very broad market. Services can be anything from Web-based email to inventory control and database processing. Because the service provider hosts both the application and the data, the end user is free to use the service from anywhere. 3-tier Architecture of cloud computing has been illustrated in figure -1.

In case of public cloud services provisioning at SaaS layer creates number of issues among which security and privacy are most critical aspects when considering adoption of cloud computing.

SaaS also faces challenges on the outsourcing of services, data, applications and processes in case confidentiality and sensitivity.

An idea to reduce the risk for data and applications at SaaS layer of public cloud is to use multiple distinct clouds simultaneously. In this paper four distinct cloud models are provided which can offer services to users according to their security and privacy benefits.

Cloud Types

There are four types of clouds: private cloud, public cloud, community cloud and hybrid cloud from the physical location of user's point of view.

Private cloud: A *private* cloud is one which is setup by single organization and installed services on its own data center. A private cloud is a proprietary network or a data center that supplies hosted services to a limited number of people. When a service provider uses public cloud resources to create their private cloud, the result is called a virtual private cloud. The types of cloud has been illustrated in figure 2.

Public cloud: A *Public* cloud services are offered by third-party cloud service providers and involve resource provisioning outside of the user's premises. A public cloud sells services to anyone on the Internet. Currently, Amazon Web Services is the largest public cloud provider.

Community cloud: The *Community* cloud can offer services to the cluster of organizations.

Hybrid cloud: A *Hybrid* cloud is the combination of any two or more types of above mentioned cloud types.

A cloud can be of any type but the goal of cloud computing is to provide easy, scalable access to computing resources and IT services.

Single Cloud

Cloud computing is a conversational expression used to describe a variety of different types of

Figure 1. 3-tier Architecture of cloud computing

	Security			Feasibility			Regulation
	Integrity	Confidentiality	Availability	Applicability	Business-Readiness	Ease of Use	Compliance
Replication of Application							
Dual Execution	+	- -	+	+	+	0	-
n Clouds Approach	++	- -	++	+	+	-	- -
Processor and Verifier	+	-	0	-	-	-	-
Partition of Application Systems into Tiers	+	-	0	++	++	++	0
Partition of Application Logic into Fragments							
Obfuscating Splitting	0	+	-	0	0	-	++
Trusted/Public Domain Splitting	++	+	0	-	-	- -	+
Homomorphic Encryption	++	++	0	- -	- -	-	++
Secure Multi-Party Computation	++	++	-	- -	- -	-	++
Partition of Application Data into Fragments							
Cryptographic Data Splitting	++	++	-	-	0	-	++
Database Splitting	0	+	0	-	+	-	+

(++) strong improvement; (+) little improvement; (0) no change; (-) little aggravation; (- -) strong aggravation

Figure 2. Types of clouds

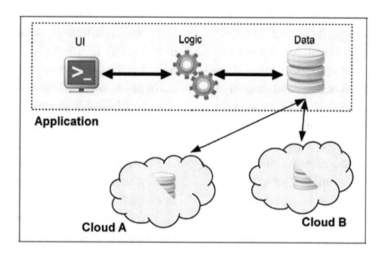

computing concepts that involve a large number of computers connected through a real-time communication network such as the Internet. Cloud computing is a term without a commonly accepted demonstrable scientific or technical definition. In science, cloud computing is a synonym for distributed computing over a network and means the ability to run a program on many connected computers at the same time. The phrase is also more commonly used to refer to network-based services which appear to be provided by real server hardware, which are in fact served by virtual hardware, simulated by software running on one or more real machines. Such virtual servers do not physically exist and can therefore be moved around and scaled up (or down) on the necessity without affecting the end user. Single cloud means a network which alone provides facilities to all user requests and also manages software and hardware to the users.

Challenging Issues in Single Cloud

Single cloud creates a large number of security issues and challenges (J. M. Bohli, Jensen, Gruschka, Schwenk, & Iacono, 2011). A list of security threats to Single cloud are presented in (Hubbard & Sutton, 2010). These challenges are ranged

from the required trust in the cloud provider and attacks on cloud interfaces to misusing the cloud services for attacks on other systems. The main problem that the Single cloud implicitly contains is that of secure outsourcing of sensitive as well as business-critical data and processes. When considering using a cloud service, the user must be aware of the fact that all data given to the cloud provider leave the own control and protection on the data. Even if deploying data-processing applications to the cloud (via IaaS or PaaS),a cloud provider gains full control on these processes. Hence, a strong trust relationship between the cloud service provider and the cloud user is considered a general backbone in cloud computing. Depending on the political context this trust may touch legal devoir. For instance, Italian operation of law requires that government data of Italian citizens, if collected by official agencies, have to remain within Italy. Thus, using a cloud service provider from outside of Italy for realizing an e-government service provided to Italian citizens would immediately violate this promise. Hence, the cloud users must trust the cloud service provider hosting their data within the borders of the country and never copying them to an off-country location (not even for backup or in case of local failure) nor providing access to the data to entities from abroad. An intruder that has access to the cloud storage component is able to take snapshots or alter data in the storage. This might be done single time, many times, or regularly. An intruder that also has access to the processing logic of the cloud can also alter the functions and their input and output data. Even though in the most of the cases it may be legitimate to assume a cloud service provider to be honest and handling the customers' affairs in a respectful and responsible manner, there still remains a risk of malicious employees of the cloud service provider, successful attacks and compromisation by third parties, or of actions ordered by an evidence. In (Gruschka & Iacono, 2009), an overview of security mistakes and intrusions on cloud computing infrastructures are given. Some examples and more recent advances are briefly discussed in the following research papers:- Ristenpart et al. (Ristenpart, Tromer, Shacham, & Savage, 2009; Zhang, Juels, Reiter, & Ristenpart, 2012), presented some attack techniques for the virtualization of the Amazon EC2 IaaS service infrastructure. In their approach, the intruder allocates new virtual machines until one runs on the same physical machine as the victim's machine. Then, the intruder can perform cross-VM side channel attacks to learn or alter the victim's data. The authors present strategies to reach the desired victim machine with a high probability, and show how to expose this position for extracting secret data, for example a cryptographic key, from the victim's VM. Finally, they propose blinding techniques to stop cross-VM side-channel intrusion. In (Gruschka & Iacono, 2009), a drawback in the management interface of Amazon's EC2 was found. The Simple object access protocol (SOAP) based interface uses XML Signature as defined in web security for integrity protection and authenticity verification. (Gruschka & Iacono, 2009) discovered that the EC2 implementation for signature verification is penetrable to the Signature Wrapping intrusion (McIntosh & Austel, 2005). In this attack, the attacker—who eavesdropped a lawful request message—can add a second

arbitrary operation to the message while keeping the original signature. Due to the fault in the EC2 framework, the modification of the message is not detected and the injected operation is executed on behalf of the lawful user and billed to the victim's account. A major incident in a SaaS cloud happened in 2009 with Google Docs (Kincaid, 2009). Google Docs allows users to edit documents (such as text, spreadsheet, presentation etc.) online and share these documents with other users. However, this system had the following demerits: Once a document was shared with anyone, it was accessible for everyone the document owner has ever shared documents with before. For this technical problem, not even any criminal implication was required to get unauthorized access to confidential data. Recent attacks have proved that cloud systems of major cloud service providers may contain severe security faults indifferent types of clouds (Bugiel, Nürnberger, Pöppelmann, Sadeghi, & Schneider, 2011; Somorovsky et al., 2011). As can be seen from this review of the related work on cloud system attacks, the cloud computing illustration contains an implicit risk of working in a compromised cloud system. If an attacker is able to penetrate the cloud system itself, all data and all processes of all users operating on that cloud system may become subject to malicious actions in an avalanche manner. Hence, the cloud computing mechanism requires an in-depth reconsideration on what security requirements might be affected by such an exploitation event. For the common case of a single cloud provider hosting and processing all of its user's data, an intrusion would immediately affect all security requirements. Integrity, confidentiality and Accessibility of data and processes may become violated, and further malicious actions may be performed on behalf of the cloud user's identity. These cloud security challenges and risks triggered a lot of research activities, resulting in a quantity of proposals targeting the various cloud security threats. Alongside with these security challenges, the cloud mechanism comes with a new set of unique features that open the path toward novel security approaches, techniques and architectures. One promising concept makes use of multiple distinct clouds simultaneously to overcome the above listed problems or challenges.

DATA INTEGRITY

One of the most important challenge related to cloud security risks is data integrity. The data stored in the cloud may suffer from damage during transition operations from or to the cloud storage provider. Cachinet al. gives examples of the risk of attacks from both inside and outside the cloud service provider, such as the recently attacked Red Hat Linux.

Although this protocol solves the problem from a cloud storage point of view, Cachinet says that they remain concerned about the users view, due to the fact that users trust the cloud as a single reliable domain or as a private cloud without being aware of the protection protocols used in the cloud provider's servers. As a solution, Cachinet al. suggests that Byzantine fault-tolerant protocol for multiple clouds.

DATA INTRUSION

According to Garfinkel, another security fear that may occur with a cloud service provider, such as the Amazon cloud service, is a hacked password or data intrusion. If someone gets access to an Amazon account password, they will be able to access all the information of account and resources. Thus the stolen password allows the intruder to erase all the information inside any virtual machine object for the stolen user account, alter it, or even disable its services. Furthermore, there is a possibility for the user's email (Amazon username) to be hacked for a discussion of the probable risks of email), and since Amazon allows a lost password

to be reset by email, the hacker may still be able to log in to the account after receiving the new reset password.

Service Availability

Various kinds of services will be available through this cloud computing paradigm like as we seen in the picture in so many ways data will be accessed by the users in less cost and it has divided into service types like IaaS, PaaS and SaaS. So if service is available in the cloud computing architecture it must be shown to users and they will be used according to their choices.

Migration toward Multi-Cloud Architecture

The terms "multi-clouds" or "interclouds" or "cloud-of-clouds" that were introduced by Vukolic These terms suggest that cloud computing paradigm should not be ended with a single cloud. Using their illustration, a cloudy sky consolidated different colors and shapes of clouds which provide directions to different implementations and administrative domains. Recent research has focused on the multi-cloud environment (Abu-Libdeh, Princehouse, & Weatherspoon, 2010) which control multiple clouds and avoids dependency on only single cloud. Cachin et al. identify two layers in the multi-cloud environmental architecture: the base or first layer is the inner-cloud while the upper or second layer is the inter-cloud. In the upper layer, the Byzantine fault tolerance finds its place. Now we will first summarize the previous work on Byzantine protocols over the last three decades.

Byzantine Protocols

In cloud computing paradigm, any fault in software or hardware is known as Byzantine fault that usually relate to improper behavior and intrusion sufferance. With these it also includes arbitrary and crash faults. Much research has been done in the field of Byzantine fault tolerance (BFT) protocol from its first introduction. Although BFT research has received a great deal of attention, it still incurs from the limitations of practical adoption and remains peripheral in distributed systems. The relationship between BFT and cloud computing has been calibrated, and many infer that in the last few years, it has been considered one of the major roles of the distributed system agenda. Even, many peoples describe BFT as being of only "purely academic interest" for a cloud service. This lack of interest in BFT is quite different to the level of interest shown in the mechanisms for sustaining crash faults that are used in large-scale systems. Causes that lower the acceptance of BFT are such as Byzantine fault-tolerant data is stolen from the cloud provider. Regarding service availability risk or loss of data, if we replicate the data into different cloud providers, we could dissertate that the data loss risk will be reduced. If one cloud service provider fails, we can still access our data that is available in other cloud service providers.

Architecture of DepSky

The DepSky architecture is made of four clouds and each cloud uses its own particular interface. The DepSky algorithm should be available in the client's machines as a software library to communicate with each cloud (Figure 3). All of these four clouds are storage clouds, so there are no codes to be executed. The DepSky algorithm library permits reading and writing operations with the storage clouds.

DepSky Data Model: As the DepSky system interact with different cloud service providers, the DepSky library interact with different cloud interface providers and hence, the data format is accepted by each cloud. The DepSky data model is made up of three abstraction levels: the conceptual data unit, a generic data unit, and the data unit implementation. The DepSky Architecture of multicloud has been illustrated in figure 3.

DepSKy System Model: The DepSky system model consists of three parts: readers, writers and four cloud storage providers, where readers and writers are the client's tasks. Bessani etal. Dif-

Figure 3. DepSky Architecture of multicloud

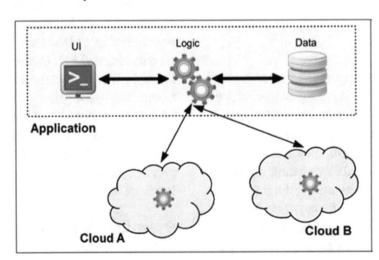

ferentiate readers and writers for cloud storage. Readers can fiasco arbitrarily (for example, they can fail by crashing, they can fail from time to time and then display any behavior) while, writers fails by crashing only.

ARCHITECTURES OF MULTICLOUD

The basic underlying idea is to use several isolated clouds at the same time to reduce the risks of malicious data manipulation, manifestation, and process tampering. By integrating multiple distinct clouds, the trust retention can be lowered to an assumption of non collaborating cloud service providers. Ahead, this setting makes it much difficult for an external intruder to access or tamper hosted data or applications of a specific cloud user. The idea of using multiple clouds has been proposed by Bernstein and Celesti (Bernstein, Ludvigson, Sankar, Diamond, & Morrow, 2009; Celesti, Tusa, Villari, & Puliafito, 2010). But previous work on multi-cloud did not focused on security. Since then, other views considering the security effects have been proposed. These approaches are operating on distinct cloud service levels, are partially combined with cryptographic methods and goals different usage scenarios. In this Chapter, we introduce a model of different architectural models for distributing resources to multiple cloud service providers. These models are used to discuss the security advantages and also to classify existing approaches. In our model, we distinguish the following 4 architectural models:

- *Repetition of applications*: This approach allows to receive multiple results of one operation performed in different clouds and to compare them within the own premise (see Section 4). This accredits the user to get evidence on the integrity of the result.
- *Partition of System architecture into layers*: This scheme of multicloud allows to separate the security logic from the data

(see Section 5). This gives superfluous protection against data leakage due to errors in the application logic.

- *Partition of Security features into segments*: This approach allows dividing and distributing the security logic to distinct clouds (see Section 6). This has two benefits. First, no cloud service provider learns the complete security logic and secondly, no cloud service provider knows about overall calculated results of data. Thus, this leads to data and application confidentiality.
- *Distributing of data into fragments*: This approach allows distributing fine-grained parts of the data to distinct clouds (see Section 7). In this approach no any cloud service provider has all the access rights so data confidentiality is increased to large extent. Now every introduced multi cloud architecture model provides individual security benefits, which map to different application scenarios and their security necessities. However, these patterns can be combined to optimize security features but this combined architecture must required large amount of time for deployment and execution.

Now in the following sections four distinct multi cloud architectures are discussed in details and their benefits and demerits are also described.

REPETITION OF APPLICATION

In the cloud computing it is very difficult to technically prove that the operation performed by cloud is correct and nobody do not alter it nor do they tamper. This gives guarantee on the basis of level of trust between the cloud customer and the cloud provider and on the contractual regulations made between them such as SLAs, applicable laws and regulations of the involved jurisdictional territory. But even if the data is kept secure by cloud service provider and customer it is also possible that data may be compromised by third party. To solve this internal problem, multiple distinct cloud scan be deployed for executing multiple copies of the same application (see Figure4). The same operation is executed by distinct clouds and then compares the obtained results; the cloud user gets confirmation on the integrity of the result. The Replication of applications in multicloud architectures has been illustrated in Figure 4.

In such a setting, the required trust toward the cloud service provider can be lowered dramatically. Instead of trusting only on cloud service provider, the cloud user only needs to believe on the assumption that the cloud providers do not collaborate with malicious party. If n is number of clouds then **n > 1**. All of the n adopted clouds perform the same task. Assume further that f denotes the number of malicious clouds and that n-f > f the majority of the clouds are honest. The correct result can then be obtained by the cloud user by comparing the results and taking the majority as the correct one. There are other methods of deriving the correct result, for instance using the TurpinCoan algorithm (Wisner, Leong, & Tan, 2005) for solving the General Byzantine Agreement problem. Instead of having the cloud user

performing the verification task, another viable approach consists in having one cloud monitoring the execution of the other clouds. For instance, Cloud A may announce intermediate results of its computations to an associated monitoring process running at Cloud B. This way, Cloud B can verify that Cloud A makes progress and sticks to the computation intended by the cloud user. As an extension of this approach, Cloud B may run a model checker service that verifies the execution path taken by Cloud A on-the-fly, allowing for immediate detection of irregularities. This architecture enables to verify the integrity of results obtained from tasks deployed to the cloud. On the other hand, it needs to be noted that it does not provide any protection in respect to the confidentiality of data or processes. On the contrary, this approach might have a negative impact on the confidentiality because—due to the deployment of multiple clouds—the risk rises that one of them is malicious or compromised. To implement protection against an unauthorized access to data and logic this architecture needs to be combined with the architecture described in Section 5.The idea of resource replication can be found in many other disciplines. In the design of dependable systems, for example, it is used to

Figure 4. Replication of applications in multicloud architectures

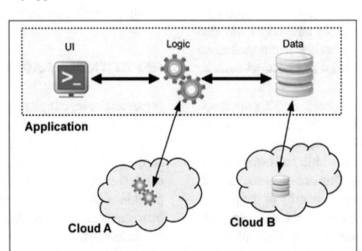

increase the robustness of the system especially against system failures (Koren & Krishna, 2010). In economic business processes—and especially in the management of supply chains—single-source suppliers are avoided to lower the dependency on suppliers and increase the flexibility of the business process (Wisner et al., 2005). In all these cases, the additional overhead introduced by doing things multiple times is accepted in favor of other goals resulting from this replication. This architectural concept can be applied to all three cloud layers. A case study at the SaaS-layer is discussed in Section 4.1.

Case Studies: Replicating of Application Tasks

Imagine a cloud provider named Instant Reporting that provides the service of creating annual accounting reports automatically out of a given set of business data. This is a very typical scenario of cloud usage, because such a report has to be published by all commercial entities once a year. Hence, the resources required to create such reports are only necessary for a small period of time every year. Thus, by using a third-party cloud service for this, in-house resources can be omitted, which would run idle most of the year. On the other side, by sharing its service capabilities among a large set of companies—all of which have to create their reports at different times of the year—a cloud service provider gains large benefits from providing such a shared service "on the cloud." However, as promising as this scenario seems to be in terms of using the cloud computing paradigm, it contains a fundamental flaw: The cloud customers cannot verify that the annual report created by the cloud service is correct. There might have been accidental or intentional modifications of the source data for the report, or the processing logic that creates the reports from the source data might contain errors. In the worst case, the cloud system itself was compromised (e.g., by a malicious competitor) and all reports are

slightly modified so that they look conclusive but contain slightly reduced profit margins, intended to make a competing company look bad—or even insolvent.4.1.1 Dual Execution In such a situation, a first and trivial approach for verification might be that a cloud customer triggers the creation of its annual accounting report more than once. For instance, instead of giving the same request to one cloud provider only (called Cloud A hereafter), a second cloud provider (called Cloud B) that offers an equivalent type of service is invoked in parallel. By placing the same request at Clouds A and B, a cloud user can immediately identify whether his request was processed differently in Clouds A and B. Hence, this way, a secret exploitation of either side's service implementation would be detected. However, besides the doubled costs of placing the same request twice, this approach additionally relies on the existence of at least two different cloud providers with equivalent service offerings and comparable type of result. Depending on the type of cloud resources used, this is either easily the case—as even today there already exist many different cloud providers offering equivalent services(see Section 1)—or difficult in cases in which very specific resources are demanded.

n Clouds Approach

A more advanced, but also more complex approach comes from the distributed algorithms discipline: the Byzantine Agreement Protocol. Assume the existence of n cloud providers, of which f collaborate maliciously against the cloud user, with $n > 3f$. In that case, each of the n clouds performs the computational task given by the cloud user. Then, all cloud providers collaboratively run a distributed algorithm that solves the General Byzantine Agreement problem (e.g., the TurpinCoan (Coan & Turpin, 1984) or Exponential Information Gathering (Lynch, 1996) algorithms). After that it is guaranteed that all non malicious cloud providers know the correct result of the computation. Hence, in the final step, the result is communicated back to the cloud user via a Secure Broadcast algorithm (e.g., plain flooding, with the cloud user taking the majority as the result). Hence, the cloud user can determine the correct result even in presence off malicious clouds.

Processor and Verifier

Instead of having Clouds A and B perform the very same request, another viable approach consists in having one cloud provider "monitor" the execution of the other cloud provider. For instance, Cloud A may announce intermediate results of its computations to a monitoring process run at Cloud B. This way, Cloud B can verify that Cloud A makes progress and sticks to the computation intended by the cloud customer. As an extension of this approach, Cloud B may run a model checker service that verifies the execution path taken by Cloud A on-the-fly, allowing for immediate detection of irregularities. One of the major benefits of this approach consists in its flexibility. Cloud B does not have to know all details of the execution run at Cloud A—especially not about the data values processed—but is able to detect and report anomalies to the cloud customer immediately. However, the guarantees given by this approach strongly depend on the type, number, and verifiability of the intermediate results given to Cloud B.

PARTITION OF SYSTEM ARCHITECTURE INTO LAYERS

The architectural pattern described in the previous Section 4 enables the cloud user to get some evidence on the integrity of the computations performed on a third-party's resources or services. The architecture introduced in this section targets the risk of undesired data leakage. It answers the question on how a cloud user can be sure that the data access is implemented and enforced effectively and that errors in the application logic do not affect the user's data? To limit the risk of undesired data leakage due to application logic flaws, the separation of the application system's tiers and their delegation to distinct clouds is proposed (see Figure 5). In case of an application failure, the data are not immediately at risk since it is physically separated and protected by an independent access control scheme. Moreover, the cloud user has the choice to select a particular—probably specially trusted—cloud provider for data storage services and a different cloud provider for applications. It needs to be noted, that the security services provided by this architecture can only be fully exploited if the execution of the application logic on the data is performed on the cloud user's system. Only in this case, the application provider does not learn anything on the users' data. Partition of system architecture into layers has been illustrated in figure 5.

Thus, the SaaS-based delivery of an application to the user side in conjunction with the controlled access to the user's data performed from the same user's system is the most far reaching instantiation. Besides the introduced overhead due to the additionally involved cloud, this architecture requires, moreover, standardized interfaces to couple applications with data services provided by distinct parties. Also generic data services might serve for a wide range of applications there will be the need for application specific services as well. The partitioning of application systems into tiers and distributing the tiers to distinct clouds provides some coarse grained protection against data leakage in the presence off laws in application design or implementation. This architectural concept can be applied to all three cloud layers. In the next section, a case study at the SaaS-layer is discussed.

Case Study

Assume a SaaS-based service named PhotOrga, which allows its users to upload and manage their photos as well as share them with their family, friends, and other contacts. For this purpose, Pho-

Figure 5. Partition of system architecture into layers

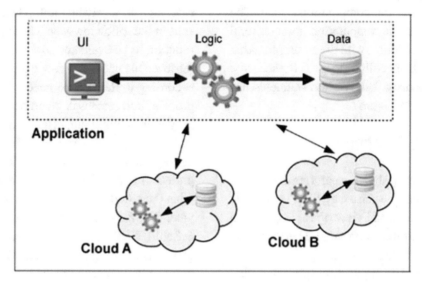

tOrga provides an adequate access control system. In such a setting, how can the user be sure that this access control system has been implemented correctly and effectively? Since the application logic andthe data storage of the PhotOrga system are tightly integrated, a flaw in the application logic might have side effects on the access control to the photos. This might result in an unwanted data leakage (such as in the Google Docs case mentioned in Section 2).The separation of the application logic layer and the data persistence layer with the assignment to two distinct clouds reduces the data leakage risk in the presence of application logic flaws. Since the data are not directly accessible by the application, design or programming errors in the application do not have such a widespread effect as in the integrated scenario. From an implementation point of view, this can be realized using OAuth. When the application (on Cloud A) wants to a access a photo it creates an OAuth request and redirects the user to the storage provider (on Cloud B). The user is than asked to grant or deny this authorization request. This way the user gets more control over his data, while having a slightly higher manag-

ing effort. This scenario can be extended to a lot of other services including e-mail, documents, spreadsheets, and so forth.

PARTITION OF SECURITY FEATURES INTO SEGMENTS

This architecture variant targets the confidentiality of data and processing logic. It gives an answer to the following question: How can a cloud user avoid fully revealing the data or processing logic to the cloud provider? The data should not only be protected while in the persistent storage, but in particular when it is processed. The idea of this architecture is that the application logic needs to be partitioned into fine-grained parts and these parts are distributed to distinct clouds (see Figure 6). This approach can be instantiated in different ways depending on how the partitioning is performed. The clouds participating in the fragmented applications can be symmetric or asymmetric in terms of computing power and trust. Two concepts are common. The first involves a trusted private cloud that takes a small critical share of the computation, and a untrusted public cloud that takes most of the computational load. The second distributes the computation among several untrusted public clouds, with the assumption that these clouds will not collude to break the security. Partition of security features into segments has been illustrated in Figure 6.

Obfuscating Splitting

By this approach, application parts are distributed to different clouds in such a way, that every single cloud has only a partial view on the application and gains only limited knowledge. Therefore, this method can also hide parts of the application logic from the clouds. For application splitting, a first approach is using the existing sequential or parallel logic separation. Thus, depending on the application, every cloud provider just performs subtasks on a subset of data. An approach by Danezis and Livshits (Danezis & Livshits, 2011) is build around secure storage architecture and focusing on online service provisioning, where the service depends on the result of function evaluations on the user's data. This proposal uses the cloud as

a secure storage, with keys remaining on client side, e.g., in a private cloud. The application is split in the following way: The service sends the function to be evaluated to the client. The client retrieves his necessary raw data and processes it according to the service needs. The result and a proof of correctness is given back to the service providing public cloud. In the cloud, the remaining functionality of the service is offered based on the aggregated input of the clients. This architecture protects the detailed user data, and reveals only what the cloud needs to know to provide the service. Similarly, the Flex Cloud approach (Groß & Schill, 2012) is based on interconnecting local, private computing environments to a semi trusted public cloud for realizing complex work flows or secures distributed storage. This approach utilizes multiple resource-constrained secure computation environments ("private clouds") to form a collaborative computing environment of similar trust level, a trustworthy "community cloud." A difficult challenge of obfuscating splitting in general is the fact that there is no generic pattern for the realization. Careful analysis where the application can be split into fragments must be performed

Figure 6. Partition of security features into segments

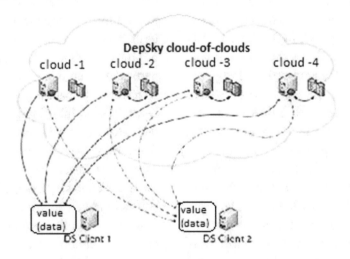

regarding its confidentiality, i.e., checking if the information that the participating cloud providers receive is really innocuous.

Multiparty Computation

Homomorphic encryption and secure multiparty computation both use cryptographic means to secure the data while it is processed. In homomorphic encryption, the user encrypts the data with his public key and uploads the cipher texts to the Cloud. The cloud can independently compute on the encrypted data to obtain an encrypted result, which only the user can decrypt. Therefore, in our scenario, homomorphic encryption uses an asymmetric fragmentation, where the user (or a small trusted private cloud) manages the keys and performs the encryption and decryption operations, while the massive computation on encrypted data is done by an untrusted public cloud. The possibility of fully homomorphic encryption supporting secure addition and multiplication of cipher texts was first suggested in (Rivest, Adleman, & Dertouzos, 1978). However, for a long time all known homomorphic encryption schemes supported efficiently only one operation(Paillier, 1999; Rivest, Shamir, & Adleman, 1978). Therefore, the recent discovery of fully homomorphic encryption by Gentry (Asharov et al., 2012; Gentry, 2009) had a tremendous impact on the cryptographic community and revived research in this field. In the case of homomorphic encryption, the cloud has the main share of work, as it operates on the encrypted inputs to compute the encrypted output. However, the algorithms are far from being practical, so the vision of clouds based on homomorphic encryption seems unreal for the foreseeable future. In addition, the applicability is limited, as for services that go beyond the outsourcing of computation, intermediate or final results need to be decrypted. This requires either interaction with the entity that holds the key(e.g., a private cloud) or the key is shared among several clouds who then assist in decrypting values that are needed in clear with a

threshold encryption scheme (Desmedt, 1998). The idea of secure multiparty computation was first presented in (Yao, 1982) as a solution to the millionaires problem: Two millionaires want to find out who is richer without disclosing any further information about their wealth. Two main variants of secure multiparty computation are known: Based on linear secret sharing (Ben-Or, Goldwasser, & Wigderson, 1988) or garbled circuits (Goldreich, Micali, & Wigderson, 1987). Schemes based on a linear secret sharing scheme work as follows: The user computes and distributes the shares to the different clouds. The clouds will jointly compute the function of interest on these shares, communicating with each other when necessary. In the end, the clouds hold shares of the result which is sent back to the user who can reconstruct the result. At least three clouds are necessary for this scheme and no two of them should collude. The approach of garbled circuits works as follows: One cloud generates a circuit that is able to compute the desired function and encrypts this circuit producing a garbled circuit, which is however still executable. Then, this cloud assists the users in encrypting their inputs accordingly. Another cloud needs now to be present to evaluate the circuit with the user's inputs. Thus, this scheme requires in general only two clouds. Although the ideas of multiparty computation are old, it is ongoing research to reduce the overhead by multiparty computation. A recent improvement, e.g., on equality and comparison of values, has lead to the constructions of programming frameworks, which can already be considered practical (Burkhart, Strasser, Many, & Dimitropoulos, 2010; Damgård, Geisler, Krøigaard, & Nielsen, 2009). An example architecture that uses garbled circuits is the Twin Clouds approach (Bugiel, Nürnberger, Sadeghi, & Schneider, 2011) that utilizes a private cloud for preparation of garbled circuits. The circuits itself is then evaluated within a high-performance commodity cloud of lower trust level-without lowering the security guarantees for the processes outsourced to the public cloud.

In all cases, using secure multiparty computation indistinct clouds guarantees the secrecy of the input data, unless the cloud providers collude to open shares or decrypt inputs. Assuming that the cloud provider itself is not malicious, but might be compromised by attacks or have single malicious employees, this collusion is hard to establish so that a good protection is given. A multiparty computation between clouds makes it possible to compute a function on data in a way that no cloud provider learns anything about the input or output data.

Case Studies

With secure multiparty computation, a number of participant scan compute functions on their input values without revealing any information on their individual inputs during the computation. Here, we consider multiparty computation to be executed between several clouds. Using secure multiparty computation can be used to better protect the secrecy of the users' data in online services available today, but also has the potential to make new services possible that do not exist today because of the user's confidentiality requirements and the lack of a trusted third party. Problems in the latter category exist in today's business environment: Multiple corporations want to do a statistical analysis of their business and market data. The result is expected to help all of them; however, for obvious reasons, no corporation wants to disclose their data to each other. If the stakeholders cannot identify a single third party trusted by all, this scenario requires multiparty computation between the private clouds of the participating corporations or outsourced to distinct public clouds. An example for a real-world application of secure multiparty computation is a sugar beet auction in Denmark (Bogetoft et al., 2009). This auction is used by farmers selling their sugar beets to the processing company Danisco. The farmers' input to the auction depends on their economic situation and productivity, which they do not want to reveal

to a competitor or to Danisco. Clearly, Danisco also does not want to give away the auction. As a trusted third party is not easily found, the easiest solution was to set up a multiparty computation between servers of the farmer's union, Danisco, and a supporting university. Although still in a research prototype stage, another application area of multiparty computation is the exchange of monitoring data and security incidents for collaborative network monitoring between several Internet providers (Bai & Devi, 2011). As network monitoring and attack detection have quite strict real-time requirements to be useful, this application requires highly efficient implementations of multiparty computation. Some algorithms are implemented in the SEPIA framework (Burkhart et al., 2010). Recent work (J.-M. Bohli, Li, & Seedorf, 2012) is considering new secrecy/efficiency tradeoffs by introducing an assisting server to support multiparty computation. The assisting server does collect some shared information, so that it might learn partial information during the computation process, but on the other hand can bring a big efficiency gain in particular for equal comparisons. Another application that has been discussed is supply chain management. In supply chain management, several companies who are part of a supply chain aim to establish an optimal supply chain. If relevant information about the supply chain, such as production cost and capacity, use of resources and labor, is shared among all companies, it is possible to find the optimal supply chain that brings the product most cost efficient to the market and, thus, finally optimizes profit for all involved companies. As the required business data are usually considered to be confidential by the companies, secure multiparty computation is a tool to compute the optimal supply chain while keeping the input data secret (Catrina & Kerschbaum, 2008). Secure multiparty computation can in principle be used to distribute any computation task on multiple clouds. Incase just one party owns the data, it is for privacy reasons not required to use more than two clouds, as we assume that the two clouds do not collude. This limits the overhead created by the multiparty computation. The task of creating the annual accounting report already mentioned in Section 4.1 can be an example if apart from data integrity the property of data secrecy is required. Especially, for highly visible stock corporations, the details of the accounting must be kept confidential. Otherwise, insider trading or other effects on the stock market are possible. However, due to the nature of the accounting report creation (only needed once a year, provider offers special software, and so on) it still might be useful to perform this task inside the cloud. In this case, using secret sharing and multiparty computation with two cloud providers offers the required properties. Other, non cryptographic ways of splitting such as obfuscation splitting is possible for many applications. For example, the calculation of earnings and expenses can be distributed to two different cloud providers. These tasks can be performed independently without any significant overhead. In this case, the amount of loss or profit-which is typically the most confidential value-remains undisclosed to the cloud providers.

DISTRIBUTION OF DATA INTO FRAGMENTS

This multicloud architecture specifies that the application data is partitioned and distributed to distinct clouds (see Figure 7).The most common forms of data storage are files and databases. Files typically contain unstructured data (e.g., pictures, text documents) and do not allow for easily splitting or exchanging parts of the data. This kind of data can only be partitioned using cryptographic methods (see Section 7.1).Databases contain data in structured form organized in columns and rows. Here, data partitioning can be performed by distributing different parts of the database (tables, rows, columns) to different cloud providers (see Section 7.2). Finally, files can also contain structured data (e.g., XML data). Here, the data can be splitted using similar approaches like for databases. XML data, for example, can be partitioned on XML element level. However, such operations are very costly. Thus, this data are commonly rather treated using cryptographic data splitting.

Figure 7. Distribution of data into fragments

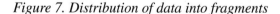
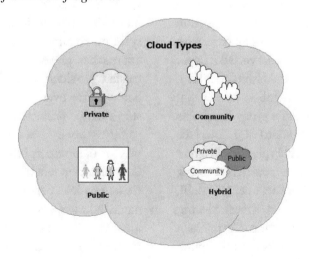

Cryptographic Data Splitting

Probably, the most basic cryptographic method to store data securely is to store the data in encrypted form. While the cryptographic key could remain at the user's premises, to increase flexibility in cloud data processing or to enable multiuser systems it is beneficial to have the key available online when needed (Pagano & Pagano, 2011). This approach, therefore, distributes key material and encrypted data into different clouds. For instance, with XML data, this can, e.g., be done inside the XML document by using XML encryption (Somorovsky et al., 2012). Distribution of data into fragments has been illustrated in figure 7.

A similar approach is taken by several solutions for secure Cloud storage: The first approach to cryptographic cloud storage (Kamara & Lauter, 2010) is a solution for encrypted key/value storage in the cloud while maintaining the ability to easily access the data. It involves searchable encryption (Abdalla et al., 2005; Curtmola, Garay, Kamara, & Ostrovsky, 2006) as the key component to achieve this. Searchable encryption allows keyword search on encrypted data if an authorized token for the keyword is provided. The keys are stored in a trusted private cloud whereas the data resides in the untrusted public cloud (see Section 6.2).One example of a relational database with encrypted data processing is CryptDB (Popa, Redfield, Zeldovich, & Balakrishnan, 2011). The database consists of a database server that stores the encrypted data and a proxy that holds the keys and provides a standard SQL interface to the user. The data are encrypted in different layers with schemes such as order-preserving encryption (Boldyreva, Chenette, Lee, & O'neill, 2009), homomorphic encryption (Rivest, Shamir, et al., 1978), searchable encryption (Curtmola et al., 2006), and a standard symmetric encryption system, such as the AES.For every SQL query, the proxy identifies and provides only the necessary keys to the server, so that exactly this query can be answered. Obviously, this implies that the

database server may learn more keys with every new query. Hence, security against persistent attackers is certainly limited here. The advantage of cryptDB lies in the fact that the database part is a standard MySQL database, and in that its efficiency is only decreased marginally, as compared to unencrypted data storage. Another option is to compute a secret sharing of the data. In a secret sharing protocol, no single cryptographic key is involved. Instead, secret sharing splits the data into multiple shares in such a way that the data can only be reconstructed if more shares than a given threshold are collected. This method integrates well with multiparty computation, as presented in Section 6.2. As discussed, multiparty computation often operates on such shares, so that the clouds that form the peers of the multiparty protocol can store their shares permanently without any loss of security.

Database Splitting

For protecting information inside databases, one has to distinguish two security goals: confidentiality of data items (e.g., a credit card number) or confidentiality of data item relationships (e.g., the items "Peter" and "AIDS" are not confidential, but their relationship is). In the first case, data splitting requires a scenario—similar to other approaches presented before—with a least one trusted provider (or additional encryption; see below). However, very often only the relationship shall be protected, and this can be achieved using just honest-but-curious providers. A typical way of database splitting is pseudonymization: One provider receives the data with some key fields (typical personal identification data like name, address, and so on) replaced by a random identifier, and the second provider receives the mapping of the identifier to the original information. This approach is used, for example, in a commercial cloud security gateway (Vijayan, 2013). For splitting a database table, there are two general approaches: Vertical fragmentation and horizontal fragmentation (Wiese, 2010). With vertical fragmentation, the columns are distributed to cloud providers in such a way that no single provider learns a confidential relationship on his own. A patient health record, for example, might be fragmented into two parts, e.g., (name, patient number) and (patient number, disease). This way, the individual providers only learn noncritical data relations. However, for real-world applications, it is a nontrivial task to find such a fragmentation. First, new relations can be learned by performing transitive combination of existing ones. Second, some relations can be concluded using external knowledge. If, in the example above, the first provider additionally learns about the relation (patient number, medication), he has technically still no knowledge about the patient's disease. However, someone with pharmaceutical background can derive the disease from the medication. Further, new relations can also be derived by combining multiple data set. For instance, using again the relation of (patient number, medication), the knowledge of a combination of medications can ease the guessing of the patient's disease. Thus, also on a row level, database splitting might be required. This is called horizontal fragmentation. Finally, database splitting can also be combined with encryption. Using key management mechanisms like mentioned before, some database columns are encrypted. The combination of encryption and splitting protects confidential columns and still allows querying database entries using plain text columns.

Case Study: Separation of Data Entities

As a case study for this multicloud architecture pattern, one can consider the reverse of what needs to be done when data sources are federated. In many cross-organization data federation projects, a common task is to harmonize distinct data sources schema wise to obtain common semantics and structure. This enables to have a combined view on the federated data. In many domains, this has been an active research and development topic in recent years. Take the federation of hospital data as an example, in which distinct medical institutions federate their data on a certain disease, as has, e.g., been the case in the EU-funded research project@neurist concerning celebral aneurysms (Rajasekaran et al., 2008). The main challenge in this case is to find a method to federate the data so that distributed data entities can be virtually correlated. In the data partition pattern, however, there already exists one common schema, because only one data source is on the centre stage. The challenge here is instead to find a partition of the data in a way that allows to distribute the data entities to distinct clouds while minimizing the amount of knowledge one cloud provider can gather by analyzing the obtained data set. By this, it might be feasible to outsource computationally intense queries to a multicloud without violating the strict security and privacy obligations attached to medical data (see also Section 8.3.1).

LEGAL ACCEPTANCES WITH MULTICLOUD ARCHITECTURES

Since legislation traditionally only slowly copes with technological paradigm shifts, there are few to none cloud specific regulations in place by now. Therefore, for cloud computing the same legal framework is applicable as for any other means of data processing. Generally, legal compliance does not distinguish between different means of technology but rather different types of information. For instance, enterprises are facing other legal requirements for the lawful processing of their tax information than for the lawful processing of their Customer Relationship Management. A one-cloud-fits-all approach does not reflect these differing compliance requirements. Multicloud architectures may be a viable solution for enterprises to address these compliance issues. Hence, this section gives a coarse-grained legal analysis on the different approaches, and their flaws and benefits in terms of compliance and privacy impact. The immanent conflict between cloud computing and the world of laws and policies results from the border less nature of clouds in contrast to the mostly national scope of legal frameworks. The most successful cloud service providers operate their clouds across national borders in multiple data centers all over the globe. Hence, they can offer high availability even in case of regional failure as well as reduced costs because of their choice of location. In contrast, the cloud customer is subject to its national legal requirements, and faces the problem to ensure legal compliance to national laws in a multinational environment. This conflict is neither new nor unique to cloud computing, but the highly dynamic and virtualized nature of clouds intensifies it as the applicability of laws relate to physical location. The legal uncertainties of cloud computing, especially in Europe with its strict data protection laws, are subject to an ongoing discussion. Nevertheless, legal experts agree that lawful cloud computing is possible as long as the adequate technical, organizational, and contractual safeguards for the specific type of information to be processed are in place. Before deciding on which cloud service type to use, be it public, private, or hybrid, IaaS, PaaS, or SaaS, the enterprise needs to conduct a risk assessment. This risk assessment is not only the best practice but also sometimes legally mandatory, e.g., in form of a Privacy Risk Assessment in the proposed European Data Protection Regulation (European, 2012). A proper risk assessment before "going cloud" means to identify one's internal processes and the relevant information involved in these processes, a risk and threat analysis, as well as identifying legal compliance requirements that have to be met and the necessary safeguards to be installed. The outcome of such a risk assessment may be that not all of enterprise's processes are suitable for a public cloud or not yet cloud ready. Usually, enterprises process varying types of information, which have different grades of sensitivity and need according

security controls. There may be business-critical information, which requires maximum availability, but is less critical in terms of confidentiality. Similarly, there may be information for which a guaranteed availability rate of 99 percent is sufficient, but a breach of confidentiality would be crucial. Legal and other compliance frameworks may ask for specific additional safeguards. For instance, for processing of medical information of US citizens, a Health Insurance Portability and Accountability Act (Act, 1996) certification may be required. Similarly, for credit card information processing, compliance to the Payment Card Industry Data Security Standard (Liu et al., 2010)(PCI DSS, (PCI Security Standards Council, 2010)) is mandatory. Further, US Federal Information Security Management Act (Congress, 2002) (FISMA of 2002, (US Congress, 2002)) and US Federal Risk and Authorization Management Program (Risk, 2012) (FedRAMP, (US General Services Administration, 2012) are relevant for processing information of US Federal Agencies. Cloud customers based in the European Union that are contracting with cloud service providers outside the European Economic Area to outsource the processing of personal identifiable information have to adhere to the EU Data Protection Directive (Directive, 1995). This includes mandatory contractual safeguards for the export of personal data, including mandatory contractual safeguards such as Standard Contractual Clauses and Binding Corporate Rules (Commission, 2010; Party, 2007). Furthermore, many national legislations require specific information to stay within the national borders of the country. This typically applies to information regarding national security, but also to information of public authorities or electronic health records. Potential cloud customers are facing several of these requirements for security controls, standards, and certifications, probably even varying per process. Identifying one cloud service provider to offer all of these options like a modular system seems impossible. Multicloud approaches may help addressing these issues. As discussed next, the compliance benefits and drawbacks of the identified multicloud architectures, in general, seem auspicious.

Repetition of Application

This approach appears to have the fewest benefits regarding legal compliance as it multiplies the necessity to identify and choose a cloud service provider perfectly tailored for the requirements of the relevant process and information. Since this could mean negotiating and concluding individual contracts with several cloud service providers, replicating a highly sensitive process or an application seems to unreasonably tie up personnel and financial resources. Therefore, this approach has its value for information and processes with low sensitivity but high availability and soundness requirements.

Partition of System Architecture into Layers

The separation of logic and data offers the possibility to store the data in the cloud with compliant controls and safeguards and to outsource the processing logic to a not specifically certified cloud with favorable price. It also allows for storing the data in a national cloud while the application logic is outsourced to a multinational one. A drawback of this approach is that the compliant separation of logic and data is only possible if the application provider does not receive the customer's data in any case. The processing needs to take place in an environment as secure and certified as the chosen storage cloud. This can either be the customer's own premise, an approach that almost annihilates the benefits of outsourcing, cost reduction, and seamless scalability of using cloud computing, because the customer needs to provision sufficient and compliant resources by himself. Alternatively, the application logic can also take place in a different tier of the compliant storage cloud, or on a different cloud with similar compliance level.

The drawback of this approach obviously is that the customer has to fully trust those cloud service providers that receive all information, logic, and data. This somewhat contradicts the initial motivation of this multicloud approach.

Partition of Security Features

Obscure Splitting and Database Splitting

These approaches are especially valuable for dealing with personal identifiable data. Segmenting personal identifiable data—if realized in a reasonable way—is a viable privacy safeguard. Best practice would be to separate the data in a way that renders the remaining data pseudonymous. Pseudonymity itself is a privacy safeguard (Fed. Republic of Germany, 2009, Section 3a). Therefore, outsourcing pseudonymized information, which is unlinkable to a specific person, does require considerable less additional safeguards as compared to non pseudonymized information. Pseudonymization based on the Obfuscated Splitting approach could be used, e.g., in Human Resources or Customer Relationship Management. A potential cloud customer would have to remove all directly identifying data in the first place, like name, social security number, credit card information, or address, and store this information separately, either on premise or in a cloud with adequately high-security controls. The remaining data can still be linked to the directly identifying data by means of an unobvious identifier (the pseudonym), which is unusable for any malicious third parties. The unlinkability of the combined pseudonymized data to a person can be ensured by performing a carefully conducted privacy risk assessment. These assessments are always constrained by the assumptions of an adversary's "reasonable means". The cloud customer has the option to outsource the pseudonymized data to a cloud service provider with fewer security controls, which may result in additional cost savings. If the customer decides to outsource the directly identifiable data to a different cloud service provider, she has to ensure that these two providers do not cooperate, e.g., by using the same IaaS provider in the backend.

Cryptographic Data Splitting and Homomorphic Encryption

As of today, this approach appears to be the most viable alternative, both from the technical and economical point of view. State-of-the-art encryption of data with adequate key management is one of the most effective means to safeguard privacy and confidentiality when outsourcing data to a cloud service provider. Nevertheless, at least in the European Union, encryption is not considered to relieve cloud customers from all of their responsibilities and legal obligations. Encrypted data keep the nature it has in its decrypted state; personally identifiable information in encrypted form is still regarded as personally identifiable information (Party, 2012)(EU Article 29 Working Party, 2012). Encryption is considered as an important technical security measure; however, some additional mandatory legal safeguards still apply. For personally identifiable data, this means that, e.g., adequate contracts for the export of data to countries outside of the European Economic Area have to be in place.

ASSESSMENTS OF MULTICLOUD ARCHITECTURES

Given the vast amount of specific approaches for realizing each of the presented multicloud architectures, it is not feasible to perform a general assessment adequately covering all of them. Furthermore, many approaches are only suitable in very special circumstances, rendering each comparison to other approaches of the same domain inadequate. However, in this section we perform a high-level assessment of all multicloud approaches presented above, focusing on their capabilities in terms of security, feasibility, and compliance, as shown in Fig. 5. Therein, the security considerations indicate an approach's general improvements and aggravations in terms of integrity, confidentiality, and availability of application logic or data, respectively. For instance, the n clouds approach is highly beneficial in terms of integrity (every deviation in execution that occurs at a single cloud provider only can immediately be detected and corrected), but quite disadvantageous in terms of confidentiality (because every cloud provider learns everything about the application logic and data). The feasibility aspect covers issues of applicability, business readiness, and ease of use. Herein, applicability means the degree of flexibility of using one approach to solve different types of problems. Business-readiness evaluates how far the research on a multicloud approach has progressed and if it is ready for real-world applications, whereas ease of use indicates the complexity of implementing the particular approach. As an example, the approaches of secure multiparty computation may be of high benefits in terms of security, but only solve a very specific type of computation problem (i.e., are limited in applicability), and are quite complex to implement (i.e., not easy to use) even if they can be applied reasonably. The compliance dimension provides a high-level indication of the impact of each approach to the legal obligations implied to the cloud customer when utilizing that approach. Comparison study of multicloud approaches with their capabilities has been illustrated in figure 8.

Application of the dual execution approach, for instance, maybe favorable in terms of security and feasibility, but requires complex contractual negotiations between the cloud customer and two different cloud providers, doubling the work load and legal obligations for the whole cloud application. Equivalently, the use of more than two different cloud providers (n clouds approach) improves on integrity and availability, but also requires n contract negotiations and risk assess-

Figure 8. Comparison study of multicloud approaches with their capabilities

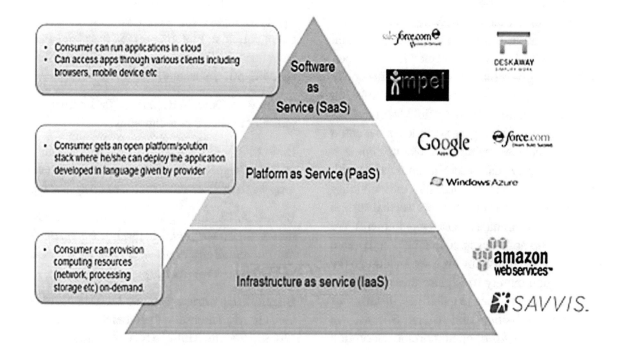

CONCLUSION

ments, amplified by the necessity to assess the risks associated with automated detection and correction of irregularities within the n parallel executions. Based on the observations subsumed in Figure 5, we can conclude that there is no such thing as a "best" approach. From a technical point of view, the use of multiple cloud providers leads to a perceived advantage in terms of security, based on the perception of shared—and thus mitigated—risks. From a compliance point of view, however, many of these advantages do not sustain, and may even lead to additional legal obligations—and hence to higher risks. The few approaches that would be beneficial in terms of both security and compliance tend to be quite limited in feasibility of application, and are not business ready yet or rather nontrivial to use in real-world settings.

The use of multiple cloud providers for gaining security and privacy benefits is nontrivial. As the approaches investigated in this paper clearly show, there is no single optimal approach to foster both security and legal compliance in an omniapplicable manner. Moreover, the approaches that are favorable from a technical perspective appear less appealing from a regulatory point of view, and vice versa. The few approaches that score sufficiently in both these dimensions lack versatility and ease of use, hence can be used in very rare circumstances only. As can be seen from the discussions of the four major multicloud approaches, each of them has its pitfalls and weak spots, either in terms of security guarantees, in terms of compliance to legal obligations, or in terms of feasibility. Given that every type of multicloud approach falls into one of these four categories, this implies a state of the art that is somewhat dissatisfying. However, two major indications for improvement can be taken from the examinations performed in this paper. First of all, given that for each type of security problem there exists at least one technical solution approach, a highly interesting field for future research lies in combining the approaches presented here. For instance, using the n clouds approach (and its integrity guarantees) in combination with sound data encryption (and its confidentiality guarantees) may result in approaches that suffice for both technical and regulatory requirements. We explicitly do not investigate this field here—due to space restrictions; however, we encourage the research community to explore these combinations, and assess their capabilities in terms of the given evaluation dimensions. Second, we identified the fields of homomorphic encryption and secure multiparty computation protocols to be highly promising in terms of both technical security and regulatory compliance. As of now, the limitations of these approaches only stem from their narrow applicability and high complexity in use. However, given their excellent properties in terms of security and compliance in multicloud architectures, we envision these fields to become the major building blocks for future generations of the multicloud computing paradigm.

REFERENCES

Abdalla, M., Bellare, M., Catalano, D., Kiltz, E., Kohno, T., Lange, T., Shi, H. (2005). *Searchable encryption revisited: Consistency properties, relation to anonymous IBE, and extensions*.

Abu-Libdeh, H., Princehouse, L., & Weatherspoon, H. (2010). *RACS: a case for cloud storage diversity*.

Act, A. (1996). Health insurance portability and accountability act of 1996. *Public Law, 104*, 191.

Asharov, G., Jain, A., López-Alt, A., Tromer, E., Vaikuntanathan, V., & Wichs, D. (2012). Multiparty computation with low communication, computation and interaction via threshold FHE. Advances in Cryptology–EUROCRYPT 2012 (pp. 483-501). Springer.

Bai, B. B., & Devi, N. R. (2011). The international journal of science & technology.

Ben-Or, M., Goldwasser, S., & Wigderson, A. (1988). *Completeness theorems for non-cryptographic fault-tolerant distributed computation*.

Bernstein, D., Ludvigson, E., Sankar, K., Diamond, S., & Morrow, M. (2009). *Blueprint for the intercloud-protocols and formats for cloud computing interoperability*.

Bogetoft, P., Christensen, D. L., Damgaard, I., Geisler, M., Jakobsen, T., Kroeigaard, M., et al. (2009). Secure Multiparty Computation Goes Live. Financial Cryptography and Data Security. In R. Dingledine and P. Golle (Eds), LNCS Vol. 5628. Springer-Verlag. doi:10.1007/978-3-642-03549-4_20

Bohli, J. M., Jensen, M., Gruschka, N., Schwenk, J., & Iacono, L. L. L. (2011). *Security prospects through cloud computing by adopting multiple clouds*.

Bohli, J.-M., Li, W., & Seedorf, J. (2012). Assisting server for secure multi-party computation Information Security Theory and Practice. Security, Privacy and Trust in Computing Systems and Ambient Intelligent Ecosystems. (pp. 144-159). Springer.

Boldyreva, A., Chenette, N., Lee, Y., & O'neill, A. (2009). Order-preserving symmetric encryption Advances in Cryptology-EUROCRYPT 2009. (pp. 224-241). Springer.

Bugiel, S., Nürnberger, S., Pöppelmann, T., Sadeghi, A.-R., & Schneider, T. (2011). *AmazonIA: when elasticity snaps back*.

Bugiel, S., Nürnberger, S., Sadeghi, A.-R., & Schneider, T. (2011). *Twin clouds: Secure cloud computing with low latency*.

Burkhart, M., Strasser, M., Many, D., & Dimitropoulos, X. (2010). SEPIA: Privacy-preserving aggregation of multi-domain network events and statistics. *Network, 1*, 101101.

Catrina, O., & Kerschbaum, F. (2008). *Fostering the uptake of secure multiparty computation in e-commerce*.

Celesti, A., Tusa, F., Villari, M., & Puliafito, A. (2010). *How to enhance cloud architectures to enable cross-federation*.

Coan, B. A., & Turpin, R. (1984). Extending Binary Byzantine Agreement to Multivalued Byzantine Agreement: DTIC Document.

Commission, E. (2010). Standard Contractual Clauses for the Transfer of Personal Data to Processors Established in Third Countries under Directive 95/ 46/EC of the European Parliament and of the Council. congress, U. (2002). Federal Information Security Management Act.

Curtmola, R., Garay, J., Kamara, S., & Ostrovsky, R. (2006). *Searchable symmetric encryption: improved definitions and efficient constructions*.

Damgård, I., Geisler, M., Krøigaard, M., & Nielsen, J. B. (2009). Asynchronous multiparty computation: Theory and implementation Public Key Cryptography–PKC 2009 (pp. 160-179%@ 3642004679): Springer.

Danezis, G., & Livshits, B. (2011). Towards Ensuring Client-Side Computational Integrity (A position paper).

Desmedt, Y. (1998). Some recent research aspects of threshold cryptography Information Security (pp. 158-173%@ 3540643826): Springer.

Directive, E. U. (1995). 95/46/EC of the European Parliament and of the Council of 24 October 1995 on the protection of individuals with regard to the processing of personal data and on the free movement of such data. *Official Journal of the EC, 23*(6).

European, C. (2012). Proposal for a regulation of the European Parliament and of the council on the protection of individuals with regard to the processing of personal data and on the free movement of such data (general data protection regulation). COM (2012) 11 final, 2012/0011 (COD), Brussels, 25 January 2012.

Gentry, C. (2009). *A fully homomorphic encryption scheme*. Stanford University.

Goldreich, O., Micali, S., & Wigderson, A. (1987). *How to play any mental game*.

Groß, S., & Schill, A. (2012). Towards user centric data governance and control in the cloud Open Problems in Network Security (pp. 132-144%@ 3642275842): Springer.

Gruschka, N., & Iacono, L. L. (2009). *Vulnerable cloud: Soap message security validation revisited*.

Hubbard, D., & Sutton, M. (2010). *Top threats to cloud computing v1. 0*. Cloud Security Alliance.

Kamara, S., & Lauter, K. (2010). Cryptographic cloud storage Financial Cryptography and Data Security (pp. 136-149%@ 364214991X): Springer.

Kincaid, J. (2009). Google privacy blunder shares your docs without permission. *TechCrunch, March*.

Koren, I., & Krishna, C. M. (2010). *Fault-tolerant systems*. Morgan Kaufmann.

Liu, J., Xiao, Y., Chen, H., Ozdemir, S., Dodle, S., & Singh, V. (2010). A survey of payment card industry data security standard. *Communications Surveys & Tutorials, IEEE, 12*(3), 287-303%@ 1553-1877X.

Lynch, N. A. (1996). *Distributed algorithms.* Morgan Kaufmann.

McIntosh, M., & Austel, P. (2005). *XML signature element wrapping attacks and countermeasures.*

Pagano, F., & Pagano, D. (2011). *Using in-memory encrypted databases on the cloud.*

Paillier, P. (1999). *Public-key cryptosystems based on composite degree residuosity classes.*

Party, E. A. W. (2007). Standard Application for Approval of Binding Corporate Rules for the Transfer of Personal Data.

Party, E. A. W. (2012). Cloud Computing.

Popa, R. A., Redfield, C., Zeldovich, N., & Balakrishnan, H. (2011). *CryptDB: protecting confidentiality with encrypted query processing.*

Rajasekaran, H., Lo Iacono, L., Hasselmeyer, P., Fingberg, J., Summers, P., Benkner, S., . . . Friedrich, C. M. (2008). *@ neurIST-Towards a System Architecture for Advanced Disease Management through Integration of Heterogeneous Data, Computing, and Complex Processing Services.*

Risk, F. (2012). Authorization Management Program (FedRAMP),". *Concept of Operations (CONOPS)", Version, 1.*

Ristenpart, T., Tromer, E., Shacham, H., & Savage, S. (2009). *Hey, you, get off of my cloud: exploring information leakage in third-party compute clouds.*

Rivest, R. L., Adleman, L., & Dertouzos, M. L. (1978). On data banks and privacy homomorphisms. *Foundations of secure computation, 4*(11), 169-180.

Rivest, R. L., Shamir, A., & Adleman, L. (1978). A method for obtaining digital signatures and public-key cryptosystems. *Communications of the ACM, 21*(2), 120-126.

Somorovsky, J., Heiderich, M., Jensen, M., Schwenk, J., Gruschka, N., & Lo Iacono, L. (2011). *All your clouds are belong to us: security analysis of cloud management interfaces.*

Somorovsky, J., Meyer, C., Tran, T., Sbeiti, M., Schwenk, J., & Wietfeld, C. (2012). *SeC2: Secure Mobile Solution for Distributed Public Cloud Storages.*

Vijayan, J. (2013). Vendors tap into cloud security concerns with new encryption tools.

Wiese, L. (2010). Horizontal fragmentation for data outsourcing with formula-based confidentiality constraints Advances in Information and Computer Security. (pp. 101-116). Springer.

Wisner, J. D., Leong, G. K., & Tan, K. C. (2005). Principles of Supply Chain Management–A Balanced Approach, 2005. *South-Western, Mason, Ohio, 442.*

Yao, A. C. (1982). *Protocols for secure computations.*

Zhang, Y., Juels, A., Reiter, M. K., & Ristenpart, T. (2012). *Cross-VM side channels and their use to extract private keys.*

KEY TERMS AND DEFINITIONS

Cloud Computing: A model for delivering IT services in which resources are retrieved from the internet through web-based tools and applications rather than a direct connection to a server.

Hybrid Cloud: A *Hybrid* cloud is the combination of any two or more types of above mentioned cloud types.

IaaS: Infrastructure is a Service, is used to provide network for connecting users and servers and also provides virtual machines to start, stop, access and configure virtual servers and storage blocks.

Multicloud: It is the concomitant use of two or more cloud services to minimize the risk of widespread data loss or downtime due to a localized component failure in a cloud computing environment.

PaaS: Platform is a Service, in this model a platform is provided to users which typically include operating system, programming languages, execution environments, databases, queues and web servers.

Private Cloud: A *private* cloud is one which is setup by single organization and installed services on its own data center. A private cloud is a proprietary network or a data center that supplies hosted services to a limited number of people.

Chapter 12
Hard Clues in Soft Environments:
The Cloud's Influence on Digital Forensics

Andrea Atzeni
Politecnico di Torino, Italy

Paolo Smiraglia
Politecnico di Torino, Italy

Andrea Siringo
Former Student at Politecnico di Torino, Italy

ABSTRACT

Cloud forensics is an open and important area of research due to the growing interest in cloud technology. The increasing frequency of digital investigations brings with it the need for studying specific scenarios in the area of forensics, both when evidence are inside the cloud and when the cloud can be used as platform to perform the investigations. In this chapter we highlight the problems digital forensics must deal with in the Cloud. We introduce historical roots of digital forensics, as well as an overall background about the Cloud and we provide possible meanings of cloud forensics, based on available definitions. Since the cloud introduces different architectural paradigm that affects all the phases of a forensics investigation, in this survey we detail many security issues digital forensics have to face in a cloud environment. We describe when and what available solutions exist and, on the contrary, the still open problems, and we discuss possible future directions in this field.

INTRODUCTION

Cloud computing is of great interest to private and government organizations, always looking for ways to get fast and effective results and to lower the production costs. The Cloud model may enable low costs for accessing computational and storage resources. Due to the implementation of the pay-on-demand model, the economic costs of cloud resources are strictly related to their real usage. Moreover, cloud resources are managed through a web browser, so access and configuration are easy.

DOI: 10.4018/978-1-4666-8387-7.ch012

Given these encouraging premises, market predictions foresee an annual increase for the Cloud of 23.5% in 2013-2016 (from International Data Corporation (IDC) (Gens & Shirer, 2013) and similar by Gartner (Columbus, 2013)). According to other survey results (KPMG International, 2013), half of the companies who currently do not use cloud-based services expressed the intention to adopt them by 2015.

However, despite the will to adopt cloud-based solutions, the same survey highlights that many companies are still worried about security and reliability concerns. These include, for example, data loss and theft of intellectual properties, violation of user privacy, law and regulations compliance and any security risk that may cause service interruption.

As real cases demonstrate, cloud architectures may be involved in both ends of cyber-attacks. For instance, as reported by C. Metz (Metz, 2009), in 2009 Amazon was the victim of a DDoS attack while in 2011 the Amazon cloud was used to breach the PlayStation Network (Galante, Kharif, & Alpeyev, 2011). So the characteristic of flexibility, which is distinctive of the cloud and a source of benefits for companies, can also be exploited to facilitate illicit acts and distribute illegal material. Moreover, in case of attack the volatile nature of cloud provisioned resources may make possible subsequent investigations difficult. So, security solutions need to be specifically developed or adapted for the cloud domain.

In case of a security breach, it is necessary to perform an investigation to clarify who carried out the attack and how the system was infringed. Here the digital forensics practices which have been developed in recent decades come into play. This discipline was born to assist the police in managing the use of electronic devices in criminal acts. It takes care to obtain evidence from any device capable of storing, such as a computer, a smartphone or even a digital camera.

Effectively, digital forensics is the set of best practices used to ensure that the digital evidence extracted from the devices is unaltered. To avoid contamination and subsequent loss of integrity and/or of authenticity, appropriate methods and tools must be adopted at all stages of evidence processing, from seizure of the devices on which the data is stored to the presentation of the results of the analysis performed on the data.

In this chapter we will discuss possible solutions which can be implemented to solve problems arising when an investigation needs to cope with cloud computing architectures. For the sake of clarity, we will introduce concepts and methods of digital forensic followed by distinctive features of cloud computing. Then we will discuss problems deriving by the use of digital forensics in the cloud. Finally, we will detail solutions for some of the technical problems, concluding with open issues and future directions.

BACKGROUND

This section will introduce the key concepts necessary to understand the rest of this chapter. Digital forensic science and the Cloud computing model will be defined. Using these two definitions cloud forensics, a recently emerged branch of digital forensics science, will be presented.

Digital Forensics

Forensic science is the set of scientific methods for examining and gathering information about the past in order to support investigations. Digital forensics is a branch of this science and focuses on the identification and acquisition of digital evidence from electronic devices like laptops and smartphones as well as digital cameras and MP3 readers. It is defined digital evidence any "*information of probative value stored or transmitted in digital form*" (Scientific Working Group on Digital Evidence (SWGDE), International Organization on Digital Evidence (IOCE), 2000). In order to consider digital evidence (referred to simply as "evidence" from now on) as valid proof, there are a number of requirements.

Firstly, evidence should be authentic. This means that it is necessary to identify the full causal chain, i.e. the generation of the evidence starting from the final illegal violation back to the initial criminal action. An example of a causal chain may be:

1. The attacker Mallory gets the malicious executable from the FTP server reachable at the IP address 126.12.34.15
2. Mallory installs the malicious executable on the victim host by exploiting an email-based fishing attack
3. Through the malicious executable, Mallory accesses the victim host and executes the attack under investigation

During digital evidence handling, accidental corruption is extremely easy. Therefore, to ensure integrity, evidence must be treated with specific tools and techniques. For instance, evidence should be gathered from seized devices through write-blocker tools and forensics analysis should be executed on a copy (named forensic copy) and not directly on the original evidence. When evidences are obtained from seized devices, in most cases they are in raw format, represented as a sequence of bytes. In these cases, a correct data interpretation should be performed to ensure evidence correctness. Evidence should be complete. This means that all the information related to them, for instance the sources of the malicious executable, should be also gathered. Finally, evidences are legally permissible if they are obtained through legally accepted procedures and tools.

Performing a digital forensics investigation may involve several entities. For instance, in July 2014, an international task force leaded by the prosecutor M. Michelozzi uncovered a network of paedophiles who shared pornographic material over the internet (ANSA, 2014). In such a scenario, the adoption of a standardised modus operandi significantly improves the investigation effectiveness. So, the creation of harmonised guidelines was subject of many efforts during recent decades. In 2001, Budapest hosted the first European international convention on cybercrime, also known as "Budapest Convention of Cybercrime" (Council of Europe, 2001). The goal of this meeting was the harmonisation of national laws on cyber criminality, the investigation techniques improvement and finally the increasing of cooperation among nations on these topics. In 2008, Italy ratified Budapest treaty with law n. 48/2008 (Italian Parliament, 2008). Meanwhile, in UK, the Association of Chief Police Officers (ACPO) formalised the best practices for digital evidence management in a report titled "Good Practice Guide for Computer-Based Electronic Evidence" (Wilkinson & Haagman, 2007). In another initiative at European level, the Data Protection and Cybercrime Division of Council of Europe (COE) produced a guide in March 2013 (Jones, George, Merida, Rasmussen, & Volzow, 2013) with the goal of supporting and guiding in identification and handling of digital evidence. In the other side of the ocean, in United States, the National Institute of Standards and Technologies (NIST) in cooperation with National Institute of Justice (NIJ) published in 2004 a guide (Hart, Ashcroft, & Daniels, 2004) for enforcing law in examination of evidence.

Some agreed terms and procedures on the matter were defined in these and other groups. In 2001, an official definition of digital forensics science was released in a technical report produced by a working group of the first Digital Forensics Research Workshop (DFRWS). By citing the report, digital forensics science is "the use of scientifically derived and proven methods toward the preservation, collection, validation, identification, analysis, interpretation, documentation and presentation of digital evidence derived from digital sources for the purpose of facilitating or furthering the reconstruction of events found to be criminal, or helping to anticipate unauthorized actions shown to be disruptive to planned operations" (Palmer, 2001). As stated within this definition, a digital forensics investigative process is a sequence of several steps. Technical literature groups these steps in three main stages. The first, commonly named securing, is the phase when detectives identify the convicted devices and secure the evidence to preserve integrity. The second phase is named analysis. This comprises all the operations necessary to rebuild the event under investigation starting from the gathered evidence. Finally, the third and last phase is the documentation. In this phase, all the conclusions produced by previous phases are joined in a report. Thus, the investigation result is ready and may be provided, for example, to the judge.

Cloud Computing

Cloud computing, referred with the term "Cloud" in the following, is an emergent computing model. It facilitates easy access to remote resources, like computation and storage, which are provided by a third party, named Cloud Service Provider (CSP), by adopting the pay-on-demand paradigm.

In scientific and technical literature, several Cloud Computing definitions are available. The NIST proposes one of the most cited: "a model for enabling ubiquitous, convenient, on-demand network access to a shared pool of configurable computing resources (e.g., networks, servers, storage, applications, and services) that can be rapidly provisioned and released with minimal management effort or service provider interaction" (Mell & Grance, 2011). Three models of the Cloud service provisioning are defined in the same NIST document: Software-as-a-Service (SaaS), Platform-as-a-Service (PaaS) and Infrastructure-as-a-Server (IaaS).

In the SaaS model, users access cloud-based resources neither installing nor configuring any additional software. Examples of the SaaS model are the webmail service provided by Google and the remote storage provided by Dropbox. In the former case, users have access to a full-featured email client which is accessible via any device equipped with a standard web browser. In the latter case, users are allowed to store and retrieve files remotely, without any knowledge in the field of the remote storage management.

In the PaaS model, CSP provides application deployment environments (like the Java servlet container) that cloud users may adopt to deploy their own application. In this manner, users may spend the 100% of their time in application development and rely on CSP for the management of the deployment framework. Nowadays, examples of PaaS services could be Google Apps Engine, Amazon Elastic Beanstalk and Windows Azure.

In the IaaS model, the CSP provides infrastructural assets (e.g. computation, storage, and network) in the form of virtualised resources. A typical example of an IaaS system is the so called Virtual Private Server (VPS). This is simply a virtual machine hosted on the physical infrastructure owned by the CSP. Cloud users are allowed to install and configure any kind of software in this virtual machine. Two examples of the most adopted IaaS providers are Amazon AWS and Rackspace.

A different categorisation for the Cloud infrastructure is based on the deployment schema. Four possible models exist: private, community, public and hybrid (or cloud of clouds).

In a "private cloud", a single entity consumes the provided resources. In a typical private cloud scenario, an organisation purchases a set of VPS to move its IT infrastructure on the Cloud. In a "community cloud" a limited number of entities share a cloud-based resource, for example when members of a project's consortium share a code versioning platform hosted on the Cloud. In a "public cloud" there are no limitations about who can access a cloud resource (e.g. public webmail). Finally, any composition of private, community and public cloud is defined "hybrid cloud" or "cloud of clouds" as, for example, any organisation that organises its IT infrastructure on different Cloud models. A common example scenario is that the organisation's web site is deployed on a server and this server is shared with other organisations that are members of the same consortium, and the organization has a remote document repository that is configured in a specific (different) VPS.

Cloud Forensics

The highly distributed nature of the cloud, the massive use of resource virtualization and the access to remote services, create many barriers to the use of traditional digital forensics best practices. Cloud forensics, a new branch of digital forensics, is emerging for this reason. Such new branch groups all the forensics procedures applicable to a cloud environment, including also the traditional ones that have been adapted whenever possible.

One of the first formal definitions of cloud forensics was provided by Ruan in 2012. By directly citing from the work:

Cloud forensics is the application of digital forensic science in cloud computing environments. Technically it consists of a hybrid forensic approach (e.g., remote, virtual, network, live, large-scale, thin-client, thick-client) towards the generation of digital evidence. Organizationally it involves interactions among cloud actors (i.e., cloud provider, cloud consumer, cloud broker, cloud carrier, cloud auditor) for the purpose of facilitating both internal and external investigations. Legally it often implies multi-jurisdictional and multi-tenant situations (Ruan & Carthy, Cloud Computing Reference Architecture and Its Forensic Implications: A Preliminary Analysis, 2012).

In scientific community, several researches highlighted that cloud computing model may have a strong impact on digital forensics investigations. In Biggs et al. (Biggs & Vidalis, 2009), the authors point out that in absence of an international regulation on cybercrime, the impact of cloud computing on digital forensics will be acute and the number of crimes that will go unpunished will be great. In (Birk & Wegener, 2011), and similarly in (Taylor, Haggerty, Gresty, & Lamb, 2011), the treatment on cloud forensics is technically focused on the impossibility for the investigators to apply traditional approaches to evidence collection and evidence recovery, due to decentralized nature of data processing in the cloud. In 2014, NIST published in the IR-8006 document (Dykstra, et al., 2014) a summary of the research performed by the NIST Cloud Computing Forensic Science Working Group. In this publication, authors aggregate, categorise and discuss the forensics challenges faced by experts while reacting to incidents in a cloud-computing ecosystem. These issues will be detailed and discussed in the next sections.

ISSUES IN CLOUD COMPUTING

Often traditional digital forensics procedures cannot be plainly applied to the cloud environment. In the following we will illustrate the differences between traditional digital forensics and cloud forensics. Our purpose is to bring out challenges introduced by the cloud computing model in this field. In particular, we will highlight in which stages of a cloud forensics investigation (i.e. securing, analysis and documentation) cloud challenges have more relevance.

First of all, the Cloud provides a different architectural paradigm that affects all the phases of a forensics investigation. As previously defined, the entity providing resources through cloud model is called Cloud Service Provider (CSP). Since CSP is the owner of the Cloud infrastructure, it is the only entity capable to access both physical and logical resources. In computer security field this position may be considered as potential source of attacks. Thus, security administrators tend to provide mechanisms to limit a similar unbounded access. This is a tremendous threat, because the unrestricted access to all the resources allows to circumvent the security systems without being noticed, making possible to hide malicious or unfair activities.

Furthermore, from the cloud users' privacy perspective, the CSP may act as a powerful honest but curious attacker. I.e. the CSP can exploit its super-user permissions to collect or access some users' private data without producing any evidence to demonstrate the abuse.

This scenario may get even worse considering that in most cases the trustiness of a provider is simply based on its reputation (e.g. "It's trusted because it's Google!") and not on some public verifiable indicators (e.g. "It's trusted because it's Google... and I'm able to verify it with cryptography!").

Despite the fact that auditability is a crucial element for providing trust, widely used cloud providers still not provide adequate transparency, as reported in survey results published in 2010 by Fujitsu Labs (Fujitsu, 2010). Presently, CSP is often assumed as a trusted party, but we advise that future security researches address this complex point, mitigating the opportunity for the CSP to perform illicit actions with very few limitations.

On the other hand, honest CSPs are fundamental for carrying out digital investigations. For instance, CSP cooperation is mandatory for accessing specific types of proofs (e.g. file system metadata) or to execute some operations involving physical devices (e.g. forensic copy of evidence). Making CSP active part of the investigation means including it within the chain of custody. In forensics science the chain of custody is the data source (e.g. a document) containing all the information related to the evidence handling occurred during the investigation. For instance, it could include the references about who executed the devices seizure and the list of the performed analysis.

Any "ring" in the chain of custody must be intact to ensure the validity of a forensics activity. This is mandatory to allow the use of digital investigation results as legal proofs. Therefore, including within the chain critical elements like the CSP could put at risk the overall investigation. By citing the ACPO directives (Wilkinson & Haagman, 2007) technical staff operating on behalf of CSP in forensics investigations must have all the required skills to avoid unintentional data corruption. Of course, this is another aspect complex to verify when a third party is involved.

Securing Phase

The securing phase is the first part of the digital forensics process. This phase must ensure that all the investigation relevant material does not suffer changes during the investigative process. This is the stage of a forensics investigation activity mostly affected by the cloud computing model. In traditional forensics, during this phase incriminated devices are seized and evidences included on them are identified, extracted and safety collected. Differently, in cloud environment, the access to physical devices is not easily feasible and requires the cooperation of the CSP. Such constraint introduces several issues, described in next sections.

Data Collection

Typically, the first phase of a forensics investigation is the seizure of indicted devices. For example, a police officer can physically confiscate a laptop. The highly distributed nature of the Cloud makes this kind of operations very complicated or even not feasible, because within the cloud logical resources like virtual machines or storage buckets are mapped and fragmented over several physical devices. Moreover, these devices are spread in multiple data centres. In this scenario, the confiscation of physical devices hosting the logical resources may be a maze, due to the lack of a direct logical to physical mapping. Furthermore, volatile nature of logical resource could make impossible the acquisition of certain kind of data. For instance, as stated by Birk et al. (Birk & Wegener, 2011) and Guo et al. (Guo, Jin, & Shang, 2012), some parts of the memory content can be no longer available once a virtual machine is destroyed.

In order to protect the evidence integrity against unintentional corruption, all the forensic analyses are performed over clones that are generated through a process called forensic copy. Such process copies the data contained within indicted devices without any modification or interpretation of the original data structure. The original data structure is protected by specific tools called write blocker, which disable all writing capabilities of the source device. A forensic copy requires physical access to the device, but, as stated by Ruan et al. (Ruan, Carthy, Kechadi, & Crosbie, 2011), honest CSPs intentionally hide physical data location in order to facilitate data movement and replication. Of course, this makes challenging a physical contact to the required device.

Beside technical aspects, the abstraction of the physical layer and the Cloud elastic nature is a challenge for the legislative field. The logical resources can be located on different countries to ensure availability, resiliency and performance, but each different country may obey to a different legal regulation. In this cross-border scenario, forensic investigation can be hampered by transnational bureaucracy (Taylor, Haggerty, Gresty, & Lamb, 2011) or may induce investigators in unintentional law violations (Biggs & Vidalis, 2009).

In digital investigations, a fast reaction is of uttermost importance to avoid evidence destruction. However, in practice a quick answer faces two challenges: 1) the police researches must be compliant with all the involved jurisdictions; 2) a cross-border task force of detectives must be ar-

ranged. The required time to do so may be relevant, making impossible fast reactions. Therefore, as stated by Wang et al. (Wang, 2010), such a different cadence can put at stake the validity and the efficiency of the whole investigation process.

Multi-Tenancy in the Cloud

In cloud computing, physical resources like storage and primary memory (RAM) are frequently shared by several users. This may present two different types of problem: contamination of data between different applications and leakage of private information. Moreover, Ristenpart (Ristenpart, Tromer, Shacham, & Savage, 2009) has shown that resource sharing could be also vehicle of attack. In particular, it allows the implementation of a side-channel to collect other tenants' data. This is possible when tenants' virtual machines are placed under the same hypervisor as the attacker, by exploiting shared communication channels.

Live Forensics and Virtualization

Live forensics is the whole of techniques allowing the retrieving of data that may be lost by switching off the indicted devices. It allows data collection from running systems without causing data corruption.

In traditional digital forensics, live techniques can be directly applied on a real system. However, this is not easily feasible if the target system is, for instance, a virtual machine deployed upon a cloud. Nance et al. (Nance, Bishop, & Hay, 2009) proposed a process called Virtual Machine Introspection (VMI) to allow live forensics also in virtual environments. Such a process enables access to volatile content inside the virtual machines (e.g. process list, encryption keys loaded in RAM). A key role is played by the cloud node hypervisor – also known as Virtual Machine Manager (VMM) – that is the software in charge to map physical and logical resources. Hypervisor is one of the elements under direct control of the CSP, and it is not directly accessible without the CSP collaboration. Therefore, the issue of the CSP trust emerges again.

Data Deletion

Within electronic devices, data are stored as sequences of blocks. When files are deleted, the list of occupied memory blocks is erased, making such blocks again available. From the operating system perspective, this means that files are no longer available, but in case of forensics analysis this is not true: until data blocks are not overwritten, their content is still available and total or partial file rebuild is possible through forensic tools (e.g. TestDisk (CGSecurity, 2014)).

Performing secure data erasure is easily feasible in offline scenario due to the physical accessibility of memory devices and the availability of several tools like shred (Wikimedia Foundation, Inc., 2014) or Eraser (Eraser, 2013). On the contrary, in a highly distributed and third party owned environment like the Cloud performing secure data deletion is far from easy, raising a problem when required by authorised users.

Cloud Logging

Logging is the process of collecting traces, commonly named logs, about events occurring in a system. For instance, logs can keep tracks about users' login and logout, installed software and viewed web pages. Investigators can rebuild past history of a system through logs. Therefore having "good logs" could be considered a requirement for an effective forensic analysis. In order to be "good", each log entry should be as much detailed as possible. For instance, in addition to the minimal accepted information set (timestamp and event description) each log entry should include further information like processes, user and group IDs.

The format used to organise such information with each entry is one of the main issues related

to the logs analysis. In a simple system like a personal laptop, the log sources are limited in number; therefore, the analysis can be manually executed. On the contrary, in sophisticated cloud architectures logs are generated by several applications, each one potentially using its own storage format. In such a scenario the amount of logs to be analysed could be huge. So, tools like log analysers are a mandatory aid for investigators. Unfortunately, the efficiency of these tools could be undermined by the absence of a common format and rules for structuring the information within the logs.

In addition, there are other issues that can create problems in the cloud forensic activity. For instance, as highlighted by Marty (Marty, 2011), cloud-based applications store logs (when enabled) on several locations and their availability can be limited to a restricted time frame. So, investigators may spend much time and effort to find them all. Furthermore, investigators should access information contained within the logs taking care of the privacy of the users not under investigation and by avoiding third party brokering (e.g. from cloud service provider). This care is important to reduce risks related to malicious or involuntary data manipulation.

Analysis Phase

During analysis phase, all the collected data are analysed and a detailed chain of custody is developed and maintained. While in securing phase cloud related issues require a specific treatment, this phase requires limited modification in respect of traditional digital forensics.

Data Amount

Once seized, devices and relative data need to be safety stored for future analysis. Due to the enhancements in storage technology field and to the lowering of the costs per gigabyte, the quantity of data per user is expected to grow. If in traditional forensics this aspect introduces some troubles, for instance related to the amount of time required for the analysis, in cloud computing the problem can degenerate. Thanks to the Cloud, any user have available an almost unlimited storage space. Therefore, an eventual forensics analysis on an "infinite" data set could require a great number of resources in terms of time, computation and storage. A preliminary approach to mitigate this issue could be the employment of cloud-based resources, but also in this case the cloud service provider should be included within the chain of custody. Furthermore, acquiring or performing operations on remotely available big data can be a bottleneck from the network perspective.

Cloud and Cryptography

In many cases, cloud users should be obliged to encrypt their data before pushing them on the cloud for organization policies or legal constraints. Moreover, in some cases (Amazon, Inc., 2014), cloud service providers inform users that cryptography is used only in the backbone infrastructure. Thus, the protection of personal data is up to final user (e.g. by applying security best practices). Pushing protected data on the cloud, for instance with cryptography, ensures privacy preserving also in case of absence of protection from the CSP, but form the perspective of a forensic investigations it can be a stopping hindrance.

In traditional forensics, the content of a seized device is "frozen" by disabling writing capabilities. Moreover, in order to check data integrity and to identify eventual corruptions, before starting every analysis a checksum like MD5 or SHA2 is calculated. In cloud forensics, checksum computation of indicted data is a critical point. This because direct access to physical devices is not allowed, hence the involvement of the cloud service provider is required also in this case.

Presentation Phase

In judicial process, evidences collected during investigation are presented to the judge together with a report about techniques and methods adopted during the forensics activity. As presented by Grispos et al. (Grispos, Storer, & Glisson, 2012), in United States and United Kingdom scientific depositions are executed taking into account the so called Daubert's guidelines. These guidelines, coming from the judgement "Daubert v. Merrel Dow Pharmaceutical" (Cornell University Law School, 2014), define a set of criteria for evaluating the legal relevance of a scientific method (Orofino, 1996). These criteria include scientific verifiability and falsifiability level of the method as well as the error rate. Moreover, the method should be under continuous monitoring by scientific community and generally accepted by major experts in such field. It is realistic to assume that evaluations of digital forensics techniques and methods are performed following Daubert's guidelines. Cloud computing influence in this phase introduces some challenges mostly related to the immaturity of this new forensics branch. For instance, standard dataset representing a typical cloud data are still not available, therefore execution of tests for evaluating the error rate is not feasible in a standard way.

SOLUTIONS

Some of the cloud's problems are real points to be addressed while some other are just matter of perception. A fundamental step for this technology affirmation is to increase the trust in cloud computing perceived by users. To achieve this, services hosted in the cloud must decrease psychological and technical scaring factors. In our discussion, we will leave out of scope the "soft trust" (Varadharajan, 2009), i.e. the trust influenced by subjective human perceptions, emotions, human interactions and exchange of experience, as well as "brand" faithfulness.

On the contrary, we will focus on preventive technical controls, like encryption, authentication and access control and in general, any countermeasure to mitigate or prevent the occurrence of an attack. These controls that establish trust in the cloud from a technical point of view are known as "hard trust" mechanisms (complementary to the "soft" ones). Specifically, the most relevant properties that impacts trust in the cloud are security, privacy, accountability, auditability.

Securing Phase

In the cloud model, physical seizure of the storage devices is often difficult and sometimes impossible. Therefore, it is not possible to make a forensic copy of the entire device. Thus, usual digital forensics guidelines are not automatically applicable, since both technical and legislative issues emerge. The next sections will discuss possible solutions.

Multi-Tenancy in the Cloud

Contamination between different applications can be avoided if all the instances involved in a cloud service are isolated, as stated by Delport (Delport, Kohn, & Olivier, Isolating a cloud instance for a digital forensic investigation, 2011). Indeed, cloud architecture achieves some isolation by design, helping to prevent malicious manipulation of the collected evidences. Another problem, the information leakage of private information, can be avoided if careful data collection methods are applied to ensure that information gathered is not related to non-implicated users.

In order to address issues related to instance isolation, Delport et al. (Delport & Olivier, Cloud Separation: Stuck Inside the Cloud, 2012) exposed

characteristics and methods to achieve effective isolation within the cloud. In particular, the following properties are needed:

- Location: knowledge of the physical location of the instance. This information can often be derived from cloud management software.
- Restricted communications: the instance cannot send or receive messages to or from the outside world. A firewall may be placed in the node, or alternatively the firewall used to control the Cloud can be used for this task as well.
- Collection: the evidence can be retrieved from the instance.
- Contamination: the evidence must not be contaminated during the process of isolation.
- Separation: information not related to the incident investigated must not be isolated. The instance to be examined must be the only one present in the node. For example, this can be achieved by moving the instance investigated on an isolated node or by moving the instances not under investigation to different nodes.

The service deployment patterns may significantly impact on how the isolation is carried out. In a private cloud all data belongs to a single organization, so privacy concerns are reduced if the investigation is internally performed by an employee. Confinement is only applied to ensure the eligibility of the data, obtained by the protection of evidence from unauthorized manipulations. On the contrary, if the investigation has to be conducted by an external organization, any data not involved must remain private. In this respect, each cloud model requires data isolation at a different level of abstraction.

In an IaaS service, different instances usually belong to different users. Each instance can be seen as a separate computer that can tamper with possible evidence or contaminate evidences found in other instances. In this case, the virtual machine must be isolated. In a PaaS service, the platform that characterizes instances is known and made available by the cloud service supplier. Here the focus is on installed software and data. Therefore, data and applications must be isolated, while the behaviour of the platform is known and can be controlled, and so does not require further isolation. In an SaaS service, different instances differ in application data and configuration, so these are the parts of the instance that require isolation.

As said above, an instance which is investigated has to be separated from the rest of the cloud to ensure isolation, i.e. it must be located in a cloud node containing only the instance under investigation. This can be achieved following two possible approaches. In the former, only the instance under investigation migrates to a new cloud node (e.g. sandbox node) while in the latter, the elements that are migrated to a new node are all the instances not under investigation. Although the first approach seems more rational since it is less resource expensive, it can be easily identified by the attacker who may react by compromising the attack evidence.

Delport et al. (Delport & Olivier, Cloud Separation: Stuck Inside the Cloud, 2012) dealt with the problem of the isolation of a set of logically inter-linked instances. Many instances can be linked together to provide a service forming a single logical resource, for example to improve service availability. In this case, a possible solution is the migration of all connected instances from source nodes to a different set of nodes. The destination nodes must be logically separate from the rest of the cloud. This separation can be realised using separate virtual networks for different sets of nodes, or by creating an internal sub-cloud infrastructure. Alternatively, separation can also be achieved by migrating to an outside cloud, accessible by investigators only.

Data Recovery in the Cloud

Dykstra (Dykstra & Sherman, Acquiring forensic evidence from infrastructure-as-a-service cloud computing: Exploring and evaluating tools, trust, and techniques, 2012) presents another approach to address the problem of the Cloud's trust, in particular, how valid information can be extracted from IaaS systems.

In a traditional digital investigation, investigators require confidence about tools used and steps performed. For example, they require that the write blocker is working as intended or (in case of live analysis) the operating system and the computer hardware has not been maliciously modified. In the case of cloud computing, more layers can be considered, depending on which method is used to obtain the data. According to Dykstra, in an IaaS environment six layers can be defined. Starting from the lowest, in terms of abstraction, these are communication network, hardware, host operating system, virtualization system, guest operating systems and finally guest applications. Depending on the level used, methods to get the data may differ and so may the trust requirements: a higher level requires more trust, since all the layers below need to be trusted. Additionally, the service supplier has to be trusted if a public cloud is used.

For each layer, Table 1 describes the IaaS environment, the forensics data acquisition methods and the required levels of trust. On the base of the layers under control, different tools may be used, ranging from basic remote access client, to classical forensics tools, like EnCase (Guidance Software, Inc., 2014) and FTK (AccessData Group, Inc., 2014), to direct request to the service provider, which is nowadays the most common way for digital investigations (although not always desirable due to the CSP influence).

Dykstra et al. (Dykstra & Sherman, Design and implementation of FROST: Digital forensic tools for the OpenStack cloud computing platform,

Table 1. Correspondence between layers and required trust

Layer	Cloud Layer	Acquisition Method	Trust Required
6	Guest	Application/data	Depends on data Guest operating systems (OS, hypervisor, host OS, hardware, network
5	Guest OS	Remote forensics software	Guest OS, hypervisor, host OS, hardware, network
4	Virtualisation	Introspection	Hypervisor, host OS, hardware, network
3	Host OS	Access virtual disk	Host OS, hardware, network
2	Hardware	Access physical disk	Hardware, network
1	Network	Packet capture	Network

2013) developed an alternative solution to reduce CSP involvement in forensic investigations. They proposed a management plane: via a web interface and an API it exports some management functions for the firewall and for the VM customer life cycle. In this way, the user can access log files, disk images and sniffed network packets on demand, without the intervention of the service provider. On the other side, this solution implies customer collaboration to access valid forensic data, requires a trusted logger and hypervisor, and requires a management plane protected with adequate access control mechanisms and secured connections.

Moreover, Merkle trees (Wikimedia Foundation, Inc., 2014) are adopted for both the firewall and API logs. This is to allow separate logs from different services related to IaaS customers and, at the same time, to ensure integrity. The use of these structures minimises the quantity of control data to transmit. For the two different targets (firewall and API) there are two trees with the same function: for each system user a sub-tree is created under each of the two main trees. The four parameters VM identifier, year, month and day, organise the tree structure, and the logs are stored as leaves.

Volatile Data Recovery in the Cloud

As indicated by Birk (Birk & Wegener, 2011), some IaaS services do not offer persistent storage space for a VM. In this case, the use of VMI

(Virtual Machine Introspection) can prevent the loss of important data. This solution consists in performing continuous synchronization of volatile data (e.g. RAM memory content, internal system files) on a persistent storage. The instance of the VM has to be running for the synchronization. This method is also known as proactive data collection, in contrast with the reactive collection that takes place during the first phase of the investigative process in traditional digital forensic workflow. The user can use the appropriate APIs to synchronize a set of data on external storage at regular intervals. This approach is not reliable if the VM has been tampered with or the user wants to conceal evidence of his actions. However, the need for a collaborative end user can be diminished if the CSP exploits the method for automated and regular collection of volatile data (e.g. through the VMI and the defined API).

Logging in the Cloud

A study by Zafarullah et al. (Zafarullah, Anwar, & Anwar, 2011) examines the well-known IaaS framework Eucalyptus (Eucalyptus System, Inc., 2014). This work identifies the information made available by default in the system logs if the platform is attacked. The study points out log entries created by RSyslog (Gerhards, 2014), Snort (Cisco, 2014) and other applications generating logs that are relevant in forensic investigations. The idea is to monitor and track all the internal and external Eucalyptus interactions that can be generated by known cloud vulnerabilities and attacks. This is done by simulating DoS/DDoS attacks on the Cloud Controller component that provides the public HTTP interface and the web based API interface. Within the logs useful information is recorded like the IP address of the attacker, the number of HTTP requests and relative timestamp, the HTTP request/response and a fingerprint of the operating system and web browser used by the attacker.

A problem noted by the authors is that Eucalyptus does not support exporting logs to a remote syslog server. This means that logs remain localized only in the machine where they were created, potentially vulnerable. Even though in the most recent architectures (e.g. OpenStack) this problem was solved, log decentralization in the cloud is one of the problems mentioned by Marty in his work (Marty, 2011), as well as the obstacles given by the nature of the cloud model (e.g. the already-mentioned virtualised multi-tenancy). So, to achieve effective and efficient log usage the log architecture should provide the following characteristics:

- Centralization of all logs, even if created at various levels of abstraction
- Storage of scalable logs
- Fast data access and retrieval
- Support for different types of log format
- Correlation analysis of the data extracted from the logs
- Retention of log records
- Archiving and restoring of old logs on demand
- Access control system to the log data to maintain log segregation
- Preservation of the log integrity
- Audit trail for the log access

The accomplishment of all these properties is difficult, because each component, from operating systems to applications, has to provide logs. In simpler cases (e.g. operating system, databases)

the software normally produces effective logs, and the main problem is the optimization of the records. On the contrary, in applications bigger problems arise, because logging capabilities are application-specific. In the worst case, the application may ever be developed with no capability for providing any log.

The available logs must then be made comparable and filtered, on the base of the required use. For example, Apache creates records for errors, regular access, and access to resources. Since the user needs can be different on a case by case basis, the logging system must be flexible and allow different data organisations (e.g. transcribe all of them into a single file or separate them by type) at different levels of granularity (even ignore and delete part of them if not useful to the logging system user).

Finally, coordinate logs must be securely transmitted to the centralised structure, (e.g. the communication takes place in encrypted form in order to preserve logs integrity and confidentiality). Moreover, the transmission should minimize the bandwidth consumption, and uphold time coherency between the logs (e.g. the clocks of the various components of the infrastructure have to be synchronized each other). All these properties are essential to later analysis to the logs derived from different sources.

The native implementation of the TLS protocol in a syslog daemon, as described in (Miao, Ma, & Salowey, 2009), is quite complex. So, a suitable tool is to provide secure communication is log-shuttle (Heroku, Inc., 2014). This is an open source Unix program to transport logs using HTTPS. In particular, the program is responsible for creating a secure communication channel between two syslog daemons.

The log records are not defined by agree international standard. So, some guidelines would be helpful to determine the most useful information on the base of the use case under analysis. As a general rule, the application status should be recorded at the end of each function regardless the result is positive or negative. In this way, the application activity can be recreated in any case.

For the purposes of an investigation the information about the state of the applications (errors or bugs, critical conditions, performed updates, modifications to configuration, application installation) are important. Moreover, this information should be complemented by storing all logins and logout attempts, both remote and local, failed access to resources, the changes to passwords and permissions and all actions performed by privileged users, in order to possibly point out suspect behaviour.

The minimum information provided should indicate who triggered the event, and what/when/why the event happened. In addition to the log semantic, also the log syntax should be defined. This would allow for normalisation, i.e. the process of subdividing each log record in understandable and unambiguous sub-parts. In this way, the log can be interpreted either by a computer or by a human user, facilitating the use in the analysis phase.

There are several proposals for standardization, including the open source project Lumberjack (Robertson & Bartos, 2013) that implements the Common Event Expression (CEE) proposal (MITRE, 2013). The CEE framework defines the specifications for all components involved in every step of event management system cycle, as well as their description, coding and transport.

Systems designed for log management in a distributed environment exists, and can meet one or more of the cloud required features. For example, Amazon makes available to its customers Cloud Trail (Amazon, Inc., 2014), a service to record information related to the AWS services API calls and to centralize all log into a storage space on the user section of the cloud. The information provided reflect those noted above (who triggered the event, what, when and why, and that the event is happening).

Pape et al. (Pape, Reissmann, & Rieger, 2013) have created a prototype for the correlation, aggregation, condensation and automatic log of system messages. These operations are performed to facilitate the analysis and storage of log data generated by virtual machines, which can produce large quantities of information. After normalization of data originating from different sources, logging information is sent to a correlation engine that analyses the messages, consolidates them in order to reduce quantity of data with no information loss, and then makes them persistent. The normalization process enables correlation of messages generated by different sources (e.g. syslog and possibly others). The prototype exports a RESTful web service interface easily accessible by CSPs.

Event logs are fundamental in digital forensics investigation because they allow investigators to rebuild past history of the system under investigation. In addition, logging could be useful to increase the trustiness of the cloud. Ko et al. (Ko, et al., 2011) describe a conceptual model called TrustCloud. This model is designed to increase accountability and auditability of the cloud in order to have more information about cloud transactions and positively impacting user confidence. A file based logging system keeps track of the whole files' life from creation to destruction. Compared to traditional server approaches the customer's focus is on data security rather than server protection. The proposed framework is based on five levels of accountability: system, data, workflows, policies, laws and regulations.

The system layer is the lowest level of the framework. It is responsible for finding the file-centric information in the operating system, the file system and the internal communication network of the Cloud. The logs that normally an operating system creates (e.g. system events) should be complemented by other data to keep history of file system accesses (e.g. tracing read/write calls). In this way, the logging system can track the correspondence between virtual and physical location of the files. Also, the exchange of data and files over the cloud internal network is important information to record, since it makes possible to record the files life cycle within the infrastructure.

The data layer facilitates the data-centric logging through the use of the provenance. This term refers to a collection of metadata that describes the history of an object, that is, all the processes and interactions that have contributed to the actual status. The adoption of this mechanism in the cloud requires the effective management of the huge amount of the provenance data, e.g. through the development of an efficient querying system. An adequate access control system has to be provided as well, since these data may contain confidential information and data manipulation or corruption must be avoided.

The workflow layer is focused on audit trails and specific cloud services data logs. This layer's goal is to extend the control to cover maintenance, upgrades and patching history. For example, an anomalous increment in cloud resource usage is a sensible trigger to activate accurate monitoring sensors, looking for suspicious activity and irregularities. This process must also apply when each component used must be compliant with specific service quality levels (as common in a service-oriented architecture).

Finally, policies, law and regulations layers require the record of data processed, accessed, stored or transmitted, in addition to detailed information about how, why, where, when and by whom the operations have been made. This information is necessary to made data available only when company policies or regulatory requirements authorize the access.

Implementing all or partially a TrustCloud model would decrease the present diffidence in cloud solutions, thus can foster cloud diffusion among most security aware users.

Data Deletion

In the case a secure data erasure have to be done (e.g. to accomplish organisation security policies) users can adopt cryptography-based solutions ensuring the data unavailability. For instance, Cachin et al. (Cachin, Haralambiev, Hsiao, & Sorniotti, 2013) proposed an approach to perform secure data erasure based on the destruction of cryptographic keys used to encrypt data. In this way, even if data are still present in memory, the unavailability of cryptographic keys makes them no longer accessible. In this case, a forensics analysis would be not feasible or very unlikely, e.g. by attempting a probably unsuccessful brute force attack.

Cloud Time Synchronization

During the securing phase, one of the most fragile operations is the record of the device system time and the difference with an external time reference. Precise time records are vital to correlate information from different sources and to reconstruct a temporal succession. Thus, a protocol for time synchronization of different nodes is a requirement in the cloud environment.

The most used algorithm for synchronizing computer clocks within a packet switching network is the Network Time Protocol (NTP) (Mills, 1992). NTP adopts Coordinated Universal Time (UTC) and is therefore time-zone independent. It can synchronize the computer clocks over the Internet within a margin of ten milliseconds. This accuracy significantly improves in a LAN, where the margin of less than two hundreds milliseconds is guaranteed.

As analysed by Bernstein (Bernstein, Ludvigson, Sankar, Diamond, & Morrow, 2009), the NTP protocol is enough to keep synchronized nodes and obtain accurate information in many cloud-based scenarios. However, for special applications the latency present in distributed systems like the cloud may be unacceptable. The digital forensics is one of these special cases, since the recording nodes require accurate reconstruction of the events sequence. In this scenario, Bernstein shows how to use the Precision Time Protocol (National Instruments, 2013) to enable a less-than-a-microsecond accuracy.

Live Forensics in the Cloud

The hypervisor is the host operating system that allocate computational resources (memory, CPU, disk I/O, network) to guest operating systems. Since it acts as broker between hardware resources and guests, the hypervisor processed all data when they come and go to physical devices.

Garfinkel and Rosenblum (Garfinkel & Rosenblum, 2003) developed the Virtual Machine Introspection (VMI), i.e. a method to use data obtained through the hypervisor for analysis. This technology can be used in the cloud framework to inspect the contents of the virtual machines without compromising normal operations. The exact approach depends on the virtualization platform used. For example, the work of Garfinkel and Rosenblum was designed to work with VMWare.

Payne et al. (Payne, De Carbone, & Lee, 2007) extended the support for VMI to the well-known hypervisor Xen. In detail, authors developed an abstract architecture for virtual machines monitoring called XenAccess, subsequently evolved in LibVMI project (Google, Inc., 2014). LibVMI library focuses on reading and writing the memory of the virtual machines. This library enables applications to securely access the memory status, the CPU registers and the disk activity of the guest operating systems. In this way, since the memory can be read while normal virtual machine operations are on-going, it is possible to create copies (snapshots) of the memory to be analysed later on. However, the VM should be paused to ensure the

security and integrity of the snapshot. Otherwise, the snapshot may be inconsistent, since the system main memory is continuously changing. Anyway, this is not a big issue since all hypervisors provide the "pause" functionality.

A snapshot can register both RAM and disks state of a virtual machine storing only the differences from the base image. This data can subsequently be used to restore the last virtual machine condition. A relevant snapshot must be stored as a persistent object in the structure of the provider, as well as any data a user wants to save before closing the virtual machine. Some providers supply this service, for example Amazon Simple Storage Service (S3) (Amazon, Inc., 2014) and Elastic Block Storage (EBS) (Amazon, Inc., 2014).

In practice, a number of possible ways to acquire a snapshot exists. For example, recent versions of LibVMI get memory snapshots by using Kernel-based Virtual Machine (KVM). However, this feature is experimental and limited to specific versions of QEMU (the system that provides the virtualized infrastructure used by KVM). Another possibility come from the project LiveCloudKd (MoonSols Ltd., 2012) for the Microsoft Hyper-V platform. In this case, a debugger works on the Microsoft Windows kernel in the virtual machine and allows to hold the VM and to copy its memory. Another project, HyperTaskMgr (MoonSols Ltd., 2011), can show all virtual machines running on a Hyper-V system. Furthermore, it can provide information on running processes and associated dynamically loadable libraries (DLL). Moreover, it can influence execution by elevating permissions granted to a process and stopping its execution.

VMI and monitoring software can also be exploited as defence from malicious software. Ando et al. (Ando, Kadobayashi, & Shinoda, 2007) modified a Linux distribution for the event-driven memory snapshot. The heuristic developed in this project can detect unknown malware that cannot be discovered through known signature detection.

Lempereur et al. (Lempereur, Merabti, & Shi, 2010) illustrate a framework useful to evaluate automatically live acquisition forensics tools on different platforms. The impact of the tools on the state of the system can be evaluated as well. The analysis is performed using pairs of VMs initialized in parallel. In one of these, some techniques are used for live analysis. Subsequently, the framework creates copies of the pleadings of both virtual machines. The impact estimation is given by comparing differences between bits present in the two copies.

Krishnan et al. (Krishnan, Snow, & Monrose, 2010) propose a forensic platform to seamlessly monitor and log the accesses to the data within a virtualized environment. They use the functionalities exposed by a hypervisor. The project monitors the disk data access and it allows following the accesses done by different processes, even if the data are copied in central memory. Theese observations are then recorded on an audit log to reconstruct the events and the changes. The authors claim this tool can provide malware behaviour profiles.

The cloud is a highly distributed environment, thus requires correlating information from different sources as well as information collected by different hypervisors. More information sources than the nodes and its virtual machines have to be considered to achieve this goal. Poisel et al. (Poisel, Malzer, & Tjoa, 2013) address as example the OpenStack platform (OpenStack Foundation, 2014) whose central architectural elements are the message queue and the database. All operations performed are coordinated through the use of these two components. In this case, the supplemental information comes from the metadata analysis of the data flow generated in the Cloud.

Analysis Phase

As said, the elasticity and distributed structure of the cloud can represent an obstacle for the analysis phase. However, the solution of these problems can often be found by taking advantage of the cloud characteristics.

Data Analysis

The amount of data to be analysed during forensics investigation tends to increase as consequence of the constant increment of the low-cost storage space. So, the cloud computing power must be used as well to allow scalability. In particular, this means to enrich existing instruments by the use of cloud functionalities. For example, Sleuth Kit developers exploited the potentiality of MapReduce implemented in Hadoop (The Apache Software Foundation, 2014) to analyse disk images on the cloud (Carrier, 2014). Hadoop is an open source project for developing reliable and scalable software for distributed computing. The framework uses a programming model based on the map and reduces functions. The first deals with the application of a function to a set of input data and generates a set of values. The second works on the latter set of data generated by the map and combines them. In this way, a complex problem is divided into simpler sub problems. Finally, the results of these sub problems are eventually recombined for solving the original problem.

Wen et al. (Wen, Man, Le, & Shi, 2013) proposes another framework that exploits the characteristics of Hadoop to facilitate digital forensics. The infrastructure is designed to investigate large quantities of data. In particular, it allows the use and deployment of interoperable tools for digital forensics. The goal is the creation and customization of a data processing workflow. The framework assessment has been carried out on a prototype by using Amazon EC2. This service has emphasized the savings in terms of time for an increasing number of nodes, thanks to the optimization of the process carried out by the workflow engine and the use of parallelization obtained by MapReduce.

Integrity Verification

The characteristics of the cloud infrastructure can be exploited also to facilitate the integrity check on large quantities of data. In a forensic process, the integrity is an unavoidable requirement that ensures the evidence validity. The control of this feature can possibly be made many times. Possibly, every time there is a shift of custody of the forensic copy and every time the seized data are analysed. The integrity can be ensured by computing a fresh hash from the seized data and by comparing the result with the hash of the original data. This process can be laborious in the Cloud, because data are distributed on different servers and the quantity of storage to be analysed may be very large.

Hegarty et al. (Hegarty, Merabti, Shi, & Askwith, 2011) propose a mechanism to reduce the quantity of data transmitted. Their approach is a signature detection cloud system. This technique compares a set of known files' signature with the files in the cloud. Any finding indicates the presence of interesting files in the system. This technique obtains signatures of the appropriate length from the first n bits of a MD5 digest. The length is tuned on the base of the number of files to be scanned and the number of signatures. The application of this method in cloud environment (as well as in any distributed system) requires that the analysis system is distributed as well.

Documentation Phase

The chain of custody refers to both the physical devices and the data contained therein. It is a fundamental point to consider for all documented evidences produced during an investigation. Keeping a chain of custody that follows the traditional digital forensics guidelines may not be feasible in a cloud environment. For a number of reasons, police officers can not seize all devices that could contain the data of interest unless the investigation involves a private cloud of modest size. For example, bureaucratic requirements for the seizure may be slow to be satisfied, causing an investigation delay. Thus, in a cloud investigation only data may be available, without corresponding physical

devices. However, honest service providers have interest to make available a valid chain of custody, since are required to ensure the integrity of the original data. An acceptable digital equivalent can be built implementing a safe system of provenance, as proposed by Dykstra et al. (Dykstra & Sherman, Understanding issues in cloud forensics: two hypothetical case studies, 2011).

The provenance (or source) can be implemented through a set of metadata which describes the history of an object. The data provided by provenance may include what action has been done on an object, by whom, how, when, and in what environment has been accomplished (Ram & Liu, 2007). The provenance can be described as a directed acyclic graph. The nodes of the graph represent objects such as files and processes of the data set. These are further annotated with attributes, for example name and path for command line arguments or environment variables for processes. An arc between two nodes indicates the dependence between objects, that is, the derivation of an object from another. The starting one is defined as ancestor of the ending node. Each version of an object has its own distinct node withithe graph. The provenance graph is acyclic because a file cannot appear among the ancestors of itself. The provenance differs significantly from a simple log: the former describes the history of the origin of an object; the latter is a list of entries for default actions related to a specific application.

The provenance information can be exploited in cloud computing in many ways. Bates et al. (Bates, Mood, Valafar, & Butler, 2013) use them as a basis for a fine grained access control system. Davidson et al. (Davidson & Freire, 2008) propose the use of provenance to validate the processes output and verify their integrity. Provenance can also be used as a source of evidences in addition to information provided by the logging system. In particular, it helps to reconstruct the sequence of actions performed in the Cloud (Lu, Lin, Liang, & Shen, 2010).

A cloud computing system must provide the following characteristics to natively support the collection of provenance (Zhang, Kirchberg, Ko, & Lee, 2011).

- Provenance data consistency: an object and its provenance must be closely related, i.e. there must be consistency between them.
- Atomicity: the provenance the data that describes must be stored in a single logic operation. Atomicity and consistency together ensure that the provenance describes data with full coverage and accuracy. I.e. they achieve the feature of provenance data-coupling.
- Causal sorting: the system tracks the causal relationship between the objects in the provenance graph. If an object A is an ancestor of B then all the ancestors of A are also ancestors of B. The system has to ensure that the ancestors of an object and related provenances are consistent before including them in the graph. A violation of this feature could lead to inconsistent arcs (e.g. without a destination) and storage of incomplete information.
- Long-term persistence: the provenance of an object must be kept even if the related object is removed to avoid disconnected graphs. The provenance of an object removed from the storage system can only be deleted if it is no longer part of the chain of derivation of any other object. I.e. if the deleted object has no descendant.
- Query efficiency: data provenance must be easily queried. For example, this is useful when a user wants to access a set of objects whose provenance satisfies some specific criteria. The efficiency of the querying system is a priority since the amount of data for the graph structure in a cloud can be very large.
- Storage structures and calculation coordination: automatic provenance computation

should be possible since many providers offer both computing and storage services. Provenance information can be extracted by the interaction between the services and the cloud storage operations.

- Interface for the inclusion of provenance: users who create file locally and upload them to the Cloud should possibly be able to add provenance information. The CSPs should provide an interface or API for the purpose.

Many systems of storage and management of the provenance have been proposed in literature. For example, Muniswamy-Reddy (Muniswamy-Reddy & Seltzer, 2010) proposed the Provenance Aware Storage System (PASS) to automatically collect the provenance data in a local computer. The system facilitates the organization of provenance in different levels of abstraction (e.g. application, operating system). The PASS reaches this goal through components integrating various application provenance supports. Macko et al. (Macko, Chiarini, & Seltzer, 2011) developed an implementation of this system that collects the provenance of a virtual machine via an accordingly amended hypervisor.

The provenance information must be adequately protected, since provenance data can be source of evidences and/or contain sensitive information. In some scenarios, these data must be kept confidential, e.g. if a cloud service is a health care system. In these cases, information must not be available to everyone and a separate access control system for service data and for provenance data is required. Furthermore, the system must also ensure that the provenance information remain intact throughout their life cycle, and it must ensure that information stored are not falsifiable without detection and they cannot be repudiated by who generate them after being stored into the system.

There are some articles in the literature concerning provenance security. Lu et al. (Lu, Lin, Liang, & Shen, 2010) describe a framework for managing the provenance data shared among many users of a cloud storage service. Their model is composed by three kinds of entities: the users, the service provider and the system administrator. The latter is a complex entity representing a reliable third party. The administrator is responsible for the management of the secure provenance system, e.g. he/she have to register new users and investigate disputes that may occur. This scheme allows anonymous data access. Furthermore, it ensures integrity and confidentiality through the use of encryption and data signing. In this framework, the service provider verifies the signature before storing them. If a dispute arises concerning the data stored, the service provider can allow anonymous access to the system administrator. In this manner the administrator can figure out the user who created the disputed data, since he/she possesses the master key that derived all private authentication keys.

OPEN ISSUES

Despite methods and approaches presented in previous section, some problems still remain open in cloud forensics field. One of the main concerns the difficulty for finding deleted data, which is the basic operation of the investigative process. The problem is due to the multi-tenancy architecture, which has in the resource elasticity one of its strengths. Resource elasticity means that the memory space made available after the data deletion can be overwritten (at least partially) in a short time. The redundancy of data across multiple data centres would be helpful in this context, but even this possibility is not a significant aid in case the cloud provider adopts stringent policy on erasing data. The traditional forensic research methods for recovering deleted data in physical devices can not be used in absence of some conditions. I.e., if no metadata or other evidence can link the recoverable data (e.g. file fragments or complete files) to the investigation in progress, e.g. through

metadata associated to memory locations. This could confirm if the last data stored in a given area of a device is of interest to the investigators, and therefore make admissible the recovery after the deletion from the file system.

The problems related to the deletion of date can be legally relevant and requires great attention, up to the involvement of the European Parliament on the matter. In this scenario, the legislator must find the right balance among the users and investigators needs. Furthermore, there are common practice and law background must be produced when investigators accesses data located in other jurisdictions. Currently, these questions are under study and need further analysis. They are often mentioned in recent literature (Biggs & Vidalis, 2009), (Ruan, Carthy, Kechadi, & Crosbie, 2011) and (Zafarullah, Anwar, & Anwar, 2011) but at the moment there is only one work analysing in detail the impact of U.S. legislation in the investigation process in the Cloud (Orton, Alva, & Endicott-Popovsky, 2012). This article represents an important step toward formalization of a forensics procedure that meets the eligibility requirement for evidences However, these guidelines need to be re-tuned for different countries and different legislation.

With regard to cross-border legal issues, Biggs (Biggs & Vidalis, 2009) assumed as the only solution the introduction of legislation shared worldwide, tuned specifically for investigations in the cloud. According to the authors, only a new shared protocol can enable fast actions and facilitate the investigations. Noteworthy, problems related to the multi-jurisdictional nature of data are not unique to the cloud environment, but they are addressed also in different context (Orton, Alva, & Endicott-Popovsky, 2012). A first step in EU has been made by the European Convention on Cybercrime, a.k.a. the Budapest Convention. This is an international treaty on crimes committed via the Internet and other computer networks that aims to strengthen international cooperation. It was ratified also from the United States, Japan,

Australia, as well as by most EU countries, but its practical application as well as its worldwide adoption are still incomplete.

FUTURE WORK

Some mentioned solutions are simply proposals, without a proper follow-up of experimental studies, as in the cases of provenance and chain of custody, as suggested by Dykstra and Sherman (Dykstra & Sherman, Understanding issues in cloud forensics: two hypothetical case studies, 2011) or in the proactive data collection made by Birk and Wegener (Birk & Wegener, 2011).

In case of provenance, some studies addressed how to obtain a model for the safe cloud collection and preservation. These studies assume that the main features of a chain of custody are integrity and authenticity. However, several of the proposed solutions are only models without a real implementation, as in the case of *DataPROVE* (Zhang, Kirchberg, Ko, & Lee, 2011).

So, practical experiments in this field are required to understand the exact extent of the problem and the exact proposals pros and cons. The lack of experimental data makes not possible to apply Daubert's standards (Cornell University Law School, 2014), so there is no assessment method for the validity of a scientific process in a legal case. As analysed by Orton (Orton, Alva, & Endicott-Popovsky, 2012) the main challenges to address are related to 1)the knowledge of the techniques used by the scientific community, 2) the knowledge of the error rate, 3) the forensic community acceptance of the methods used to link a cloud data to a particular individual.

Future work aim will be to develop sound and widely accepted cloud specific guidelines, so that evidences obtained from the Cloud will be used in a legal trial with less subjectivity and variance.

CONCLUSION

Cloud's characteristics impose changes in digital forensics investigation process. Techniques and methodologies referred to as "best practices" in traditional digital forensics often can not be directly reused in case of cloud investigation. For this reason in recent years raised the cloud forensics, a new branch of digital forensics specific for this case. As evidenced by Ruan (Ruan & Carthy, Cloud Computing Reference Architecture and Its Forensic Implications: A Preliminary Analysis, 2012), cloud forensics development is along three main lines: technical, organizational and legal.

In our discussion, we focused mostly on the technical field. Our work highlighted the problems faced by forensics in the cloud, describing the requirement, the state of the art and future directions, with particular care on the problems that arise in the securing phase of the investigative process. In this stage, it is particularly important to adopt cloud tuned methods to ensure that the data collected have sound characteristics. Only in this case investigators can keep substantial and reliable evidence. Inly in this case investigators can use evidences in the subsequent analysis phase, and so in the course of a process.

Some important steps of the investigation process have not yet been solved in research field but have been indicated as relevant by researchers of the area. We have pointed out issues in order to obtain the characteristics of authenticity, integrity, completeness, truthfulness and eligibility of evidence. Most relevant issues concern integrity of the data acquired from the cloud, the assurance that the original data are not manipulated by unauthorized persons during the course of the investigation, the deployment of a proper chain of custody, the user's trust in the infrastructure, the construction of a logging system suitable for the cloud environment.

Also the CSP level of trust will be a relevant research field, since in order to consider VM's data valid as legal proofs, investigators must trust the CSP, but CSP rarely provides indicators attesting their internals like, for example, information about the status of the VMM software (e.g. bug fixes, running version), making this step hazardous from a trust point of view.

These issues make difficult normal investigative procedures, in cases where it is impossible to physically seize the storage media for the purpose of obtaining evidence.

Thus, the researchers and experts challenge is to find solutions and to create a process of investigation technically sound and widely accepted by both industry experts and legal forces, by enriching and experimenting proposed theoretical methods, and by testing presently implemented on real case scenarios.

REFERENCES

Forensic Toolkit (2014). AccessData Group, Inc. Retrieved from http://www.accessdata.com/solutions/digital-forensics/ftk

Amazon, S3. (2014). *Amazon.com.* Retrieved from http://aws.amazon.com/s3/

Amazon EBS. (2014). *Amazon Inc.* Retrieved from http://aws.amazon.com/ebs/

AWS CloudTrail. (2014). Amazon, Inc. Retrieved from http://aws.amazon.com/cloudtrail/

AWS Security Center. (2014). Amazon, Inc. Retrieved from http://aws.amazon.com/security/

Ando, R., Kadobayashi, Y., & Shinoda, Y. (2007). Synchronous pseudo physical memory snapshot and forensics on paravirtualized vmm using split kernel module. *Information Security and Cryptology (ICISC'07)*, 131-143.

ANSA. (2014). *Pedofilia, sgominata rete in Italia e 11 Paesi.* Retrieved from http://www.ansa.it/sito/notizie/cronaca/2014/07/11/pedofilia-sgominata-rete-in-italia-e-11-paesi_8c7a9210-ad9d-4a82-af3a-85e609c205ec.html

Bates, A., Mood, B., Valafar, M., & Butler, K. (2013). Towards secure provenance-based access control in cloud environments. *Proceedings of the third ACM conference on Data and application security and privacy* (pp. 277-284). San Antonio (TX, USA): ACM. doi:10.1145/2435349.2435389

Bernstein, D., Ludvigson, E., Sankar, K., Diamond, S., & Morrow, M. (2009). Blueprint for the intercloud-protocols and formats for cloud computing interoperability. *4th International Conference on Internet and Web Applications and Services (ICIW'09)* (pp. 328-336). Venice (Italy): IEEE. doi:10.1109/ICIW.2009.55

Biggs, S., & Vidalis, S. (2009). Cloud computing: The impact on digital forensic investigations. *International Conference for Internet Technology and Secured Transactions (ICITST'09)* (pp. 1-6). IEEE. doi:10.1109/ICITST.2009.5402561

Birk, D., & Wegener, C. (2011). Technical issues of forensic investigations in cloud computing environments. *6th International Workshop on Systematic Approaches to Digital Forensic Engineering (SADFE'11)* (pp. 1-10). IEEE. doi:10.1109/SADFE.2011.17

Cachin, C., Haralambiev, K., Hsiao, H.-C., & Sorniotti, A. (2013). Policy-based secure deletion. *Proceedings of the 2013 ACM SIGSAC conference on Computer & communications security* (pp. 259-270). ACM. doi:10.1145/2508859.2516690

Carrier, B. (2014). *Sleuth Kit Hadoop Framework.* Retrieved from http://www.sleuthkit.org/tsk_hadoop/

TestDisk. (2014). *CGSecurity*. Retrieved from http://www.cgsecurity.org/wiki/TestDisk

Columbus, L. (2013). *Gartner Predicts Infrastructure Services Will Accelerate Cloud Computing Growth*. Retrieved from http://www.forbes.com/sites/louiscolumbus/2013/02/19/gartner-predicts-infrastructure-services-will-accelerate-cloud-computing-growth/

Cornell University Law School. (2014). *Daubert v. Merrell Dow Pharmaceuticals*. Retrieved from http://www.law.cornell.edu/supct/html/92-102.ZS.html

Council of Europe. (2001, November 23). *Convention on Cybercrime*. Retrieved from http://conventions.coe.int/Treaty/EN/Treaties/Html/185.htm

Davidson, S., & Freire, J. (2008). Provenance and scientific workflows: challenges and opportunities. *Proceedings of the 2008 ACM SIGMOD international conference on Management of data* (pp. 1345-1350). Vancouver (Canada): ACM. doi:10.1145/1376616.1376772

Delport, W., Kohn, M., & Olivier, M. (2011). Isolating a cloud instance for a digital forensic investigation. *Proceedings of Information Security South Africa Conference (ISSA'11)*, (pp. 15-17). Johannesburg, South Africa.

Delport, W., & Olivier, M. (2012). Cloud Separation: Stuck Inside the Cloud. *9th International Conference on Trust, Privacy and Security in Digital Business* (pp. 36-49). Vienna (Austria): Springer. doi:10.1007/978-3-642-32287-7_4

Dykstra, J., Gowe, L., Jackson, R., Reemelin, O. S., Rojas, E., & Ruan, K. S. et al. (2014). *NIST IR 8006 - NIST Cloud Computing Forensic Science Challenges (DRAFT)*. NIST.

Dykstra, J., & Sherman, A. (2011). Understanding issues in cloud forensics: two hypothetical case studies. *Proceedings of the 2011 ADSFL Conference on Digital Forensics, Security, and Law (ADSFL'11)*, (pp. 19-31). Richmond VA, USA.

Dykstra, J., & Sherman, A. (2012). Acquiring forensic evidence from infrastructure-as-a-service cloud computing: Exploring and evaluating tools, trust, and techniques. Proceedings of 12th Annual Digital Forensics Research Work Shop (DFRWS'12), (pp. S90-S98). Washington DC, USA.

Dykstra, J., & Sherman, A. (2013). Design and implementation of FROST: Digital forensic tools for the OpenStack cloud computing platform. *Proceedings of 13th Annual Digital Forensics Research Work Shop (DFRWS'13)*, (pp. S87-S95). Monterey (CA, USA).

Eraser. (2013). *Eraser*. Retrieved from http://eraser.heidi.ie/

Eucalyptus | Open Source Private Cloud Software. (2014). *Eucalyptus System, Inc.* Retrieved from https://www.eucalyptus.com/

Galante, J., Kharif, O., & Alpeyev, P. (2011). *Sony Network Breach Shows Amazon Cloud's Appeal for Hackers*. Retrieved from http://www.bloomberg.com/news/2011-05-15/sony-attack-shows-amazon-s-cloud-service-lures-hackers-at-pennies-an-hour.html

Garfinkel, T., & Rosenblum, M. (2003). A Virtual Machine Introspection Based Architecture for Intrusion Detection. *Proceedings of the 10th Network and Distributed System Security Symposium (NDSS'03)*, (pp. 191-206). San Diego, CA, USA.

Gens, F., & Shirer, M. (2013). *IDC Forecasts Worldwide Public IT Cloud Services Spending to Reach Nearly $108 Billion by 2017 as Focus Shifts from Savings to Innovation*. Retrieved from http://www.idc.com/getdoc.jsp?containerId=prUS24298013

Gerhards, R. (2014). *RSyslog*. Retrieved from http://www.rsyslog.com/

Google, Inc. (2014). *vmitools*. Retrieved from https://code.google.com/p/vmitools/

Grispos, G., Storer, T., & Glisson, W. (2012). Calm before the storm: The challenges of cloud computing in digital forensics. *International Journal of Digital Crime and Forensics*, *4*(2), 28–48. doi:10.4018/jdcf.2012040103

Guidance Software, Inc. (2014). *EnCase Forensic v7.10: The Fastest, Most Comprehensive Forensic Solution Available*. Retrieved from https://www.guidancesoftware.com/products/Pages/encase-forensic/overview.aspx

Guo, H., Jin, B., & Shang, T. (2012). Forensic investigations in Cloud environments. *Proceedings of 2012 International Conference on Computer Science and Information Processing (CSIP'12)* (pp. 248-251). IEEE.

Hart, S. V., Ashcroft, J., & Daniels, D. J. (2004). Forensic examination of digital evidence: a guide for law enforcement. Washington DC (USA): U.S. National Institute of Justice (NIJ).

Hegarty, R., Merabti, M., Shi, Q., & Askwith, B. (2011). Forensic Analysis of Distributed Service Oriented Computing Platforms. *Proceedings of 12th Annual PostGraduate Symposium on the Convergence fo Telecommunications, Networking and Broadcasting (PGNet'11)*. Liverpool (UK).

Log Shuttle. (2014). *Heroku, Inc*. Retrieved from http://www.log-shuttle.io/

Italian Parliament. (2008). *L48/2008* - Ratifica ed esecuzione della Convenzione del Consiglio d'Europa sulla criminalità informatica, fatta a Budapest il 23 novembre 2001, e norme di adeguamento dell'ordinamento interno. [Ratification and implementation of the Council of Europe Convention on Cybercrime, signed in Budapest on 23 November 2001 and the rules of adapting internal.] Retrieved from http://www.parlamento.it/parlam/leggi/08048l.htm

Jones, N., George, E., Merida, F. I., Rasmussen, U., & Volzow, V. (2013). *Electronic evidence guide - A basic guide for police officers, prosecutors and judges*. Strasburg, France: Council of Europe - Data Protection and Cybercrime Division.

Ko, R. K., Jagadpramana, P., Mowbray, M., Pearson, S., Kirchberg, M., & Liang, Q. et al. (2011). TrustCloud: A framework for accountability and trust in cloud computing. *Proceedings of 2011 IEEE World Congress on Services (SERVICES'11)* (pp. 584-588). Washington (DC, USA): IEEE. doi:10.1109/SERVICES.2011.91

KPMG International. (2013). *The cloud takes shape - Global coud survey: the implementation challenge*. Retrieved from http://www.kpmg.com/Global/en/IssuesAndInsights/ArticlesPublications/cloud-service-providers-survey/Documents/the-cloud-takes-shape-v4.pdf

Krishnan, S., Snow, K. Z., & Monrose, F. (2010). Trail of bytes: efficient support for forensic analysis. *Proceedings of the 17th ACM conference on Computer and Communications Security (CCS'10)* (pp. 50-60). Chicago (IL, USA): ACM. doi:10.1145/1866307.1866314

Lempereur, B., Merabti, M., & Shi, Q. (2010). Pypette: A framework for the automated evaluation of live digital forensic techniques. *International Journal of Digital Crime andForensics (IJDCF)*, 31-46.

Lu, R., Lin, X., Liang, X., & Shen, X. S. (2010). Secure provenance: the essential of bread and butter of data forensics in cloud computing. *Proceedings of the 5th ACM Symposium on Information, Computer and Communications Security (ASIACCS'10)* (pp. 282-292). Beijin (China): ACM. doi:10.1145/1755688.1755723

Macko, P., Chiarini, M., & Seltzer, M. (2011). Collecting Provenance via the Xen Hypervisor. *Proceeding of 3rd USENIX Workshop on the Theory and Practice of Provenance (TaPP'11)*. Heraklion (Greece).

Marty, R. (2011). Cloud application logging for forensics. *Proceedings of the 2011 ACM Symposium on Applied Computing* (pp. 178-184). ACM. doi:10.1145/1982185.1982226

Mell, P., & Grance, T. (2011). The NIST definition of cloud computing. NIST - Computer Security Division, Information Technology Laboratory.

Metz, C. (2009). DDoS attack rains down on Amazon cloud - Code haven tumbles from sky. *The Register*. Retrieved from http://www.theregister.co.uk/2009/10/05/amazon_bitbucket_outage/

Miao, F., Ma, Y., & Salowey, J. (2009). *Transport Layer Security (TLS) Transport Mapping for Syslog (RFC-5425)*. IETF. doi:10.17487/rfc5425

Mills, D. (1992). *Network Time Protocol (Version 3) - Specification, Implementation and Analysis (RFC 1305)*. IETF. doi:10.17487/rfc1305

Common Event Expression - A Unified Event Language for Interoperability. (2013). *MITRE*. Retrieved from https://cee.mitre.org/

NEW UTILITY: MoonSols HyperTaskMgr v1.0. (2011). *MoonSols Ltd*. Retrieved from http://www.moonsols.com/2011/07/19/new-utility-moonsols-hypertaskmgr-v1-0/

LiveCloudKd. (2012). MoonSols Ltd. Retrieved from http://moonsols.com/2010/08/12/live-cloudkd

Muniswamy-Reddy, K.-K., & Seltzer, M. (2010). Provenance as first class cloud data. *Operating Systems Review*, *43*(4), 11–16. doi:10.1145/1713254.1713258

Nance, K., Bishop, M., & Hay, B. (2009). Investigating the implications of virtual machine introspection for digital forensics. *International Conference on Availability, Reliability and Security (ARES'09)* (pp. 1024-1029). IEEE. doi:10.1109/ARES.2009.173

National Instruments. (2013). *Introduction to Distributed Clock Synchronization and the IEEE 1588 Precision Time Protocol*. Retrieved from http://www.ni.com/white-paper/2822/en/

OpenStack Foundation. (2014). *OpenStack | Open source software for building private and public clouds*. Retrieved from http://www.openstack.org/

Orofino, S. (1996). Daubert v. Merrell Dow Pharmaceuticals, Inc.: the battle over admissibility standards for scientific evidence in court. *Journal of Undergraduate Sciences*, 109-111.

Orton, I., Alva, A., & Endicott-Popovsky, B. (2012). Legal process and requirements for cloud forensic investigations. In *Cybercrime and Cloud Forensics*. IGI Global.

Palmer, G. (2001). A road map for digital forensic research. *1st Digital Forensic Research Workshop (DFRWS'01)*, (pp. 27-30). Utica, New York, USA.

Pape, C., Reissmann, S., & Rieger, S. (2013). RESTful Correlation and Consolidation of Distributed Logging Data in Cloud Environments. *Proceedings of the 8th International Conference on Internet and Web Applications and Services (ICIW'13)*, (pp. 194-199). Rome, Italy.

Payne, B. D., De Carbone, M. D., & Lee, W. (2007). Secure and flexible monitoring of virtual machines. *Proceedings of 23th Annual Computer Security Applications Conference (ACSAC'07)*, (pp. 385-397). Miami Beach, FL, USA. doi:10.1109/ACSAC.2007.10

Personal data in the cloud- A global survey of consumer attitudes. (2010). *Fujitsu.*

Poisel, R., Malzer, E., & Tjoa, S. (2013). Evidence and cloud computing: The virtual machine introspection approach. *Journal of Wireless Mobile Networks, Ubiquitous Computing, and Dependable Applications (JoWUA)*, 135-152.

Ram, S., & Liu, J. (2007). Understanding the semantics of data provenance to support active conceptual modeling. In P. P. Chen, & W. L. Y, Active conceptual modeling of learning (pp. 17-29). Springer. doi:10.1007/978-3-540-77503-4_3

Ristenpart, T., Tromer, E., Shacham, H., & Savage, S. (2009). Hey, you, get off of my cloud: exploring information leakage in third-party compute clouds. *Proceedings of the 16th ACM conference on Computer and Communications Security (CCS'09)* (pp. 199-212). Chicago (IL, USA): ACM. doi:10.1145/1653662.1653687

Robertson, k., & Bartos, M. (2013). *Lumberjack Project.* Retrieved from https://fedorahosted.org/lumberjack/

Ruan, K., & Carthy, J. (2012). Cloud Computing Reference Architecture and Its Forensic Implications: A Preliminary Analysis. *Proceedings of 4rt International Conference on Digital Forensics and Cyber Crime (ICDF2C'12)*, (pp. 1-21). Lafayette, IN, USA. doi:10.1007/978-3-642-39891-9_1

Ruan, K., Carthy, J., Kechadi, T., & Crosbie, M. (2011). Cloud forensics. In *Advances in digital forensics VII* (pp. 35–46). Springer. doi:10.1007/978-3-642-24212-0_3

Scientific Working Group on Digital Evidence (SWGDE), International Organization on Digital Evidence (IOCE). (2000). *Digital Evidence: Standards and Principles.* Retrieved from http://www.fbi.gov/about-us/lab/forensic-science-communications/fsc/april2000/swgde.htm

Snort. (2014). *Cisco.* Retrieved from https://www.snort.org/

Taylor, M., Haggerty, J., Gresty, D., & Lamb, D. (2011). Forensic investigation of cloud computing systems. In *Network Security* (pp. 4–10). Elsevier.

Welcome to Apache Hadoop! (2014). *The Apache Software Foundation.* Retrieved from http://hadoop.apache.org/

Varadharajan, V. (2009). A note on trust-enhanced security. *IEEE Security and Privacy, 7*(3), 57–59. doi:10.1109/MSP.2009.59

Wang, K. (2010). Using a local search warrant to acquire evidence stored overseas via the internet. *Advances in Digital Forensics, VI*, 37–48.

Wen, Y., Man, X., Le, K., & Shi, W. (2013). Forensics-as-a-Service (FaaS): Computer Forensic Workflow Management and Processing Using Cloud. *Proceedings of the 4th International Conference on Cloud Computing, GRIDs, and Virtualization (COMPUTING'13)*, (pp. 208-214). Valencia, Spain.

Merkle tree. (2014, September). *Wikimedia Foundation, Inc.* Retrieved from Wikipedia: http://en.wikipedia.org/wiki/Merkle_tree

Shred (Unix). (2014, September). *Wikimedia Foundation, Inc.* Retrieved from Wikipedia: http://en.wikipedia.org/wiki/Shred_%28Unix%29

Wilkinson, S., & Haagman, D. (2007). *Good practice guide for computer-based electronic evidence. Association of Chief Police Officers.* ACPO.

Zafarullah, Z., Anwar, F., & Anwar, Z. (2011). Digital forensics for eucalyptus. Proceedings of Frontiers of Information Technology (FIT'11), (pp. 110-116). Islamabad, Pakistan. doi:10.1109/FIT.2011.28

Zhang, O. Q., Kirchberg, M., Ko, R. K., & Lee, B. S. (2011). How to track your data: The case for cloud computing provenance. *Proceedings of the 3rd International Cloud Computing Technology and Science (CloudCom'11)* (pp. 446-453). Athens (Greece): IEEE. doi:10.1109/CloudCom.2011.66

KEY TERMS AND DEFINITIONS

Analysis Phase: The part of the digital forensics process in which all the collected data are analysed and tracked.

Chain of Custody: The data source containing all the information related to the evidence handling occurred during the investigation. The evidence handling addresses both the physical devices and the data contained therein.

Cloud Computing: A computing model that facilitates easy access to remote resources (e.g. computation power and storage) provided by a third party (Cloud Service Provider or CSP) adopting the pay-on-demand paradigm.

Digital Forensics: A branch of forensics that focuses on the identification and acquisition of digital evidence from electronic devices like laptops and smartphones.

Forensics: The set of scientific methods for examining and gathering information about the past in order to support investigations.

Presentation Phase: The phase of the digital forensics for preparing evidences collected during investigation to be presented to the judge. It comprises the development of a report about techniques and methods adopted during the forensics activity.

Securing Phase: The first part of the digital forensics process. This phase must ensure that all the investigation relevant material does not suffer changes during the investigative process.

Chapter 13
Security Challenges for Cloud Computing Development Framework in Saudi Arabia

Lawan A. Mohammed
King Fahd University of Petroleum and Minerals, Saudi Arabia

Kashif Munir
King Fahd University of Petroleum and Minerals, Saudi Arabia

ABSTRACT

In recent years, cloud computing or on-demand computing technologies and applications have become ubiquitous, permeating every aspect of our personal and professional lives. Governments and enterprises are now adopting cloud technologies for numerous applications to increase their operational efficiency, improve their responsiveness and competitiveness. For these reasons, the requirements for developing cloud applications have increased. Despite having many advantages for IT organizations, cloud has some issues that must be consider during its deployment. The main concerns are security, privacy and trust. These issues arise during the deployment of mostly public cloud infrastructure. In this chapter, security, privacy and trust issues of cloud computing deployment in Saudi Arabia were identified and the solutions to overcome these problems were discussed.

1. INTRODUCTION

Cloud computing is a new paradigm in the world of Information Technology Advancement. Considerable amount of cloud computing technology is already being used and developed in various flavors. Cloud Computing provides efficient network login to an appropriate pool of computing resources which can be provided and released with just nominal assiduity and service

providers reciprocity as reported in Armbrust et al.(2009) and Toby et al. (2009). The resources can be network servers, applications, platforms, infrastructure segments and services. Cloud computing delivers services autonomously based on demand and provides sufficient network access, data resource environment and effectual flexibility. This technology is used for more efficient and cost-effective computing by centralizing storage, memory, computing capacity of PC's and servers.

DOI: 10.4018/978-1-4666-8387-7.ch013

Industry experts believe that this trend will only continue to grow and develop even further in the coming few years. Thus, cloud computing affects people, process and technology of the enterprise. In spite of having benefits with Cloud computing paradigm such as efficiency, flexibility, easy set up and overall reduction in IT cost (Sultan, 2010), cloud computing paradigm could raise privacy and confidentiality risks. "Not all types of cloud computing raise the same privacy and confidentiality risks. Some believe that much of the computing activity occurring today entirely on computers owned and controlled locally by users will shift to the cloud in the future" (Gellman, 2009). In Cloud computing, users connect to the CLOUD, which appears as a single entity as opposed to the traditional way of connecting to multiple servers located on company premises. Public Private Partnership these days is a usually adopted pattern of governance to meet the diverse needs of their citizens with confidence and providing quality of these services. Cloud Computing Technology can also act as a facilitator between public and private partnership. In such cases there is a possibility that an external party can be involved in providing Cloud Services having partial control over the data storage, processing and transmission of data and privacy regulations become relevant (Ruiter & Warnier, 2011). Cloud computing has significant implications for the privacy of personal information as well as for the confidentiality of business and governmental information. A survey by EDUCAUSE involving 372 of its member institutions revealed that a great proportion of the respondents with use cases that involved cloud-based services reported that data privacy risks and data security risks were among their top barriers to overcome.

In this chapter, we study how cloud computing can benefit governments and enterprises in KSA. We discuss the cloud computing environment and explore how enterprises may take advantage of clouds not only in terms of cost but also in terms of efficiency, reliability, portability, flexibility, and security. We also discuss challenges including risks and problems associated with cloud computing. The rest of this chapter is organized as follows: In next section, we give a brief overview on cloud computing models, in section 3 we explore the benefits of cloud computing in KSA (Kingdom of Saudi Arabia). Section 4 presents security challenges associated with cloud computing and some counter measures to be taken. It include a simple survey to assess the perception of secure cloud computing environment by some selected IT related organizations in KSA. Section 5 provides some general recommendations, Finally, section 6 concludes the chapter.

2. CLOUD COMPUTING MODELS

Various efforts were made in order to find an appropriate definition for cloud computing.

For instance, Hays defined it as on-demand computing, software as services or the Internet as a platform (Hayes, 2008). However, this definition seems to be general and does not give a comprehensive technical view. In an effort to give a more descriptive definition, Armbrust and colleagues defined cloud computing as applications that deliver services over the Internet where the hardware and software systems in the datacenter provide these services (Armbrust et al., 2009). In this definition, cloud refers to the hardware and software in the datacenters, and the applications can be defined as software as a service (SAAS). Based on these definitions, it can be noticed that cloud computing helps in adopting IT services without considering the infrastructure and hardware required running these services. In terms of classification, cloud computing systems are classified as public cloud, private cloud, community cloud and hybrid cloud as described in: Dimitrios & Dimitrios (2012), Subashini & Kavitha (2011), and Ahmed & Manal, (2011). These classes are known as deployment models and they describe the scope of services offered on the cloud to the customers.

- **Public Cloud:** In public clouds the infrastructure and other cloud services are made available to the general public over the Internet. The cloud is owned and managed by a CSP who offers services to consumers on a pay-per-use basis. Public cloud users are by default treated as untrustworthy; therefore, security and privacy are big concerns about this type of cloud (Jansen & Grance, 2011). Many popular cloud services are public including Amazon EC2, Google App Engine and Salesforce.com.
- **Private Cloud:** In private clouds the computing resources are operated exclusively by one organization. It may be managed by the organization itself or a CSP. Private clouds are considered to be more secure than public clouds since their users are trusted individuals inside the organization. The other two deployment models, community clouds and hybrid clouds, fall between public and private clouds (Jansen & Grance, 2011).
- **Community Clouds:** Community clouds are similar to private clouds but the cloud infrastructure and computing resources are shared by several organizations that have the same mission, policy and security requirements (Mell & Grance, 2011). An example of a community cloud is the educational cloud used by universities and institutes around the world to provide education and research services.
- **Hybrid Clouds:** In hybrid clouds, the cloud infrastructure consists of a combination of two or more public, private or community cloud components. The cloud components are bound together by standardized technology and managed as a single unit, yet each cloud remains a unique entity

(Dimitrios & Dimitrios, 2012) and (Mell & Grance2011). Hybrid clouds allow organizations to optimize their resources, so the critical core activities can be run under the control of the private component of the hybrid cloud while other auxiliary tasks may be outsourced to the public component. Figure 1 below shows different cloud deployment.

3. BENEFITS OF CLOUD COMPUTING IN KSA

Since cloud computing is still young in KSA, the, most important aspect is the deployment procedures. If deployed properly and to the extent necessary, working with data in the cloud can vastly benefit all types of businesses in the Kingdom. What's important today is the development of standards in the area of security, interoperability and data protection and portability to ensure information is protected; clouds and the computing applications they support can work together; and content can be moved within and among different clouds without jeopardizing access to or integrity of the data. Some of the key values for the deployment of secured cloud computing are as follows:

- **Reduce spending on technology infrastructure -** Cloud computing is probably the most cost efficient method to use, maintain and upgrade. Traditional desktop software costs companies a lot in terms of finance. Adding up the licensing fees for multiple users can prove to be very expensive for the establishment concerned. The cloud, on the other hand, is available at much cheaper rates and hence, can significantly lower the company's IT expenses. Besides, there are many one-time-payment, pay-as-you-go and other scalable options available, which makes it very reasonable for the company in question.

Figure 1. Cloud computing mode

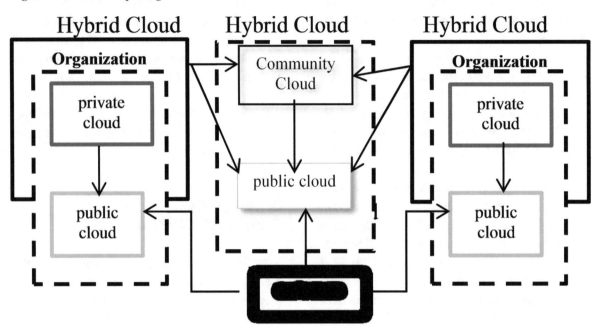

- **Almost Unlimited Storage** - Storing information in the cloud gives almost unlimited storage capacity. Hence, no more need to worry about running out of storage space or increasing current storage space availability.
- **Backup and Recovery -** Since all data is stored in the cloud, backing it up and restoring the same is relatively much easier than storing the same on a physical device. Furthermore, most cloud services are usually competent enough to handle recovery of information. Hence, this makes the entire process of backup and recovery much simpler than other traditional methods of data storage.
- **Automatic Software Integration -** In the cloud, software integration is usually something that occurs automatically. This means that there is no need to take additional efforts to customize and integrate applications as per preferences. This aspect usually takes care of itself. Not only that, cloud computing allows customizing options with great ease. Hence, one can handpick just those services and software applications that will best suit particular enterprise.
- **Globalize your workforce on the cheap** - Once registered in the cloud, one can access the information from anywhere, where there is an Internet connection. This convenient feature lets one move beyond time zone and geographic location issues.
- **Streamline processes.** Get more work done in less time with less people.
- **Reduce capital costs.** There's no need to spend big money on hardware, software or licensing fees.
- **Improve accessibility.** You have access anytime, anywhere, making your life so much easier.

- **Monitor projects more effectively.** Stay within budget and ahead of completion cycle times.
- **Less personnel training is needed.** It takes fewer people to do more work on a cloud, with a minimal learning curve on hardware and software issues.
- **Minimize licensing new software.** Stretch and grow without the need to buy expensive software licenses or programs.
- **Improve flexibility.** You can change direction without serious "people" or "financial" issues at stake.

4. SECURITY CHALLENGES IN CLOUD COMPUTING ENVIRONMENT

Cloud computing security sometimes referred to simply as "cloud security" is an evolving subdomain of computer security, network security, and, more broadly, information security. It refers to a broad set of policies, technologies, and controls deployed to protect data, applications, and the associated infrastructure of cloud computing. There are a number of security issues/concerns associated with cloud computing but these issues fall into two broad categories:

1. Security issues faced by cloud providers (organizations providing Software-, Platform-, or Infrastructure-as-a-Service via the cloud) and security issues faced by their customers (WebSphere, 2009).
2. Security issues faced by their customers. In most cases, the provider must ensure that their infrastructure is secure and that their clients' data and applications are protected while the customer must ensure that the provider has taken the proper security measures to protect their information (Thunderclouds, 2011).

The extensive use of virtualization in implementing cloud infrastructure brings unique security concerns for customers or tenants of a public cloud service. Virtualization alters the relationship between the OS and underlying hardware - be it computing, storage or even networking. This introduces an additional layer - virtualization - that itself must be properly configured, managed and secured. Specific concerns include the potential to compromise the virtualization software, or "hypervisor". While these concerns are largely theoretical, they do exist (Winkler, 2011). IT companies stores or centralizes their data on servers present on their premises. Slowly, organizations start sharing these servers with other business organizations in shared service centers (SSC). With passing years; they started outsourcing to third parties. With the advances in IT, Cloud Computing becomes the new paradigm for modern organizations.

In a nutshell, cloud computing is hugely beneficial for the enterprise and while still evolving, will be around for the long haul. It is therefore vital that those who embrace it adopt a long term security strategy or risk falling short. Although economically viable, cloud computing may turn into a very expensive venture for those who neglect to implement and maintain a solid security practice for their virtual environment. It is the time for researchers in this field to get together and think about how to address these issues. Different cloud models as described in figure 1, require different security solution:

4.1 Survey

A simple survey is conducted to assess the perception of secure cloud computing implementation in Saudi Arabia. A random sampling frame of IT related practitioners in Saudi Arabia were selected as participants to this survey. The result of the survey is shown in figure 3. The organizations involved in the survey are Education, bank, govern-

Figure 2. Cloud computing models and security requirements

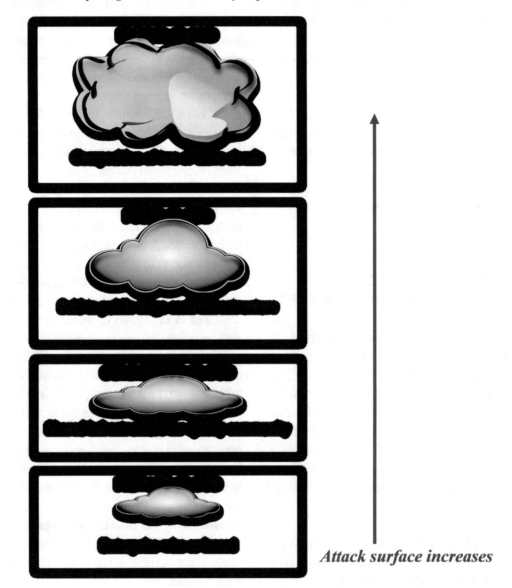

ment and wireless and mobile services providers. Five questions in the survey form are as follows:

Q1. My organization does not use cloud computing applications that are not thoroughly scrutinized for security risks and loopholes.

Q2. My organization always conducts assessments of cloud computing resources before deployment.

Q3. My organization is proactive in assessing information that is too sensitive be stored in the cloud.

Q4. My organization's security leaders are most responsible for securing our organization's safe use of cloud computing resources.

Q5. In my organization, cloud computing presents a more secure environment than on premises computing.

Figure 3. Perception about secure cloud computing in KSA

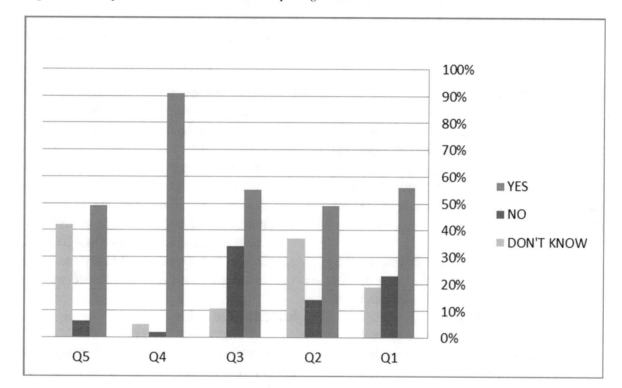

The survey reveals the following key important issues:

- *42% of the participant did not know whether cloud computing presents a more secure environment than on premises computing.*
- *34% of the participant did not agree that their organization is proactive in assessing information that is too sensitive be stored in the cloud.*
- *37% of respondents said they don't know if their organization always conducts assessments of cloud computing resources before deployment.*

While individual threats continue to pose risk, it is the combination of them, along with the speed at which attacks may be launched, that provide the greatest danger. This increasingly complex threat landscape is comprised of:

- *External threats* that come from the increasing sophistication of cybercrime, state-sponsored espionage, activism moving online, and attacks on systems used to manage critical infrastructure in the real world.
- *Regulatory threats* that come as regulators grapple to implement legislation calling for greater transparency about incidents and security preparedness, all the while increasing requirements for data privacy.
- *Internal threats* that come as technology continues to develop at "tweetneck" speed,

introducing new benefits but also raising the risk temperature as businesses adopt them without fully assessing the security implications.

External Threats

Since businesses can expect to see a continuing increase in the frequency, sophistication and effectiveness of attacks, they require the capability to respond more quickly and effectively. Consider these five actions to prepare for today's external threats:

1. Ensure standard security policies and procedures, such as an acceptable use policy for employee-owned computing devices, are in place across the business.
2. Develop your cyber-resilience by establishing a cybersecurity governance function gather and share attack intelligence, assess your own resilience and develop a comprehensive response plan.
3. Consider getting involved and shaping local cybersecurity initiatives, sharing incident data, and working with other organizations and industry bodies to build the foundations of resilience.
4. Monitor the threat landscape for further developments.
5. Increase business leadership involvement in all of the above this is a business issue, not something solely for information security.

Regulatory Threats

Regulators and legislators the world over are trying to figure out the rules and statutes for an ever-changing environment. Clearly, changes that are business-friendly and allow innovation will be welcome, as will those that harmonize regulations across jurisdictions. There is always the danger, however, that increased regulation will bring with it an increased cost of compliance, particularly for the unprepared. Businesses can take these steps to better prepare themselves to respond to these regulatory threats:

1. Adopt and practice a structured and systematic approach to assessing risk and meeting data breach and other transparency requirements.
2. Monitor legislative and regulatory developments on a continuing basis and amend your data protection framework and information management procedures to reflect any changes, including privacy-related controls.
3. Join and participate in industry and other associations to assess and influence policies.

Internal Threats

Whether it's one person's error that isn't caught in time, or an old server that wasn't upgraded because the plan was cut back, the result ends up the same. Whether it's accidental, deliberate or malicious, the incident's cost could easily be immensely out of proportion to the cost of prevention.

However, internal threats are more than internal mistakes or deliberate abuse; they also come from the introduction of new technology, underinvestment in security functions, and the pace of technological changes. A business can counter these internal threats by:

1. Adopting business-wide information security governance and integrate it with other risk and governance efforts within the organization.
2. Improve the integration of security across the business and elevate security reporting to a level with other governance, risk and compliance (GRC) areas.
3. Understand your organization's risk appetite and ensure the value of continuous security investment meets the business need and is

well spent; engage business leaders in this so they understand the implications of any zero-budget planning.

4. Take ownership of coordinating the contracting and provisioning of business relationships with outsourcers, offshorers and supply chain and cloud providers. How secure are your suppliers?

5. Monitor new business initiatives and get information security involved early, as an enabler.

5. SECURITY REQUIREMENTS

Generally, the security requirements for cloud computing can be roughly divided into two main categories; *network security requirements* and *user security requirements*.

5.1 Network Security Requirements

Cloud computing aims to provide users with computer-supported capabilities anywhere and anytime. In order to achieve this, an increasing number of intelligent devices/nodes are required, whether portable or embedded in the user's environment. In addition, these devices need to connect and communicate with each other as well as with the network service provider. In any system where security matters the correct identification and verification of users is paramount. Authentication is equally important when allowing a user access to a physically secure space as it is when granting access to a secure file space. Its purpose is to ensure that each entity is correctly matched to its corresponding privileges. If someone is not accurately identified then their identification is left unverified. Unauthorized access to data and resources is a real possibility. Major security requirements, such as authorization, auditing and non-repudiation all hinge on the accurate identification and verification of users in such networking environment.

In cloud computing environment, the risk of someone fraudulently performing input using authorized user's login details is greater and, for reasons such as this, access to these workspaces and the computers within them may require more physical and information security measures than the normal wired network environment. Moreover, one of the main difficulties in designing a secure cloud computing environment is in ensuring that the functionality of the environment is not over constrained by security. In general, the security requirement can be categorized into two: the physical security of the environment and the security of information within this environment.

The network security requirement for cloud computing environment should include the following points:

1. Prevent threats from traditional networks such as: viruses, the system attacks, invasion, etc.;

2. To ensure data integrity and confidentiality when transmission in different networks (cellular networks, wireless or cable networks);

3. Establish invasion detection with context-aware function, preventing system in a dynamic environment.

The following are some key issues related to network security as highlighted by Cloud Security Alliance (CSA, 2010):

- **Insecure Application Programming Interfaces** - Cloud Computing providers expose a set of software interfaces or APIs that customers use to manage and interact with cloud services. Provisioning, management, orchestration, and monitoring are all performed using these interfaces. The security and availability of general cloud services is dependent upon the security of these basic APIs. From authentication and access control to encryption and activity monitoring, these interfaces must be designed to protect against both accidental and malicious attempts to circumvent policy. Furthermore, organizations and third parties often build upon these interfaces to offer value-added services to their customers. This introduces the complexity of the new layered API; it also increases risk, as organizations may be required to relinquish their credentials to third parties in order to enable their agency.

- **Shared Technology Vulnerabilities** - IaaS vendors deliver their services in a scalable way by sharing infrastructure. Often, the underlying components that make up this infrastructure (*e.g.,* CPU caches, GPUs, etc.) were not designed to offer strong isolation properties for a multi-tenant architecture. To address this gap, a virtualization hypervisor mediates access between guest operating systems and the physical compute resources. Still, even hypervisors have exhibited flaws that have enabled guest operating systems to gain inappropriate levels of control or influence on the underlying platform. A defense in depth strategy is recommended, and should include compute, storage, and network security enforcement and monitoring. Strong compartmentalization should be employed to ensure that individual customers do not impact the operations of other tenants running on the same cloud provider. Customers should not have access to any other tenant's actual or residual data, network traffic, etc.

5.2 User Security Requirements

In cloud computing, some security requirements include the following: Entity Authentication. Intruders personate legitimate users to get information; Authorization of User. Invaders steal legitimate user's authorization to carry out illegal activities; Confidentiality. Information of sensors

transmission might be illegally intercepted; Data Integrity. Invaders intercepted data may modify damage data integrity. In general, the following keys are important:

- **Privacy Issues** - User privacy is one of the big challenges for deploying cloud computing services on a significant scale. Further, privacy in any computing environment is considered to be one of the fundamental security concerns that are explicitly identified by a series of laws (see http://www.techlawjournal.com/cong107/Privacy). In environments with significant concentration of "invisible" computing devices gathering and collecting the identities, locations and transaction information of users, users should rightly be concerned with their privacy. Considerable research has been undertaken to develop user's privacy. Examples include identity management technologies, personal assistants or agents administering the privacy preferences of their owners, or the linking of data generated to the location or proximity in order to avoid their uncontrolled spread and exploitation (Johann, 2005). Similar user privacy issues were discussed in (Al-Muhtadi et al., 2002) which include location privacy, connection anonymity and confidentiality. Other important privacy issues that need to be addressed in described in (Kui &Wenjing, 2007).

- **Malicious Insiders** - The threat of a malicious insider is well-known to most organizations. This threat is amplified for consumers of cloud services by the convergence of IT services and customers under a single management domain, combined with a general lack of transparency into provider process and procedure. For example, a provider may not reveal how it grants employees access to physical and virtual assets, how it monitors these employees, or how it analyzes and reports on policy compliance. To complicate matters, there is often little or no visibility into the hiring standards and practices for cloud employees. This kind of situation clearly creates an attractive opportunity for an adversary ranging from the hobbyist hacker, to organized crime, to corporate espionage, or even nation-state sponsored intrusion. The level of access granted could enable such an adversary to harvest confidential data or gain complete control over the cloud services with little or no risk of detection.

- **User's Authentication Service** - Authentication is the security service that enables communication partners to verify the identity of their peer entities or a process whereby one party is assured of the identity of the second party involved in a protocol, and that the second party actually participated (is active at, or immediately prior to, the time the evidence is acquired). Entity authentication plays an important role in ensuring data secrecy and authenticity because of its goals of allowing any pair of communicating parties to mutually verify each other's identity.

- **Data Loss/Leakage -** There are many ways to compromise data. Deletion or alteration of records without a backup of the original content is an obvious example. Unlinking a record from a larger context may render it unrecoverable, as can storage on unreliable media. Loss of an encoding key may result in effective destruction. Finally, unauthorized parties must be prevented from gaining access to sensitive data. The threat of data compromise increases in the cloud, due to the number of and interactions between risks and challenges which are ei-

ther unique to cloud, or more dangerous because of the architectural or operational characteristics of the cloud environment.

- **Abuse and Nefarious Use of Cloud Computing** – IaaS providers offer their customers the illusion of unlimited compute, network, and storage capacity. — often coupled with a 'frictionless' registration process where anyone with a valid credit card can register and immediately begin using cloud services. Some providers even offer free limited trial periods. By abusing the relative anonymity behind these registration and usage models, spammers, malicious code authors, and other criminals have been able to conduct their activities with relative impunity. PaaS providers have traditionally suffered most from this kind of attacks; however, recent evidence shows that hackers have begun to target IaaS vendors as well. Future areas of concern include password and key cracking, DDOS, launching dynamic attack points, hosting malicious data, botnet command and control, building rainbow tables, and CAPTCHA solving farms.

- **Account, Service & Traffic Hijacking** - Account or service hijacking is not new. Attack methods such as phishing, fraud, and exploitation of software vulnerabilities still achieve results. Credentials and passwords are often reused, which amplifies the impact of such attacks. Cloud solutions add a new threat to the landscape. If an attacker gains access to your credentials, they can eavesdrop on your activities and transactions, manipulate data, return falsified information, and redirect your clients to illegitimate sites. Your account or service instances may become a new base for the attacker. From here, they may leverage the power of your reputation to launch subsequent attacks.

5.3 Security Measures and Practices

This section highlights some countermeasure against the some of the major threats discussed in this chapter.

Protection against Hackers and Other Network Breaches

The best practices for protecting against hackers, viruses, spyware and other network threats are essentially the same best practices used to defend the perimeter of large offices. The difference is that many types of security measures must be applied on each individual mobile and remote device, instead of once at the gateway to the network. The more commonly used defenses include:

- Security patch management products.
- Personal firewalls
- Anti-virus and anti-spyware tools

Other technologies that are emerging as supplements to these defenses include local intrusion protection and "day-zero protection."

Protection against Theft and Loss of Data

Data encryption is becoming an increasingly critical technology for protecting financial institutions, government agencies, and other similar industries where confidential data is routinely stored on laptops. Data encryption products encode data stored to disk and other storage media, so that even if a laptop or storage device is lost or stolen, the contents cannot be deciphered.

Protecting Access to the Network

If mobile systems are compromised, hackers have an opportunity to use those systems to penetrate the central corporate network. For this reason, compliance checking and Network Access Control (NAC) are seen as essential technologies to protect enterprise information assets. These technologies monitor mobile systems to see if they remain in compliance with corporate policies, and block access to the corporate network if they do not. Strong authentication is another best practice to help ensure safe mobile computing. Mobile employees must log onto the network using a security token, smart card or other authentication device in addition to a user ID and password. This makes it harder for an outsider to gain access merely by discovering a password or stealing a laptop.

Privacy Problem

To address the privacy problems in cloud computing, it is vital to implement a strong communication protocol. Example of such protocol was proposed in (Al-Muhtadi, et. al., 2002) known as the Mist for pervasive computing. Mist facilitates the separation of location from identity. This allows authorized entities to access services while protecting their location privacy. A brief overview of how Mist works is given below. Mist consists of a privacy- preserving hierarchy of *Mist Routers* that form an overlay network. The system facilitates private communication by routing packets using a *hop-by-hop, handle-based routing* protocol. The system uses public key cryptography in the initial setup of these handles. The technique makes communication infeasible to trace by eavesdroppers and untrusted third parties. A handle is an identifier that is unique per Mist Router. Every incoming packet has an "incoming handle" that is used by the Mist Router to identify the next hop to which to forward the packet. The incoming handle is replaced by an outgoing handle before the packet is transmitted to the next hop. This hop-by-hop routing protocol allows a Mist Router to forward the packet to the next hop, while hiding the original source and final destination. In effect, this process creates "virtual circuits" over which data can flow securely and privately.

Security Policies

It is important in cloud computing to have a flexible and convenient method for defining and managing security policies in a dynamic and flexible fashion. Policy Management tools provide administrators the ability to specify, implement, and enforce rules to exercise greater control over the behavior of entities in their systems. Currently, most network policies are implemented by systems administrators using tools based on scripting applications (Mundy et. al., 1999) that iterate through lists of low-level interfaces and change values of entity-specific system variables. The policy management software maintains an exhaustive database of corresponding device and resource interfaces. With the proliferation of heterogeneous device-specific and vendor-specific interfaces, these tools may need to be updated frequently to accommodate new hardware or software, and the system typically becomes difficult to manage.

Since most policy management tools deal with these low-level interfaces, administrators may not have a clear picture of the ramifications of their policy management actions. Dependencies among objects can lead to unexpected side effects and undesirable behavior (Loscocco & Smalley, 2001). Further, the disclosure of security policies may be a breach of security. For example, knowing whether the system is on the lookout for an intruder could actually be a secret. Thus, unauthorized personnel should not be able to know what the security policy might become under a certain circumstance.

Governments and other non-profit organization worldwide have been recognizing the need for regulations and compliance laws/acts. Examples of such act and organizations are the Sarbanes-Oxyley Act (SOX), Health Insurance Portability and Accountability Act (HIPAA), Gramm-Leach-Bliley Act (GLBA), European Union Detectives etc.

5.4 General Recommendations

This section provides some recommended security measures that agencies can discuss both internally and with vendors that are transparent about their security measures. Organizations should decide which issues are most relevant based on the agency's intended use of cloud computing.

- **Required cloud deployment model.** Organization need to decide the type of cloud deployment model required; are they considering using a potentially less secure public cloud, a potentially more secure hybrid cloud or community cloud, or a potentially most secure private cloud.
- **Sensitivity of stored data.** Data to be stored or processed in the cloud should be classified as either sensitive, private, or data that is publicly available to all users For example, the sensitivity may increase if storing a significant amount of data, or storing a variety of data that if compromised would facilitate identity theft.
- **The type of encryption algorithms needed.** The ability to encrypt data while it is being processed by the vendor's computers is still an emerging technology and is an area of current research by industry and academia. Is the encryption deemed strong enough to protect my data for the duration of time that my data is sensitive? For example, cloud computing processing power has already been used to significantly re-

duce the time and cost of using brute force techniques to crack and recover relatively weak passwords either stored as SHA1 hashes or used as Wi-Fi Protected Access (WPA) pre-shared keys.

- **Vendor's remote monitoring and management.** What role does the vendor plays; does the vendor monitor, administer or manage the computers that store or process my data? If yes, is this performed remotely from foreign countries or not? Can the vendor provide patch compliance reports and other details about the security of workstations used to perform this work, and what controls prevent the vendor's employees from using untrustworthy personally owned laptops?

- **Personal monitoring and management.** The ability for the client to use existing tools for integrity checking, compliance checking, security monitoring and network management, to obtain visibility of all systems regardless of whether these systems are located locally or in the cloud.

- **Gateway technologies.** The use of appropriate technologies by the vendor to create a secure gateway environment. Examples include firewalls, traffic flow filters, content filters, antivirus software and data diodes where appropriate.

- **User authentication.** The type of identity and access management systems used. Examples include two factor authentication, synchronisation with the agency's Active Directory and other federated single sign-on.

- **Tamper proof.** To ensure that network cabling are professionally installed to internationally acceptable standards, to help avoid the vendor's employees from accidentally connecting cables to the wrong computers, and to help readily highlight any deliberate attempts by the vendor's employees to tamper with the cabling.

- **Training of employees.** Employees should possess the required qualifications, certifications and regular information security awareness training to know how to use the systems in a secure manner and to identify potential security incidents.

6. CONCLUSION

This chapter discusses some of the major security problems associated with cloud computing. It discusses the advantages companies can derive from cloud computing, but emphasis that any new technology should not be endorsed or adopted without adequate evaluation. Information security and data privacy are at greater risk anytime these assets are stored with a third-party. Policies must be developed, used, and enforced to ensure all cloud computing applications meet an organization's standard for security and are in keeping with both departmental and corporate strategic goals.

REFERENCES

Ahmed, Y., & Manal, A. (2011). Security Issues in Cloud Computing. GSTF International Journal on Computing, 1(3).

Al-Muhtadi, J., Campbell, R., Kapadia, A., Mickunas, D., & Yi, S. (2002). Routing Through the Mist: Privacy Preserving Communication in Ubiquitous Computing Environments. Proceedings of *International Conference of Distributed Computing Systems (ICDCS 2002)*, Vienna, Austria. doi:10.1109/ICDCS.2002.1022244

Armbrust, M. A., Fox, R., Griffith, A., Joseph, R., Katz, A., & Konwinski, G. et al. (2009). *Above the Clouds: A Berkeley View of Cloud Computing*. UC Berkeley Reliable Adaptive Distributed Systems Laboratory.

CSA. (2010). Cloud Security Alliance. Retrieved from http://www.cloudsecurityalliance.org/top-threats

Dimitrios, Z., & Dimitrios, L. (2012). Addressing cloud computing security issues. *Future Generation Computer Systems*, *28*(3), 583–592. doi:10.1016/j.future.2010.12.006

Gellman, R. (2009). Privacy in the Clouds: Risks to Privacy and Confidentiality. Proceedings of *Cloud Computing, World Privacy Forum*, USA.

Cloud Computing - Building a Framework for Successful Transition. (2009). *GTSI Group*. [White Paper].

Hayes, B. (2008). Cloud computing. *Communications of the ACM*, *51*(7), 9–11. doi:10.1145/1364782.1364786

Jansen, W., & Grance, T. (2011). Guidelines on Security and Privacy in Public Cloud Computing. *NIST Draft Special Publication* 800-144. Retrieved from http://csrc.nist.gov/publications/drafts/800-144/Draft-SP-800-144_cloud-computing.pdf

Johann, C. (2005). Privacy in Pervasive Computing Environments – A Contradiction in Terms? *IEEE Technology and Society Magazine*, 24–33.

Kui, R. (2007). Privacy-enhanced, Attack-resilient Access Control in Pervasive Computing Environments with Optional Context Authentication Capability. *Mobile Networks and Applications*, *12*(1), 79–92. doi:10.1007/s11036-006-0008-7

Loscocco, P., & Smalley, S. (2001). Integrating Flexible Support for Security Policies into the Linux Operating System. *Proceedings of the FREENIX Track of the 2001 USENIX*.

Mell, P., & Grance, T. (2011). The NIST Definition of Cloud Computing. NIST Special Publication 800-145. Retrieved from http://csrc.nist.gov/publications/nistpubs/800-145/SP800-145.pdf

Mundy, R., Partain, D., & Stewart, B. (1999, April). Introduction to SNMPv3. *RFC 2570*.

Ramgovind. S., Eloff, M.M., & Smith, E. (2010, August 2–4). The Management of Security in Cloud Computing. Proceedings of *Information Security for South Africa* (ISSA), Sandton, Johannesburg.

Ruiter, J., & Warnier, M. (2011). Privacy regulations for cloud computing, compliance and implementation in theory and practice. In S. Gutwirth, Y. Poullet, P. de Hert, & R. Leenes (Eds.), *Computers, Privacy and Data Protection: an Element of Choice* (pp. 293–314). Springer. doi:10.1007/978-94-007-0641-5_17

Subashini, S., & Kavitha, V. (2011). A survey on security issues in service delivery models of cloud computing. *Journal of Network and Computer Applications*, *34*(1), 1–11. doi:10.1016/j.jnca.2010.07.006

Sultan, N. (2010). Cloud computing for education: A new dawn? *International Journal of Information Management*, *30*(2), 109–116. doi:10.1016/j.ijinfomgt.2009.09.004

Toby, V., Anthony, V., & Robert, E. (2009). Cloud Computing, A Practical Approach.

Extending SOA into the Private Cloud with WebSphere CloudBurst Appliance and WebSphere Application Server HyperVisor Edition. (2009). *WebSphere*. Retrieved from http://www.websphereusergroup.org/cms/websphere_virtual_enterprise/119583/monthly_focus:_websphere_in_the_clouds

Wik, P. (2011). Thunderclouds – Managing SOA-Cloud Risk. *Service Technology Magazine*. 2011-10.

Winkler, V. (2011). *Securing the Cloud: Cloud Computer Security Techniques and Tactics.* Elsevier.

KEY TERMS AND DEFINITIONS

Access Control: Set of security measures to determine who should have access to the system or part of the system. It is a counter measure against unauthorized access.

Authentication: The process of determining whether someone or something is, in fact, who or what it is declared to be before accessing or using a computer system.

Computer Fraud: Any act using computer or network resources and services to defraud people, companies, or government agencies of money, revenue, or Internet access.

Cybersecurity: The body of technologies, processes and practices designed to protect networks, computers, programs and data from attack, damage or unauthorized access.

Malicious Insider: This is an employee, contractor or sub-contractor with access to whole or part of the computer systems who may be disgruntled or feel obligated to steal intellectual property.

Network Security: Security mechanism dealing with protection of the networking system as a whole and sustain its capability to provide connectivity between the communicating entities.

Traffic Hijacking: Intentional redirection of internet traffic. Attackers take advantage of traffic routing announcements between networks using Border Gateway Protocol being trust-based.

301

Chapter 14
Big Data Security:
Challenges, Recommendations and Solutions

Fatima-Zahra Benjelloun
Ibn Tofail University, Morocco

Ayoub Ait Lahcen
Ibn Tofail University, Morocco

ABSTRACT

The value of Big Data is now being recognized by many industries and governments. The efficient mining of Big Data enables to improve the competitive advantage of companies and to add value for many social and economic sectors. In fact, important projects with huge investments were launched by several governments to extract the maximum benefit from Big Data. The private sector has also deployed important efforts to maximize profits and optimize resources. However, Big Data sharing brings new information security and privacy issues. Traditional technologies and methods are no longer appropriate and lack of performance when applied in Big Data context. This chapter presents Big Data security challenges and a state of the art in methods, mechanisms and solutions used to protect data-intensive information systems.

INTRODUCTION

The value of Big Data is now being recognized by many industries and governments. In fact, the efficient mining of Big Data enables to improve the competitive advantage and to add value for many sectors (economic, social, medical, scientific research and so on).

Big Data is mainly defined by its *3Vs* fundamental characteristics. The *3Vs* include *Velocity*

(data are growing and changing in a rapid way), *Variety* (data come in different and multiple formats) and *Volume* (huge amount of data is generated every second) (Wu, Zhu, Wu, & Ding, 2014). According to (Berman, 2013) these three characteristics must coexist to confirm that a source is a Big Data source. If one of these three *Vs* does not apply, we cannot discuss about Big Data.

(Berman, 2013) and (Katal, Wazid, & Goudar, 2013) indicate that more *Vs* and other character-

DOI: 10.4018/978-1-4666-8387-7.ch014

istics have been added by some Big Data actors to better define it: *Vision* (the defined purpose of Big Data mining), *Verification* (processed data comply to some specifications), *Validation* (the purpose is fulfilled), *Value* (pertinent information can be extracted for the benefit of many sectors), *Complexity* (it is difficult to organize and analyse Big data because of evolving data relationships) and *Immutability* (collected and stored Big Data can be permanent if well managed).

Beside this, some argue when defining Big Data, that any huge amount of digital data sets that we can no longer collect and process adequately, through the existing infrastructures and technologies, are by nature Big Data.

In this chapter, we are interested in security challenges faced in Big Data context. We present also a state of the art in several methods, mechanisms and solutions used to protect information systems that handle large data sets.

Big Data security has many common points with the security of traditional information systems (where data are structured). However, Big Data security requires more powerful tools, appropriate methods and advanced technologies for rapid data analysis. It requires also a new security management model that handles in parallel internal data (data produced by internal systems and processes within an organization) and external data (e.g., data collected from other companies or external web sites). Regarding those points, many questions can be raised: i) How to manage and process securely large, unstructured and heterogeneous types of data sets? ii) How to integrate security mechanisms into distributed platforms while ensuring a good performance level (e.g., efficient storage, rapid processing and real-time analysis)? iii) How to analyse massive data streams without compromising data confidentiality and privacy?

This chapter presents first these challenges in detail. Then, it discusses various solutions and recommendations proposed to protect data-intensive information systems.

SECURITY CHALLENGES IN BIG DATA CONTEXT

As mentioned by (Kim, Kim, & Chung, 2013), security in Big Data context includes three main aspects: information security, security monitoring and data security. For (Lu et al., 2013), managing security in a distributed environment means to ensure Big Data management, system integrity and cyberspace security.

Generally, Big Data security aims to ensure a real-time monitoring to detect vulnerabilities, security threats and abnormal behaviours; a granular role-based access control; a robust protection of confidential information and a generation of security performance indicators. It supports rapid decision-making in a security incident case. The following sections identify and explain a number of challenges to achieve these goals.

Big Data Nature

Because of Big Data velocity and huge volumes, it is difficult to protect all data. Indeed, adding security layers may slow system performances and affect dynamic analysis. Thus, access control and data protection are two "BIG" security problems (Kim et al., 2013). Furthermore, it is difficult to handle data classification and management of large digital disparate sources. Even though that the cost by GB has diminished, Big Data security requires important investments. In addition to all that, Big Data is most of the time stored and transferred across multiple Clouds and distributed worldwide systems. Sharing data over many networks increase security risks.

The Need to Share Information

In globalization context, business models have to face holistic competition across the world. Thus, enterprises need to build a sustainable advantage through collaboration with many entities, data monetization, and appropriate dynamic data sharing.

For data sharing, digital ecosystems are based on multiple heterogeneous platforms. Such ecosystems aim to ensure real time data access for many partners, clients, providers and employees. They rely on multiple connections with different levels of securities. Data sharing associated to advanced analytics techniques brings multiple security threats such us: discovering confidential information (e.g., process and method of productions) or illegal access to networks' traffics. In fact, by establishing relations between extracted data from different sources, it is possible to identify individuals in spite of data anonymization (e.g., by using correlation attacks, arbitrary identification, intended identification attacks, etc.).

For instance, in health sector, massive amounts of medical data are shared between hospitals and pharmaceutical laboratories for research and analysis purposes. Such sharing may affect patient's privacy even if all the medical records are anonymized, by finding for instance correlations between medical records and mutual health insurances (Shin, Sahama, & Gajanayake, 2013).

Multiple Security Requirements

In Big Data context, one challenge is to handle information security while managing massive and rapid data streams. Thus, security tools should be flexible and easily scalable to simplify the integration of future technological evolutions and to handle applications requirements' changes.

There is a need to find a balance between multiple security requirements, privacy obligations, system performance and rapid dynamic analysis on divers large data sets (data in motion or static, private and public, local or shared, etc.).

Inadequate Traditional Solutions

Traditional Security techniques, such as some types of data encryption, slow the performance and are time-consuming in Big Data context. Furthermore, they are not efficient. Indeed, just small data partitions are processed for security purposes. So most of the time, security's attacks are detected after the spread of the damage (Lu et al., 2013). Big Data platforms imply the management of various applications and multiple parallel computations. Therefore, the performance is a key element for data sharing and real-time analysis in such environments.

New Security Tools Lack of Maturity

The combination of multiple technologies may bring hidden risks that are most of the time not evaluated or under-estimated. In addition, new security tools lack maturity. So, Big Data platforms may incorporate new security risk and vulnerabilities that are not fully assessed.

At the same time, data value is concentrated on various clusters and data centres. Those rich data mines are very attractive for commerce, governments and industrials. They constitute a target of several attacks and penetrations. Furthermore, most of security risks come from employees, partners and end-point users (more than a third-part). Hence, it is important to deploy advanced security mechanisms to protect Big Data clusters

(Ring, 2013; Jensen, 2013). Regarding this point, data owners have the responsibilities to set clear security clauses and policies to be respected by outsources.

Data Anonymization

To ensure data privacy and security, data anonymization should be achieved without affecting system performance (e.g., real-time analysis) or data quality. However, traditional anonymization techniques are based on several iterations and time consuming computations. Several iterations may affects data consistency and slow down system performance specially when handling huge heterogeneous data sets. In addition, it is difficult to process and analyse anonymized Big Data (they need costly computations).

Compatibility with Big Data Technologies

Some security techniques are incompatible with commonly used Big Data technologies like MapRecude paradigm. To ensure security and privacy of Big Data, it is not enough just to choose powerful technologies and security mechanisms. It is also mandatory to verify their compatibility with the organization Big Data requirements and existing infrastructure components (Zhao et al., 2014).

Information Reliability and Quality

The reliability of data analysis results depends on data quality and integrity (Alvaro, Pratyusa, & Sreeranga, 2013). Therefore, it is important to verify Big Data sources authenticity and integrity before analysing data. Since the huge volumes of data sets are generated every second, it is difficult to assess the authenticity and integrity of all various data sources.

In addition, to extract reliable and complete information from Big Data sources, the analysts have to deal with incomplete and heterogeneous data streams coming from different sources in different formats. They have to filter data (e.g., eliminating noises, errors, spams, and so on). They have also to organize and contextualize data (e.g., adding geo-location data) before performing any analysis.

Compliance to Security Laws Regulations and Policies

Private organizations and government agencies have to respect many security laws and industrial standards that aim to enhance the management of digital data security and to protect confidentiality (e.g., delete personal data if no more used, data protection through its life cycle, transactions archiving for legal purposes, citizens' right to access and modify their data). However, some ICTs may involve entities across many countries. So enterprises have to deal with multiple laws and regulations (Tankard, 2012).

Furthermore, Big Data analytics may be in conflict with some privacy principles. For example, analysts can correlate many different data sets from different entities to reveal personal or sensible data even with anonymization techniques. Consequently, such analysis may enable to identify individuals or to discover confidential information (Alvaro et al., 2013).

Need of Big Data Experts

In the era of Big Data, data analysis is a key factor to prevent and detect security incidents. However, several surveys confirm that a number of enterprises are not aware of the importance to recruit data scientists for advanced security analysis. In fact, to ensure Big Data security, organizations should rely on a multi-disciplinary team with data scientists, mathematicians and security best practices programmers (Constantine, 2014).

Big Data Security on Social Networks

Huge amount of photos, videos, user's comments and clicks are generated from social networks (SNs). They are usually the first source of information for different entities (Sykora, Jackson, O'Brien, & Elayan, 2013).

Big Data on SNs constitute a valuable mine for governments to better manage national security risks. Indeed, some governments analyse SNs Big Data in order to supervise public opinions (e.g., voting intentions, emotions, feelings about a project or an event). They can prevent terrorist and security attacks and assess citizens' satisfaction regarding public services.

In addition, dynamic analysis of SNs enables crisis committees to optimize and ensure a rapid crisis management like in disasters cases. The goal is to detect rapidly abnormal patterns and to ensure a real-time monitoring of alarming events.

BIG DATA SECURITY SOLUTIONS

Nowadays, with the spread of social networks, distributed systems, multiple connections, mobile devices, the security of a Big Data information system become the responsibility of all actors (e.g., managers, security chiefs, auditors, end-users and customers). In fact, most of security threats come from inside users and employees. Thus, it is convenient to raise the security awareness of all parties and to promote security best practices of all the connected entities of the digital ecosystem. It is not sufficient just to integrate security technologies. The collaboration of all actors is required to eliminate the weak link of the system chain and to ensure compliance to security laws and policies.

There exist various security models, mechanisms and solutions for Big Data. However, most of them are not well known or mature. Many research projects are currently struggling to enhance their performances (Mahmood & Afzal, 2013). In the following sections, we present some important ones.

Security Foundations for Big Data Projects

For any Big Data project, it is important to consider the strategic priorities related to security and to establish clear organizational guidelines for choosing associated technologies (in term of reliability, performance, maturity, scalability, overall cost including maintenance cost). It is also important to consider the constraints related to the integration, the existing infrastructure, the available and planned budget for Big Data security management.

The goal is to ensure agility across all the security systems, solutions, processes and procedures. Organizational agility is important to enable organizations to face rapid changes in terms of new security's requirements: legal changes, new partners and customers, environment and market's changes, technological updates and innovations, new security risks and so on.

After the establishment of security values, strategies and management models, it is important to deduce and establish clear security policies, guidelines, user agreements as well as security contractual clauses to respect when outsourcing Big Data services. All security strategies and policies should take in consideration many factors: First of all, it is essential to establish Big Data classification and management principles guided by a long term vision. In fact, data classification is mandatory to determine sensitive data and valuable information to protect, to define data owners with their security policies, requirements and responsibilities. Then, the security strategy should be based on the assessment of security risks related to the different Big Data management process (e.g., data generation, storage, transfer, exchange, access, deletion, modification and so on). Finally, a security level has to be determined for each data category according to the organizational strategy. In fact, (Bodei, Degano, Ferrari, Galletta, & Mezzetti, 2012) recommends identifying data attributes to protect and to encrypt at the beginning of the system conception phase.

Furthermore, the organization has to keep track of legal changes to update the organizational policies and procedures. To ensure continuous legal compliance, it is important to involve the legal department in the development of Big Data projects and in the upgrading of all the security policies, including calendar duration of personal information, access permission, data transfer abroad, data access and exchange between many stakeholders with different security requirements, integration of contractual security requirements, data conservation or destruction.

Risk Analysis Related to Multiple Technologies

It is important to study and assess security risks related to the mix of multiple technologies inside a Big Data platform. It is not sufficient to evaluate security risks related to each used technology. In fact, the integration of disparate technologies for multiple purposes may bring hidden risks and unknown security threats.

In addition, with the increasing spread of the Cloud and the BYOD (Bring Your Own Device), it important to consider security threats related to the distributed environments and the use of non-normalized mobile and personal devices for professional purposes. For this point, (Ring, 2013) recommends to protect the multi-disparate endpoints with an extra security layer. Furthermore, the mobile devices should be normalized to fulfil organizational and industrial security standards.

Choosing Adequate Security Solutions

To enhance Big Data security, organizations rely on advanced dynamic security analysis. The goal is to extract and analyse in real-time or nearly real-time security events and related users actions in order to enhance online and transactional security and to prevent fraudulent attacks.

Such dynamic analysis on the generated Big Data helps to detect timely security incidents, to identify abnormal customers' behaviours, to monitor security threats, to discover known and new cyber-attack patterns and so on. Hence, dynamic analysis on Big Data enables an improved prevention and rapid reactivity to take good decisions for security. In parallel, the analysis of the generated statics from applications and programs allows to produce security performance indicators and to monitor and secure programs' behaviours.

(Kim et al., 2013) recommends protecting the data values instead of the data themselves. In fact, it is too difficult, and nearly impossible to protect huge data sets. Furthermore, Big Data security analysis techniques are based on the attributes' information. Thus, the data owners or operators have the responsibility to define, select and protect only important attributes that they consider valuable for their use cases. To protect such important data attributes in Big Data context, (Kim et al., 2013) presents the following:

- Evaluate the importance of the attributes, compare and evaluate the correlations between them.
- Filter and define the valuable attributes to protect.
- Choose security mechanisms to protect the relevant attributes according to the data owner or the organization policies.

Several analytical solutions are available to secure Big Data such as Accenture, HP, IBM, CISCO, Unisys, EADS security solutions. They brings different level of performance and several benefits like: enable Agile decision-making and rapid reaction through real-time surveillance and monitoring; detect dynamic attacks with enhanced reliability (low false-positive rate) thanks to the analysis of active and passive security information; provide Full visibility of the network status and applications' security problems.

(Mahmood & Afzal, 2013) identifies the deployment phases of Big Data Analytics solutions. First of all, it recommends identifying strategic priorities and Big Data security analysis goals. Then, the organizational priorities should provide guideline to develop a more detailed strategy for Big Data analysis platform's deployment. The purpose is to optimize the selection of security solutions according to the strategic goals, the triple constraints (overall cost, quality, duration of the implementation), the added value and the available features (performance, reliability, scalability and so on). Regarding organizational strategy, it recommends to adopt a centralized Big Data management for better security outcomes.

Before Big Data analysis, one pre-requisite is to consider the integrity and authenticity of data sources. Indeed, Big Data sources may contain errors, noises, incomplete data, or data without context information. Consequently, it is essential to filter and prepare data and to add context data before applying analysis techniques.

Anonymization of Confidential or Personal Data

Data anonymization is a recognized technique used to protect data privacy across the Cloud and the distributed systems. Several models and solutions are used to implement this technique such as: Sub-tree data anonymization, t-closeness, m-invariance, k-anonymity and l-diversity.

Sub-tree techniques are based on two methods: Top-Down Specialization (TDS) and Bottom-Up Generalization (BUG). However, those methods are not scalable. There is a lack of performance when such methods are used for certain anonymization parameters. They cannot scale when applied to anonymize Big Data on distributed systems.

In order to improve the anonymization of valuable information extracted from large data sets, (Zhang et al., 2014) suggests a hybrid approach that combines both anonymization techniques TDS and BUG. This approach selects and applies automatically one of the two techniques that are suitable for the use case parameters. Thus, this hybrid approach provides efficiency, performance and scalability required to anonymize huge databases. It is supported by newly adapted programs to handle MapReduce paradigm. It enables to reduce computation time in the distributed systems or the Cloud.

Big Data processing and analysis are based most of the time on much iteration to have reliable and precise results, which may slow computations and the performance of security solutions. Regarding this, (Zhang et al., 2014) proposes a method based on one-iteration for operations generalization. The goal is to enhance parallelism capacities, the performance and the scalability of anonymization techniques.

Currently, many projects are working to develop new techniques and to improve existing ones to protect privacy. As an example, some projects are based on privacy preservation aware analysis and scheduling techniques of large data set.

Data Cryptography

Data Encryption is a common solution used to ensure data and Big Data confidentiality. Many researches were conducted to improve the performance and the reliability of traditional techniques or to create new ways for Big Data encryption techniques.

Unlike some traditional techniques for encryption, Homomorphic Cryptography enables computation even on encrypted data. Consequently, this technique ensures information confidentiality while allowing extracting useful insight through some possible analysis and computations on the encrypted data.

Regarding this solution, (Chen & Huang, 2013) proposes an adapted platform to handle MapReduce computations in the case of Homomorphic Cryptography. To ensure performance of the cryptographic solutions in distributed environments, (Liu et al., 2013) suggests a new approach for key exchange called CBHKE (Cloud Background Hierarchical Key Exchange). It is a secured solution that is more rapid than its predecessor techniques (IKE and CCBKE). It is based on an iterative strategy to an Authenticate Key Exchange (AKE) through two phases (layer by layer). However, new approaches with enhanced performance are still needed to improve the encryption of large data sets on distributed systems.

Centralized Security Management

(Kasim, Hung, & Li, 2012) recommend storing data on the Cloud rather than mobile devices. The goal is to take advantage of the normalized and standard compliance infrastructure and centralized security mechanisms of the Cloud. Indeed, the Cloud platforms are regularly updated and continuously monitored for an enhanced security.

However, "Zero risk" is hard to achieve. In fact, data security relies on the hand of the Cloud outsourcers and operators. In addition, the Cloud is very attractive for attackers as it is a centralized mine of valuable data. Data owners and managers should be aware of the security risks and define clear data access policies. They have to ensure that the required security level is ensured when outsourcing Big Data management, storage or processing.

Furthermore, it is essential to change the traditional governance concept where only security managers and chiefs, are accountable. It is more convenient to adopt a centralized security governance to meet the challenges of securing Big Data sources on distributed environments. The organization should involve all the stakeholders connected to its ecosystem including employees, managers, ISR, operators, users, customers, partners, suppliers, outsources and so on. The goal is to make all the parties accountable for security management to enhance the adoption of security best practices and to ensure standard and law compliance. Users should be aware threats, regulations and policies.

As an example, partners have to respect data access and confidentiality policies. Users have to update regularly their systems, to make sure that their mobile devices respect standards and recommended security practices and regulations. Users have also to avoid installing non reliable components (e.g., counterfeit software, software without a valid license). On the other hand, programmers, architectures and designers of Big Data applications have to integrate security and privacy requirements though out all the development life cycle. The outsourcers should be made accountable for Big Data security through clear security clauses.

Data Confidentiality and Data Access Monitoring

There is an increasing spread of security threats because of the increasing data exchange over distributed systems and the Cloud. To face these security challenges, (Tankard, 2012) proposes to enhance the control by integrating controls at data level and during storage phase. In fact, it has proved that controls at application and system levels are not sufficient.

In addition, access controls have to be well granulated to limit the access by role and responsibilities. There exist many techniques to ensure access control and data confidentiality such as ICP, certificates, smart-cards, federated identity management, multi-factors authentication.

For example, Law Enforcement Agencies (LEA) of USA have launched INDECT project in order to implement a secured infrastructure for a secured data exchange between agencies and other members (Stoianov, Uruena, Niemiec, Machnik, & Maestro, 2013). The solution includes:

- A public Key Infrastructure (PKI) with three levels (certification authority, users and machines). The PKI provides access control based on a multi-factor authentication and the security level required for each data type. For instance, access to highly confidential applications requires a valid certificate and a password.
- A Federated Identity Management is a concept used by the INDECT platform to enhance access control and security. This type of federated management is delegated to an Identity Provider (IdP) within a monitored trust domain. It is based on two security tools: certificates and smart-cards. Those tools are used to store user certificates issued by the PKI to encrypt and sign documents and emails.
- An INDECT Block Cipher IBC algorithm is a new algorithm for asymmetric cryptography. It was developed and used to encrypt databases, communication sessions (TLS-SSL) and VPN tunnels. The goal is to ensure a high level of data confidentiality.
- Secured communications based on VPN and TLS-SSL protocols. Those mechanisms are used to protect access to Big Data servers.

Authentication mechanisms are most of the time, complex and heavy to handle across distributed clusters and large data sets. For this reason, (Zhao et al., 2014) suggests a model for security on G-Hadoop that integrates several security solutions. It is based on Signe Sign On (SSO) concept that simplifies users authentication and the computation of MapReduce functions. Thus, this model enables users to access different clusters with the same account identifier. Furthermore, privacy is protected through encrypted connections based on SSL protocol, Public Key Cryptography and valid certificates for authentication. Hence, this model offers an efficient access control and a protection against hackers and attackers (e.g., MITM attacks, version rollback, delay attack) and deny access to fraudulent or untruthful entities.

(Mansfield-Devine, 2012) recommends to involve not just security chiefs but also to make responsible all end users for a better access control. It suggests also combining different types of controls inside multi-silo environments (e.g., archives, data loss prevention, access control, logs).

Security Surveillance and Monitoring

It is important to ensure a continuous surveillance in order to detect in real time security incidents, threats and abnormal behaviours. To ensure Big Data security surveillance, some solutions are available such as: Data Loss Prevention (DLP), Security Information and Event Management (SIEM) and dynamic analysis of security events. Such solutions are based on consolidation and correlations methods between multiple data sources, and on contextualization tools (to add context as data attribute to the extracted data). It is also important to conduct regular audits and to verify the respect of security policies and recommended best practices by users and employees.

EXAMPLE: SECURITY OF SMART GRID BIG DATA

This section presents security challenges and solutions regarding Big Dada processed in Smart Grid infrastructures.

Giving the growing power demand, a Smart Grid gather and process huge data sets generated daily (e.g., consumers' behaviours and habits) to ensure an efficient and cost-effective production and distribution of electricity. Unlike traditional electrical grid, Smart Grid is based on advanced technologies and enables bidirectional power flow between connected devices. However, Smart Grid infrastructures are vulnerable and face many security threats. In fact, data are transferred massively in this context and security attacks may have serious and large scale impacts (e.g., regional or national interruption in power supply, important economic loss, disruption of public services, low service quality in hospitals, etc.).

Hence, securing Big Data of Smart Grid infrastructures is fundamental to protect grid system performances, to ensure reliable coordination between control centres and equipments, and to enhance the safety of all system operations.

Smart Grid Security Challenges

Security challenges that are facing critical large scale infrastructures can be classified according to various parameters. (Pathan, 2014) recommends a holistic multi-layered security approach to deal with this issue at all grid levels (i.e., physical, cybernetics and data). In fact, Smart Grid environment incorporates many distributed subsystems and end-points, including distributed sensors and actuators, ever-growing number of Intelligent Electronic Devices (IED) with different power requirements (e.g., electric vehicles and smart homes), electric generators and control applications. In addition, these subsystems and end-points have multiple bidirectional communications between each other.

This complexity increases anomalies, human errors and system vulnerabilities that can be exploited by security attackers. As an example, the governor control system (GC) of a Smart Grid ensures the steady operation of all power generators. It detects by sensors the speed and the frequency deviation of generators and rapidly adjusts their operations. Attackers may succeed to access one point of network communications and change values recorded by the generators sensors. Thus, such type of communication intrusion and malicious modification of data, could affect power flow inside the grid and compromise the decision making process supervised by the Optimal Power Flow (OPF).

Moreover, attackers may use Grid utilities and smart meters to get private information, which compromises consumer privacy (Stimmel, 2014).

Since Smart Grid system incorporates multiple interconnected subsystems. There is a risk of cascading failures. In fact, any attack to one of the subsystems may compromise the security of the other ones. Thus, it is crucial to secure the overall Smart Grid system, including the physical components, the cyber space and the data generated and transmitted through the grid networks.

Security Solutions for Smart Grid

Big Data security management in Smart Grid environment aims to ensure data confidentiality, integrity and availability for efficient and reliable grid operations. To increase Smart Grid attacks-resilience and response to the previous cited challenges, several solutions and research efforts have been made.

Considering the cascading failure aspect and the complexity of the Smart Grid system, it is recommended to adopt multi-layered approach. This helps to secure not only data layer but also all the other layers: physicals, networks, hosts, data stores, applications, policies and regulations.

For instance, at the physical layer, it is important to ensure the security of equipments, consumer devices, substations, sensors, control centres and so on. Concerning the cyber layer, it is recommended to secure network communications and eliminate weak points from the cyber topology (e.g., bad intrusion detection algorithms). Regarding the data layer, it is crucial to ensure granular access control and granular audits (Alvaro A. C., Pratyusa K. M., & Sreeranga P. R., 2013).

A successful security management of Smart Grid system should incorporate real-time security monitoring. Big Data analytics algorithms are one of the powerful solutions recommended to face such issue. Those algorithms drive improved predictions and more precise analysis. They are often based on Machine Learning techniques and use not only traditional security logs and events, but also performance and costumers' data to recognize and prevent malicious behaviours (Khorshed, Ali, & Wasimi, 2014).

Real-time monitoring can be part in mitigation strategy to help security decision making. It assists security analysts to decide if a preventive or remedial action should be taken (e.g., change user roles or privileges, suspend suspicious access, correct network configurations). The list of actions depends on the nature of incident and its impact. They can be implemented through an automatically or semi-automatically process. Ensuring continuous updates of such strategy is a good practice. This helps integrating new security solutions, new laws as well as emerging security practices and models.

Considering the complexity and evolving nature of cybercrimes, it is important to promote continuous commitment and timely sharing of security information between all Smart Grid partners, utilities, and specialized organizations in cybercrimes (Bughin, J., Chui, M., & Manyika, J. 2010).

It is well known that security techniques are not sufficient in any industry. They have to be guided by legal actions and regulations in order to protect the valuable data and other assets. Therefore, security requirements, policies, regulations and standards should be updated regularly to consider evolving security issues.

CONCLUSION

Big Data applications promise interesting opportunities for many sectors. In fact, extracting valuable insight and information from disparate large data sources enables to improve the competitive advantage of organizations. For instance, the analysis of data streams or archives (e.g., using predictive or identification models) can help to optimize production processes, to enhance services with added value and to adapt them to customers' needs. However, Big Data sharing and analysis rise many security issues and increase privacy threats. This chapter presents some of the important Big Data security challenges and describes related solutions and recommendations. Because it is nearly impossible to secure very large data sets, it is more practical to protect the data value and its key attributes instead of the data itself, to analyse security risks of combining different evolving Big Data technologies and to choose security tools according to the goals of the Big Data project.

REFERENCES

Alvaro, A. C., Pratyusa, K. M., & Sreeranga, P. R. (2013). Big data analytics for security. *IEEE Security and Privacy, 11*(6), 74–76. doi:10.1109/MSP.2013.138

Berman, J. J. (2013). *Principles of big data: Preparing, sharing, and analyzing complex information.* San Francisco, CA: Morgan Kaufmann Publishers Inc.

Bodei, C., Degano, P., Ferrari, G. L., Galletta, L., & Mezzetti, G. (2012). Formalising security in ubiquitous and cloud scenarios. In A. Cortesi, N. Chaki, K. Saeed, & S. Wierzchon (Eds.), *Computer information systems and industrial management: Proceedings of the 11th IFIP TC 8 International Conference (LNCS)* (Vol. 7564, pp. 1-29). Berlin, Germany: Springer. doi:10.1007/978-3-642-33260-9_1

Bughin, J., Chui, M., & Manyika, J. (2010). Clouds, big data, and smart assets: Ten tech-enabled business trends to watch. Retrieved from http://www.mckinsey.com/insights/high_tech_tele-coms_internet/clouds_big_data_and_smart_as-sets_ten_tech-enabled_business_trends_to_watch

Chen, X., & Huang, Q. (2013). The data protection of mapreduce using homomorphic encryption. In *Proceedings of the 4th IEEE International Conference on Software Engineering and Service Science* (pp. 419-421). Beijing, China: IEEE.

Constantine, C. (2014). Big data: An information security context. *Network Security, 2014*(1), 18–19. doi:10.1016/S1353-4858(14)70010-8

Jensen, M. (2013). Challenges of privacy protection in big data analytics. In *Proceedings of IEEE International Congress on Big Data* (pp. 235-238). Washington, DC: IEEE Computer Society. doi:10.1109/BigData.Congress.2013.39

Kasim, H., Hung, T., & Li, X. (2012). Data value chain as a service framework: For enabling data handling, data security and data analysis in the cloud. *In Proceedings of the 18th IEEE International Conference on Parallel and Distributed Systems* (pp. 804-809). Washington, DC: IEEE Computer Society. doi:10.1109/ICPADS.2012.131

Katal, A., Wazid, M., & Goudar, R. (2013). Big data: Issues, challenges, tools and good practices. In *Proceedings of the Sixth International Conference on Contemporary* Computing (pp. 404-409). Noida, India: IEEE. doi:10.1109/IC3.2013.6612229

Khorshed, M. T., Ali, A. B., & Wasimi, S. A. (2014). Combating Cyber Attacks in Cloud Systems Using Machine Learning. In S. Nepal & M. Pathan (Eds.), *Security, Privacy and Trust in Cloud Systems* (pp. 407–431). Berlin, Germany: Springer. doi:10.1007/978-3-642-38586-5_14

Kim, S. H., Kim, N. U., & Chung, T. M. (2013). Attribute relationship evaluation methodology for big data security. In *Proceedings of the International Conference on IT Convergence and Security* (pp. 1-4). Macao, China: IEEE. doi:10.1109/ICITCS.2013.6717808

Liu, C., Zhang, X., Liu, C., Yang, Y., Ranjan, R., Georgakopoulos, D., & Chen, J. (2013). An iterative hierarchical key exchange scheme for secure scheduling of big data applications in cloud computing. In *Proceedings of the 12th IEEE International Conference on Trust, Security and Privacy in Computing and Communications* (pp. 9-16). Washington, DC: IEEE Computer Society. doi:10.1109/TrustCom.2013.65

Lu, T., Guo, X., Xu, B., Zhao, L., Peng, Y., & Yang, H. (2013). Next big thing in big data: The security of the ict supply chain. In *Proceedings of the International Conference on Social Computing* (pp. 1066-1073). Washington, DC: IEEE Computer Society. doi:10.1109/SocialCom.2013.172

Mahmood, T., & Afzal, U. (2013). Security analytics: Big data analytics for cybersecurity: A review of trends, techniques and tools. *In Proceedings of the 2nd National Conference on Information Assurance* (pp. 129-134). Rawalpindi, Pakistan: IEEE. doi:10.1109/NCIA.2013.6725337

Mansfield-Devine, S. (2012). Using big data to reduce security risks. *Computer Fraud & Security*, (8): 3–4.

Pathan, A. S. K. (2014). *The state of the art in intrusion prevention and detection*. Boca Raton, FL: Auerbach Publications. doi:10.1201/b16390

Ring, T. (2013). It's megatrends: The security impact. *Network Security, 2013*(7), 5–8. doi:10.1016/S1353-4858(13)70080-1

Shin, D., Sahama, T., & Gajanayake, R. (2013). Secured e-health data retrieval in daas and big data. In *Proceedings of the 15th IEEE international conference on e-health networking, applications services* (pp. 255-259). Lisbon, Portugal: IEEE. doi:10.1109/HealthCom.2013.6720677

Stimmel, C. L. (2014). *Big data analytics strategies for the smart grid.* Boca Raton, FL: Auerbach Publications. doi:10.1201/b17228

Stoianov, N., Uruena, M., Niemiec, M., Machnik, P., & Maestro, G. (2012). *Security Infrastructures: Towards the INDECT System Security.* Paper presented at the 5th International Conference on Multimedia Communication Services & Security (MCSS), Krakow, Poland. doi:10.1007/978-3-642-30721-8_30

Sykora, M., Jackson, T., O'Brien, A., & Elayan, S. (2013). National security and social media monitoring: A presentation of the emotive and related systems. In *Proceedings of the European Intelligence and Security Informatics Conference* (pp. 172-175). Uppsala, Sweden: IEEE. doi:10.1109/EISIC.2013.38

Tankard, C. (2012). Big data security. *Network Security*, (7): 5–8.

Wu, X., Zhu, X., Wu, G.-Q., & Ding, W. (2014). Data mining with big data. *IEEE Transactions on Knowledge and Data Engineering, 26*(1), 97–107. doi:10.1109/TKDE.2013.109

Zhang, X., Liu, C., Nepal, S., Yang, C., Dou, W., & Chen, J. (2014). A hybrid approach for scalable sub-tree anonymization over big data using mapreduce on cloud. *Journal of Computer and System Sciences, 80*(5), 1008–1020. doi:10.1016/j.jcss.2014.02.007

Zhao, J., Wang, L., Tao, J., Chen, J., Sun, W., & Ranjan, R. et al. (2014). A security framework in g-hadoop for big data computing across distributed cloud data centres. *Journal of Computer and System Sciences, 80*(5), 994–1007.

KEY TERMS AND DEFINITIONS

Anonymization: Anonymization is the process of protecting data privacy across information systems. Several models and methods are used to implement it such as: t-closeness, m-invariance, k-anonymity and l-diversity.

Authentication: Authentication aims to test and ensure, with a certain probability, that particular data are authentic, i.e., they have not been changed.

Big Data: Big Data is mainly defined by its *3Vs* fundamental characteristics. The *3Vs* include *Velocity* (data are growing and changing in a rapid way), *Variety* (data come in different and multiple formats) and *Volume* (huge amount of data is generated every second).

Confidentiality: Confidentiality is a property that ensures that data is not made disclosed to unauthorized persons. It enforces predefined rules while accessing the protected data.

Encryption: Encryption relies on the use of encryption algorithms to transform data into encrypted forms. The purpose is to make them unreadable to those who do not possess the encryption key(s).

Privacy: Privacy is the ability of individuals to seclude information about themselves. In other words, they selectively control its dissemination.

Security Management: Security management is a part of the overall management system of an organization. It aims to handle, implement, monitor, maintain, and enhance data security.

Chapter 15
Access Control Framework for Cloud Computing

Kashif Munir
King Fahd University of Petroleum and Minerals, Saudi Arabia

Lawan A. Mohammed
King Fahd University of Petroleum and Minerals, Saudi Arabia

ABSTRACT

Access control is generally a rule or procedure that allows, denies, restricts or limit access to system's resources. It may, as well, monitor and record all attempts made to access a system. Access Control may also identify users attempting to access unauthorized resources. It is a mechanism which is very much important for protection in computer security. Various access control models are in use, including the most common Mandatory Access Control (MAC), Discretionary Access Control (DAC) and Role Based Access Control (RBAC). All these models are known as identity based access control models. In all these access control models, user (subjects) and resources (objects) are identified by unique names. Identification may be done directly or through roles assigned to the subjects. These access control methods are effective in unchangeable distributed system, where there are only a set of Users with a known set of services. For this reason, we propose a framework which is well suited to many situations in cloud computing where users or applications can be clearly separated according to their job functions. In this chapter, we proposes a role based access control framework with various features including security of sensitive data, authorization policy and secure data from hackers. Our proposed role based access control algorithm provides tailored and fine level of user access control services without adding complexity, and supports access privileges updates dynamically when a user's role is added or updated.

INTRODUCTION

Cloud computing describes a new delivery model for IT services based on the Internet, and it typically involves over-the-Internet provision of dynamically scalable and often virtualized resources. It is a byproduct and consequence of the ease-of-access to remote computing sites provided by the Internet. This frequently takes the form of web-based tools or applications that users can access and use through a web browser as if it is a program installed locally on their own computer (Armbrust et. al, 2009).

DOI: 10.4018/978-1-4666-8387-7.ch015

In the "cloud", all data processing tasks are handled by a large number of distributed computers, end-users get access to the computer and storage systems through network on their demand. Enterprise Data Center is responsible for handling customer' task which is from customer' computer, so that it can provide data services for all kinds of users who use variety of different devices through just one data center and allow anyone who has the right Internet links to get access to the cloud applications (Arnold, 2008).

Aside from the huge marketing efforts, cloud security has been criticized for its unknown privacy and security protection. There could be benefits from a security perspective since most customers utilizing cloud may not have the expertise to safeguarding their information assets using traditional IT approaches, and using cloud services could mitigate this problem. On the other side, companies hosting the cloud services have in general full control over the services they provide. They could control and monitor data essentially at will. It has been noted by the research community that confidentiality and auditability are one of the top 10 obstacles to the growth of cloud computing (Armbrust et. al, 2009(b)).

As the goal of Cloud Computing is to share resources among the cloud service consumers, cloud partners, and cloud vendors in the cloud value chain. There has been a growing trend to use the cloud for large-scale data storage. However, the multi-tenant nature of the cloud is vulnerable to data leaks, threats, and malicious attacks. Therefore, it is important for enterprises to have strong access control policies in place to maintain the privacy and confidentiality of data in the cloud. The cloud computing platform is highly dynamic and diverse. Current access control techniques, like firewalls and VLAN, are not exactly well-suited to meet the challenges of cloud computing environment. They were originally designed to support IT systems in an enterprise environment. In addition, any weak access control mechanisms in the cloud can lead to major data breaches.

For instance, a few years back a massive data breach took place on the server of Utah Department Technology Services (DTS) as reported in *InformationWeek* (http://www.darkreading.com/risk-management/utahs-medicaid-data-breach-worse-than-expected/d/d-id/1103823). A hacker group from Eastern Europe succeeded in accessing the servers of DTS, compromising 181,604 Medicaid recipients and the Social Security numbers of 25,096 individual clients. The reason behind this massive breach is believed to be a configuration issue at the authentication level when DTS moved its claims to a new server. The hacker took advantage of this busy situation and managed to infiltrate the system, which contained sensitive user information like client names, addresses, birth dates, SSNs, physicians' names, national provider identifiers, addresses, tax identification numbers, and procedure codes designed for billing purposes. The Utah Department of Technology Services had proper access controls, policies, and procedures in place to secure sensitive data. However, in this particular case, a configuration error occurred while entering the password into the system. The hacker got access to the password of the system administrator, and as a result accessed the personal information of thousands of users. The biggest lesson from this incident is that even if the data is encrypted, a flaw in authentication system could render a system vulnerable. Enterprises should be sure to limit access to control policies, enforcing privileges and permissions for secure management of sensitive user data in the cloud. In another cloud computing survey conducted by *PC Connection* (PCConnection, 2013), it was mentioned that in 2011, 174 million records were compromised, costing organizations an average of $5.5 million—or $194 per compromised record.

According to the *Ponemon Institute* (Ponemon, 2013) Research Report of 2013 findings, organizations have improved their security practices around cloud use when compared to 2010 responses. However, only about half of respondents had positive perceptions about how their organizations are adopting cloud security best practices and creating confidence in cloud services used within their organization. In summary, the research showed that:

- While the use of SaaS and IaaS services has increased and security practices have improved since 2010, only half of organizations (51 percent for SaaS and 49 percent for IaaS) are evaluating these services in terms of security prior to deployment. And only about half are confident in the security of those services (53 percent confident in SaaS and 50 percent confident in IaaS).
- Fifty percent of respondents say they are confident they know all cloud computing services in use in their organization. While just at half, this is an improvement over the 2010 response of 45 percent.
- Only 50 percent of the respondents say they are engaging their security team (always or most of the time) in determining the use of cloud services. This is a slight decrease from 2010 (which was 51 percent).

To manage cloud security in today's world, you need a solution that helps you address threats to your data and infrastructure, as well as the major challenges of cloud computing. These include:

- Changing attackers and threats—Attacks aren't coming just from isolated hackers now. More and more, organized crime is driving well-resourced, sophisticated, targeted attacks for financial gain.
- Evolving architecture technologies—with the growth of virtualization and rise in cloud adoption, perimeters and their controls within the data center are in flux, and data is no longer easily constrained or physically isolated and protected.
- Consumerization of IT—As mobile devices and technologies continue to become more common, employees want to use per-

sonally owned devices to access enterprise applications, data, and cloud services.

As the popularity of cloud computing increases, more and more organizations want to migrate their data and applications to cloud computing. As a result the main concern for all cloud service providers is to provide security to their information and to their data. For that the identity of all the users must be known to the cloud provider administrator. To solve the security problem of cloud computing, one should first solve the user access. By implementing role based access control (RBAC) cost and complexity of security can be reduced (Rao & Vijay, 2009). With RBAC, the administrators grant permissions to the roles that he created according to job functions performed in an organization, and then assign users to the roles on the basis of their specific job responsibilities. To access the cloud computing resources user first have to register themselves into one or more classes and get credentials to identify themselves (R.S. Sandhu, et.al, 1996). In a cloud numbers of systems are implementing RBAC. Each system has its own user accounts or system accounts with credentials. As the environment grows, number of accounts will also increase which leads to the increase of credentials. And all this is managed by system administrator.

For these reasons, security in cloud computing is still ongoing issue. This chapter intends to focus on the access control aspect of cloud security, and provide a RBAC framework to protect data in cloud. First we will look at the history of access control models, then we propose a framework for RBAC for cloud computing.

HISTORY OF ACCESS CONTROL MODELS

In present day, people rely less and less on personal face-to-face contact as they need to use computer and telecommunication technology to access information both at home, office, shops etc. Therefore this signifies the importance of protecting information from unauthorized access. The aspect of protecting information by authenticating users to ensure authorized access is commonly known as the *Access Control System* (ACS).

In the 1970s, under the sponsorship of the US Department of Defence, work on developing models for secure information systems where carried out. Bell and La Padula published a paper that modeled computer security after military secrecy methods (Bell, 1973) and Biba published another based on integrity (Biba, 1977). One of the constrains of Bell La Padula model is that it was developed in the context of military secure systems and assumed the existence of a method of classifying the security levels of users and information. The concept of "mandatory access control" is not appropriate for commercial information systems as there is no application of security classifications to data and security clearance accorded to employees in commercial organizations.

There has been further research but these are largely deviations based on the above two models, like the Clark-Wilson model (Clark, 1987). In 1983, the US Government introduce the Trusted System Evaluation Criteria (TSEC) to provide computer manufacturers with a set of guidelines and an evaluation system for the development of trusted computer systems, (known as the Orange Book). This prompted commercial and government organizations to turn to TSEC as a guideline for the development of secure information systems. The European Community produced a set of criteria called the ITSEC. It is common for manufacturers to build the criteria spelt out into their new commercial product. The drawback of TSEC and ITSEC is that their specifications are limited to the use of mathematical concepts to achieve the objective of maintaining secrecy and integrity, by introducing concepts like mandatory and discretionary access controls. There are no specifications for the development of access devices and it is largely left to technologist.

Currently there are several types of access devices. Generally, they are fall into one of the following categories:

1. Verification of something known, like password, PIN. This category is known as *codeword*. Details are provided in the next subsection.
2. Verification of something possessed, like smart card. This is refers to as *token*. Token has some drawbacks, as there are many cases of forgery of tokens, people have also been known to be complacent in their handling of the token.
3. Verification of some unique features of our body. This is known as *biometric*. One of the limitation of this method is that it is very expensive to implement, moreover, it is also not common therefore cannot fit into our daily life style.

CODEWORDS

Identification is an essential part of securing information processing systems and networks. Source identification can be achieved by the use of either secret key or public key cryptosystems (to be discussed later). In general, it is the process of obtaining assurance that the identity of some participant in a networking scenario is as claimed. For example, when a user seeks the services of a computer, the computer needs to make sure that the user is not forging a false identity. The classical solution to this is through the use of *passwords*. The National Computer Security Centre defines the probability of guessing a particular password as:

$$P = \frac{LXR}{S}$$

where, L is the password lifetime (The maximum amount of time it can be used before it must be changed). *R* is the guess rate (the number of guesses per unit time that it is possible to make). *S* is the password space (the total number of unique passwords that can be used). *S* is defined in turn as $S = A^M$, where *A* is the number of characters in the alphabet (the set of characters that may be used in a password), and *M* is the password length.

If we assume that most people restrict their passwords to upper and lowercase letters, numbers, and punctuation. *A* takes a value of about 92. Now, let us assume that a password lifetime is up to one year, and that a password can be tried at a rate of 1,000 per second (a reasonable value on many of today's architectures).

As we lower our estimate of *A* (for example, it would probably be more realistic to assume only letters and numbers, for a value of 62) or increase our estimate of *R* (to account for faster processors), these probabilities only gets worse. Manipulating our equation also gives us a procedure for determining the minimum acceptable password length for a given system:

1. Establish an acceptable password lifetime *L* (a typical value might be one month).
2. Establish an acceptable probability *P* (the probability might be no more than 1 in 1,000,000).
3. Solve for the size of the password space *S*, using the equation derived from the previous one:

$$S = \frac{L\,X\,R}{P}$$

Determine the length of the password, M, from the equation:

$$M = \frac{logS}{\log A}$$

Using this procedure with *L* equals to 1 month, *R* equals to 1,000 guesses/second, *A* equals to 92, and *P* equals to 1 in 1,000,000, we end up with *M* equals to 7.85, which rounds up to 8. Thus the minimum acceptable password length to insure no better than 1 in 1,000,000 chance of guessing the password is eight characters. There are other means for securing codewords one of the most effective is known one-way function.

Cryptographic Algorithms

Cryptography is the method of converting data from a human readable form to a modified form, and then back to its original readable form, to make unauthorized access difficult. Cryptography is needed to make electronic transactions as trustworthy and legally binding as physical communication.

Different access control mechanisms with high level of security have been developed. So one may like to know the role of encryption techniques in such system. One of its use is, of course, its standard application – the protection of data transmitted across conventional links. Generally, cryptography is used in the following ways:

*   Ensure data privacy, by encrypting data
*   Ensures data integrity, by recognizing if data has been manipulated in an unauthorized way
*   Ensures data uniqueness by checking that data is "original", and not a "copy" of the "original". The sender attaches a unique identifier to the "original" data. This unique identifier is then checked by the receiver of the data.

The original data may be in a human-readable form, such as a text file, or it may be in a computer-readable form, such as a database, spreadsheet or graphics file. The original data is called unencrypted data or plain text. The modified data is called encrypted data or cipher text. The process of converting the unencrypted data is called encryption. The process of converting encrypted data to unencrypted data is called decryption. Cryptography can be classified as either conventional or asymmetric, depending on the type of keys used.

In order to convert the data, you need to have an encryption algorithm and a key. If the same key is used for both encryption and decryption that key is called a secret key and the algorithm is called a symmetric algorithm. Symmetric algorithms include DES, Triple DES, Rijndael, RC2, RC4, IDEA, Blowfish, CAST, Red Pike and a host of others.

If different keys are used for encryption and decryption, the algorithm is called an asymmetric algorithm. Some of these algorithms include RSA, DSA and Diffie-Hellman as well as El Gamal and various forms of Elliptic Curve Cryptography (ECC). Asymmetric algorithms involve extremely complex mathematics typically involving the factoring of large prime numbers. Asymmetric algorithms are typically stronger than a short key length symmetric algorithm but because of their complexity they are used in signing a message or a certificate. They not ordinarily used for data transmission encryption.

RELATED WORK

For providing secure and reliable cloud computing one should first secure the cloud resources from unauthorized access. Now a day's many cloud computing platforms implementing role based access control. Still lots of researches are going on to secure RBAC in cloud. Georgia institute of Technology introduced a middleware security platform CASA which provides security with user bio information or location information (Covington. et.al, 2000). For context-information modeling SOCAM proposes OWL, which consists of several components (Gu et.al, 2004). (Kom-

lenovic et. al, 2011) proposes distributed access for role based access control. Their approach uses directed graph, access matrix. If there is limit on number of users and permission than access matrix is an optimal choice and if it is variable then directed graph. (Ching-Ching & Kamalendu, 2008) proposes distributed authorization caching technique which helps to improve performance, scalability of an authorization system . (Ei Ei & Thin, 2011) combines RBAC and Attribute based access control system and proposes a new framework ARBAC which supports both mandatory and discretionary needs.

ROLE BASED ACCESS CONTROL (RBAC)

Role Based Access Control (RBAC) is a method that offers a satisfactory level of safety & security for organizational resources & data because of rules & policies put into effect for the user in the form of login & password. However, the description is not limited to the organization resources but gives security and protection for users' personal information and actions.

There are two main user attributes i.e. presence & location (Takabi & Joshi, 2010). Presence is linked with the real-time communication systems such as: Instant Message and (IM) and Voice over IP (VoIP), where it gives the required explanation about users category all through the communication and even after that also, tells the status as idle or active, online or offline and for specific tasks it is done in the form of writing documents or email.

The current application Role Based Access Control RBAC offers Authentication, Authorization and Auditing for users using the cloud computing as follows:

- **Authentication:** Cloud computing authentication includes validating the identity of users or systems. For example, facility to service authentication engages in certifying the access demand to the information which served by another service.

- **Authorization:** After the authentication process, the system will put security rules to bring legitimate users.
- **Auditing:** Auditing is a process that involves reviewing & examining the records of authorization & authentication to check over organizations compliance with set security standards & policies in order to evade system breaches.

According to (Mather, et,al, 1996) RBAC will go through five stages as follow:

- **Provisioning and deprovisioning:** User will be authorized to access to the information based on the organization & role. This process is long as every user is to be provided with an identity. Nevertheless, cloud management uses techniques such as identity Management as a Service (IDaaS).
- **Authentication and Authorization:** A significant authentication and authorization infrastructure will be requisite to make a custom authentication and authorization representation that fulfills the business goals.
- **Self-Service:** Facilitating self-service in the identity management will improvise the identity management systems. Users can reset their information like password and uphold their data from any location.
- **Password Management:** Single Sign on (SSO) support system is to access cloud-base services. Password management comprises of how the password will be stored in the cloud database.
- **Compliance and Audit:** Here, the access will be scrutinized & tracked to monitor the security breaches in the system. This process also assists to audit the fulfillment to diverse access control policies, periodic auditing and reporting.

PROPOSED FRAMEWORK

In this chapter, we propose a *Role-Based Access Control* (RBAC) model suitable for cloud computing environment. RBAC model is defined in terms of three model components-Core RBAC, Hierarchical RBAC and Constraint RBAC Core RBAC includes sets of six basic data elements called users (U), roles(R), objects (0), operations (Ops), permissions (P) and sessions (Sessions). The basic concept of RBAC is that users are assigned to roles rather than users. Through a set of maps, this model makes the role and a group of related operations manage each other, the user belongs to roles has the right to execute corresponding actions which are associated to these roles (Blaze et al, 1998).

Role-Based Access Control, introduced by Ferraiolo and Kuhn, has become the predominant model for advanced access control because it reduces the complexity and cost of security administration in large networked applications (Kong and Li, 2007). With RBAC, system administrators create roles according to the job functions performed in an organization, grant permissions to those roles, and then assign users to the roles on the basis of their specific job responsibilities and qualifications (Sandhu et al., 1996). Role based access control (RBAC) introduces the concept of "role" between the users and the operations of objects.

The researcher's framework attempts to solve the above-mentioned problems. The proposed architecture is shown in Figure 1. The following terminologies were used in our model:

- *AC*: Access Control
- *UC*: Usage Control
- *PPN*: Privacy Policy Negotiation

The following are the access control elements used in our model:

Figure 1. Proposed framework

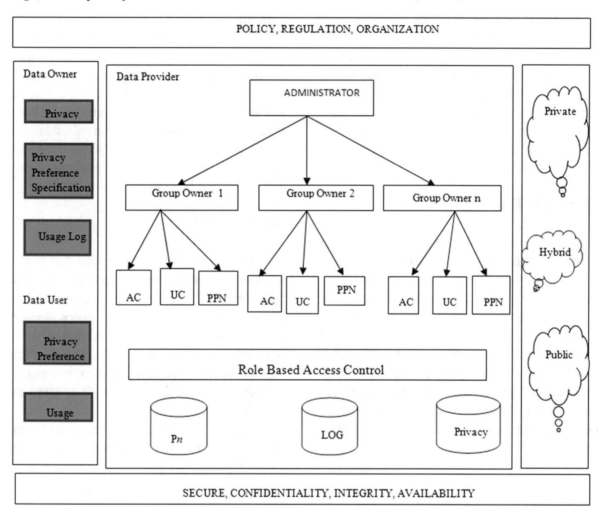

A. *Data administrator:* In a cloud, various services like the data services, applications services, and VM services can be created by the cloud users and stored in the storage allocations in the.

B. *Data users:* Cloud users can access their services and data post receipt of the data owner's permission.

C. *Cloud Service Providers (CSP):* Users can operate the cloud, its components and services according to the rules defined by cloud service providers.

Administrator: The administrator has all the rights to authorize the user and give him/her access rights according to policy. The administrator also keeps one's information confidential from unauthorized users. All the groups are controlled by the administrator. It is only with his approval that users and groups can be added or deleted.

D. *Group:* Every group has its own group owner who will control access, and assign privacy privileges to the users. If any user tries to access sensitive data, he/she has to take permission from the group owner first. The group owner will first check the user's credentials and if that user has the rights to access the resource concerned. It is only after that verification that the group owner will send a key to the user's email id. Only with that key, will the user access sensitive resources. One user can be placed within several groups. There can be two possible cases with this framework.

Scenario # 1

If a user is present in a number of groups and the access rights that are given to him/her are different. In this case, we will take the optimistic approach. High priority will be given to less restriction. For example, if a user is present in group 1 as well as in group 4, and if within group 1, he is assigned FULL ACCESS while in group 4, he gets READ ONLY rights, then, he will be eligible for FULL ACCESS. If the access rights are for sensitive data, then, that user will have to consult his group owner first and only after that can he access that resource.

The algorithm for scenario 1 is given as Algorithm 1.

The algorithm first checks, the number of groups in which the user is present. That count is stored in variable C. For loop, this count is stored in an array named list [length(C)]. D is a variable that is used to store the access rights of a user. If the user is present in one group only, then, the designated access rights will be given. If the user is present in number of group then access rights will be decided according to less restriction.

Scenario # 2

How will shareable resources be handled in this framework? For instance, if one user has access rights to read that resource and another user has access rights to write on that resource at same time, the researcher suggests synchronization. If one user is accessing some resource then other user will have to wait to access same resource.

The algorithm for Scenario #2 is given as Algorithm 2.

In the entry section, user i first raises a flag indicating a desire to access the resource. Then

Algorithm 1.

```
 [Initialize]. Set A: = 1, B: = Number of User's Group, access: = 'No Access',
list
    [Length (C)]:= Groups of Users, D.
If B = 0, then access: = 'User's Access' and Exit.
If B = 1, then access: = 'User's Access in Group' and Exit.
Repeat Steps 5 to 10 while A ≤ B:
D: = list [A].getUserAccessInGroup.
If D = 'Full Access', then access: = 'Full Access' and Exit.
If D = 'Read/Write', then access: = 'Read/Write'.
If D = 'Read' and access ≠ 'Read/Write', then access: = 'Read'.
If D = 'NO Access' and access ≠ 'Read/Write' and access ≠ 'Read', then access:=
    'No Access'.
Set A: = A+1.
[End of Step 4 Loop]
Exit.
```

Algorithm 2.

```
do{
flag[i]=TRUE;
turn=j;
while(flag[j]&&turn==j);
flag[i] = FALSE;
remainder section
} while (TRUE);
```

the turn is set to j to allow the other user to access the resource, if user j so desires. While the loop is a busy loop (notice the semicolon at the end), which makes user i wait for as long as user j has his turn, and accessing the resource user i lowers the flag[i] in the exit section, allowing user j to continue if he has been waiting.

Framework Features

The proposed framework helps to secure the system more efficiently with the following features.

- Security of Sensitive information: The proposed framework helps to secure information that is private or sensitive to the user. When a user wants to access the sensitive information first, an email is sent to the group owner, who then, checks the user's credentials to see if he has access rights to use the data or not. If he does have the requisite right, then, an email with security key will be sent to the user, and using this, the user can access that sensitive information.
- Security from hackers: Sometimes a user leaves his account open and anyone can access that account. If a hacker wants to access any private information then, the group owner gets intimated that private data is being misused leading to him blocking the access to that data.

- Addition of user or group dynamically: This framework helps to add or update users and groups, dynamically. For example, if a user is no longer working in an organization, a user's access rights will be changed and then, this framework will update these changes dynamically.

SECURITY POLICIES

The need to prove that data and files are authentic is always important, but that requirement is particularly compelling when organizations must show compliance with laws and regulations. This includes situations related to:

- *Regulated industries*, where companies need to document, for example, how they comply with Health Insurance Portability and Accountability Act or HIPAA rules for protecting personally identifiable health information, SEC 17a-4 requirements for retaining data on securities transactions, and 21 CFR Part 11 requirements for protecting records required by the FDA.
- *Financial information*, used for SEC reporting and compliance with Sarbanes-Oxley (SOX) and other investor protection regulations.
- *Documents with legal and contractual implications*, whose admissibility as evidence needs to be protected.
- *Intellectual property*, such as engineering and patent documents, trade secrets and business plans, whose date and provenance might need to be proved in court.
- *Records management applications*, where documents and files might need to be retrieved and validated after years or even decades.

CONCLUSION

In conclusion, today's business environment is very attracted by cloud computing paradigm because of providing services in a very effective way. On top of commodity hardware there is a virtualization layer which is drive force and helps cloud providers to respond promptly to cloud user requests.

Instead of all these advantages of cloud computing, there is still a question mark on its usage. Security and privacy are main challenges from storage and processing of sensitive data due to multi-tenancy feature of cloud computing. For the efficient use of cloud computing providing proper security is very important. Cloud computing security begins with implementing Identity and Access Management to ensure Authentication, Authorization and Auditing.

Cloud computing is so named because the information being accessed is found in the "clouds", and does not require a user to be in a specific place to gain access to it. cloud computing structure allows access to information as long as an electronic device has access to the web.

In this chapter, we present the RBAC framework that protects the sensitive information in the cloud, specifies the privacy policies for the private cloud; and protects the data from hackers. Two scenarios has been presented. Scenario 1 deals with what if is present in a number of groups and the access rights that are given to him/her are different whereas scenario 2 deals with shareable resources be handled in this framework. Algorithm has been presented to support the scenarios.

REFERENCES

Armbrust, M., Armando, F., Rean, G., Anthony, D. J., Katz, R. H., Konwinski, A., et al. (2009b). Above the Clouds: A Berkeley View of Cloud Computing. *Tech. Report UCB/EECS-2009-28.*

Armbrust. M., Fox A., Griffith, R., Joseph, A. D., Katz, R., Konwinski, A., Lee, G., Patterson, D., Rabkin, A., Stoica, I., & Zaharia, M. (2009a). *Above the Clouds: A View of Cloud Computing* [EB/OL]. UC Berkeley. Retrieved from https://www.eecs.berkeley.edu/Pubs/TechRpts/2009/EECS-2009-28.pdf.

Arnold, S. (2008, July-August). *Cloud computing and the issue of privacy. KM World.* Retrieved from http://www.kmworld.com

Bell, D., & LaPadula, J. (1973). Secure Computer System: Mathematical foundation and model, Mitre Corp, MTR 2547, 2.

Biba, R. R. (1977). Integrity Considerations for Secure Computer Systems: Unified exposition and multics interpretation. *Mitre Corp., MTR 3153.*

Blaze, M., Feigen, B., & Keromytis, J. (1998). A.D. keynote: trust management for public-key infrastructures. In: Christianaon, B., Crispo, B., Willian, S., et al. (Eds.) Security Protocols International Workshop. Berlin: Springer-Verglag.

Ching – Ching. L, Kamalendu. B. (2008). Distributed Authorization Cache. Proceedings of Security & Management, pp. 381-386.

Clark, D., & Wilson, D. (1987). A Comparison of Commercial and Military Computer Security Policies", *IEEE Symposium on security and privacy.* doi:10.1109/SP.1987.10001

Overcoming the Security Challenges of the Cloud: Best Practices for Keeping Your Data and Your Organization Safe. (2013, May 13). *PC Connection.* Retrieved from http://www.pc-connection.com/~/media/PDFs/Brands/C/Cisco/Survey/25240_PCC_CloudSurvey.pdf

Covington, M. J., Moyer, M. J., & Ahamad, M. (2000, October). Generalized role-based access control for securing future application. NISSC, pp. 40–51.

Ei Ei, M., Thinn, T. N. (2011). The privacy-aware access control system using attribute-and role-based access control in private cloud. *IEEE International conference on Broadband Network and Multimedia Technology, pp. 447-451.*

Gu, T., Pung, H. K., & Zhang, D. Q. (2004). *A Middleware for Building Context-Aware Mobile Services. Proceedings of IEEE Vehicular Technology Conference, VTC.*

Kong, G., & Li, J. (2007). Research on RBAC-based separation of duty constraints. *Journal of Information and Computing Science, 20,* 235–24.

Marko, K., Mahesh, T., & Toutik, Z. (2011). An Empirical Assessment of Approaches to Distributed Enforcement in Role Based Access Control. *Proceedings of ACM conference on Data & Application Security & Privacy, pp. 1-29.*

Mather, T., Kumarasuwamy, S., & Latif, S. (2009). Cloud Security and Privacy. O'Rielly.

Maxwell, J. C. (3 Ed.). (2009). A Treatise on Electricity and Magnetism, 2. Oxford: Clarendon, 1892.

Ponemon (2013, December 21). Security of Cloud Computing Users Study. Retrieved from http://www.ca.com/kr/~/media/Files/IndustryAnalystReports/2012-security-of-cloud-computer-users-final1.pdf

Rao, M., & Vijay, S. (2009). Cloud Computing and the Lessons from the Past. The 18th IEEE international Workshops on Enabling Technologies: Infrastructures for Collaborative Enterprises, pp. 57-62, 2009.

Sandhu, R. S., Coyne, E. I., Feinstein, H. L., & Youman, C. E. (1996, February). Role based access control models. *IEEE Computer, 29*(2), 38–47. doi:10.1109/2.485845

Sandhu, R. S., Coyne, E. J., Feinstein, H. L., & Youman, C. E. (1996, February). Role based access control models. *IEEE Computer, 29*(2), 38–47. doi:10.1109/2.485845

Takabi, H., Joshi, J. B. D. (2010, November). Security and privacy challenges in cloud computing environment. *IEEE Journal on Security and Privacy, 8(6), pp. 24-31.*

KEY TERMS AND DEFINITIONS

Algorithm: A self-contained step-by-step set of operations to be performed.

Authentication: The act of confirming the truth of an attribute of a single piece of data (datum) or entity.

Confidentiality: A set of rules or a promise that limits access or places restrictions on certain types of information.

Framework: An abstraction in which software providing generic functionality can be selectively changed by additional user-written code, thus providing application-specific software.

Role-Based Access Control: An approach to restricting system access to authorized users.

Security Policy: A definition of what it means to *be secure* for a system, organization or other entity.

Security: The degree of resistance to, or protection from, harm. It applies to any vulnerable and valuable asset, such as a person, dwelling, community, nation, or organization.

Chapter 16
Big Data:
An Emerging Field of Data Engineering

Piyush Kumar Shukla
University Institute of Technology RGPV, India

Madhuvan Dixit
Millennium Institute of Technology, India

ABSTRACT

In this chapter, Big Data provide large-volume, complex structure, heterogeneous and irregular growing data sets include multiple and autonomous different resources. In this chapter, With the growing improvement of networking sites, image information storing capacity become big issue too, Big Data concept are most growing expanding in all technical area and knowledge engineering domains, including physical, medical and paramedical sciences. Here a data-driven method consist demand-driven aggregation of information and knowledge mining and analysis, user interest prototyping, security and privacy aspects has been presented.

INTRODUCTION

Big data is concept more uses from various companies. Some examples are related with oil and gas refineries and mining industries, online social networks, multimedia data and business related transactions. More amount of data collected from different increasingly efficient data storing various devices as well as stored on fast-growing mass storage, people are keep to search to find solutions to collect and process the information more efficiently, and to find various values from the mass at the same time. When referring to big data research strategy problems, people often

support the 4 v's -- volume, velocity, variety, and value. These pose support more brand-new challenges to computer scientists nowadays (Ahmed & Karypis, 2012).

In 2004, Wal-Mart claimed to have the very large data warehouse with approx 500 terabytes storage. In 2009, eBay announce storage amounted to eight PB. Two years later, the Yahoo warehouse totaled 170 PB. Since the rise of digitization, various technical enterprises have amassed burgeoning amounts of digital information, including trillions of bytes of data about their customers, suppliers and operations (Aral & Walker, 2012). Information volume is also growing exponentially

DOI: 10.4018/978-1-4666-8387-7.ch016

due to the spread of machine-oriented data (data records, web-log files, sensors information) and from growing human involvement within the social networks.

Basically the growth of information will never stop. As per the 2011 IDC Digital Universe Study, 130 EB of data were created and stored in 2006. The amount grew to 1,327 EB in 2011 and is projected to grow at 43.6% to 7,913 EB in 2016. The growth of information constitutes the "Big Data" concept – a technological concept bring about by the rapid rate of data expands and parallel generalization in technology that have given rise to an contribution of software and hardware products that are enabling users to analyze this information to produce new and more granular desire levels of information (Machanavajjhala & Reiter, 2012). A decade of Digital Universe Growth: Storage in Exabytes has been illustrated in Figure 1.

According to McKinsey, Big Data, perform to datasets whose sizes are beyond the ability of database software product to acquire, store, manage and study. There is no explicit definition of how big an image dataset should be in order to be considered large Big Data. New technology has to be manages this Big Data concept. Basically, IDC defines Big Data technologies considered as a new generation of database technologies and architectures designed to extract data value from large volumes of a wide variety of data. According to Reilly, "Big data is information which is exceeds the processing capacity of traditional database products. Basically, information is too big, moves too fast, or does not assemble the structures of desired database architectures. To gain value from these databases resource, there must be different way to process it" (Machanavajjhala & Reiter, 2012).

CHARACTERISTICS OF BIG DATA

Big Data is not just about the volume of information but also includes information variety and velocity. Together, these three parameters form the three Vs of Big Data theory. Volume is synonymous form of the "big" in the term, "Big Data". Volume is a relative term – some smaller-sized industries are likely to have mere gigabytes or terabytes of information storage as opposed to the PB or EB of data that big data global enterprises have. Data volume will continue to expand, regardless of the organization's capacity. There is a natural definition for companies to store data of all categories: account data, biomedical data, research data and so on. Many of these organization datasets are within the terabytes range today but in early days they could be reach PB or even EB (Aral & Walker, 2012). Data can come from a variety of resources and in a variety of category. With the expansion of

Figure 1. A decade of Digital Universe Growth: Storage in Exabytes (Machanavajjhala & Reiter, 2012)

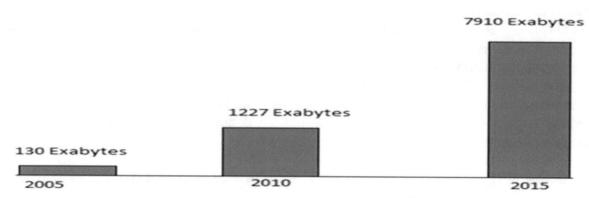

Figure 2. The 3 Vs of Big Data (Bollen, Mao, & Zeng, 2011)

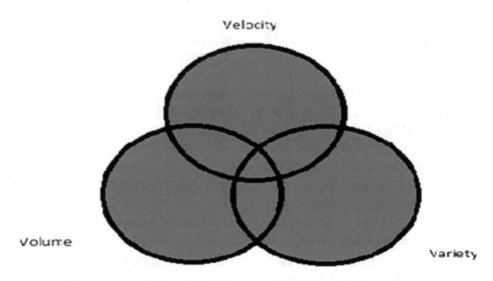

sensors, various smart devices such smart phone as well as social networking sites, information in an organization has become more complex because it includes not only structured and complex relational information, but also semi-structured, heterogeneous and unstructured information. The 3 Vs of Big Data has been illustrated in figure 2.

Structured data: This type expresses information which is categorized into a relational scheme. The information configuration and consistency permits it to respond to simple queries to achieve at usable data, based on an industry attributes and experimental.

Semi-structured data: It is a form of structured information that does not confirm to an explicit and fixed overall database. The information is extendable self-describing and includes tags to enforce hierarchies of data records and fields within the information. Examples include weblogs and social network.

Unstructured data: This type of information consists of formats which cannot easily be indexed into relational database tables for analysis or querying structures. Examples include images, multimedia such as audio and video files (Banerjee & Agarwal, 2012).

The three data types has been illustrated in figure 3. The velocity of information in terms of the regularity of its generation and delivery is also a feature of big data. Traditionally velocity typically considers that how quickly the information achieved and is stored, and how rapidly it can be retrieved. In Big Data, velocity should also be performed to information in motion. The various data streams and the increase in digital network deployment have led to a flow of data at a pace that has made it impossible for conventional systems to handle (Banerjee & Agarwal, 2012).

For handling the three Vs helps organizations retrieve the cost of Big Data. The cost comes in move the three Vs into the three Is:

1. Informed intuition: for predicting likely future possibility and what course of actions is apply likely to be more successful.
2. Intelligence: what is happening now in real duration and predicting the action to take.
3. Insight: reviewing what has happened and determining the action to take.

The convergence across business task area has ushered in a new desired economic system

Figure 3. The three data types (Banerjee & Agarwal, 2012)

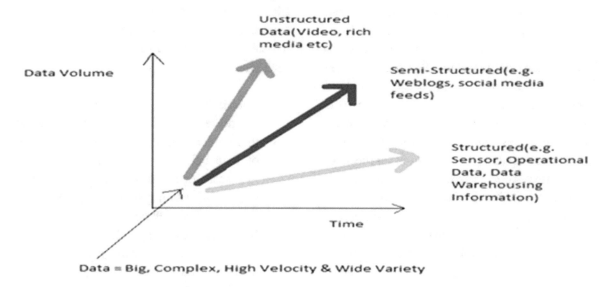

that is exploring relationships among producers, distributors and services. In an enhancing complex world, business verticals are collaborated and what happens in one direction has a direct impact on other directions (Machanavajjhala & Reiter, 2012). Within an industry, this complexity makes it more difficult for business expertise to rely solely on experience to make accurate decisions. They need to rely on good information services for their rights. For placing information at the center of the business executions to allow higher access to new contrast, industries will then be support to compete more efficiently (Banerjee & Agarwal, 2012).

Following three aspects have come together to drive Big Data:

1. The technologies to incorporate and interrogate Big Data have designed to a point where their deployments are more desirable.
2. The underline value of the desired infrastructure switch to power the study has fallen dramatically and making it economic to calculate the information.

3. The competitive pressure on industry has improved to the point where most conventional strategies are offering only marginal advantages.

For years, industries have occupied structured information and used bulk processes in batch to place compress of the information into conventional databases. The analysis of such type of information is retrospective and the investigations apply on the image datasets are on past patterns of business transactions.

RELATED WORK

File system is the basic foundation of upper application layer (Alam, Ha, & Lee, 2012). With the continuous growth of internet based applications, information is growing speedily. So the large-scale data storage became the task of the industries and various research areas. Because of the limit on the extension of storage limit, traditional storage system is more difficult to achieve the big data storage system. So have to use the concept of distributed file system (DFS) to transfer system load to multiple sections (Aral & Walker, 2012). By classifying hard disks on multiple nodes into a centralized storage system, distributed file system supports polymeric storage capacity and I/O bandwidth and easy to extension according to the system scale. Generally speaking, the mainstream distributed file systems such as GFS, HDFS, separately store metadata and application data because of the different characteristics of store and access (Birney, 2012). Divide and rule can increase the performance of the entire file system significantly. Despite these advantages, distributed file system still has many shortcomings when it faces growth of information, complex several of storage needs. Then these shortcomings are more paid and more attention, and become the find research focus today (Bughin, Chui, & Manyika, 2010).

1. Small Files Problem: Distributed file systems, such as GFS and HDFS are examined for larger files. But most of the information on the internet represent by the more frequency of small files, and more storage access for small files in the given application (Centola, 2010).

   a. Small file retrieve frequency is higher, need to retrieve the local disk for many times, so the performance of I/O is low;
   b. Small files will form a large amount of data about data, which can assist the management and access performance of metadata server, and cause overall performance may be degradation;
   c. Because the file is relatively small, easy to apply file fragmentation resulting in a waste of storage space;
   d. To maintain a link for each file can easily lead to network overheads;

In (Chang, Bai, & Zhu, 2009), the different files belong to same directory will write into the same block as much as possible. This will support increase the work speed distributed by MapReduce in the future.

2. Load Balancing Algorithm: In order to make the different stations can be a very good to complete the work together, a different of load balancing procedure is proposed to discard or avoid unbalanced load, data traffic congestion system and long reaction time. The load balancing procedure (Chen, Sivakumar, & Kargupta, 2004) can be implements by two ways. The I/O request is equally distributed on each storage media station by the right I/O scheduling approach, so each node can be a very better task, and situation that a part of the stations are overloaded, but another part of the station are light load will not be maintained. Another way is to maintain after what happened. When load of information, imbalance concept has emerged, it can be discarded effectively by migration or copy (Chang et al., 2009). In general, load balancing procedure through many years research has been relatively mature, usually divided into two types: static load balancing algorithm and dynamic load balancing algorithm. Static load algorithm has nothing to do with the recent state of the system. It assigns the job by experience or pre-established system (Chang et al., 2009). This procedure is easy, and spends little. But it does not assume the dynamic changes of the strategy status information, so it has blindness. It is mainly perfect for smaller and homogeneous service strategy. Classical static load balancing procedure includes polling procedure, ratio algorithm, priority algorithm (Chen et al., 2004). Dynamic load

balancing procedure assigns the I/O task or adjust the load between nodes according to the recent load of the system. Classical load balancing procedure contains minimum connection procedure, weighted least connection procedure, destination address procedure, source address algorithm. Dynamic load balancing procedure can be divided into centralized and distributed system. Load balancing algorithm in the distributed file strategy can also be divided into sender starting approach and recipient starting approach (Chang et al., 2009). Sender starting method initiates load distribution activities by extreme point, by which part of the overloaded stations is sent to light load stations, is suitable for the system as a complete in light load condition, because of more light load stations in system, light load station is simple to found, so frequent migration won't done (Chen et al., 2004).

We selected four different contributions that together represent shows state-of-the-art research in Big Data approach, and that support a broadly overview of the distinguishable and its prediction to the future. Other work in Big Data Mining can be found in the main conferences as KDD, ECML-PKDD, or international journals as "Data Mining and Knowledge Discovery" (Papadimitriou & Sun, 2008).

- Scaling Big Data Mining Infrastructure: This chapter represents insights about concern Big Data mining infrastructures, and the most experience of doing analytics at face book. It shows that due to the current level of the data mining methods. Most of the time is consumed in task to the application of data mining tools, and turning approaches into robust solutions (Chen et al., 2004; Luo, Ding, & Huang, 2012).
- Mining Heterogeneous Information Networks: A Structural Analysis method

by Yizhou Sun and Jiawei Han. This chapter represents that heterogeneous data network is a new and promising research in Big Data Mining research. It assumes interconnected, multi-typed information, including the relational database information, as heterogeneous information (Bollen et al., 2011; Chang et al., 2009).

- Big Graph Mining: Algorithms, procedures and discoveries by U Kang and Christos Faloutsos. This chapter represents a concepts of mining big data graphs, showing some find in the Web Graph and facebook social network. The chapter gives inspirational next research instructions for big graph mining (Papadimitriou & Sun, 2008).

DIMENSIONS OF GENERALIZED BIG DATA

There are no comprehensive Big Data technology standards in place today. The main reason is that the Big Data analytics projects companies are taking on are typically complex and diverse in nature. A proven comprehensive Big Data certification and standards are not yet in place although some vendors such as IBM and EMC have announced certification programs centers on providing training for their Hadoop-based products.

Hadoop is almost synonymous with the term "Big Data" in the industry and is popular for handling huge volumes of unstructured data. The Hadoop Distributed File System enables a highly scalable, redundant data storage and processing environment that can be used to execute different types of large-scale computing projects. For large volume structured data processing, enterprises use analytical databases such as EMC's Green plum and Teradata's Aster Data Systems. Many of these appliances offer connectors or plug-ins for integration with Hadoop systems.

Big Data technology can be broken down into two major components – the hardware component and the software component, as shown in the figure below. The hardware component refers to the component and infrastructure layer. The software component can be further divided into data organization and management software, analytics and discovery software, and decision support and automation software. A Big Data Technology Stack has been illustrated in Figure 4.

Infrastructure: Infrastructure is the foundation of the Big Data technology stack. The main components of any data storage infrastructure - industry standard x86 servers and networking bandwidth of 10 Gbps - may be extended to a Big Data storage facility. Storage systems are also becoming more flexible and are being designed in a scale-out fashion, enabling the scaling of system performance and capacity. In-memory computing is supported by increased capabilities in system memory delivered at lower prices, making multi-gigabytes (even multi-terabytes) memory more affordable. In many instances, Not AND (NAND) flash memory boards are deployed, together with traditional Dynamic Random Access Memory (DRAM), producing a more cost-effective and improved performance (Birney, 2012).

Data organization and management: This layer refers to the software that processes and prepares all types of structured and unstructured data for analysis. This layer extracts, cleanses, normalizes and integrates data. Two framework namely as Extended Relational Database Management System and the NoSQL database management system, have been developed to manage the different types of information. Extended RDBMS is generally optimized for scale and speed in processing huge relational information (i.e., structured data) sets, adopting approaches such as using columnar data stores to reduce the number of table scans (columnar database) and exploiting massively parallel processing (MPP) frameworks. On the other hand, the NoSQL database management system (NoSQL DBMS) grew out of the realization that SQL's transactional qualities and detailed indexing are not suitable for the processing of unstructured files. (More discussion on NoSQL DBMS can be found in the segment on Technology Outlook.) (Bollen et al., 2011).

Data Analytics and Discovery: This layer comprises two data analytics software segments – software that supports offline, ad hoc, discovery and deep analytics, and software that supports dynamic real-time analysis and automated, rule-

Figure 4. Big Data Technology Stack (Sun, 2008)

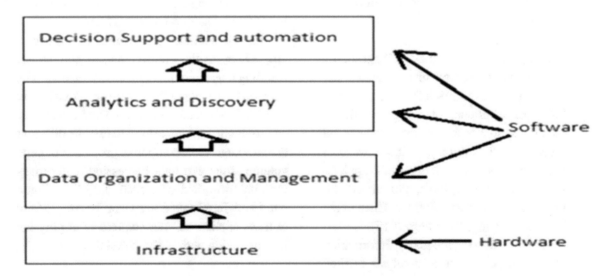

based transactional decision making (Luo et al., 2012). The tools can also be categorized by the type of data being analyzed, such as text, audio and video. The tools within this layer can also be at different levels of sophistication. There are tools that allow for highly complex and predictive analysis as well as tools that simply help with basic data aggregation and trend reporting. In any case, the usage of the tools is not mutually exclusive – there can be a set of tools with different features residing in a system to enable Big Data analytics (Bughin et al., 2010).

Decision support and automation interface: The process of data analysis usually involves a closed-loop decision making model which, at the minimum, includes steps such as track, analyze, decide and act (Banerjee & Agarwal, 2012). To support decision making and to ensure that an action is taken, based on data analysis, is not a trivial matter. From a technology perspective, additional functionalities such as decision capture and retention are required to support collaboration and risk management (Michel, 2012).

There are two decision support and automation software categories: transactional decision management and project-based decision management software. The former is automated, embedded within applications, real-time and rules-based in nature. It enables the use of outputs to prescribe or enforce rules, methods and processes. Examples include fraud detection, securities trading, airline pricing optimization, product recommendation and network monitoring. Project- based decision management is typically standalone, ad hoc and exploratory in nature. It can be used for forecasting and estimation of trends. Examples include applications for customer segmentation for targeted marketing, product development and weather forecasting (Campbell, 2008).

BIG DATA MODEL

Big Data is a recent concept used to identify the image datasets that due to their very large size, we cannot handle them with the typical image data mining software methods. Instead of explaining "Big Data" as datasets of a desired large size, for instance in the order of magnitude of PB, the concept is linked to the idea that the image dataset is too large to be handled without using recent methods or technologies. The McKinsey Global Institute released a desired report on Big Data topic (Michel, 2012) that analyses the business exposures that concern big data opens a value of $400 billion in the United States health care, $150 billion in European government or improving the operating margin of companies by 65 percent. Big Data analytics is becoming an important method to improve efficiency and quality in industry, and its importance is moving to improve in the next years. There are two important strategies for dealing with big data concept, first is sampling and second is distributed system. Sampling is based in the idea that if the dataset is too big and we cannot use all the instances, we can obtain a desired solution using a subset of the instances. A good sampling approach will try to choose the best instances, to have a good achievement using a small quantity of memory. An alternative to sampling is the use of probabilistic methods. Backstrom, Boldi, Ugander and Vigna (Campbell, 2008) evaluated the average distance of friends links in FB. They iterated the practical that Stanley Milgram did in 1967(Papadimitriou & Sun, 2008), where he challenged audience to send letters to specific people around United States using only direct acquaintances. Milgram acquired a number between 4.2 and 5.1, so the notion of six levels of separation was confirmed. The practical using

FB shows four levels of distinguish pattern. For run these practical, these researchers used Hyper-ANF, a software tool by Boldi and Vigna (Chu et al., 2007). Basically, ANF is a fast and scalable technique for big data mining in massive graphs (Chu et al., 2007) which computes approximations to the neighborhood mapping of nodes in massive graphs. The neighborhood mapping of a node n and distance h is explained as the number of points at a certain distance h reachable from node n. This mapping is evaluated using the set of points that can be reachable from h − 1 using probabilistic counter desired data structures. The number of users of Facebook is more than 700 million users, but they managed to evaluate the average distance between two peoples on FB only using one PC. The map-reduce approaches started in Google Inc, as a technique to perform crawling of the web. Basically, Hadoop is an open-source implementation of map-reduce method in Yahoo! and is being used in moreover non-streaming image big data analysis. The map-reduce technique divides procedures in two main steps: map and reduce. The input data is split into more datasets and each split is send to a map, which will transform the image data. The result of the map will be combined in reducers that will produce the result of the algorithm. Finally, we would like to apply the work that GP is doing using image Big Data theory to enhance life in progressive countries. A Big Data Approach has been illustrated in Figure 5.

GP is a UN initiative, which is launched in 2011, which provide the mapping as an innovative experiments, and that is based on image Big Data mining. They pursue a main strategy that consists of 1) researching techniques and methods for analyzing real-time data to detect emerging vulnerabilities; 2) assembling open source technique product for analyzing real-time information and sharing ideas; and 3) establishing an integrated, to pilot the method. GP describe the main objectives Big Data applies to progressive countries in their White chapter "Big Data for Development: Challenges & Opportunities":

- Early warning: finding drawbacks in the usage of media.
- Real-time awareness: policies with a grained representation of reality.
- Real-time feedback: using this feedback make the desired necessary changes.

Figure 5. Big Data Approach (Chu et al., 2007)

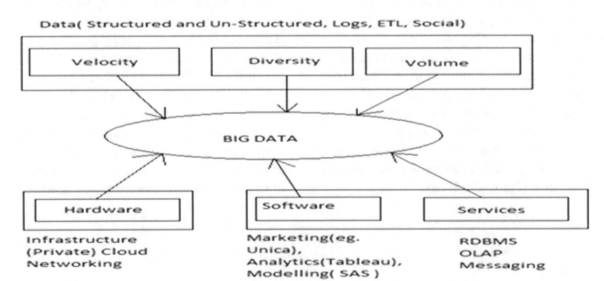

The Big Data mining approach is not limited to the industrialized real world, as mobiles are more spreading in progressive countries. It is calculated then there are over 7 billion cell phones, and that 750% are situated in developing countries.

BIG DATA PROCESSING FRAMEWORK

Big data and cloud computing is receiving more interest from both company and academia nowadays. They have been currently entitled as important strategies by Australian Government. To address the big data problems, cloud computing is faith to be the most important platform. In Australia, various big companies such as Vodafone Mobile and News Corporation are already moving their business information and its processing jobs to Amazon cloud such as Amazon Web Services (AWS). Email systems of concern Australian universities are using cloud computing as the backbone. To tackle the large amount of information in scientific applications, CERN, for example, is already putting the processing of petabytes of information into cloud computing resources. There has been a lot of research regarding scientific approach of cloud computing. For big data tasks within cloud computing, information security is a problem that should always be properly addressed. In fact, information security is biggest reasons why people are reluctant in using cloud computing. Therefore, more effective and efficient security techniques are directly in need to support people establish their confidence in all-around cloud computing. Data integrity is always an essential part in information security, and there is no exception for cloud data computing. Client-side verification is as important as server-side security. As data in most big data applications are strictly dynamic in nature, we will focus on verification of dynamic information. A large proportion of the important updates are very small but very frequent. For instance, in 2010 Twitter is generating

every day up to 12 terabytes of data, composed of tweets with maximum of 150 characters. Business strategy transactions and loggings are also good instances. The dataset in these big data scenario are very large in size and require large-scale processing capabilities. Hence, the requirements are not only in security, but also in better efficiency. There are 3 parties in an integrity verification scenario: client, CSS and TPA. The client node stores information on CSS, while TPA's objective is to justify the integrity of client's node data stored on CSS. Although the three forms a robust and efficient triangle, each of the two authority are only semi-trusted by each other as shown in figure 1. New security enhance may appear while verifying information integrity, which is why we need a good architecture to address this problem systematically. The main framework of a remote integrity justification station with support for dynamic information updates can be analyzed in the following steps:

Setup, data are upload -> Authorization of TPA -> Challenge the integrity proof -> Proof for verification -> Updated for data upload -> Updated for metadata upload -> Verification of updated data

The relationship and order of following steps has been illustrated in figure 6. We now explore in detail how these steps task and why they are essential to integrity justification of cloud information storage.

Setup and upload data: In cloud environment, user information is stored remotely on CSS. In order to justify the information without accessing them, the client station will need to setup verification data about data, namely homomorphic linear authenticator (HLA) or homomorphic verifiable tag (HVT), based on homomorphic signatures (Chu et al., 2007). Then, these metadata will be setup to uploaded and exist alongside with the original datasets. These are computed from the original information; they must be small in size in comparison to the original dataset for practical purpose.

Figure 6. A brief outline of integrity justification over big data in cloud computing

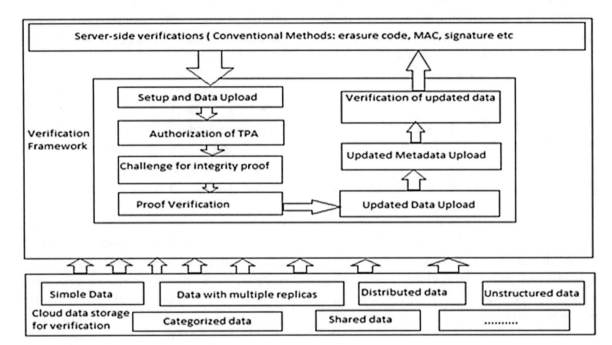

Authorization for TPA: This step is not essential in a two-party strategy where clients justify their information for themselves, but it is essential when users require a semi-trusted TPA to verify the information on their behalf. If a third party can infinitely ask for integrity verify over a certain piece of information, there will always be security risks in existence such as plaintext extraction level.

Challenge and justification of data storage: This step is where the main task is integrity verification to be fulfilled. The client station will send a challenge message to the server level, and server node will evaluate a response over the pre-stored information (HLA) and the challenge message. The client station can then verify the response to find out whether the information is intact. The structure has public verifiability if this justification can be done without the help of client's secret key. If the information storage is static, the complete process would have been ended. Therefore, as discussed earlier, data are always dynamic in many big data

contexts nature. In these scenarios, we will need the rest of the steps to complete the framework.

Data update Occurs in dynamic data aspects. The client station needs to apply updates to some of the cloud information storage. The updates could be roughly classified in insert, delete and modification; if the data is stored in separate blocks with different size for efficiency purpose, there will be more different types of updates to address here.

Metadata update: In order to keep the data storage stay justifiable without accessing all the information stored and/or re-running the entire desired setup phase, the client station will need to extend the verification metadata, according with the existing keys.

Verification of updated data: This is also an essential step in dynamic information aspect. As the CSS is not completely verifiable, the client station needs to verify the information update process to see if the extending of both user information and verification metadata have been performed successfully in order to ensure the updated information can still be verified accurately in the future.

DATA MINING CHALLENGES WITH BIG DATA

HACE Theorem is describe as Big Data initiate with large-capacity, heterogeneous, autonomous resources with distributed manner, and searches to explore more complex and evolving links among information. For an learning database system to manage Big Data feature, the essential step is to move up to the more exceptionally huge volume of information and provide extra treatments for the properties featured by the HACE method. The Big Data processing layout, which consists three tiers from considerations on data accessing and computing (Tier I), data security and privacy (Tier II), and Big Data mining procedures (Tier III). The issues at Tier I focus on data retrieving and arithmetic computing methods. Because Big Data are stored at different sites and information volumes may improve, an effective computing platform will have to take distributed huge-scale information volume into aspect for computing procedure. For example, data mining procedures accept all data to be loaded into the primary memory, however, is becoming a clear technical issue for Big Data because moving information across different sites is more expensive, even if we do have a large primary memory to hold all information for computing.

The issues at Tier II center around semantic and task knowledge for various Big Data applications. Such data can support additional advantages to the mining process, as well as add technical issues to the Big Data access (Tier I) and mining procedures (Tier III). For example, depending on various domain applications, the data security and data sharing approaches between data producers and data consumers can be differ. Sharing sensor network information for applications such as water quality monitoring may not be discouraged, while releasing and sharing mobile user's site data is clearly not acceptable for majority applications. The application domains can also support additional information to guide Big Data mining method. For example, in market transactions data, each transaction is taken as independent. On the other hand, users are linked and share different structures. The knowledgeable information is then represented by user communities, leaders in each group, and social influence modeling, and so on.

BIG DATA MINING PLATFORM

In the big data mining, information sharing is not only a promise of each stage, but also a objective of Big Data processing.

Tier First-Big Data Mining: In typical big data mining methods, the mining approaches require computing resources for information analysis and desired comparisons. For small scale big data mining tasks, a single PC, that contains hard disk and processors, is necessary and sufficient to accept the big data mining objectives. Common solutions are to provide on parallel computing process, (Chu et al., 2007).

For Big Data Mining method, because data scale is far beyond the length which is a single PC can handle, a Big Data layout will rely on cluster computers with a more high-performance parallel computing, with a data mining task being deployed by running some parallel programming approach, on a large number of parallel computing points. The role of the software component is to design sure that a single big data mining work domain, such as finding the best match of an image data query from a given database, is subdivide into many small task domains each of which task is running on computing nodes. In fact, for decades, many companies have been making decisions based on transactional information stored in relational databases. Big Data mining provides opportunities to go traditional databases to rely on less structured information: weblogs, social site, web-mail, sensors, and photographs that can be mined for useful data. Major business companies, such IBM, Oracle, google and so on, have all properties their own products to support customers acquire and organize these diverse information sources and coordinate with customers information to search new insights and capitalize on relationships.

Tier Second- Big Data Layout and Application Knowledge: Processing layout and data application in Big Data specify to numerous aspects that are related to the protocols, user knowledge, and work domain information. The two most important aspects at this tier consists 1) data sharing and privacy; and 2) task and application knowledge. The former support answers to resolve given concerns on how information is shared;

Information Sharing and Data Privacy: Data sharing is an objective for all systems involving different parties. While the motivation for sharing is clear, a real-world concern is that Big Data approach are related to sensitive data, such as banking transactions and medical records. Simple information exchanges do not resolve privacy concerns. To protect privacy, two common methods are to 1) access to the information, such as adding access control to the information entries, and 2) anonymize data fields. For the first method, common challenges are to create secured certification mechanisms, such that no sensitive information can be misconducted by individuals. For data anonymization, the main objective is to supply randomness into the information to ensure a number of privacy objectives. For example, the most generalize k-anonymity privacy measure is to insist that each individual in the database must be different from k-1. Common anonymization techniques are to use suppression, generalization, and permutation to generate an edited version of the information, which is, in fact, some uncertain information.

Domain and Application Knowledge: Domain and application knowledge supports essential data for designing Big Data algorithms. In a simple case, task knowledge can support to identify right features for modeling the underlying data. The domain knowledge can also support design business objectives by using Big Data techniques. For example, stock market data are a domain that generates a more quantity of data, in every single second. The market continuously evolves and is impacted by distinguish factors, such as domestic and international news, government reports and so on. A Big Data mining task is to design a Big Data mining system to assume the movement of the market in the next one or two minutes. Such systems, even if the prediction accuracy is slightly better than generalize random guess, will bring significant business costs to the developers.

Tier Third-Big Data Mining Algorithms:

Local Space Learning and Prototype Fusion for Multiple Data Sources: Big Data applications are characterized with different sources and decentralized information controls, distributed information resources to a centralized location for big data mining is contribute due to the information transmission cost and privacy fields. On the other hands, although we can always carry out different big data mining processes at different distributed location. Under such a given circumstance, a Big Data system has to perform an information exchange and image fusion approach to ensure that all various distributed location can work to achieve a desired global optimization. Big Data technique and correlations are the suitable steps to verify that techniques or patterns found from multiple information sources can be meet the desired global data mining objective. More basically, the global data mining can be featured with a general two-stage phase, at data model and at knowledge phases. At the data level, each local site can implement the data history based on the local data sources and interchange the statistics between different sites to achieve an accurate global data distribution level. A Big Data processing framework has been illustrated in Figure 7.

However, Big Data mining complexity is represented in many criteria, including complex heterogeneous data types, complex semantic associations in data and complex link networks among data. The value of Big Data is in its complexity.

SECURITY AND UNCERTAINTY ISSUES IN BIG DATA

An important and challenging uncertainty domain may be the pattern problem. Patterns are variables of sets endowed with a partial order relation. Examples of patterns are item sets, trees and graphs. The structured pattern problem is as follows. A set of examples of the form (t, y) is given, where y is a discrete class and t is a specific pattern. The objective is to produce from these examples a prototype y = f(t) that will predict the labels y of next pattern examples Most standard methods of classification can only deal with vector information, but one of many possible pattern.

Having described the multiple phases in the Big Data analysis pipeline, we now turn to some common challenges that underlie many, and sometimes all, of these phases. These are shown as five boxes in the second row of Figure 1.

(a) Heterogeneity and Incompleteness: When humans consume information, a great deal of heterogeneity is comfortably tolerated. In fact, the nuance and richness of natural language can provide valuable depth. However, machine analysis algorithms expect homogeneous data, and cannot understand nuance. In consequence, data must be carefully structured as a first step in (or prior to) data analysis. Consider, for example, a patient who has multiple medical procedures at a hospital. We could create one record per medical procedure or laboratory test, one record for the entire hospital stay, or one record for all lifetime hospital interactions of this patient. With anything other than the first design, the number of medical procedures and lab tests per record would be different for each patient. The

Figure 7. A Big Data processing framework

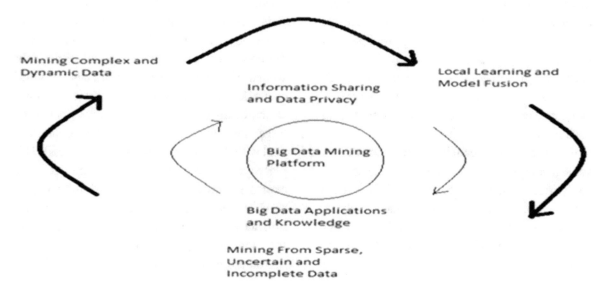

three design choices listed have successively less structure and, conversely, successively greater variety. Greater structure is likely to be required by many (traditional) data analysis systems. However, the less structured design is likely to be more effective for many purposes – for example questions relating to disease progression over time will require an expensive join operation with the first two designs, but can be avoided with the latter. However, computer systems work most effectively if they can hold different items that are all identical in size and layout. Efficient presentation, fetch, analysis of semi-structured data require further work.

Consider an electronic health record database design that has fields for birth date, occupation, and blood type for each patient. What do we do if one or more of these pieces of information is not provided by a patient? Obviously, the health record is still placed in the database, but with the corresponding attribute values being set to NULL. A data analysis that looks to classify patients by, say, occupation, must take into account patients for which this information is not known. Worse, these patients with unknown occupations can be ignored in the analysis only if we have reason to believe that they are otherwise statistically similar to the patients with known occupation for the analysis performed. For example, if unemployed patients are more likely to hide their employment status, analysis results may be skewed in that it considers a more employed population mix than exists, and hence potentially one that has differences in occupation-related health-profiles.

Even after data cleaning and error correction, some incompleteness and some errors in data are likely to remain. This incompleteness and these errors must be managed during data analysis. Doing this correctly is a challenge. Recent work on managing probabilistic data suggests one way to make progress.

(b) Scale: Of course, the first thing anyone thinks of with Big Data mining is its length. After all, the word "large" is there in the very most name. Managing large and increasing volumes of information has been an important issue for many past years. In the past, this challenge task was initiated by processors getting more faster, to provide us with the sources needed to cope with increasing volumes of information. There is a fundamental shift on the way now: information volume is scaling fastest than compute mentioned resources, and CPU speeds are going static. First, over the last five years the processor based technology has made an evolutionary dramatic shift – instead of processors doubling their clock cycle frequency every 24-36 months, due to power level constraints, clock cycle speeds have largely stable and processors are being make with increasing several of cores. These unprecedented modifications require us to rethink how we represent, build and operate data processing elements.

The second shift that is on the way is the move towards cloud computing resources, which now aggregates different disparate workloads with varying objective goals into very big level clusters. This level of sharing of resources on expensive and large clusters requires new ways of determining how to run and execute data processing jobs so that we can meet the goals of each workload cost-effectively, and to deal with system failures, which occur more frequently as we operate on larger and larger clusters (that are required to deal with the rapid growth in data volumes). This places a premium on declarative approaches to expressing programs, even those doing complex machine learning tasks, since global optimization across multiple users programs is necessary for good overall performance. Reliance on user-driven program optimizations is likely to lead to poor cluster utilization, since users are unaware of other users programs. System-driven holistic optimization requires programs to be sufficiently transparent, e.g., as in relational database systems, where declarative query languages are designed with this in mind.

(c) Timeliness: The flip side of size is speed. The larger the data set to be processed, the longer it will take to analyze. The design of a system that effectively deals with size is likely also to result in a system that can process a given size of data set faster. However, it is not just this speed that is usually meant when one speaks of velocity in the aspect of Big Data. Instead of, there is an acquisition rate challenge, and a timeliness challenge described next.

(d) Privacy Detail: The privacy of data is another more aspect, and one that update in the in spite of Big Data Mining. For electronic health information records, there are strictly rules governing what can and cannot be done. Consequently, there is more great public fear regarding the inappropriate use of desired information, particularly joining of data from multiple resources. Managing privacy is more effectively both a technical and a sociological situation.

Consider, data gleaned from different location-based services. These new given architectures accept user to share his/her location with the service provider, resulting in obvious privacy concerns. In general, Barabási et al. showed that there is a close correlation between people's identities and their movement patterns (Borgatti, Mehra, Brass, & Labianca, 2009). Note that hiding a user location is much more challenging than hiding his/her identity. This is because with location-based services, the location of the user is needed for an information access, while the identity of the user is not necessary.

There are many additional challenging research problems. For example, we do not know yet how to share private data while limiting disclosure and ensuring sufficient data utility in the shared data. The existing paradigm of differential privacy is a very important step in the right direction, but it unfortunately reduces information content too far in order to be useful in most practical cases. In addition, real data is not static but gets larger and changes over time; none of the prevailing techniques results in any useful content being released in this scenario. Yet another very important direction is to rethink security for information sharing in Big Data use cases. Many online services today require us to share private information (think of Facebook applications), but beyond record-level access control we do not understand what it means to share data, how the shared data can be linked, and how to give users fine-grained control over this sharing.

(e) Human Collaboration: In spite of the tremendous advances produce in technical analysis, there remain many different patterns that humans can easily find but computer procedure has a hard time searching. Indeed, CAPTCHAs emerge precisely this fact to tell human web users apart from computer generated programs. Generally, analytics for Big Data will not be all computed rather it will be designed more explicitly to have a human in the loop. The new sub-field of visual impact analytics is applying to do this, at least with respect to modeling and analysis step in pipeline. There is similar value to human input at all steps of the analysis pipeline.

In today's world, it often takes different experts from multiple domains to really understand what is going on. A Big Data analysis strategy must support input value from different human experts and sharable exploration of conclusions. These different experts may be classified in space and time when it is more expensive to assemble an entire group together in one space. The information system has to access this different distributed expert input value and support their collaboration.

A popular method of harnessing human ingenuity to solve given problems is through crowd sourcing. Wikipedia is the online encyclopedia is perhaps the best known example of crowd sourced information. We are relying upon information provided by unvented strangers. Most often, what they say is correct. Therefore, we should assume there to be individuals who have other motives and abilities some may have a reason to support false data in an intentional attempt to mislead. While most such bugs will be detected and corrected by others in the crowd, we need techniques to facilitate this. We also need a architecture to use in result of such crowd-sourced information with conflicting statements.

CONCLUSION

Process by real-world techniques and industrial shareholders and initialized by national society, Managing and Big Data mining have expose to be a challenge yet very compelling task. The term Big Data support concerns about data sizes. The privacy concerns, errors and noise can be represented into the data, to produce altered information copies. Implementing a secure and sound data sharing rules is a major concern. The key challenge is to represent global prototype by combining locally founded patterns to form a display. This requires securely designed methods to analyze prototype correlations between distributed locations, and fake decisions from different resources to gain an accurate prototype out of the Big Data. At the system level, the efficient challenge is that a Big Data mining paradigm needs to assume complex links between space samples, prototypes, and information data resources, along with their evolving different with time duration and other factors. A system necessary to be secure designed so that unstructured information can be linked through their complex links to form useful information patterns, and the progress of data sizes and product relationships should support form legitimate information patterns to assume the trend and bright future. We regard Big Data as a growing trend and the need for Big Data mining approach is arising in all engineering task domains. With Big Data approaches, we will enjoy fully be able to support most relevant and most desired accurate social feedback to better understand our social society at real-time. We can further expose the active participation of the public audiences in the information production group for societal events. The natural era of Big Data has arrived.

SUMMARY

We have proposed a years of Big Data. Through better analysis of the big volumes of information that are becoming available, there is the more potential for making faster advances in many desired scientific area and improving the profitability and grow of many enterprises. Therefore, many technical issues which described in this chapter must be specified before this potential can be more realized. The main issues include not the issues of scale, but also heterogeneity level, lack of layout, error-handling, security, timeliness and visualization at all levels of the analysis processing from data acquisition stage to conclusion interpretation. These technical issues are more common across a large distinguish of application task area. Furthermore, these issues will acquire transformation conclusions, and will not be specified naturally by the future generation of products. We also must support and fundamental experiments towards addressing these technical issues.

REFERENCES

Ahmed, R., & Karypis, G. (2012). Algorithms for mining the evolution of conserved relational states in dynamic networks. *Knowledge and Information Systems, 33*(3), 603-630.

Alam, M. H., Ha, J., & Lee, S. (2012). Novel approaches to crawling important pages early. *Knowledge and Information Systems, 33*(3), 707-734.

Aral, S., & Walker, D. (2012). Identifying influential and susceptible members of social networks. *Science, 337*(6092), 337-341.

Banerjee, S., & Agarwal, N. (2012). Analyzing collective behavior from blogs using swarm intelligence. *Knowledge and Information Systems, 33*(3), 523-547.

Birney, E. (2012). The making of ENCODE: lessons for big-data projects. *Nature, 489*(7414), 49-51.

Bollen, J., Mao, H., & Zeng, X. (2011). Twitter mood predicts the stock market. *Journal of Computational Science, 2*(1), 1-8.

Borgatti, S. P., Mehra, A., Brass, D. J., & Labianca, G. (2009). Network analysis in the social sciences. *Science, 323*(5916), 892-895.

Bughin, J., Chui, M., & Manyika, J. (2010). Clouds, big data, and smart assets: Ten tech-enabled business trends to watch. *The McKinsey Quarterly, 56*(1), 75–86.

Campbell, P. (2008). Editorial on special issue on big data: Community cleverness required. *Nature, 455*(7209), 1. doi:10.1038/455001a PMID:18769385

Centola, D. (2010). The spread of behavior in an online social network experiment. *Science, 329*(5996), 1194-1197.

Chang, E. Y., Bai, H., & Zhu, K. (2009). *Parallel algorithms for mining large-scale rich-media data.*

Chen, R., Sivakumar, K., & Kargupta, H. (2004). Collective mining of Bayesian networks from distributed heterogeneous data. *Knowledge and Information Systems, 6*(2), 164-187.

Chu, C., Kim, S. K., Lin, Y. A., Yu, Y., Bradski, G., Ng, A. Y., & Olukotun, K. (2007). Map-reduce for machine learning on multicore. Advances in neural information processing systems, 19, 281.

Luo, D., Ding, C. H. Q., & Huang, H. (2012). *Parallelization with Multiplicative Algorithms for Big Data Mining.*

Machanavajjhala, A., & Reiter, J. P. (2012). Big privacy: protecting confidentiality in big data. *XRDS: Crossroads, The ACM Magazine for Students, 19*(1), 20-23.

Michel, F. (2012). How Many Photos Are Uploaded to Flickr Every Day and Month? Papadimitriou, S., & Sun, J. (2008). *Disco: Distributed co-clustering with map-reduce: A case study towards petabyte-scale end-to-end mining.*

KEY TERMS AND DEFINITIONS

Autonomous Sources: Autonomous describes things that function separately or independently. Once you move out of your parents' house, and get your own job, you will be an *autonomous* member of the family.

Big Data: Big data is a broad term for data sets so large or complex that traditional data processing applications are inadequate.

Big Data Mining: Big data analytics enables organizations to analyze a mix of structured, semi-structured and unstructured data in search of valuable business information and insights.

Big Data Model: Big data is a collection of data from traditional and digital sources inside and outside your company that represents a source for ongoing discovery and analysis.

Data Analytics: Data analytics refers to qualitative and quantitative techniques and processes used to enhance productivity and business gain.

Data Mining: Data mining is the analysis of data for relationships that have not previously been discovered.

Heterogeneity: Heterogeneity is a word that signifies diversity. A classroom consisting of people from lots of different backgrounds would be considered having the quality of heterogeneity.

Chapter 17
Achieving Efficient Purging in Transparent per-file Secure Wiping Extensions

Wasim Ahmad Bhat
University of Kashmir, India

ABSTRACT

According to a recent Cloud Security Alliance Report, insider attacks are the third biggest threat in Cloud Security. A malicious-insider can access the low-level device, and recover the sensitive and confidential information which had been deleted by the customer with a belief that the data no more exists physically. Though proposals for secure deletion of data exist, specifically transparent per-file secure wiping extensions, however, they are not efficient and reliable. In this chapter, we propose an efficient and reliable transparent per-file-wiping filesystem extension called restfs. Instead of overwriting at file level which is found in existing wiping extensions, restfs overwrites at block level to exploit the behavior of filesystems for efficiency and reliability. We empirically evaluated the efficiency of restfs using Postmark benchmark and results indicate that restfs can save 28-98% of block overwrites which otherwise need necessarily to be performed in existing wiping extensions. In addition, it can also reduce the number of write commands issued to the disk by 88%.

INTRODUCTION

The intrusion of digital technologies into every aspect of our day to day life is continuously creating voluminous amounts of confidential and sensitive digital information which is stored in the form of directories and files. This sensitive and confidential information, which when deleted with a belief that the information has been physically erased, can be recovered even by novice users.

Following are some of the incidents that are the consequence of this misbelief and had happened in recent past.

In 2004, a customer database and the current access codes to the supposedly secure intranet of one of Europe's largest financial services groups was left on a hard disk offered for sale on eBay (Leyden, 2004). In 2006, flash drives containing classified US military secrets in the form of deleted files turned up for sale in a bazaar in

DOI: 10.4018/978-1-4666-8387-7.ch017

Afghanistan (Leyden, 2006). And in 2009, the highly sensitive details of a US military missile air defense system were found on a secondhand hard drive bought on eBay (The-Daily-Mail, 2009). The situation is even worse than it seems, as the non-sanitization of storage devices continues. In 2009, a fifth study was published in an ongoing research program which was being conducted into the levels and types of information that remain on computer hard disks that have been offered for sale on the secondhand market (Jones, Valli, & Dabibi, 2009). The study revealed that over a period of five years there were clear indications that the number of disks that contain information relating to organizations and individuals is reducing. Unfortunately, it also found that because of the increasing volume of storage capacity of the disk, the quantity of non-sanitized data appears to be increasing.

Operating systems give an illusion of file deletion by just invalidating the filename and stripping it of allocated data blocks. As such, the contents of data blocks associated with a file remain there even after its deletion, unless and until these blocks get reallocated to some other file and finally get overwritten with new data. This policy is adopted as a trade-off between performance and security. Though, this allows users to recover files deleted accidentally; unfortunately, this poses a serious security threat as the files deleted intentionally can also be recovered (Rosenbaum, 2000).

In case of Cloud Service Provider, who to cut costs, conserve resources and maintain efficiency, stores more than one customer's data on a server, the hazards are magnified. As a result, more confidential but believed to be deleted data is at risk of breach via after-deletion data recovery.

There are generally two techniques to ensure secure deletion of data; 1) wiping, and 2) encryption.

Secure Deletion Using Encryption

Secure deletion using encryption can employ various encryption techniques to encrypt data before it is stored on disk and to decrypt it on its retrieval. This solution protects both deleted as well as non-deleted data. However, it suffers from several problems (C. P. Wright, Dave, & Zadok, 2003): 1) All encryption systems suffer from cumbersome and costly management of keys, 2) Encryption adds CPU overheads for most of filesystem operations, 3) Keys could be lost or broken and thus, a compromised key allows recovery of both live and deleted data, 4) Using per-file keys adds more overhead and key management costs, 5) At last, strong encryption is not allowed in some countries.

Secure Deletion Using Wiping

Secure deletion using wiping works by overwriting the meta-data and data pertaining to a file when it is deleted. In its simplest form, the filesystem or the storage media can be overwritten in its entirety and the process can be accomplished by user applications or assisted at hardware level. Unfortunately, this process is inconvenient as it erases the live data also and thus is applicable only when whole disk or filesystem sanitization is required. The most applicable and desired wiping procedure is transparent per-file wiping which can be performed at two levels of an operating system: 1) User-mode level, & 2) Filesystem level. User-mode transparent per-file wiping can be implemented by modifying the library or adding extensions to it, to support overwriting on deletion. However, this solution demands library modification, does not work with statically linked binaries, can't overwrite all the meta-data belonging to the file and can be bypassed easily. As such, it is not a feasible solution to transparent per-file wiping. In contrast, at filesystem level, all the filesystem operations can be intercepted and thus complete wiping can be guaranteed. Although many transparent per-file secure wiping filesystem extensions have been proposed, unfortunately they are not efficient (number of disk blocks to be wiped and number of disk writes issued) and/ or reliable (sustainability across system crash).

Because existing transparent per-file secure wiping filesystem extensions work at file level, they are not able to exploit the behavior of filesystems at block level for efficiency which includes 1) skipping the overwriting of a recently deallocated block which got re-allocated to some new file, and 2) ordering of possibly unordered deallocated blocks and then coalescing the consecutive blocks to reduce the number of write commands. This chapter proposes overwriting at block level to exploit these possibilities in order to perform efficient wiping via a transparent per-file secure wiping filesystem extension called *restfs*. *restfs* also uses traditional logging mechanism for blocks to be overwritten in order to ensure reliable wiping across system crashes. *restfs* is currently implemented for ext2 filesystem only though it is design compatible with all filesystems which export block allocation map of a file to VFS. On empirical evaluation of *restfs* using *Postmark* benchmark, we found that *restfs* can save 28-98% of disk block overwrites which otherwise need necessarily to be performed in existing wiping extensions. In addition, it can also reduce the number of write commands issued to disk by 88%.

BACKGROUND AND RELATED WORK

Wiping Myths

In 1992, it was reported that Magnetic Force Microscope (MFM) can be used to reconstruct the magnetic structure of a sample magnetic surface (Gomez, Adly, Mayergoyz, & Burke, 1992). Also, in 2000, a technique was introduced that uses a spin-stand to collect several concentric and radial magnetic surface images, which can be processed to form a single surface image (Mayergoyz, Serpico, Krafft, & Tse, 2000). These techniques make it possible to recover overwritten data if we accept the proposition that the head positioning system is not accurate enough that the data written to a drive may not be written back to the precise location of the original data. This track misalignment has been argued to make possible the process of identifying traces of data from earlier magnetic patterns alongside the current track. The basis of this belief is that the actual value stored is closer to 0.95 when a zero (0) is overwritten with one (1), and a value 1.05 when one (1) is overwritten with one (1). As such, using these techniques the data overwritten once or twice may be recovered by subtracting what is expected to be read from a storage location from what is actually read. In 1996, based on this proposition, Peter Gutmann developed a 35-pass data overwriting scheme for secure data deletion (Gutmann, 1996). The basic idea was to flip each magnetic domain on the disk back and forth as much as possible, without writing the same pattern twice in a row and to saturate the disk surface to the greatest depth possible. NIST recommends that the magnetic media be degaussed or overwritten at least three times (Grance, Stevens, & Myers, 2003). The Department of Defence Document DoD522.22M suggests overwrite with a character, its compliment, then a random character, as well as other software-based overwrite methods (Diesburg & Wang, 2010).

In 2008, a study demonstrated that correctly wiped data cannot be reasonably retrieved even if it is of a small size or found only over small parts of the hard drive due to the enhancements in magnetic drive technologies such as advanced encoding schemes (PRML and EPRML), Zone Bit Recording (ZBR) and so on (C. Wright, Kleiman, & Sundhar R.S., 2008). The purpose of the paper was a categorical settlement to the controversy surrounding the misconceptions involving the belief that data can be recovered following a wipe procedure. In general, a single wipe procedure is enough to make any reasonable data recovery using software and hardware techniques impossible.

Existing Per-File Secure Wiping Proposals

In order to achieve transparent per-file secure wiping, the filesystem level is most appropriate as it is able to intercept every filesystem operation and does not require any modification in user level libraries or applications. Many transparent per-file secure wiping extensions have surfaced from time to time to ensure secure data deletion.

In 2001, Bauer et al. (Bauer & Priyantha, 2001) modified ext2 filesystem to asynchronously overwrite data on *unlink()* and *truncate()* operations. However, this technique has some drawbacks such as source code modification can break stability and reliability of a filesystem, modification should be made in every filesystem and the wiping cannot sustain across crashes.

In 2005, automatic instrumentation of filesystem source using *FiST* (Zadok & Nieh, 2000) to add purging support was demonstrated by Joukov et al. (Joukov & Zadok, 2005) to save the manual work of source modification. In case, the source was not available the wiping extension, called *purgefs*, instruments a null-pass *vnode* stackable filesystem, called base0fs, to add purging extension as a stackable filesystem. *purgefs* supports many overwrite policies and can overwrite both synchronously and asynchronously. In asynchronous mode, *purgefs* can remap the data pages to a temporary file and overwrite them using a kernel thread. However, *purgefs* also suffers from reliability problem as wiping can't sustain across system crashes.

In 2006, Joukov et al. (Joukov, Papaxenopoulos, & Zadok, 2006) proposed another *FiST* extension called *FoSgen* which is similar to *purgefs* in instrumentation, i.e., if source of filesystem to be instrumented is not available, the *FiST* creates a stackable filesystem. However, *FoSgen* differs from *purgefs* in operation as it moves the files to be deleted (or truncated) to a special directory called *ForSecureDeletion* and invokes the user mode shred tool that overwrites the files. In case

of truncation, *FoSgen* creates a new file with same name as original file and copies a portion of the original file to the new one while deleting the original. Due to Trash Bin like functionality in *FoSgen*, the wiping does sustain across system crashes.

However, *purgefs* (Joukov & Zadok, 2005) & *FoSgen* (Joukov et al., 2006) overwrite at file level and are not able to exploit the behavior of filesystems at block level for efficiency. Although, modification by Bauer et al. (Bauer & Priyantha, 2001) does work at block level but it makes no effort to exploit it for efficiency.

DESIGN OF *RESTFS* FILESYSTEM

restfs is a stackable filesystem that is designed to overcome the problems found in existing secure data deletion extensions. The design goals of *restfs* include efficiency and reliability in overwriting the meta-data and user data of a file when *unlink()* or *truncate()* operation is called. All the purging extensions discussed so far suffer from these problems. In order to achieve its efficiency and reliability, *restfs* exploits the behavior of filesystems at block level.

Possibilities Exploited for Efficiency

It can be safely argued that a filesystem under heavy workload has a good probability that the blocks de-allocated may be re-allocated to some other file and finally may get overwritten with new data. The wiping extensions can exploit this possibility in a filesystem to save some block overwrites.

Moreover, there is a possibility that many fragmented files are to be purged. As such, there are good chances that the fragments of two or more files to be purged may be placed consecutively on the disk. The overwriting can be done efficiently if all the individual overwrites to consecutive fragments are merged as a single overwrite. Even in case of two or more non-fragmented files to be purged there is a possibility that their content is placed next to each other on disk. Therefore, the overwriting can be efficient if the individual overwrites are merged as a single overwrite (Ganger & Kaashoek, 1997).

These efficiency patches are either not possible in *purgefs* (Joukov & Zadok, 2005) & *FoSgen* (Joukov et al., 2006) as they overwrite at file level or are not considered by Bauer et al. (Bauer & Priyantha, 2001). Nevertheless, *restfs* considers these possible scenarios to achieve efficiency during secure data deletion and operates at block level to achieve it. Figure 1 shows these two possibilities exploited by *restfs* for efficiency.

Ensuring Reliability in Wiping

The wiping is guaranteed across system crashes only in *FoSgen* (Joukov et al., 2006) wherein the deleted files are moved to a special directory and shredded there. As *restfs* works at block level, thus to ensure the reliability of wiping across system crashes it logs the block numbers identifying the blocks to be wiped.

The Mechanism

To accomplish its intended task, *restfs* during *unlink()* operation exports the block allocation map of the file (to be deleted) to user space to

Figure 1. Possibilities exploited by restfs for efficiency

file1 (blocks allocated)

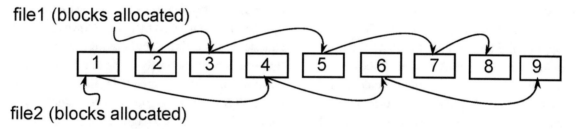

file2 (blocks allocated)

After file1 and file2 are deleted, the current purging techniques will overwrite blocks in the sequence 2,3,5,7 & 8 followed by 1,4,6 & 9. restFS can overwrite in an efficient manner by sorting the de-allocated blocks and creating number of long sequences; in this case 1,2,3,5,6,7,8 & 9.

file1 (blocks de-allocated 2,3,5,7,8)

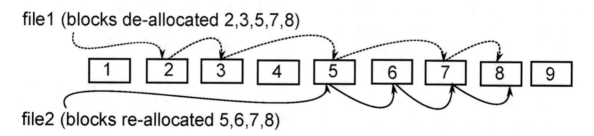

file2 (blocks re-allocated 5,6,7,8)

When file1 is deleted and file2 is created (appended), the current purging techniques will overwrite blocks 2,3,5,7 & 8 and then the re-allocated blocks 5,7 & 8 will be written again with new data. restFS can save block overwrites of these re-allocated blocks. Thus, blocks overwritten in this case will be 2 & 3 only.

be processed by a user level daemon which logs them into a per-filesystem log. Also, the meta-data is synchronously overwritten within the *unlink()* call after being exported to the user level daemon. The daemon sorts the block numbers and tries to reduce the number of overwrites by creating a number of long sequences of consecutive blocks for overwriting. This design decision helps in reducing the frequency and number of write commands issued to the disk. In addition, *restfs* exports the information about the blocks newly allocated to a file during *write()* call. Using this information, the daemon ignores the overwriting of those de-allocated blocks which are present on the over-write list but have been re-allocated. This design decision helps in reducing the number of blocks to be overwritten. Furthermore, during truncation operation only the information about the blocks which are de-allocated (or allocated in case of size extension) is exported. This saves the copying of data that may be required during truncation in *FoSgen* (Joukov et al., 2006).

Thus, the efficiency of *restfs* is achieved by reducing 1) the number of data blocks to be over-written, 2) the number of write commands issued to the disk, and 3) the frequency of disk writes.

Finally, the reliability of wiping across system crashes is accomplished by creating per-filesystem persistent log of de-allocated blocks that are to be overwritten. The log is created only for the blocks to be overwritten and not for the newly allocated blocks. The newly allocated blocks are read by daemon and corresponding blocks are searched in the log for their removal to save some block overwrites. This decision to let user level daemon create the log simplifies the implementation of *restfs* kernel module and achieves faster execution of filesystem operations (*unlink()* and *truncate()*).

Overwriting Policy

The overwriting policy is left up to the user level daemon for flexibility. The daemon can overwrite instantly as soon as information is passed to it (preferably in case of removable devices) or delay the process. Also, the daemon can be configured to overwrite instantly for small files. Likewise, it can be configured to overwrite instantly the header and/or footer of files to further reduce the window of insecurity. This makes overwriting policy re-configurable without any need to remount the *restfs* module.

IMPLEMENTATION OF *RESTFS* FILESYSTEM

The design of *restfs* relies on the capability of below mounted filesystem to export the list of data blocks associated with a file. Unfortunately, VFS does not provide a generic routine for such filesystems to export this information. In addition, there is no corresponding VFS routine for truncate operation to be hooked by *restfs*. However, *restfs* can accomplish this task by hooking a VFS routine that sets the attributes for a file and look for the possible file size change. This limited capability of VFS has been argued before (Zadok, Iyer, Joukov, Sivathanu, & Wright, 2006). We believe that the filesystem research community will come up with some solutions and remedies. Having said that, we implemented *restfs* for ext2 filesystem as it exports the information needed by *restfs* and is widely used in secure deletion research papers.

Kernel Module for Ext2 Filesystem

restfs is implemented as a Linux Loadable Kernel Module (LKM) by instrumenting a null-pass vnode stackable filesystem called *base0fs* (Joukov & Zadok, 2005). *restfs* performs reliable and efficient secure data deletion when inserted between VFS and below mounted ext2 filesystem. There are actually only two filesystem operations that need to be intercepted for secure deletion of data: *unlink()* (called to delete a file) and *truncate()* (called to change the file size). However, because *restfs* also exports the newly allocated blocks, we need to intercept *write()* filesystem operation also.

When *restfs* is loaded, it creates a directory entry in */proc* filesystem of the name *restfs*. After this, when *restfs* is mounted on top of some native filesystem, it checks for ext2 filesystem and then creates a directory entry in */proc/restfs/* having name same as that of mount point of the below mounted ext2 filesystem. Under this directory, 3 files namely *config, dealloc* and *alloc* are created. *config* file exports the configuration data of ext2 filesystem like device name, block size and so on; *dealloc* file exports the list of blocks de-allocated and *alloc* file exports the list of blocks newly allocated. The */proc/restfs/<mount-point>/alloc* is populated in *restfs write()* call as this is the main function that may add some new data blocks to an existing file. Similarly, */proc/restfs/<mount-point>/dealloc* is populated in *restfs unlink()* call. However, as mentioned earlier that there is no corresponding operation provided by VFS for *truncate()* operation, *restfs* hooks *setattr()* call

which is immediately called after *truncate()* and other operations to reflect metadata changes. *restfs setattr()* populates *dealloc* or *alloc* file depending upon whether the new file size is lesser or greater than previous size. Figure 2 depicts the behavior of *restfs()* during *unlink()* operation when mounted on top of ext2 filesystem.

User-Level Daemon for Ext2 Filesystem

The *restfs* daemon is a Linux service that reads */proc/restfs/<mount-point>/config* file to know the device file and block size of ext2 filesystem on top of which *restfs* is mounted. After this, the daemon keeps reading both *alloc* and *dealloc* files and creates a persistent log file per-filesystem. Depending upon the overwriting policy of daemon, it can overwrite instantly or delay the process. Finally, the daemon removes the entry from the log after it validates that the block overwrite has

Figure 2. Behavior of restfs during unlink() operation

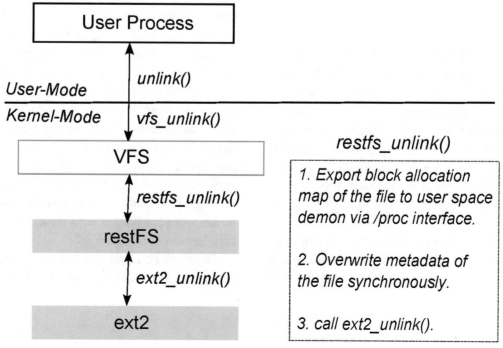

been committed to disk by checking */proc/sys/vm/block_dump* file for the specified block.

In all cases, it sorts the log and creates longest possible lists of consecutive blocks. In any case, as soon as some new block is added to */proc/restfs/<mount-point>/alloc* list, the daemon reads it, checks for its existence in persistent log of blocks to be overwritten and if found, removes it from the log. Moreover, the clean-up process of */proc/restfs/<mount-point>/alloc* and */proc/restfs/<mount-point>/dealloc* is done by user level daemon. Figure 3 shows the working of user level daemon of *restfs*.

One may argue how the design of *restfs* is different from (Bauer & Priyantha, 2001). Design of (Bauer & Priyantha, 2001) mainly differs from *restfs* in 5 aspects; 1) it modifies source code of ext2 filesystem, 2) it doesn't exploit the behavior of filesystem at block level for efficiency, 3) it does nothing to make wiping reliable, 4) it uses kernel daemon, and 5) the design is not compatible with other filesystems.

EXPERIMENT

Goal

restfs only processes *unlink()*, *truncate()* and *write()* filesystem calls and does a minimal amount of work of exporting allocation map of a file to user space. As such, the performance overhead of *restfs* for CPU bound workloads is naturally negligible. Also, because *restfs* does not overwrite data, either synchronously or asynchronously, within *unlink() & truncate()* calls, it adds no performance overhead to I/O bound workloads. However, it does overwrite meta-data synchronously within *unlink() and truncate()* call, but the overhead is negligible and affordable. Therefore, we didn't evaluate *restfs* for performance overhead incurred

during CPU bound and I/O bound workloads, rather the experiment was aimed to validate the efficiency of *restfs*.

We evaluated *restfs* for its efficiency to 1) reduce the number of blocks to be overwritten by skipping the blocks among recently deallocated which were reallocated, and 2) reduce the frequency and number of writes to disk. Agrawal et al. (Agrawal, Bolosky, Douceur, & Lorch, 2007) found that large files account for a large fraction of space but most files are 4 KB or smaller. They also argued that although the absolute count of files per filesystem will grow significantly over time, but this general shape of the distribution will not change significantly. As such, we evaluated *restfs* for large number of random read/write and create/delete operations on large number of small files. To accomplish this, we used I/O intensive workload simulator called *Postmark* (Katcher, 1997).

Environment

The experiment was conducted on an Intel based PC with Intel Core i3 CPU 550 @ 3.20 GHz with total 4MB cache, and 2GB DDR3 1333MHz SDRAM. The magnetic disk drive used was a 320 GB SATA drive with on board cache of 8 MB and 15.3 ms of reported average access time. The drive was partitioned into a 20 GB primary partition to host Fedora Core 14 operating system running 2.6.35.14-95.fc.14.i686 kernel version. Another 20 GB primary partition was used to mount ext2 filesystem with *restfs* on top. Furthermore, the evaluation was done with Linux running at run-level 1 to reduce the random effect of other applications and daemons. Also, the experiment was repeated atleast 5 times and the average of results were considered with standard deviation less than 4% of the average.

Postmark performs a series of file appends, reads, creations and deletions. We ran *Postmark*

Figure 3. Working of user level daemon of restfs

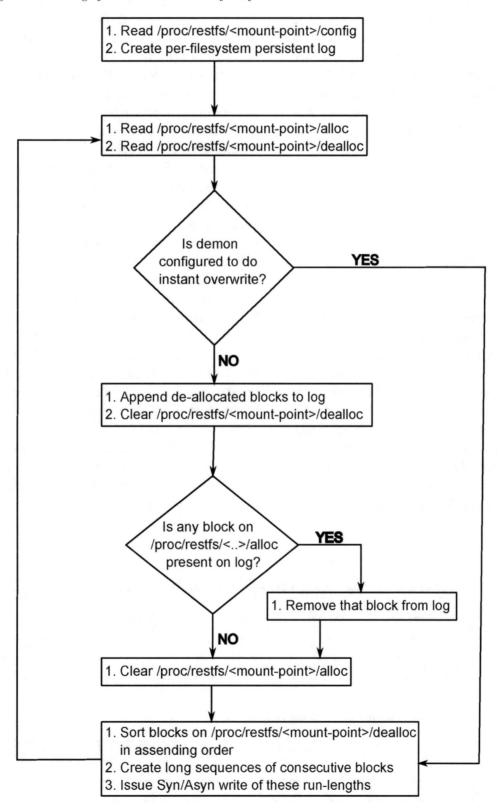

in its default configuration in which it initially created a pool of 500 files between 500-10 K bytes and then performed 500 transactions. In each transaction there is an equal probability of create/delete and read/write operations. Finally, it deleted all the files. Table 1 shows the statistics gathered from *Postmark*. Furthermore, *restfs* daemon was configured in delay-overwrite mode.

RESULTS AND DISCUSSION

We intercepted and analyzed the information exported by *restfs* kernel module and processing done by user level daemon during the execution of *Postmark* benchmark.

First, the results indicate that most of the blocks de-allocated during transactions got re-allocated. The number of de-allocated blocks that got re-allocated was 98%. This means, if during transactions all de-allocated blocks would have been over-written for secure deletion, almost all of these blocks would still have been over-written with some new data. Indeed, this is what would happen in existing wiping extensions. Further, in total, at the completion of *Postmark* benchmark (which deletes all the files that were created), the results indicate that 28% of the total de-allocated

blocks were re-allocated. This 71% loss in efficiency is due to the fact that at the completion of *Postmark* no new blocks are allocated. This indicates that, using *restfs* a minimum of 28% of block over-writes can be saved. Both results do not consider the blocks allocated during the creation of initial pool of 500 files. Table 2 shows the evaluation of efficiency of *restfs* to reduce number of block overwrites.

Second, the deallocated blocks which were not re-allocated and needed to be overwritten, were sorted. The sorted list was used to find a number of run lengths of consecutive blocks. These run lengths were overwritten one at a time and hence, reduced the number and frequency of disk writes issued. The results indicate that there was no gain at all during transactions as very few de-allocated blocks were left unallocated. However, in total, at the completion of *Postmark*, the save increased to 88%. This huge growth in efficiency is due to the fact that at the completion of *Postmark* large number of blocks were de-allocated. Table 3 shows the evaluation of efficiency of *restfs* to reduce number of disk writes. The table indicates that without using *restfs*, 530 commands are issued to disk wherein each command writes to small number of consecutive blocks as would have happened in case of existing wiping extensions. While as using

Table 1. Postmark benchmark report

	Initial Pool	During Transactions Only	After Transactions Only	Total
Files Created	500	264	55	764
Files Read	55	243	55	243
Files Appended	55	257	55	257
Files Deleted	55	236	528	764

Table 2. Efficiency to reduce number of block overwrites

	During Transactions Only	Total
Blocks unlinked	446	1547
Unlinked blocks reallocated	437	437

Table 3. Efficiency to reduce number of disk writes

	During Transactions Only	**Total**
Unlinks issued	236	764
Non-sequential disk writes before coalescing	9	530
Non-sequential disk writes after coalescing	9	62
%age of issued disk write commands saved	0%	88%

restfs, just 62 commands are issued wherein each command writes to large number of consecutive blocks. In both cases, the total amount of data and number of blocks written is same. The gain is in reduction in number and frequency of disk write commands issued in addition to reduced random disk arm seeks.

It is worth mentioning here that these two efficiency patches are complimentary. This means that if there are many de-allocated blocks and new blocks are being allocated, large number of block overwrites are saved as the de-allocated blocks get re-allocated. However, because very few de-allocated blocks are left un-allocated, there is no saving in number of disk writes. Similarly, if there are many de-allocated blocks and no new blocks are allocated, there is no saving in block overwrites but a large number of disk writes are saved. This fact is depicted by Table 2 and Table 3.

CONCLUSION

We can conclude that to counter the after-deletion recovery threat in Cloud Security, the secure wiping of data can be employed on transparent per-file basis. Furthermore, to ensure reliability and efficiency in transparent per-file wiping, instead at file level, overwriting must be done at block level. To support our argument, we designed and implemented a stackable filesystem called *restfs*. *restfs* is design compatible with any filesystem that exports block allocation map of a file to VFS and is currently implemented for ext2 filesystem.

The reliability of *restfs* exploits logging of deallocated blocks for sustainability of purging across system crashes. While as, the efficiency of *restfs* exploits probability of reallocation of recently deallocated blocks to reduce number of blocks to be overwritten, and ordering and coalescing the consecutive deallocated blocks to reduce the number of disk writes issued.

To validate, we employed *Postmark* benchmark to exercise ext2 filesystem and results indicate that *restfs* saves a minimum of 28% (and maximum of 98%) of data blocks that needed to be overwritten in existing extensions and reduces the number of disk writes issued by 88%.

REFERENCES

Agrawal, N., Bolosky, W. J., Douceur, J. R., & Lorch, J. R. (2007, October). A five-year study of file-system metadata. *Transactions on Storage*, *3*(3), 338–346. doi:10.1145/1288783.1288788

Bauer, S., & Priyantha, N. B. (2001). Secure data deletion for linux filesystems. In *Proceedings of the 10th conference on usenix security symposium*, 10. (pp. 12–12). Berkeley, CA, USA: USENIX Association.

Diesburg, S. M., & Wang, A. I. A. (2010, December). A survey of confidential data storage and deletion methods. *ACM Computing Surveys*, *43*(1), 1–37. doi:10.1145/1824795.1824797

Ganger, G. R., & Kaashoek, M. F. (1997). Embedded inodes and explicit grouping: exploiting disk bandwidth for small files. In *Proceedings of the annual conference on usenix annual technical conference* (pp. 1–1). Berkeley, CA, USA: USENIX Association.

Gomez, R., Adly, A., Mayergoyz, I., & Burke, E. (1992, September). Magnetic force scanning tunneling microscope imaging of overwritten data. *IEEE Transactions on Magnetics*, *28*(5), 3141–3143. doi:10.1109/20.179738

Grance, T., Stevens, M., & Myers, M. (2003). Guide to selecting information security products (2nd Ed.). National Institute of Standards and Technology (NIST).

Gutmann, P. (1996). Secure deletion of data from magnetic and solid-state memory. In *Proceedings of the 6th conference on usenix security symposium, focusing on applications of cryptography* Vol. 6 (pp. 8–8). Berkeley, CA, USA: USENIX Association.

Jones, A., Valli, C., & Dabibi, G. (2009). The 2009 analysis of information remaining on usb storage devices offered for sale on the second hand market. Proceedings of Australian digital forensics conference (p. 61).

Joukov, N., Papaxenopoulos, H., & Zadok, E. (2006). Secure deletion myths, issues, and solutions. In *Proceedings of the second acm workshop on storage security and survivability* (pp. 61–66). New York, NY, USA: ACM. doi:10.1145/1179559.1179571

Joukov, N., & Zadok, E. (2005). Secure data deletion for linux filesystems. *Proceedings of the 3rd IEEE security in storage workshop (SISW '05)* (pp. 12–12). San Francisco, CA: IEEE

Katcher, J. (1997). Postmark: A new filesystem benchmark (Tech. Rep. No. TR3022). Network Appliance.

Leyden, J. (2004). Oops! firm accidentally eBays customer database. *The Register*.

Leyden, J. (2006). Afghan market sells us military flash drives bazaar security breach. *The Register*.

Mayergoyz, I. D., Serpico, C., Krafft, C., & Tse, C. (2000). Magnetic imaging on a spin-stand. *Journal of Applied Physics*, *87*(9), 6824–6826. doi:10.1063/1.372854

Rosenbaum, J. (2000). In defense of the delete key.

Computer hard drive sold on eBay had details of top secret US missile defense system. (2009). *The-Daily-Mail*.

Wright, C., Kleiman, D., & Sundhar, R. S. S. (2008). Overwriting hard drive data: The great wiping controversy. In Proceedings of the Information Systems Security (p. 243-257). Berkeley, CA, USA: Springer Berlin. doi:10.1007/978-3-540-89862-7_21

Wright, C. P., Dave, J., & Zadok, E. (2003, October). Cryptographic filesystems performance: What you don't know can hurt you. In *Proceedings of the 2nd IEEE International Security in Storage Workshop*. IEEE Computer Society. doi:10.1109/SISW.2003.10005

Zadok, E., Iyer, R., Joukov, N., Sivathanu, G., & Wright, C. P. (2006, May). On incremental filesystem development. *Transactions on Storage*, *2*(2), 161–196. doi:10.1145/1149976.1149979

Zadok, E., & Nieh, J. (2000). Fist: a language for stackable filesystems. In *Proceedings of the annual conference on usenix annual technical conference* (pp. 5–5). Berkeley, CA, USA: USENIX Association.

KEY TERMS AND DEFINITIONS

Daemon-Process: A background process.

ext2: Second Extended (ext2) filesystem is a filesystem for Linux kernel.

LKM: Linux Kernel Module (LKM) is a kernel-level plugin that extends the capability of a base-kernel.

Metadata: The data structure that defines the specification of a filesystem.

Secure-Deletion: It is a process of overwriting the data to completely destroy all remnants of digital data on a storage device.

Stackable-Filesystem: It is an abstraction layer at kernel level below VFS and above a concrete filesystem which allows pre- and post-processing of filesystem operations.

VFS: A Virtual File System (VFS) is an abstraction layer at kernel level above all concrete filesystems that allows user processes to access different underlying filesystems in a uniform way.

Chapter 18
Reliability, Fault Tolerance, and Quality-of-Service in Cloud Computing:
Analysing Characteristics

Piyush Kumar Shukla
University Institute of Technology RGPV, India

Gaurav Singh
Motilal Nehru National Institute of Technology, India

ABSTRACT

In this chapter we are focusing on reliability, fault tolerance and quality of service in cloud computing. The flexible and scalable property of dynamically fetching and relinquishing computing resources in a cost-effective and device-independent manner with minimal management effort or service provider interaction the demand for Cloud computing paradigm has increased dramatically in last few years. Though lots of enhancement took place, cloud computing paradigm is still subject to a large number of system failures. As a result, there is an increasing concern among community regarding the reliability and availability of Cloud computing services. Dynamically provisioning of resources allows cloud computing environment to meet casually varying resource and service requirements of cloud customer applications. Quality of Service (QoS) plays an important role in the affective allocation of resources and has been widely investigated in the Cloud Computing paradigm.

1. INTRODUCTION

Cloud computing can be viewed as a model of equipping computing resources such as hardware, system software and applications as a reliable service over internet in a convenient, flexible and scalable manner. Often, this computer resources

that is hardware, system software and applications are referred as Infrastructure as a Service (IaaS), Platform as a Service (PaaS) and Software as a service (IaaS), respectively. It (Buyya, Yeo, Venugopal, Broberg, & Brandic, 2009; Expósito et al., 2013) offers cost effective and effortless outsourcing of resources in dynamic service environments

DOI: 10.4018/978-1-4666-8387-7.ch018

to consumers and also facilitates the construction of service based applications equipped with the latest advancement of diverse research areas, such as Grid Computing, Service-oriented computing, business processes and virtualization.

Cloud computing providers often employs two different models to offer these services, utility computing model and Pay per Use model. Utility computing model is similar to how traditional utility services (such as water, electricity) are consumed. Whereas in Pay per Use model users are allowed to pay on the basis of number of type of service (characterized on basis of parameters like CPU cores, memory, and disk capacity)they use (A Vouk, 2008; Randles, Lamb, & Taleb-Bendiab, 2010). Payper Use model is useful in cloud resource provisioning to satisfy the SaaS user's needs with reducing cost and maximizing the profit of the SaaS provider. Another major concern for cloud resource providers is how to reduce energy consumption and thereby decreasing operating costs and maximizing the revenue of cloud provider (Berl et al., 2010; Kim, Beloglazov, & Buyya, 2009; Srikantaiah, Kansal, & Zhao, 2008).Therefore, how to serve request of the cloud services user to meet Quality of Service (QoS) needs, fault resistant reliable services and maximize the profit of the SaaS provider and cloud resource provider becomes a concern to be addressed in cloud computing environment urgently(Li, 2012).

In order to achieve its goal, Cloud, require a novel infrastructure that incorporates a high-level monitoring approach to support autonomous, on demand deployment and decommission of service instances. For this, Clouds rely greatly, on virtualization of resources to provide management combined with separation of users. Virtual appliances are employed to encapsulate a complete software system (e.g. operating system, software libraries and the deployable services themselves) prepared

for execution in virtual machines (VM)(Kertész et al., 2013). Cloud management is responsible for all resources used by all the applications deployed in the cloud.

Cloud computing and networking can be viewed as the two different important keys in future Internet (FI) vision, where Internet connection of objects and federation of infrastructures become of high importance (Papagianni et al., 2013). For many cloud computing applications, network performance is a key factor in cloud computing performance to meet QoS delivery, which is directly linked to the network performance and provisioning model adopted for computational resources. Thus, in cloud paradigm the convergence between cloud computing and networking is more a requirement than a desire in order to facilitate the efficient realization of cloud computing paradigm. Providers need to consider the dynamic provisioning, configuration, reconfiguration, and optimization of both computing resources (e.g., servers) as well as networking resources to meet their objectives.

2. CLOUD COMPUTING ARCHITECTURE

Cloud computing environment supposed to furnish its huge pool of computing resources that encompasses processing power, memory, and development platform and platform to its users. This demand of sharing drives architecture of cloud computing to support convenient, efficient and flexible on demand services to users.

Architecture of cloud system comprised of different components connected in a loosely manner. These components can be broadly categorized into two parts as a front end and back end. Generally, users input and output device that includes PC, smart phone, tablet, etc. are referred as front end.

Also applications and interfaces e.g. web browser that are required to access cloud services are components of front end. Traditional cloud computing architecture is depicted in Figure 1 below.

Whereas, cloud and all the resources required to provide cloud computing services are referred to as back end. Cloud back end comprises four distinct layers as illustrated in Figure 1 (Fox et al., 2009). Physical resources such as servers, storage and network switches comprise the lowest-layer in the stack. On top of physical layer is the Infrastructure-as-a-Service (IaaS) layer where virtualization and system management tools are embedded. Front and back end are linked through a network may be via Internet Intranet or Inter-cloud. Cloud Computing Architecture has been illustrated in Figure 1.

Typically, in cloud deployment, the data centers and virtualization technology are employed

to utilize the maximum physical resources. The layer above the IaaS is the Platform-as-a-Service (PaaS) which contains all user-level middleware tools that provide an environment to simplify application development and deployment (e.g., web 2.0 interfaces, libraries and programming languages).Layer on top of the PaaS layer where user-level applications (e.g., social networks and scientific models) are built and hosted referred as the Software-as-a-Service (SaaS). Security, protocols and control mechanisms are also implemented at Back end.

The fundamental model of cloud computing architecture is to separate powerful computation from user devices so that users can enjoy almost all services with simple, light-weighted devices with input/output and communication capacities enough to access to cloud systems for their demanded services as shown in Figure 2. Users

Figure 1. Cloud Computing Architecture

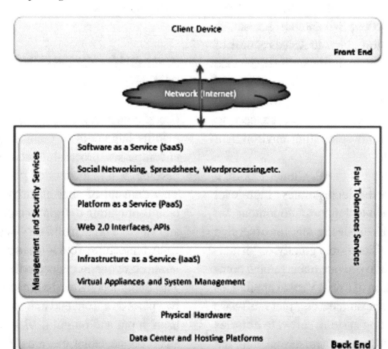

access the cloud computing environment using output device has been illustrated in Figure 1.

User demand a service using his input device, this demand then will be transmitted to a cloud system over network. After receiving demand cloud system processes the demand using powerful resources and returns a result efficiently to the user output device. Similarly, users are allowed to store their data in the cloud and make use of applications embedded in cloud system to process their data and retrieve them if needed regardless of their locations. Cloud systems let it be possible that users can enjoy complex, various and novel services without being limited by their own equipment.

Challenges

In a general, cloud service architecture, on demand of service, cloud assigns resources to service the user by taking into account the server loading, service type, location of users, and so on. In memory oriented service the current usage depends on the previous one, hence, it is essential to load the service status, stored in the previously hosted

server, of previous usage before proceeding. To encounter this server would store the image file of the virtual machine in its storage to ensure that the user resume it services with the same settings. In case if the user wants to access virtual machine from location far away from the server then the connection would be forced to point to the server which stores the image file. Thus, it necessitates the cloud system to assign the previous server, where service was processed, to host him. Consequently, result deduced from user operations will be transmitted along a very long path to the output device of the user. As a result QoS may be affected as more and more streams are transmitted through the backbone, the bandwidth of the backbone would be almost exhausted.

To address this, researchers had proposed multiple clouds environment, interoperability of clouds, resource allocation scheme, service migration and many more. Multiple clouds environment had been proposed in (Houidi, Mechtri, Louati, & Zeghlache, 2011) which focus on the cloud service provisioning from multiple cloud providers. A five-level model to assess the maturity of cloud to cloud interoperability was presented

Figure 2. Users access the cloud computing environment using output device

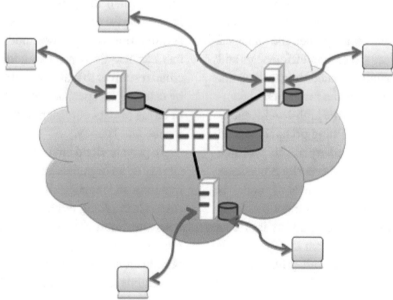

by (Dowell, Barreto, Michael, & Shing, 2011). A resource allocation scheme for efficient on demand resource allocation had been proposed in (Marshall, Keahey, & Freeman, 2011). There had been some researches about service migration (Oikonomou & Stavrakakis, 2010) which lack the considerations of the characteristics of cloud computing. A scheme called dual migration to monitor users location as well as to move the contents onto the server closest to the user is proposed by Researchers (Lai, Yang, Lin, & Shieh, 2012). Therefore, a user can enjoy services by means of the great capacity of the closest server.

3. TYPES OF CLOUDS

Cloud environments (Sotomayor, Montero, Llorente, & Foster, 2009) can be categorized into private clouds, public clouds, hybrid clouds and community clouds on the basis of the way in which the clouds can be deployed. Different types of cloud are explained in brief in following subsections.

Private Cloud

As name implies, the infrastructure of a private cloud is an internal data centre of an organization which is privately owned not available to the public. Computing resources are pooled and managed internally which leads to greater efficiencies and can be applied dynamically according to demand. It facilitates internal users the fundamental computing resources as well as the high-level security and control mechanisms. Being privately owned private cloud allows the enterprise to continue to follow own workflow and security procedures which ensures that the correct level of "code" is executing. Also private clouds are not burdened by network bandwidth and availability issues or potential security exposures that may be associated with public clouds. Overall private clouds

can offer the provider and user greater control, security, and resilience.

Public Cloud

A public cloud is one in which a third-party provider makes resources, such as applications and other computing resources available to the general public via the Internet. The cloud service provider is responsible for setting up the hardware, software, applications, and networking resources. A public cloud service has advantages associated with such as flexibility, extensibility, pay-per-use and inexpensive to use, but it is often more expensive than a private data center if resources are used for several years. Also public clouds do not imply that the user's data is public. In many cases, access control mechanisms are required before the user can make use of cloud resources. It is made available to the general public or a wide industry group.

Hybrid Cloud

The private cloud platform owned by each enterprise integrates various resources such as computing and storage in a server, which can be re-configured when and as required. This flexibility, which the private cloud provides shows how powerful and valuable it is when deployed in combination with public cloud. In hybrid cloud, one can use its private in addition with public cloud resources to make capital out of investments by catering for specific application requirements in terms of data confidentiality, security, performance and latency.

In private cloud environment, it is the responsibility of an organization who purchased it, is to maintain and manage all resources. According to research in (Kang et al., 2008) the peak load of a private cloud is much larger than average, but transient. The big spikes are not predictable. If a private cloud attempts to satisfy all the workload constraints, the transit peak load would force the owner to invest more hardware resources in the private cloud. This leads to over provisioning and waste of hardware resources in most of the time. The pay-as-you-go public cloud model can be utilized in such scenario without making any redundant resources in the private cloud. To deal with the spike workload problem in a cost consideration aspect, the public cloud resources are dynamically added into a private cloud, and become a hybrid cloud environment. As the public cloud resources can be dynamically moved in and out according to different requirements. Only the period during which the public cloud handles the overloading tasks can cost extra money which is far less than investing more in purchasing resources. Therefore, the hybrid cloud model helps reduce hardware cost and the operation cost if a private cloud already exists. To achieve this, the workload has to be split and distributed to the private cloud and the public cloud, or simply the hybrid cloud (Bittencourt & Madeira, 2011). A hybrid cloud is a combination of public and private clouds bound together by either standardized or proprietary technology that enables data and application portability. With hybrid cloud deployment model, the users benefited by lower over provisioning factor, more efficient provisioning, better performance and less hardware cost (Subramanian, 2011). One of the result of evolution of hybrid cloud is a cloud federation (Casola, Rak, & Villano, 2010) which aims to cost-effective assets and resources optimization among heterogeneous environments where clouds can cooperate together with the goal of obtaining unbounded computation resources, hence new business opportunities. Federation brings together different cloud flavors, external and internal resources. Thus, any organization can select a public computing environment on demand when its private cloud reaches a particular workload threshold.

Community Cloud

A community cloud can be a private cloud purchased by a single user to support a community of users, or a hybrid cloud with the costs spread over a few users of the cloud. A community cloud is often set up as a sandbox environment where community users can test their applications, or access cloud resources. Community cloud are used and controlled by a group of organizations with a shared interest. In other words, it is a private cloud purchased by a single user to support a community of users where fees may be charged to subsidiaries.

4. RELIABILITY AND FAULT-TOLERANCE

With the flexibility and scalability characteristic in dynamically obtaining and releasing computing resources in a cost-effective and device-independent manner with minimal management effort or service provider interaction the demand for Cloud computing paradigm has increased dramatically in last few years. While lots of improvement taken place, cloud computing paradigm is still subject to a large number of system failures. As a result, there is an increasing concern among community regarding the reliability and availability of Cloud computing services. Moreover, the highly complex nature of the underlying resources makes it more vulnerable to a large number of failures even for carefully engineered data centres (Barroso, Clidaras, & Hölzle, 2013). These failures had an impact on the overall reliability and availability of the Cloud computing service. As a result, an effective means to encounter failures even that are unknown and unpredictable in numbers has becomes of urgent need to both the users as well as the service providers to ensure correct and continuous system operation. Fault tolerance serves as a technique to assure user's reliability and availability.

In general, a failure refers to error or condition in which the system to achieve its intended functionality or the expected behavior. There may be many reason behind a Failure may happen by various reasons that is due to reaching an invalid system state, network failure, etc,. The belief cause for an error is a fault that represents a fundamental impairment in the system. Thus, Fault tolerance is the ability of the system to perform its function even in the presence of failures. It serves as one of the means to improve the overall system's dependability. In particular, it contributes significantly in increasing system's reliability and availability. Cloud computing environment faults that appear as failures to the end users can be categorized into two types similarly to other distributed systems (Piuri, 2013):

- Crash faults that cause the system components to completely stop functioning or remain inactive during failures (e.g., power outage, hard disk crash)
- Byzantine faults that leads the system components to behave arbitrarily or maliciously during failure, causing the system to behave unpredictably incorrect.

To implement fault tolerant system the most important is to clearly understand and determine what constitutes the correct system behavior so that specifications on its failure characteristics can be provided. Failure in any layer in the cloud architecture at particular instance has an impact on the services offered by the layers above it. That is if failures occur in the IaaS layer or the physical hardware then its impact is significantly high; hence, it is more important to characterize typical hardware faults and develop corresponding fault tolerance techniques.

The key observations derived from one of the study of failure behaviour of various server components and hardware repair behaviour based on the statistical information (Gill, Jain, & Nagappan, 2011; Vishwanath & Nagappan, 2010) is as follows.

- 8% of the machines that are subject to repair events has the average number of repair is2 i.e., 2 per machine. The annual failure rate (AFR) is therefore around 8%.
- An amount spent on repair cost for an 8% AFRwere 2.5 million dollars approximately.
- About 78% of total faults/replacements were detected on hard disks, 5% on RAID controllers and 3% due to memory failures. 13% of replacements were due to a collection of components. This implies that Hard disks are clearly the most failure-prone hardware components and the most significant reason behind server failures.
- About 5% of servers experience a disk failure in less than 1 year from the date when it is purchased, 12% when the machines are 1 year old, and 25% of the servers see hard disk failures when it is 2 years old.
- Interestingly, factors such as age of the server, its configuration, location within the rack and workload run on the machine were not found to be a significant indicator for failures.

It can be inferred from these statistics that robust fault tolerance mechanisms must be employed to improve the reliability of hard disks (assuming independent component failures) in order to reduce the number of failures. Furthermore, use of hard disks that have already experienced a failure should be reduced to meet the high availability and reliability requirements.

In order to model failure behavior of cloud computing it is also important to consider failure behavior of the network. And to characterize the network failure behavior it is important to understand the overall network topology and various network components involved in constructing a data center. Similarly to the study on failure behavior of servers, a large scale study on the network failures in data centers is performed in (Gill et al., 2011). A link failure happens when the connection between two devices on a specific interface is down and a device failure happens when the device is not routing/forwarding packets correctly (e.g., due to power outage or hardware crash). Key observations derived from this study are as follows:

- With failure probability of 1 in 5 load balancers are least reliable among all the network devices, and ToRs are most reliable with a failure rate of less than 5%. The root causes for failures in LBs are mainly the software bugs and configuration errors as opposed to the hardware errors for other devices.

- The links forwarding traffic from LBs have highest failure rates whereas links higher in the topology and links connecting redundant devices have second highest failure rates.

- The estimated median number of packets lost during a failure is 59K and median number of bytes is 25MB.

- Network redundancy reduces the median impact of failures (in terms of number of lost bytes) by only 40%. This observation is against the common belief that network redundancy completely masks failures from applications.

- Therefore, the overall data center network reliability is about 99.99% for 80% of the links and 60% of the devices.

The most widely adopted methods to achieve fault tolerance against crash faults and byzantine faults are as follows:

- Checking and monitoring: In this technique the system is constantly monitored at runtime to validate, verify and ensure that correct system specifications are being met. This technique plays an important role in failure detection and subsequent reconfiguration and easy to implement.

- Checkpoint and restart: When the system undergoes a failure, it is restored to the previously known correct state captured and saved based on pre-defined parameters using the latest checkpoint information instead of restarting the system from start.

- Replication: Critical system components are mirrored using additional hardware, software and network resources in such a manner that a copy of the critical components is available even after a failure happens. Replication mechanisms are mainly applied in two formats: active and passive. In active replication, all the replicas are simultaneously active and each replica processes the same request at the same time. This ensures that all the replicas have the same system state at any given point of time and it can continue to deliver its service even in case of a single replica failure. Whereas, in passive replication, only one primary replica processes the requests while the backup replicas only save the system state during normal execution periods. Backup replicas are invoked only when the primary replica fails.

Fault tolerance mechanisms are varyingly successful in tolerating faults according to study (Ayari, Barbaron, Lefevre & Primet, 2008). For example, a passively replicated system can handle only crash faults whereas actively replicated system using 3+1 replicas are capable of overcoming byzantine faults. In general, mechanisms that handles failures at a finer granularity, offering higher performance guarantees but at cost of higher amount of resources (Jhawar, Piuri, & Santambrogio, 2012). Therefore, in the design of fault tolerance mechanisms one must take into account a number of factors such as implementation complexity, resource costs, resilience, and performance metrics, and achieve a fine balance of the following parameters:

- Fault tolerance model: This factor measures the resilience level of the fault tolerance technique that means at what par it can tolerate failures or error in the system. It can also be understood as a robustness of failure detection protocols, strength of the failover level and state synchronization method.

- Resource consumption: It takes into account the amount and cost of resources incorporates to realize a fault tolerance mechanism. This factor is normally subject to the depth of the failure detection and recovery mechanisms involved in terms of CPU, memory, bandwidth, I/O, and so on.

- Performance: The impact of the fault tolerance procedure on the end-to-end quality of service (QoS) both during failure and failure-free periods is measured by this factor. This impact is often characterized using, replica launch latency fault detection latency and failure recovery latency, and other application-dependent metrics such as bandwidth, latency, and loss rate.

5. QUALITY OF SERVICE

Dynamically provisioning of resources allows cloud computing environment to meet casually varying resource and service requirements of cloud customer applications. Quality of Service (QoS) plays an important role in the affective allocation of resources and has been widely investigated in the Cloud Computing paradigm. Not only in cloud, QoS has been an issue in many of the Distributed Computing paradigms, such as Grid computing and High Performance Computing. Quality of Service (QoS)provides a level of assurance against the application requirements that ensure a certain level of reliability, availability and performance of a service and can also cover other aspects of service quality such as security and dependability. QoS is primarily concerned with the management

and performance of resources such as processors memory, storage and networks in Cloud Computing. The QoS is sometimes used as a quality measure, with many different definitions instead of referring to the ability to reserve resources.

QoS models are associated with End-Users and Providers (and often Brokers) and include resource capacity planning via the use of schedulers and load balancers and utilize Service Level Agreements (SLA)(Armstrong & Djemame, 2009). SLAs is a legal binding contract upon QoS between an End-User and Provider and define End-User resource requirements and execution environment guarantees to provide End-User what that they are receiving the exact services they have payed for.

Multiple providers of cloud offers different services on their own terms employing own security levels, system platforms and management systems. Users often face difficulty while finding best services to meet their objectives. Cloud service broker are specialized expert to provide intermediary role between providers and consumers of cloud and assist purchaser of cloud services to find the appropriate cloud offering as well as in deployment and management of applications on cloud. Cloud brokers helps in negotiating the best deals and relationships between cloud consumers and cloud providers. Specialized tools are used by brokers to identify the most appropriate cloud resource and map the requirements of application to it. They can also be dynamic by automatically routing data, applications and infrastructure needs based on some QoS criteria like availability, reliability, latency, price etc. In an attempt to provide broker solutions Researchers have (Salehi & Buyya, 2010) proposed a user level broker using two market oriented scheduling policies. The proposed broker increases the computational capacity of the local resources by employing resources from an IaaS provider. Researchers(Yang, Zhou, Liang, He, & Sun, 2010) qcr4w introduced a service oriented broker that claims guarantee data transmission and uniform mechanism for arranging resources via broker to maintain certain level of services to users. Cloud Quality of Service management Strategy(C-QoSMS) framework has been proposed by Researchers (Ganghishetti & Wankar, 2011) which needs to be included in the cloud service broker. By adding C-QoSMS component in the cloud broker provides the capacity to the customer to select a cloud provider based on the QoS criteria specified in the SLA in minimum searching time.

It is also important to know that there are different types of cloud users with different types of applications with different set of personalized preferences or QoCS requirements. Some applications require considerable computing and storage power while others have strong need for execution time. Reliability, Availability, Execution Time, Reputation, and Tariff are the commonly used QoS criteria for services selection (Lin, Sheu, Chang, & Yuan, 2011). The goal of the cloud users' is to process their services successfully and meet their performance, security, deadline and cost target. This implies that the success of the underlying business motto of the cloud users rely on determining the best fitted cloud service for a personalized application.

Cloud service typically comes with various levels of services and performance characteristics and to fulfill its promises to provide high quality, on-demand services with service-oriented architecture often makes Quality of Cloud Service (QoCS) high variance. This let the difficulty for the users to compare these cloud services and select them to meet their QoCS requirements. To address this Researcher (Wang, Liu, Sun, Zou& Yang, 2014) propose an accurate evaluation approach of QoCS in service-oriented cloud computing by employing fuzzy synthetic decision to asses cloud service providers according to cloud users' preferences. Also, cloud service with consistently good QoCS performance is usually more recommendable than a QoCS performance having large variance. So, due to any unpredictable behavior of network such as bandwidth, time and many other factors may impact the quality of these

cloud services. Hence, in the evaluation of cloud service performance consistency should be taken into account as an important criterion.

The deadline constraint problem is another important QoS criterion that can be viewed as a resource selection problem to fit the user's demand in terms of execution time. Such a problem is similar to the service discovery problem in the domain of web service composition. Researchers introduced the linear integer programming (LIP) model in order to address the service selection problem by maximizing the utility value which is a weighted sum of user-defined QoS attributes (Ardagna & Pernici, 2007). They applied LIP-based approaches for service matching, ranking and selection. LIP-based approaches are prone to high computational complexity associated with the growth of the size of web services. This kind of scheduling problem with QoS constraints are modeled as a variation of multi-dimension multi choice knapsack problem (MMKP) (Parra-Hernandez & Dimopoulos, 2005), which has been proven to be NP-complete (Martello & Toth, 1990).To encounter this Researcher(Wang, Chang, Lo& Lee, 2013) propose an adaptive scheduling algorithm called Adaptive Scheduling with QoS Satisfaction (*AsQ*) for hybrid cloud environments. The *AsQ*aims to fit the deadline constraints of the submitted jobs and to reduce the cost for renting public cloud resources if using a public cloud is necessary. The AsQ attempts to maximize the utilization rate of the private cloud and to minimize the renting cost of the public cloud.

6. CONCLUSION

In this Chapter, the current consensus of what Cloud Computing is, the confusion surrounding the different cloud computing deployment model viz., Public, Private, Hybrid and Community cloud, traditional cloud computing architecture and the relevance of reliability, fault tolerance and QoS in Clouds have been discussed. Fault tolerance is a critical means of assuring reliability QoS criteria in cloud computing. In other words, Fault tolerance is concerned with all the methods required to enable a system to tolerate software faults at the runtime. It ensures the correct functioning and continuous operation of cloud system. We discussed the different failure attributes of typical Cloud-based services caused largely due to crash faults and byzantine faults and fault tolerance mechanisms to encounter these failures. We also described various study conducted that addresses user's reliability and availability concerns. Quality of services (QoS) is the ability to render different priority to different applications, users, or data flows, or to guarantee a certain level performance data flow. To meet the requirements of both cloud users and service providers, role of resource broker is discussed. In this Chapter, we also discussed the QoS measures covering its research challenges, tools used for implementing QoS in cloud computing. The motivation behind, concepts, technology, researches and the state of QoS in Cloud Computing have been reviewed.

REFERENCES

Ardagna, D., & Pernici, B. (2007). Adaptive service composition in flexible processes. *Software Engineering, IEEE Transactions on, 33*(6), 369-384.

Armstrong, D., & Djemame, K. (2009). *Towards quality of service in the cloud.*

Ayari, N., Barbaron, D., Lefevre, L., & Primet, P. (2008). Fault tolerance for highly available internet services: concepts, approaches, and issues. *Communications Surveys & Tutorials, IEEE, 10*(2), 34-46.

Barroso, L. A., Clidaras, J., & Hölzle, U. (2013). The datacenter as a computer: An introduction to the design of warehouse-scale machines. *Synthesis lectures on computer architecture, 8*(3), 1-15.

Berl, A., Gelenbe, E., Di Girolamo, M., Giuliani, G., De Meer, H., Dang, M. Q., & Pentikousis, K. (2010). Energy-efficient cloud computing. *The computer journal, 53*(7), 1045-1051.

Bittencourt, L. F., & Madeira, E. R. M. (2011). HCOC: a cost optimization algorithm for workflow scheduling in hybrid clouds. *Journal of Internet Services and Applications, 2*(3), 207-227.

Buyya, R., Yeo, C. S., Venugopal, S., Broberg, J., & Brandic, I. (2009). Cloud computing and emerging IT platforms: Vision, hype, and reality for delivering computing as the 5th utility. *Future Generation computer systems, 25*(6), 599-616.

Casola, V., Rak, M., & Villano, U. (2010). *Identity federation in cloud computing.*

Dowell, S., Barreto, A., Michael, J. B., & Shing, M.-T. (2011). Cloud to cloud interoperability.

Expósito, R. R., Taboada, G. L., Ramos, S., González-Domínguez, J., Touriño, J., & Doallo, R. (2013). Analysis of I/O performance on an amazon EC2 cluster compute and high I/O platform. *Journal of grid computing, 11*(4), 613-631.

Fox, A., Griffith, R., Joseph, A., Katz, R., Konwinski, A., Lee, G., et al. (2009). Above the clouds: A Berkeley view of cloud computing. University of California, Berkeley, Rep. UCB/EECS, 28, 13.

Ganghishetti, P., & Wankar, R. (2011). Quality of Service Design in Clouds. *CSI Communications, 35*(2), 12–15.

Gill, P., Jain, N., & Nagappan, N. (2011). Understanding network failures in data centers: measurement, analysis, and implications.

Houidi, I., Mechtri, M., Louati, W., & Zeghlache, D. (2011). Cloud service delivery across multiple cloud platforms.

Jhawar, R., Piuri, V., & Santambrogio, M. (2012). A comprehensive conceptual system-level approach to fault tolerance in cloud computing.

Kang, X., Zhang, H., Jiang, G., Chen, H., Meng, X., & Yoshihira, K. (2008). Measurement, modeling, and analysis of internet video sharing site workload: *A case study.*

Kertész, A., Kecskemeti, G., Oriol, M., Kotcauer, P., Acs, S., Rodríguez, M., . . . Franch, X. (2013). Enhancing federated cloud management with an integrated service monitoring approach. *Journal of grid computing, 11*(4), 699-720.

Kim, K. H., Beloglazov, A., & Buyya, R. (2009). Power-aware provisioning of cloud resources for real-time services.

Lai, W. K., Yang, K.-T., Lin, Y.-C., & Shieh, C.-S. (2012). Dual migration for improved efficiency in cloud service Intelligent Information and Database Systems (pp. 216-225). Springer.

Li, C. (2012). Optimal resource provisioning for cloud computing environment. *The Journal of Supercomputing, 62*(2), 989-1022.

Lin, C.-F., Sheu, R.-K., Chang, Y.-S., & Yuan, S.-M. (2011). A relaxable service selection algorithm for QoS-based web service composition. *Information and Software Technology, 53*(12), 1370-1381.

Marshall, P., Keahey, K., & Freeman, T. (2011). Improving utilization of infrastructure clouds.

Martello, S., & Toth, P. (1990). *Knapsack problems: Algorithms and computer interpretations.* Hoboken, NJ: Wiley-Interscience.

Oikonomou, K., & Stavrakakis, I. (2010). Scalable service migration in autonomic network environments. *Selected Areas in Communications, IEEE Journal on, 28*(1), 84-94.

Papagianni, C., Leivadeas, A., Papavassiliou, S., Maglaris, V., Cervello-Pastor, C., & Monje, A. (2013). On the optimal allocation of virtual resources in cloud computing networks. *Computers, IEEE Transactions on, 62*(6), 1060-1071.

Parra-Hernandez, R., & Dimopoulos, N. J. (2005). A new heuristic for solving the multichoice multidimensional knapsack problem. *Systems, Man and Cybernetics, Part A: Systems and Humans, IEEE Transactions on, 35*(5), 708-717.

Piuri, R. J. V. (2013). Fault Tolerance and Resilience in Cloud Computing Environments. In J. Vacca (Ed.), *Computer and information Security Handbook* (2nd Ed.). Morgan Kaufmann.

Randles, M., Lamb, D., & Taleb-Bendiab, A. (2010). *A comparative study into distributed load balancing algorithms for cloud computing.*

Salehi, M. A., & Buyya, R. (2010). Adapting market-oriented scheduling policies for cloud computing Algorithms and Architectures for Parallel Processing (pp. 351-362). Springer.

Sotomayor, B., Montero, R. S., Llorente, I. M., & Foster, I. (2009). Virtual infrastructure management in private and hybrid clouds. *Internet computing, IEEE, 13*(5), 14-22.

Srikantaiah, S., Kansal, A., & Zhao, F. (2008). *Energy aware consolidation for cloud computing.*

Subramanian, K. (2011). *Hybrid clouds.* Retrieved from http://emea. trendmicro. com/imperia/md/content/uk/cloud-security/wp01_hybridcloud-krish_110624us. pdf

Vishwanath, K. V., & Nagappan, N. (2010). Characterizing cloud computing hardware reliability.

A Vouk, M. (2008). Cloud computing–issues, research and implementations. *CIT. Journal of Computing and Information Technology, 16*(4), 235-246.

Wang, S., Liu, Z., Sun, Q., Zou, H., & Yang, F. (2014). Towards an accurate evaluation of quality of cloud service in service-oriented cloud computing. *Journal of Intelligent Manufacturing, 25*(2), 283-291.

Wang, W.-J., Chang, Y.-S., Lo, W.-T., & Lee, Y.-K. (2013). Adaptive scheduling for parallel tasks with QoS satisfaction for hybrid cloud environments. *The Journal of Supercomputing, 66*(2), 783-811.

Yang, Y., Zhou, Y., Liang, L., He, D., & Sun, Z. (2010). A service-oriented broker for bulk data transfer in cloud computing.

KEY TERMS AND DEFINITIONS

Cloud Computing: A model for delivering IT services in which resources are retrieved from the internet through web-based tools and applications rather than a direct connection to a server.

Fault Tolerance: It is the property that enables a system to continue operating properly in the event of failure of some of its components.

Quality of Service (QoS): Quality of service (QoS) generally refers to a network's capability to achieve maximum bandwidth and deal with other network performance elements like latency, error rate and uptime. Quality of service also involves controlling and managing network resources by setting priorities for explicit types of data (files, audio and video) on the network or cloud.

Virtualization: Virtualization, in computing, is the creation of a virtual (rather than actual) version of something, such as a hardware platform, operating system, a storage device or network resources.

Compilation of References

A Security Analysis of Cloud Computing (2009). Cloud-computing.sys. Retrieved from http://cloudcomputing. sys- con.com/node/1203943

A Vouk, M. (2008). Cloud computing–issues, research and implementations. *CIT. Journal of Computing and Information Technology, 16*(4), 235-246.

Abaza, A., Ross, A., Hebert, C., Harrison, M. A. F., & Nixon, M. S. (2013). A Survey on Ear Biometrics. *ACM Computing Surveys, 45*(2), 1–35. doi:10.1145/2431211.2431221

Abdalla, M., Bellare, M., Catalano, D., Kiltz, E., Kohno, T., Lange, T., Shi, H. (2005). *Searchable encryption revisited: Consistency properties, relation to anonymous IBE, and extensions.*

Abu-Libdeh, H., Princehouse, L., & Weatherspoon, H. (2010). *RACS: a case for cloud storage diversity.*

Act, A. (1996). Health insurance portability and accountability act of 1996. *Public Law, 104*, 191.

Agrawal, N., Bolosky, W. J., Douceur, J. R., & Lorch, J. R. (2007, October). A five-year study of file-system metadata. *Transactions on Storage, 3*(3), 338-346. doi:10.1145/1288783.1288788

Ahmed, R., & Karypis, G. (2012). Algorithms for mining the evolution of conserved relational states in dynamic networks. *Knowledge and Information Systems, 33*(3), 603-630.

Ahmed, Y., & Manal, A. (2011). Security Issues in Cloud Computing. GSTF International Journal on Computing, 1(3).

Alabool, H. M., & Mahmood, A. K. (2013). Trust -Based Service Selection in Public Cloud Computing Using Fuzzy Modified VIKOR Method. *Australian Journal of Basic and Applied Sciences, 7*(9), 211–220.

Alam, M. H., Ha, J., & Lee, S. (2012). Novel approaches to crawling important pages early. *Knowledge and Information Systems, 33*(3), 707-734.

Alam, B., Doja, M. N., Alam, M., & Malhotra, S. (2013). Security issues analysis for cloud computing. *International Journal of Computer Science and Information Security, 11*(9), 117–125.

Al-Aqrabi, H., Liu, L., Xu, J., Hill, R., Antonopoulos, N., & Zhan, Y. (2012, April). Investigation of IT security and compliance challenges in Security-as-a-Service for cloud computing. 15th *IEEE International Symposium on Object/Component/Service-Oriented Real-Time Distributed Computing Workshops.* (pp. 124-129). doi:10.1109/ISORCW.2012.31

Alhamad, M., Dillon, T., & Chang, E. (2011). A Trust-Evaluation Metric for Cloud applications. *International Journal of Machine Learning and Computing, 1*(4), 416–421. doi:10.7763/IJMLC.2011.V1.62

Al-Muhtadi, J., Campbell, R., Kapadia, A., Mickunas, D., & Yi, S. (2002). Routing Through the Mist: Privacy Preserving Communication in Ubiquitous Computing Environments. Proceedings of *International Conference of Distributed Computing Systems (ICDCS 2002)*, Vienna, Austria. doi:10.1109/ICDCS.2002.1022244

Alshammari, H. (2014). Privacy and security concerns in cloud computing. *International Journal of Computer Science and Information Security, 12*(3), 1–4.

Alvaro, A. C., Pratyusa, K. M., & Sreeranga, P. R. (2013). Big data analytics for security. *IEEE Security and Privacy, 11*(6), 74–76. doi:10.1109/MSP.2013.138

Alzain, M. A., Pardede, E., Soh, B., & Thom, J. A. (2012). Cloud Computing Security: From Single to Multi-Cloud. In *Proceedings of 45th Hawaii International Conference on System Science.* (pp. 5490-5499). Maui, HI: IEEE. doi:10.1109/HICSS.2012.153

Alzain, M. A., Soh, B., & Pardede, E. (2011). MCDB: Using Multi Cloud to Ensure Security in Cloud Computing, In *Proceedings of IEEE 9th International Conference on Dependable, Autonomic & Secure Computing.* (pp. 784-791). Sydney, NSW: IEEE. doi:10.1109/DASC.2011.133

Alzain, M. A., Soh, B., & Pardede, E. (2012). A New Approach Using Redundancy Technique to Improve Security in Cloud Computing, In *Proceedings of International Conference on Cyber Security, Cyber Warfare & Digital Forensic.* (pp. 230-235). Kuala Lumpur: IEEE. doi:10.1109/CyberSec.2012.6246174

Amazon EBS. (2014). *Amazon Inc.* Retrieved from http://aws.amazon.com/ebs/

Amazon Virtual Private Cloud. (2012). Amazon.com. Retrieved from http://aws.amazon.com/vpc/

Amazon, S3. (2014). *Amazon.com.* Retrieved from http://aws.amazon.com/s3/

Anderson, J. (2015). Lincoln school district to become largest in state to provide computers to all students from elementary grades up. *OMaha World-Herald.*

Ando, R., Kadobayashi, Y., & Shinoda, Y. (2007). Synchronous pseudo physical memory snapshot and forensics on paravirtualized vmm using split kernel module. *Information Security and Cryptology (ICISC'07),* 131-143.

ANSA. (2014). *Pedofilia, sgominata rete in Italia e 11 Paesi.* Retrieved from http://www.ansa.it/sito/notizie/cronaca/2014/07/11/pedofilia-sgominata-rete-in-italia-e-11-paesi_8c7a9210-ad9d-4a82-af3a-85e609c205ec.html

Aral, S., & Walker, D. (2012). Identifying influential and susceptible members of social networks. *Science, 337*(6092), 337-341.

Ardagna, D., & Pernici, B. (2007). Adaptive service composition in flexible processes. *Software Engineering, IEEE Transactions on, 33*(6), 369-384.

Armbrust, M., Armando, F., Rean, G., Anthony, D. J., Katz, R. H., Konwinski, A., et al. (2009b). Above the Clouds: A Berkeley View of Cloud Computing. *Tech. Report UCB/EECS-2009-28.*

Armbrust, M., Fox, A., Griffith, R., & Anthony, D. Joseph, Katz R. H., Konwinski A., Lee G., Patterson D. A., Rabkin A., S. Ion and Zaharia M., (2009). Above the clouds: A Berkeley view of cloud computing. *EECS Department, University of California, Berkeley.*

Armbrust, M., Fox, A., Griffth, R., et al. (2009). Above the clouds: A Berkeley View of Cloud Computing. EECS Department University of California Berkeley. Retrieved from http://www.eecs.berkeley.edu/Pubs/TechRpts/2009/EECS-2009-28.pdf

Armbrust. M., Fox A., Griffith, R., Joseph, A. D., Katz, R., Konwinski, A., Lee, G., Patterson, D., Rabkin, A., Stoica, I., & Zaharia, M. (2009a). *Above the Clouds: A View of Cloud Computing* [EB/OL]. UC Berkeley. Retrieved from https://www.eecs.berkeley.edu/Pubs/TechRpts/2009/EECS-2009-28.pdf.

Armbrust, M. A., Fox, R., Griffith, A., Joseph, R., Katz, A., & Konwinski, G. et al. (2009). *Above the Clouds: A Berkeley View of Cloud Computing.* UC Berkeley Reliable Adaptive Distributed Systems Laboratory.

Armbrust, M., Stoica, I., Zaharia, M., Fox, A., Griffith, R., & Joseph, A. D. et al. (2010). A view of cloud computing. *Communications of the ACM, 53*(4), 50–58. doi:10.1145/1721654.1721672

Armstrong, D., & Djemame, K. (2009). *Towards quality of service in the cloud.*

Arnold, S. (2008, July-August). *Cloud computing and the issue of privacy. KM World.* Retrieved from http://www.kmworld.com

Asharov, G., Jain, A., López-Alt, A., Tromer, E., Vaikuntanathan, V., & Wichs, D. (2012). Multiparty computation with low communication, computation and interaction via threshold FHE. Advances in Cryptology–EUROCRYPT 2012 (pp. 483-501). Springer.

Aslam, U., Ullah, I., & Ansari, S. (2010). Open source private cloud computing. *Interdisciplinary Journal of Contemporary Research in Business*, 2(7), 399-399-407

AWS CloudTrail. (2014). Amazon, Inc. Retrieved from http://aws.amazon.com/cloudtrail/

AWS Security Center. (2014). Amazon, Inc. Retrieved from http://aws.amazon.com/security/

Ayanoglu, E. (1993). Performance improvement in the broadband networks using forward error correction for lost packets recovery. *Journal of High-Speed Networks*, *1*, 287–303.

Ayanoglu, E. (1996). Forward error control for MPEG-2 video transport in a wireless ATM LAN. *Proceedings of IEEEICIP*, *2*, 833–836.

Ayari, N., Barbaron, D., Lefevre, L., & Primet, P. (2008). Fault tolerance for highly available internet services: concepts, approaches, and issues. *Communications Surveys & Tutorials, IEEE*, *10*(2), 34-46.

Azzedin, F., Ridha, A., & Rizvi, A. (2007). Fuzzy Trust for Peer-to-Peer Based Systems. World Academy of Science, Engineering and Technology, 123-127.

Babcock, C. (2014). 9 Cloud Trends for 2015. *InformationWeek*.

Baber, M., & Chauhan, M. (2011). A Tale of Migration to Cloud Computing for SharingExperiences and Observations, Proceedings of the *2nd International Workshop on Software Engineering for Cloud Computing 2011*. Retrieved from http://delivery.acm.org.ezproxy.apollolibrary.com

Babu, M. S., & Sekhar, M. C. (2013). Enterprise Risk Management Integrated framework for Cloud Computing. *International Journal of Advanced Networking & Applications*, *5*(3), 1939–1950.

Bai, B. B., & Devi, N. R. (2011). The international journal of science & technology.

Bai, Y., & Wang, D. (2006). Fundamentals of Fuzzy Logic Control – Fuzzy Sets, Fuzzy Rules and Defuzzifications. In Y. Bai, D. Wang, & H. Zhuang, Advanced Fuzzy Logic Technologies in Industrial Applications (pp. 17-36). Springer London.

Baier, A. (1986). Trust and antitrust. *Ethics*, *96*(2), 231–260. doi:10.1086/292745

Baltzan, P., & Phillips, A. (2012). *Business Driven Technology*. New York, NY: McGraw-Hill Irwin.

Banerjee, S., & Agarwal, N. (2012). Analyzing collective behavior from blogs using swarm intelligence. *Knowledge and Information Systems*, *33*(3), 523-547.

Banerjee, P., Friedrich, R., Bash, C., Goldsack, P., Huberman, B., & Manley, J. et al. (2010). Everything as a Service: Powering the New Information Economy. *IEEE Computer*, *44*(3), 36–43. doi:10.1109/MC.2011.67

Barroso, L. A., Clidaras, J., & Hölzle, U. (2013). The datacenter as a computer: An introduction to the design of warehouse-scale machines. *Synthesis lectures on computer architecture*, *8*(3), 1-15.

Bates, A., Mood, B., Valafar, M., & Butler, K. (2013). Towards secure provenance-based access control in cloud environments. *Proceedings of the third ACM conference on Data and application security and privacy* (pp. 277-284). San Antonio (TX, USA): ACM. doi:10.1145/2435349.2435389

Bauer, S., & Priyantha, N. B. (2001). Secure data deletion for linux filesystems. In *Proceedings of the 10th conference on usenix security symposium*, 10. (pp. 12–12). Berkeley, CA, USA: USENIX Association.

Bell, D., & LaPadula, J. (1973). Secure Computer System: Mathematical foundation and model, Mitre Corp, MTR 2547, 2.

Bellido, L., & Fernández, D. & Pastor. (1996). Architectural Issues for Multimedia Cooperative Systems. *Proceedings of the 3rd International Workshop on Protocols for Multimedia Systems (PROMS)*. (pp. 33-47).

Ben-Or, M., Goldwasser, S., & Wigderson, A. (1988). *Completeness theorems for non-cryptographic fault-tolerant distributed computation*.

Berl, A., Gelenbe, E., Di Girolamo, M., Giuliani, G., De Meer, H., Dang, M. Q., & Pentikousis, K. (2010). Energy-efficient cloud computing. *The computer journal*, *53*(7), 1045-1051.

Berman, J. J. (2013). *Principles of big data: Preparing, sharing, and analyzing complex information.* San Francisco, CA: Morgan Kaufmann Publishers Inc.

Bernstein, D., Ludvigson, E., Sankar, K., Diamond, S., & Morrow, M. (2009). *Blueprint for the intercloud-protocols and formats for cloud computing interoperability.*

Bernstein, D., Ludvigson, E., Sankar, K., Diamond, S., & Morrow, M. (2009). Blueprint for the intercloud-protocols and formats for cloud computing interoperability.*4th International Conference on Internet and Web Applications and Services (ICIW'09)* (pp. 328-336). Venice (Italy): IEEE. doi:10.1109/ICIW.2009.55

Best, S. J., Krueger, B. S., & Ladewig, J. (2008). The effect of risk perceptions on online political participatory decisions. *Journal of Information Technology & Politics, 4*(1), 5–17. doi:10.1300/J516v04n01_02

Bhaskar, P. R., Admela, J., Dimitrios, K., & Goeleven, Y. (2011). Architectural requirements for cloud computing systems: An enterprise cloud approach. *Journal of Grid Computing,* 3–26.

Bially, T., Gold, B., & Seneff, S. (1980). A technique for adaptive voice flow control in integrated packet networks. *IEEE Transactions on Communications, 28*(3), 325–333. doi:10.1109/TCOM.1980.1094677

Biba, R. R. (1977). Integrity Considerations for Secure Computer Systems: Unified exposition and multics interpretation. *Mitre Corp., MTR 3153.*

Biggs, S., & Vidalis, S. (2009). Cloud computing: The impact on digital forensic investigations.*International Conference for Internet Technology and Secured Transactions (ICITST'09)* (pp. 1-6). IEEE. doi:10.1109/ICITST.2009.5402561

Bikram. B (2009). Safe on the Cloud. A Perspective into Security Concerns of Cloud Computing, 4, 34-35.

Birk, D., & Wegener, C. (2011). Technical issues of forensic investigations in cloud computing environments.*6th International Workshop on Systematic Approaches to Digital Forensic Engineering (SADFE'11)* (pp. 1-10). IEEE. doi:10.1109/SADFE.2011.17

Birney, E. (2012). The making of ENCODE: lessons for big-data projects. *Nature, 489*(7414), 49-51.

Bisong, A., & Rahman, S. M. (2011). An Overview of the Security Concerns in Enterprise Cloud Computing. *International Journal of Network Security & Its Applications, 3*(1), 30–45. doi:10.5121/ijnsa.2011.3103

Bittencourt, L. F., & Madeira, E. R. M. (2011). HCOC: a cost optimization algorithm for workflow scheduling in hybrid clouds. *Journal of Internet Services and Applications, 2*(3), 207-227.

Blaze, M., Feigen, B., & Keromytis, J. (1998). A.D. keynote: trust management for public-key infrastructures. In: Christianaon, B., Crispo, B., Willian, S., et al. (Eds.) Security Protocols International Workshop. Berlin: Springer-Verglag.

Blumenthal, M. S. (2011). Is security lost in the clouds? *Communications & Stratégies, 81*(1), 69–86.

Bodei, C., Degano, P., Ferrari, G. L., Galletta, L., & Mezzetti, G. (2012). Formalising security in ubiquitous and cloud scenarios. In A. Cortesi, N. Chaki, K. Saeed, & S. Wierzchon (Eds.), *Computer information systems and industrial management: Proceedings of the 11th IFIP TC 8 International Conference (LNCS)* (Vol. 7564, pp. 1-29). Berlin, Germany: Springer. doi:10.1007/978-3-642-33260-9_1

Bogetoft, P., Christensen, D. L., Damgaard, I., Geisler, M., Jakobsen, T., Kroeigaard, M., et al. (2009). Secure Multiparty Computation Goes Live. Financial Cryptography and Data Security. In R. Dingledine and P. Golle (Eds), LNCS Vol. 5628. Springer-Verlag. doi:10.1007/978-3-642-03549-4_20

Bohli, J. M., Jensen, M., Gruschka, N., Schwenk, J., & Iacono, L. L. L. (2011). *Security prospects through cloud computing by adopting multiple clouds.*

Bohli, J.-M., Li, W., & Seedorf, J. (2012). Assisting server for secure multi-party computation Information Security Theory and Practice. Security, Privacy and Trust in Computing Systems and Ambient Intelligent Ecosystems. (pp. 144-159). Springer.

Böhm, M., Koleva, G., Leimeister, S., Riedl, C., & Krcmar, H. (2010). Towards a generic value network for cloud computing. In Economics of Grids, Clouds, Systems, and Services. (pp. 129-140). Springer Berlin Heidelberg. doi:10.1007/978-3-642-15681-6_10

Bojkovic, Z. S. (1995). Image decomposition and compression in digital multimedia systems.*Proceedings of IX Int. Conference on signal processing applications and technology, ICSPAT.* Boston, USA. (pp.940-944).

Bojkovic, Z. S. (1996). Multimedia communication system: modeling, standardization, requirements.*Proceedings of International Conference on multimedia technology and digital telecommunication services, ICOMPT.* Budapest, Hungary. (pp. 5-13)

Boldyreva, A., Chenette, N., Lee, Y., & O'neill, A. (2009). Order-preserving symmetric encryption Advances in Cryptology-EUROCRYPT 2009. (pp. 224-241). Springer.

Bollen, J., Mao, H., & Zeng, X. (2011). Twitter mood predicts the stock market. *Journal of Computational Science, 2*(1), 1-8.

Boneh, D., Gentry, C., Lynn, B., & Shacham, H. (2003). Aggregate and Verifiably Encrypted Signatures from Bilinear Maps. In E. Biham (Ed.), *Advances in Cryptology.* Lecture Notes in Computer ScienceHeidelberg: Springer. doi:10.1007/3-540-39200-9_26

Borgatti, S. P., Mehra, A., Brass, D. J., & Labianca, G. (2009). Network analysis in the social sciences. *Science, 323*(5916), 892-895.

Boss, G., Malladi, P., Quan, D., et al. (2010). *IBM Cloud Computing White Book.* Retrieved from http://www-01.ibm.com/software/cn/Tivoli/ao/reg.html

Brad, R., (2009, April). Protecting Against Insider Attacks. *GIAC (GCIH) Gold Certification.* SANS Institute InfoSec Reading Room.

Brady, P. (1990). A model for generating on-off patterns in two-way communications. *The Bell System Technical Journal, 48*(7), 2445–2472. doi:10.1002/j.1538-7305.1969.tb01181.x

Brodkin, J. (2008, August). Loss of customer data spurs closure of online storage service. *Network World.*

Brooks, C. (2009). *Amazon EC2 Attack Prompts Customer Support Changes.* Tech Target.

Bruegger, B. P., Hühnlein, D., & Schwenk, J. (2008). *TLS-Federation-a Secure and Relying-Party-Friendly Approach for Federated Identity Management* (pp. 93–106). BIOSIG.

Bughin, J., Chui, M., & Manyika, J. (2010). Clouds, big data, and smart assets: Ten tech-enabled business trends to watch. Retrieved from http://www.mckinsey.com/insights/high_tech_telecoms_internet/clouds_big_data_and_smart_assets_ten_tech-enabled_business_trends_to_watch

Bughin, J., Chui, M., & Manyika, J. (2010). Clouds, big data, and smart assets: Ten tech-enabled business trends to watch. *The McKinsey Quarterly, 56*(1), 75–86.

Bugiel, S., Nürnberger, S., Pöppelmann, T., Sadeghi, A.-R., & Schneider, T. (2011). *AmazonIA: when elasticity snaps back.*

Bugiel, S., Nürnberger, S., Sadeghi, A.-R., & Schneider, T. (2011). *Twin clouds: Secure cloud computing with low latency.*

Burge, M., & Burger, W. (2002). Ear biometrics in Computer Vision, *InProceedings of International Conference of Pattern Recognition.* (pp. 822-826).

Burkhart, M., Strasser, M., Many, D., & Dimitropoulos, X. (2010). SEPIA: Privacy-preserving aggregation of multi-domain network events and statistics. *Network, 1*, 101101.

Buyya, R., Yeo, C. S., Venugopal, S., Broberg, J., & Brandic, I. (2009). Cloud computing and emerging IT platforms: Vision, hype, and reality for delivering computing as the 5th utility. *Future Generation computer systems, 25*(6), 599-616.

Cachin, C., Haralambiev, K., Hsiao, H.-C., & Sorniotti, A. (2013). Policy-based secure deletion.*Proceedings of the 2013 ACM SIGSAC conference on Computer & communications security* (pp. 259-270). ACM. doi:10.1145/2508859.2516690

Calore, M. (2009, January). Ma.gnolia suffers major data loss, site taken offline. *Wired.*

Campbell, P. (2008). Editorial on special issue on big data: Community cleverness required. *Nature, 455*(7209), 1. doi:10.1038/455001a PMID:18769385

Canny, J. (1986). A Computational Approach to Edge Detection. *IEEE Transactions on Pattern Analysis, 8*(6), 679–698.

Cappelli, D. M., Moore, A. P., Trzeciak, R. F., & Shimeall, T. J. (2008). *Common Sense Guide to Prevention and Detection of Insider Threats. CERT Insider Threat Study Team.* Carnegie Mellon University.

Carbo, J., Molina, J., & Davila, J. (2003). Trust Management Through Fuzzy Reputation. *International Journal of Cooperative Information System, 12*(1), 135–155. doi:10.1142/S0218843003000681

Carrier, B. (2014). *Sleuth Kit Hadoop Framework.* Retrieved from http://www.sleuthkit.org/tsk_hadoop/

Casola, V., Rak, M., & Villano, U. (2010). *Identity federation in cloud computing.*

Castle, L. (2015). *Creating a New IT at Fairfield University.* Mobile Enterprise.

Catrina, O., & Kerschbaum, F. (2008). *Fostering the uptake of secure multiparty computation in e-commerce.*

Celesti, A., Tusa, F., Villari, M., & Puliafito, A. (2010). *How to enhance cloud architectures to enable cross-federation.*

Centola, D. (2010). The spread of behavior in an online social network experiment. *Science, 329*(5996), 1194-1197.

Chakrabarti, A. (2007). Managing Trust in the Grid. In A. Chakrabarti, Grid Computing Security (pp. 218-221). Springer-Verlag Berlin Heidelberg. doi:10.1007/978-3-540-44493-0_10

Chakraborty, R., Ramireddy, S., Raghu, T. S., & Rao, H. R. (2010). The information assurance practices of cloud computing vendors. *IT Professional Magazine,* 12(4), 29-29-37

Chandrareddy, J. B., & Mahesh, G. U. (2012).Cloud Zones: Security and Privacy Issues in Cloud Computing", Asian Journal of Information Technology 11(3), 83-93- ISSN-1682-3915-

Chang, E. Y., Bai, H., & Zhu, K. (2009). *Parallel algorithms for mining large-scale rich-media data.*

Chang, E., Dillon, T., & Calder, D. (2008, May). Human system interaction with confident computing. The mega trend. In *Human System Interactions, 2008 Conference* (pp. 1-11).

Chang, Znati, T.F. (n. d.). ADVANCES IN DISTRIBUTED MULTIMEDIA SYSTEMS.

Chao-Chih, C., Lihua, Y., & Albert, G., Greenberg, Chen-Nee C., Prasant M. (2011). Routing-as-a-Service (RaaS): A framework for tenant-directed route control in data center, *InProceedings of 30ᵗʰ IEEE international conference of INFOCOM.* (pp. 1386-1394).

Chao-yang, Z. (2011). An Improved Binary Image Watermarking Algorithm Based on Singular Value Decomposition. *Proceedings of International Symposium on Intelligence Information Processing and Trusted Computing.* Hubei, China. doi:10.1109/IPTC.2011.70

Chaudhuri, A. (2011). Enabling Effective IT Governance: Leveraging ISO/IEC 38500: 2008 and COBIT to Achieve Business–IT Alignment. *EDPACS, 44*(2), 1–18. doi:10.1080/07366981.2011.599278

Chaudhuri, A., Solms, S. H., & Chaudhuri, D. (2011). Auditing Security Risks in Virtual IT Systems. *ISACA Journal, 1,* 16.

Chen, R., Sivakumar, K., & Kargupta, H. (2004). Collective mining of Bayesian networks from distributed heterogeneous data. *Knowledge and Information Systems, 6*(2), 164-187.

Chen, Y., Paxson, V., & Katz, R. H. (2010). What's new about cloud computing security. *Technical Report No. UCB/EECS-2010-5.* Retrieved from http://www.eecs.berkeley.edu/Pubs/TechRpts/2010/EECS-2010-5.html

Chen, X., & Huang, Q. (2013). The data protection of mapreduce using homomorphic encryption. In *Proceedings of the 4th IEEE International Conference on Software Engineering and Service Science* (pp. 419-421). Beijing, China: IEEE.

Chevrie, F., & Guély, F. (1998). *Fuzzy Logic. Cahier Technique no. 191.* France: Groupe Schneider.

Ching – Ching. L, Kamalendu. B. (2008). Distributed Authorization Cache. Proceedings of Security & Management, pp. 381-386.

Choo, K. (2010). Cloud computing: Challenges and future directions. *Trends & Issues in Crime & Criminal Justice,* (400), 1-6

Chow, R., Golle, P., Jakobsson, M., Shi, E., Staddon, J., Masuoka, R., & Molina, J. (2009, November). Controlling data in the cloud: outsourcing computation without outsourcing control. In *Proceedings of the 2009 ACM workshop on Cloud computing security.* (pp. 85-90). doi:10.1145/1655008.1655020

Chow, R., Jakobsson, M., Masuoka, R., Molina, J., Niu, Y., Shi, E., & Song, Z. (2010, October). Authentication in the clouds: a framework and its application to mobile users.*InProceedings of the 2010 ACM workshop on Cloud computing security workshop.* (pp. 1-6). doi:10.1145/1866835.1866837

Chu, C., Kim, S. K., Lin, Y. A., Yu, Y., Bradski, G., Ng, A. Y., & Olukotun, K. (2007). Map-reduce for machine learning on multicore. Advances in neural information processing systems, 19, 281.

Clark, D., & Wilson, D. (1987). A Comparison of Commercial and Military Computer Security Policies", *IEEE Symposium on security and privacy.* doi:10.1109/SP.1987.10001

Clarke, G. (2009, March 16). Microsoft's Azure Cloud Suffers First Crash. *The Register.*

Clement, L., Hately, A., von Riegen, C., & Rogers, T. (2004). *UDDI Version 3.0. 2, UDDI Spec Technical Committee Draft.* OASIS UDDI Spec TC.

Cloud 101: Developing a Cloud-Computing Strategy for Higher Education. (2012). *Cisco.*

Cloud Computing: Benefits, Risks, and Recommendations. (2009). European Network and Information Security Agency. Retrieved from http://www.enisa.europa.eu/act/rm/files/deliverables/cloud-computing-risk-assessment

Cloud Computing - Building a Framework for Successful Transition. (2009). *GTSI Group.* [White Paper].

Cloud Computing: Business Benefits With Security, Governance and Assurance Perspectives. (2009). *ISACA.* Retrieved from http://www.isaca.org/Knowledge-Center/Research/ResearchDeliverables/Pages/Cloud-Computing-Business-Benefits-With-Security-Governance-and-Assurance-Perspective.aspx

Cloud Computing and Security. (2010). A Natural Match. *Trusted Computing Group.* http://www.trustedcomputing-group.org

Cloud Governance: Questions Boards of Directors Need to Ask. (2013). ISACA. Retrieved from http://www.isaca.org/Knowledge-Center/Research/ResearchDeliverables/Pages/Cloud-Governance-Questions-Boards-of-Directors-Need-to-Ask.aspx

Cloud Security Questions? Here are some answers (2010). Cloudcomputing.sys. http://cloudcomputing.sys-con.com/node/1330353

Cloud Security Toolkit, Cloud Security 101. (2012, February). Healthcare Information and Management Systems Society

Coan, B. A., & Turpin, R. (1984). Extending Binary Byzantine Agreement to Multivalued Byzantine Agreement: DTIC Document.

Cohen, A., Daubechies, I., & Feauveau, J. C. (1992). Biorthogonal bases of compactly supported wavelets. *Communications on Pure and Applied Mathematics,* *45*(5), 485–560. doi:10.1002/cpa.3160450502

Columbus, L. (2013). *Gartner Predicts Infrastructure Services Will Accelerate Cloud Computing Growth.* Retrieved from http://www.forbes.com/sites/louiscolumbus/2013/02/19/gartner-predicts-infrastructure-services-will-accelerate-cloud-computing-growth/

Commission, E. (2010). Standard Contractual Clauses for the Transfer of Personal Data to Processors Established in Third Countries under Directive 95/ 46/EC of the European Parliament and of the Council. congress, U. (2002). Federal Information Security Management Act.

Common Event Expression - A Unified Event Language for Interoperability. (2013). *MITRE.* Retrieved from https://cee.mitre.org/

Computer hard drive sold on eBay had details of top secret US missile defense system. (2009). *The-Daily-Mail.*

Constantine, A. Papandreou. (1998). Architecture of a multimedia communication system for technical documentation in a modern factory. In Computers in Industry. (pp. 83–93). Elsevier.

Constantine, C. (2014). Big data: An information security context. *Network Security, 2014*(1), 18–19. doi:10.1016/S1353-4858(14)70010-8

Controlling Data in the Cloud (2009). Outsourcing Computation Without Outsourcing Control. Retrieved from http://www.parc.com/content/attachments/ControllingDataInTheCloud- CCSW-09.pdf

Cornell University Law School. (2014). *Daubert v. Merrell Dow Pharmaceuticals*. Retrieved from http://www.law.cornell.edu/supct/html/92-102.ZS.html

Corporate governance of information technology. (2008). International Organization for Standardization IEC 38500:2008-s. Retrieved from http://www.iso.org/iso/catalogue_detail?csnumber=51639

Council of Europe. (2001, November 23). *Convention on Cybercrime*. Retrieved from http://conventions.coe.int/Treaty/EN/Treaties/Html/185.htm

Covington, M. J., Moyer, M. J., & Ahamad, M. (2000, October). Generalized role-based access control for securing future application. NISSC, pp. 40–51.

Cox, R. V., Haskell, B. G., LeCun, Y., Shahraray, B., & Rabiner, L. (1998). On the applications of multimedia processing to communications. *Proceedings of the IEEE*, *86*(5), 755–824. doi:10.1109/5.664272

CSA. (2010). Cloud Security Alliance. Retrieved from http://www.cloudsecurityalliance.org/topthreats

CSA. (2013). Cloud Controls Matrix v3.0: Cloud Security Alliance. Retrieved from https://cloudsecurityalliance.org/download/cloud-controls-matrix-v3/

Curtmola, R., Garay, J., Kamara, S., & Ostrovsky, R. (2006). *Searchable symmetric encryption: improved definitions and efficient constructions*.

Da Silva, C. M. R., da Silva, J. L. C., Rodrigues, R. B., do Nascimento, L. M., & Garcia, V. C. (2013). Systematic mapping study on security threats in cloud computing. *International Journal of Computer Science and Information Security*, *11*(3), 55–64.

Daly, J. (2013). The State of Cloud Computing in Higher Education. *EdTechMagazine*.

Damgård, I., Geisler, M., Krøigaard, M., & Nielsen, J. B. (2009). Asynchronous multiparty computation: Theory and implementation Public Key Cryptography–PKC 2009 (pp. 160-179% @ 3642004679): Springer.

Danchev, D. (2009). Zeus crimeware using Amazon's EC2 as command and control server. *ZDnet*. Retrieved from http://blogs.zdnet.com/security/?p=5110

Danezis, G., & Livshits, B. (2011). Towards Ensuring Client-Side Computational Integrity (A position paper).

Data as a service. (2014, December 11). Wikipedia. Retrieved from http://en.wikipedia.org/wiki/Data_as_a_service

Davidson, S., & Freire, J. (2008). Provenance and scientific workflows: challenges and opportunities. *Proceedings of the 2008 ACM SIGMOD international conference on Management of data* (pp. 1345-1350). Vancouver (Canada): ACM. doi:10.1145/1376616.1376772

Delport, W., Kohn, M., & Olivier, M. (2011). Isolating a cloud instance for a digital forensic investigation. *Proceedings of Information Security South Africa Conference (ISSA'11)*, (pp. 15-17). Johannesburg, South Africa.

Delport, W., & Olivier, M. (2012). Cloud Separation: Stuck Inside the Cloud. *9th International Conference on Trust, Privacy and Security in Digital Business* (pp. 36-49). Vienna (Austria): Springer. doi:10.1007/978-3-642-32287-7_4

Desmedt, Y. (1998). Some recent research aspects of threshold cryptography Information Security (pp. 158-173% @ 3540643826): Springer.

Diesburg, S. M., & Wang, A. I. A. (2010, December). A survey of confidential data storage and deletion methods. *ACM Computing Surveys*, *43*(1), 1–37. doi:10.1145/1824795.1824797

Dikaiakos, M. D., Katsaros, D., Mehra, P., Pallis, G., & Vakali, A. (2009). Cloud Computing: Distributed Internet Computing for IT and Scientific Research. *IEEE Internet Computing*, *13*(5), 10–13. doi:10.1109/MIC.2009.103

Dimitrios, Z., & Dimitrios, L. (2012). Addressing cloud computing security issues. *Future Generation Computer Systems*, *28*(3), 583–592. doi:10.1016/j.future.2010.12.006

Dinesha, H. A. (2012). Multi-level Authentication Technique for Accessing Cloud Services. *InProceedings of IEEE Computing, Communication and Applications (ICCCA)*. (pp. 1-4). doi:10.1109/ICCCA.2012.6179130

Directive, E. U. (1995). 95/46/EC of the European Parliament and of the Council of 24 October 1995 on the protection of individuals with regard to the processing of personal data and on the free movement of such data. *Official Journal of the EC, 23*(6).

Dowell, S., Barreto, A., Michael, J. B., & Shing, M.-T. (2011). Cloud to cloud interoperability.

Dugad, R., Ratakonda, K., & Ahuja, N. (1998). A New Wavelet-based Scheme for Watermarking Images. *Proceedings of International Conference on Image Processing*, Chicago, IL, USA. doi:10.1109/ICIP.1998.723406

Dunn, J. E. (2010). Ultra-secure Firefox Offered to UK Bank Users. *Techworld.*

Dutta, R. (2009). *Planning for Single SignOn.* [White Paper]. MIEL e-Security Pvt

Dykstra, J., & Sherman, A. (2012). Acquiring forensic evidence from infrastructure-as-a-service cloud computing: Exploring and evaluating tools, trust, and techniques. Proceedings of 12th Annual Digital Forensics Research Work Shop (DFRWS'12), (pp. S90-S98). Washington DC, USA.

Dykstra, J., & Sherman, A. (2013). Design and implementation of FROST: Digital forensic tools for the OpenStack cloud computing platform. *Proceedings of 13th Annual Digital Forensics Research Work Shop (DFRWS'13)*, (pp. S87-S95). Monterey (CA, USA).

Dykstra, J., Gowe, L., Jackson, R., Reemelin, O. S., Rojas, E., & Ruan, K. S. et al. (2014). *NIST IR 8006 - NIST Cloud Computing Forensic Science Challenges (DRAFT)*. NIST.

Dykstra, J., & Sherman, A. (2011). Understanding issues in cloud forensics: two hypothetical case studies. *Proceedings of the 2011 ADSFL Conference on Digital Forensics, Security, and Law (ADSFL'11)*, (pp. 19-31). Richmond VA, USA.

Ei Ei, M., Thinn, T. N. (2011). The privacy-aware access control system using attribute-and role-based access control in private cloud. *IEEE International conference on Broadband Network and Multimedia Technology, pp. 447-451.*

Eisenhauer, M. P. (2005). *Privacy and Security Law Issues in Off-shore Outsourcing Transactions* (pp. 15). Atlanta, Georgia: Hunton & Williams.

Eludiora, S., Abiona, O., Oluwatope, A., Oluwaranti, A., Onime, C., & Kehinde, L. (2011). A user identity management protocol for cloud computing paradigm. *International Journal of Communications, Network and System Sciences*, 4(3), 152-152-163

Eraser. (2013). *Eraser*. Retrieved from http://eraser.heidi.ie/

Eucalyptus | Open Source Private Cloud Software. (2014). *Eucalyptus System, Inc.* Retrieved from https://www.eucalyptus.com/

European, C. (2012). Proposal for a regulation of the European Parliament and of the council on the protection of individuals with regard to the processing of personal data and on the free movement of such data (general data protection regulation). COM (2012) 11 final, 2012/0011 (COD), Brussels, 25 January 2012.

Expósito, R. R., Taboada, G. L., Ramos, S., González-Domínguez, J., Touriño, J., & Doallo, R. (2013). Analysis of I/O performance on an amazon EC2 cluster compute and high I/O platform. *Journal of grid computing, 11*(4), 613-631.

Extending SOA into the Private Cloud with WebSphere CloudBurst Appliance and WebSphere Application Server HyperVisor Edition. (2009). *WebSphere*. Retrieved from http://www.webspheremusergroup.org/cms/websphere_virtual_enterprise/119583/monthly_focus:_websphere_in_the_clouds

Feng D.G., Zhang, et al. (2011). Research on Cloud Computing Security. *Journal of Software*, 71–82.

Ferguson, T. (2009). Salesforce.com outage hits thousands of businesses. *CNET*. Retrieved from http://news. cnet.com/8301-1001_3-10136540-92. html

Ferrie, P. (2007). *Attacks on more virtual machine emulators*. Symantec Technology Exchange.

FIRE. Future Internet Research and Experimentation. (2014). Retrieved from http://cordis.europa.eu/fp7/ict/fire

Fletcher, K. K. (2010). Cloud Security requirements analysis and security policy development using a high-order object-oriented modeling. Master of science, Computer Science, Missouri University of Science and Technology, 13.

Florence, L. (2015). *Universities struggle to effectively implement cloud-based technologies*. The Daily Texan.

Forensic Toolkit (2014). AccessData Group, Inc. Retrieved from http://www.accessdata.com/solutions/digital-forensics/ftk

Fox, A., Griffith, R., Joseph, A., Katz, R., Konwinski, A., Lee, G., et al. (2009). Above the clouds: A Berkeley view of cloud computing. University of California, Berkeley, Rep. UCB/EECS, 28, 13.

Frei, S., Duebendorfer, T., Ollmann, G., & May, M. (2008). *Understanding the web browser threat. TIK*. ETH Zurich.

G.711 *ITU-T Recommendation G.711: Pulse code modulation (PCM) of voice frequencies* (1988). Retrieved from https://www.itu.int/rec/T-REC-G.711

Gajek, S., Jensen, M., Liao, L., & Schwenk, J. (2009, July). Analysis of signature wrapping attacks and countermeasures. In *Web Services, 2009. ICWS 2009. IEEE International Conference.* (pp. 575-582). IEEE. doi:10.1109/ICWS.2009.12

Gajek, S., Schwenk, J., & Chen, X. (2008). On the insecurity of Microsoft's identity metasystem cardspace. *Horst Görtz Institute for IT-Security, Tech. Rep. HGI TR-2008-004*.

Gajek, S., Jager, T., Manulis, M., & Schwenk, J. (2008). A browser-based kerberos authentication scheme. In *Computer Security-ESORICS 2008* (pp. 115–129). Springer Berlin Heidelberg. doi:10.1007/978-3-540-88313-5_8

Gajek, S., Schwenk, J., Steiner, M., & Xuan, C. (2009). Risks of the CardSpace protocol. In *Information Security.* (pp. 278–293). Springer Berlin Heidelberg. doi:10.1007/978-3-642-04474-8_23

Galante, J., Kharif, O., & Alpeyev, P. (2011). *Sony Network Breach Shows Amazon Cloud's Appeal for Hackers*. Retrieved from http://www.bloomberg.com/news/2011-05-15/sony-attack-shows-amazon-s-cloud-service-lures-hackers-at-pennies-an-hour.html

Gambetta, D. (2000). Can we trust trust. *Trust: Making and breaking cooperative relations*, (pp. 213-237).

Ganger, G. R., & Kaashoek, M. F. (1997). Embedded inodes and explicit grouping: exploiting disk bandwidth for small files. In *Proceedings of the annual conference on usenix annual technical conference* (pp. 1–1). Berkeley, CA, USA: USENIX Association.

Ganghishetti, P., & Wankar, R. (2011). Quality of Service Design in Clouds. *CSI Communications, 35*(2), 12–15.

Garfinkel, S. L. (2007). An evaluation of Amazon's grid computing services: EC2, S3, and SQS.

Garfinkel, T., & Rosenblum, M. (2003). A Virtual Machine Introspection Based Architecture for Intrusion Detection. *Proceedings of the 10th Network and Distributed System Security Symposium (NDSS'03)*, (pp. 191-206). San Diego, CA, USA.

Garfinkel, T., & Rosenblum, M. (2005). *When Virtual is Harder than Real*. HotOS.

Gellman, R. (2009). Privacy in the Clouds: Risks to Privacy and Confidentiality. Proceedings of *Cloud Computing, World Privacy Forum*, USA.

Gellman, R. (2012, August). Privacy in the clouds: risks to privacy and confidentiality from cloud computing. In *Proceedings of the World privacy forum.*

Gens, F., & Shirer, M. (2013). *IDC Forecasts Worldwide Public IT Cloud Services Spending to Reach Nearly $108 Billion by 2017 as Focus Shifts from Savings to Innovation*. Retrieved from http://www.idc.com/getdoc.jsp?containerId=prUS24298013

Gentry, C. (2009). *A fully homomorphic encryption scheme*. Stanford University.

Gerhards, R. (2014). *RSyslog*. Retrieved from http://www.rsyslog.com/

Gharshi, R. S. (2013, July). Enhancing Security in Cloud Storage using ECC Algorithm. *International Journal of Science and Research, 2*(7).

Giff, S. (2000). The Influence of Metaphor, Smart Cards and Interface Dialogue on Trust in eCommerce. *MSc project*.

Gill, P., Jain, N., & Nagappan, N. (2011). Understanding network failures in data centers: measurement, analysis, and implications.

Giordanelli, R., & Mastroianni, C. (2010). *The cloud computing paradigm: Characteristics, opportunities and research issues. Istituto di Calcolo e Reti ad Alte Prestazioni*. ICAR.

Godsey, M. (2015). The Deconstruction of the K-12 Teacher. *The Atlantic*.

Gold, B. (1977). Digital speech networks. *Proceedings of the IEEE, 65*(12), 1630–1658. doi:10.1109/PROC.1977.10806

Goldreich, O., Micali, S., & Wigderson, A. (1987). *How to play any mental game*.

Gomez, R., Adly, A., Mayergoyz, I., & Burke, E. (1992, September). Magnetic force scanning tunneling microscope imaging of overwritten data. *IEEE Transactions on Magnetics, 28*(5), 3141–3143. doi:10.1109/20.179738

Goodin, D. (2011). Salesforce.com outage exposes cloud's dark linings.

Google, Inc. (2014). *vmitools*. Retrieved from https://code.google.com/p/vmitools/

Grance, T., Stevens, M., & Myers, M. (2003). Guide to selecting information security products (2nd Ed.). National Institute of Standards and Technology (NIST).

Greenberg, A. (2009, July 13). IBM's blindfolded calculator. *Forbes*.

Griffiths, N. (2006). A Fuzzy Approach to Reasoning with Trust, Distrust and Insufficient Trust. *Proceedings of the 10th international conference on Cooperative Information Agents*. (pp. 360-374). Springer-Verlag Berlin Heidelberg. doi:10.1007/11839354_26

Grimes, J., Jaeger, P., & Lin, J. (2011). Weathering the Storm: The Policy Implications of Cloud Computing [Online]. Retrieved from ischools.org/images/iConferences/CloudAbstract13109F INAL.pdf

Grispos, G., Storer, T., & Glisson, W. (2012). Calm before the storm: The challenges of cloud computing in digital forensics. *International Journal of Digital Crime and Forensics, 4*(2), 28–48. doi:10.4018/jdcf.2012040103

Grobauer, B., Walloschek, T., & Stocker, E. (2011). Understanding Cloud Computing Vulnerabilities. *Security & Privacy, IEEE, 9*(2), 50–57. doi:10.1109/MSP.2010.115

Groß, S., & Schill, A. (2012). Towards user centric data governance and control in the cloud Open Problems in Network Security (pp. 132-144%@ 3642275842): Springer.

Groß, T. (2003, December). Security analysis of the SAML single sign-on browser/artifact profile. In *Computer Security Applications Conference, 2003. Proceedings. 19th Annual.* (pp. 298-307). IEEE. doi:10.1109/CSAC.2003.1254334

Gruschka, N., & Iacono, L. L. (2009). *Vulnerable cloud: Soap message security validation revisited.*

Gruschka, N., & Iacono, L. L. (2009, July). Vulnerable cloud: Soap message security validation revisited. In *Web Services, 2009. ICWS 2009. IEEE International Conference.* (pp. 625-631).

Gruschka, N., & Iacono, L. L. (2009, July). Vulnerable cloud: Soap message security validation revisited. Proceedings of *Web Services, 2009. ICWS 2009. IEEE International Conference on* (pp. 625-631).

Gu, T., Pung, H. K., & Zhang, D. Q. (2004). *A Middleware for Building Context-Aware Mobile Services. Proceedings of IEEE Vehicular Technology Conference, VTC.*

Guidance Software, Inc. (2014). *EnCase Forensic v7.10: The Fastest, Most Comprehensive Forensic Solution Available*. Retrieved from https://www.guidancesoftware.com/products/Pages/encase-forensic/overview.aspx

Gunderloy, M. (2008, January 13). Who Protects Your Cloud Data?, Web Worker Daily.

Guo, H., Jin, B., & Shang, T. (2012). Forensic investigations in Cloud environments. *Proceedings of 2012 International Conference on Computer Science and Information Processing (CSIP'12)* (pp. 248-251). IEEE.

Gutmann, P. (1996). Secure deletion of data from magnetic and solid-state memory. In *Proceedings of the 6th conference on usenix security symposium, focusing on applications of cryptography* Vol. 6 (pp. 8–8). Berkeley, CA, USA: USENIX Association.

H.261 *ITU-T Recommendation H.261: Video codec for audiovisual services at p x 64 kbit/s* (March 1993). Retrieved from https://www.ece.cmu.edu/~ece796/documents/Intro_H26x.doc

H.310 *ITU-T Recommendation H.310: Broadband audio-visual communications systems and terminal equipment* (1996). Retrieved from https://www.ece.cmu.edu/~ece796/documents/H323V2NC-final.DOC

H.321 *ITU-T Recommendation H.321: Adaptation of H.320 Visual Telephone Terminals to B-ISDN Environments* (1996). Retrieved from https://www.itu.int/rec/T-REC-H.321-199603-S/en

Hamlen, K., Kantarcioglu, M., Khan, L., & Thuraisingham, B. (2010). Security Issues for Cloud Computing. *International Journal of Information Security and Privacy, 4*(2), 39–51. doi:10.4018/jisp.2010040103

Han, S., & Xing, J. (2011). Ensuring Data Storage Security Through a Novel Third Party Auditor Scheme in Cloud Computing, In *Proceedings of IEEE International Conference on Cloud Computing & Intelligence Systems.* (pp. 264-268). Beijing, China: IEEE. doi:10.1109/CCIS.2011.6045072

Hanzo, L., Cherriman, P., & Streit, J. (2001). *Wireless Video Communications.* NY: IEEE. doi:10.1109/9780470547083

Hart, S. V., Ashcroft, J., & Daniels, D. J. (2004). Forensic examination of digital evidence: a guide for law enforcement. Washington DC (USA): U.S. National Institute of Justice (NIJ).

Hayes, B. (2008). Cloud computing. *Communications of the ACM, 51*(7), 9–11. doi:10.1145/1364782.1364786

Hegarty, R., Merabti, M., Shi, Q., & Askwith, B. (2011). Forensic Analysis of Distributed Service Oriented Computing Platforms. *Proceedings of 12th Annual Post-Graduate Symposium on the Convergence fo Telecommunications, Networking and Broadcasting (PGNet'11).* Liverpool (UK).

Hemant, P., Chawande, N. P., Sonule, A., & Wani, H. (2011). Development of Servers in Cloud Computing to Solve Issue Related to Security and Backup, In *Proceedings of IEEE International Conference on Cloud Computing & Intelligence System.* (pp. 158-163). Beijing, China: IEEE. doi:10.1109/CCIS.2011.6045052

Herold, B. (2014). Kansas Suspends State Tests Following Cyber Attacks. *Education Week.*

HIPAA Best Practices Checklist: Best Practices That Go Beyond Compliance to Mitigate Risks. (2010). Iron Mountain.

Homma, T. (1995). MPEG contribution: Report of the adhoc group on MPEG-2 applications for multi-view point pictures. *ISO/IEC SC29/WG11 Doc.* 861.

Horwath, C., Chan, W., Leung, E., & Pili, H. (2012). Enterprise Risk Management for Cloud Computing. *Thought Leadership in ERM, Committee of Sponsoring Organizations of the Treadway Commission (COSO) research paper,* (pp. 3-32).

Houidi, I., Mechtri, M., Louati, W., & Zeghlache, D. (2011). Cloud service delivery across multiple cloud platforms.

Hubbard, D., & Sutton, M. (2010). *Top threats to cloud computing v1. 0.* Cloud Security Alliance.

Huynh, T. D. (2009, March). A personalized framework for trust assessment. In *Proceedings of the 2009 ACM symposium on Applied Computing* (pp. 1302-1307). ACM. doi:10.1145/1529282.1529574

Hype Cycle for Cloud Computing. (2013). Gartner Inc. Retrieved from https://www.gartner.com/doc/2573318/hype-cycle-cloud-computing-

IBM Cloud Services (Part I). (2015). Seeking Alpha.

Inoue, H., Miyazaki, A., & Katsura, T. (2000). A Digital watermark for Images Using the Wavelet Transform. *Integrated Computer-Aided Engineering, 7*(2), 105–115.

Irakoze, I. (2013). Cloud-Based Mobile Applications.

ISO/IEC IS 13818-1. *Generic coding of moving pictures and associated audio, Part 1: System,* 1995. Retrieved from https://www.iso.org/iso/iso_catalogue/catalogue.../catalogue_tc_browse.html

ISO/IEC JTC1/SC29/WG11, Doc. N4030. (2001, March). *MPEG-4 Overview v18.0,* Singapore.

ISO/IEC JTC1/SC29/WG11, Doc.N3752. (2000). *Overview of the MPEG-7 standard,* La Baule. Retrieved from https:// 193.226.6.174/IT2002/pdf/L3.pdf

ISO/IEC N4041. (2001). *MPEG-21 Overview*, Singapore. Retrieved from https:// itscj.ipsj.or.jp/sc29/ open/29view/29n43211.doc

Italian Parliament. (2008). *L48/2008* - Ratifica ed esecuzione della Convenzione del Consiglio d'Europa sulla criminalità informatica, fatta a Budapest il 23 novembre 2001, e norme di adeguamento dell'ordinamento interno. [Ratification and implementation of the Council of Europe Convention on Cybercrime, signed in Budapest on 23 November 2001 and the rules of adapting internal.] Retrieved from http://www.parlamento.it/parlam/leggi/08048l.htm

ITU-T Recommendation H.261, Video codec for audiovisual services at px64 kbit/s. (n. d.). Retrieved from https:// www.itu.int/rec/T-REC-H.261-199303-I/en

Jackson, S. (2014) Data breach could affect 30,000 Iowa State students. *The Des Moines Register*.

Jackson, C. (2010). *8 Cloud Security Concepts You Should Know*. Network World.

Jacobs, D., & Aulbach, S. (2007, March). *Ruminations on Multi-Tenant Databases*, 103, 514–521. BTW.

Jaeger, P. T., & Fleischmann, K. R. (2013). Public libraries, values, trust, and e-government. *Information technology and Libraries, 26*(4), 34-43.

Jain, A. K. Flynn Patrick, Ross Arun A. (2008). Handbook of Biometrics. New York, Springer.

Jain, A. K., Pankanti, S., Prabhakar, S., & Hong, L. (2004), Biometrics: a grand challenge. *Proceedings of 17th International Conference on Pattern Recognition*, 2, (pp. 935-942).

James, L., Wayman. (2001). Fundamentals of biometric authentication technologies. *International Journal of Imaging and Graphics, 1*(93). doi:10.1142/ S0219467801000086

Jamil, D., & Zaki, H. (2011). Cloud Computing Security. *International Journal of Engineering Science and Technology, 3*(4), 3478–3483.

Jansen, W., & Grance, T. (2011). Guidelines on Security and Privacy in Public Cloud Computing. *NIST Draft Special Publication* 800-144. Retrieved from http://csrc. nist.gov/publications/drafts/800-144/Draft-SP-800-144_ cloud-computing.pdf

Jansen, W., & Grance, T. (2011). Guidelines on security and privacy in public cloud computing. *NIST* publication. (pp.144, 800).

Jansen, W. (2010). *Directions in security metrics research*. Diane Publishing.

Jantz, R. L. (1987). Anthropological dermatoglyphic research. *Annual Review of Anthropology, 16*(1), 161–177. doi:10.1146/annurev.an.16.100187.001113

Jantz, R. L. (1997). Variation among European populations in summary finger ridge count variables. *Journal of Annual Human Biology, 24*(2), 97–108. doi:10.1080/03014469700004842 PMID:9074746

Jayant, N. (1993). High quality networking of audio-visual information. *IEEE Communications Magazine, 31*(9), 84–95. doi:10.1109/35.236275

Jensen, M., & Schwenk, J. (2009, March). The accountability problem of flooding attacks in service-oriented architectures. In *Availability, Reliability and Security, 2009. ARES'09. International Conference*. (pp. 25-32). doi:10.1109/ARES.2009.11

Jensen, M., Gruschka, N., & Luttenberger, N. (2008, March). The impact of flooding attacks on network-based services. In *Availability, Reliability and Security, 2008. ARES 08. Third International Conference*. (pp. 509-513). doi:10.1109/ARES.2008.16

Jensen, M., Gruschka, N., et al. (2008). The impact of flooding Attacks on network based services. Proceedings of the *IEEE International conference on Availiabilty, Reliability and Security*.

Jensen, M., Schwenk, J., Gruschka, N., & Iacono, L. L. (2009, September). On technical security issues in cloud computing. In *Cloud Computing, 2009. CLOUD'09. IEEE International Conference*. (pp. 109-116). doi:10.1109/ CLOUD.2009.60

Jensen, M., Sehwenk, J., et al. (2009). On Technical Security Issues iCloud Computing. Proceedings of *International conference on cloud Computing*.

Jensen, M. (2013). Challenges of privacy protection in big data analytics. In *Proceedings of IEEE International Congress on Big Data* (pp. 235-238). Washington, DC: IEEE Computer Society. doi:10.1109/BigData.Congress.2013.39

Jensen, M., Gruschka, N., & Herkenhöner, R. (2009). A survey of attacks on web services. *Computer Science-Research and Development*, *24*(4), 185–197. doi:10.1007/s00450-009-0092-6

Jhawar, R., Piuri, V., & Santambrogio, M. (2012). A comprehensive conceptual system-level approach to fault tolerance in cloud computing.

Jivanadham, L. B., Islam, A. K. M. M., Katayama, Y., Komaki, S., & Baharun, S. (2013). Cloud Cognitive Authenticator (CCA): A public cloud computing authentication mechanism.*InProceedings of International IEEE Conference on In Informatics, Electronics & Vision (ICIEV)* (pp. 1-6). doi:10.1109/ICIEV.2013.6572626

Johann, C. (2005). Privacy in Pervasive Computing Environments – A Contradiction in Terms? *IEEE Technology and Society Magazine*, 24–33.

Jones, A., Valli, C., & Dabibi, G. (2009). The 2009 analysis of information remaining on usb storage devices offered for sale on the second hand market. Proceedings of Australian digital forensics conference (p. 61).

Jones, N., George, E., Merida, F. I., Rasmussen, U., & Volzow, V. (2013). *Electronic evidence guide - A basic guide for police officers, prosecutors and judges*. Strasburg, France: Council of Europe - Data Protection and Cybercrime Division.

Joshi, S., Udupi, V., & Joshi, D. (2012). A Novel Neural Network Approach for Digital Image Data Encryption/Decryption. Proceedings of *IEEE International Conference on Power, Signals, Controls and Computation*, Kerala, India. doi:10.1109/EPSCICON.2012.6175229

Joukov, N., & Zadok, E. (2005). Secure data deletion for linux filesystems. *Proceedings of the 3rd IEEE security in storage workshop (SISW '05)* (pp. 12–12). San Francisco, CA: IEEE

Joukov, N., Papaxenopoulos, H., & Zadok, E. (2006). Secure deletion myths, issues, and solutions. In *Proceedings of the second acm workshop on storage security and survivability* (pp. 61–66). New York, NY, USA: ACM. doi:10.1145/1179559.1179571

JPEG2000. (2014, April 14) Retrieved from www.jpeg.org/jpeg2000/index.html

Kalpana, P. (2012). Cloud Computing–Wave of the Future. *International Journal of Electronics Communication and Computer Engineering*, *3*(3).

Kamara, S., & Lauter, K. (2010). Cryptographic cloud storage Financial Cryptography and Data Security (pp. 136-149%@ 364214991X): Springer.

Kandukuri, B. R., Paturi, V. R., & Rakshit, A. (2009, September). Cloud security issues. In *Services Computing, 2009. SCC'09. IEEE International Conference.* (pp. 517-520). doi:10.1109/SCC.2009.84

Kang, X., Zhang, H., Jiang, G., Chen, H., Meng, X., & Yoshihira, K. (2008). Measurement, modeling, and analysis of internet video sharing site workload*: A case study*.

Karger, P. A. (2009, March). Securing virtual machine monitors: what is needed? In *Proceedings of the 4th International Symposium on Information, Computer, and Communications Security* (p. 1). ACM. doi:10.1145/1533057.1533059

Karlsson, G. Asynchronous transfer of video. *SICS Research Report R95:14, Sweden*.

Kashif, M., & Sellapan, P. (2012, December). *Security Threats\Attacks present in Cloud Environment*. International Journal of Computer Science and Network Security, 12(12), 107-114. Retrieved from http://paper.ijcsns.org/07_book/201212/20121217

Kasim, H., Hung, T., & Li, X. (2012). Data value chain as a service framework: For enabling data handling, data security and data analysis in the cloud.*InProceedings of the 18th IEEE International Conference on Parallel and Distributed Systems* (pp. 804-809). Washington, DC: IEEE Computer Society. doi:10.1109/ICPADS.2012.131

Katal, A., Wazid, M., & Goudar, R. (2013). Big data: Issues, challenges, tools and good practices. In *Proceedings of the Sixth International Conference on Contemporary* Computing (pp. 404-409). Noida, India: IEEE. doi:10.1109/IC3.2013.6612229

Katcher, J. (1997). Postmark: A new filesystem benchmark (Tech. Rep. No. TR3022). Network Appliance.

Katz, N. (2010, February 18). Austin Plane Crash: Pilot Joseph Andrew Stack May Have Targeted IRS Offices. Says FBI. *CBS News*.

Keleta, Y., Eloff, J. H. P., & Venter, H. S. (2005). *Proposing a Secure XACML architecture ensuring privacy and trust. Research in Progress Paper.* University of Pretoria.

Kerner, S. M. (2010). Mozilla Confirms Security Threat from Malicious Firefox Add-Ons, eSecurity Planet, February 5, 2010.

Kertész, A., Kecskemeti, G., Oriol, M., Kotcauer, P., Acs, S., Rodríguez, M., . . . Franch, X. (2013). Enhancing federated cloud management with an integrated service monitoring approach. *Journal of grid computing, 11*(4), 699-720.

Khade, P., & Narnaware, M. (2012). Practical Approach for Image Encryption/Scrambling using 3D Arnolds Cat Map. *Advances in Communication, Network, and Computing, 108,* 398–404.

Khalid, S. (2000). *Introduction to Data Compression.* New York: Morgan Kaufmann Publishers.

Khorshed, M. T., Ali, A. B., & Wasimi, S. A. (2014). Combating Cyber Attacks in Cloud Systems Using Machine Learning. In S. Nepal & M. Pathan (Eds.), *Security, Privacy and Trust in Cloud Systems* (pp. 407–431). Berlin, Germany: Springer. doi:10.1007/978-3-642-38586-5_14

Kim, J., & Hong, S. (2011). One-Source Multi-Use System having Function of Consolidated User Authentication. Proceedings of *JCICT & The first Yellow Sea International Conference on Ubiquitous Computing.*

Kim, K. H., Beloglazov, A., & Buyya, R. (2009). Power-aware provisioning of cloud resources for real-time services.

Kim, S. H., Kim, N. U., & Chung, T. M. (2013). Attribute relationship evaluation methodology for big data security. In *Proceedings of the International Conference on IT Convergence and Security* (pp. 1-4). Macao, China: IEEE. doi:10.1109/ICITCS.2013.6717808

Kincaid, J. (2009). Google privacy blunder shares your docs without permission. *TechCrunch, March.*

King, S. T., & Chen, P. M. (2006, May). SubVirt: Implementing malware with virtual machines. In *Security and Privacy, 2006 IEEE Symposium.* (pp. 14).

Koenen, R., & Pereira, F. (2000). *MPEG-7:* A standardized description of audiovisual content. *Signal Processing Image Communication, 16*(1-2), 5–13. doi:10.1016/S0923-5965(00)00014-X

Koide, M., & Keiichi Iwamura, K. (2010). Scalable Authentication for Various Representations of JPEG 2000 Images. In p*roceedings of 17th International Conference on Image Processing,* Hong Kong. doi:10.1109/ICIP.2010.5650709

Kong, G., & Li, J. (2007). Research on RBAC-based separation of duty constraints. *Journal of Information and Computing Science, 20,* 235–24.

Ko, R. K., Jagadpramana, P., Mowbray, M., Pearson, S., Kirchberg, M., & Liang, Q. et al. (2011). TrustCloud: A framework for accountability and trust in cloud computing. *Proceedings of 2011 IEEE World Congress on Services (SERVICES'11)* (pp. 584-588). Washington (DC, USA): IEEE. doi:10.1109/SERVICES.2011.91

Koren, I., & Krishna, C. M. (2010). *Fault-tolerant systems.* Morgan Kaufmann.

Kormann, D. P., & Rubin, A. D. (2000). Risks of the passport single signon protocol. *Computer Networks, 33*(1), 51–58. doi:10.1016/S1389-1286(00)00048-7

Kosko, B. (1986). Fuzzy cognitive maps. *International Journal of Man-Machine Studies, 24*(1), 65–75. doi:10.1016/S0020-7373(86)80040-2

Kowalski, E., Conway, T., Keverline, S., Williams, M., Cappelli, D., Willke, B., & Moore, A. (2008). Insider threat study: Illicit cyber activity in the government sector. *US Department of Homeland Security, US Secret Service, CERT, and the Software Engineering Institute (Carnegie Mellon University), Tech. Rep.*

KPMG International. (2013). *The cloud takes shape - Global coud survey: the implementation challenge.* Retrieved from http://www.kpmg.com/Global/en/IssuesAndInsights/ArticlesPublications/cloud-service-providers-survey/Documents/the-cloud-takes-shape-v4.pdf

Krebs, B. (2007, November 6). Salesforce.com Acknowledges Data Loss. *The Washington Post,* 8-10.

Krigsma, M. (2008, February 15). Amazon S3 Web Services Down. Bad, Bad News for Customers, ZDNET.

Krishnan, S., Snow, K. Z., & Monrose, F. (2010). Trail of bytes: efficient support for forensic analysis. *Proceedings of the 17th ACM conference on Computer and Communications Security (CCS'10)* (pp. 50-60). Chicago (IL, USA): ACM. doi:10.1145/1866307.1866314

Kroenke, D. M. (2013). *Experiencing MIS*. Boston, MA: Pearson.

Kruger, D., & Anschutz, T. (2013). A new approach in IT security. *Healthcare Financial Management Association*, *67*(2), 104–106. PMID:23413677

Kui, R. (2007). Privacy-enhanced, Attack-resilient Access Control in Pervasive Computing Environments with Optional Context Authentication Capability. *Mobile Networks and Applications*, *12*(1), 79–92. doi:10.1007/s11036-006-0008-7

Kumar, P., Nitin, V., Shah, K., Shukla, S. S. P., & Chauhan, D. S. (2011). A Novel Approach for Security in Cloud Computing using Hidden Markov Model and Clustering. In *Proceedings of Information & Communication Technologies*. (pp. 810–815). Mumbai, India: IEEE. doi:10.1109/WICT.2011.6141351

Kumar, S., & Saxena, A. (2011). Data Integrity Proofs in Cloud Storage. In *Proceedings of Third International Conference on Communication Systems and Networks*. (pp. 1-4). Bangalore, India: IEEE.

Kung, C., Chao, S., Yan, Y., & Kung, C. (2009). A Robust Watermarking and Image Authentication Scheme used for Digital Content Application. *Journal of Multimedia*, *4*(3), 112–119. doi:10.4304/jmm.4.3.112-119

La'Quata Sumter, R. (2010). Cloud Computing: Security Risk Classification. ACMSE Oxford, USA.

Lai, W. K., Yang, K.-T., Lin, Y.-C., & Shieh, C.-S. (2012). Dual migration for improved efficiency in cloud service Intelligent Information and Database Systems (pp. 216-225). Springer.

Leavitt, N. (2009). Is cloud computing really ready for prime time? *Computer*, *42*(1), 15–20. doi:10.1109/MC.2009.20

Lempereur, B., Merabti, M., & Shi, Q. (2010). Pypette: A framework for the automated evaluation of live digital forensic techniques. *International Journal of Digital Crime and Forensics (IJDCF)*, 31-46.

Lenk, A., Klems, M., Nimis, J., Tai, S., & Sandholm, T. (2009, May). What's inside the Cloud? An architectural map of the Cloud landscape. *InProceedings of the 2009 ICSE Workshop on Software Engineering Challenges of Cloud Computing*, 23-31. IEEE Computer Society. doi:10.1109/CLOUD.2009.5071529

Levien, R. (2009). Attack-resistant trust metrics. In *Computing with Social Trust*. (pp. 121–132). Springer London. doi:10.1007/978-1-84800-356-9_5

Leyden, J. (2004). Oops! firm accidentally eBays customer database. *The Register*.

Leyden, J. (2006). Afghan market sells us military flash drives bazaar security breach. *The Register*.

Li, C. (2012). Optimal resource provisioning for cloud computing environment. *The Journal of Supercomputing*, *62*(2), 989-1022.

Li, H., Tian, X., Wei, W., & Sun, C. (2012). A Deep Understanding of Cloud Computing Security. In Network Computing and Information Security. (pp. 98-105). Springer Berlin Heidelberg.

Li, S., Wang, J., & Gao, X. (2008). The Fast Realization of Image Scrambling Algorithm using Multi-Dimensional Orthogonal Transform. Proceedings of Congress on Image and Signal Processing, Sanya, China. doi:10.1109/CISP.2008.433

Lieberman, B. (2013). *Testing the Waters: Mobile and Cloud Computing for Education*. Intel.

Li, H., Pincus, M., & Rego, S. O. (2008). Market reaction to events surrounding the Sarbanes-Oxley Act of 2002 and earnings management. *The Journal of Law & Economics*, *51*(1), 111–134. doi:10.1086/588597

Lim, S., Moon, H., Chae, S., Yongwha Chung, Y., & Pan, S. (2009). JPEG 2000 and Digital Watermarking Technique Using in Medical Image. *Proceedings of 3rdInternational Conference on Secure Software Integration and Reliability Improvement*, Shanghai, China. doi:10.1109/SSIRI.2009.45

Lin, C.-F., Sheu, R.-K., Chang, Y.-S., & Yuan, S.-M. (2011). A relaxable service selection algorithm for QoS-based web service composition. *Information and Software Technology, 53*(12), 1370-1381.

Lin, S., & Costello, D. Jr. (1983). *Error Control Coding: Fundamentals and Applications*. NJ: Prentice Hall.

Listanti, M., & Villani, F. (1983, February). An X.25 compatible protocol for packet voice communications. *Computer Communications, 6*(1), 23–31. doi:10.1016/0140-3664(83)90172-X

Liu, J., Xiao, Y., Chen, H., Ozdemir, S., Dodle, S., & Singh, V. (2010). A survey of payment card industry data security standard. *Communications Surveys & Tutorials, IEEE, 12*(3), 287-303%@ 1553-1877X.

Liu, C., Zhang, X., Liu, C., Yang, Y., Ranjan, R., Georga-kopoulos, D., & Chen, J. (2013). An iterative hierarchical key exchange scheme for secure scheduling of big data applications in cloud computing. In *Proceedings of the 12th IEEE International Conference on Trust, Security and Privacy in Computing and Communications* (pp. 9-16). Washington, DC: IEEE Computer Society. doi:10.1109/TrustCom.2013.65

LiveCloudKd . (2012). MoonSols Ltd. Retrieved from http://moonsols.com/2010/08/12/livecloudkd

Li, W., Ping, L., Qiu, Q., & Zhang, Q. (2012). Research on Trust Management Strategies in Cloud Computing Environment. *Journal of Computer Information Systems, 8*(4), 1757–1763.

Log Shuttle. (2014). *Heroku, Inc.* Retrieved from http://www.log-shuttle.io/

Lombardi, F., & Di Pietro, R. (2011). Secure virtualization for cloud computing. *Journal of Network and Computer Applications, 34*(4), 1113–1122. doi:10.1016/j.jnca.2010.06.008

Loscocco, P., & Smalley, S. (2001). Integrating Flexible Support for Security Policies into the Linux Operating System. *Proceedings of the FREENIX Track of the 2001 USENIX.*

Luo, D., Ding, C. H. Q., & Huang, H. (2012). *Parallelization with Multiplicative Algorithms for Big Data Mining.*

Lu, R., Lin, X., Liang, X., & Shen, X. S. (2010). Secure provenance: the essential of bread and butter of data forensics in cloud computing. *Proceedings of the 5th ACM Symposium on Information, Computer and Communications Security (ASIACCS'10)* (pp. 282-292). Beijin (China): ACM. doi:10.1145/1755688.1755723

Lu, T., Guo, X., Xu, B., Zhao, L., Peng, Y., & Yang, H. (2013). Next big thing in big data: The security of the ict supply chain. In *Proceedings of the International Conference on Social Computing* (pp. 1066-1073). Washington, DC: IEEE Computer Society. doi:10.1109/SocialCom.2013.172

Lynch, N. A. (1996). *Distributed algorithms*. Morgan Kaufmann.

Machanavajjhala, A., & Reiter, J. P. (2012). Big privacy: protecting confidentiality in big data. *XRDS: Crossroads, The ACM Magazine for Students, 19*(1), 20-23.

Macko, P., Chiarini, M., & Seltzer, M. (2011). Collecting Provenance via the Xen Hypervisor. *Proceeding of 3rd USENIX Workshop on the Theory and Practice of Provenance (TaPP'11)*. Heraklion (Greece).

Mahmood, T., & Afzal, U. (2013). Security analytics: Big data analytics for cybersecurity: A review of trends, techniques and tools. *In Proceedings of the 2nd National Conference on Information Assurance* (pp. 129-134). Rawalpindi, Pakistan: IEEE. doi:10.1109/NCIA.2013.6725337

Mahmood, Z. (2011). Data Location and Security Issues in Cloud Computing. In *Proceedings of International Conference on Emerging Intelligent Data and Web Computing*. (pp. 49-54). Tirana: IEEE. doi:10.1109/EIDWT.2011.16

Mairal, C., & Agueh, M. (2010). Scalable and robust JPEG 2000 images and video transmission system for multiple wireless receivers. *Proceedings of Latin-American Conference on Communications*. Paris, France. doi:10.1109/LATINCOM.2010.5641128

Mallat, S. (1989). A Theory for Multiresolution Signal Decomposition: The Wavelet Representation. *IEEE Transactions on Pattern Analysis and Machine Intelligence, 11*(7), 674–693. doi:10.1109/34.192463

Mansfield-Devine, S. (2012). Using big data to reduce security risks. *Computer Fraud & Security*, (8): 3–4.

Marko, K., Mahesh, T., & Toutik, Z. (2011). An Empirical Assessment of Approaches to Distributed Enforcement in Role Based Access Control. *Proceedings of ACM conference on Data & Application Security & Privacy, pp. 1-29.*

Marshall, P., Keahey, K., & Freeman, T. (2011). Improving utilization of infrastructure clouds.

Martello, S., & Toth, P. (1990). *Knapsack problems: Algorithms and computer interpretations*. Hoboken, NJ: Wiley-Interscience.

Martinez-Ruiz, M., Artes-Rodriguez, A., Diaz-Rico, J. A., & Fuentes, J. B. (2010). New initiatives for imagery transmission over a tactical data link. A case study: JPEG2000 compressed images transmitted in a Link-16 network method and results. Proceedings of Military Communications Conference, San Jose, CA, USA. doi:10.1109/MILCOM.2010.5680102

Marty, R. (2011). Cloud application logging for forensics. *Proceedings of the 2011 ACM Symposium on Applied Computing* (pp. 178-184). ACM. doi:10.1145/1982185.1982226

Mather, T., Kumarasuwamy, S., & Latif, S. (2009). Cloud Security and Privacy. O'Rielly.

Mathisen (2011, May 31-June 3). Security Challenges and Solutions in Cloud Computing. Proceedings of 5th IEEE International Conference on Digital Ecosystems and Technologies. Daejeon, Korea.

MathWorks. (n. d.). *MathWorks*. Retrieved from www.mathworks.in: http://www.mathworks.in/help/fuzzy/fuzzy-inference-process.html

Maxwell, J. C. (3 Ed.). (2009). A Treatise on Electricity and Magnetism, 2. Oxford: Clarendon, 1892.

Mayergoyz, I. D., Serpico, C., Krafft, C., & Tse, C. (2000). Magnetic imaging on a spin-stand. *Journal of Applied Physics*, *87*(9), 6824–6826. doi:10.1063/1.372854

McIntosh, M., & Austel, P. (2005). *XML signature element wrapping attacks and countermeasures.*

McMillan, R. (2007, November 6). Salesforce.com warns customers of phishing scam. *PC Magazine, IDG News Network*.

McMillan, R. (2009, September 17). Misdirected Spyware Infects Ohio Hospital. *PC Magazine, IDG News Service*.

McMillan, R. (2009). *Hackers find a home in Amazon's EC2 cloud. Infoworld*. IDG News Network.

Mehta, M. (2015). The Wisdom of the PaaS Crowd. *Forbes*.

Mell, P., & Grance, T. (2009, October 7). The NIST Definition of Cloud Computing. *National Institute of Standards and Technology*. Retrieved from www.csrc.nist.gov

Mell, P., & Grance, T. (2011). The NIST definition of cloud computing (draft). *National Institute of Standards and Technology.*http://csrc.nist.gov/publications/drafts/800–145/Draft-SP-800-145_cloud-definition.pdf.

Mell, P., & Grance, T. (2011). The NIST Definition of Cloud Computing. *National Institute of Standards and Technology*. Retrieved from http://csrc.nist.gov/publications/nistpubs/800-145/SP800-145.pdf

Mell, P., & Grance, T. (2011). The NIST definition of cloud computing. NIST - Computer Security Division, Information Technology Laboratory.

Mell, P., & Grance, T. (2011). The NIST Definition of Cloud Computing. NIST Special Publication 800-145. Retrieved from http://csrc.nist.gov/publications/nistpubs/800-145/SP800-145.pdf

Memon, Q. (2013). Smarter Healthcare Collaborative Network. In K. Pathan Al-Sakib, M. Monowar Muhammad, Md. Fadlullah Zubair (Eds.), Building Next-Generation Converged Networks: Theory and Practice (451–474). Florida: CRC Press.

Memon, Q. (2006). A New Approach to Video Security over Networks. *International Journal of Computer Applications in Technology*, *25*(1), 72–83. doi:10.1504/IJCAT.2006.008670

Mendel, J. (1995, March). Fuzzy Logic Systems for Engineering: A Tutorial. *Proceedings of the IEEE*, (pp. 345-377). doi:10.1109/5.364485

Merkle tree. (2014, September). *Wikimedia Foundation, Inc.* Retrieved from Wikipedia: http://en.wikipedia.org/wiki/Merkle_tree

Merriman, P. (2000). *Video over DSL architecture* (pp. 250–257). Alcatel Telecommunications Review.

Metz, C. (2009). DDoS attack rains down on Amazon cloud - Code haven tumbles from sky. *The Register.* Retrieved from http://www.theregister.co.uk/2009/10/05/amazon_bitbucket_outage/

Metz, C. (2009). *DDoS attack rains down on Amazon cloud.* The Register.

Miao, F., Ma, Y., & Salowey, J. (2009). *Transport Layer Security (TLS) Transport Mapping for Syslog (RFC-5425).* IETF. doi:10.17487/rfc5425

Michel, F. (2012). How Many Photos Are Uploaded to Flickr Every Day and Month? Papadimitriou, S., & Sun, J. (2008). *Disco: Distributed co-clustering with map-reduce: A case study towards petabyte-scale end-to-end mining.*

Miller, R. (2009, June 11). Lightning Strike Triggers Amazon EC2 Outage. *Data Center Knowledge.*

Miller, R. (2013). Major outage for Amazon S3 and EC2. *Data Center Knowledge.*

Miller, B. (1988). *Everything you need to know about biometric identification. Personal Identification News.* Washington, DC: Warfel &Miller, Inc.

Mills, D. (1992). *Network Time Protocol (Version 3) - Specification, Implementation and Analysis (RFC 1305).* IETF. doi:10.17487/rfc1305

Minoli, D. (n. d.). Optimal packet length for packet voice communication. *IEEE Transactions on Communications, COM-27,* 607–611.

MobilityFirst Future Internet Architecture Project. (2013). Retrieved from http://mobilityfirst.winlab.rutgers.edu

Mongan, K. (2011). Cloud computing the storm is coming. *Accountancy Ireland, 43*(3), 58-58-60.

Mouftah, H. T. (1992). Multimedia communications: An overview. *IEEE Communications Magazine, 30,* 18–19.

Mowbray, M., & Pearson, S. (2009, June 16-19). A client-based privacy manager for cloud computing. Proceedings of *Fourth International Conference on Communication System Software and Middleware (ComsWare).* Dublin, Ireland. doi:10.1145/1621890.1621897

Mui, L., Mohtashemi, M., & Halberstadt, A. (2002). A Computational Model of Trust and Reputation. *Proceedings of the 35th Annual Hawaii International Conference on System Sciences.* IEEE. doi:10.1109/HICSS.2002.994181

Mukhin, V., & Volokyta, A. (2011, September 15-17). Security Risk Analysis for Cloud Computing Systems. Proceedings of the *6th IEEE International Conference on Intelligent Data Acquisition and Advanced Computing Systems: Technology and Applications.* Prague, Czech Republic.

Mundy, R., Partain, D., & Stewart, B. (1999, April). Introduction to SNMPv3. *RFC 2570.*

Muniswamy-Reddy, K.-K., & Seltzer, M. (2010). Provenance as first class cloud data. *Operating Systems Review, 43*(4), 11–16. doi:10.1145/1713254.1713258

Musheer Ahmad, A., Haque, E., & Farooq, O. (2011). A Noise Resilient Scrambling Scheme for Noisy Transmission Channel. *Proceedings of International Conference on Multimedia, Signal Processing and Communication Technologies,* Aligarh, India.

Named Data Networking Project. (2014). Retrieved from http://www.nameddata.net

Nance, K., Bishop, M., & Hay, B. (2009). Investigating the implications of virtual machine introspection for digital forensics. *International Conference on Availability, Reliability and Security (ARES'09)* (pp. 1024-1029). IEEE. doi:10.1109/ARES.2009.173

National Instruments. (2013). *Introduction to Distributed Clock Synchronization and the IEEE 1588 Precision Time Protocol.* Retrieved from http://www.ni.com/white-paper/2822/en/

NEBULA Project. (2013). Retrieved from http://nebula.cis.upenn.edu

NEW UTILITY: MoonSols HyperTaskMgr v1.0. (2011). *MoonSols Ltd.* Retrieved from http://www.moonsols.com/2011/07/19/new-utility-moonsols-hypertaskmgr-v1-0/

Nielsen, J. (1999). *Trust or bust: Communicating trustworthiness in web design*. Jacob Nielsen's Alertbox.

Ni, J., Yang, T., & Tsang, D. H. K. (1996). CBR transportation on VBR MPEG-2 video traffic for video-on-demand in ATM networks. *Proceedings of the IEEE, ICC*, Dallas, Texas, USA. (pp. 1391–1395).

Ning, G., Jiamao, L., & Xiaolu, C. (2006, January). *Theory and Practice R & D of Web Services*. (pp. 10). Machinery Industry Press.

Nissenbaum, H. (1999). Can trust be secured online? A theoretical perspective.

Nooteboom, B. (2007). Social capital, institutions and trust. *Review of Social Economy*, *65*(1), 29–53. doi:10.1080/00346760601132154

NSF Future Internet Architecture Project. (2013). Retrieved from http://www.nets-fia.net

NSF NeTS FIND Initiative. (2013). Retrieved from http://www.nets-find.net

Oberheide, J., Cooke, E., & Jahanian, F. (2008, February). Empirical exploitation of live virtual machine migration. In *Proc. of BlackHat DC convention*.

Oikonomou, K., & Stavrakakis, I. (2010). Scalable service migration in autonomic network environments. *Selected Areas in Communications, IEEE Journal on, 28*(1), 84-94.

Okubo, S., Dunstan, S., Morrison, G., Nilsson, M., Radha, H., Skran, D. L., & Thom, G. (1997). ITU-T Standardization of Audiovisual Communication Systems in ATM and LAN Environments. *IEEE Journal on Selected Areas in Communications*, *15*(6), 965–982. doi:10.1109/49.611153

Okuhara, M., et al. (2009). Security Architecture for Cloud Computing. *Fujitsu*. www.fujitsu.com/downloads/MAG/vol46-4/paper09.pdf

O'Neil, M. (2014). Data Breaches Put a Dent in Colleges' Finances as Well as Reputations. *The Chronicle*.

Onwubiko, C. (2010). Security issues to cloud computing. In Cloud Computing. (pp. 271-288). London: Springer.

Onwubiko, C. (2010). Security issues to cloud computing. In *Cloud Computing* (pp. 271–288). Springer London. doi:10.1007/978-1-84996-241-4_16

OpenStack Foundation. (2014). *OpenStack | Open source software for building private and public clouds*. Retrieved from http://www.openstack.org/

Ormandy, T. (2007). *An empirical study into the security exposure to hosts of hostile virtualized environments*.

Orofino, S. (1996). Daubert v. Merrell Dow Pharmaceuticals, Inc.: the battle over admissibility standards for scientific evidence in court. *Journal of Undergraduate Sciences*, 109-111.

Orton, I., Alva, A., & Endicott-Popovsky, B. (2012). Legal process and requirements for cloud forensic investigations. In *Cybercrime and Cloud Forensics*. IGI Global.

Orzessek, M., & Sommer, P. (1998). *ATM and MPEG-2. Integrating digital video into broadband networks*. Upper Saddle River: Prentice Hall PTR.

Orzessek, M., & Sommer, P. (2006). *ATM and MPEG-2 integration of digital video into broadband networks. Prentice HallPTR*. Upper Saddle River: New Jersy.

Osterwalder, D. (2001). Trust through evaluation and certification? *Social Science Computer Review*, *19*(1), 32–46. doi:10.1177/089443930101900104

Overby, S. (2010, April). How to Negotiate a Better Cloud Computing Contract. *CIO*.

Overcoming the Security Challenges of the Cloud: Best Practices for Keeping Your Data and Your Organization Safe. (2013, May 13). *PCConnection*. Retrieved from http://www.pcconnection.com/~/media/PDFs/Brands/C/Cisco/Survey/25240_PCC_CloudSurvey.pdf

Overview of Security processes. (2008, September). *Amazon Web Services*. Retrieved from http://aws.amazon.com

Pagano, F., & Pagano, D. (2011). *Using in-memory encrypted databases on the cloud*.

Paillier, P. (1999). *Public-key cryptosystems based on composite degree residuosity classes*.

Pal, S., Khatua, S., Chaki, N., & Sanyal, S. (2011). A new trusted and collaborative agent based approach for ensuring cloud security. *arXiv preprint arXiv:1108.4100*.

Palmer, G. (2001). A road map for digital forensic research. *1st Digital Forensic Research Workshop (DFRWS'01)*, (pp. 27-30). Utica, New York, USA.

Papagianni, C., Leivadeas, A., Papavassiliou, S., Maglaris, V., Cervello-Pastor, C., & Monje, A. (2013). On the optimal allocation of virtual resources in cloud computing networks. *Computers, IEEE Transactions on, 62*(6), 1060-1071.

Pape, C., Reissmann, S., & Rieger, S. (2013). RESTful Correlation and Consolidation of Distributed Logging Data in Cloud Environments. *Proceedings of the 8th International Conference on Internet and Web Applications and Services (ICIW'13)*, (pp. 194-199). Rome, Italy.

Parra-Hernandez, R., & Dimopoulos, N. J. (2005). A new heuristic for solving the multichoice multidimensional knapsack problem. *Systems, Man and Cybernetics, Part A: Systems and Humans, IEEE Transactions on, 35*(5), 708-717.

Party, E. A. W. (2007). Standard Application for Approval of Binding Corporate Rules for the Transfer of Personal Data.

Party, E. A. W. (2012). Cloud Computing.

Pastor, E., Fernández, D., & Bellido, L. (1995). Cooperative Learning Over Broadband Networks. *6th Joint European Networking Conference (JENC6)*, Tel-Aviv.

Patel, S. C., Umrao, L. S., & Singh, R. S. (2012). Policy-based Framework for Access Control in Cloud Computing. In *International Conference on Recent Trends in Engineering & Technology (ICRTET2012)*. (pp. 142-146).

Pathan, A. S. K. (2014). *The state of the art in intrusion prevention and detection*. Boca Raton, FL: Auerbach Publications. doi:10.1201/b16390

Patr, D. W., DaSilva, L. A., & Frost, V. S. (1989). Priority discarding of speech in integrated packet networks. *IEEE Journal on Selected Areas in Communications, 7*(5), 644–656. doi:10.1109/49.32328

Payne, B. D., De Carbone, M. D., & Lee, W. (2007). Secure and flexible monitoring of virtual machines. *Proceedings of 23th Annual Computer Security Applications Conference (ACSAC'07)*, (pp. 385-397). Miami Beach, FL, USA. doi:10.1109/ACSAC.2007.10

Pearson, S., Casassa, M., Mont, & Crane, S. (2005, March 18). *Analysis of Trust Properties and Related Impact of Trusted Platforms*. Trusted Systems Laboratory. HP Laboratories, Bristol.

Pearson, S. (2009, May). Taking account of privacy when designing cloud computing services. In *Proceedings of the 2009 ICSE Workshop on Software Engineering Challenges of Cloud Computing* (pp. 44-52). IEEE Computer Society. doi:10.1109/CLOUD.2009.5071532

Pearson, S., Mont, M. C., & Crane, S. (2005). Persistent and dynamic trust: analysis and the related impact of trusted platforms. In *Trust management* (pp. 355–363). Springer Berlin Heidelberg. doi:10.1007/11429760_24

Pearson, S., & Yee, G. (Eds.). (2013). *Privacy and Security for cloud Computing. In series Computer Communications and Networks*. New York: Springer London Heidelberg. doi:10.1007/978-1-4471-4189-1

Pentland, A., Moghaddam, B., & Starner, T. (1994). View-Based and Modular Eigen spaces for Face Recognition. *Proceedings of the IEEE Computer Vision and Pattern Recognition, Seattle*, Washington. (pp. 84-91). doi:10.1109/CVPR.1994.323814

Pereira, F. (2004). . *Signal Processing Image Communication, 15*, 269–270.

Personal data in the cloud- A global survey of consumer attitudes. (2010). *Fujitsu.*

Phadikar, A., & Maity, S. P. (2010). Roi based error concealment of compressed object based image using QIM data hiding and wavelet transform. *IEEE Transactions on Consumer Electronics, 56*(2), 971–979. doi:10.1109/TCE.2010.5506028

Piuri, R. J. V. (2013). Fault Tolerance and Resilience in Cloud Computing Environments. In J. Vacca (Ed.), *Computer and information Security Handbook* (2nd Ed.). Morgan Kaufmann.

Poisel, R., Malzer, E., & Tjoa, S. (2013). Evidence and cloud computing: The virtual machine introspection approach. *Journal of Wireless Mobile Networks, Ubiquitous Computing, and Dependable Applications (JoWUA)*, 135-152.

Ponemon (2011, April). Security of cloud computing providers study. *CA Technologies.*http://www.ca.com/~/media/Files/ IndustryResearch/security-of-cloud-computing-providers-final-april-2011.pdf

Ponemon (2013, December 21). Security of Cloud Computing Users Study. Retrieved from http://www.ca.com/kr/~/media/Files/IndustryAnalystReports/2012-security-of-cloud-computer-users-final1.pdf

Popa, R. A., Redfield, C., Zeldovich, N., & Balakrishnan, H. (2011). *CryptDB: protecting confidentiality with encrypted query processing.*

Provos, N., McNamee, D., Mavrommatis, P., Wang, K., & Modadugu, N. (2007, April). The ghost in the browser analysis of web-based malware. In *Proceedings of the first conference on First Workshop on Hot Topics in Understanding Botnets.* (pp. 4).

Provos, N., Rajab, M. A., & Mavrommatis, P. (2009). Cybercrime 2.0: When the cloud turns dark. *Communications of the ACM, 52*(4), 42–47. doi:10.1145/1498765.1498782 PMID:21218176

Pun, K. H., & Moon, Y. S. (2004). Recent advances in ear biometrics. In *Proceedings of the Automatic Ear and Gesture Recognition*, 164–169.

Puri, A. (1993). *Video coding using the MPEG-2 compression standard.* (pp. 1701–1713). Boston: SPIE/VCIP.

Qu, C., & Buyya, R. (2014). A Cloud Trust Evaluation System using Hierarchical Fuzzy Inference System for Service Selection. Proceedings of *IEEE 28th International Conference on Advanced Information Networking and Applications.* (pp. 850-857). IEEE Computer Society.

Qurban, M., & Takis, K. (1995). Block median filters. Proceedings of *International Symposium on OE/Aerospace Sensing and Dual Use Photonics*, Orlando, FL, USA.

Rajasekaran, H., Lo Iacono, L., Hasselmeyer, P., Fingberg, J., Summers, P., Benkner, S., . . . Friedrich, C. M. (2008). *@ neurIST-Towards a System Architecture for Advanced Disease Management through Integration of Heterogeneous Data, Computing, and Complex Processing Services.*

Ram, S., & Liu, J. (2007). Understanding the semantics of data provenance to support active conceptual modeling. In P. P. Chen, & W. L. Y, Active conceptual modeling of learning (pp. 17-29). Springer. doi:10.1007/978-3-540-77503-4_3

Ramgovin, S., Eloff, M.M., Smith, E. (2010). *The* Management of Security in Cloud Computing. *In proceedings of the IEEE Cloud Computing.* (pp. 1-7).

Ramgovind. S., Eloff, M.M., & Smith, E. (2010, August 2–4). The Management of Security in Cloud Computing. Proceedings of *Information Security for South Africa* (ISSA), Sandton, Johannesburg.

Randles, M., Lamb, D., & Taleb-Bendiab, A. (2010). *A comparative study into distributed load balancing algorithms for cloud computing.*

Rao, M., & Vijay, S. (2009). Cloud Computing and the Lessons from the Past. The 18th IEEE international Workshops on Enabling Technologies: Infrastructures for Collaborative Enterprises, pp. 57-62, 2009.

Rashmi, .G.Sahoo, .S.Mehfuz (2013, August). Securing Software as a Service Model of Cloud Computing: Issues and Solutions. *International Journal on Cloud Computing: Services and Architecture*, Vol.3, No.4.

Ring, T. (2013). It's megatrends: The security impact. *Network Security, 2013*(7), 5–8. doi:10.1016/S1353-4858(13)70080-1

Risk, F. (2012). Authorization Management Program (FedRAMP),". *Concept of Operations (CONOPS)", Version, 1.*

Ristenpart, T., Tromer, E., Shacham, H., & Savage, S. (2009). *Hey, you, get off of my cloud: exploring information leakage in third-party compute clouds.*

Ristenpart, T., Tromer, E., Shacham, H., & Savage, S. (2009, November). Hey, you, get off of my cloud: exploring information leakage in third-party compute clouds. In *Proceedings of the 16th ACM conference on Computer and communications security.* (pp. 199-212). doi:10.1145/1653662.1653687

Rivest, R. L., Adleman, L., & Dertouzos, M. L. (1978). On data banks and privacy homomorphisms. *Foundations of secure computation, 4*(11), 169-180.

Rivest, R. L., Shamir, A., & Adleman, L. (1978). A method for obtaining digital signatures and public-key cryptosystems. *Communications of the ACM, 21*(2), 120-126.

Robertson, k., & Bartos, M. (2013). *Lumberjack Project.* Retrieved from https://fedorahosted.org/lumberjack/

Rong, C., & Cheng, H. (2012). A Secure Data Access Mechanism for Cloud Tenants. *In Proceedings of the Cloud Computing, GRIDs, and Virtualization.*

Rosenbaum, J. (2000). In defense of the delete key.

Rosenberg, J., Kraut, R. E., Gomez, L., & Buzzard, C. A. (1992). Multimedia communications for users. *IEEE Communications Magazine, 30*(5), 20–36. doi:10.1109/35.137476

Rousseau, D., Sitkin, S., Burt, R. & Camerer, C. (1998). Not so Different after All: A Crossdiscipline View of Trust. *Academy of Management Review, 23*(3), pp. 393-404.

Ruan, K., & Carthy, J. (2012). Cloud Computing Reference Architecture and Its Forensic Implications: A Preliminary Analysis. *Proceedings of 4rt International Conference on Digital Forensics and Cyber Crime (ICDF2C'12),* (pp. 1-21). Lafayette, IN, USA. doi:10.1007/978-3-642-39891-9_1

Ruan, K., Carthy, J., Kechadi, T., & Crosbie, M. (2011). Cloud forensics. In *Advances in digital forensics VII* (pp. 35–46). Springer. doi:10.1007/978-3-642-24212-0_3

Rubin, A. D. (1995, June). Independent One-Time Passwords. *USENIX UNIX Security Symposium,* Salt Lake City, Utah.

Ruiter, J., & Warnier, M. (2011). Privacy regulations for cloud computing, compliance and implementation in theory and practice. In S. Gutwirth, Y. Poullet, P. de Hert, & R. Leenes (Eds.), *Computers, Privacy and Data Protection: an Element of Choice* (pp. 293–314). Springer. doi:10.1007/978-94-007-0641-5_17

Ruohomaa, S., & Kutvonen, L. (2005). Trust Management Survey. In P. Herrmann, V. Issarny, & S. Shiu, Trust Management. (pp. 77-92). Springer Berlin Heidelberg. doi:10.1007/11429760_6

Rustan, J. (2012). The Risks in the Cloud. *Foster Rapid Innovation in Computational Science and Information Management.*

Sabater, J., & Sierra, C. (2001). Regret: a reputation model for gregarious societies. *Proceedings of the Fifth International Conference on Autonomous Agents.* (pp. 194-195). New York: ACM. doi:10.1145/375735.376110

Salehi, M. A., & Buyya, R. (2010). Adapting market-oriented scheduling policies for cloud computing Algorithms and Architectures for Parallel Processing (pp. 351-362). Springer.

Sandhu, R. S., Coyne, E. I., Feinstein, H. L., & Youman, C. E. (1996, February). Role based access control models. *IEEE Computer, 29*(2), 38–47. doi:10.1109/2.485845

Sathishkumar, G., Ramachandran, S., & Bagan, K. (2012). Image Encryption Using Random Pixel Permutation by Chaotic Mapping. *Proceedings of IEEE Symposium on Computers and Informatics.* Penang, Malaysia.

Scavo, T. (2009). SAML V2. 0 Holder-of-Key Assertion Profile Version 1.0. OASIS, 2009.

Schelkens, P., Skodras, A., & Ebrahimi, T. (2009). *The JPEG 2000 Suite.* NJ: Wiley Series. doi:10.1002/9780470744635

Schreiber, T. (2004). *Session Riding a Widespread Vulnerability in Today's Web Applications.* [White Paper]. Retrieved from http://www.securenet.de/papers/Session_Riding.pdf

Schwenk, J., Liao, L., & Gajek, S. (2008). Stronger bindings for saml assertions and saml artifacts. In *Proceedings of the 5th ACM CCS Workshop on Secure Web Services (SWS'08).* (pp. 11-20).

Scientific Working Group on Digital Evidence (SWGDE), International Organization on Digital Evidence (IOCE). (2000). *Digital Evidence: Standards and Principles.* Retrieved from http://www.fbi.gov/about-us/lab/forensic-science-communications/fsc/april2000/swgde.htm

Security Guidance for Critical Areas of Focus in Cloud Computing V3.0. (2011). *CSA.* Retrieved from http://www.cloudsecurityalliance.org/guidance/csaguide.v3.0.pdf

Security guidance for critical areas of focus in cloud computing. (2009). *Cloud Security Alliance.* Retrieved from http://www.cloudsecurityalliance.org

Security Within a Virtualized Environment: A New Layer in Layered Security. *Reflex Security*. retrieved http://www.vmware.com/files/pdf/partners/security/securityvirtualizedwhitepaper.pdf

Security Intelligence: Can "Big Data Analytics Overcome Our Blind Spots? (2012). LogRhythm.

Servetto, S. D., & Nahrstedt, K. (2001). Broadcast quality video over IP. *IEEE Transactions on Multimedia*, *3*(1), 162–173. doi:10.1109/6046.909603

Shah, M. A., Baker, M., Mogul, J. C., & Swaminathan, R. (2007). Auditing to Keep Online Storage Services Honest. In Proceedings of HotOS. (pp. 1-5). Berkeley, California.

Shah, A. (2008). Kernel-based Virtualization with KVM. *Linux Magazine*, *86*, 37–39.

Shamir, A. (1979). How to share a secret. *Communications of the ACM*, *22*(11), 612–613. doi:10.1145/359168.359176

Sharda, R., Dursun, D., & Turban, E. (2014). *Business Intelligence A Managerial Perspective on Analytics*. Boston, MA: Pearson.

Shawish, A., & Salama, M. (2014). Cloud Computing: Paradigms and Technologies. In Inter-cooperative Collective Intelligence: Techniques and Applications (pp. 39-67). Springer Berlin Heidelberg.

Shelton, T. (2005). *Remote Heap Overflow*. ID: ACS-SEC-2005-11-25 - 0x1, http://packetstormsecurity.org/0512- advisories/ACSSEC-2005-11-25-0x1.txt

Shen, Z., Li, L., Yan, F., & Wu, X. (2010). Cloud Computing System Based on Trusted Computing Platform. *Proceedings of Intelligent Computation Technology and Automation*, *1*, 942–945.

Shimanek, A. E. (2000). Do You Want Milk with Those Cookies: Complying with the Safe Harbor Privacy Principles. *The Journal of Corporation Law*, *26*, 455.

Shin, D., & Ahn, G. J. (2005). Role-based privilege and trust management. *Computer Systems Science and Engineering*, *20*(6), 401.

Shin, D., Sahama, T., & Gajanayake, R. (2013). Secured e-health data retrieval in daas and big data. In *Proceedings of the 15th IEEE international conference on e-health networking, applications services* (pp. 255-259). Lisbon, Portugal: IEEE. doi:10.1109/HealthCom.2013.6720677

Shred (Unix). (2014, September). *Wikimedia Foundation, Inc.* Retrieved from Wikipedia: http://en.wikipedia.org/wiki/Shred_%28Unix%29

Shrivastava, A., Kundu, A., Surat, S., & Majumdar, A. K. (2008). Credit Card Fraud Detection Using Hidden Markov Model. *IEEE Transactions on Dependable and Secure Computing*, *5*(1), 37–48. doi:10.1109/TDSC.2007.70228

Sidron, J., & Gotal, J. S. (1988). PARIS: An approach to integrated high speed private networks. *International Journal of Digital Analog Cable System*, *1*(2), 77–85. doi:10.1002/dac.4520010208

Singh, M., & Singh, S. (2012). Design and Implementation of Multi-tier Authentication Scheme in Cloud, International *Journal of Computer Science Issues*.

Singh, S., & Morley, C. (2009, November). Young Australians' privacy, security and trust in internet banking. In *Proceedings of the 21st Annual Conference of the Australian Computer-Human Interaction Special Interest Group: Design: Open 24/7*. (pp. 121-128). doi:10.1145/1738826.1738846

Sitkin, S. B., & Roth, N. L. (1993). Explaining the limited effectiveness of legalistic "remedies" for trust/distrust. *Organization Science*, *4*(3), 367–392. doi:10.1287/orsc.4.3.367

Skodras, A. N., Christopoulos, C. A., & Ebrahimi, T. (2000). JPEG2000: the upcoming still image compression standard. *Proceedings of the 11th Portuguese Conference on Pattern Recognition*, Porto, Portugal. (pp. 359-366).

Slaviero, M. (2009). BlackHat Presentation Demo Vids: Amazon, part 4 of 5. *AMIBomb*. Retrieved from http://www. sensepost. com/blog/3797. html

Slaviero, M. (2009, August 8). BlackHat presentation demo vids: Amazon, part 4 of 5. *AMIBomb*.

Slemko, M. (2001). Microsoft passport to trouble.

Snort. (2014). *Cisco*. Retrieved from https://www.snort.org/

Somorovsky, J., Heiderich, M., Jensen, M., Schwenk, J., Gruschka, N., & Lo Iacono, L. (2011). *All your clouds are belong to us: security analysis of cloud management interfaces*.

Somorovsky, J., Meyer, C., Tran, T., Sbeiti, M., Schwenk, J., & Wietfeld, C. (2012). *SeC2: Secure Mobile Solution for Distributed Public Cloud Storages.*

Song, S., Hwang, K., Zhou, R., & Kwok, Y.-K. (2005). Trusted P2P Transactions with Fuzzy Reputation Aggregation. *IEEE Internet Computing, 9*(6), 24–34. doi:10.1109/MIC.2005.136

Sotomayor, B., Montero, R. S., Llorente, I. M., & Foster, I. (2009). Virtual infrastructure management in private and hybrid clouds. *Internet computing, IEEE, 13*(5), 14-22.

Srikantaiah, S., Kansal, A., & Zhao, F. (2008). *Energy aware consolidation for cloud computing.*

Stallings, W. (2006). The Whirlpool secure hash function. *Cryptologia, 30*(1), 55–67. doi:10.1080/01611190500380090

Stimmel, C. L. (2014). *Big data analytics strategies for the smart grid.* Boca Raton, FL: Auerbach Publications. doi:10.1201/b17228

Stoianov, N., Uruena, M., Niemiec, M., Machnik, P., & Maestro, G. (2012). *Security Infrastructures: Towards the INDECT System Security.* Paper presented at the 5th International Conference on Multimedia Communication Services & Security (MCSS), Krakow, Poland. doi:10.1007/978-3-642-30721-8_30

Subashini, S., & Kavitha, V. (2011). A survey on security issues in service delivery models of cloud computing. *Journal of Network and Computer Applications, 34*(1), 1–11. doi:10.1016/j.jnca.2010.07.006

Subramanian, K. (2011). *Hybrid clouds.* Retrieved from http://emea. trendmicro. com/imperia/md/content/uk/cloud-security/wp01_hybridcloud-krish_110624us. pdf

Sultan, N. (2010). Cloud computing for education: A new dawn? *International Journal of Information Management, 30*(2), 109–116. doi:10.1016/j.ijinfomgt.2009.09.004

Sun, Q., & Zhang, Z. (2006). A Standardized JPEG2000 Image Authentication Solution based on Digital Signature and Watermarking". Proceedings of China Communications, Beijing, China.

Sun, X., Chang, G., & Li, F. (2011). A Trust Management Model to enhance security of Cloud Computing Environments. *Second International Conference on Networking and Distributed Computing.* (pp. 244-248). IEEE Computer Society. doi:10.1109/ICNDC.2011.56

Sutter, J. D. (2009). Twitter Hack Raises Questions about 'Cloud Computing'. *CNN.*

Swamp Computing a.k.a. Cloud Computing. (2009, December 28). Web Security Journal.

Sykora, M., Jackson, T., O'Brien, A., & Elayan, S. (2013). National security and social media monitoring: A presentation of the emotive and related systems. In *Proceedings of the European Intelligence and Security Informatics Conference* (pp. 172-175). Uppsala, Sweden: IEEE. doi:10.1109/EISIC.2013.38

Takabi, H., Joshi, J. B. D. (2010, November). Security and privacy challenges in cloud computing environment. *IEEE Journal on Security and Privacy, 8(6), pp. 24-31.*

Takabi, H., Joshi, J. B., & Ahn, G. J. (2010, July). Securecloud: Towards a comprehensive security framework for cloud computing environments. Proceedings of Computer Software and Applications Conference Workshops (COMPSACW), 2010 IEEE 34th Annual. (pp. 393-398).

Tang, Z., & Zhang, X. (2011). Secure Image Encryption without Size Limitation using Arnold Transform and Random Strategies. *Journal of Multimedia, 6*(2), 202–206. doi:10.4304/jmm.6.2.202-206

Tankard, C. (2012). Big data security. *Network Security,* (7): 5–8.

Taylor, M., Haggerty, J., Gresty, D., & Lamb, D. (2011). Forensic investigation of cloud computing systems. In *Network Security* (pp. 4–10). Elsevier.

TestDisk. (2014). *CGSecurity.* Retrieved from http://www.cgsecurity.org/wiki/TestDisk

The FP7 4WARD Project. (2014). Retrieved from http://www.4ward-project.eu/

Toby, V., Anthony, V., & Robert, E. (2009). Cloud Computing, A Practical Approach.

Top 7 threats to cloud computing (2010). *HELP NET SECURITY*. Retrieved from http://www.net-security.org/secworld.php?id=8943

Top Threats to Cloud Computing. (2010). *Cloud Security Alliance*. Retrieved from http://www.cloudsecurity-alliance.org/topthreats/csathreats.v1.0.pdf

Tripathi & Mishra, A. (2011, September 14-16). Cloud computing security considerations. Proceedings of *IEEE conference signal processing, communication and computing*. Xi'an, Shaanxi, China.

Tsai, P., Hu, Y., Yeh, H., & Shih, W. (2012). Watermarking for Multi-resolution Image Authentication. *International Journal of Security and Its Applications*, 6(2), 161–166.

Tseng, B. L., & Anastassiou, D. (1996). Multi view point video coding with MPEG-2 compatibility. *IEEE Transactions CSVT*, 6, 414-419.

Turk, M., & Pentland, A. (1991) Face Recognition Using Eigenfaces, *IEEE Conference on Computer Vision and Pattern Recognition*, Maui, Hawaii, USA, 586-591

Turk, M., & Pentland, A. (1991). Eigenfaces for Recognition. *Journal of Cognitive Neuroscience*, 3(1), 71–86. doi:10.1162/jocn.1991.3.1.71 PMID:23964806

Twitter Email Account Hack Highlights Cloud Dangers. (2009, July 23). *Infosecurity Magazine*. Retrieved from http://www.infosecurity-magazine.com/view/2668/twitteremail-account-hack-highlights-cloud-dangers-/

Un, S., Jho, N. S., Kim, Y. H., & Choi, D. S. (2009). Cloud computing security technology. *ETRI*, 24(4), 79–88.

UTSA announces creation of Open Cloud Institute. (2015The University of Texas at San Antonio.

Varadharajan, V. (2009). A note on trust-enhanced security. *IEEE Security and Privacy*, 7(3), 57–59. doi:10.1109/MSP.2009.59

Varalakshmi, P., & Deventhiran, H. (2012). Integrity Checking for Cloud Environment Using Encryption Algorithm. In *Proceedings of International Conference on Recent Trends in Information Technology*. (pp. 228-232). Chennai, Tamil Nadu: IEEE. doi:10.1109/ICRTIT.2012.6206833

Verhoeyen, M. (2000). *Delivering voice services over DSL* (pp. 244–249). Alcatel Telecommunications Review.

Vieira, K., Schulter, A., Westphall, C., & Westphall, C. (2009). Intrusion detection for grid and cloud computing. *IT Professional*, (4): 38–43.

Vijayan, J. (2013). Vendors tap into cloud security concerns with new encryption tools.

Virtualization-Aware Security for the Cloud. (2010). VMware vShield Product brochure. Retrieved from http://www.vmware.com/files/pdf/vmware-vshield_br-en.pdf>

Vishwanath, K. V., & Nagappan, N. (2010). Characterizing cloud computing hardware reliability.

VMware Hosted Products and Patches for ESX and ESXi. (n. d.). VMware Security Advisory. http://www.vmware.com/security/advisories/VMSA-2009-0006.html

Vu, Q. H., Pham, T. V., Truong, H. L., Dustdar, S., & Asal, R. (2012, March). Demods: A description model for data-as-a-service. DEMODS: A Description Model for Data-As-A-Service, IEEE 26th Conference on Advanced Information Networking and Applications. (pp. 605–612). doi:10.1109/AINA.2012.91

Wainewright, P. (2010). Many degrees of multi-tenancy. *ZDNET*.

Wang, P., Ku, C. C., & Wang, T. C. (2011). *A New Fingerprint Authentication Scheme Based on Secret-Splitting for Enhanced Cloud Security*, 183-196.

Wang, S., Liu, Z., Sun, Q., Zou, H., & Yang, F. (2014). Towards an accurate evaluation of quality of cloud service in service-oriented cloud computing. *Journal of Intelligent Manufacturing, 25*(2), 283-291.

Wang, W.-J., Chang, Y.-S., Lo, W.-T., & Lee, Y.-K. (2013). Adaptive scheduling for parallel tasks with QoS satisfaction for hybrid cloud environments. *The Journal of Supercomputing, 66*(2), 783-811.

Wang, C., Wang, Q., Ren, K., Cao, N., & Lou, W. (2012). Toward secure and dependable storage services in cloud computing. *Services Computing. IEEE Transactions, 5*(2), 220–232.

Wang, K. (2010). Using a local search warrant to acquire evidence stored overseas via the internet. *Advances in Digital Forensics, VI*, 37–48.

Wang, Y., & Lin, K. J. (2008). Reputation-oriented trustworthy computing in e-commerce environments. *IEEE Internet Computing, 12*(4), 55–59. doi:10.1109/MIC.2008.84

Wang, Y., & Zhu, Q. (1998). Error control and concealment for video communication: A Review. *Proceedings of the IEEE, 86*(5), 974–996. doi:10.1109/5.664283

Wayman, J., Jain, A. K., Maltoni, D., & Maio, D. (2005). An introduction to biometric authentication systems. In Biometric Systems, 1-20). Springer London. doi:10.1007/1-84628-064-8_1

Wayne, A. Jansen (2011). Cloud Hooks: Security and Privacy Issues in Cloud Computing. Proceedings of *44th Hawaii International Conference on System*.

Wayne, A., & Jansen, (2011) "Cloud Hooks: Security and Privacy Issues in Cloud Computing", NIST, *Proceedings of the 44th Hawaii International Conference on System Sciences*. (pp. 1530-1605)

Weaver, D. (2015). *Six Advantages of Cloud Computing in Education*. Technology in the Classroom.

Wei, J., Zhang, X., Ammons, G., Bala, V., & Ning, P. (2009, November). Managing security of virtual machine images in a cloud environment. In *Proceedings of the 2009 ACM workshop on Cloud computing security*. (pp. 91-96). doi:10.1145/1655008.1655021

Welcome to Apache Hadoop! (2014). *The Apache Software Foundation*. Retrieved from http://hadoop.apache.org/

Wen, J., Wang, J., Feng, F., & Zhang, B. (2009). A Reversible Authentication Scheme for JPEG2000 Images. *Proceedings of Ninth International Conference on Electronic Measurement & Instruments*. Beijing, China. doi:10.1109/ICEMI.2009.5274015

Wen, Y., Man, X., Le, K., & Shi, W. (2013). Forensics-as-a-Service (FaaS): Computer Forensic Workflow Management and Processing Using Cloud. *Proceedings of the 4th International Conference on Cloud Computing, GRIDs, and Virtualization (COMPUTING'13)*, (pp. 208-214). Valencia, Spain.

What cloud computing really means. InfoWorld (2007). *Infoworld*. Retrieved from http://www.infoworld.com/d/cloud-computing/what-cloud-computing-really-means-031?page=0,0

Whitney, L. (2009). Amazon EC2 cloud service hit by botnet, outage. *CNET News, 11*.

Wiese, L. (2010). Horizontal fragmentation for data outsourcing with formula-based confidentiality constraints Advances in Information and Computer Security. (pp. 101-116). Springer.

Wik, P. (2011). Thunderclouds – Managing SOA-Cloud Risk. *Service Technology Magazine*. 2011-10.

Wik, P. (2011, November). Thunderclouds: *Managing SOA-Cloud Risk. Service Technology Magazine*.

Wilkinson, S., & Haagman, D. (2007). *Good practice guide for computer-based electronic evidence. Association of Chief Police Officers*. ACPO.

Winkler, V. (2011). *Securing the Cloud: Cloud Computer Security Techniques and Tactics*. Elsevier.

Wisner, J. D., Leong, G. K., & Tan, K. C. (2005). Principles of Supply Chain Management–A Balanced Approach, 2005. *South-Western, Mason, Ohio, 442*.

Wolf, L. C., Griwadz, C., & Steinmetz, R. (1997). Multimedia communication. *Proceedings of the IEEE, 85*(12), 1915–1933. doi:10.1109/5.650175

Woodside, J. M. (2010). A BI 2.0 Application Architecture for Healthcare Data Mining Services in the Cloud. Proceedings of *The World Congress in Computer Science, Computer Engineering & Applied Computing - International Data Mining Conference*.

Woodside, J. M., Allabun, N., & Amiri, S. (2014). Bring Your Own Technology (BYOT) to Education. Proceedings of The 5th International Multi-Conference on Complexity. Informatics and Cybernetics.

Woodside, J. M., & Amiri, S. (2014). Bring Your Own Technology (BYOT) to Education. *Journal of Informatics, Systems, and Cybernetics, 12*(3), 38–40.

Wright, C., Kleiman, D., & Sundhar, R. S. S. (2008). Overwriting hard drive data: The great wiping controversy. In Proceedings of the Information Systems Security (p. 243-257). Berkeley, CA, USA: Springer Berlin. doi:10.1007/978-3-540-89862-7_21

Wright, C. P., Dave, J., & Zadok, E. (2003, October). Cryptographic filesystems performance: What you don't know can hurt you. In *Proceedings of the 2nd IEEE International Security in Storage Workshop*. IEEE Computer Society. doi:10.1109/SISW.2003.10005

Wu, X., Zhu, X., Wu, G.-Q., & Ding, W. (2014). Data mining with big data. *IEEE Transactions on Knowledge and Data Engineering*, 26(1), 97–107. doi:10.1109/TKDE.2013.109

Yang, Y., Zhou, Y., Liang, L., He, D., & Sun, Z. (2010). A service-oriented broker for bulk data transfer in cloud computing.

Yang, S. J., Lai, P. C., & Li, J. (2013). Design Role-Based Multi-tenancy Access Control Scheme for Cloud Services, *International Symposium on Biometrics and Security Technologies (ISBAST)*, *(pp.273-279*. doi:10.1109/ISBAST.2013.48

Yan, S., & Lin, Q. (2010). Partial Encryption of JPEG2000 Images Based on EBCOT. *Proceedings of International Conference on Intelligent Control and Information Processing*, China. doi:10.1109/ICICIP.2010.5565304

Yao, A. C. (1982). *Protocols for secure computations.*

Yassin, A. A., Hai, J., Ibrahim, A., & Deqing, Z. (2012). Anonymous Password Authentication Scheme by Using Digital Signature and Fingerprint in Cloud Computing, *InProceedings of the Cloud and Green Computing (CGC)*. (pp. 282–289). doi:10.1109/CGC.2012.91

You, P., Peng, Y., Liu, W., & Xue, S. (2012). Security Issues and Solutions in Cloud Computing. In *Proceedings of 32nd International Conference on Distributed Computing System Workshops*. (pp. 573-577). Macau, China: IEEE. doi:10.1109/ICDCSW.2012.20

Yuan, J., Yu S. (2013). Efficient privacy-preserving biometric identification in cloud computing, Proceedings of *IEEE INFOCOM*. (pp. 2652–2660).

Yuizono, T., Wang, Y., Satoh, K., & Nakayama, S. (2002). Study on individual recognition for ear images by using genetic local search, In *Proceedings of the Congress on Evolutionary Computation*. (pp. 237–242). doi:10.1109/CEC.2002.1006240

Yu, Z., Zhe, Z., Haibing, Y., Wenjie, P., & Yunpeng, Z. (2010). A Chaos-Based Image Encryption Algorithm Using Wavelet Transform.*Proceedings of International Conference on Advanced Computer Control*, China.

Zadeh, L. (1965, June). Fuzzy Sets. *Information and Control*, 8(3), 338–353. doi:10.1016/S0019-9958(65)90241-X

Zadok, E., Iyer, R., Joukov, N., Sivathanu, G., & Wright, C. P. (2006, May). On incremental filesystem development. *Transactions on Storage*, 2(2), 161–196. doi:10.1145/1149976.1149979

Zadok, E., & Nieh, J. (2000). Fist: a language for stackable filesystems. In *Proceedings of the annual conference on usenix annual technical conference* (pp. 5–5). Berkeley, CA, USA: USENIX Association.

Zafarullah, Z., Anwar, F., & Anwar, Z. (2011). Digital forensics for eucalyptus. Proceedings of Frontiers of Information Technology (FIT'11), (pp. 110-116). Islamabad, Pakistan. doi:10.1109/FIT.2011.28

Zahia, Z., Bessalah, H., Tarabet, A., & Kholladi, M. (2008). A new selective encryption technique of JPEG2000 codestream for medical images transmission. *Proceedings of International Conference on Telecommunications and Informatics*. US.

Zakaria, G., & Maes, P. (2000). Trust Management through Reputation Mechanisms. In Applied Artificial Intelligence. (pp. 881-907). doi:10.1080/08839510050144868

Zalaznick, M. (2013). *Cyberattacks on the rise in higher education*. University Business.

Zalewski, M. Browser security handbook, 2008.

Zetter, K. (2009, April). FBI defends disruptive raid on Texas data centers. *Wired*. Retrieved from http://www.wired.com/threatlevel/2009/04/data-centers-ra

Zhang, S., Zhang, S., & Chen, X. (2010). Cloud Computing Research and Development Trend. Proceedings of Second International Conference on Future Networks, ICFN 2010. (pp. 93). doi:10.1109/ICFN.2010.58

Zhang, Y., Juels, A., Reiter, M. K., & Ristenpart, T. (2012). *Cross-VM side channels and their use to extract private keys.*

Zhang, O. Q., Kirchberg, M., Ko, R. K., & Lee, B. S. (2011). How to track your data: The case for cloud computing provenance.*Proceedings of the 3rd International Cloud Computing Technology and Science (CloudCom'11)* (pp. 446-453). Athens (Greece): IEEE. doi:10.1109/CloudCom.2011.66

Zhang, Q., Cheng, L., & Boutaba, R. (2010). Cloud computing: State-of-the-art and Research Challenges. *Journal of Internet Services and Applications*, *1*(1), 7–18. doi:10.1007/s13174-010-0007-6

Zhang, X., Liu, C., Nepal, S., Yang, C., Dou, W., & Chen, J. (2014). A hybrid approach for scalable sub-tree anonymization over big data using mapreduce on cloud. *Journal of Computer and System Sciences*, *80*(5), 1008–1020. doi:10.1016/j.jcss.2014.02.007

Zhang, Y. (1997). MPEG-2 video services for wireless ATM networks. *IEEE Journal on Selected Areas in Communications*, *15*(1), 119–128. doi:10.1109/49.553683

Zhang, Y., & Joshi, J. (2009). *Access control and trust management for emerging multidomain environments.* (pp. 421–452). Emerald Group Publishing.

Zhao, J., Wang, L., Tao, J., Chen, J., Sun, W., & Ranjan, R. et al. (2014). A security framework in g-hadoop for big data computing across distributed cloud data centres. *Journal of Computer and System Sciences*, *80*(5), 994–1007.

Ziegler, C. N., & Lausen, G. (2004, March). Spreading activation models for trust propagation. In *e-Technology, e-Commerce and e-Service, 2004. EEE'04*. (pp. 83-97). IEEE. doi:10.1109/EEE.2004.1287293

About the Contributors

Kashif Munir received his BSc degree in Mathematics and Physics from Islamia University Bahawalpur, Pakistan in 1999. He received his MSc degree in Information Technology from University Sains Malaysia in 2001. He also obtained another MS degree in Software Engineering from University of Malaya, Malaysia in 2005. He completed his PhD in Informatics from Malaysia University of Science and Technology, Malaysia. His research interests are in the areas of Cloud Computing Security, Software Engineering, and Project Management. He has published journal, conference papers and book chapters. Kashif Munir has been in the field of higher education since 2002. After an initial teaching experience with courses in Stamford College, Malaysia for around four years, he later relocated to Saudi Arabia. He has been working as lecturer with King Fahd University for 8 years.

Mubarak S. Almutairi is currently the Dean of Hafr Albatin Community College, King Fahd University of Petroleum & Minerals (KFUPM). He received the B.Sc. degree in systems engineering from King Fahd University of Petroleum & Minerals, Dhahran, Saudi Arabia, in 1997, the M.A.Sc. degree in industrial and systems engineering from the University of Florida, Gainesville, Florida, USA, in 2003, and the Ph.D. degree in systems design engineering from the University of Waterloo, Waterloo, Canada, in 2007. From 1997 to 2000, he was an industrial engineer with the Saudi Arabia Oil Company (Aramco). He is currently an assistant professor in the computer science and engineering department at Hafr Albatin Community College, Hafr Albatin, Saudi Arabia. His research interests include decision analysis, expert systems, information security, fuzzy logic, trust, and e-commerce. Dr. Almutairi is a recipient of three research grants in the field of ITC. He has edited a book and published journal, conference papers, and book chapters. He is serving as a member of the KFUPM board. He is a member of IEEE (USA), senior member IIE (USA), ASNT (USA), ASEE (USA), and SCE (Saudi Arabia). He is also the recipient of the distinguished teaching award of the University of Waterloo for the year 2007.

Lawan A. Mohammed received his BSC (ED) degree in Mathematics and Education from Ahmadu Bello University, Zaria, Nigeria. He received his MSc degree in Operational Research from University Putra Malaysia. He also obtained an MSc degree in Computer Science from DeMontfort University, UK. He completed his PhD degree in Computer and Communication Systems Engineering from University Putra Malaysia in 2004. His PhD research area was in the field of secure network communication particularly in the design of authentication protocol for both wired and wireless network.

***

Ali Imam Abidi completed his B.Tech. in Department of Computer Science & Engineering from BBDNITM, Lucknow affiliated to UPTU, Lucknow in 2008. He earned avid corporate experience working with MNCs like Infosys Ltd., Mysore and Pune, Primecall Consultancies etc. for 2 years. He has worked on Govt. of India sponsored Design Studio for MSMEs project with the National Institute of Design, Ahmedabad, premier design institute of India and worldwide until 2012. Currently he is pursuing Ph.D. from Department of Computer Science & Engineering, Indian Institute of Technology (B.H.U.) Varanasi, starting from 2012. His research interests include areas like Computer Vision, Deformable Image Registration, Biomedical Imaging, Multimedia Biometrics, Computational aspects of Telemedicine etc.

Mahendra Kumar Ahirwar received his Bachelor's degree in Information Technology from PCST, Bhopal in 2011 and Master of Engineering in Computer Science and Engineering from University Institute of Technology-RGPV, Bhopal, Madhya Pradesh, India. At present, he is working as an Assistant Professor in Department of Computer Science & Engineering, University Institute of Technology-RGPV, Bhopal, Madhya Pradesh, India.

Ayoub Ait Lahcen is an Assistant Professor of Computer Engineering at the ENSA Kenitra, a Moroccan engineering school, and a researcher at both LGS laboratory (ENSA Kenitra) and LRIT laboratory (Mohammed V Agdal University, Morocco). Prior to that, he got a Swiss Government Scholarship to work during an academic year, as a postdoctoral researcher, with the Software Engineering Group of the University of Fribourg, Switzerland. He received the Ph.D. degree in computer science from both Nice Sophia Antipolis University, France (prepared at INRIA Sophia Antipolis Research Center, in the Zenith team) and Mohammed V Agdal University (prepared at LRIT laboratory). He received a "Best Paper Award" at MOPAS 2010. He was awarded a Moroccan Research Excellence Scholarship for Ph.D. candidates and a Merit Scholarship for his Master in Computer Science and Telecommunications.

Andrea Atzeni is a Senior Research Assistant at the Dipartimento di Automatica e Informatica, Politecnico di Torino, in the TORSEC Security group. In the last twelve years he participated in a number of large scale European research projects, even as Politecnico di Torino's technical leader. His work addressed, among others, definition of security requirements, investigation and modelisation of user expectation on security and privacy, specification of functional and security architectures, development of cross-domain usable security, risk analysis and threat modeling for complex cross-domain systems, legal and technical issues for using cross-border authentication services, mobile malware analysis and detection, digital forensics.

Wasim A. Bhat (wab.cs@uok.edu.in) is working as Assistant Professor at Department of Computer Sciences, University of Kashmir. His research interests include Operating Systems, specifically Filesystems & Storage subsystems, with focus on design considerations.

Kirti Raj Bhatele received Bachelor's degree in Information Technology in 2010 from RITS Bhopal and M.Tech (Information Technology) in 2012 from TIT, RGPV, Bhopal. M.P. India. Currently he is working as an Assistant Prof. (Contract) in Department of Computer Science & Engineering, UIT-RGPV Bhopal. He has published six papers in International journal and Conferences. His Research Interest lies in Network Security, Image Processing etc.

Satarupa Biswas received her B.E. degree from Tripura Institute of Technology and M.Tech degree from Tripura University. Her areas of interests are cloud Computing and Mobile Computing.

Fatima-Zahra Benjelloun is a Ph.D. candidate in computer science at the ENSA Kenitra, Morocco. She received the M.B.A's degree in the Management of Information Technology and another M.B.A's degree in E-Business from Laval University, Quebec, Canada. Prior to that, she received an engineer's degree in computer science from Al Akhawayn University, Ifrane, Morocco. She is a certified Project Management Professional (PMP) and an ISO 27001 Provisional Auditor of Information Systems. She has worked as a consultant in the Management of Information Security field in several ministries of Quebec City from 2006 to 2011. Her research interests include Big Data, security, and privacy.

Rajanpreet Kaur Chahal completed her B.Tech in Computer Science and Engineering from Punjab Technical University, Jallandhar, Punjab, India in 2012 and is pursuing a Masters in Computer Science and Engineering from Panjab University, Chandigarh, India. She is currently a Research Scholar in Panjab University working on trust issues in cloud computing. Her research interests include cloud computing, distributed systems, and issue of trust evaluation in distributed systems.

Abhik Chaudhuri MBA (IIM), PMP, ITIL Expert, ITSM, certified in COBIT foundation, IBM-accredited Senior IT Specialist, is currently in 12th year of IT Consulting profession, working with Tata Consultancy Services and specializing in Cloud Security, IT Governance Risk Management and Compliance, Green IT initiatives, Service Management, IT Infrastructure Service Delivery, IT Process Management, Program / Project Management. He has implemented robust security features in enterprise resource planning (ERP) systems of reputed clients in the United States, Europe and Australia. He has worked with the Corporate Controller and external auditors for quarterly IT security audits. Abhik has multiple publications in reputed international Journals (ISACA, EDPACS, LNCS Springer). He has performed collaborative research as mentioned below - - Working group member for preparing Cloud Security Alliance's (CSA, USA) Cloud Controls Matrix Framework v1.2 - Contributing Author of Cloud Security Guidance V3 (CSA, USA). - Peer reviewer for CSA's SecaaS Implementation Guidance, Category 2: Data Loss Prevention. He is an Editorial Board member of EDPACS Journal (Taylor & Francis, USA). (Link - http://www.tandfonline.com/action/journalInformation?show=editorialBoard&journalCode=uedp20) Abhik has also contributed as Expert Reviewer for following initiatives - - Expert Reviewer for book titled "Controls and Assurance in the Cloud: Using COBIT 5" published by ISACA USA; April 2014 - SME Reviewer for Dan Swanson's popular book "IT Auditing – Raising the Bar" (published by IT Governance Company, U.K.) - Reviewer for IBM Press. Abhik can be reached at abhik.chaudhuri@gmail.com.

Madhuvan Dixit received M.Tech degree from Patel Institute of Technology, Bhopal (M.P). He is working as an Associate Professor in the Department of Computer Science Engineering, Millennium Institute of Technology & Science, Bhopal, M.P.He is a member of IJITE, IJSPR. He is having eleven years of teaching experience and one years of experience in the field of Software development. He has written many research papers in various International &National Journals & Conferences.

Sumit Jaiswal received his M.Tech degree from NIT Durgapur in 2013, presently he is pursuing a PhD in Computer Science and Engineering from IIT (BHU), Varanasi. His Research interest include Information Security, Network Security, Cryptography and Cloud Computing Security.

Santosh Kumar completed his B. Tech. in Department of Computer Science and Engineering from Ajay Kumar Garg Engineering, Ghaziabad, Uttar Pradesh Technical University (UPTU) in 2008 and M. Tech. in Computer Science & Engineering from Birla Institute of Technology, Mesra, Ranchi (Jharkhand, India) in 2012. Currently he is pursuing Ph.D. from Department of computer science and engineering Indian Institute of Technology (B.H.U.) Varanasi. His research interests span a wide range of spectrum including Computer Vision, pattern recognition, digital image processing, digital video processing, Swarm Intelligence, bio-inspired computing, Artificial Intelligence, operating systems and theoretical computer science.

Abhishek Majumer received his B.E. degree in Computer Science & Engineering from the National Institute of Technology, Agartala, and M.Tech. degree in Information Technology from Tezpur University, Assam in 2006 and 2008 respectively. He is currently working as an Assistant Professor in the Department of Computer Science & Engineering, Tripura University (A Central University), Suryamaninagar, India. His areas of interest are Wireless Network and Cloud Computing.

Qurban A Memon has contributed at levels of teaching, research, and community service in the area of electrical and computer engineering. Currently, he is working as Associate Professor at UAE University, College of Engineering. He has authored/co-authored over eighty publications in his academic career. He has executed research grants and development projects in the area of microcontroller based systems; and networks. He has served as a reviewer of many international journals and conferences as well as session chair at various conferences. His research interests include intelligent systems and networks.

Marwan Omar serves as a full time faculty member of computer science and IT at Nawroz University, Duhok, Iraq. Omar is recognized for his information security expertise and knowledge and holds a security + certification from Comptia. Research interests are: cyber security, mobile security, open source software, and cloud computing.

Sellappan Palaniappan is currently the acting provost and the dean of the School of Science and Engineering at Malaysia University of Science and Technology (MUST). Prior to joining MUST, he was an associate professor at the Faculty of Computer Science and Information Technology, University of Malaya. He earned a PhD in interdisciplinary information science from the University of Pittsburgh and an MS in computer science from the University of London. Dr. Palaniappan is a recipient of several government research grants and has published numerous journals, conference papers, and information technology (IT) books. He is also an external examiner/assessor for several public and private universities. He was a member of the IEEE (United States), Chartered Engineering Council (United Kingdom), and British Computer Society (United Kingdom), and is currently a member of the Malaysian National Computer Confederation (MNCC).

Subhash Chandra Patel received his M.Tech. degree in Information Security from the Guru Gobind Singh Indraprashtha University, New Delhi in 2010. Currently, he is pursuing a Ph.D. in the Department of Computer Engineering at the IIT (BHU), Varanasi, India. He is working on Cloud Computing. His research interests include Cloud Computing Security and Information Security.

Sudipta Roy received his MCA degree from Birla Institute of Technology, Meshra and M.Tech degree in Software Engineering from Jadavpur University. He completed his PhD degree from Department of Information Technology, Assam University. He is currently working as an Associate Professor in the Department of Information Technology, Assam University (A Central University), Silchar, India. His area of interest is Image Processing and Cloud Computing.

Piyush Kumar Shukla received Bachelor's degree in Electronics & Communication Engineering, LNCT, Bhopal in 2001, M. Tech (Computer Science & Engineering) in 2005 from SATI, Vidisha and Ph.D. (Computer Science & Engineering) in 2013 from RGPV, Bhopal. M.P. India. He is a member of IEEE, IACSIT. Currently he is working as an Assistant Prof. in Department of Computer Science & Engineering, UIT-RGPV Bhopal. He is also I/C of PG Courses in DoCSE, UIT, RGPV. He has published more than 40 Research Papers in various International & National Journals & Conferences. He has written more than 10 chapters for IGI Global/ Elsevier/ Springer Book Series, which are either published or under publications. He has Published papers in SCI/SCIE Indexed Journals.

Gaurav Singh received his Master of Engineering in Computer Science and Engineering from ABV-IIITM, Gwalior, Madhya Pradesh, India. At present, he is working as an Assistant Professor in Department of Computer Science & Engineering, Department, Motilal Nehru National Institute of Technology, Allahabad, Uttar Pradesh-211004, India.

Ravi Shankar Singh received a Ph.D. in Computer Science and Engineering from the Institute of Technology, Banaras Hindu University, India in 2010. He is working as Assistant Professor in IIT (BHU) since 2004. His research interest includes Data Structures, Algorithms, and High Performance Computing.

Sarbjeet Singh received his B.Tech degree in Computer Science and Engineering from Punjab Technical University, Jallandhar, Punjab, India in 2001 and M.E. degree is Software Engineering from Thapar University, Patiala, India in 2003. He also received a Ph.D degree in Computer Science and Engineering from Thapar University, Patiala, India in 2009, working on grid security systems architecture. Currently he is Associate Professor in Computer Science and Engineering at UIET, Panjab University, Chandigarh, India. He has more than 30 research publications in international journals and conferences to his credit. His research interests include parallel and distributed systems, distributed security architectures, distributed services like grid and web services, privacy and trust related issues in distributed environments. Dr. Singh is a life member of Computer Society of India and Indian Society for Technical Education.

Sanjay Kumar Singh completed his B. Tech. in Computer Engg., M. Tech. in Computer Applications and Ph.D. in Computer Science and Engineering. Currently he is an associated professor at the Department of Computer Science and Engineering, IIT BHU, Varanasi. He is a Certified Novell Engineer

(CNE) from Novell Netware, USA and a Certified Novell Administrator (CNA) from Novell Netware, USA. He is a member of LIMSTE, IEE, International Association of Engineers and ISCE. His research areas include Biometrics, Computer Vision, Image Processing, Video Processing, Pattern Recognition and Artificial Intelligence. He has over 50 national and international journal publications, book chapters and conference papers.

Andrea Siringo obtained his MSc degree in Computer Engineering in 2014 at Politecnico di Torino. The thesis of his final exam was focused on digital forensics in cloud environment and the related issues to accomplish a forensically sound process with respect to well known best practices. His main topics of interest during his studies have been networking, distributed systems, and computer security. As a technology enthusiast, he is also interested in mobile and web programming. He is currently working as a mobile software developer.

Paolo Smiraglia was student at Politecnico di Torino. He obtained his MSc degree in 2010 with a thesis focused on "Trusted Computing" and "Cloud Computing" technologies. After graduating, Paolo Smiraglia started his research activity on IT security at Politecnico di Torino as a research assistant. Main topics of his research are cloud security, logging, and digital identity management. Paolo Smiraglia is currently a member of the Politecnico di Torino's IT research group.

Joseph M. Woodside is an assistant professor of business intelligence and analytics (http://cbia. stetson.edu) in the Department of Decision and Information Sciences in the School of Business Administration at Stetson University. Dr. Woodside has over 10 years of professional industry experience in healthcare, information systems, business intelligence and analytics. Dr. Woodside is also helping lead the Center for Business Intelligence and Analytics, partnering leading organizations together with Stetson University to link faculty and student talent resources, conduct focused research projects, provide input for curriculum, advance educational benefits and drive industry innovation.

Index

Become an IRMA Member

Members of the **Information Resources Management Association (IRMA)** understand the importance of community within their field of study. The Information Resources Management Association is an ideal venue through which professionals, students, and academicians can convene and share the latest industry innovations and scholarly research that is changing the field of information science and technology. Become a member today and enjoy the benefits of membership as well as the opportunity to collaborate and network with fellow experts in the field.

IRMA Membership Benefits:

- **One FREE Journal Subscription**
- **30% Off Additional Journal Subscriptions**
- **20% Off Book Purchases**
- Updates on the latest events and research on Information Resources Management through the IRMA-L listserv.
- Updates on new open access and downloadable content added to Research IRM.
- A copy of the Information Technology Management Newsletter twice a year.
- A certificate of membership.

IRMA Membership $195

Scan code to visit irma-international.org and begin by selecting your free journal subscription.

Membership is good for one full year.

www.irma-international.org

Printed in the United States
By Bookmasters